SOVEREIGN VIRTUE

SOVEREIGN VIRTUE

The Theory and Practice of Equality

RONALD DWORKIN

Harvard University Press

Cambridge, Massachusetts

London, England

2000

Library of Congress Cataloging-in-Publication Data

Dworkin, R. M.
Sovereign virtue : the theory and practice of equality / Ronald Dworkin.
p. cm.
Includes bibliographical references and index.
ISBN 0-674-00219-9 (alk. paper)
1. Equality.   I. Title.

JC575 .D86 2000
305—dc21   00-020071

For Betsy, as always

Contents

∧

SOVEREIGN VIRTUE

Introduction:
Does Equality Matter?

⬥

I

Equality is the endangered species of political ideals. Even a few decades ago any politician who claimed to be liberal, or even centrist, endorsed a truly egalitarian society as at least a utopian goal. But now even self-described left-of-center politicians reject the very ideal of equality. They say they represent a "new" liberalism or a "third way" of government, and though they emphatically reject the "old right's" creed of callousness, which leaves people's fates entirely to the verdict of an often cruel market, they also reject what they call the "old left's" stubborn assumption that citizens should share equally in their nation's wealth.

Can we turn our backs on equality? No government is legitimate that does not show equal concern for the fate of all those citizens over whom it claims dominion and from whom it claims allegiance. Equal concern is the sovereign virtue of political community—without it government is only tyranny—and when a nation's wealth is very unequally distributed, as the wealth of even very prosperous nations now is, then its equal concern is suspect. For the distribution of wealth is the product of a legal order: a citizen's wealth massively depends on which laws his community has enacted—not only its laws governing ownership, theft, contract, and tort, but its welfare law, tax law, labor law, civil rights law, environmental regulation law, and laws of practically everything else. When government enacts or sustains one set of such laws rather than another, it is not only predictable that some citizens' lives will be worsened by its choice but also, to a considerable degree, which citizens these will be. In the prosperous democracies it is predictable, whenever government curtails welfare programs or declines to expand them, that its decision will keep the lives of poor people bleak. We must be prepared to explain, to those who suffer in that way, why they have nevertheless been treated with the equal concern that is their right. Perhaps we can—that depends on what genuine equal concern requires, which is the subject of this book. But if we cannot, we must act to redeem our political virtue, and what we can and must then do is also this book's subject.

The "new" left does not reject equal concern: when it rejects equality as an ideal, it means to reject only a particular conception of what equal concern requires. It saddles the "old" left with the idea that genuine equality among citizens holds only when everyone has the same wealth, cradle to grave, no matter whether he chooses to work or what work he chooses—that government must constantly take from the ants and give to the grasshoppers. But no one, I think, would seriously propose this as a political ideal: flat, indiscriminate equality is not just a weak political value, or one that is easily overridden by other values. It is no value at all: there is nothing to be said for a world in which those who choose leisure, though they could work, are rewarded with the produce of the industrious.

But if equal concern does not mean that government must insure that everyone has the same wealth, no matter what, then what does it mean? There is no straightforward or uncontroversial answer to that question. Equality is a contested concept: people who praise or disparage it disagree about what it is they are praising or disparaging. The correct account of equality is itself a difficult philosophical issue: philosophers have defended a variety of answers, many of which are discussed in this book. Would it not be wise, then, to follow the new fashion and abandon the ideal altogether, for just that reason? If we cannot agree whether true equality means equality of opportunity, for example, or of outcome, or something altogether different, then why should we continue to puzzle about what it is? Why not just ask, directly, whether a decent society should aim that its citizens have the same wealth, or that they have the same opportunities, or only that each has sufficient wealth to meet minimal needs? Why not forget about equality in the abstract, and focus instead on these apparently more precise questions?

But if equal concern is a precondition of political legitimacy—a precondition of the majority's right to enforce its laws against those who think them unwise or even unjust—we cannot set aside the issue of what that equal concern requires. Would it be enough for a community to secure a minimal level of nutrition, housing, and medical care for everyone, and then to take no further interest in whether some citizens have vastly more wealth than others? We must ask: would that policy satisfy the demand of equal concern for those who still cannot even dream of lives that some of their fellow citizens take for granted?

That might seem a pointless or at least premature question. The prosperous democracies are very far from providing even a decent minimal life for everyone—though some come closer to that goal than others—and we might therefore think it wise to concentrate on urging that lesser requirement and ignore, at least for the foreseeable future, the more demanding one of full equality. But once it is conceded that the comfortable members of a community do not owe their uncomfortable fellow citizens equality, but only some decent minimum standard of living, then too much is allowed to turn on the essentially subjective question of how minimum a standard is decent, and contemporary history suggests that the comfortable are unlikely to give a generous answer to that question. So even in the present lamentable state of affairs, it would be unwise to abandon the question whether equality, not simply some lessening of inequality, must be a legitimate community's goal.

This book argues that equal concern requires that government aim at a form of material equality that I have called equality of resources, though other names might be equally appropriate. The argument is divided into two parts. Part I begins in large theoretical issues and uses examples mainly in the standard philosophical way—as artificial cases invented to illustrate and test theoretical hypotheses. Part II, on the contrary, begins in contemporary and heated political controversies, including national debates over health care provision, welfare programs, electoral reform, affirmative action, genetic experimentation, euthanasia, and homosexuality. The discussions of this part work inside-out, from these critical political issues toward theoretical structures that seem appropriately to bear on and help to adjudicate them. Some of these discussions, like that of Chapter 11, carry the argument into considerable detail, attempting to supply not just a structure for confronting a particular issue but facts needed to apply that structure. Others aim only to show the structure, that is, to show what facts we need.

The difference between the two parts lies in mode of presentation, not in the overall level of abstraction or complexity that is reached. In particular, the second part does not consist merely in applications of theories elaborated in the first: several of the "inside-out" chapters make important theoretical advances on the earlier "outside-in" ones. Chapter 10, on campaign finance reform, for example, makes more articulate the account of democracy latent in the earlier chapters, and though Chapters 8 and 9, on medical care and welfare reform, are extended examples of the hypothetical insurance device described in Chapter 2, they carry the theoretical elaboration of that device further.

I emphasize the interdependence of political theory and practical controversy because I believe it essential that political philosophy respond to politics. I do not mean that political philosophers should avoid theoretical complexity, nor do I claim that this book does that. We should not hesitate to follow an argument that begins in practical politics into whatever abstract acres of political philosophy, or even philosophy in its more general parts, that we are driven to explore before we achieve what strikes us as a satisfactory intellectual resolution, or at least as satisfactory a resolution as we feel able to reach. But it is important that the argument that ends in general philosophy should have begun in our life and experience, because only then is it likely to have the right shape, not only finally to help us, but also finally to satisfy us that the problems we have followed into the clouds are, even intellectually, genuine not spurious.

II

I emphasize the book's inside-out character for a further reason as well: to introduce a more philosophical level of the argument that is mainly indistinct in these pages but that I propose to develop in detail in a later book that will be based in part on the John Dewey Lectures that I gave at Columbia University, in the autumn of 1998, under the title "Justice for Hedgehogs." In those lectures I argued that a theory of political morality, such as the theory developed in this book, should be located in a more general account of the humane values of ethics and morality, of the status and integrity of value, and of the character and possibility of objective truth.[1] We should hope for a plausible theory of all the central political values—of democracy, liberty, and civil society as well as of equality—that shows each of these growing out of and reflected in all the others, an account that conceives equality, for example, not only as compatible with liberty but as a value that someone who prized liberty would therefore also prize. We should hope, moreover, for a theory of all these that show them reflecting even more basic commitments about the value of a human life and about each person's responsibility to realize that value in his own life.

These aims are contrary in spirit to two of the most powerful contemporary influences on liberal theory—the political liberalism of John Rawls and the value pluralism of Isaiah Berlin—and the consequences of that contrary spirit emerge in this book. Berlin insisted that important political values are in dramatic conflict—he particularly emphasized the conflict between liberty and equality—but Chapters 3 and 5, among others, strive to dissipate such conflicts and to integrate those values. Rawls's social-contract device is designed to insulate political morality from ethical assumptions and controversies about the character of a good life. But this book's argument makes no use of any social contract: it hopes to find whatever support its political claims may claim not in any unanimous agreement or consent, even hypothetical, but rather in the more general ethical values to which it appeals—to the structure of a good life described in Chapter 6, for example, and to the principles of personal responsibility described in Chapters 7, 8, and 9. The contrast is exemplified, in Chapter 9, in the distinction between two designs for welfare provision: Rawls's difference principle, which prescinds from any consideration of individual responsibility, and the hypothetical insurance approach, which attempts to make as much turn on such responsibility as possible.

Two principles of ethical individualism seem to me fundamental to any such comprehensive liberal theory, and together they shape and support the account of equality defended in this book. The first is the principle of equal importance: it is important, from an objective point of view, that human lives be successful rather than wasted, and this is equally important, from that objective point of view, for each human life. The second is the principle of special responsibility: though we must all recognize the equal objective importance of the success of a human life, one person has a special and final responsibility for that success—the person whose life it is.

The principle of equal importance does not claim that human beings are the same or equal in anything: not that they are equally rational or good, or that the lives they create are equally valuable. The equality in question attaches not to any property of people but to the importance that their lives come to something rather than being wasted. The consequences of that importance for the rightness or wrongness of anyone's behavior is, moreover, a further question. Many philosophers accept what is often called a principle of beneficence: that individual people have a moral obligation always to act with as much concern for the fate of everyone else in the world as for their own fate or that of their family and friends. Some philosophers who accept that principle conclude that people must always act so as maximally to benefit all other people, on average, in the world; other philosophers conclude that people must act so as maximally to benefit the worst-off people in the world. But though the principle of equal importance is consistent with any such principle of beneficence, no such principle follows from it. True, if I accept the principle of equal importance, I cannot offer, as a reason why I may devote more of my attention to my children than to yours, that it is objectively more important that my children prosper than that yours do. But I may have other justifications for my special concern for my own daughter: for example, that she is my daughter. But the principle of equal importance does require people to act with equal concern toward some groups of people in certain circumstances. A political community that exercises dominion over its own citizens, and demands from them allegiance and obedience to its laws, must take up an impartial, objective attitude toward them all, and each of its citizens must vote, and its officials must enact laws and form governmental policies, with that responsibility in mind. Equal concern, as I said, is the special and indispensable virtue of sovereigns.

The second principle of ethical individualism, the principle of special responsibility, is neither metaphysical nor sociological. It does not deny that psychology or biology can provide persuasive causal explanations of why different people choose to live as they do choose, or that such choices are influenced by culture or education or material circumstance. The principle is rather relational: it insists that so far as choices are to be made about the kind of life a person lives, within whatever range of choice is permitted by resource and culture, he is responsible for making those choices himself. The principle does not endorse any choice of ethical value. It does not contemn a life that is traditional and unexciting, or one that is novel and eccentric, so long as that life has not been forced upon someone by the judgment of others that it is the right life for him to lead.

This book's argument—the answer it gives to the challenge of equal concern—is dominated by these two principles acting in concert. The first principle requires government to adopt laws and policies that insure that its citizens' fates are, so far as government can achieve this, insensitive to who they otherwise are—their economic backgrounds, gender, race, or particular sets of skills and handicaps. The second principle demands that government work, again so far as it can achieve this, to make their fates sensitive to the choices they have made. The central doctrines and devices that the book endorses—the choice of impersonal and personal resources as the metric of equality, of opportunity costs for others as the measure of anyone's holding of impersonal resources, and of a hypothetical insurance market as the model for redistributive taxation—can all be seen as shaped by these twin demands. I make no assumption that people choose their convictions or preferences, or their personality more generally, any more than they choose their race or physical or mental abilities. But I do assume an ethics which supposes—as almost all of us in our own lives do suppose—that we are responsible for the consequences of the choices we make out of those convictions or preferences or personality.

I said earlier that many politicians are now anxious to endorse what they call a "new" liberalism, or a "third" way between the old rigidities of right and left. These descriptions are often criticized as merely slogans lacking substance. The criticism is generally justified, but the appeal of the slogans nevertheless suggests something important. The old egalitarians insisted that a political community has a collective responsibility to show equal concern for all its citizens, but they defined that equal concern in a way that ignored those citizens' personal responsibilities. Conservatives—new and old—insisted on that personal responsibility, but they have defined it so as to ignore the collective responsibility. The choice between these two mistakes is an unnecessary as well as an unattractive one. If the argument that follows is sound, we can achieve a unified account of equality and responsibility that respects both. If that is the third way then it should be our way.

III

Several of the chapters were published earlier—the first two chapters, for example, in 1981. They have been the subject of extended comment by others, and for that reason I have decided to revise them here only in minor—typographical or stylistic—ways. But I have benefited very much from criticism, and though I discuss some of that criticism directly in only one chapter—Chapter 7—I hope that its impact will also be evident in the chapters of Part II that were written for this volume or were first published after commentary on the earlier chapters had appeared.

I

THEORY

I

Equality of Welfare

⚹

I. Two Theories of Equality

Equality is a popular but mysterious political ideal. People can become equal (or at least more equal) in one way with the consequence that they become unequal (or more unequal) in others. If people have equal income, for example, they will almost certainly differ in the amount of satisfaction they find in their lives. It does not follow, of course, that equality is worthless as an ideal. But it is necessary to state, more exactly than is commonly done, what form of equality is finally important.

This is not a linguistic or even conceptual question. It does not call for a definition of the word "equal" or an analysis of how that word is used in ordinary language. It requires that we distinguish various conceptions of equality, in order to decide which of these conceptions (or which combination) states an attractive political ideal, if any does. That exercise may be described, somewhat differently, using a distinction I have drawn in other contexts. There is a difference between treating people equally, with respect to one or another commodity or opportunity, and treating them as equals. Someone who argues that people should be more equal in income claims that a community that achieves equality of income is one that really treats people as equals. Someone who urges that people should instead be equally happy offers a different and competing theory about what society deserves that title. The question is then: which of the many different theories of that sort is the best theory?

In this chapter and the next I discuss one aspect of that question, which might be called the problem of distributional equality. Suppose some community must choose between alternative schemes for distributing money and other resources to individuals. Which of the possible schemes treats people as equals? This is only one aspect of the more general problem of equality, because it sets aside a variety of issues that might be called, by way of contrast, issues about political equality. Distributional equality, as I describe it, is not concerned with the distribution of political power, for example, or with individual rights other than rights to some amount or share of resources. It is obvious, I think, that these questions I throw together under the label of political equality are not so independent from issues of distributional equality as the distinction might suggest. Someone who can play no role in determining, for example, whether an environment he cherishes should be preserved from pollution is poorer than someone who can play an important role in that decision. But it nevertheless seems likely that a full theory of equality, embracing a range of issues including political and distributional equality, is best approached by accepting initial, even though somewhat arbitrary, distinctions among these issues.

I shall consider two general theories of distributional equality. The first (which I shall call equality of welfare) holds that a distributional scheme treats people as equals when it distributes or transfers resources among them until no further transfer would leave them more equal in welfare. The second (equality of resources) holds that it treats them as equals when it distributes or transfers so that no further transfer would leave their shares of the total resources more equal. Each of these two theories, as I have just stated them, is very abstract, because, as we shall see, there are many different interpretations of what welfare is, and also different theories about what would count as equality of resources. Nevertheless, even in this abstract form, it should be plain that the two theories will offer different advice in many concrete cases.

Suppose, for example, that a man of some wealth has several children, one of whom is blind, another a playboy with expensive tastes, a third a prospective politician with expensive ambitions, another a poet with humble needs, another a sculptor who works in expensive material, and so forth. How shall he draw his will? If he takes equality of welfare as his goal, then he will take these differences among his children into account, so that he will not leave them equal shares. Of course he will have to decide on some interpretation of welfare and whether, for example, expensive tastes should figure in his calculations in the same way as handicaps or expensive ambitions. But if, on the contrary, he takes equality of resources as his goal, then, assuming his children have roughly equal wealth already, he may well decide that his goal requires an equal division of his wealth. In any case the questions he will put to himself will then be very different.

It is true that the distinction between the two abstract theories will be less clear-cut in an ordinary political context, particularly when officials have very little information about the actual tastes and ambitions of particular citizens. If a welfare-egalitarian knows nothing of this sort about a large group of citizens, he may sensibly decide that his best strategy for securing equality of welfare would be to establish equality of income. But the theoretical difference between the two abstract theories of equality nevertheless remains important in politics, for a variety of reasons. Officials often do have sufficient general information about the distribution of tastes and handicaps to justify general adjustments to equality of resources (for example by special tax allowances) if their goal is equality of welfare. Even when they do not, some economic structures they might devise would be antecedently better calculated to reduce inequality of welfare under conditions of uncertainty, and others to reduce inequality of resources. But the main importance of the issue I now raise is theoretical. Egalitarians must decide whether the equality they seek is equality of resources or welfare, or some combination or something very different, in order plausibly to argue that equality is worth having at all.

I do not mean that only pure egalitarians need take any interest in this question. For even those who do not think that equality is the whole story in political morality usually concede that it is part of the story, so that it is at least a point in favor of some political arrangement, even if not decisive or even central, that it reduces inequality. People who assign equality even this modest weight must nevertheless identify what counts as equality. I must emphasize, however, that the two abstract conceptions of equality I shall consider do not exhaust the possible theories of equality, even in combination. There are other important theories that can be captured only artificially by either of these. Several philosophers, for example, hold meritocratic theories of distributional equality, some of which appeal to what is often called equality of opportunity. This claim takes different forms; but one prominent form holds that people are denied equality when their superior position in either welfare or resources is counted against them in the competition for university places or jobs, for example.

Nevertheless the claims of both equality of welfare and equality of resources are both familiar and apparent, and it is these that I shall consider. In this chapter I examine, and on the whole reject, various versions of the former claim. In Chapter 2 I shall develop and endorse a particular version of the latter. I might perhaps add two more caveats. It is widely believed that certain people (for example criminals) do not deserve distributional equality. I do not consider that question, though I do raise some questions about merit or desert in considering what distributional equality is. John Rawls (among others) has questioned whether distributional equality might not require deviations from an equal base when this is in the interests of the then worst-off group, so that, for example, equality of welfare is best served when the worst-off have less welfare than others but more than they would otherwise have. I discuss this claim in the next chapter, with respect to equality of resources, but not in this one, where I propose that equality in welfare is not a desirable political goal even when inequality in welfare would not improve the position of the worst-off.

II. A First Look

There is an immediate appeal in the idea that insofar as equality is important, it must ultimately be equality of welfare that counts. For the concept of welfare was invented or at least adopted by economists precisely to describe what is fundamental in life rather than what is merely instrumental. It was adopted, in fact, to provide a metric for assigning a proper value to resources: resources are valuable so far as they produce welfare. If we decide on equality, but then define equality in terms of resources unconnected with the welfare they bring, then we seem to be mistaking means for ends and indulging a fetishistic fascination for what we ought to treat only as instrumental. If we want genuinely to treat people as equals (or so it may seem), then we must contrive to make their lives equally desirable to them or give them the means to do so, not simply to make the figures in their bank accounts the same.

This immediate attraction of equality of welfare is supported by one aspect of the domestic example I described. When the question arises how wealth should be distributed among children, for example, those who are seriously physically or mentally handicapped do seem to have, in all fairness, a claim to more than others. The ideal of equality of welfare may seem a plausible explanation of why this is so. Because they are handicapped, the blind need more resources to achieve equal welfare. But the same domestic example also provides at least an initially troublesome problem for that ideal. For most people would resist the conclusion that those who have expensive tastes are, for that reason, entitled to a larger share than others. Someone with champagne tastes (as we might describe his condition) also needs more resources to achieve welfare equal to those who prefer beer. But it does not seem fair that he should have more resources on that account. The case of the prospective politician, who needs a great deal of money to achieve his ambitions to do good, or the ambitious sculptor, who needs more expensive materials than the poet, perhaps falls in between. Their case for a larger share of their parent's resources seems stronger than the case of the child with expensive tastes, but weaker than the case of the child who is blind.

The question therefore arises whether the ideal of equality in welfare can be accepted in part, as an ideal that has a place, but not the only place, in a general theory of equality. The theory as a whole might then provide that the handicapped must have more resources, because their welfare will otherwise be lower than it could be, but not the man of champagne tastes. There are a number of ways in which that compromise within the idea of equality might be constructed. We might, for example, accept that in principle social resources should be distributed so that people are as equal in welfare as possible, but provide, by way of exception, that no account should be taken of differences in welfare traceable to certain sources, such as differences in tastes for drink. That gives equality of welfare the dominant place, but it prunes the ideal of certain distinct and unappealing consequences. Or we might, at the other extreme, accept only that differences in welfare from certain specified sources, such as handicaps, should be minimized. On this account equality of welfare would play only a part—perhaps a very minor part—in any general theory of equality, whose main political force must then come from a very different direction.

I shall postpone, until later in this chapter, the question of how far such compromises or combinations or qualifications are in fact available and attractive, and also postpone until then consideration of the particular problems of expensive tastes and handicaps. But I want to single out and set aside in advance one form of objection to the feasibility of compromises of equality of welfare. It might be objected, against any such compromise, that the concept of welfare is insufficiently clear to permit the necessary distinctions. We cannot tell (it might be said) how much any welfare differences between two people who have equal wealth are in fact traceable to differences in the cost of their tastes or in the adequacy of their physical or mental powers, for example. So any theory that embraces equality of welfare must pay attention to people's welfare as a whole rather than welfare derived or lost through any particular source. Obviously, there is much in this sort of objection, though how strong the objection is must depend on the form of compromise proposed. I want, however, to set aside all objections about the feasibility of distinguishing welfare sources.

I also want to set aside the more general objection, that the concept of welfare is itself, even apart from distinctions as to source, too vague or impractical to provide the basis for any theory of equality. I said earlier that there are many different interpretations or conceptions of welfare, and that a theory of equality of welfare that uses one of these will have very different consequences, and will require a very different theoretical support, from a theory that uses another. Some philosophers think of welfare as a matter of pleasure or enjoyment or some other conscious state, for example, while others think of it as success in achieving one's plans. We shall later have to identify the leading conceptions of welfare and look at the different conceptions of equality of welfare they supply. But we may notice, in advance, that each of the familiar conceptions of welfare raises obvious conceptual and practical problems about testing and comparing the welfare levels of different people. Each of them has the consequence that comparisons of welfare will often be indeterminate: it will often be the case that of two people neither will have less welfare, but that their welfare will not be equal. It does not follow, however, that the ideal of equality of welfare, on any interpretation, is either incoherent or useless. For that ideal states the political principle that, so far as is possible, no one should have less welfare than anyone else. If that principle is sound, then the ideal of equality of welfare may sensibly leave open the practical problem of how decisions should be made when the comparison of welfare makes sense but its result is unclear. It may also sensibly concede that there will be several cases in which the comparison is even theoretically pointless. Provided these cases are not too numerous, the ideal remains both practically and theoretically important.

III. Conceptions of Equality of Welfare

There are several theories in the field about what welfare is, and therefore several conceptions of equality of welfare. I shall divide what I consider the most prominent and plausible such theories into two main groups, without, however, supposing that all the theories in the literature can fit comfortably into one or the other. The first group I shall call success theories of welfare.

These suppose that a person's welfare is a matter of his success in fulfilling his preferences, goals, and ambitions, and so equality of success, as a conception of equality of welfare, recommends distribution and transfer of resources until no further transfer can decrease the extent to which people differ in such success. But since people have different sorts of preferences, different versions of equality of success are in principle available.

People have, first, what I shall call political preferences, though I use that term in a way that is both narrower and more extended than the way it is often used. I mean preferences about how the goods, resources, and opportunities of the community should be distributed to others. These preferences may be either formal political theories of the familiar sort, such as the theory that goods should be distributed in accordance with merit or desert, or more informal preferences that are not theories at all, such as the preference many people have that those they like or feel special sympathy for should have more than others. Second, people have what I shall call impersonal preferences, which are preferences about things other than their own or other people's lives or situations. Some people care very much about the advance of scientific knowledge, for example, even though it will not be they (or any person they know) who will make the advance, while others care equally deeply about the conservation of certain kinds of beauty they will never see. Third, people have what I shall call personal preferences, by which I mean their preferences about their own experiences or situation. (I do not deny that these types of preferences might overlap, or that some preferences will resist classification into any of the three categories. Fortunately my arguments will not require the contrary assumption.)

The most unrestricted form of equality of success that I shall consider holds that redistribution should continue until, so far as this is possible, people are equal in the degree to which all their various preferences are fulfilled. I shall then consider the more restricted version that only nonpolitical preferences should be counted in this calculation, and then the still more restricted version that only personal preferences should count. More complex versions of equality of success, which combine the satisfaction of some but not all preferences from the different groups, are of course available, though I hope that the arguments I make will not require me to identify and consider such combinations.

The second class of theories of welfare I shall call conscious-state theories. Equality of welfare linked to that sort of theory holds that distribution should attempt to leave people as equal as possible in some aspect or quality of their conscious life. Different conceptions of that ideal are constructed by choosing different accounts or descriptions of the state in question. Bentham and other early utilitarians took welfare to consist in pleasure and the avoidance of pain; equality of welfare, so conceived, would require distribution that tended to make people equal in their balance of pleasure over pain. But most utilitarians and other partisans of the conscious-state conception of welfare believe that "pleasure" and "pain" are much too narrow to represent the full range of conscious states that should be included. For example, "pleasure," which suggests a specific kind of sensuous glow, poorly describes the experience produced by a harrowing piece of drama or poetry, an experience people nevertheless sometimes aim to have, and "pain" does not easily capture boredom or unease or depression.

I do not wish to discuss the issues this dispute raises. Instead I shall use the words "enjoyment" and "dissatisfaction" indiscriminately to name the full range of desirable and undesirable conscious states or emotions that any version of a conscious-state conception of equality of welfare might suppose to matter. This usage gives those words, of course, a broader sense than they have in ordinary language, but I intend that broad sense, provided only that they must name conscious states that people might aim to have or avoid for their own sakes, and states that are introspectively identifiable.

People often gain enjoyment or suffer dissatisfaction directly, from sensuous stimulation through sex or food or sun or cold or steel. But they also gain enjoyment or suffer dissatisfaction through the fulfillment or defeat of their preferences of different sorts. So there are unrestricted and restricted versions of the conscious-state conception of equality of welfare parallel to the versions I distinguished of conceptions of equality of success. One version aims to make people more equal in enjoyment without restriction as to source, another only in the enjoyment they take directly and from nonpolitical preferences, and another in the enjoyment they take directly and from personal preferences only. As in the case of equality of success, more discriminating versions that combine enjoyment from subdivisions of these different sorts of preferences are also available.

I shall also consider, though only very briefly, a third class of conceptions of equality of welfare, which I shall call objective conceptions. Many subdivisions and further classifications among these three classes of conceptions, beyond those I have just noticed, would have to be considered in any full account of possible theories of welfare, and there are theories of welfare not represented in this list at all. But these seem the most plausible candidates for constructing theories of distribution. I shall just mention, however, two sorts of complexities that we should at least bear in mind. First, many of the conceptions and versions I have distinguished raise the question of whether equality in that conception is reached when people are in fact equal in welfare so conceived, or rather when they would be equal if they were fully informed of the relevant facts. Does someone attain a given level of success, for purposes of equality of success, when he believes that his preferences have been fulfilled to a given degree, or rather when he would believe that if he knew the facts? I shall try, when questions of that sort might affect the argument, either to discuss both possibilities or to assume the version that seems to me in context more plausible. Second, many of the conceptions I shall discuss raise problems about time. People's preferences change, for example, so that the question of how far someone's preferences for his life have been fulfilled overall will depend on which set of his preferences is chosen as relevant, or which function of the different preferences he has at different times. I do not believe that any of these temporal problems affects the various points that I shall make, but readers who do should consider whether my arguments hold against alternate versions.

There is, however, a further preliminary question that must detain us longer. We can distinguish two different questions. (1) Is someone's overall welfare—his essential well-being—really just a matter of the amount of his success in fulfilling his preferences (or just a matter of his enjoyment)? (2) Does distributional equality really require aiming to leave people equal in that success (or enjoyment)? The first of these questions takes a certain view of the connection between theories of welfare, such as those I described, and the concept of welfare itself. It supposes that this connection is rather like the connection between theories or conceptions of justice and the concept of justice itself. We agree that justice is an important moral and political ideal, and we ask ourselves which of the different theories about what justice actually consists in is the best such theory. So we might suppose that (for one or another purpose) the welfare of persons, conceived as their essential well-being, is an important moral and political concept, and then ask ourselves which of the traditional theories (or new theories we might deploy) is the best theory of what welfare, so conceived, actually is.

But the second question does not, in itself, require that we confront—or even acknowledge the sense of—that last question. We may believe that genuine equality requires that people be made equal in their success (or enjoyment) without believing that essential well-being, properly understood, is just a matter of success (or enjoyment). We may, indeed, believe that equality requires equality in success even if we are skeptical about the whole idea of essential well-being, considered to be a deep or further fact about people conceptually independent from their success or enjoyment. That is, we may accept equality of success as an attractive political ideal even if we reject the very sense of the question whether two people who are equal in success are equal in essential well-being. And we may do so even if we deny that this question is analogous to the question whether producing the highest possible average utility makes an institution just.

I make these remarks because it is important to distinguish between two strategies that someone anxious to defend a particular conception of equality of welfare might use. He might begin, first, by accepting the idea of welfare as essential well-being, and then take, as at least the tentative premise of his argument, the proposition that genuine equality requires people to be equal in essential well-being. He might then argue for a particular theory of welfare (success, for example) as the best theory of what essential well-being consists in, and so conclude that equality requires that people be made equal in success. Or, second, he might argue for some conception of equality of welfare, such as equality of success, in a more direct way. He might take no position on the question whether essential well-being consists in success, or even on the prior question whether that question makes sense. He might argue that, in any case, equality of success is required for reasons of fairness, or for some other reasons having to do with the analysis of equality that are independent of any theory about the sense or content of essential well-being.

Is it therefore necessary to consider both of these strategies in assessing the case for any particular conception of equality of welfare? I think not, because the defeat of the second strategy (at least in a certain way) must count as a defeat of the first as well. I do not mean myself to claim that the idea of essential well-being, as a concept admitting of different conceptions, is nonsense, so that the first strategy, shorn of nonsense, is just the second. On the contrary, I think that idea, at least as defined by certain contexts, is an important one, and the question of where a person's essential well-being lies, when properly conceived, is sometimes, in those contexts, a question of profound importance. Nor do I think it follows from the conclusion that people should not be made equal in some particular conception of welfare, that this is a poor conception of welfare (conceived as essential well-being). I mean rather to deny something like the opposite claim: that if some conception is a good conception of welfare, it follows that people should be made equal in welfare so conceived. This does not follow. I might accept, for example, that people are equal in essential well-being when each is roughly equally successful in achieving a certain set of his preferences, without thereby conceding that an advance toward that situation is even pro tanto an advance toward genuine distributional equality. Even if I initially accept both propositions, I should abandon the latter if I am then persuaded that there are good reasons of political morality for not making people equal in that sort of success, and that these reasons hold whether or not the former proposition is sound. So any arguments capable of defeating the second strategy, by showing that there are strong reasons of political morality why distribution should not aim to make people equal in success, must also count as strong arguments against the first strategy, though not, of course, as arguments defeating the interim conclusion of that strategy: that essential well-being consists in success. In what follows I shall try to oppose the second strategy in this manner.

IV. Success Theories

I want now to examine equality of welfare conceived in the various ways I have described, beginning with the group of theories I called success theories. As I said, I do not intend to make much of the practical difficulties (as such) of applying these or any other conceptions of equality of welfare. If any society dedicated itself to achieving any version of equality of success (or of enjoyment), it could do at best only a rough job, and could have only a rough idea of how well it was doing. Some differences in success would be beyond the reach of political action, and some could be eliminated only by procedures too expensive of other values. Equality of welfare so conceived could be taken only as the ideal of equality, to be used as a standard for deciding which of different practical political arrangements seemed most or least likely to advance that ideal on the whole as a matter of antecedent tendency. But precisely for that reason it is important to test the different conceptions of equality of welfare as ideals. Our question is: If (impossibly) we could achieve equality of welfare in some one of these conceptions, would it be desirable, in the name of equality, to do so?

Political Preferences

I shall begin by considering equality of success in the widest and most unrestricted sense I distinguished, that is, equality in the fulfillment of people's preferences when these include political as well as other forms of preferences. We should notice a threshold difficulty in applying this conception of equality in a community in which some people themselves hold, as a matter of their own political preferences, exactly the same theory. Officials could not know whether such a person's political preferences were fulfilled until they knew whether their distribution fulfilled everyone's preferences equally, including his political preferences, and there is danger of a circle here. But I shall assume that equality of welfare, so conceived, might be reached in such a society by trial and error. Resources might be distributed and redistributed until everyone pronounced himself satisfied that equality of success on the widest conception had been achieved.

We should also notice, however, a further threshold difficulty: that it would probably prove impossible to reach a reasonable degree of equality in this conception even by trial-and-error methods in a community whose members held very different and very deeply felt political theories about justice in distribution. For any distribution of goods we might arrange, some group, passionately committed to a different distribution for reasons of political theory, might be profoundly dissatisfied no matter how well they fared personally, while others might be very pleased because they held political theories that approved the result. But because I propose to ignore practical or contingent difficulties, I shall assume a society in which it is possible to achieve rough equality in the amount by which people's unrestricted preferences were fulfilled, that is roughly equal success on this wide conception, either because people all hold roughly the same political theories, or because, though they disagree, anyone's dissatisfaction with a solution on political grounds could be made up by favoritism in his personal situation, without arousing so much antagonism in others as to defeat equality so conceived for that reason.

This latter possibility—that people who lose out because their political theories are rejected could be given more goods for themselves by way of compensation—makes this conception of equality of welfare immediately unattractive, however. Even people otherwise attracted to the idea of equality of welfare, on any conception, would presumably not wish to count gains or losses in welfare traceable to, for example, racial prejudice. So I assume that almost everyone would wish to qualify equality of success at least by stipulating that a bigot should not have more goods than others in virtue of the fact that he would disapprove a situation in which blacks have as much as whites unless his own position were sufficiently favored to make up the difference.

But it is unclear why this stipulation should not apply to all political theories that are in conflict with the general ideal of equality of success, and not just to racial bigotry. It should apply equally to people who think that aristocrats should have more than plebs, or to meritocrats who think that, as a matter of political morality, those who are more talented should have more. Indeed, it should apply even to egalitarians who think that people should be equal in resources or enjoyment or in the success each has in his personal life rather than in the fulfillment of all his preferences, including his political preferences. These "wrong" egalitarian theories will of course seem more respectable to officials who have accepted the latter conception of equality than will bigoted or meritocratic theories. But it still seems odd that even wrong egalitarians should have extra resources credited to their personal account just to make up for the fact that their overall approval of the situation would otherwise be lower than those who hold the political theory assumed to be correct, and on which any claims the former might make to extra resources must in some sense rely. It seems odd (among other reasons) because a good society is one that treats the conception of equality that society endorses, not simply as a preference some people might have, and therefore as a source of fulfillment others might be denied who should then be compensated in other ways, but as a matter of justice that should be accepted by everyone because it is right. Such a society will not compensate people for having preferences that its fundamental political institutions declare it is wrong for them to have.

The reason why racial bigotry should not count, as a justification for giving the bigot more in personal goods, is that this political theory or attitude is condemned by the proper conception of equality, not that the bigot is necessarily insincere or unreflective or personally wicked. But then other forms of nonegalitarian political theory, and even misconceived forms of egalitarian theory, should be discounted in the same way. Suppose, moreover, that no one has a nonegalitarian or wrong-egalitarian political theory of any formal sort, but that some people are merely selfish and have no political convictions even in the extended sense, so that their overall approval of the state of affairs after any distribution is just a matter of their own private situation, while others are benevolent, so that their overall approval is increased by, say, the elimination of poverty in the society. Unless we refuse to take that benevolence into account, as a positive source of success in meeting the preferences overall of those who are benevolent, we shall end once again by giving those who are selfish more for themselves, to compensate for the success others have from that benevolence. But it is surely a mark against any conception of equality that it recommends a distribution in which people have more for themselves the more they disapprove or are unmoved by equality.

Consider, finally, a different situation. Suppose no one holds, in any case very deeply, any formal political theory, but each is generally benevolent. Many people, however, by way of what I called a political theory in the extended sense, sympathize especially with the situation of one group of those less fortunate than themselves—say, orphans—and have special preferences that these be looked after well. If these preferences are allowed to count, this must have one or the other of two results. Either orphans will, just for this reason, receive somewhat better treatment than equality would itself have required in the absence of these special preferences, at the inevitable expense of other groups—including those disadvantaged in other ways, such as, say, cripples; or, if this is ruled out on egalitarian grounds, those who care more about orphans than about cripples will be given extra resources to make up for the failure to fulfill this discrete preference (which extra resources they then may or may not contribute to orphans). Neither of these results does credit to an egalitarian theory.

So we have good reason to reject the unrestricted conception of equality of success, by eliminating from the calculation of comparative success both formal and informal political preferences, at least for communities whose members differ in these political preferences, which is to say for almost all actual communities with which we might be concerned. We might just pause to consider, however, whether we must reject that conception for all other communities as well. Imagine a community in which people by and large hold the same political preferences. If these common preferences endorse equality of success, including success in political preferences, then that theory for all practical purposes collapses into the more restricted theory that people should succeed equally in their nonpolitical preferences. For if a distribution is reached that everyone regards with roughly equal overall approval, and the force of individual political convictions, in each person's judgment of how well he regards it, is simply to approve the result because everyone else does regard it equally, then the distribution must be one in which each person regards his own impersonal and personal preferences as equally fulfilled as well. Suppose Arthur is less satisfied with his impersonal and personal situation than Betsy. Arthur can have, by hypothesis, no political theory or attitude that could justify or require a distribution in which he is less satisfied in this way than Betsy is, so Arthur can have no reason to regard the distribution with as much general or overall approval, combining political, impersonal, and personal assessments, as Betsy does.

But suppose the shared political theory is not the ideal of equality of overall approval, but some other, nonegalitarian theory that could provide such a reason. Suppose everyone accepts a caste theory, so that though Amartya is somewhat poorer than others, the distribution leaves his preferences as a whole equally fulfilled because he believes that he, as a member of a lower caste, should have less, so that his preferences as a whole would be worse fulfilled if he had more. Bimal, from a higher caste, would also be less satisfied overall if Amartya had any more. In this situation, unrestricted equality of success does recommend a distribution that no other conception of equality of welfare would. But it is unacceptable for that very reason. An inegalitarian political system does not become just simply because everyone wrongly believes it to be.

Unrestricted equality of success is acceptable only when the political preferences that people happen to have are sound rather than simply popular, which means, of course, that it is in the end an empty ideal, useful only when it rubber-stamps a distribution already and independently shown to be just through some more restricted conception of equality of success or through some other political ideal altogether. Suppose someone denies this and argues that it is good, in and of itself, when everyone approves of a political system highly and equally no matter what that system is. This seems so arbitrary, and so far removed from ordinary political values, as to call into question whether he understands what a political theory is or is for. In any case he does not state an interpretation of equality, let alone an attractive one.

Impersonal Preferences

We must surely restrict equality of success still further by eliminating, from the calculation it proposes, at least some of what I called people's impersonal preferences. For it is plainly not required by equality that people should be equal, even insofar as distribution can achieve this, in the degree to which all their nonpolitical hopes are realized. Suppose Charles very much and very deeply hoped that life would be discovered on Mars, or that the Great American Novel would be written within his lifetime, or that the coast of Martha's Vineyard would not be eroded by the ocean as it inevitably continues to be. Equality does not require that funds be taken from others, who have more easily fulfilled hopes about how the world will go, and transferred to Charles so that he can, by satisfying other preferences he has, decrease the overall inequality in the degree to which his and their nonpolitical preferences are fulfilled.

Should any impersonal preferences be salvaged from the further restriction this suggests? It might be said that the various impersonal preferences I just took as examples are all impossible dreams or, in any case, all dreams that the government can do nothing to fulfill. But I cannot see why that matters. If it is right to aim to decrease inequality in disappointment in all genuine nonpolitical aims or preferences, then the government should do what it can in that direction, and though it cannot bring it about that there is life on Mars, it can at least partially compensate Charles for his failed hopes by allowing him to be more successful otherwise. In any case, I might have easily taken as examples hopes people have that are not impossible, or even particularly difficult, for government to realize. Suppose Charles hopes that no distinctive species will ever become extinct, not because he enjoys looking at a variety of plants and animals, or even because he thinks others do, but just because he believes that the world goes worse when any such species is lost. He would overwhelmingly prefer that a very useful dam not be built at the cost of losing the snail darter. (He has not set out deliberately to cultivate his views about the importance of species. If he had, then this might be thought to raise the special issues about deliberate cultivation of expensive tastes that I shall consider later. He just finds he has these views.) But after the political process has considered the issue and reached its decision, the dam is built. Charles's disappointment is now so great (and he cares so little about everything else) that only the payment of a vast sum of public money, which he could use to lobby against further crimes against species, could bring his welfare, conceived as the fulfillment of all nonpolitical preferences, back to the general level of the community as a whole. I do not think that equality requires that transfer, nor do I believe that many, even of those who find appeal in the general ideal of equality of welfare, will think so either.

Of course equality does require that Charles have a certain place in the political process I described. He must have an equal vote in selecting the officials who will make the decision, and an equal opportunity to express his opinions about the decision these officials should take. It is at least arguable, moreover, that the officials should take his disappointment into account, perhaps even weighted for its intensity, in the general cost-benefit balancing they undertake in deciding whether the dam should be built all things considered, that his dissatisfaction should count in a Benthamite calculation and be weighted against the gains to others that the dam would bring. We might wish to go beyond this, perhaps, and say that if the community faces a continuing series of decisions that pit economic efficiency against species preservation, it should not take these decisions discretely, through separate cost-benefit calculations each of which Charles would lose, but as a series in which the community should defer to his opinion at least once. But none of this comes near arguing that the community treats Charles as an equal only if it recognizes his eccentric position in a different way, by undertaking to insure, so far as it can, that his success in finding all his nonpolitical preferences fulfilled remains as high as everyone else's when the series of decisions is completed, no matter how singular his impersonal preferences are. Indeed this proposition contradicts rather than enforces what conventional ideals of political equality recommend, because if the community acknowledged that responsibility, Charles' opinions would very probably play a role far beyond what these traditional ideas provide for them.

But someone might still protest that my arguments depend on assigning to people impersonal preferences that are in the circumstances unreasonable, or, rather, unreasonable to expect the community to honor by compensating for their failure. My arguments do not, it might be said, suggest that reasonable impersonal preferences should not be honored in that way. But this introduces a very different idea into the discussion. For we now need an independent theory about when an impersonal preference is reasonable or when it is reasonable to compensate for one. It seems likely that such a theory will assume that a certain fair share of social resources should be devoted to the concerns of each individual, so that a claim for compensation might be appropriate when this fair share is not in fact put at his disposal, but not if deciding as he wishes or compensating him for his disappointment would invade the fair share of others. We shall consider, later in this section, the consequences of using the idea of fair shares in this way within a theory of equality of success. It is enough to notice now that some such major refinement would be necessary before any impersonal preferences would qualify for the calculation of equality of success.

Nor does it seem implausible to restrict a conception of equality of welfare to success in achieving personal, as distinct from both all political and all impersonal, ambitions. For that distinction is appealing in other ways. Of course people do care, and often care very deeply, about their political and impersonal preferences. But it does not seem callous to say that insofar as government has either the right or the duty to make people equal, it has the right or the duty to make them equal in their personal situation or circumstances, including their political power, rather than in the degree to which their differing political convictions are accepted by the community, or in the degree to which their differing visions of an ideal world are realized. On the contrary, that more limited aim of equality seems the proper aim for a liberal state, though it remains to see what making people equal in their personal circumstances could mean.

Equality of Personal Success

Relative success.   We should therefore consider the most restricted form of equality of success that I shall discuss, which requires that distribution be arranged so that people are as nearly equal as distribution can make them in the degree to which each person's preferences about his own life and circumstances are fulfilled. This conception of equality of welfare presupposes a particular but plausible theory of philosophical psychology. It supposes that people are active agents who distinguish between success or failure in making the choices and decisions open to them personally, on the one hand, and their overall approval or disapproval of the world in general, on the other, and seek to make their own lives as valuable as possible according to their own conception of what makes a life better or worse, while recognizing, perhaps, moral constraints on the pursuit of that goal and competing goals taken from their impersonal preferences. There is no doubt a measure of idealization in this picture; it may never be a fully accurate description of any person's behavior, and it may require significant qualification in many cases. But it seems a better model against which to describe and interpret what people are than the leading and perhaps more familiar alternatives.

So I shall not quarrel with this psychological theory. But we must notice at once a difficulty in the suggestion that the resources of a community should be distributed, so far as possible, to make people equal in the success they have in making their lives valuable in their own eyes. People make their choices, about what sort of a life to lead, against a background of assumptions about the rough type and quantity of resources they will have available with which to lead different sorts of lives. They take that background into account in deciding how much of what kind of experience or personal relationship or achievement of one sort must be sacrificed for experiences or relationships or achievements of another. They therefore need some sense of what resources will be at their disposal under various alternatives before they can fashion anything like the plan for their lives of the sort that this restricted conception of equality of success assumes that they have, at least roughly, already created. Some of these resources are natural: people need to make assumptions about their expected life span, health, talents, and capacities, and how these compare with those of others. But they also need to make assumptions about the resources they will have of just the sort society would allocate under any scheme of equality of welfare: wealth, opportunities, and so on. But if someone needs a sense of what wealth and opportunities will be available to him under a certain life before he chooses it, then a scheme for distribution of wealth cannot simply measure what a person should receive by figuring the expense of the life he has chosen.

There is therefore again danger of a fatal circle here. But I propose to set that problem aside, as another instance of the kind of technical problem that I promised not to labor. So I shall suppose, once again, that the problem can be solved in a trial-and-error way. Suppose a society in which people in fact have equal resources. It is discovered that some are much more satisfied than others with the way their lives are going. So resources are taken from some and given to others, on a trial-and-error basis, until it is true that, if people were fully informed about all the facts of their situation, and each was asked how successful he believed himself to be at fulfilling the plans he had formed given the level of resources he now has, each person would indicate roughly the same level or degree of success.

But this "solution" of the practical difficulty I describe brings to the surface a theoretical problem to which the practical difficulty points. People put different values on personal success and failure, not only as contrasted with their political and moral convictions and their impersonal goals, but just as part of their personal circumstances or situation. At least they do in one sense of success and failure. For we must now notice an important distinction I have so far neglected. People (at least as conceived in the way just described) choose plans or schemes for their lives against a background of natural and physical resources they have available, in virtue of which they have discrete goals and make discrete choices. They choose one occupation or job over another, live in one community rather than another, seek out one sort of lover or friend, identify with one group or set of groups, develop one set of skills, take up one set of hobbies or interests, and so forth. Of course, even those people who come closest to the ideal of that model do not make all these choices deliberately in the light of some overall scheme, and perhaps make none of them entirely deliberately. Luck and occasion and habit will play important roles. But once the choices they do make have been made, these choices define a set of preferences, and we can ask how far someone has succeeded or failed at fulfilling whatever preferences he has fixed in that way. That (I shall say) is the question of his relative success—his success at meeting the discrete goals he has set for himself.

But people make these choices, form these preferences, in the light of a different and more comprehensive ambition, the ambition to make something valuable of the only life they have to lead. It is, I think, misleading to describe this comprehensive ambition as itself only another preference people have. It is too fundamental to fit comfortably under that name; and it is also too lacking in content. Preferences represent the result of a decision, of a process of making what one wants more concrete. But the ambition to find value in life is not chosen as against alternatives, for there is no alternative in the ordinary sense. Ambition does not make plans more concrete; it is simply the condition of having any plans at all. Once someone has settled on even a tentative or partial scheme for his own life, once his discrete preferences have been fixed in that way, then he can measure his own relative success in a fairly mechanical way, by matching his situation to that scheme. But he cannot tell whether his life has succeeded or failed in finding value simply by matching his achievements to any set target in that way. He must evaluate his life as a whole to discover the value that it has, and this is a judgment that must bring to bear convictions that, however inarticulate these are, and however reluctant he might be to call them this, are best described as philosophical convictions about what can give meaning or value to any particular human life. I shall call the value that someone in this way attributes to his life his judgment of that life's overall success.

People disagree about how important relative success is in achieving overall success. One person might think that the fact that he is likely to be very successful at a particular career (or love affair or sport or other activity) counts strongly in favor of his choosing or pursuing it. If he is uncertain whether to be an artist or lawyer, but believes he would be a brilliant lawyer and only a good artist, he might regard that consideration as decisive for the law. Someone else might weigh relative success much less. He might, in the same circumstances, prefer to be a good artist to being a brilliant lawyer, because he thinks art so much more important than anything lawyers do.

This fact—that people value relative success differently in this way—is relevant here for the following reason. The basic, immediate appeal of equality of welfare, in the abstract form in which I first set it out, lies in the idea that welfare is what really matters to people, as distinct from money and goods, which matter to them only instrumentally, so far as these are useful in producing welfare. Equality of welfare proposes, that is, to make people equal in what is really and fundamentally important to them all. Our earlier conclusion, that in any event the fulfillment of political and impersonal preferences should not figure in any calculation aimed at making people equal in welfare through distribution, might well be thought to damage that appeal. For it restricts the preferences that people are meant to fulfill in equal degree to what I have called personal preferences, and people do not care equally about the fulfillment of their personal preferences as opposed to their political convictions and impersonal goals. Some care more about their personal preferences, as opposed to their other preferences, than others do. But a substantial part of the immediate appeal I describe remains, though the point would now be put slightly differently. Equality of welfare (it might now be said) makes people equal in what they all value equally and fundamentally so far as their own personal situations or circumstances are concerned.

But even that remaining claim is forfeit if equality of welfare is construed as making people equal, so far as distribution can achieve this, in their relative success, that is, in the degree to which they achieve the goals they fix for themselves. On this conception, money is given to one rather than another, or taken from one for another, in order to achieve equality in a respect some value more than others and some value very little indeed, at the cost of inequality in what some value more. A person of very limited talents might choose a very limited life in which his prospects of success are high because it is so important to be successful at something. Another person will choose almost impossible goals because for him the meaning is the challenge. Equality of relative success proposes to distribute resources— presumably much fewer to the first of these two and much more to the second—so that each has an equal chance of success in meeting these very different kinds of goals.

Suppose someone now replies that the appeal of equality of welfare does not lie where I located it. Its purpose is not to make people equal in what they do value fundamentally, even for their own lives, but rather in what they should value fundamentally. But this change in the claims for equality of welfare achieves nothing. For it is absurd to suppose that people should find value only in relative success without regard to the intrinsic value or importance of the life at which they are relatively successful. Perhaps some people—those with grave handicaps—are so restricted in what they can do that they must choose just so as to be able to be minimally successful at something. But most people should aim to do more than what they would be, relatively, most successful in doing.

Overall success.   This discussion might be thought to suggest a better interpretation of equality of welfare, namely equality of overall rather than relative success. But if we are to explore equality of welfare in that conception we must make a distinction not necessary (or in any case not so plainly necessary) in comparing relative success. We must distinguish a person's own judgment of his overall success (or, if we prefer, the judgment he would make if fully informed of the pertinent ordinary sorts of facts) from the objective judgment of how much overall success in fact he has. A person's own judgment (even if fully informed of the facts) will reflect his own philosophical convictions about what gives value to life, and these might be, from the standpoint of the objective judgment, confused or inaccurate or just wrong. I shall suppose, here, that equality of overall success means equality in people's overall success as judged by themselves, from the standpoint of their own perhaps differing philosophical beliefs. I shall later consider, under the title of objective theories of welfare, the different conception that requires equality in the success of their lives judged in some more objective way.

So let us now alter the exercise we have imagined. Now we rearrange resources, as far as we are able, so that when we have finished, each person would, at least if fully informed, offer the same assessment, not of his relative success in achieving the goals he selected for himself, but of his overall success in leading a valuable life. But we must take care in describing just what we take that latter opinion to be. For there are many different beliefs each of which might possibly be thought to count as an assessment of one's own overall success, and it is of crucial importance to decide which of these, if any, should play a role in rearranging resources in the name of equality. Nor can we find much guidance in the literature either of welfare economics or of utilitarianism, which are the natural places to look. For most of those writers who argue or assume that welfare consists in the fulfillment of preferences seem to have had relative rather than overall success in mind, and in any case have not discussed the problems raised by the latter idea when the two ideas are separated. The language they use—the language of preferences (or wants or desires)—seems too crude to express the special, comprehensive judgment of the value of a life as a whole.

We might begin by distinguishing the question of how valuable someone believes his life has been, taken as a whole, from the question of how much he wants his life to continue. These are certainly different matters. Some people, to be sure, wish their life to end, or are in any case almost indifferent whether it continues, because they regard it as a failure. But others wish to die just because they think their life has been too brilliant to tarnish with a slow decline. And others think that a successful life can be made more successful by the timely use of suicide as a creative act. People can want to end, that is, a life they are proud to have led. Can we say at least that if someone wishes to die he must regard the future life he would otherwise lead as having no or little value? This will certainly be so in most cases, but the connection is nevertheless, I think, contingent. He may only think that though his future life would be quite successful, his life as a whole would be more successful if it ended now. Nor does it follow from the fact that someone very much wishes to continue living, for as long as he can imagine, that he thinks that his life is a successful life, or even that his future life will be especially successful. He may, on the contrary, want to live longer because he thinks his life has been unsuccessful, because he needs more time to do anything worth doing, though it is more likely that he simply fears death. The distinction I want to make can be summarized, perhaps, this way. Someone's preferences about the length of his life are just that, preferences that are like his choices of jobs and lovers, fixed as part of the dominating exercise of deciding what life, given background assumptions about resources, would be the most valuable life all things considered. They are not in themselves judgments of overall success or failure.

Can we make a further distinction between the value someone finds in his own life and the value he believes it has *for* him? I am not sure what that latter phrase would mean as part of this contrast. We sometimes say that a person puts a low value on his own life when we mean, not that he is not proud of the life he has or will lead, but rather that he counts the value of that life low compared with the value he puts on his duty or the lives of others. But we are now considering something different, not the value someone puts on his own life as compared with his moral or impersonal values, but the value he puts on that life as part of the assessment of his own situation.

Perhaps "the value of someone's life for him" means only the intensity of his preference that his life continue. If so, the distinction between the value someone finds in his life and its value for him is the distinction we have already discussed. But someone who uses that phrase may have in mind something more complex and more elusive than that. He may mean to distinguish someone's judgment about the value of any single human life (or indeed human life in general) to the universe as a whole from that person's judgment from the inside, from the standpoint of someone charged with making something valuable of his own life. If so, then it is the latter judgment with which we are now concerned. Or he may mean to distinguish someone's judgment of his own success in that assignment, given his talents and opportunities, from his judgment of whether it was good for him to have had the talents and opportunities and convictions that made him the person whose life would have most value lived that way. It is not hard to imagine lives that illustrate the distinction so understood. It is in fact a cliché that great artists often work, not out of enjoyment (even in the widest sense of enjoyment), but rather in constant misery simply because it is not possible for them not to write poetry or music or paint. A poet who says this may well think that a life he spent in any other way would be, in the most fundamental sense, a failure. But he might well think that the conspiracy of talents and beliefs that made this true was bad for him, meaning only that his life would be more enjoyable if he lacked these talents or did not have the belief, which he could not however shake, that a life of creating poetry in misery and despair was all things considered the most valuable life for him to lead. Suppose we then ask him the dark question only philosophers and sentimental novelists ask: Would it have been better for you if you had never been born? If he says yes, as he might in some moods, we would know what he meant, and it would not be that he has done nothing valuable with his life. If the distinction between someone's judgment of the value of his life and his judgment of the value it has for him is taken in this way, then it is the former judgment I mean by his judgment of his overall success. But if the distinction cannot be taken in this way, or in any of the other ways I have considered, then I do not understand it, and suspect that it is no distinction at all.

These scrappy remarks are intended to clarify the comparison we must intend when we propose that people should be equal in their overall success. We cannot carry out this comparison simply by discovering two people's own fixed preferences and then matching their situations to these preferences. That is only a comparison of their relative success. We must invite them to make (or ourselves make from their point of view) an overall rather than a relative judgment that takes fixed preferences as part of what is judged rather than the standard of assessment. If we ask them to make that assessment themselves, however, and then try to compare the assessments each makes, we may discover the following difficulty. Suppose we ask Jack and Jill each to evaluate the overall success of his or her own life, and we make plain, by a variety of distinctions, what we mean by overall success as distinct from relative success, enjoyment, how much they wish their lives to continue, and so forth. And we provide them with a set of labels, from "total failure" to "very great success" with several stops in between, from which to choose. We have no guarantee that each will use any of these labels to make the same judgment that the other makes in using the same label. Jack may use one or more of the labels with a different meaning from the meaning Jill uses, and they may be using different scales in judging the intervals between these labels. Jack might suppose, for example, that there is a vast difference between "great success" and "very great success," while Jill understands these terms to enforce only a marginal difference; so that both might use the latter label to report judgments that we, on the basis of further conversation with them, would come to believe were in fact very different judgments. This difficulty, so described, is a difficulty in translation, and I shall suppose that we could in principle conquer it, at least for speakers of our own language, by the further conversations just mentioned.

But of course all this assumes that there is indeed a single kind of overall judgment that we are asking Jack and Jill each to make (or that we propose to make from their standpoint, on their behalf) and that this judgment is in fact a judgment about the inherent value of their life and therefore different from a judgment of relative success or a judgment about how much a person wants his life to continue or how much enjoyment he finds in it. Many people are, of course, skeptical about such judgments so interpreted. If they are right, then the judgments we ask Jack and Jill to make are meaningless judgments. But then equality of overall success is itself meaningless for that reason. (Though someone might still propose, for reasons we need not explore, that people should nevertheless be equal in the character of each's illusion.) If we assume that the skeptics are wrong, however (or even that equality of illusion is the true aim), then equality of overall success must suddenly seem a peculiar goal indeed, at least in the following circumstances.

Suppose that Jack and Jill have equal resources and that they are otherwise roughly similar in every way except in respect of the beliefs I am about to mention. They are both healthy, neither handicapped, both reasonably successful in their chosen occupations, neither outstandingly accomplished or creative. They take roughly the same enjoyment from their day-to-day life. But Jack (who has been much influenced by genre painting) thinks that any ordinary life fully engaged in projects is a life of value, while Jill (perhaps because she has taken Nietzsche to heart) is much more demanding. Jack thinks, for example, that the life of a busy peasant who achieves very little and leaves nothing behind is full of value, while Jill thinks that such a life is only full of failure. If each is asked to assess the overall value of his or her own life, Jack would rate his high and Jill hers low. But there is surely no reason in that fact for transferring resources from Jack to Jill provided only that Jill would then rate her life, while still of little overall success, a bit higher.

It might seem that the difficulty this example exposes arises only from the fact that our procedures attempt to compare judgments of value reached on the basis of very different theories about what gives value to life, which is like comparing apples and oranges. Someone might object that we would do better if we asked Jack and Jill each to make comparative judgments using their own standards for each comparison, and then compared these comparative judgments in some way that would neutralize the difference in their philosophical convictions. This is, I think, a mistake, but we should explore the suggestion nevertheless. We might ask Jack, for example, to compare the value, in his eyes, of his present life with the value of the life he would have under whatever conditions of physical and mental power and whatever collection of material resources and opportunities at his disposal he would take to be ideal. Or we might ask him to compare in this way his present life with the life he would have under what he would take to be the worst conditions. We might ask him how far his life is better than the life he would have if he had no or very few resources or opportunities. We would then put the same questions to Jill. Or we might ask each a rather different sort of question, not asking them to imagine different material circumstances, but rather to compare their present lives with lives in which each would find no value at all.[1] We might ask each how far his or her life exceeded, in its value, that life. And so on. Once some one of these questions (or perhaps some weighted group of them) had been selected as for some reason especially appropriate for the purpose, equality of overall success, as a political ideal, would recommend redistribution until either the proportion or the flat amount hypothetically reported by way of answer was as close to the same in all cases as could be achieved in that way.

I should say at once that there is room for doubt, at least, whether all or possibly even any of these various questions could actually be answered, or be answered by any but the most philosophically inclined respondents. I shall set the doubts aside, however, and assume that people generally have a sufficient grasp of theories of value to be able intelligently to answer them. But of course the different comparisons the different questions prompted might, if each was harnessed to the ideal of equality of overall success, yield different recommendations for redistribution. Suppose, for example, that Jack thought his present life much better than the worst life he could imagine, but also much worse than the best life, while Jill thought her life not much better than the worst and not much worse than the best. Then the direction of redistribution would depend on which of these two comparisons was thought more important for comparing levels of overall success. Even if all the answers to all the questions we could invent pointed in the same direction for redistribution, we should still have to show that at least one of these questions was the right question to ask.

When we look more closely at the questions I listed, however, they turn out to be very much the wrong questions. Suppose Jack and Jill (who, as I imagined, are now roughly equal in resources and enjoyment and relative success in their chosen lives) do disagree radically in judgments about how much more valuable their lives would be if they had everything they could have, for example. Jack believes that with all these resources he could solve the riddle of the origin of the universe, which would be the greatest imaginable achievement for human beings, while Jill believes that riddle unsolvable and has no comparable dream in hand. So Jack believes his present life is only a small fraction as good as what it could ideally be, but Jill believes her life is not that much worse than what it could possibly be. Surely we have no reason of equality here for transferring resources from Jill to Jack (destroying their assumed equality of resources and enjoyment and relative success) even if such a transfer would cause Jack to rank his new life as having come somewhat closer to his ideal solving-the-riddle life.

Suppose that Jack considers his present life much more valuable than any life he would consider to have no value at all, while Jill thinks her life just barely better, on any flat scale of value in life, than a life she would think had absolutely no value, but that this is for the reason already suggested. Jack

considers any life fully engaged and active, with as much day-to-day enjoyment as his has, of enormous value, something to be treasured and protected and pursued. He can imagine a life about which he would be indifferent, but it is a life so impoverished that he has no trouble reporting that his
life is better than that by a very long chalk. Jill has roughly as much day-to-
day pleasure or enjoyment. She is not depressive, but rather very demanding
in her idea of what life could be deemed a really successful life. She cannot
say, when asked seriously to consider this grave question in a philosophical
mood, that she thinks her life, for all its apparent richness, is in fact a life of
much real value; she can easily imagine a life that she would believe had
absolutely no value and cannot say that she honestly thinks her life is really,
all things considered, much more valuable than that one. Once again it
seems implausible that equality demands that resources be transferred from
Jack to Jill.

   Why are all these comparative questions so plainly the wrong questions to
ask? Because we have not in fact escaped, in switching from flat questions to
comparative ones, the difficulty we found in the former. Because the differences between Jack and Jill we have noticed are still differences in their
beliefs but not differences in their lives. They are differences in their speculative fantasies about how good or bad their lives would be under very different and bizarre circumstances, or differences in their philosophical convictions about what could give great value to any life; but not, for that reason, a
difference in what their lives now are. Each of the judgments Jack or Jill
makes, in responding to the different questions we put to them, can be
considered a judgment about the value or overall success of their lives. But
they are not all the *same* judgment, and none of the judgments we have so
far described seems appropriate for a theory of equality of overall success.

   I want now to suggest a comparison of the overall success in people's lives,
very different from the comparisons suggested in all these questions, that
does seem to be connected, at least, to problems of distributional equality.
Differences in people's judgments about how well their lives are going overall are differences in their lives, rather than simply differences in their beliefs,
only when they are differences not in fantasy or conviction but in fulfillment, which is, I take it, a matter of measuring personal success or failure
against some standard of what *should* have been, not merely of what conceivably *might* have been. The important, and presently pertinent, comparison seems to me this. The more that people can reasonably regret not having
done something with their lives, the less overall success their lives have had.

"Reasonably," of course, carries much weight here. But it is all necessary. No one can reasonably regret that he has not had the life that someone with supernatural physical or mental powers, or the life span of Methuselah, would have had. So no one has a less successful life, all things considered, just because he thinks that such a life would be infinitely more valuable, in the philosophical way, than the life he has. But people can reasonably regret that they have not had the normal powers or the normal span of life that most people have. No one can reasonably regret that he has not had the life that someone with an unfairly large share of the world's resources would have led, so no one person's life is less successful than another's because the first thinks his life would be much more valuable in those circumstances while the other does not. But people can reasonably regret not having whatever share of material resources they are entitled to have.

Perhaps the point is now clear. Any proposed account of equality of overall success that does not make the idea of reasonable regret (or some similar idea) pivotal in this way is irrelevant to a sensible theory of equality in distribution. It may develop a concept of overall success useful for some purpose, but not for this purpose. But any proposed account that does make this idea pivotal must include, in its description of equality of overall success, assumptions about what a fair distribution would be, and that means that equality of overall success cannot be used to justify or constitute a theory of fair distribution. I do not mean simply that equality of success could not be applied in some cases without having an independent theory of fair distribution as a supplement for such cases. If the point were only that, then it would show only that equality of overall success could not be the whole story in a theory of distribution. The point is more striking. Equality of overall success cannot be stated as an attractive ideal at all without making the idea of reasonable regret central. But that idea requires an independent theory of fair shares of social resources (this might, for example, be the theory that everyone is entitled to an equal share of resources) which would contradict equality of overall success not in some cases only, but altogether.

Suppose someone contests this important conclusion in the following way. He concedes that the aim of equality of success, properly conceived, is to make people equal in what they have reasonably to regret. But he believes that the idea of reasonable regret can be elucidated in some way that does not require any theory of fair share of resources *other than* some version or refinement of the equal-success theory itself. He might propose the following. People cannot reasonably regret that they are not leading the life of someone with supernatural powers, or the life of a successful sadist, or a life in which they have resources such that, with those resources, they could achieve a life with less reasonably to regret than others can have with the resources then left for them. This will not do, however. We aim to make people equal in what they have reasonably to regret. Suppose (as before) that Jack and Jill have equal resources. Jack has (as we saw) grand ambitions and, though he does not believe himself entitled to anything in particular, will always regret not having more than he does. We want to know whether Jack and Jill are nevertheless equal in what they have *reasonably* to regret. On the proposed test, we must ask Jack (or ask ourselves from his point of view) how far the life he can now lead falls short of the life he would lead if he had (among other things) the amount of resources such that if he had those resources he would have the same amount reasonably to regret as others would then have. Jack cannot answer that question (nor can we). He can pick some different distribution at random—say, a distribution in which he has a million dollars more and others in the aggregate a million less. But he cannot tell whether his new-distribution life is the proper baseline against which to measure his present life without knowing whether the reasonable regret he would feel with one more million is no more than others would reasonably regret with what they could then have, and he cannot tell this without picking some *further* new distribution at random (in which, perhaps, he has two million more) against which to compute his regret at the one-million-more life. And so on into infinite regress. We cannot, of course, repair this failure (as we tried to repair other failures) by some trial-and-error device. For the problem is not that we can offer no noncircular algorithm for reaching an initial distribution to test, but rather that we can offer no method for testing any distribution however reached.[2]

I conclude that reasonable regret cannot itself figure in the distributional assumptions against which the decision whether some regret is reasonable is to be made. Nor can I think of any other conception or refinement of equality of overall success that can fill that role. If so, then the goal of making people equal in what they have reasonably to regret is self-contradictory in the way I described. I do not mean that comparisons of fulfillment—of how far different people have been able to make a success of their lives in their own eyes—have no place in discussions of equality. Many differences in overall regret—many occasions that people have properly to regret what they have not done—flow from handicaps or bad luck or weakness of will or sudden changes, too late for anything but regret, in people's perceptions of what they really take to be valuable. But it is perhaps the final evil of a genuinely unequal distribution of resources that some people have reason for regret just in the fact that they have been cheated of the chance others have had to make something valuable of their lives. The ideas of fulfillment and of reason for regret are competent to express this final argument against inequality only because they are ideas that reflect, in their assumptions, what inequality independently is.

I cannot, of course, prove that no one will invent a test or metric for overall success that will be both pertinent to equality and independent of prior assumptions about equality in distribution. For that reason I considered a fairly wide variety of suggested tests of this sort, hoping to show why I think it unlikely that one can be found. Certainly nothing that I am aware of in the present literature will do. But now suppose someone defending equality of overall success concedes that no such distribution-independent test can be found. I have been assuming that he must then concede that equality of overall success is useless as a distinct political goal because, insofar as it recommends changes from the independent distribution it assumes to be fair, it must recommend distributions it condemns as unfair. But is this too quick a conclusion?

Suppose he argues that we must distinguish between the measure and the means of achieving equality of overall success. He might suggest, for example, that a fair distribution for purposes of computing some person's present overall success is an equal distribution of resources. We compute Jack's and Jill's overall success by asking how far each regards his or her life as less successful than the best life he or she could have if resources were shared equally in society. If Jack's overall success, so measured, is greater than Jill's, we transfer resources from Jack to Jill so far as we can thus reduce the difference. It is true that Jack and Jill will not then have equal resources. Jill will have more resources than Jack. But they will be (more) equal in overall success as measured in the proper, reasonable-regret-oriented, way. There is no contradiction in using the idea of equal resources internally, within the metric for determining overall success, and then actually distributing so as to achieve equality of overall success rather than equality of resources.

But this reply misses the point. The reasonable-regret metric for determining overall success makes assumptions about what distribution is fair, about the distribution to which people are *entitled*. If that metric assumes that a fair distribution is an equal distribution of resources, and Jill is then given more than an equal share, she is given more than the theoretical argument supposedly justifying the transfer says is her fair share. Of course Jill might not complain about having more than the share of resources to which she is, by hypothesis, entitled. But Jack will complain about having less than the justification assumes he is entitled to have, and the only way to give Jill more than that share is to give Jack (or someone else) less.

V. Equality of Enjoyment

I now propose to discuss the second group of conceptions of equality of welfare that I distinguished at the outset, which take equality of welfare to consist in equal amounts or degrees of a conscious state. I shall simplify this discussion, as I said there, by taking the concept of enjoyment to stand for a particularly broad version of the conscious state or states in question. Fortunately, this discussion can be simplified in another way as well, for much of the argument I used in considering unrestricted versions of equality of success apply to unrestricted versions of equality of enjoyment as well.

People gain enjoyment, as I said, from the satisfaction of their political and impersonal preferences as well as directly and from their personal preferences, and they suffer dissatisfaction when these political and impersonal preferences are defeated. But the same considerations that argue for a restricted form of equality of success, which does not count success or failure in achieving these preferences in the calculations that theory recommends, argue for similar restrictions in equality of enjoyment. So I shall assume that equality of enjoyment, as a theory of equality in distribution, holds that resources should be distributed, so far as possible, so that people are equal in the enjoyment they take directly and from their beliefs that their personal preferences are achieved.

My first argument against this restricted version of equality of enjoyment is also modeled on the argument I used against equality of relative success. The main appeal of a restricted form of equality of enjoyment lies in the claim that it makes people equal in what they all value equally and fundamentally so far as their personal position is concerned. But that appeal cannot be sustained, because in fact people differ in the importance each attaches to enjoyment even in the widest sense that leaves that term a description of conscious states. When they are made equal in that one respect, they become unequal in other respects many value much more.

For almost everyone, pain or dissatisfaction is an evil and makes life less desirable and valuable. For almost everyone, pleasure or enjoyment of some other form is of value, and contributes to the desirability of life. Conscious states of some such form, positive and negative, figure as components of everyone's conception of the good life, but *only* as components, because almost no one pursues only enjoyment or will make any large sacrifice of something else he values to avoid a small amount of pain. And different people give even these conscious states very different weight. Two scholars, for example, may both value creative work, but one may be willing to give up more, by way of social pleasure or the enjoyments of reputation or the satisfaction that comes from completing a piece of research well done, to do work that is in fact more original.

Someone might now object that the first scholar does not value enjoyment less but rather finds it in a different source—not in the delights of society or the glow of fame but in the deeper satisfactions of the pursuit of genuine discovery. But this is plainly not necessarily or even usually so. Some of the most ambitious scholars (and artists and statesmen and athletes) set off in a direction that they predict will bring them only failure, and they know that they will find no delight or satisfaction just in the fact that they are aiming high, but only misery in how far they have fallen short. They may truly say (in the spirit of the poet whose views I described earlier) that they wish that some goal or project had not occurred to them or fallen in their path, or that they did not have the talents that made it necessary for them to pursue it, because then their lives would have been more satisfactory, more enjoyable all things considered. It perverts their report, misunderstands their complex situation, to say that they have actually found more enjoyment in the life they have led. For it is exactly their point that they have led that life in spite of, rather than for, the quality of the conscious life it has brought them.

Now of course not many people are dedicated to some ambition in that particularly strenuous way. But most of us, I think, are dedicated to something whose value to us is not exhausted or captured in the enjoyment its realization will bring, and some are dedicated to more things in that way, or more strongly dedicated, than others. Even when we do enjoy what we have or have done, we often enjoy it because we think it valuable, not vice versa. And we sometimes choose, in the same manner, though not to the same dramatic degree as the most ambitious scholar, a life that we believe will bring less enjoyment because it is in other ways a better life to lead. This is evident, I think, in a psychological fact that in some ways illustrates a different point, but is nevertheless relevant. Suppose you had a genuine choice (which, once made, you would forget) between a life in which you in fact achieved some goal important to you, though you did not realize that you had, and a different life in which you falsely believed that you had achieved that goal and therefore had the enjoyment or satisfaction flowing from that belief.[3] If you make the former choice, as many would, then you rank enjoyment, however described, as less important than something else.

Suppose someone now says, however, that equality of enjoyment is an attractive political goal, not because people all do value that state equally and fundamentally, when they decide what is important for themselves, but rather because they ought to do so. He says, not that the ambitious scholar I described really values enjoyment, but rather that he is mistaken, perhaps even irrational, because he does not. Someone making this objection, that is, abandons what I said is the immediate appeal of any conception of equality of welfare, which is that it claims to make people equal in what they value equally and fundamentally. He argues that the appeal of that political ideal is rather that it makes people equal in what they ought to value equally and fundamentally.

We have, I think, two answers. First, he is wrong in his view about what people ought to value. He is wrong in supposing either that the most valuable life is a life of maximum enjoyment, no matter how generously that conscious state is described, or that everyone ought to hold that view of what is the best life. Second, even if that theory about what people ought to value is more plausible than I think, even if it is in fact true, a political theory of equality based on that conception of the good life is an unattractive theory for a society in which many if not most people reject that conception, and some reject it as alien to their most profound beliefs about the goodness of their own lives.

We may, moreover, find a second argument against the restricted form of equality of enjoyment in the arguments we considered against equality of overall success. Though I have emphasized the error in supposing that ambitious people all take enjoyment in their strenuous lives, or pursue those lives for the sake of the enjoyment they will bring, it is nevertheless true that people of ambition often find dissatisfaction in the failure of their grand aims, and in their regret that they do not have the additional resources of talent and means that would make success more likely, whether or not they hold political theories that suppose that they are entitled to more than they have. Though this was not part of my story of Jack and Jill, we might vary that story to suppose, for example, that Jack found keen disappointment and day-to-day dissatisfaction in the fact that he did not have solving-the-riddle talents and means. But it would seem as wrong to transfer resources to him on account of that greater dissatisfaction as on account of his lower success ratio measured in that way. No one, I think, would want to aim at counting more than the dissatisfaction he found in reasonable regret. But if the arguments I offered earlier are sound, introducing the idea of reasonable regret for the sake of that limitation would introduce a different and inconsistent theory of distribution into the very statement of and justification for equality of enjoyment.

VI. Objective Theories of Welfare

The conceptions of equality of welfare thus far considered are all subjective in the following sense. They may each be enforced without asking whether a person's own consistent and informed evaluation of how far he meets the deployed standard of welfare is correct. Of course the arguments in favor of choosing one or another conception of equality of welfare may assume that people are wrong in what they take to be important, or even in what they would take to be important if fully informed of the pertinent facts. We considered, for example, the argument in favor of equality of enjoyment that people ought to value enjoyment as fundamentally important to their lives, in spite of the fact that many do not. But even if the conscious-state conception is defended in that way, it may be applied without any evaluation of the enjoyment in question. It directs officials to produce the distribution such that each person takes equal enjoyment in the life he leads, without asking whether people are right to take enjoyment in what they then would.

Equality of overall success in the form we considered it is also subjective in that way. It aims to make people equal in (as we should now say) the amount or degree by which each person could reasonably regret that he was not leading a life he would deem to be a life of greater value. That judgment is in certain ways, it is true, nonsubjective. It imposes constraints on reasonable regret that the person in question might himself reject, for example. If that person's assessment of what gives value to life changes over the course of his life, the judgment requires some amalgamation or selection among his different judgments. But the judgment does not allow the computation of someone's reasonable regret to be based on assessments of value in life that are wholly foreign to him, that he would reject even if fully informed of the ordinary facts.

I should now mention a version of equality of overall success that is more objective in just that way, however. Someone might propose that people be made equal in the amount of regret they should have about their present lives. On this revised test officials would have to ask whether someone who in fact does not value friendship, for example, and believes his life good though it is solitary and without love, and believes this in spite of the fact that he is aware of the comforts and joy that others find in friendship, is wrong. If so, then resources might be transferred to him, either directly or through special education for him about the values of friendship, on the ground that his overall success is low even though he would count it high, at least before the special education takes hold.

Now we may well object that officials have no business relying on their own judgments about what gives value to life in redistributing wealth. We might believe that such a scheme for redistribution invades autonomy or is in some other way foreign to the correct liberal principles. But we need not consider these objections, because this more objective version of equality of overall success meets the same argument we used against the more subjective version. Any pertinent test of what someone should regret about the life he is in fact leading, even on the best rather than his own theory about what gives value to life, must rely on assumptions about what resources an individual is entitled to have at his disposal in leading any life at all. So the objective version, like the subjective version, must assume an independent theory of fair distribution, and has no more power to justify giving some people more and others less than what they are entitled to have under that theory. Both versions are self-defeating insofar as they recommend any changes in a distribution independently, under some other theory of distribution, shown to be fair.

I should just mention, though very briefly, another putative conception of equality of welfare that might also be considered an objective conception. This supposes that a person's welfare consists in the resources available to him, broadly conceived, so as to include physical and mental competence, education, and opportunities as well as material resources; or, on some versions, more narrowly conceived so as to include only those that are in fact, whatever people think, most important. It holds that two people occupy the same welfare level if they are both healthy, mentally sound, well educated, and equally wealthy even though one is for some reason malcontent and even though one makes much less of these resources than the other. This is an objective theory in the sense that it refuses to accept a person's own judgment about his welfare, but rather insists that his welfare is established by at least certain kinds of basic resources at his command.

Equality of welfare, so interpreted, requires only that people be equal in the designated resources. This version of equality of welfare is therefore not different from equality of resources or at least equality in some resources. It is rather a statement of equality of resources in the (misleading) language of welfare. The abstract statement of equality of resources, of course, as I said, leaves open the question of what counts as a resource and how equality of resources is to be measured. These are the complex questions left for Chapter 2. But there is no reason to think that these questions will be easier to answer if we tack on to the ideal of equality of resources the rider that if people are equal in resources, on the correct conception of that ideal they will also be equal in some objective concept of welfare.

VII. An Ecumenical Suggestion

I must now consider what might seem a wise and ecumenical suggestion. Perhaps an attractive conception of equality of welfare can be found, not exclusively in one or another of the different conceptions we have now inspected and dismissed, but in some judicious and complex mix of these. In that case the strategy I followed in the last three sections might be the misleading and fallacious strategy of divide and conquer, rejecting each conception of equality of welfare by supposing that unless that conception tells the whole story it may be wholly ignored. Perhaps the ideal of equality of welfare may be considered fairly only by treating the different unrestricted and restricted versions of equality of success and equality of enjoyment each as strands to be considered in a complex package rather than as isolated theories.

It would be foolish to say, in advance, that no new conception of equality of welfare could be described that would make that ideal attractive. We must wait to see what new conceptions are presented. But it is perhaps not foolish to suppose that no successful conception could be formed using the conceptions we considered as components in some larger package. In any case my arguments were intended to reduce confidence in that project. I did not argue simply that no one of the versions I discussed is satisfactory on its own, or that each leads to unappealing consequences if unchecked by some other. If my arguments had been of that character, they would indeed invite the suggestion that these conceptions might be combined so as to supplement or check the shortcomings of each alone. But I meant to support a more radical criticism: that we have no reason to accept any of these versions of equality of welfare as a theory of distributional equality, even pro tanto.

It is of course desirable, in some sense at least, that people's overall success be improved, though philosophers and politicians might disagree whether the subjective or objective versions of that goal should be controlling when the two conflict. But, for reasons explained, neither version can provide other than an idle or self-defeating principle of equality in distribution. Nor, for the same reasons, can either figure as useful components in some complex package of conceptions of equality of welfare. Insofar as equality of overall success figured, even as one component among many, it would figure because some independent test of fair distribution was assumed, and it could not recommend, nor could the package overall, any deviation from that independent test.

The other conceptions of equality of welfare we considered we rejected for different reasons. We found no reason to support the idea that a community should accept the goal of making people more equal in any one of these different ways even when it could do so without damage to any of the others. If that is so then it is unlikely that it should accept the goal of making people more equal in some way that is a composite or compromise among these different ways. Combinations and trade-offs are appropriate when a set of competing goals or principles, each of which has independent appeal, cannot all be satisfied at once. They are not appropriate when no goal or principle has been shown to have independent appeal, at least as a theory of equality, at all.

VIII. Expensive Tastes

I said at the outset that equality of welfare, even as stated simply in the abstract, without specifying any of the conceptions we later distinguished, seems to produce initially troubling counterexamples. The most prominent of these is the problem of expensive tastes (a term I shall use, most often, to include expensive ambitions as well). Equality of welfare seems to recommend that those with champagne tastes, who need more income simply to achieve the same level of welfare as those with less expensive tastes, should have more income on that account. But this seems counterintuitive, and I said that someone generally attracted to the ideal would nevertheless wish to limit or qualify it so that his theory did not have that consequence. I want to return to that suggestion now, not because the problem of expensive tastes is of practical importance in politics, but for two different reasons. First, many readers initially attracted to some conception of equality of welfare may suspect that the arguments I directed against their favorite conception, in the last several sections, would have less force if a limitation or qualification suitable to exclude the expensive-tastes consequence had been built into my description of that conception. I think that this suspicion, if indeed it exists, is mistaken, but it is nevertheless worthwhile to consider, for this reason alone, whether such a limitation is in fact possible. Second, there will be readers who are left unpersuaded by my earlier arguments, but would nevertheless abandon their favorite conception of equality of welfare if they believed that it could not in fact be qualified so as to avoid that consequence.

We must be careful to distinguish, when we consider possible qualifications of any such conception, the compromise of a principle from its contradiction. A compromise reflects the weight of some independent and competing principle; a contradiction is a qualification that reflects instead the denial of the original principle itself. The question I want to press is this: Can the principle of equality of welfare be compromised (under any interpretation of what equality of welfare is) in such a way as to block the initially counterintuitive results of that principle, like the proposition that people with champagne tastes should have more resources? Or is any qualification capable of barring those results rather a contradiction that concedes the final irrelevance of the principle?

Imagine that a particular society has managed to achieve equality of welfare in some chosen conception of that ideal. Suppose also that it has achieved this through a distribution that in fact (perhaps just by coincidence) gives everyone equal wealth. Now suppose that someone (Louis) sets out deliberately to cultivate some taste or ambition he does not now have, but which will be expensive in the sense that once it has been cultivated he will not have as much welfare on the chosen conception as he had before unless he acquires more wealth. These new tastes may be tastes in food and drink: Arrow's well-known example of tastes for plovers' eggs and pre-phylloxera claret.[4] Or they may (more plausibly) be tastes for sports, such as skiing, from which one derives pleasure only after acquiring some skill; or, in the same vein, for opera; or for a life dedicated to creative art or exploring or politics. Can Louis be denied extra wealth, taken from those who acquire less expensive tastes (or simply keep those they already have), without contradicting the ideal of equality of welfare that his community has embraced?

Let us first consider how we might explain what Louis has done. No doubt people often put themselves in the way of new tastes carelessly or on whim, without considering whether they will really be better off if they acquire these tastes, or even perversely, knowing that they will be worse off. Even when they think they would be better off, they might be mistaken. But I want to suppose that Louis is not only acting deliberately rather than inadvertently, but is also acting on the basis of the kind of judgment I said people often make when they form and change their preferences. He is trying to make his life a better life in some way. This does not make his claim for extra resources any more appealing or less counterintuitive, I think. On the contrary, the fact that he is acting so deliberately in his own interests seems to make his claim, if anything, less appealing than the claim of someone who tries an expensive experience on a whim, for the pleasure of the moment, and then finds that he is hooked.

Louis will, of course, have his own ideas of what makes a life better, of where his own essential well-being lies. If his society has chosen one of the discrete conceptions of welfare, such as enjoyment or relative success, however, as the welfare in which people should be equal, then Louis cannot think that his own well-being consists in the maximum amount of welfare in that conception. If he did, his behavior would make no sense. This means that one possibly appealing description of what he has done must be wrong. Many people, first hearing this story, might assume that Louis cultivates expensive tastes in order to steal a march on others, so that it would "reward" improper efforts if he were to receive more income. But if stealing a march means acquiring more welfare than others in the chosen conception, then this is impossible. Of course someone might pretend to like plovers' eggs, though he hates them in fact, in order to gain more income, and then spend that income secretly buying more hens' eggs and thus more enjoyment than others can afford. But the problem of expensive tastes is not the problem of fraud—that problem must be handled separately in any society based on equality of welfare because someone could, after all, pretend to be crippled. If Louis sets out to acquire a taste for plovers' eggs so that, if successful, he will in fact have less welfare on the chosen conception if he does not have them, then he cannot purpose to gain some advantage in that form of welfare over others by this decision. He may of course think that he will in the end get more welfare in that conception from a dollar's worth of plovers' eggs than from a dollar's worth of hens' eggs, costly though the former are. In that case he knows that his income will be reduced if he is successful. Or he may think that he will not gain more welfare per dollar by cultivating a taste for plovers' eggs, but rather less. In that case he knows that his welfare (as always, on the chosen conception) will decline overall (though not by much in a very large community) because the total welfare that can then be produced (of which in the end he can expect only $1/n$th) will decrease. It would be absurd to think that he sets out to reduce his own welfare in order to have a larger income, either absolutely or relative to others. After all, though he may have a larger income than others, they are, by hypothesis, no worse off in the chosen conception of welfare than he is, and he is at least by some degree worse off than he would otherwise have been.

Louis does, as I said, suppose that if he cultivates his new taste his life will be better. But this is because he does not accept that the value of his life is measured just by the welfare in which his society has, for some reason, undertaken to make people equal. It is hard to see how the fact that he has this opinion can justify either the suggestion that he has acted improperly or the decision not to give him more resources but rather to leave him unequal to others in the chosen conception. The choice of that conception was society's choice, not his, and society chose that people be equal in it, not the other conception that Louis values more. After all there is no reason to think that people were equal in welfare on Louis's conception even before he developed his new taste, and he may still have less than others have of that even if he is brought back to equality in the chosen conception.

Louis thinks, as I said, that his life would be a more successful life overall—would provide less reason for regret—if he had the expensive taste or ambition even at the small cost in welfare in the chosen conception he would lose if society reestablished equality in that conception for him. Indeed he might think that his life would be more successful overall even if society did not reestablish equality for him. (People develop expensive tastes even in our own society, when they must bear the increased costs themselves.) Suppose the chosen conception is enjoyment. If Louis develops a taste for plovers' eggs, he must believe that a life of satisfying expensive tastes is a better life overall in spite of the fact that it will provide less enjoyment, and might believe it better even if it would provide much less enjoyment. These may, in fact, be plausible beliefs. Or at least they may be plausible if we substitute, for the contrived examples of plovers' eggs, the sorts of expensive tastes that people do seem to cultivate deliberately and in their own interests, such as a taste for sports that follows from developing skill, or a desire for practical power that follows taking an interest in the public weal. It is plausible to suppose that beliefs of that sort figure even in the best accounts of why people in our own economy develop the less admirable expensive tastes—champagne tastes—that figure in the usual examples. For if someone like Louis wishes to lead the life of people in *New York* magazine ads, this must be because he supposes that a life in which rare and costly goods are savored is a life better because it knows a greater variety of pleasure, or more sophisticated pleasures, or, indeed, simply pleasures that others do not know, in spite of containing less pleasure overall.

This explanation of Louis's behavior challenges the importance of the distinction we have thus far been assuming between expensive tastes that are deliberately cultivated and other aspects of personality or person, such as native desires or socially imposed tastes, that affect people's welfare. For the explanation suggests that such tastes are often cultivated in response to beliefs—beliefs about what sort of life is overall more successful—and such beliefs are not themselves cultivated or chosen. Not, that is, in any sense that provides a reason for ignoring differences in welfare caused by these beliefs in a community otherwise committed to evening out differences in welfare. I do not mean that beliefs are afflictions, like blindness, that people find that they have and are stuck with. People reason about their theories of what gives value to life in something of the same way in which they reason about other sorts of beliefs. But they do not choose that a life of service to others, for example, or a life of creative art or scholarship, or a life of exquisite flavors, be the most valuable sort of life for them to lead, and therefore do not choose that they shall believe that it is. We may still distinguish between the voluntary decision someone makes to become a person with certain tastes, or to lead the sort of life likely to have that consequence, and his discovery of tastes and ambitions that he just has. But the distinction is less important than is sometimes thought, because that decision is rarely if ever voluntary all the way down.

If Louis's society aimed to make people equal, not in one of the discrete conceptions of welfare we have thus far been assuming in his story, such as enjoyment or relative success, but in subjective overall success, then we would need a somewhat different account of why he would develop expensive tastes, and of whether it would be fair to deny him extra resources. I argued earlier that any attractive version of equality of overall success must provide a place for the idea of reasonable regret, and that this idea in turn presupposes some independent nonwelfare theory defining a fair distribution of resources. If this is right, then no one could claim extra resources for expensive tastes in a community ostensibly governed by equality of overall success. If his share of resources is fair before he cultivates his new taste, his share remains fair after he has done so. But since I want to offer independent arguments in this section, I shall assume that my earlier arguments are unsound, and that an attractive subjective version of equality of overall success can be developed that is not self-defeating in that way.

But then, since the chosen conception is now overall success, we can no longer say that Louis acts as he does because he believes his life would be more successful overall though less successful on the chosen conception. Suppose that before Louis conceived his expensive taste he was satisfied that his life was roughly as successful overall as everyone else's. He then came to believe that his life would be more valuable if he cultivated some expensive hobby, for example. We must ask what he now thinks about the value of the life he had before he formed that belief. He may think that, though his earlier life was just as good as he thought it was, and would remain so if he could not pursue his new hobby, it would be much better if he could. In that case the problem of expensive tastes does not arise. For Louis is claiming additional resources in order to have more welfare than others on the chosen conception, and he does not have even a prima facie claim to that. But he may instead have changed his beliefs about how valuable his life was. He may have read more widely, or reflected more deeply, and come to the conclusion that his former life, for all its former appeal to him, was in fact a worthless and insipid life. He wants to cultivate new and more challenging tastes to repair the defects in his life, as he now understands them. He asks only the resources necessary to make his life as valuable, in his eyes after they have been opened, as other people find their lives. How can a society committed to equality in this respect deny him these resources? It cannot say that he was wrong to continue to reflect on how best to live. An unexamined life is for that very reason a poor life. If Louis had reached his present opinions about value in life before the initial distribution, he would have received then the resources he now seeks. Why should he be refused them now, and be condemned to a life he finds less valuable than everyone else finds his?[5]

We might summarize the position we have reached in this way. If the chosen conception is one of the discrete conceptions we considered, other than overall success, then Louis is attempting to improve his welfare on some other conception he values more, while retaining equality in the chosen conception. But if the chosen conception is what really matters for equality, and if in any case others may already have more welfare in the conception Louis prefers, what ground does society have for now refusing him equality in the chosen conception? If the chosen conception is overall success (which is assumed, arguendo, not to be self-defeating), then if a claim for extra resources arises at all, it arises because Louis now believes that the earlier distribution was based on a mistake. He asks no special advantage, but only that society reach the distribution it would have reached if he had been able to see more clearly then. What ground could society have for refusing him that?

One ground perhaps suggests itself, which is the ordinary utilitarian principle that average welfare in society (which we should understand to mean welfare in the chosen conception) should be as high as possible. If society "rewards" people who develop expensive tastes by giving them extra resources with which to satisfy these tastes, then people will not be discouraged from doing so. But expensive tastes (by definition) decrease the total welfare that can be produced from a given stock of resources. So the independent principle of utility justifies a compromise with the principle of equality of welfare by recommending that people not be brought to parity of welfare if they develop expensive tastes, in order to discourage them from doing so. If the chosen conception is a discrete conception, this means that people are to be discouraged, for the sake of average utility, from bringing it about that they will need more resources to achieve the same welfare, even though they may think that their lives would be more successful if they did bring that about. If the chosen conception is overall success, judged subjectively, then people are to be discouraged from reexamining their lives in a way that might leave them dissatisfied with the value of the lives they have.

But in fact the principle of utility does not explain what needs explaining here. I can at best explain why compensating those who develop expensive tastes is inefficient. It cannot explain why the ideal of equality does not recommend doing so. It is, after all, a familiar idea in political theory that a just society will make some compromise between efficiency and distribution. It will sometimes tolerate less than perfect equality in order to improve average utility. But the compromise intuitively demanded by the problem of expensive tastes is not such a compromise between efficiency and equality. It is rather a compromise within the idea of equality. Our difficulty is not that, though we believe that equality requires us to pay Louis more because he has forced himself to like champagne, we must deny him equality in order to protect the overall stock of utility. Expensive tastes are embarrassing for the theory that equality means equality of welfare precisely because we believe that equality, considered in itself and apart from questions of efficiency, condemns rather than recommends compensating for deliberately cultivated expensive tastes.

I should also point out, parenthetically, that it is far from plain that the utilitarian principle, by itself, can even provide an explanation of what it does purport to explain, which is why a society that does wish to compromise equality for efficiency would select expensive tastes as the point of sacrifice for equality. Refusing to compensate people who develop expensive tastes will protest average utility only if it succeeds in discouraging at least some people from developing such tastes who would otherwise do so. It is impossible to predict how much of such experimentation would take place in a society dedicated to equality of welfare even without this kind of deterrence, or how effective the deterrence would be. (After all, people develop expensive tastes even in our own society when they do not receive extra resources when they do.) It is also impossible to predict the long-term consequences for utility under any particular assumptions about the success of the deterrence. Any society bent on using noncompensation as a deterrent must set a fairly articulate policy that stipulates reasonably clearly when people whose tastes and ambitions change will be compensated and when they will not be. How would the policy distinguish, for example, between tastes that are deliberately cultivated and those that simply steal up on people? What level of expense—what level of efficiency in producing enjoyment, for example, per dollar cost—would be stipulated as making a taste expensive rather than inexpensive? Beer may very well be less expensive, in this sense, than champagne, but it is also more expensive than water. Suppose the community responds to these difficulties by refusing to compensate for new tastes if people take any positive steps to acquire them or even act in a way that they should know makes their acquisition more likely, whenever these tastes are any more expensive than the tastes, if any, that they replace. If this policy succeeds in discouraging experimentation in tastes to any marked degree, then it might well end, for all we know, in a dull, conformist, unimaginative, and otherwise unattractive community, and a community with a less long-term utility as well. There are many reasons for predicting that latter consequence, but I shall mention only the two most obvious. First, some tastes that are expensive when taken up only by a few people become inexpensive—produce more utility per dollar than present tastes—when they become very popular through the example of those few. Second, a society that does become dull and conformist is a society in which no one takes much pleasure in anything, or cares very deeply about achieving the goals that have been taken mechanically from others rather than developed for himself. It is of course not plain that this policy of noncompensation tacked to a general principle of compensation for tastes acquired in a less voluntary way would have these consequences. But that is because no hypothesis about what levels of utility would be achieved by such a society, so different from our own, is worth much, which hardly recommends this explanation of why an equality of welfare society that is also utilitarian would refuse compensation.

So the supposed utilitarian justification of our intuitive conviction, that equality does not require that those who deliberately cultivate expensive tastes have equal welfare after they have done so, fails on two grounds. We still lack a justification for that conviction. But suppose someone now argues in the following way. It is true that people do not choose their beliefs about what would make their lives overall more successful. But they do choose whether and how far to act on these beliefs. Louis knows, or at least ought to know, that if he cultivates some expensive taste in a society dedicated to equality of enjoyment, for example, and is compensated, then that will decrease the enjoyment available for others. If, knowing this, he chooses the more expensive life, then he does not *deserve* compensation. He is no longer a member of the company of those who deserve equal enjoyment in their lives.

Louis has a choice. He may choose to keep the presently equal resources I said he had, and settle for a life with the enjoyment he now has but without the tastes or ambitions he proposes to cultivate. Or he may keep his present resources and settle for a life that *he* deems more successful overall than his present life, but one that contains less enjoyment. It is quite unfair that he should have a third choice, that he should be able, at the expense of others, to lead a life that is more expensive than theirs at no sacrifice of enjoyment to himself just because he would, quite naturally, consider *that* life a more successful life overall than either of the other two. The reason why Louis does not deserve compensation is not that the more expensive life he might choose is necessarily a worse life. He might be right in thinking that enjoyment is not all that matters, and that a life poorer in enjoyment may be, just from the personal standpoint, a more successful life overall. We say only that the first two choices are rightly his, but that the third is not.

I myself find this argument both powerful and appealing. It is also an important argument for the following reason. The objection to allowing Louis the third choice described is most naturally put this way. Louis should be free (at least within the limits allowed by a defensible form of paternalism) to make the best sort of life he can with his fair share of social resources. But he should not be free to trespass on the fair shares of others, because that would be unfair to them. But of course once the point is put that way it cannot stand simply as an argument for a compromise to equality of welfare tailored to the problem of expensive tastes. For the idea of fair shares cannot then mean simply shares that give people equal welfare on the chosen conception, because that is exactly the conception to which Louis appeals in asking for extra resources. If fair shares are shares fixed independently of that conception, however, then any compromise using the idea of fair shares becomes a contradiction.

Can the idea of fair shares be defined for this purpose in some way that does not make the shares that produce equal welfare in the chosen conception automatically fair shares, but nevertheless uses that conception in some way that avoids contradicting it? Suppose someone's fair share is taken to be the share that produces equal welfare in that conception, or would produce it if the person in question had not deliberately cultivated an expensive taste. This will not help, as we saw, if the chosen conception is overall success, and if Louis believes that the life he would lead if he did not cultivate new tastes would be a life of less overall success than others believe their lives to be. Even if the chosen conception is one of the discrete conceptions, such as enjoyment, defining fair shares in this way will not help. The argument I said I found powerful uses the idea of fair shares not simply to describe the limitation on equality of welfare it recommends, but also to justify that limitation. It proposes to explain why, in spite of the various objections I made earlier in this section, independent and noncontradictory considerations of fairness justify a compromise of equality of welfare. But if the definition of fair shares just assumes that the compromise in question is for some unspecified reason fair, then the appeal to fair shares can itself provide no justification that is not immediately circular. If the idea of fair shares is to do any work, then it must appeal to some independent account of fairness in distribution, and any independent account contradicts the conception to which it is attached, as I said, because it occupies all the space that conception claims for itself. I might add that I think that the most plausible independent account, which I myself had in mind when I said that the argument against Louis's third choice was powerful, is some conception of equality of resources (though of course there are others available, including, for example, the principle that resources are fairly distributed when those with more merit have more).

Perhaps ingenuity could produce some explanation or interpretation of the argument in question—that Louis does not deserve more resources just because he has chosen a more expensive life—which does not use this idea of fair shares or any similar ideas. But any such account would, I suspect, fall before the following further example. Imagine now a society newly dedicated to equality of enjoyment in which, when resources are redistributed in order to achieve equality of enjoyment, Jude has far less money than anyone else because his wants are so simple and so inexpensively satisfied. But one day (perhaps after reading Hemingway) he decides that his life, for all its richness in enjoyment, is a life of less overall success than it might be, and proposes to cultivate a new taste for some challenging sport, such as bullfighting. Suppose that after he does so he finds himself seriously frustrated by his lack of funds with which, for example, to travel to Spain, and asks for more funds through a further redistribution after which he would still, as things fall out, have less than anyone else. Do we now have any grounds for saying that he is undeserving of the increase, when we know that if it is denied he will have both fewer funds and less enjoyment than anyone else? I doubt anyone will want to say this. But if so then we cannot say that the reason Louis is undeserving of an increase is simply that the taste he has cultivated is expensive. Jude's new taste may be just as expensive. The difference is that Louis asks that more than an equal share of social resources be put at the disposal of his life while Jude asks only that something closer to an equal share be put at the disposal of his. We need the idea of fair shares (in this particular case the idea of an equal share of resources) in order to express the force of this difference.

Suppose that if Jude is given more funds and can travel to Spain he will have not merely as much as but *more* welfare than anyone else, in whatever conception has been chosen, including overall success, though he will still have much less money than anyone else. Does equality now require that he be denied the additional money? If not, then Jude's case makes an even stronger point. Not only may Jude reestablish equality of welfare in spite of the expensive taste he has deliberately cultivated. He may even succeed, by developing such a taste, in having more welfare than others. In both cases it is the idea of equality of resources that is doing the work.

I hope the moral of this long section is clear. If someone begins anxious to defend some version or conception of equality of welfare, but also wishes to resist the consequence that those who develop expensive tastes should have more, he will come, in the end, to a very different theory of equality. He will find that he must presuppose some other theory that makes his conception of equality of welfare either idle or self-defeating. That is, of course, exactly the conclusion that we reached in studying certain of these conceptions separately. It remains to consider, in the next section, whether there are strong reasons for nevertheless trying to find some small room for equality of welfare within a general and different theory of equality.

IX. Handicaps

I conceded, at the beginning, the immediate appeal of the idea that genuine equality is equality of welfare. One aspect of that immediate appeal may easily have survived the various doubts I have raised, which is apparent power of equality of welfare to explain why people with physical or mental handicaps (or with other special needs) should have extra resources. Surely (it might still be said) this is because they are able to achieve less of something that falls within the general ambit of "welfare" than others are on the same share of resources. Perhaps we care about the handicapped because they are able to achieve less enjoyment or relative or overall success, or perhaps it is some discrete combination of these, or all of them. But some tug toward equality of welfare under some interpretation must be part of our intuitions about the handicapped. If so, then this fact might be thought to show that any final theory of equality must provide at least some space for equality of welfare, though perhaps only as a supplement to or qualification of another theory of equality, if only to capture the provisions we insist on making for those who are unfortunate in this particular way.

But it is far from clear that some welfare concept is needed to explain why the handicapped should sometimes have more material resources than the healthy. In the next chapter I shall describe a different approach to the problem of handicaps which does not rely on welfare comparisons but which might explain this equally as well. There is no reason to assume, in advance of considering this and other suggestions, that only a welfare-based theory of equality can provide the account that is necessary. In fact (and moreover) a welfare-based theory can provide only a less satisfactory account than might at first appear. The argument we are now considering is that equality of welfare deserves a place, at least, in any general theory of equality, because it so accurately captures our intuitions about how the handicapped should be treated in the name of equality. But is this true? It does seem plausible to say, on any conception of welfare, that people with severe handicaps are likely, as a class, to have less welfare than others. But this is of course true only statistically. In many cases those with handicaps have in consequence less income, and therefore do not have even equal material resources with others. And some people with appalling handicaps need extra income just to survive. But many people with serious handicaps have high levels of welfare on any conception—higher than many others who are not handicapped. That is true, for example, of Tiny Tim and Scrooge. Tim is happier than Scrooge, approves the way the world is going more, is more successful in his own eyes, and so forth.

The intuition I spoke of, however, that those with handicaps should have extra resources, is not limited to those among the handicapped who do in fact have lower-than-average welfare on some conception. If Tim had as much money as Scrooge (when perhaps Tim's welfare would be greater than Scrooge's by an even larger margin) but Tim nevertheless did not have enough money to afford physiotherapy, many of us would think him entitled to extra resources for that purpose. Now of course we might believe this only because our intuitions have been schooled by the statistical fact. On this hypothesis, we feel that the handicapped as a group should have more because their welfare is as a group lower, and we then apply the general intuition to individual cases without checking to see whether the general rule holds. But I do not find that a persuasive account of why we feel as we do. If, when we know that someone handicapped is not particularly low in welfare, we still believe that he is entitled to extra resources in virtue of that handicap, then this belief is poorly explained by supposing that we have lost the power to discriminate.

So our beliefs about the handicapped are not in fact justified so accurately or powerfully by the idea of equality of welfare as to suggest that any general theory must on that account include some measure of that ideal. The lower-welfare explanation of these beliefs has further shortcomings as well. Suppose that the welfare (on any interpretation) of an entirely paralyzed but conscious person is vastly less than the welfare of anyone else in the community, that putting more and more money at his disposal would steadily increase his welfare but only by very small amounts, and that if he had at his disposal all the resources beyond those needed simply to keep the others alive he would still have vastly less welfare than they. Equality of welfare would recommend this radical transfer, that is, until the latter situation was reached. But it is not plain to me (or, I think, to others) that equality, considered just on its own, and without regard to the kinds of considerations that sometimes might be thought to override it, really does require or even recommend that radical transfer under these circumstances.

I do not claim (as this last observation recognizes) that any community that embraced equality of welfare in principle would then be committed to the radical transfer. Some other principle the community also accepted (for example the principle of utility) might recommend some compromise with equality here. But where should the line be drawn? It might, perhaps, be left to the practical politics of intuition to draw such a line. But then the victim of total paralysis might well receive nothing at all. The equality principle would in itself offer no reason for the community's accepting an initial utility loss to do him some good that would not also apply to doing him more good, at least in the circumstances I describe in which the marginal utility to him of further transfers does not much decline. The principle would offer almost no guidance to the community here, beyond a call for help equally strident over the whole range of possible transfers to this victim, a call too impractical to honor in full and too unstructured for principled compromise.

Now suppose different facts. There is an expensive piece of equipment that would enable a paraplegic to lead a much more normal life, and the community can afford that equipment at great but not crippling sacrifice to its other needs and projects. The community votes to levy a special tax to provide this machine for him. But he is an excellent and dedicated violinist, and he replies that he would rather have a superb Stradivarius, which he could purchase with the same funds. Can the community properly refuse to honor that choice?[6] On any of the conceptions of welfare we might choose, the paraplegic's welfare might in fact be increased more by owning the violin than by having the machine. Even if he knew all the facts he would prefer to have it, it would bring him more enjoyment, make his life both relatively and overall more successful in his own eyes and objectively. The independent principle of utility would recommend the same choice, of course.

But these facts would be embarrassing to a scheme that was not committed generally to equality of welfare, and allowed that ideal only a limited place in order to handle the special problem of handicaps. For consider someone else, not handicapped, who has a low level of welfare on all the same conceptions. He takes little enjoyment from his life, counts it a failure, and so forth, just because, though he has the same amount of wealth as everyone else not handicapped, that is not enough to buy the Stradivarius he covets above all else. If the paraplegic is allowed to use his extra funds to buy the violin, that other person might properly complain. The paraplegic treats the transfer, not as the occasion to remove or mitigate his handicap, but simply as an opportunity to increase his welfare in other ways, and the other violin-lover would seem to have, in his low state of welfare, as much claim to do that as the paraplegic has. But if the community denies the handicapped person that use of his extra funds, and requires him to buy the machine instead, its position seems perverse. It grants extra funds to him just on the ground that this will increase his lower-than-average welfare, and yet denies him the right to increase his welfare, with those funds, as much as he can.

X. Welfarism

If I am right in the various arguments I have made here, then equality of welfare is not so coherent or attractive an ideal as it is often taken to be. We therefore have reason to consider with some care the alternative ideal of equality of resources. But it is worth stopping now to consider very briefly whether the arguments I have made against equality of welfare might be effective against other forms of welfarism and, in particular, how far they might be effective against utilitarianism. (I am using Amartya Sen's account of welfarism as the general theory that the justice of distributions must be defined exclusively by stipulating some function of individual welfare.)[7]

The different versions of equality of welfare that we have been studying are varieties of welfarism. Utilitarianism, which calls for some maximizing function over some conception of welfare, is another, or rather, another group. Two kinds of justification are in principle available for any form of welfarism. A welfarist theory can be defended on the teleological ground that the stipulated function of the stipulated conception of welfare is something good in itself that ought to be produced for its own sake. Or it can be defended as a particular conception of equality, as a particular theory about when people are being treated as equals. The distinction between these two types of grounds is reasonably clear, I think, in the case of utilitarianism.

That theory can be supported in a direct teleological way: not only is pain bad in itself but pleasure (or some other conception of positive welfare) is good in itself, and the more there is of it, the better. Or it can be supported as a conception of equality. It is then understood as the theory that people are treated as equals when and only when their pleasures and pains (or components of some other conception of welfare) are taken into account quantitatively only, each in that sense to count as one and only one. Of course this egalitarian version of utilitarianism cannot, as the teleological version can, purport to supply all of a plausible general political or moral theory. The egalitarian utilitarian would have to explain why it is not as good to aim at maximum average misery as maximum average happiness, for example, or why there is anything to regret in a natural disaster that kills thousands though it improves the situation of a few. But he might find this explanation either in a further political principle, which holds that those who aim at others' misery or failure do not show these others the concern to which human beings, at least, are entitled, or in a distinct morality of outcomes which holds that death or pain or some other kind of suffering is bad in itself, but which uses neither the same conception nor the same metric of welfare as his egalitarian utilitarianism deploys.

The arguments we considered against equality of welfare would seem, at least on a first look, equally effective against utilitarianism when it is understood in that second way, that is, as a conception of equality. Once again we should proceed by stating different interpretations of utilitarianism composed by taking different conceptions of welfare as the maximands for a given community. And once again it will seem implausible only to take gains and losses in enjoyment, for example, or in relative success, as the measure of when people are being treated as equals, because people value welfare in these particular conceptions differently. Nor will it be helpful to take gains and losses in overall success, interpreted either subjectively or objectively, as the measure, because, as we saw, these conceptions of welfare depend on already having accepted a different, independent test of when people are being treated as equals.

These various arguments are plainly beside the point, however, when utilitarianism is supported in the first way, that is, as the teleological theory that welfare on some conception is inherently good in itself. Against that argument my claim, that people cannot be treated as equals by making them equal in some dimension they value unequally, is irrelevant, because what is then in question is only whether welfare on that conception is good in itself.

I might add that I think that the teleological ground of utilitarianism, which my arguments do not touch, is much less appealing than the egalitarian ground, which they do. It is the egalitarian ground, I think, rather than the teleological ground, that accounts for whatever appeal utilitarian arguments still have for modern politicians and lawyers.

The distinction between these two types of grounds for welfarist theories might seem less plausible when applied to forms of welfarism other than utilitarianism. But it is available at least in principle, I think, and we can construct a teleological defense of at least some conceptions of equality of welfare. Someone might say that it is simply a good thing when people have the same amount of enjoyment, for example, whether or not everyone agrees that enjoyment is fundamentally important in their own lives, or even, perhaps, whether they ought to agree that it is important in that way. The arguments I have offered do not reach equality of welfare taken to be a theory about treating people as equals. Equality of welfare, so conceived, is weaker than we might initially have thought. Is equality of resources stronger?

2

Equality of Resources

⋏

I. The Auction

In Chapter 1 we considered the claims of equality of welfare as an interpretation of treating people as equals. Here we shall consider the competing
claims of equality of resources. But we shall be occupied, for the most part,
simply in defining a suitable conception of equality of resources, and not in
defending it except as such definition provides a defense. I shall assume, for
this purpose, that equality of resources is a matter of equality in whatever
resources are owned privately by individuals. Equality of political power,
including equality of power over publicly or commonly owned resources, is
therefore treated as a different issue, reserved for discussion on another
occasion. This distinction is, of course, arbitrary on any number of grounds.
From the standpoint of any sophisticated economic theory, an individual's
command over public resources forms part of his private resources. Someone who has power to influence public decisions about the quality of the air
he or she breathes, for example, is richer than someone who does not. So an
overall theory of equality must find a means of integrating private resources
and political power.

Private ownership, moreover, is not a single, unique relationship between
a person and a material resource, but an open-textured relationship many
aspects of which must be fixed politically. So the question of what division
of resources is an equal division must to some degree include the question of
what powers someone who is assigned a resource thereby gains, and that in
turn must include the further question of his right to veto whatever changes
in those powers might be threatened through politics. Here, however, I shall
for the most part assume that the general dimensions of ownership are

sufficiently well understood that the question of what pattern of private ownership constitutes an equal division of private resources can be discussed independently of these complications.

I argue that an equal division of resources presupposes an economic market of some form, mainly as an analytical device but also, to a certain extent, as an actual political institution. That claim may seem sufficiently paradoxical to justify the following preliminary comments. The idea of a market for goods has figured in political and economic theory, since the eighteenth century, in two rather different ways. It has been celebrated, first, as a device for both defining and achieving certain communitywide goals variously described as prosperity, efficiency, and overall utility. It has been hailed, second, as a necessary condition of individual liberty, the condition under which free men and women may exercise individual initiative and choice so that their fates lie in their own hands. The market, that is, has been defended both through arguments of policy, which appeal to the overall, communitywide gains it produces, and through arguments of principle, which appeal instead to some supposed right to liberty.

But the economic market, whether defended in either or both of these ways, has during this same period come to be regarded as the enemy of equality, largely because the forms of economic market systems developed and enforced in industrial countries have permitted and indeed encouraged vast inequality in property. Both political philosophers and ordinary citizens have therefore pictured equality as the antagonist or victim of the values of efficiency and liberty supposedly served by the market, so that wise and moderate politics consists in striking some balance or trade-off between equality and these other values, either by imposing constraints on the market as an economic environment, or by replacing it, in part or altogether, with a different economic system.

I shall try to suggest, on the contrary, that the idea of an economic market, as a device for setting prices for a vast variety of goods and services, must be at the center of any attractive theoretical development of equality of resources. The main point can be shown most quickly by constructing a reasonably simple exercise in equality of resources, deliberately artificial so as to abstract from problems we shall have to face later. Suppose a number of shipwreck survivors are washed up on a desert island that has abundant resources and no native population, and any likely rescue is many years away. These immigrants accept the principle that no one is antecedently entitled to any of these resources, but that they shall instead be divided equally among them. (They do not yet realize, let us say, that it might be wise to keep some resources as owned in common by any state they might create.) They also accept (at least provisionally) the following test of an equal division of resources, which I shall call the envy test. No division of resources is an equal division if, once the division is complete, any immigrant would prefer someone else's bundle of resources to his own bundle.[1]

Now suppose some one immigrant is elected to achieve the division according to that principle. It is unlikely that he can succeed simply by physically dividing the resources of the island into n identical bundles of resources. The number of each kind of the nondivisible resources, like milking cows, might not be an exact multiple of n, and even in the case of divisible resources, like arable land, some parcels of land would be better than others, and some better for one use than for another. Suppose, however, that by a great deal of trial and error and care the divider could create n bundles of resources, each of which was somewhat different from the others but was nevertheless such that he could assign one to each immigrant and no one would in fact envy anyone else's bundle.

The distribution might still fail to satisfy the immigrants as an equal distribution, for a reason that is not caught by the envy test. Suppose (to put the point in a dramatic way) the divider achieved his result by transforming all the available resources into a very large stock of plovers' eggs and pre-phylloxera claret (either by magic or by trade with a neighboring island that enters the story only for that reason) and divides this glut into identical bundles of baskets and bottles. Many of the immigrants—let us say all but one—are delighted. But if that one hates plovers' eggs and pre-phylloxera claret he will feel that he has not been treated as an equal in the division of resources. The envy test is met—he does not prefer any one's bundle to his own—but he prefers what he would have had under some fairer treatment of the initially available resources.

A similar, though less dramatic, piece of unfairness might be produced even without magic or bizarre trades. For the combination of resources which composes each bundle the divider creates will favor some tastes over others, compared with different combinations he might have composed. That is, different sets of n bundles might be created by trial and error, each of which would pass the envy test, so that for any such set that the divider chooses, someone will prefer that he had chosen a different set, even though that person would not prefer a different bundle within that set. Trades after the initial distribution may, of course, improve that person's position. But they will be unlikely to bring him to the position he would have had under the set of bundles he would have preferred, because some others will begin with a bundle they prefer to the bundle they would have had in that set, and so will have no reason to trade to that bundle.

So the divider needs a device that will attack two distinct foci of arbitrariness and possible unfairness. The envy test cannot be satisfied by any simple mechanical division of resources. If any more complex division can be found that will satisfy it, many such might be found, so that the choice among these would be arbitrary. The same solution will by now have occurred to all readers. The divider needs some form of auction or other market procedure in order to respond to these problems. I shall describe a reasonably straightforward procedure that would seem acceptable if it could be made to work, though as I shall describe it would be impossibly expensive of time. Suppose the divider hands each of the immigrants an equal and large number of clamshells, which are sufficiently numerous and in themselves valued by no one, to use as counters in a market of the following sort. Each distinct item on the island (not including the immigrants themselves) is listed as a lot to be sold, unless someone notifies the auctioneer (as the divider has now become) of his or her desire to bid for some part of an item, including part, for example, of some piece of land, in which case that part becomes itself a distinct lot. The auctioneer then proposes a set of prices for each lot and discovers whether that set of prices clears all markets, that is, whether there is only one purchaser at that price and all lots are sold. If not, then the auctioneer adjusts his prices until he reaches a set that does clear the markets.[2] But the process does not stop then, because each of the immigrants remains free to change his bids even when an initially market-clearing set of prices is reached, or even to propose different lots. But let us suppose that in time even this leisurely process comes to an end, everyone declares himself satisfied, and goods are distributed accordingly.[3]

Now the envy test will have been met. No one will envy another's set of purchases because, by hypothesis, he could have purchased that bundle with his clamshells instead of his own bundle. Nor is the choice of sets of bundles arbitrary. Many people will be able to imagine a different set of bundles meeting the no-envy test that might have been established, but the actual set of bundles has the merit that each person played, through his purchases against an initially equal stock of counters, an equal role in determining the set of bundles actually chosen. No one is in the position of the person in our earlier example who found himself with nothing but what he hated. Of course, luck plays a certain role in determining how satisfied anyone is with the outcome, against other possibilities he might envision. If plovers' eggs and old claret were the only resources to auction, then the person who hated these would be as badly off as in our earlier example. He would be unlucky that the immigrants had not washed up on an island with more of what he wanted (though lucky, of course, that it did not have even less). But he could not complain that the division of the actual resources they found was unequal.

He might think himself lucky or unlucky in other ways as well. It would be a matter of luck, for example, how many others shared various of his tastes. If his tastes or ambitions proved relatively popular, this circumstance might work in his favor in the auction, if there were economies of scale in the production of what he wanted; or against him, if what he wanted was scarce. If the immigrants had decided to establish a regime of equality of welfare instead of equality of resources, then these various pieces of good or bad luck would be shared with others, because distribution would be based, not on any auction of the sort I described, in which luck plays this role, but on a strategy of evening out differences in whatever concept of welfare had been chosen. Equality of resources, however, offers no similar reason for correcting for the contingencies that determine how expensive or frustrating someone's preferences turn out to be.[4]

Under equality of welfare, people are meant to decide what sorts of lives they want independently of information relevant to determining how much their choices will reduce or enhance the ability of others to have what they want. That sort of information becomes relevant only at a second, political level at which administrators then gather all the choices made at the first level to see what distribution will give each of these choices equal success under some concept of welfare taken as the correct dimension of success. Under equality of resources, however, people decide what sorts of lives to pursue against a background of information about the actual cost their choices impose on other people and hence on the total stock of resources that may fairly be used by them. The information left to an independent political level under equality of welfare is therefore brought to the initial level of individual choice under equality of resources. The elements of luck in the auction just described are in fact pieces of information of a crucial sort; information that is acquired and used in that process of choice.

So the contingent facts of raw material and the distribution of tastes are not grounds on which someone might challenge a distribution as unequal.

They are rather background facts that determine what equality of resources, in these circumstances, is. Under equality of resources, no test for calculating what equality requires can be abstracted from these background facts and used to test them. The market character of the auction is not simply a convenient or ad hoc device for resolving technical problems that arise for equality of resources in very simple exercises like our desert island case. It is an institutionalized form of the process of discovery and adaptation that is at the center of the ethics of that ideal. Equality of resources supposes that the resources devoted to each person's life should be equal. That goal needs a metric. The auction proposes what the envy test in fact assumes, that the true measure of the social resources devoted to the life of one person is fixed by asking how important, in fact, that resource is for others. It insists that the cost, measured in that way, figures in each person's sense of what is rightly his and in each person's judgment of what life he should lead, given that command of justice. Anyone who insists that equality is violated by any particular profile of initial tastes, therefore, must reject equality of resources and fall back on equality of welfare.

Of course it is sovereign in this argument, and in this connection between the market and equality of resources, that people enter the market on equal terms. The desert island auction would not have avoided envy, and would have no appeal as a solution to the problem of dividing the resources equally, if the immigrants had struggled ashore with different amounts of money in their pockets, which they were free to use in the auction, or if some had stolen clamshells from others. We must not lose sight of that fact, either in the argument that follows or in any reflections on the application of that argument to contemporary economic systems. But neither should we lose sight, in our dismay over the inequities of those systems, of the important theoretical connection between the market and the concept of equality of resources.

There are, of course, other and very different sorts of objections that might be made to the use of an auction, even an equal auction of the sort I described. It might be said, for example, that the fairness of an auction supposes that the preferences people bring to the auction, or form in its course, are authentic—the true preferences of the agent rather than preferences imposed upon him by the economic system itself. Perhaps an auction of any sort, in which one person bids against another, imposes an illegitimate assumption that what is valuable in life is individual ownership of something rather than more cooperative enterprises of the community or some group within it as a whole. Insofar as this (in part mysterious) objection is pertinent here, however, it is an objection against the idea of private ownership over an extensive domain of resources, which is better considered under the title of political equality, not an objection to the claim that a market of some sort must figure in any satisfactory account of what equality in private ownership is.

II. The Project

Since the device of an equal auction seems promising as a technique for achieving an attractive interpretation of equality of resources in a simple context, like the desert island, the question arises whether it will prove useful in developing a more general account of that ideal. We should ask whether the device could be elaborated to provide a scheme for developing or testing equality of resources in a community that has a dynamic economy, with labor, investment, and trade. What structure must an auction take in such an economy—what adjustments or supplements must be made to the production and trade that would follow such an auction—in order that the results continue to satisfy our initial requirement that an equal share of the resources be available to each citizen?

Our interest in this question is threefold. First, the project provides an important test of the coherence and completeness of the idea of equality of resources. Suppose no auction or pattern of post-auction trade could be described whose results could be accepted as equality in any society much more complex or less artificial than a simple economy of consumption; or that no auction could produce equality without constraints and restrictions that violate independent principles of justice. This would tend to suggest, at least, that there is no coherent ideal of equality of resources or that the ideal is not politically attractive after all.

We might discover, on the contrary, less comprehensive gaps or defects in the idea. Suppose, for example, that the design for the auction we develop does not uniquely determine a particular distribution, even given a stipulated set of initial resources and a stipulated population with fixed interests and ambitions, but is instead capable of producing significantly different outcomes depending on the order of decisions, arbitrary choices about the composition of the initial list of options, or other contingencies. We might conclude that the ideal of equality of resources embraces a variety of distributions, each of which satisfies the ideal, and that the ideal is therefore partially indeterminate. This would show limitations on the power of the ideal to discriminate between certain distributions, but it would not for that reason show that the ideal is either incoherent or practically impotent. So it is worth trying to develop the idea of an equal auction as a test of the theoretical standing and power of the political ideal.

Second, a fully developed description of an equal auction, adequate for a more complex society, might provide a standard for judging institutions and distributions in the real world. Of course no complex, organic society would have, in its history, anything remotely comparable to an equal auction. But we can nevertheless ask, for any actual distribution, whether it falls within the class of distributions that might have been produced by such an auction over a defensible description of initial resources, or, if it does not, how far it differs from or falls short of the closest distribution within this class. The device of the auction might provide, in other words, a standard for judging how far an actual distribution, however it has been achieved, approaches equality of resources at any particular time.

Third, the device might be useful in the design of actual political institutions. Under certain (perhaps very limited) circumstances, when the conditions for an equal auction are at least roughly met, then an actual auction might be the best means of reaching or preserving equality of resources in the real world. This will be true, particularly, when the results of such an auction are antecedently indeterminate in the way just described, so that any result the auction reaches will respect equality of resources even though it is not known, in advance, which result would be reached. In such a case it may be fairer to conduct an actual auction than to choose, through some other political means, one rather than another of the results that an auction might produce. Even in such a case it will rarely be possible or desirable to conduct an actual auction in the design our theoretical investigations recommend. But it may be possible to design an auction surrogate—an economic or political institution having sufficient of the characteristics of a theoretical equal auction that the arguments of fairness recommending an actual auction were it feasible also recommend the surrogate. The economic markets of many countries can be interpreted, even as they stand, as forms of auctions. (So, too, can many forms of democratic political process.) Once we have developed a satisfactory model of an actual auction (to the extent we can) we can use that model to test these institutions, and reform them to bring them closer to the model.

Nevertheless our project is in the main, in the discussion here, entirely theoretical. Our interest is primarily in the design of an ideal, and of a device to picture that ideal and test its coherence, completeness, and appeal. We shall therefore ignore practical difficulties, like problems of gathering information, that do not impeach these theoretical goals, and also make simplifying counterfactual assumptions that do not subvert them. But we should try to notice which simplifications we are making, because they will be of importance, particularly as to the third and most practical application of our projects, at any later stage, at which we consider second-best compromises of our ideal in the real world.

III. Luck and Insurance

If the auction is successful as described, then equality of resources holds for the moment among the immigrants. But perhaps only for the moment, because if they are left alone, once the auction is completed, to produce and trade as they wish, then the envy test will shortly fail. Some may be more skillful than others at producing what others want and will trade to get. Some may like to work, or to work in a way that will produce more to trade, while others may like not to work or prefer to work at what will bring them less. Some will stay healthy while others fall sick, or lightning will strike the farms of others but avoid theirs. For any of these and dozens of other reasons some people will prefer the bundle others have in, say, five years, to their own.

We must ask whether (or rather how far) such developments are consistent with equality of resources, and I shall begin by considering the character and impact of luck on the immigrants' post-auction fortunes. I shall distinguish, at least for the moment, between two kinds of luck. Option luck is a matter of how deliberate and calculated gambles turn out—whether someone gains or loses through accepting an isolated risk he or she should have anticipated and might have declined. Brute luck is a matter of how risks fall out that are not in that sense deliberate gambles. If I buy a stock on the exchange that rises, then my option luck is good. If I am hit by a falling meteorite whose course could not have been predicted, then my bad luck is brute (even though I could have moved just before it struck if I had had any reason to know where it would strike). Obviously the difference between these two forms of luck can be represented as a matter of degree, and we may be uncertain how to describe a particular piece of bad luck. If someone develops cancer in the course of a normal life, and there is no particular decision to which we can point as a gamble risking the disease, then we will say that he has suffered brute bad luck. But if he smoked cigarettes heavily then we may prefer to say that he took an unsuccessful gamble.

Insurance, so far as it is available, provides a link between brute and option luck, because the decision to buy or reject catastrophe insurance is a calculated gamble. Of course, insurance does not erase the distinction. Someone who buys medical insurance and is hit by an unexpected meteorite still suffers brute bad luck, because he is worse off than if he had bought insurance and not needed it. But he has had better option luck than if he had not bought the insurance, because his situation is better in virtue of his not having run the gamble of refusing to insure.

Is it consistent with equality of resources that people should have different income or wealth in virtue of differing option luck? Suppose some of the immigrants plant valuable but risky crops while others play it safer, and that some of the former buy insurance against uncongenial weather while others do not. Skill will play a part in determining which of these various programs succeed, of course, and we shall consider the problems this raises later. But option luck will also play a part. Does its role threaten or invade equality of resources?

Consider, first, the differences in wealth between those who play it safe and those who gamble and succeed. Some people enjoy, while others hate, risks; but this particular difference in personality is comprehended in a more general difference between the kinds of lives that different people wish to lead. The life chosen by someone who gambles contains, as an element, the factor of risk; someone who chooses not to gamble has decided that he prefers a safer life. We have already decided that people should pay the price of the life they have decided to lead, measured in what others give up in order that they can do so. That was the point of the auction as a device to establish initial equality of resources. But the price of a safer life, measured in this way, is precisely forgoing any chance of the gains whose prospect induces others to gamble. So we have no reason to object, against the background of our earlier decisions, to a result in which those who decline to gamble have less than some of those who do not.

But we must also compare the situation of those who gamble and win with that of those who gamble and lose. We cannot say that the latter have chosen a different life and must sacrifice gains accordingly; for they have chosen the same lives as those who won. But we can say that the possibility of loss was part of the life they chose—that it was the fair price of the possibility of gain. For we might have designed our initial auction so that people could purchase (for example) lottery tickets with their clamshells. But the price of those tickets would have been some amount of other resources (fixed by the odds and the gambling preferences of others) that the shells would otherwise have bought, and which will be wholly forgone if the ticket does not win.

The same point can be made by considering the arguments for redistribution from winners to losers after the event. If winners were made to share their winnings with losers, then no one would gamble, as individuals, and the kind of life preferred by both those who in the end win and those who lose would be unavailable. Of course, it is not a good argument, against someone who urges redistribution in order to achieve equality of resources, that redistribution would make some forms of life less attractive or even impossible. For the demands of equality (we assume in this chapter) are prior to other desiderata, including variety in the kinds of life available to people. (Equality will in any case make certain kinds of lives—a life of economic and political domination of others, for example—impossible.) In the present case, however, the difference is apparent. For the effect of redistribution from winners to losers in gambles would be to deprive both of lives they prefer, which indicates, not simply that this would produce an unwanted curtailment of available forms of life, but that it would deprive them of an equal voice in the construction of lots to be auctioned, like the man who hated both plovers' eggs and claret but was confronted only with bundles of both. Winners and losers all wanted gambles to be in the mix, either originally or as represented by resources with which they can take risks later, and the chance of losing is the correct price, measured on the metric we have been using, of a life that includes gambles with a chance of gain.

We may, of course, have special reasons for forbidding certain forms of gambles. We may have paternalistic reasons for limiting how much any individual may risk, for example. We may also have reasons based in a theory of political equality for forbidding someone to gamble with his freedom or his religious or political rights. The present point is more limited. We have no general reason for forbidding gambles altogether in the bare fact that in the event winners will control more resources than losers, any more than in the fact that winners will have more than those who do not gamble. Our initial principle, that equality of resources requires that people pay the true cost of the lives they lead, warrants rather than condemns these differences.

We may (if we wish) adjust our envy test to record that conclusion. We may say that in computing the extent of someone's resources over his life, for the purpose of asking whether anyone else envies those resources, any resources gained through a successful gamble should be represented by the opportunity to take the gamble at the odds in force, and comparable adjustments made to the resources of those who have lost through gambles. The main point of this artificial construction of the envy test, however, would be to remind us that the argument in favor of allowing differences in option luck to affect income and wealth assumes that everyone has in principle the same gambles available to him. Someone who never had the opportunity to run a similar risk, and would have taken the opportunity had it been available, will still envy some of those who did have it.

Nor does the argument yet confront the case of brute bad luck. If two people lead roughly the same lives, but one goes suddenly blind, then we cannot explain the resulting differences in their incomes either by saying that one took risks that the other chose not to take, or that we could not redistribute without denying both the lives they prefer. For the accident has (we assume) nothing to do with choices in the pertinent sense. It is not necessary to the life either has chosen that he run the risk of going blind without redistribution of funds from the other. This is a fortiori so if one is born blind and the other sighted.

But the possibility of insurance provides, as I suggested, a link between the two kinds of luck. For suppose insurance against blindness is available, in the initial auction, at whatever level of coverage the policyholder chooses to buy. And also suppose that two sighted people have, at the time of the auction, equal chance of suffering an accident that will blind them, and know that they have. Now if one chooses to spend part of his initial resources for such insurance and the other does not, or if one buys more coverage than the other, then this difference will reflect their different opinions about the relative value of different forms or components of their prospective lives. It may reflect the fact that one puts more value on sight than the other; or, differently, that one would count monetary compensation for the loss of his sight as worthless in the face of such a tragedy while the other, more practical, would fix his mind on the aids and special training that such money might buy; or simply that one minds or values risk differently from the other, and would, for example, rather try for a brilliant life that would collapse under catastrophe than a life guarded at the cost of resources necessary to make it brilliant.

But in any case the bare idea of equality of resources, apart from any paternalistic additions, would not argue for redistribution from the person who had insured to the person who had not if, horribly, they were both blinded in the same accident. For the availability of insurance would mean that, though both had had brute bad luck, the difference between them was a matter of option luck, and the arguments we entertained against disturbing the results of option luck under conditions of equal antecedent risk hold here as well. But then the situation cannot be different if the person who decided not to insure is the only one to be blinded. For once again the difference is a difference in option luck against a background of equal opportunity to insure or not. If neither had been blinded, the man who had insured against blindness would have been the loser. His option luck would have been bad—though it seems bizarre to put it this way—because he spent resources that, as things turned out, would have been better spent otherwise. But he would have no claim, in that event, from the man who did not insure and also survived unhurt.

So if the condition just stated were met—if everyone had an equal risk of suffering some catastrophe that would leave him or her handicapped, and everyone knew roughly what the odds were and had ample opportunity to insure—then handicaps would pose no special problem for equality of resources. But of course that condition is not met. Some people are born with handicaps, or develop them before they have either sufficient knowledge or funds to insure on their own behalf. They cannot buy insurance after the event. Even handicaps that develop later in life, against which people do have the opportunity to insure, are not randomly distributed through the population, but follow genetic tracks, so that sophisticated insurers would charge some people higher premiums for the same coverage before the event. Nevertheless the idea of a market in insurance provides a counterfactual guide through which equality of resources might face the problem of handicaps in the real world.

Suppose we can make sense of and even give a rough answer to the following question. If (contrary to fact) everyone had at the appropriate age the same risk of developing physical or mental handicaps in the future (which assumes that no one has developed these yet) but the total number of handicaps remained what it is, how much insurance coverage against these handicaps would the average member of the community purchase? We might then say that but for (uninsurable) brute luck that has altered these equal odds, the average person would have purchased insurance at that level, and compensate those who do develop handicaps accordingly, out of some fund collected by taxation or other compulsory process but designed to match the fund that would have been provided through premiums if the odds had been equal. Those who develop handicaps will then have more resources at their command than others, but the extent of their extra resources will be fixed by the market decisions that people would supposedly have made if circumstances had been more equal than they are. Of course, this argument does involve the fictitious assumption that everyone who suffers handicaps would have bought the average amount of insurance, and we may wish to refine the argument and the strategy so that no longer holds.[5] But it does not seem an unreasonable assumption for this purpose as it stands.

Can we answer the counterfactual question with sufficient confidence to develop a program of compensation of that sort? We face a threshold difficulty of some importance. People can decide how much of their resources to devote to insurance against a particular catastrophe only with some idea of the life they hope to lead, because only then can they decide how serious a particular catastrophe would be, how far additional resources would alleviate the tragedy, and so forth. But people who are born with a particular handicap or who develop one in childhood will of course take that circumstance into account in the plans they make. So in order to decide how much insurance such a person would have bought without the handicap we must decide what sort of life he would have planned in that case. But there may be no answer, even in principle, to that question.

We do not need, however, to make counterfactual judgments that are so personalized as to embarrass us for that reason. Even if people did all have equal risk of all catastrophes, and evaluated the value and importance of insurance differently entirely as a result of their different ambitions and plans, the insurance market would nevertheless be structured through categories designating the risks against which most people would insure in a general way. After all, risks of most catastrophes are now regarded by the actual insurance market as randomly distributed, and so we might follow actual insurance practice, modified to remove the discriminations insurers make when they know that one group is more likely, perhaps for genetic reasons, to suffer a particular kind of brute bad luck. It would make sense to suppose, for example, that most people would make roughly the same assessment of the value of insurance against general handicaps, such as blindness or the loss of a limb, that affect a wide spectrum of different sorts of lives. (We might look to the actual market to discover the likelihood and the contours of more specialized insurance we might decide to use in more complex schemes, like the insurance of musicians against damage to their hands.)

We would, in any case, pay great attention to matters of technology, and be ready to adjust our sums as technology changed. People purchase insurance against catastrophes, for example, against a background of assumptions about the remedial medical technology, or special training, or mechanical aids that are in fact available, and about the cost of these remedies. People would seek insurance at a higher level against blindness, for example, if the increased recovery would enable them to purchase a newly discovered sight-substitute technology, than they would if that increased recovery simply swelled a bank account they could not, in any case, use with much satisfaction.

Of course, any judgments that the officials of a community might make about the structure of the hypothetical insurance market would be speculative and open to a variety of objections. But there is no reason to think, certainly in advance, that a practice of compensating the handicapped on the basis of such speculation would be worse, in principle, than the alternatives, and it would have the merit of aiming in the direction of the theoretical solution most congenial to equality of resources.

We might now remind ourselves of what these alternatives are. I said in Chapter 1 that the regime of equality of welfare, contrary to initial impressions, does a poor job of either explaining or guiding our impulse to compensate the severely handicapped with extra resources. It provides, in particular, no upper bound to compensation so long as any further payment would improve the welfare of the wretched; but this is not, as it might seem, generous, because it leaves the standard for actual compensation to the politics of selfishness broken by sympathy, politics that we know will supply less than any defensible hypothetical insurance market would offer.

Consider another approach to the problem of handicaps under equality of resources. Suppose we say that any person's physical and mental powers must count as part of his resources, so that someone who is born handicapped starts with less by way of resources than others have, and should be allowed to catch up, by way of transfer payments, before what remains is auctioned off in any equal market. People's powers are indeed resources, because these are used, together with material resources, in making something valuable out of one's life. Physical powers are resources for that purpose in the way that aspects of one's personality, like one's conception of what is valuable in life, are not. Nevertheless the suggestion, that a design of equality of resources should provide for an initial compensation to alleviate differences in physical or mental resources, is troublesome in a variety of ways. It requires, for example, some standard of "normal" powers to serve as the benchmark for compensation.[6] But whose powers should be taken as normal for this purpose? It suffers, moreover, from the same defect as the parallel recommendation under equality of welfare. In fact, no amount of initial compensation could make someone born blind or mentally incompetent equal in physical or mental resources with someone taken to be "normal" in these ways. So the argument provides no upper bound to initial compensation, but must leave this to a political compromise likely to be less generous, again, than what the hypothetical insurance market would command.

Quite apart from these practical and theoretical inadequacies, the suggestion is troublesome for another reason. Though powers are resources, they should not be considered resources whose ownership is to be determined through politics in accordance with some interpretation of equality of resources. They are not, that is, resources for the theory of equality in exactly the sense in which ordinary material resources are. They cannot be manipulated or transferred, even so far as technology might permit. So in this way it misdescribes the problem of handicaps to say that equality of resources must strive to make people equal in physical and mental constitution so far as this is possible. The problem is, rather, one of determining how far the ownership of independent material resources should be affected by differences that exist in physical and mental powers, and the response of our theory should speak in that vocabulary.

It might be wise (if for no other reason than as a convenient summary of the argument from time to time) to bring our story of the immigrants up to date. By way of supplement to the auction, they now establish a hypothetical insurance market that they effectuate through compulsory insurance at a fixed premium for everyone on the basis of speculations about what the average immigrant would have purchased by way of insurance had antecedent risk of various handicaps been equal. (We choose for them, that is, one of the simpler possible forms of instituting the hypothetical insurance market. We shall see, when we discuss the problem of skills, that they might well choose a more complex scheme of the sort discussed there.)

But now a question arises. Does this decision place too much weight on the distinction between handicaps, which the immigrants treat in this compensatory way, and on accidents touching preferences and ambitions (like the accidents of what material resources are in fact available and of how many other people share a particular person's taste)? The latter will also affect welfare, but they are not matters for compensation under our scheme. Would it not now be fair to treat as handicaps eccentric tastes, or tastes that are expensive or impossible to satisfy because of scarcity of some good that might have been common? We might compensate those who have these tastes by supposing that everyone had an equal chance of being in that position and then establishing a hypothetical insurance market against that possibility.

A short answer is available. Someone who is born with a serious handicap faces his life with what we concede to be fewer resources, just on that account, than others do. This circumstance justifies compensation, under a scheme devoted to equality of resources, and though the hypothetical insurance market does not right the balance—nothing can—it seeks to remedy one aspect of the resulting unfairness. But we cannot say that the person whose tastes are expensive, for whatever reason, therefore has fewer resources at his command. For we cannot state (without falling back on some version of equality of welfare) what equality in the distribution of tastes and preferences would be. Why is there less equality of resources when someone has an eccentric taste that makes goods cheaper for others, than when he shares a popular taste and so makes goods more expensive for them? The auction, bringing to bear information about the resources that actually exist and the competing preferences actually in play, is the only true measure of whether any particular person commands equal resources. If the auction has in fact been an equal auction, then the man of eccentric tastes has no less than equal material resources, and the argument that justifies a compensatory hypothetical auction in the case of handicaps has no occasion even to begin. It is true that this argument produces a certain view of the distinction between a person and his circumstances, and assigns his tastes and ambitions to his person, and his physical and mental powers to his circumstances. That is the view of a person I sketched in the introductory section, of someone who forms his ambitions with a sense of their cost to others against some presumed initial equality of economic power, and though this is different from the picture assumed by equality of welfare, it is a picture at the center of equality of resources.

In one way, however, my argument might well be thought to overstate the distinction between handicaps and at least certain sorts of what are often considered preferences. Suppose someone finds he has a craving (or obsession or lust or, in the words of an earlier psychology, a "drive") that he wishes he did not have, because it interferes with what he wants to do with his life and offers him frustration or even pain if it is not satisfied. This might indeed be some feature of his physical needs that other people would not consider a handicap at all: for example, a generous appetite for sex. But it is a "preference" (if that is the right word) that he does not want, and it makes perfect sense to say that he would be better off without it. For some people these unwanted tastes include tastes they have (perhaps unwittingly) themselves cultivated, such as a taste for a particular sport or for music of a sort difficult to obtain. They regret that they have these tastes, and believe they would be better off without them, but nevertheless find it painful to ignore them. These tastes are handicaps; though for other people they are rather an essential part of what gives value to their lives.

Now these cases do not present, for particular people, borderline cases between ambitions and handicaps (though no doubt other sorts of borderline cases could be found). The distinction required by equality of resources is the distinction between those beliefs and attitudes that define what a successful life would be like, which the ideal assigns to the person, and those features of body or mind or personality which provide means or impediments to that success, which the ideal assigns to the person's circumstances. Those who see their sexual desires or their taste for opera as unwanted disadvantages will class these features of their body or mind or personality firmly as the latter. These are, for them, handicaps, and are therefore suitable for the regime proposed for handicaps generally. We may imagine that everyone has an equal chance of acquiring such a craving by accident. (Of course, for each person the content of a craving that would have that consequence would be different. We are supposing here, not the risk of any particular craving, but the risk of whatever craving would interfere with set goals in that way.) We may then ask—with as much or as little intelligibility as in the case of blindness—whether people generally would purchase insurance against that risk, and if so at what premium and what level of coverage. It seems unlikely that many people would purchase such insurance, at the rates of premium likely to govern if they sought it, except in the case of cravings so severe and disabling as to fall under the category of mental disease. But that is a different matter. The important point, presently, is that the idea of an insurance market is available here, because we can imagine people who have such a craving not having it, without thereby imagining them to have a different conception of what they want from life than what in fact they do want. So the idea of the imaginary insurance auction provides at once a device for identifying cravings and distinguishing them from positive features of personality, and also for bringing these cravings within the general regime designed for handicaps.

IV. Labor and Wages

Equality of resources, once established by the auction, and corrected to provide for handicaps, would be disturbed by production and trade. If one of the immigrants, for example, was specially proficient at producing tomatoes, he might trade his surplus for more than anyone else could acquire, in which case others would begin to envy his bundle of resources. Suppose we wished to create a society in which the division of resources would be continuously equal, in spite of different kinds and degrees of production and trade. Can we adapt our auction so as to produce such a society?

We should begin by considering a different sequence after which people would envy each other's resources, and the division might be thought no longer to be equal. Suppose all the immigrants are in fact sufficiently equal in talent at the few modes of production that the resources allow each to produce roughly the same goods from the same set of resources. Nevertheless they wish to lead their lives in different ways, and they in fact acquire different bundles of resources in the initial auction and use them differently thereafter. Adrian chooses resources and works them with the single-minded ambition of producing as much of what others value as possible; and so, at the end of a year, his total stock of goods is larger than anyone else's. Each of the other immigrants would now prefer Adrian's stock to his own; but by hypothesis none of them would have been willing to lead his life so as to produce them. If we look for envy at particular points in time, then each envies Adrian's resources at the end of the year, and the division is therefore not equal. But if we look at envy differently, as a matter of resources over an entire life, and we include a person's occupation as part of the bundle of his goods, then no one envies Adrian's bundle, and the distribution cannot be said to be unequal on that account.

Surely we should take the second, synoptic, point of view. Our final aim is that an equal share of resources be devoted to the lives of each person, and we have chosen the auction as the right way to measure the value of what is made available to a person, through his decision, for that purpose. If Bruce chooses to acquire land for use as a tennis court, then the question is raised how much his account should be charged, in the reckoning whether an equal share has been put to his use, in virtue of that choice, and it is right that his account should be charged the amount that others would have been willing to pay had the land been devoted to their purposes instead. The appeal of the auction, as a device for picturing equality of resources, is precisely that it enforces that metric. But this scheme will fail, and the device disappoint us, unless Adrian is able to bid a price for the same land that reflects his intention to work rather than play on it and so to acquire whatever gain would prompt him to make that decision. Otherwise those who want tomatoes and would pay Adrian his price for them will not be able to bid indirectly, through Adrian's decision, against Bruce, who will then secure his tennis court at a price that, because it is too low, defeats equality of resources. This is not, I should add, an argument from efficiency as distinct from fairness, but rather an argument that in the circumstances described, in which talents are equal, efficiency simply is fairness, at least as fairness is conceived under equality of resources. If Adrian is willing to spend his life at drudgery, in return for the profit he will make at prices that others will pay for what he produces, then the land on which he would drudge should not be used for a tennis court instead, unless its value as a tennis court is greater as measured by someone's willingness to invade an initially equal stock of abstract resources.

Now this is to look at the matter entirely from the standpoint of those who want Adrian's tomatoes, a standpoint that treats Adrian only as a means. But we reach the same conclusion if we look at the matter from his point of view as well. If someone chooses to have something inexpensive in his life, under a regime of equality of resources, then he will have more left over for the rest of what he wants. Someone who accepts Algerian wine may use it to wash down plovers' eggs. But a decision to produce one thing rather than another with land, or to use the land for leisure rather than production, is also the choice of something for one's life, and this may be inexpensive as well. Suppose Adrian is desperate for plovers' eggs but would rather work hard at tilling his land than settle for less than champagne. The total may be no more expensive, measured in terms of what his decisions cost others, than a life of leisure and grape juice. If he earns enough by working hard, or by working at work that no one else wants to do, to satisfy all his expensive tastes, then his choice for his own life costs the rest of the community no more than if his tastes were simpler and his industry less. So we have no more reason to deny him hard work and high consumption than to deny him less work and frugality. The choice should be indifferent under equality of resources, so long as no one envies the total package of work plus consumption that he chooses—so long as no one envies, that is, his life as a whole. Of course, Adrian might actually enjoy his hard work, so that he makes no sacrifice. He prefers working hard to anything else. But his preference cannot provide any argument, under equality of resources, that he should gain less in money or other goods by his work than if he hated every minute of it, any more than it argues against charging someone a low price for lettuce, which he actually prefers to truffles.

So we must apply the envy test diachronically: it requires that no one envy the bundle of occupation and resources at the disposal of anyone else over time, though someone may envy another's bundle at any particular time. It would therefore violate equality of resources if the community were to redistribute Adrian's wealth, say, at the end of each year. If everyone had equal talents (as we have been assuming just now), the initial auction would produce continuing equality of resources even though bank-account wealth became more and more unequal as years passed.

Is that unlikely condition—that everyone has equal talent—absolutely necessary to that conclusion? Would the auction produce continuing equality of resources if (as in the real world) talents for producing differed sharply from person to person? Now the envy test would fail, even interpreted diachronically. Claude (who likes farming but has a black thumb) would not bid enough for farming land to take that land from Adrian; or, if he did, he would have to settle for less in the rest of his life. But he would then envy the package of Adrian's occupation and wealth. If we interpret occupation in a manner sensitive to the joys of craft, then Adrian's occupation, which must then be described as skillful, craftsmanlike farming, is simply unavailable to Claude. If we interpret occupation in a more censuslike fashion, then Claude may undertake Adrian's occupation, but he cannot have the further resources that Adrian has along with it. So if we continue to insist that the envy test is a necessary condition of equality of resources, then our initial auction will not insure continuing equality, in the real world of unequal talents for production.

But it may now be objected that we should not insist on the envy test at this point, even in principle, for the following reason. We are moving too close to the goal that people must not envy each other, which is different from the requirement that they must not envy one another's bundles of resources. People may envy each other for a variety of reasons: some are physically more attractive, some more easily satisfied with their condition, some better liked by others, some more intelligent or able in different ways, and so on. Of course, under a regime of equality of welfare each of these differences would be taken into account, and transfers made to erase their welfare consequences so far as possible or feasible. But the point of equality of resources is fundamentally different: it is that people should have the same external resources at their command to make of them what, given these various features and talents, they can. That point is satisfied by an initial auction, but since people are different it is neither necessary nor desirable that resources should remain equal thereafter, and quite impossible that all envy should be eliminated by political distribution. If one person, by dint of superior effort or talent, uses his equal share to create more than another, he is entitled to profit thereby, because his gain is not made at the expense of someone else who does less with his share. We recognized that, just now, when we conceded that superior industry should be rewarded, so that Adrian, who worked hard, should be allowed to keep the rewards of his effort.

Now this objection harbors many mistakes, but they all come to this: it confuses equality of resources with the fundamentally different idea sometimes called equality of opportunity. It is not true, in the first place, that someone who does more with his initial share does not, in so doing, lessen the value of what others have. If Adrian were not so successful at agriculture, then Claude's own efforts would be rewarded more, because people would buy his inferior produce having no better alternative. If Adrian were not so successful and hence so rich he would not be able to pay so much for wine, and Claude, with his smaller fortune, would be able to buy more at a lower price. These are simply the most obvious consequences of the fact that the immigrants form one economy, after the initial auction, rather than a set of distinct economies. Of course these consequences also follow from the situation we discussed a moment ago. If Adrian and Bruce have the same talents, but Adrian chooses to work harder or differently and acquires more money, then this circumstance may also decrease the value of Claude's share to him. The difference between these two circumstances, if there is one, lies elsewhere; but it is important to reject the claim, instinct in some arguments for equality of opportunity, that if people start with equal shares the prosperity of one does no damage to the other.

Nor is it true that if we aim at a result in which those with less talent do not envy the circumstances of those with more talent we have destroyed the distinction between envying others and envying what they have. For Adrian has two things that Claude would prefer to have which belong to Adrian's circumstances rather than his person. The desires and needs of other people provide Adrian but not Claude with a satisfying occupation, and Adrian has more money than Claude can have. Perhaps nothing that can be done, by way of political structure or distribution, to erase these differences and remove the envy entirely. We cannot, for example, alter the tastes of other people by electrical means so as to make them value more what Claude can produce and value less what Adrian can produce. But the fact that we could not and should not do this provides no argument against other schemes, such as schemes of education that would allow Claude to find satisfaction in his work or of taxation that would redistribute some of Adrian's wealth to him, and we could fairly describe these schemes as aiming to remove Claude's envy of what Adrian has rather than his envy of what Adrian is.

Important as these points are, it is more important still to identify and correct another mistake that the present objection makes. It misunderstands our earlier conclusion, that when talents are roughly equal the auction provides continuing equality of resources, and so misses the important distinction between that case and the present argument. The objection supposes that we reached that conclusion because we accept, as the basis of equality of resources, what we might call the starting-gate theory of fairness: that if people start in the same circumstances and do not cheat or steal from one another, then it is fair that people keep what they gain through their own skill. But the starting-gate theory of fairness is very far from equality of resources. Indeed it is hardly a coherent political theory at all.

The starting-gate theory holds that justice requires equal initial resources. But it also holds that justice requires laissez-faire thereafter, in accordance, presumably, with some version of the Lockean theory that people acquire property by mixing their labor with goods or something of that sort. But these two principles cannot live comfortably together. Equality can have no greater force in justifying initial equal holdings when the immigrants land— against the competing view that all property should be available for Lockean acquisition at that time—than later in justifying redistributions when wealth becomes unequal because people's productive talents are different. The same point may be put the other way around. The theory of Lockean acquisition (or whatever other theory of justice in acquisition is supposed to justify the laissez-faire component in a starting-gate theory) can have no less force in governing the initial distribution than it has in justifying title through talent and effort later. If the theory is sound later, then why does it not command a Lockean process of acquisition in the first instance, rather than an equal distribution of all there is? The moment when the immigrants first land is, after all, an arbitrary point in their lives at which to locate any one-shot requirement that they each have an equal share of any available resources. If that requirement holds then, it must also hold on the tenth anniversary of that date, which is, in the words of the banal and important cliché, the first day in the rest of their lives. So if justice requires an equal auction when they land, it must require a fresh, equal auction from time to time thereafter; and if justice requires laissez-faire thereafter, it must require it when they land.

Suppose someone replies that there is an important difference between the initial distribution of resources and any later redistribution. When the immigrants land, no one owns any of the resources, and the principle of equality therefore dictates equal initial shares. But later, after the initial resources have been auctioned, they are each owned in some way by someone, so that the principle of equality is superseded by respect for people's rights in property or something of that sort. This reply begs the question straightway. For we are considering precisely whether a system of ownership should be established in the first instance that has that consequence, or whether a different system of ownership should be chosen that explicitly makes any acquisition subject to schemes of redistribution later. If the latter sort of system is chosen at the outset, then no one can later complain that redistribution is ruled out by his property rights alone. I do not mean that no theory of justice can consistently distinguish between justice in initial acquisition and justice in transfer on the ground that anyone may do what he wants with property that is already his. Robert Nozick's theory, for example, does just that.[7] This is consistent, because his theory of justice in initial acquisition purports to justify a system of property rights which have that consequence: justice in transfer, that is, flows from the rights that the theory of acquisition claims are acquired in acquiring property. But the theory of initial acquisition on which the starting-gate theory relies, which is equality of resources, does not even purport to justify a characterization of property that necessarily includes absolute control without limit of time thereafter.

So the starting-gate theory, that the immigrants should start off equal in resources but grow prosperous or lean through their own efforts thereafter, is an indefensible combination of very different theories of justice. Something like that combination makes sense in games, such as Monopoly, whose point is to allow luck and skill to play a highly circumscribed and, in the last analysis, arbitrary role; but it cannot hold together a political theory. Our own principle, that if people of equal talent choose different lives it is unfair to redistribute halfway through those lives, makes no appeal to the starting-gate theory. It is based on the very different idea that the equality in question is equality of resources devoted to whole lives. This principle offers a clear answer to the question that embarrasses the present objection. Our theory does not suppose that an equal division of resources is appropriate at one moment in someone's life but not at any other. It argues only that resources available to him at any moment must be a function of resources available or consumed by him at others, so that the explanation of why someone has less money now may be that he has consumed expensive leisure earlier. Nothing like that explanation is available to explain why Claude, who has worked as hard and in the same way as Adrian, should have less in virtue of the fact that he is less skillful.

So we must reject the starting-gate theory and recognize that the requirements of equality (in the real world at least) pull in opposite directions. On the one hand we must, on pain of violating equality, allow the distribution of resources at any particular moment to be (as we might say) ambition-sensitive. It must, that is, reflect the cost or benefit to others of the choices people make so that, for example, those who choose to invest rather than consume, or to consume less expensively rather than more, or to work in more rather than less profitable ways must be permitted to retain the gains that flow from these decisions in an equal auction followed by free trade. But on the other hand, we must not allow the distribution of resources at any moment to be endowment-sensitive, that is, to be affected by differences in ability of the sort that produce income differences in a laissez-faire economy among people with the same ambitions. Can we devise some formula that offers a practical, or even a theoretical, compromise between these two apparently competing requirements?

We might mention, but only to dismiss, one possible response. Suppose we allow our initial auction to include, as resources to be auctioned, the labor of the immigrants themselves, so that each immigrant can bid for the right to control part or all of his own or other people's labor. Special skills would accrue to the benefit, not of the laborer himself, but of the community as a whole, like any other valuable resource the immigrants found when they landed. Except in unusual cases, since people begin with equal resources for bidding, each agent would bid enough to secure his own labor. But the result would be that each would have to spend his life in close to the commercially most profitable manner he could or, at least if he is talented, suffer some very serious deprivation if he did not. For since Adrian, for example, is able to produce prodigious income from farming, others would be willing to bid a large amount to have the right to his labor and the vegetables thereof, and if he outbids them, but chooses to write indifferent poetry instead of farming full-time, he will have spent a large part of his initial endowment on a right that will bring him little financial benefit. That is indeed the slavery of the talented.

We cannot permit this, but it is worth pausing to ask what grounds we have for barring it. Shall we say that since a person owns his own mind and body, he owns the talents that are only capacities thereof, and therefore owns the fruit of those talents? This is, of course, a series of non sequiturs. It is also a familiar argument in favor of the laissez-faire labor market we have decided is a violation of equality of resources when people are unequal in talent. But we could not accept it in any case, because it uses the idea of prepolitical entitlement based on something other than equality, and that is inconsistent with the premise of the scheme of equality of resources we have developed.

So we must look elsewhere for the ground of our objection to taking people's labor as a resource for the auction. We need not, in fact, look very far; for the principle that people should not be penalized for talent is simply part of the same principle we relied on in rejecting the apparently opposite idea, that people should be allowed to retain the benefits of superior talent. The envy test forbids both of these results. If Adrian is treated as owning whatever his talents enable him to produce, then Claude envies the package of resources, including occupation, that Adrian has over his life considered as a whole. But if Adrian is required to purchase leisure time or the right to a less productive occupation at the cost of other resources, then Adrian will envy Claude's package. If equality of resources is understood to include some plausible version of the envy test as a necessary condition of an equal distribution, then the role of talent must be neutralized in a way that no simple addition to the stock of goods to be auctioned can accomplish.

We should turn, therefore, to a more familiar idea: the periodic redistribution of resources through some form of income tax.[8] We want to develop a scheme of redistribution, so far as we are able, that will neutralize the effects of differential talents, yet preserve the consequences of one person's choosing an occupation, in response to his sense of what he wants to do with his life, that is more expensive for the community than the choice another makes. An income tax is a plausible device for this purpose because it leaves intact the possibility of choosing a life in which sacrifices are constantly made and discipline steadily imposed for the sake of financial success and the further resources it brings, though of course it neither endorses nor condemns that choice. But it also acknowledges the role of genetic luck in such a life. The accommodation it makes is a compromise; but it is a compromise of two requirements of equality, in the face of both practical and conceptual uncertainty how to satisfy these requirements, not a compromise of equality for the sake of some independent value such as efficiency.

But of course the appeal of a tax depends on our ability to fix rates of taxation that will make that compromise accurately. It might be helpful, in that aim, if we were able to find some way of identifying, in any person's wealth at any particular time, the component traceable to differential talents as distinguished from differential ambitions. We might then try to devise a tax that would recapture, for redistribution, just this component. But we cannot hope to identify such a component, even given perfect information about people's personalities. For we will be thwarted by the reciprocal influence that talents and ambitions exercise on each other. Talents are nurtured and developed, not discovered full-blown, and people choose which talents to develop in response to their beliefs about what sort of person it is best to be. But people also wish to develop and use the talents they have, not simply because they prefer a life of relative success, but because the exercise of talent is enjoyable and perhaps also out of a sense that an unused talent is a waste. Someone with a good eye or a skilled hand conceives a picture of what would make his life valuable that someone more clumsy would not.

So we cannot hope to fix the rates of our income tax so as to redistribute exactly that part of each person's income that is attributable to his talent as distinguished from his ambitions. Talents and ambitions are too closely intertwined. Can we do better by proceeding on a slightly different tack? Can we aim to fix rates so as to leave each person with the income he would have had if, counterfactually, all talents for production had been equal? No, because it is impossible to say, in any relevant way, what sort of world that would be. We should have to decide what sort and level of talent everyone would have equally, and then what income people exploiting those talents to different degrees of effort would reach. Should we stipulate that in that world everyone would have the talents that the most talented people in the real world now have? Do we mean, by "the most talented people," the people who are able to earn the most money in the actual world if they work single-mindedly for money? But in a world in which everyone could hit a high inside pitch or play sexy roles in films with equal authority, there would probably be no baseball or films; in any case no one would be paid much for exercising such talents. Nor would any other description of the talents everyone would be supposed to have in equal degree be any more help.

But though this crude counterfactual exercise must fail, it suggests a more promising exercise. Let us review our situation. We want to find some way to distinguish fair from unfair differences in wealth generated by differences in occupation. Unfair differences are those traceable to genetic luck, to talents that make some people prosperous but are denied to others who would exploit them to the full if they had them. But if this is right, then the problem of differential talents is in certain ways like the problem of handicaps we have already considered.

V. Underemployment Insurance

Though skills are different from handicaps, the difference can be understood as one of degree: we may say that someone who cannot play basketball like Wilt Chamberlain, paint like Piero, or make money like Geneen, suffers from an (especially common) handicap. This description emphasizes one aspect of skills, which is their genetic and, hence, luck component, at the expense of hiding the more intimate and reciprocal play we noticed between skills and ambitions. But it also points to one theoretical solution to the problem of identifying at least the minimum requirements of a fair redistribution policy responding to differences in skill. We may capitalize on the similarities between handicaps and relative lack of skill to propose that the level of compensation for the latter be fixed, in principle, by asking how much insurance someone would have bought, in an insurance subauction with initially equal resources, against the possibility of not having a particular level of some skill.

Of course, there is no actual insurance market against lack of what we ordinarily take to be skill, as there is an insurance market against catastrophes that result in handicap. For one thing, a person's level of skills is sufficiently fixed and known, at least roughly, before that person enters the insurance market, so that lack of skill is primarily a matter of history rather than one of future contingency. (There are other reasons as well, which we shall have to identify in a moment.) But let us nevertheless try to frame a hypothetical question something like the questions we asked in the case of handicaps. Suppose an imaginary world in which, though the distribution of skills over the community were in the aggregate what it actually is, people for some reason all had the same antecedent chance of suffering the consequences of lacking any particular set of these skills, and were all in a position to buy insurance against these consequences at the same premium structure. How much insurance would each buy at what cost? If we can make sense of that question, and answer it even by fixing rough lower limits on average, then we shall have a device for fixing at least the lower bounds of a tax-and-redistribution program satisfying the demands of equality of resources.

There are several ways in which we might construct a hypothetical or imaginary insurance market of that sort. We might try to imagine, for example, that people are ignorant of the skills they actually have, though they know how many people will turn out to have each skill, and therefore what their own chances are. People might then be supposed to insure against turning out to lack some particular skill at some particular level, either a very precise skill like the ability to capture September light at dusk in oil, or a more general skill, like a very good memory or a quick way with numbers. This model would be very like the model we constructed for handicaps, and would therefore provide theoretical continuity for our theory as a whole. We might even propose to integrate the two hypothetical insurance markets by taking seriously the suggestion that the lack of some skill is just another handicap, and simply asking how many so-called skills would find their way into a general market for catastrophe insurance.

But this model for the hypothetical insurance market for skills is subject to a certain objection. We noticed, in considering the hypothetical insurance market for handicaps, the following difficulty. There is a certain indeterminacy in the issue of what ambitions and tastes someone who is handicapped would have if he were not, and this indeterminacy infects the question of how much of what insurance he would then buy. The indeterminacy is manageable in the case of ordinary handicaps, because generalizations are nevertheless possible. But it would not be manageable in the case of skills, because if we suppose that no one has any idea what talents he has, we have stipulated away too much of his personality to leave any intelligible base for speculation about his ambitions, even in a general or average way. The connection between talents and ambitions, which I described much earlier, is much closer than that between ambitions and handicaps—it is, for one thing, reciprocal—and much too close to permit that sort of counterfactual speculation.

So let us suppose, not that people are wholly ignorant of what talents they have, but rather that for some other reason they do not have any sound basis for predicting their economic rent—what income the talents they do have can produce, or even whether the economic situation will be such that these talents will find any employment. There are, of course, many different ways of imagining such a state of affairs, and it does not much matter, for present purposes, which we select. So let us fall back on our immigrants once again. Suppose that before the initial auction has begun, information about the tastes, ambitions, talents, and attitudes toward risk of each of the immigrants, as well as information about the raw materials and technology available, is delivered to a computer. It then predicts not only the results of the auction but also the projected income structure—the number of people earning each level of income—that will follow the auction once production and trade begin, on the assumption that there will be no income tax.

Now the computer is asked a further hypothetical question. Assume each immigrant knows the projected income structure but is ignorant of the computer's data base, except for its information about himself, and is therefore radically uncertain what income level his own talents would permit him to occupy. He supposes, in fact, that he has the same chance as anyone else of occupying any particular level of income in the economy, though he takes the number projected for that level into account. Assume that there is no monopoly in insurance, and insurance firms offer policies of the following sort. Insurance is provided against failing to have an opportunity to earn whatever level of income, within the projected structure, the policyholder names, in which case the insurance company will pay the policyholder the difference between that coverage level and the income he does in fact have an opportunity to earn.[9] Premiums will vary with the level of coverage chosen, must be the same for everyone at any particular coverage level, and will be paid, not out of the policyholder's initial stock of resources (or clamshells), but rather from future earnings after the auction at fixed periods. How much of such insurance would the immigrants, on average, buy, at what specified level of income coverage, and at what cost?

That problem seems amenable, at least in principle, to the various types of analysis that economists devote to problems of decision making under uncertainty, and there is no reason to doubt that the computer could furnish an answer. Even without the computer's information and powers, we can make some general observations about what it is likely to predict. Economists make a rough distinction between two kinds of decisions under uncertainty. An insurance problem is posed when a small cost purchases reimbursement for an unlikely but serious loss. A gambling problem is posed when a small cost purchases a small chance of a large gain. Let us define a financially advantageous bet of either of these types as a bet such that the cost of the bet is less than the amount of the return if "successful"—if the covered risk eventuates or if the bet is won—discounted by the improbability of success. Insurance for a dollar premium that pays ten dollars in the event of a loss that is as likely as not to occur, or a ten-to-one bet that a fair coin flip will come up heads, are financially advantageous bets. A bet is financially disadvantageous if the cost of the bet exceeds the expected return so calculated. Let us say that someone is risk-neutral if he will accept any financially advantageous bet and reject any financially disadvantageous bet, no matter what the size or other character of the bet.

Commercial insurance companies and commercial bookmakers will offer only financially disadvantageous bets, of course, because their income must equal not only the expected return to the policyholders and bettors but also their costs, including opportunity costs. So if everyone were risk-neutral no one would buy insurance or bet on the numbers or pools. But almost no one is risk-neutral over the full range of his utility curve: for almost everyone the marginal utility of more money declines over at least part of the graph that pictures how his welfare behaves as a function of his income. It is fairly easy to see how this explains the phenomenon of commercial insurance (though of course any explanation of why rates for particular policies are what they are would require more detailed information about these utility functions and would be much more complex). Suppose there is a one-in-ten chance that my $50,000 house will burn down in the next year, and I am offered full insurance at a cost of $6,000. I am offered the choice, that is, between a certainty of $44,000 (if I purchase insurance) and a gamble with an expected return of $45,000 (if I do not). If the loss of my house would be more than nine times as serious as the loss of $6,000 (because, for example, I could not find or borrow enough money to build a suitable house, my marriage would dissolve, and my children become delinquent) then it is worth my while to buy the insurance, though it is a financially disadvantageous bet. It is much harder to explain gambles. (Kenneth Arrow, discussing gambling, quoted the preacher who reached a sticky point in theology and said that the problem was a very difficult one which the congregation should face firmly and then pass on.) It is perhaps necessary to suppose that gamblers either mistake the actual odds (because they think that luck is a lady) or attach value to uncertainty for its own sake; and though both these assumptions hold sometimes, it seems doubtful that they hold sufficiently often to explain how popular gambling is.

What can be said, against this background, about the two hypothetical insurance markets we have described? Our insurance market for handicaps is sufficiently like ordinary insurance markets and requires no special comment. But the hypothetical insurance market we just described for talents is different, in part because it seems, at first blush, to allow for decisions that look much more like gambles than insurance. For it might seem that many immigrants would leap at the chance to buy a policy that would protect them against not having the very highest income projected for the economy, and would pay them, if they do not, the difference between the great income and what they can actually earn. But in fact that policy would be a very poor wager indeed.[10] We take it as given that insurance at that level would be a financially disadvantageous bet. Otherwise it would not be offered by the insurance firm. So if it is a good bet, it is good on grounds of expected welfare rather than financial grounds, as is my insurance policy on my house. But the bet is much more likely to be silly than sound in welfare terms.

Since (unlike lottery tickets generally) the chances of "winning" are extremely high—very few immigrants will turn out to have that maximum earning power—the cost of the premium will be extremely high as well.[11] It will approach the value of the projected return if the risk eventuates. So someone who buys this insurance faces an extremely high chance of gaining very little. Suppose he loses, however; suppose he is one of those who does have the maximum earning power. He is now in much worse position than if he had never insured, because he must now work at close to his top earning capacity just to pay the high premium for his insurance on which he collected nothing—just, that is, to break even. He will be a slave to his maximum earning power.[12]

Now just how bad a bargain this is will depend upon facts not specified, including the question of how many people can be expected to have the talents necessary to earn at the highest level. But it is likely to be a very bad bargain in any case. It is very different from the situation that apparently tempts large numbers of people to make financially disadvantageous bets on vast lotteries, which is the prospect of a small chance of a large fortune in return for a very small certain cost. This insurance decision would be the very different financially disadvantageous bet of a very small chance of a very great loss in return for the very large chance of a very small gain, and nothing in the literature of the psychology of gambling (except perhaps the literature of Russian roulette) supports the idea that bets of that character would be popular.

Nor does the explanation of why people purchase ordinary financially disadvantageous insurance policies offer any support. I buy insurance on my house because the marginal utility loss of an uncompensated fire is so much greater than the utility cost of the premium. But considerations of marginal utility would if anything condemn rather than support any immigrant's bet that he would not have the skills necessary to earn the highest income. For that bet pits the almost certain prospect of a tiny and probably unnoticeable welfare gain against the tiny chance of an enormous welfare loss on financially disadvantageous terms. Of course, we make assumptions in presuming that almost no one would have a utility curve that would make that bet sensible in welfare terms. But it does seem plausible that almost no one would.

Does this argument prove too much? Does it prove that insurance against lacking skills, on the model we described, would almost always be a bad buy for almost everyone? If so, it would seem to follow that the hypothetical insurance device could not, after all, provide reasonable guides for redistribution through income tax. Or, perhaps worse, it might suggest that no such redistribution would ever be justified. But in fact the argument does not have this consequence, because the lower the income level chosen as the covered risk, the better the argument becomes that most people given the chance to buy insurance on equal terms would in fact buy at that level. The argument becomes compelling, I think, well above the level of income presently used to trigger transfer payments for unemployment or minimum wage levels in either Britain or the United States.

The argument becomes stronger, as the chosen income level declines, for the following reasons. First, as the level declines, the odds that any particular person will have the talents necessary to earn that income at full stretch improve and, for a substantial section of income levels in normal economies, improve faster than the rate of that decline. Many more than twice as many people have the abilities necessary to earn the amount earned in the fiftieth percentile than in the ninety-ninth percentile of a normal income distribution. So the premium falls, and falls, at least over a considerable range, at a rate faster than the rate of the coverage. So, correspondingly, do the odds against "winning," of course, but the situation grows steadily closer to the normal case of insurance, in which people incur a small certain loss to prevent an unlikely great loss whose marginal utility costs are serious enough to justify a financially disadvantageous transaction. For even though the financial loss in falling from, say, the seventieth to the sixtieth percentile in income is vastly greater than the loss in falling from the fortieth to the thirtieth, the welfare consequences will probably, on average, be much worse for the latter drop.

As the income level covered drops, moreover, so the penalties of "losing" the insurance bet, by turning out to have the abilities to earn at least that income, diminish in importance and, once again, at what seems likely to be a faster rate. Someone who "loses" in this sense must work hard enough to cover his premium before he is free to make the trade-offs between work and consumption he would have been free to make if he had not insured. If the level of coverage is high, then this will enslave the insured, not simply because the premium is high, but because it is extremely unlikely that his talents will much surpass the level that he has chosen, which means that he must indeed work at full stretch, and that he will not have much choice about what kind of work to do. Only one form of work, and that full-time, will be likely to produce the income needed to pay the premium that is now his albatross. So his penalty has special welfare disadvantages not measurable in ordinary financial terms. It is these that make it appropriate to speak of his enslavement.

But as the level of coverage and hence the premium drop, these special welfare disadvantages are not simply mitigated, but entirely fall away. For it becomes likely that anyone who has the qualifications needed to earn at, say, the thirtieth percentile level will also have the talents to earn at a higher level, and so would retain a considerable freedom of choice about the character of work, and the mix of work and labor and additional consumption, that he prefers. Even if he just barely "loses" the insurance bet, and has exactly the talents needed to earn the level of income he covered, but no more, he will still probably retain a great freedom of choice. The premium will be small enough to sustain even if he works at a lower level of income than he could, particularly if he is willing to sacrifice consumer goods. There are, moreover, a greater variety of types of jobs that will produce a lower level of income than a higher (at least in most complex economies at least over a range of income levels), so that someone committed to earning as much as he can will nevertheless have more choice of work at that lower level. Even if he must work flat out and has no choice in his work, his situation is very little worse than if he had taken no insurance. For if the coverage level is so low that almost everyone must earn it to have a decent life, he would have worked that way and practically that hard anyway, and if the premium is very low, as it then would be, he would not have to work much harder to cover it. He is not much differently enslaved by his talent if he insures than he would be enslaved by his lack of talent if he did not.

The hypothetical insurance market might nevertheless produce apparent anomalies. Suppose Deborah and Ernest both purchase insurance at the sixtieth percentile level. Deborah is beautiful and could in fact earn at the ninetieth percentile as a movie star. Otherwise they have the same talents and interests, and these other talents would not earn at the sixtieth level. Ernest recovers under his policy, but Deborah does not. She is faced with the choice of a movie career, which she detests, or trying to pay the premium and the other expenses of her life from whatever salary she could earn at jobs both she and Ernest would prefer. Ernest can have both such a job and compensation under his policy, and is therefore much better off.[13] Is this advantage unfair? Deborah is, as it turns out, enslaved by her singular talent. But this is because she ran the risk described by purchasing insurance at a coverage level commanding a high premium and such that few jobs could produce income approaching that level. Ernest ran the same risk but had better option luck. The anomaly is therefore only a further (and more complex) example of the undesirable welfare risks of insurance at a high level. If Deborah and Ernest had purchased insurance at a lower level, the premium would have been lower and Deborah would have had a much better choice of jobs other than a film career. They would still fare differently, but the difference would be much less, and would (arguably) then be an appropriate mark of the fact that Deborah had an option Ernest did not. In any case, this unfairness, if it is unfairness, would disappear in any plausible translation of the hypothetical insurance market into an actual tax scheme of the sort described in the next section.

VI. Tax as Premium

Now let us assume that the computer fixes the average coverage level that would be reached in the hypothetical insurance market, and declares some premium to be the premium that level would command. The premiums would be a sufficiently small proportion of the coverage that (for the average person) the expected welfare of insuring would be higher than the expected welfare of not doing so. Can we translate that hypothetical insurance structure into a tax scheme? Can we base tax rates on the assumed premium, and then redistribute by paying those who do not have the ability to earn at the assumed coverage level the difference between that level and what they can earn?

We might assume that any tax system constructed to model the hypothetical insurance market in that way would suffer from serious defects. First, it seems unfair that everyone, rich and poor alike, should pay the same tax, but this would seem to be the consequence of modeling tax rates on hypothetical premiums. Second, the requirement that both the incidence and amount of payments from the fund depend on what the recipient could earn if willing seems inefficient and troublesome in a variety of ways. It might be very expensive to enforce that requirement, and in practice the requirement will tempt some people to cheat by hiding their abilities under a bushel. In any case, even honest people cannot know what they might earn at a given occupation without trying, and in the case of some professions, trying is impossible without half a lifetime of preparation. So a battery of new tests to discover latent talent would be necessary, and these would be vulnerable to many sorts of mistakes.

But these objections make certain assumptions about what the hypothetical insurance market would be like, and these assumptions are both unjustified and probably false. For suppose the insurance firms had offered, in place of the flat-rate premium for a given coverage that the objections assume, a premium fixed as an increasing percentage of the income the policy owner turns out to earn. The premium of someone who barely earns the average coverage amount would be less than the premium the insurance market would have fixed on a flat-rate basis, though the premium of someone who earns much more would be much greater. The insurance firms would have reason to offer this different scheme if the total premiums paid would be more, and the immigrants buying insurance would also have reason to accept it if the change increased their expected welfare under the conditions of equal risk we have stipulated. Since we assume declining marginal utility of money over the range in question, as part of the assumptions on which we speculate that insurance would be bought at all, these conditions will be met. Immigrants would prefer a "bet" under which the cost of the bet will be an increasing function of their income, and will prefer it by enough to provide profit for the insurance firms even counting the increased administrative costs of a progressive premium scheme.

The firms would also have reason to reduce what insurers call the "moral hazard" of such insurance—the risk that insurance will make the covered risk even more likely to occur or the level of recovery higher if it does—and to pass on part of their savings to policyholders as inducements to accept the necessary constraints. One technique insurers now use for that purpose is co-insurance. First-person automobile policies provide, for example, that the owner must assume the first several hundred dollars of damage before the insurer makes up the balance. Co-insurance in our story means that if one of the immigrants is unable to earn the average coverage amount, he will receive somewhat less than that amount as compensation. Of course people will buy insurance at a higher coverage level with co-insurance than without, though at a lower premium than the higher amount would otherwise attract, which means that the average coverage level would be higher than under a scheme with no co-insurance. But if substantial savings for the insurance firm would result from reducing the moral hazard (and popular resentment about welfare cheats under present welfare schemes in the United States, for example, supposes that they would), then the savings in premium along the range should also be substantial; if so, then the presumed coverage would indeed be higher under a co-insurance regime. How much co-insurance would obtain—by how much the payment to those who fail to earn the covered amount would fall short of that amount and what the effect on the premium structure and the presumed coverage level would be—depends only on information that has already been given to the computer.

The problem and the cost of accuracy in determining people's actual abilities to earn are made less pressing for the insurer by co-insurance. It sharply reduces the motives people have for not earning at least the covered amount in order to claim that they cannot earn it. But the insurer has another device for reducing the cost of accuracy enough to lower premiums and so make the device attractive to policyholders. Since policyholders will almost always have more information about their abilities and opportunities than the insurer will, there is room for joint savings by assigning the burden of proof to the policyholders. This burden will be more severe for coverage at the higher levels, I expect, than at the lower, because it is often difficult to prove that one could not have had a career for which special training or education or experience is necessary unless one has undertaken these. But if

I am right that the average coverage level would be relatively low, we need not pursue that problem. At the lower levels the proof will be easily provided by failed attempts to find employment or by evidence of less than average general physical and mental abilities, and so forth.

So the actual insurance profile the computer would predict is likely to be much more complex than the simple structure our defective tax system copied. If the immigrants translate this more complex insurance profile into a tax scheme they reach a more recognizable pattern of tax. They might establish a graduated income tax financing transfer payments in the amount of the difference between the average coverage level less the co-insurance factor and what an applicant can plausibly argue is the highest income he can in fact command. This exercise, of course, neither need nor should stop at this point. Further reflection about the hypothetical insurance market might develop further refinements or adjustments to the corresponding tax scheme. And we might decide that a tax scheme should differ from the best approximation of that hypothetical market for other reasons. We might decide that a tax scheme so closely modeled on that market is offensive to privacy, or too expensive in administrative costs, or too inefficient in other ways. We might decide, for these or other reasons, that a scheme that tied redistribution to actual earnings rather than to ability to earn, for example, was a better second-best approximation to the ideal of mimicking the insurance market than any other scheme we could develop.

But I want to put aside for now any further study of these issues, because we have carried them far enough, I think, to justify turning instead to the question waiting in the wings. Is the general approach sensible? Is a tax scheme constructed as a practical translation of a hypothetical insurance market, which assumes equal initial assets and equal risk, a proper response to the problem of differential talents under equality of resources?

It might be criticized from two standpoints: either that it does not justify enough redistribution, or that it justifies too much. The latter objection seems the weaker of the two. Recall the competing constraints we discovered. Equality requires that those who choose more expensive ways to live—which includes choosing less productive occupations measured by what others want—have less residual income in consequence. But it also requires that no one have less income simply in consequence of less native talent. Any objection that the transfer payments guided by the hypothetical insurance market are too great must show a lively danger that the first of these requirements has been given insufficient weight. But if the hypothetical insurance market justifies the selection of a particular level as the average assumed coverage, this argues strongly for the probability that any particular immigrant is ready to work at one of the occupations that could produce income at that level rather than have a lesser income, if the choice were available. Otherwise he would have run too great a risk by taking on a premium that makes sense only for someone ready to earn the income needed to support it, particularly if the average level is sufficiently low that the odds were great that he would have to do exactly that. He may be ready to do so because a wide range of occupations, suiting very different personalities, would produce that level of income, or because that level is necessary to lead what popular culture considers an acceptable style of life, or, more probably, both together. Of course, this favorable counterfactual would not, in fact, hold in the case of everyone who lacks appropriate talents, or does not find a job in the employment market for some other reason. Some such immigrants would not have taken insurance at the average coverage level even if it were available. But this presents a question of valuing the relative importance of the two constraints on a theory of redistribution for differential talents. Taking the average coverage level as decisive, which we have done, is an appropriate way of weighting them equally.[14] It supposes that it is at least no worse to err on the side of redistributing to someone who would not have insured than to deny redistribution to one who would have. Someone may be able to show that this is wrong, and thereby justify taking, as the standard for redistribution through taxation, a lower figure such that the odds are very strong, possibly even overwhelming, that any particular person would have insured at that level. But I do not know of any arguments for that view. Perhaps the difference between the average coverage level and some lower level of that sort would not be very great. Perhaps, that is, the utility curves of most people would look very much alike for the lower percentiles of possible coverage. But this is one of the legion of quasi-technical questions that I make no attempt to discuss here.

The opposite objection, that transfer payments based on the average coverage level are not enough, is more difficult to answer. It might be supported in two different ways. It might be said that the hypothetical insurance approach is the wrong approach through which to attempt to compromise the two requirements we discovered; or that the hypothetical insurance approach is the right approach but requires transfer payments at a higher level. The second argument presumably agrees with the objection just described, that the two requirements of equality in wage structure are not of equal weight, but insists that it is much worse to deny payments to someone who would have insured than to award them to someone who would not have done so. It insists, in other words, that the level of assumed coverage chosen should be some level such that it is very unlikely that anyone would have insured above that level. Once again, it is worth noticing that this level might not be much above the average coverage level. We saw, earlier, reasons why almost no one would insure at a very high income level in any case. Once again, however, I shall not explore the technical issue raised, but simply set the suggestion aside until the substantive argument, in favor of special deference to one requirement of equality in wage structure over the other, has been made.

But we must now state and consider the important argument that the hypothetical insurance market is altogether the wrong approach to the problem of reconciling these two requirements, because it undervalues the transfer payments that those whose talents are not in great demand should receive. The hypothetical insurance market approach aims to put such people in the position they would have been in had the risk of their fate been subjectively equally shared. But it does not make them as well-off in the end as those whose talents are in more demand, or as those with similar talents lucky enough to find more profitable employment. Some people (movie stars and captains of industry and first basemen) in fact earn at a rate far beyond the rate of coverage any reasonable person would choose in an insurance market, as our inspection showed. The hypothetical insurance market approach is beside the point (it might be said) exactly because it provides no answer to someone who is unable to find a job, points to the movie star, and declares, perfectly accurately, that he would do that work for that pay if asked. The fact that no one would buy coverage at a movie-star level in an equal insurance market simply underscores the injustice. The movie star had no need to buy that insurance. He won his life of luxury and glamor without it. The brute fact remains that some people have much more than others of what both desire, through no reason connected with choice. The envy test we once seemed to respect has been decisively defeated, and no defensible conception of equality can argue that equality recommends that result.

This is a powerful complaint, and there is no answer, I think, but to summarize and restate our earlier arguments to see if they can still persuade with that complaint ringing in our ears. Let us return to the immigrants. Claude cannot argue, on grounds of equality, for a world in which he has the movie star's income. The immigrants cannot create a world in which everyone who would be willing to work movie-star hours can have movie-star pay. If Claude is unhappy with his situation, even after the tax scheme is put into play, he must propose a world in which no one will have such an income and his income will be relatively (and perhaps absolutely) higher in consequence. But whichever such world he proposes will be changed not only for those who under our scheme would have more than he does, but for everyone else as well, including those who for one reason or another, including their preferences for work, leisure, and consumption, will have less. If, for example, no one can earn movie-star wages, people who wish to watch movies may perhaps find very different fare available which, rightly or wrongly, they will not regard as highly as what they now have. It is, of course, impossible to say in advance just what the consequences of any profound change in an economic system would be, and who would gain or lose in the long run. These changes could not be properly charted along any one simple dimension. They could not be measured simply in the funds or other "primary goods" available to one or another economic class, for example. For they also affect the prices and scarcity of different goods and opportunities that members of any particular class, even economic class, will value very differently from one another. That is exactly why the immigrants chose an auction, sensitive to what people in fact wanted for their lives, as their primary engine for achieving equality.

So though Claude may truly say that the difference between him and the movie star does not reflect any differences in tastes or ambitions or theories of the good, and so does not in itself implicate our first, ambition-sensitive requirement of equality in wage structure, he could not recommend any general change in relative economic positions that would not wreak wholesale and dramatic changes in the positions of others, changes which do implicate that requirement. Of course, this fact does not in itself rule out any changes that Claude might propose. On the contrary, the status quo achieved by laissez-faire production and trade from an equal start has no natural or privileged status, as I have been at pains to emphasize, particularly my argument against the starting-gate theory of equality. If Claude can show that a proper conception of equality of resources recommends some change, the fact that many people from all ranks would then be worse-off, given their particular tastes and ambitions, provides no objection, any more than the fact that Claude is worse-off without some change in itself provides an argument in favor of that change. I mean to emphasize only that Claude needs some argument in favor of the change he recommends which is independent of his own relative position. It is not enough for him to point to people, even those of the same ambitions and tastes as himself, who do better as things are.

The argument from the hypothetical insurance market is such an argument. It contrasts two worlds. In the first those who are relatively disadvantaged by the tastes and ambitions of others, vis-à-vis their own talents to produce, are known in advance and bear the full consequences of that disadvantage. In the second the same pattern of relative disadvantage holds, but everyone has subjectively an equal antecedent chance of suffering it, and so everyone has an equal opportunity of mitigating the disadvantage by insuring against it. The argument assumes that equality prefers the second world, because it is a world in which the resources of talent are in one important sense more evenly divided. The hypothetical insurance argument aims to reproduce the consequences of the second world, as nearly as it can, in an actual world. It answers those who would do better in the first world (who include many of those who would have more money at their disposal in the second) by the simple proposition that the second is a world that, on grounds independent of how things happen to work out for them given their tastes and ambitions, is more nearly equal in resources.

The availability of that argument is no bar to the production of other arguments showing how some further change would improve equality of resources still further. However, it is hard to anticipate how great a motive we should have to search for further arguments if the hypothetical insurance argument were in fact accepted and enforced in, for example, our immigrant case. That would depend, among other things, on how high a level of income could be shown to be the average coverage level in that society. It might be that wealth disparities would be so greatly reduced by the features of the economy we have already described that we would be much less troubled than we might suspect in advance by the wealth inequalities that would remain. Indeed it might be that the costs in overall efficiency of even those features would be so great that those who are prepared to compromise equality of resources either for general utility or in service of some strategy of making the worst-off as well-off as possible, would argue that even that much equality would be condemned by their more embracing conception of justice.

Of course, many of the political philosophers and theorists who object to inequality are concerned not simply with how poor those at the bottom are in absolute terms, but with what might be called the moral costs of a society with substantial wealth inequality, costs that remain, and indeed are sometimes exacerbated, when the position of the least well-off is sharply improved but the inequality remains. It would be a mistake, however, to suppose that the bizarre and mutually dependent attitudes about wealth that mark our own society—the ideas that the accumulation of wealth is a mark of a successful life and that someone who has arranged his life to acquire it is a proper object for envy rather than sympathy or concern—would find any footing in an economic system that is free of genuine poverty and that encourages people, as the initial auction encourages them, to see bank-account wealth as simply one ingredient among others of what might make a life worth living. For in our world, these attitudes are sustained and nourished by the assumption that a life dedicated to the accumulation of wealth or to the consumption of luxuries—a major part of whose appeal lies just in the fact that they are reserved for the very rich—is a valuable life for people given only one chance to live. That proposition comes as close as any theory of the good life can to naked absurdity.

It is no doubt an important question for social psychology and intellectual history how that proposition finds a footing in any society. It has, after all, been condemned in all literature or any other form of art taken seriously for very long in even deeply capitalistic communities, and though I understand the possibility that its rejection in art might be parasitic upon its unthinking acceptance in life, the protests of even the most popular forms of art nevertheless deepen the mystery. My present point is much more banal than any attempt to solve that mystery. It is simply this: that we are so ignorant about the complex genealogy of the implausible attitudes about wealth that we find among us, which those who point to the moral costs of the market system deplore, that we would do wrong to assume in advance that these same attitudes will rise in a market system whose very point is to encourage the kind of reflective examination about costs and gains under which these attitudes would seem most likely to shrivel and disappear.

But it is nevertheless important to try to discover arguments showing that equality of resources, as a distinct ideal, would recommend erasing even those wealth differentials that the hypothetical insurance argument would permit, and this project is not threatened by my uncertainty whether we should feel dismayed, or find our intuitions undermined, if we did not in fact discover any. I do not doubt that such arguments can be found, and it is part of my purpose to provoke them. But it is worth mentioning certain arguments that do not seem promising. It might be said, for example, that equality of resources would approve a different world still, in which people had in fact equal talents for production, more than either of the other two I described, so that we ought to strive to create a system in which wealth differences traceable to occupation were no greater than they would be in that world. There is an important point locked in that claim, which is that an egalitarian society ought, just in the name of equality, to devote special resources to training those whose talents, as things fall out, place them lower on the income scale. That is part of the larger question of an egalitarian theory of education, which I have not even attempted to take up here. But the more general point suffers from the fact that we could not even begin to replicate the wealth distribution that would hold in that different world without making assumptions about the mix of talents that everyone in that world would share in equal abundance, and no specification of the mix could be neutral among the various ambitions and tastes in the real world in which we attempt that replication.

Suppose someone says simply (and with creditable impatience) that equality of resources just *must* prefer a world in which people have more nearly equal wealth than they are likely to have in a world of free trade, even against a background of equal initial wealth and even as corrected by the hypothetical insurance market. To deny that (it might be said) is simply to prefer other values to equality, not to state an acceptable conception of equality itself. That is, of course, exactly what my arguments have been meant to challenge. Once we understand the importance, under equality of resources, of the requirement that any theory of distribution must be ambition-sensitive, and understand the wholesale effects of any scheme of distribution or redistribution on the lives that almost everyone in the community will want and be permitted to lead, we must regard with suspicion any flat statement that equality of resources just must be defined in a way that ignores these facts. Equality of resources is a complex ideal. It is probably (as the various arguments we have canvassed here suggest) an indeterminate ideal that accepts, within a certain range, a variety of distributions. But this much seems clear: any defensible conception of that ideal must attend to its different dimensions, and not reject out of hand the requirement that it be sensitive to the cost of one person's life to other people. The present suggestion, that genuine theories of equality must be concerned only with the quantity of disposable goods or liquid assets people command at a particular time, is a piece of preanalytic dogma that does not, in fact, protect the boundaries of the concept of equality from confusion with other concepts, but rather thwarts the attempt to picture equality as an independent and powerful political ideal.

VII. Other Theories of Justice

It is hardly worth repeating how far the remarks here fall short of a full theory of equality of resources even under simple and artificial conditions like those of the immigrant society. I have said nothing, for example, about how far equality, properly understood, constrains people from giving to others what they are entitled to keep and use for themselves. That question includes, of course, the troublesome issue whether those who have amassed wealth through sacrifices in their own lives should be allowed to pass this on as extra wealth for their children. Nor have I said anything about what accommodation an equal distribution of resources should make for radical changes in people's minds about how they wish to spend their lives. Is someone entitled to a fresh stock of resources when he rejects his former life and wants a fresh start? Suppose he is a profligate who has wasted his initial endowment and now finds himself with less than he needs to provide even for basic needs in later life.

These questions are of great theoretical interest, and of central practical importance when we come to ask what the requirement of an equal start, which in our immigrant world could be satisfied by an equal initial auction, would mean for the real world. I have also set aside for another occasion the entire issue of equality of political power, though as I noticed at the beginning it is quite illegitimate to regard political equality as an issue entirely distinct from economic equality. Nevertheless we have covered enough ground here that it might be useful to contrast the direction in which we are traveling with those taken by certain prominent theories of justice now in the field.

It should be reasonably plain how the conception of equality defended here contrasts with equality of welfare, the theory considered in Chapter 1. There is nothing in the idea of an equal initial auction, followed by trade and production constrained by taxation mimicking hypothetical insurance markets, that either aims at equality in any concept of welfare or makes convergence toward such equality likely. Indeed, there is no place in the theory, as developed so far, even for comparisons of the welfare levels of different people. The theory does make use of the idea of individual utility levels, for example in the calculations it recommends about how people would behave in certain hypothetical markets. But these calculations use only the rather antiseptic concept of utility proposed by John von Neumann and Oskar Morgenstern,[15] among others, rather than any of the more complex and judgmental conceptions of welfare that are necessary for interpersonal comparisons, whose shortcomings I discussed in Chapter 1.

There might well be interesting connections between the theory described here and some form of utilitarianism, which commands the maximization of some concept of welfare overall rather than equality in its distribution. Of course our theory as a whole could not be expected to maximize any concept of welfare across society, except under special and quite extravagant assumptions about individual utility functions. The assumption that people should enter economic activity with equal initial resources, for example, would count as a dubious theorem for a utilitarian, rather than as a cardinal axiom. Nevertheless the idea of an equal auction for goods and services, from the base of an equal abstract distribution of economic power, might seem to suggest a utilitarian strain in the theory, because an auction would promote overall utility better than a more mechanical division of available goods into equal lots. I do not think that this mild similarity, insofar as it does exist, is entirely accidental. On the contrary, utilitarianism owes part of its appeal, I think, to the fact that in certain circumstances a distribution that maximizes overall marginal utility from an intuitively fair basic distribution would also be recommended by the present conception of equality. This is even more plainly true of the wealth-maximization theory of justice, which is a cousin of utilitarianism and is presently popular among academic lawyers. This theory argues that, at least in certain circumstances, a distribution that maximizes marginal wealth is fair. The circumstances in which the wealth-maximization theory seems intuitively plausible[16] are in fact just the circumstances in which our conception of equality would probably recommend the decision that in fact maximizes wealth. The overall fit between our conception of equality and the wealth-maximization theory, indeed, is likely to be closer than the fit of our conception of equality with utilitarianism.[17] But in both cases, so far as the present argument holds, the connection is one-way only. A distribution that fits the two theories is fair because equality, and not the maximization of either utility or wealth, recommends it.

There are also at least superficial connections between the theory of equality of resources suggested here and various forms of the Lockean theory of justice in private property, particularly in Robert Nozick's distinguished and influential version. Of course the differences, even on the surface, are more striking. There is no place in a theory such as Nozick's for anything like the idea of an equal distribution of abstract economic power over all the goods under social control. But both Nozick's theory and equality of resources as described here give a prominent place to the idea of a market, and recommend the distribution that is achieved by a market suitably defined and constrained. It may be that those parts of Nozick's arguments that seem intuitively most persuasive are based on examples in which the present theory would reach very similar results.

The famous Wilt Chamberlain example is a case in point. Nozick supposes an equal distribution of wealth, followed by uncoerced trades to mutual advantage in which each of many people pays a small sum to watch Chamberlain play basketball, after which he grows rich and wealth is no longer equal. Equality of resources would not denounce that result, considered in itself. Chamberlain's wealth reflects the value to others of his leading his life as he does. His greater wealth, at the end of the process, is of course traceable mainly to his greater talent, and only in small part, we may assume, to the fact that he is willing to lead a life that others would not be willing to lead. But almost no one would have purchased, in the hypothetical insurance market we described, insurance against not having talents that would provide such wealth. That insurance would be, for almost everyone, a strikingly irrational investment. So our discussion would not justify taxing any of Chamberlain's wealth for redistribution to others not so fortunate, if we attend only to the fact, as Nozick does, that others have much less wealth than he does.

But our discussion left open, as Nozick's did not, that arguments justifying such redistribution might be found in a more thorough study of the actual circumstances in which wealth like Chamberlain's is accumulated. Suppose Chamberlain plays his game, not in a community whose only wealth disparity lies in his enormous wealth against the equal wealth of all others, each of whom has only slightly less than the most equal distribution we can imagine, but in Philadelphia in the early 1970s. Now a great many people earn less than the average presumed coverage of a plausible hypothetical insurance market for that society, so even if we assume that the complex wealth differences we find are all traceable to lack of talent rather than to lack of equal start (which is absurd), we are still required to put in place a tax system for redistribution to them, and Chamberlain will be required to contribute to that system. Indeed, since our argument justified the conclusion that premiums in the hypothetical insurance market would lie at progressive rates, based on income realized, Chamberlain would be required to contribute more than anyone else, both absolutely and as a percentage of his income. When the discussion is broadened in this way, equality of resources travels very far from the boundaries of the nightwatchman state.

The difference between the use the two theories make of the market is therefore clear enough. For Nozick the role of the market in justifying distributions is both negative and contingent. If someone has justly acquired something, and chooses to exchange it with someone else in return for the latter's goods or services, then no objection can be taken, in the name of justice, to the distribution that results. The history of the transaction insulates it from attack and, in this negative way, certifies its moral pedigree. There is no room, in this theory, for hypothetical markets of any form, except in the special case of restitution for demonstrated injustice in the past. For Nozick does not use the market (as, for example, some wealth-maximizers do) simply to define another of what he calls "patterned" theories of justice. Justice consists, not in the distribution that a fair market of rational persons would reach, but in the distribution that has actually, as a matter of historical contingency, been reached by a process that might, but need not, include any market transactions at all.

Under equality of resources the market, when it enters, enters in a more positive but also more servile way. It enters because it is endorsed by the concept of equality, as the best means of enforcing, at least up to a point, the fundamental requirement that only an equal share of social resources be devoted to the lives of each of its members, as measured by the opportunity cost of such resources to others. But the value of actual market transactions ends at just that point, and the market must be abandoned or constrained when analysis shows, from any direction, that it has failed in this task, or that an entirely different theoretical or institutional device would do better. Hypothetical markets are plainly of comparable theoretical importance to actual markets for this purpose. We are less certain about their results, but have a great deal more flexibility in their design, and the objection that they have no historical validity is simply beside the point.

I shall try to say something, finally, about the connections and differences between our conception of equality of resources and John Rawls's theory of justice. That theory is sufficiently rich to provide a question of connection at two different levels. First, how far do the arguments in favor of equality of resources, as described, follow the structure of argument Rawls deploys? How far do they depend, that is, on the hypothesis that people in the original position Rawls described would choose the principles of equality of resources behind the veil? Second—and independently—how far are the requirements of equality of resources different from the two principles of justice that Rawls suggests people in that position would in fact choose?

It is obviously better to start with the second of these questions. The comparison in point is that between equality of resources and Rawls's second principle of justice, whose main component is the "difference" principle, which requires no variation from absolute equality in "primary goods" save as works to the benefit of the worst-off economic class. (Rawls's first principle, which establishes what he calls the priority of liberty, has more to do with the topics I have set aside as belonging to political equality, discussed in Chapter 4.) The difference principle, like our conception of equality of resources, works only contingently in the direction of equality of welfare on any conception of welfare. If we distinguish broadly between theories of equality of welfare and of resources, the difference principle is an interpretation of equality of resources.

But it is nevertheless a rather different interpretation from our conception. From the standpoint of our conception, the difference principle is not sufficiently fine-tuned in a variety of ways. There is a conceded degree of arbitrariness in the choice of any description of the worst-off group, which is, in any case, a group whose fortunes can be charted only through some mythical average or representative member of that group. In particular, the structure seems insufficiently sensitive to the position of those with natural handicaps, physical or mental, who do not themselves constitute a worst-off group, because this is defined economically, and would not count as the representative or average member of any such group. Rawls calls attention to what he calls the principle of redress, which argues that compensation should be made to people so handicapped, as indeed it is, in the way I described, under our conception of equality. But he notes that the difference principle does not include the principle of redress, though it would tend in the same direction insofar as special training for the handicapped, for example, would work to the benefit of the economically worst-off class. But there is no reason to think that it would, at least in normal circumstances.

It has often been pointed out, moreover, that the difference principle is insufficiently sensitive to variations in distribution above the worst-off economic class. This complaint is sometimes illustrated with bizarre hypothetical questions. Suppose an existing economic system is in fact just. It meets the conditions of the difference principle because no further transfers of wealth to the worst-off class would in fact improve its position. Then some impending catastrophe (for example) presents officials with a choice. They can act so that the position of the representative member of the small worst-off class is worsened by a just noticeable amount or so that the position of everyone else is dramatically worsened and they become almost as poor as the worst-off. Does justice really require the much greater loss to everyone but the poorest in order to prevent a very small loss by them?

It may be a sufficient reply to such questions that circumstances of that sort are very unlikely to arise, and that in fact the fates of the various economic orders are or can easily be "chained" together so that improvements in the worst-off class will in fact be accompanied by improvement in at least the other classes just above them. But this reply does not remove the theoretical question whether, in all circumstances, it is really and exclusively the situation of the worst-off group that determines what is just.

Equality of resources, as described here, does not single out any group whose status has that position. It aims to provide a description of (or rather a set of devices for aiming at) equality of resources person by person, and the considerations of each person's history that affect what he should have, in the name of equality, do not include his membership in any economic or social class. I do not mean that our theory, even as so far detailed, claims any impressive degree of accuracy for those devices. On the contrary, even in the artificially simple case we treated, we several times had to concede speculation and compromise, and sometimes even indeterminacy, in the statement of what equality would require in particular circumstances. But the theory nevertheless proposes that equality is in principle a matter of individual right rather than one of group position. Not, of course, in the sense that each has a predetermined share at his disposal regardless of what he does or what happens to others. On the contrary, the theory ties the fates of people together in the way that the dominant devices of actual and hypothetical markets are meant to describe, but in the different sense that the theory supposes that equality defines a relation among citizens that is individualized for each, and therefore can be seen to set entitlements as much from the point of view of each person as from that of anyone else in the community. Even when our theory helps itself to the idea of an average utility curve, as it does in the construction of hypothetical insurance markets, it does so as a matter of probability judgments about particular people's particular tastes and ambitions, in the interests of giving them what they are, as individuals, entitled to have, rather than as part of any premise that equality is a matter of equality between groups. Rawls, on the other hand, assumes that the difference principle ties justice to a class, not as a matter of second-best practical accommodation to some deeper version of equality which is in principle more individualized, but because the choice in the original position, which defines what justice even at bottom is, would for practical reasons be framed in class terms from the start.[18]

It is impossible to say, a priori, whether the difference principle or equality of resources will work to achieve greater absolute equality in what Rawls calls primary goods. That would depend upon circumstances. Suppose, for example, that the tax necessary to provide the right coverage for handicaps and the unemployed has the long-term effect of discouraging investment and in this way reducing the primary-goods prospects of the representative member of the worst-off class. Certain individual members of the worst-off group who are handicapped or who are and will remain unemployed would be better off under the tax scheme (as would certain members of other classes as well), but the average or representative member of the worst-off class would be worse off. The difference principle, which looks to the worst-off group as a whole, would condemn the tax, but equality of resources would recommend it nevertheless.

In the circumstances of the familiar bizarre questions just described, when a just-noticeable loss to the representative member of the worst-off class, from a just base, could be prevented only by very substantial losses to those better off, the difference principle is committed to preventing that small loss even at that cost. Equality of resources, on the contrary, would be sensitive to quantitative differences of just the sort that those who object to Rawls's theory on that account believe should matter. If the base is an equal division of resources, this means, not that any transfer to the worst-off group would work to the long-run loss of that group, which it might or might not, but that any such transfer would be unfair to others. The fact that those at the bottom do not have more would not indicate that it is impossible to give them more, but rather that they have all that they are entitled to have. If some economic catastrophe is now threatened, a government that allows a much greater loss to fall on one citizen, in order to avert a much smaller loss to a second, would not be treating the former as an equal, because, since equality in itself requires no further special attention to the second, that government must have more concern with his fate than it has for the fate of others. So if the loss threatened to the financially worst-off is indeed really inconsequential to him, as the bizarre question assumes, then that is an end of the matter.

But it does not follow that equality of resources turns into utilitarianism in the face of examples like these. It is, in fact, sensitive to more, or at least different, quantitative information than either the difference principle or utilitarianism is. For suppose the impending catastrophe threatens the worst-off group, not with a trivial loss as in the original question, but with a substantial loss, though not as great, in aggregate, as the loss threatened to those better-off. Equality of resources must ask whether the calculations of the hypothetical insurance market, and of the tax scheme in force, took adequate account of the risk of the threat now about to materialize. It might not have. The possibility of a substantial loss from the unexpected quarter, if it had been anticipated, might have led the average buyer in that market to purchase either catastrophe or unemployment insurance at a higher level of coverage, and this fact might affect an official's present decision about how to distribute the coming loss. He might be persuaded, for example, that allowing the loss to fall on those better-off, in spite of the overall welfare loss, would reach a situation closer to the situation all would have been in had the tax scheme better reflected what people would have done in the hypothetical market with that additional information.

Such contrasts in the practical advice that the difference principle and equality of resources offer in particular circumstances are in fact myriad, and these examples are meant only to be suggestive of others. These contrasts are organized around the theoretical distinction I have already noticed. The difference principle is tuned to only one of the dimensions of equality that equality of resources recognizes. The former supposes that flat equality in primary goods, without regard to differences in ambition, taste, occupation, or consumption, let alone differences in physical condition or handicap, is basic or true equality. Since (once the priority of liberty is satisfied) justice consists in equality, and since true equality is just this flat equality, any compromise or deviation can be justified only on the grounds that it is in the interests of the only people who might properly complain of the deviation.

This unidimensional analysis of equality would plainly be unsatisfactory if applied person by person. It would fall before the argument that it is not an equal division of social resources when someone who consumes more of what others want nevertheless has as much left over as someone who consumes less; nor that someone who chooses to work at a more productive occupation, measured by what others want, should have no more resources in consequence than someone who prefers leisure. (It would fall before such arguments, that is, unless it were converted into a form of equality of welfare through the doubtful proposition that equality in primary goods, in spite of different consumption or occupational histories, is the best guarantee of equality of welfare.)

So (as Rawls makes plain) the difference principle does not tie itself to groups rather than individuals as a second-best accommodation to some deeper vision of equality that is individualistic. Any such deeper vision would condemn the difference principle as inadequate. It ties itself to groups in principle, because the idea of equality among social groups, defined in economic terms, is especially congenial to the flat interpretation of equality. Indeed, the idea of equality as equality among economic groups permits no other interpretation. Since the members of any economic group will be widely diverse in tastes, ambitions, and conceptions of the good life, these must drop away from any principle stating what true equality among groups requires, and we are left with only the requirement that they be equal on the only dimension on which they can, as groups, possibly differ. The tie between the difference principle and the group taken as its unit of social measure is close to definitional.

We must be wary in rushing from this fact to conclusions about Rawls's theory of justice as a whole. The first of his principles of justice is plainly meant to be individualistic in a way that the difference principle is not, and any evaluation of the role of the individual in the theory as a whole would require a careful analysis of that principle and of the manner in which the two principles might work in harness. But insofar as the difference principle is meant to express a theory of equality of resources, it expresses a theory different in its basic vocabulary and design from the theory sketched here. It might well be worthwhile to pursue that difference further, perhaps by elaborating and working out in more detail the differences between the consequences of the two theories in practical circumstances. But I shall turn instead to the first of the two issues of comparison I distinguished.

I have tried to show the appeal of equality of resources, as interpreted here, only by making plainer its motivation and defending its coherence and practical force. I have not tried to defend it in what might be considered a more direct way, by deducing it from more general and abstract political principles. So the question arises whether that sort of defense could be provided and, in particular, whether it could be found in Rawls's general method. The fact that equality of resources differs in various ways, some of them fundamental, from Rawls's own difference principle is not decisive against this possibility. For perhaps we might show that the people who inhabit Rawls's original position would choose, behind the veil of their ignorance, not his difference principle, but either equality of resources or some intermediate constitutional principles such that, when the veil was lifted, it would be discovered that equality of resources satisfied these principles better than the difference principle could.

I hope it is clear that I have not presented any such argument here. It is true that I have argued that an equal distribution is a distribution that would result from people's choices under certain circumstances, some of which, as in the case of the hypothetical insurance markets, require the counterfactual assumption that people are ignorant of what in fact they are very likely to know. But this argument is different from an argument from the original position in two ways. First, my arguments have been designed to permit people as much knowledge as it is possible to allow them without defeating the point of the exercise entirely. In particular, they allow people enough self-knowledge, as individuals, to keep relatively intact their sense of their own personality, and especially their theory of what is valuable in life, whereas it is central to the original position that this is exactly the knowledge people lack. Second, and more important, my arguments are constructed against the background of assumptions about what equality requires in principle. It is not intended, as Rawls's argument is intended, to establish that background. My arguments enforce rather than construct a basic design of justice, and that design must find support, if at all, elsewhere than in those arguments.

I do not mean to suggest, however, that I am simply agnostic about the project of supporting equality of resources as a political ideal by showing that people in the original position would choose it. I think that any such project must fail, or rather, that it is misconceived, because some theory of equality, like equality of resources, is necessary to explain why the original position is a useful device—or one among a number of useful devices—for considering what justice is. The project, as just described, would therefore be too self-sustaining. The device of an original position (as I have argued at length elsewhere)[19] cannot plausibly be taken as the starting point for political philosophy. It requires a deeper theory beneath it, a theory that explains why the original position has the features that it does and why the fact that people would choose particular principles in that position, if they would, certifies those principles as principles of justice. The force of the original position as a device for arguments for justice, or of any particular design of the original position for that purpose, depends, in my view, on the adequacy of an interpretation of equality of resources that supports it, not vice versa.

3

The Place of Liberty

I. Introduction: Liberty and Equality

Preface

In Chapters 1 and 2 I argued for a conception of equality according to which ideal equality consists in circumstances in which people are equal not in their welfare but in the resources at their command. What are the implications for liberty of that claim about equality?

The question is limited in two ways. First, I mean by liberty what is sometimes called negative liberty—freedom from legal constraint—not freedom or power more generally. Second, I am interested not in liberty generally, but only in the connection between liberty and distributional equality. So though I shall defend a characteristic thesis of liberalism, that people's liberty over matters of great personal concern should not be infringed, I shall defend that thesis only against challenges grounded in distributional arguments. I shall not consider moralistic or paternalistic challenges to liberalism; I shall not consider the argument, for example, that liberty in matters of religion must be abolished in order to ensure everyone's salvation. There are, of course, fundamentalist political movements, like the Moral Majority, that oppose liberalism on grounds of that sort. But distributional challenges to liberalism are, I believe, of greater political importance now than moralistic or political ones. It is a popular opinion that certain liberties, including freedom of choice in education, must be limited in order to achieve true economic equality, for example. It is also a popular opinion, though in different quarters, that other liberties, including freedom of sexual choice, must be limited in order to give the majority the moral environment it wishes to have and is entitled to have as a matter of distributional justice. I do consider arguments against liberalism of that character.

I try to defend, however, a much more general claim: that if we accept equality of resources as the best conception of distributional equality, liberty becomes an aspect of equality rather than, as it is often thought to be, an independent political ideal potentially in conflict with it. My argument for that thesis is complex, and it might be well to provide, in advance, an informal description of the main ideas the argument develops. Many of us believe that what we consider the morally important liberties—freedom of speech, religion, and conviction, and freedom of choice in important personal matters, for example—should be protected except in the most extreme circumstances, and we would be reluctant to think that these liberties should be abridged even for the sake of gains in equality. But the latter view is very hard to defend. We are willing to limit even important liberties for the sake of other goals, after all. We limit freedom of speech in various ways to protect ourselves from unwanted noise at inconvenient times, and we limit freedom of choice in education to ensure that children receive competent schooling. But if these important liberties yield to competing values of that sort, why should they not yield to the normally more imperative requirements of distributional justice?

If liberty were valuable in the way some people think art can be valuable—for its own sake, quite apart from its impact on those who enjoy it—then we might be able to understand, if not to approve, the view that liberty is of such fundamental metaphysical importance that it must be protected whatever the consequences for people. But liberty seems valuable to us only because of the consequences we think it does have for people: we think lives led under circumstances of liberty are better lives just for that reason. Can it really be more important that the liberty of some people be protected, to improve the lives those people lead, than that other people, who are already worse off, have the various resources and other opportunities that *they* need to lead decent lives? How could we defend that view? We might be tempted to dogmatism: to declare our intuition that liberty is a fundamental value that must not be sacrificed to equality, and then claim that no more can or needs to be said. But that is hollow, and too callous. If liberty is transcendently important we should be able to say something, at least, about why.

Those are among my reasons for thinking that any appealing defense of the morally important liberties must proceed in a different, less conventional way: not by insisting that liberty is more important than equality, but by showing that these liberties must be protected according to the best view of what distributional equality is, the best view of when a society's distribution of property treats each citizen with equal concern. That claim seems plausible if we accept equality of resources as the best view. Other conceptions of equality define an equal distribution through a metric that is insensitive to the distinct quality and value of liberty. Equality of welfare understood as the satisfaction of tastes and preferences, for example, defines an equal distribution as one in which people's preferences are equally satisfied, and since it is a contingent matter how much people prefer liberty to other resources they might secure by its sacrifice, it seems dubious that protecting the morally important liberties will always be justified as improving equality of welfare.

Equality of resources, on the other hand, provides an account of distributional equality that is immediately and obviously sensitive to the special character and importance of liberty. It makes an equal distribution depend not on a bare outcome that can be measured directly, like preference-satisfaction, but on a process of coordinated decisions in which people who take responsibility for their own ambitions and projects, and who accept, as part of that responsibility, that they belong to a community of equal concern, are able to identify the true costs of their own plans to other people, and so design and redesign these plans so as to use only their fair share of resources in principle available to all. Whether an actual society approaches equality of resources depends, then, on the adequacy of the process of discussion and choice it provides for that purpose. A substantial degree of liberty is necessary to make any such process adequate because the true cost to others of one person's having some resource or opportunity can be discovered only when people's ambitions and convictions are authentic and their choices and decisions reasonably well tailored to those ambitions and convictions. Neither is possible unless liberty is ample. So liberty is necessary to equality, according to this conception of equality, not on the doubtful and fragile hypothesis that people really value the important liberties more than other resources, but because liberty, whether or not people do value it above all else, is essential to any process in which equality is defined and secured. That does not make liberty instrumental to distributional equality any more than it makes the latter instrumental to liberty: the two ideas rather merge in a fuller account of when the law governing the distribution and use of resources treats everyone with equal concern.

It follows that equality of resources requires us to take a different view of political controversies, like the controversy over private education and private medicine, that are widely thought to present a stark choice between liberty and equality. If limiting freedom of choice in education and medicine really would improve equality of resources—as some limitations plainly would—then no defensible ideal of liberty would be compromised, and liberals should have no objection. But not every infringement of liberty that is said to promote equality of resources really does so, and infringing the liberties liberals are most concerned to protect—the morally most important liberties—could rarely, if ever, count as a contribution to equality so understood. Equality of resources provides a more convincing explanation of our intuitive convictions about the importance of liberty than any theory according to which liberty and equality are independent and sometimes conflicting virtues.

That is an advance summary of the issues considered and the conclusions proposed in this chapter. I must try to show, in some detail, which liberties are particularly important to an adequate process of reflection and decision in service of equality, and which liberties, on the contrary, must be limited to improve that process. I must try to show why the morally important liberties must be regarded as particularly invulnerable to such abridgment, and how far equality of resources can provide a practical guide to the steps that an unequal society might take, by limiting liberty, in the direction of greater equality. These are complex matters, and my argument is accordingly dense.

A. A Famous Conflict

Do liberty and equality often conflict, as is widely supposed? Must an egalitarian society cheat the liberty of its citizens? Or can the two virtues be reconciled, so that we can have all we should anyway want of each? If so, is this reconciliation a happy and perhaps temporary accident? Or are the two virtues tied together in some more conceptual way, so that compromising one necessarily violates the other? We shall need examples of situations in which liberty and equality are thought to conflict, and I draw these from actual political controversies in Britain and the United States.

Campaign expenditure. In 1974 Congress enacted a statute that limited the amount any one person could lawfully spend to advance the interests of a particular political candidate.[1] The statute's aim was egalitarian: a rich person, allowed to spend as much as he or she wishes in politics, will have a much larger impact on the political process than a poor person. The Supreme Court nevertheless held that the constraint violated the freedom of speech protected by the First Amendment, and declared that part of the statute unconstitutional.[2] The Court's decision has been widely challenged.[3]

Private sector in basic needs. The second issue is one lively in British politics. Britain has a national health service. People with sufficient means or who hold jobs providing the necessary health insurance as a fringe benefit may nevertheless pay for private medical care, which allows them, among other benefits, to jump the queue for treatment of painful and incapacitating disease. Some sections of the Labour Party favor abolishing private medicine, through laws that would forbid private arrangements for medical care, in the interests of equality. But most British politicians and, apparently, most of the British public reject that policy on the ground that it would violate an important part of their liberty: freedom of choice in medical care.

Minimum wage and maximum hour legislation. My third example has a more historical character, though the issue it presents is, as I shall argue much later, of continuing contemporary importance. Early in this century, U.S. state legislatures began to regulate employment contracts by limiting the hours people might be employed to work during a week or day or by stipulating minimum wages an employer might offer his employees. New York, for example, forbade bakers to work for more than sixty hours a week. Though the aims of such laws were no doubt mixed—the New York statute was defended as a health measure—the laws were widely welcomed as ameliorating the savage economic inequality many people were beginning to find intolerable. Nevertheless, the Supreme Court declared the New York regulation unconstitutional because, the Court said, it infringed another important liberty of constitutional standing: freedom of choice in contract and employment.[4] That decision is no longer followed,[5] and it is often cited as the second worst decision in the Court's history, yielding in dishonor only to *Dred Scott,* and as a minatory example of the dangers of encouraging the Justices to enforce their own views of political morality. Most of the critics of the decision seem to agree, however, that the case did present a conflict between liberty and equality; they criticize the Court only for insisting on its own preferred ranking of the two political ideals in place of the ranking the New York legislature had made.

These examples are arresting not only as cases in which liberty and equality are said to conflict, but as stories that seem to show how unimportant, for some people, equality really is. Few people would object to limits on even important freedoms if these limits served some other compelling purpose. Everyone agrees that freedom of speech may be constrained in order to prevent riots or stampedes, for example, and no one objects to regulation of medicine in the interests of health or safety. The Supreme Court, in *Lochner*, agreed that if the evidence had shown that New York's statute was justified as necessary to protect the health of bakers, the statute would be constitutional. Our examples—and the host of other political controversies they represent—are controversial only because in each case liberty is thought to conflict with equality rather than with something else.

So we may add another question to our initial list: Why should so many people think that equality counts for much less, in supposed conflicts with liberty, than other values or interests? If someone accepts that rights to liberty must yield to a variety of important competing interests, why should he not concede that, at least sometimes, equality is among these competing interests? A cynical answer suggests itself, of course: that many people reject equality because they are selfish. There is, I believe, a better (though perhaps not inconsistent) answer. Most of the people who seem to reject equality, in cases like our examples, do not actually reject it. They think equality very important indeed, but they do not think that the form in which equality is at stake in these cases is the important or genuine form of that virtue. I must explain and expand on that suggestion.

B. Two Senses of Two Ideas

We use the words "liberty" and "equality" in two senses. We use each as a flat description that carries, in itself, no suggestion of endorsement or complaint, and we also use each normatively to identify a political virtue or ideal that we do endorse. We use "liberty" in its flat sense simply to indicate the absence of constraint. Someone may say, using that sense, that liberty is reduced by laws prohibiting murder and theft, without implying that he opposes these laws. We use "liberty" in its normative sense, on the other hand, to describe the ways in which we believe people ought to be free. Americans use "liberty" in that second, normative, way when they say that liberty flourishes in their country and languishes elsewhere. They do not mean that people have more license in America, but that people are more free in the specific ways contemplated by liberty as a political virtue: to think and speak as they wish, for example.

We use "equality" in its flat sense simply to indicate sameness or identity along some specified or understood dimension without suggesting that the speaker believes sameness along that dimension is desirable. Someone can say, using that flat sense, that equality holds among people who all have the same wealth (or ability or happiness) without implying that sameness of wealth (or ability or happiness) is appropriate. We use "equality" in its normative sense, on the contrary, precisely to indicate the respect or respects in which the speaker thinks people should be the same, or treated the same way, as a matter of justice. When someone says that equality is possible only under socialism, he means that socialism is necessary, not for people to be the same in some respect or other, but to be the same in the respect he thereby declares to be the important one. Political philosophers who worry about conflicts between liberty and equality have the normative not the flat sense of these ideas in mind. They worry because they fear a conflict between political ideals, not just between descriptive properties. In any case, it is the conflict of normative ideals that I shall be exploring here.

C. Liberty: Rights Not License

Anyone who embraces liberty or equality as a normative ideal must have some opinion about the ways in which people should be free and the respects in which they should be the same or treated the same, and different people will have different opinions. Liberty and equality, in other words, are concepts that admit of different interpretations or conceptions. Whether we think liberty and equality conflict as ideals will undoubtedly depend on which conceptions of each we adopt. We can easily construct a conception of liberty such that liberty must obviously and inevitably conflict with any plausible conception of equality. An extreme anarchist conception of liberty, for example, which stipulated that people must be free to do whatever they might wish no matter what the consequences for others, would plainly conflict with equality, as it would with almost any other political virtue or goal. A society that forbids neither murder, nor theft, nor walking on the grass when that would injure common property cannot be egalitarian; nor can it be secure or prosperous or powerful or pleasant. We can also construct a conception of liberty with the opposite consequence: that liberty could never conflict with equality. If we stipulate, for example, that respecting liberty means allowing citizens to act in ways that produce and protect equality among them, then it is trivially true that liberty and equality cannot conflict.

Neither of these odd conceptions of liberty is satisfactory, however, because neither presents liberty as a distinct and compelling political ideal, as something whose sacrifice or compromise should in itself be a matter for regret. A more plausible conception of liberty will emerge from the argument later. Since the case for that conception will begin in the hypothesis that liberty and equality do not conflict, however, we must not rely on it when we are considering, in the earlier parts of this chapter, whether to accept or reject that hypothesis.

We will do better, in fact, not to rely on any one detailed conception of liberty for that purpose. We need only assume that any acceptable conception that captures the special importance of liberty will meet certain conditions, and then ask whether and in what circumstances a conception of liberty meeting those conditions will conflict with the demands of equality. I assume that any acceptable conception will reject the anarchist view of liberty as license; it will not count every constraint on the freedom of citizens to act as they might wish as an invasion of their liberty. Instead it will identify rights to certain designated freedoms as essential to liberty, and stipulate that government must not limit those freedoms without some special justification more powerful or compelling than the justification it requires for other political decisions, including constraints on other freedoms not protected by such rights. These rights will include, at a minimum, rights to freedom of conscience, commitment, speech, and religion, and to freedom of choice in matters touching central or important aspects of an agent's personal life, like employment, family arrangements, sexual privacy, and medical treatment.

Different people will add further and different rights to this list. They will rank differently the various rights they recognize, and take different views about which emergencies or urgent social goals would justify constraints on the freedoms the rights otherwise protect. But the dominant conceptions of liberty in our political community have this general structure: they protect not liberty as license but a set of discrete rights to particular freedoms. Liberty is widely thought to be in peril in our sample cases, for example, only because the freedom threatened in each case is regarded as special and protected by a right: the right to freedom of choice in speech or medical treatment or employment.

D. Equality: The Shadow over Liberty

We shall mainly be considering whether liberty, so understood, conflicts with a particular conception of equality—equality of resources—that I defended in Chapter 2. But it will be helpful first to consider the consequences of a conflict between liberty and any conception of equality, including that one. It is widely thought that if liberty and equality do conflict, an agonizing choice between the two virtues must be made. A familiar map of political argument, in fact, locates political parties or groups along a spectrum defined by the choices each makes in that situation. The spectrum runs between an absolutism of liberty at one end (liberty must never yield to equality when the two conflict) and a reverse absolutism of equality at the other. More moderate views supposedly range themselves between these two poles by assigning different relative weights to the two political virtues. But this popular topography is, I believe, deeply misleading as an account of the range of views available in our political culture. No theory that respects the basic assumptions which define that culture could subordinate equality to liberty, conceived as normative ideals, to any degree. Any genuine contest between liberty and equality is a contest liberty must lose.

I make that bold claim because I believe that we are now united in accepting the abstract egalitarian principle: government must act to make the lives of those it governs better lives, and it must show equal concern for the life of each. Anyone who accepts that abstract principle accepts equality as a political ideal, and though equality admits of different conceptions, these different conceptions are competing interpretations of that principle. So anyone who thinks that liberty and equality really do conflict on some occasion must think that protecting liberty means acting in some way that does not show equal concern for all citizens. I doubt that many of us would think, after reflection, that this could ever be justified.

I do not mean that the abstract egalitarian principle is so empty or trivial that no one could possibly deny it. On the contrary, people might conceivably have a variety of reasons for rejecting the principle altogether or for qualifying it in an important way. They might reject it altogether by denying that government should take any interest in improving the lives of citizens. Or they might hold that, from the point of view of good government, the lives of some—those of one race or caste, perhaps, or those who belong to one religion, or those who are more virtuous—are more important than the lives of others. Or they might accept the abstract egalitarian principle but qualify it by denying that it is an absolute principle. They might argue, for example, that though government should show equal concern for the lives of all its citizens, it should also attend to other values not captured in or reducible to that concern. They might think, for instance, that government should also aim to improve the nation's power and influence, for the sake of glory rather than for the good of citizens one by one; or, more plausibly, that government should aim to advance knowledge or to protect and develop art and other forms of high culture, again for the sake of knowledge or art itself, and not for the role they play in making people's lives better. In that case, they might think that on some occasions it would be best all things considered to neglect certain political acts that are recommended by the principle of equal concern in order to pursue other goals. They might think it would be best, for example, to subsidize art with funds that could otherwise be used in economic programs that would bring the distribution of wealth closer to what equal concern for all citizens would otherwise require.

The abstract egalitarian principle can theoretically be rejected outright or qualified in all these different ways. But no significant body of political opinion among us would either reject it outright or qualify it in any way that would allow liberty to win a conflict with it. Rejecting the principle altogether seems out of the question for us; it is no longer arguable, at least in public, that officials should be more concerned about the lives of some citizens than about the lives of others. Nor does it make sense to accept the abstract principle but qualify it by supposing liberty to be an independent competitor in some pluralistic catalogue of political virtues. Some people treat art as a fundamental value independent of and competitive with abstract equality. But they can sensibly think that only because they think art has value for reasons independent of the contribution it makes to the lives of those who produce or enjoy or benefit from it. People believe, that is, in art for art's sake. But liberty cannot, in the same way, have intrinsic value apart from the role liberty plays in the lives of those who have it.[6] For it seems bizarre that people's having some particular right, like the right of free speech, could be objectively valuable, in and of itself, quite apart from the consequences of that right for them. I do not mean what is evidently false: that having rights is always good for people in the narrow sense of improving their welfare. Critics of liberalism often point out that people are sometimes happier with less liberty, and wise liberals concede this. But no one could be enthusiastic for liberty, as something intrinsically valuable, who did not think that lives led under conditions of liberty were for just that reason more valuable lives, because more autonomous or more authentic, or lives of greater dignity, or better lives in some other way. So though it might seem plausible that the value of art is not exhausted by the various ways in which it makes the lives of at least some people better, a parallel claim does not seem plausible for rights like freedom of choice in speech, medical treatment, or employment.

If liberty is valuable because lives led under liberty are more valuable lives, then the egalitarian principle itself requires government to attend to liberty, because it requires government to have concern for the lives of those it governs. Then how can equality possibly conflict with an adequate conception of liberty? Only if two conditions are met together: (1) in spite of the fact that liberty is valuable to people's lives, the position of some group within the community would nevertheless be improved, on balance, by eliminating some liberty; and (2) equal concern for that group requires that this be done. Assume, for example, that poor people would have better medical care, and be better off overall, if private medicine were abolished, and that showing equal concern for them requires this. If government refuses to abolish private medicine, then, by hypothesis, the poor are left in a worse condition than equal concern would permit. Since liberty, we assume, has no value or importance except for the contribution it makes to people's lives, that result cannot be justified by citing some principle or goal unrelated to the concern government should have for its citizens. It could be justified, then, only if we accepted a principle flatly inconsistent with the egalitarian principle: that in these circumstances the lives of poor people are less important than the lives of others. Equality can coexist with art, as two independent goals that sometimes conflict, because we can accept either as a value without contradicting the other. But we cannot accept both that government must have equal concern for all lives and that it may sometimes show more concern for some than for others. That would be not pluralism but incoherence.

We should consolidate this important point. There is a dark side to the issues we are exploring, a shadow hanging over liberty. Any genuine conflict between liberty and equality—any conflict between liberty and the requirements of the best conception of the abstract egalitarian principle—is a contest that liberty must lose. We cannot reject the egalitarian principle outright, because it is absurd that government should show no concern for the lives of its citizens, and immoral that it should show more concern for the lives of some than of others. Nor is it plausible, for the reasons we just reviewed, to treat liberty as an independent value competitive with and sometimes dominant over the abstract principle. So we cannot, in good conscience, press for any right to liberty that conflicts with the demands of equality on our favored conception. Any genuine conflict is not just a philosophical discovery but an emotional defeat. We have that important reason for striving to show that no genuine conflict exists, that no right to liberty we would otherwise want to recognize would be compromised by policies our conception of equality demands.

E. Conceptions of Equality

I said earlier that genuine conflicts might arise for some conceptions of equality and not for others, and it is time to develop that remark. If I am right that the dominant tradition of modern Western political culture accepts the abstract egalitarian principle, either as absolute or in some qualified form, then arguments about political justice within that tradition must be capable of being understood as arguments about what equal concern really means or comes to. They must be capable of being understood, in other words, as interpretations or conceptions of equality in the abstract sense. In fact, most theories of justice in the contemporary literature of political philosophy can readily be understood in that way.[7]

We find many conceptions of equal concern in that literature. We find utilitarian conceptions which claim that a government shows equal concern when it takes the welfare of each member of the community into account in the same way, by identifying and pursuing policies that promise the greatest average welfare in the long run. We find laissez-faire egalitarians who argue that equal concern means not interfering in anyone's life, so that (and except as necessary in order that) people's fates depend on their own abilities, initiative, and luck.[8] We find welfare egalitarians who insist that a government treats people with equal concern only when its policies aim to make the welfare of each person as nearly equal to the welfare of others as possible. We find resource egalitarians who believe, instead, that equal concern requires policies that aim to provide each citizen, so far as this is possible, with an equal share of the resources the economic structure distributes to them, measured by fixing the value of the resources each person has as the cost to others of that person's having them.

Laissez-faire egalitarians presumably will never see a conflict between equality on their conception and the particular rights to freedom I said any acceptable conception of liberty would recognize. On their view, treating people with equal concern means letting them produce and trade under only such regulations as are necessary to protect security of person and property and the efficacy of contract, and so they will not think that equality could ever be improved by regulations on speech, by abolishing private medicine, or by maximum-hour or minimum-wage legislation. On the contrary, treating people with equal concern, on their view, requires respecting those liberties in full. But utilitarian-egalitarians must concede at least the possibility of conflict between equality on their conception and those rights to freedom. They must admit that under some circumstances, protecting freedom of speech or political association, for example, will diminish rather than improve average utility. Utilitarians, in fact, argue that enforcing the basic liberties our culture recognizes is, as things happen, the best way to maximize average welfare in the long run. I know of no good argument that this is so, however; it strikes me as a whistling-in-the-dark act of faith undertaken just to reconcile liberty with the utilitarian creed. Welfare-egalitarians might also be tempted by the same strategy; it is, however, even more dubious that protecting the traditional liberties as rights will always be the best means of making welfare equal on any sensible conception of what welfare is. A utilitarian-egalitarian or welfare-egalitarian, therefore, might well be required to disown liberty from time to time.

Can liberty and equality conflict, with that uncomfortable consequence, when we take equality of resources to be the best conception of equality? That will be our main question in the next several sections. But I must first return to an observation I made about our sample cases just before we began this brief account of concepts and conceptions of liberty and equality. I pointed out that in these cases many people seem to rank equality not only below liberty, but below a variety of other social concerns like safety and health. In my more recent argument, however, I claimed that equality has, for most of us, a near-absolute force, and that it cannot coherently be qualified by supposing that liberty ranks beside it as an independent political ideal. Do the examples contradict that claim?

We might explain the examples in various ways. Perhaps I am wrong in my view about the principled convictions most people would be willing to defend. Perhaps many more people than I think would reject the abstract egalitarian principle outright. But I offered another account of the examples that is consistent with my claim that very few people would, and I can now expand that explanation. People often use "equality," as I said, in a flat sense, to describe identity along some dimension indicated by the context, even when they do not believe that the best conception of the abstract egalitarian principle requires identity along that dimension. That linguistic fact threatens confusion when people with different conceptions of equality argue. When someone proposes that private medicine must be abolished, for example, in order to protect equality, he is plainly appealing equality in its normative sense. He believes that treating people as equals requires making their situations the same in ways that include offering them the same opportunity for medical care. Someone who rejects the proposal believes that the soundest conception of equality does not require that. If he states his view that way, then he suggests no conflict between liberty and equality. The argument is then about what equality requires, not whether equality should be subordinated to something else. But he may choose to state his position in a different way, by saying that liberty is more important than equality, in which case he means that liberty must prevail over what his opponent thinks the egalitarian principle requires. He uses equality in the flat, descriptive sense to indicate identity in a dimension his opponent, but not he, thinks crucial to equality as a political ideal. So perhaps, as I suggested, most people who say that equality must sometimes yield to liberty do not actually think that there is any genuine conflict between the two ideals as ideals. They mean only to deny that someone else's conception of normative equality is a sound conception. Even if I am right in this reading of popular opinion, of course, it does not follow that there is no conflict between the ideals. On some conceptions of equality, as I said, conflict seems likely. Our question is whether conflict arises if we accept the conception of equality I believe most attractive. We must face that philosophical issue directly; it is not decided, either way, by popular opinion or political rhetoric.

F. A Disclaimer

In the following pages I shall consider one group of arguments for the familiar conclusions that liberty and equality conflict: those drawn from the idea of distributive justice. I shall argue that if equality of resources furnishes the best conception of distributional equality, then these arguments fail. According to equality of resources, the rights to liberty we regard as fundamental are a part or aspect of distributional equality, and so are automatically protected whenever equality is achieved. The priority of liberty is secured, not at the expense of equality, but in its name. My case for that agreeable conclusion will be somewhat complex, however, and will rely in part on a vocabulary drawn from economics. It might therefore strike some readers as too clinical. For them the appeal of liberty is immediate and profound, and they are wary of argument that seems to make its place contingent on the intricacies of some dense dialectic. Nor could they accept that liberty is in some way instrumental or subordinate to equality; liberty, they think, is the condition of human dignity and is therefore of transcendent importance in its own right. I should therefore say, in advance, that my argument does not claim to supply the only or the most intuitively powerful argument for the liberties I discuss. And some liberties that others claim as rights are not supported by my arguments at all. I argue only that rights adequate to an attractive conception of liberty are given so foundational a place under equality of resources that conflicts between those rights and that view of distributional equality cannot arise. In any case, my argument is not intended to subordinate liberty to equality, but rather to show that though we often distinguish these two virtues in political argument and analysis, they are mutually reflecting aspects of a single humanist ideal. I shall return to that large and dark claim at the end of the chapter, when I hope it will be plainer what it means.[9]

II. Two Strategies

A. The Strategies Distinguished

We must try to reconcile liberty and equality, if we care for liberty, because any genuine conflict between the two is a contest liberty must lose. We should now distinguish two strategies for attempting that reconciliation: a two-step interest-based strategy and a one-step constitutive strategy. The two strategies differ in the connections they assume between the definition of an ideal distribution of resources, on the one hand, and the rights that constitute liberty on the other. The two-step strategy uses the idea of people's interests to define an ideal distribution. Each version of that strategy stipulates a particular account of how people's interests are to be identified, and what function of different people's interests an ideal distribution aims to satisfy. It does not appeal to liberty as part of that definition; it does not define people's interests in such a way that liberty is automatically, by definition, among those interests. But then, as a second and further step, it argues that, as things fall out, certain liberties are instrumentally connected to the satisfaction of interests so that protecting interests in the right proportion or according to the right formula requires establishing and respecting rights to these liberties.

We have already noticed one example of this interest strategy at work. The utilitarian conception of equality defines an ideal distribution as a distribution that promotes the highest possible average welfare in the long run. That definition leaves open the question of liberty: it does not rule out, by definition, the possibility that utility will in fact be maximized by denying all rights to liberty. But utilitarians hope to show, in the fashion of the interest strategy, that in fact, given the world as we find it, protecting freedom of choice and defending rights to speech and other fundamental liberties are the best available means of achieving the greatest possible average welfare.

The constitutive strategy, in contrast, builds liberty into the structure of its chosen conception of equality from the start. It insists that liberty must figure in the very definition of an ideal distribution, so that, for that reason, there can be no problem of reconciling liberty and equality. We have also noticed an example of this strategy at work. Laissez-faire egalitarians believe that an ideal egalitarian distribution cannot be defined except historically. The ideal distribution, on their view, is whatever distribution actually results from production and exchange conducted in the shadow of a political structure that protects the liberties they believe fundamental. So, as I said, laissez-faire egalitarians will not encounter any conflict between the liberties they are drawn to recognize and the historically generated distribution they consider ideal. They will not encounter any such conflict because, by hypothesis, any political decision that infringed their favored liberties would destroy rather than promote what they take equality to be.

Contractarian theories of justice also generally use the interest strategy for bringing liberty into the story they tell. They insist that just principles of government are those that people would agree in choosing, as in their own interest, under conditions of choice specified in the right way. An ideal distribution, for these theories, is a distribution fully meeting the principles that would be chosen in those circumstances. The appeal of any particular contractarian theory depends on how those conditions of choice are designed. In the crudest form of contractarian theory, the principles of justice are those that actual people with full knowledge of their social position, tastes, ambitions, and moral and religious convictions would agree upon as in the best interests of each, if they could assemble for that purpose. The interest strategy, for that crude version, would require demonstrating that everyone would in fact agree to principles of justice protecting liberty, or at least would agree to such principles after proper reflection. But that is very implausible. Why should members of a dominant majority of conviction, for example, agree to principles protecting the freedom of worship and choice of a minority as in the majority's interest, especially when the costs of protecting that liberty mean fewer material goods for them?

John Rawls's contractarian theory is much more complex. In its latest version, choice conditions are constructed so as to reflect, first, a conception of persons as citizens of a free and equal community, each of whom has higher-order "moral" interests in protecting his or her capacity for justice and his or her capacity rationally to form and revise conceptions of the good, and, second, principles of reasonableness suited to the political culture of Western liberal democracies. So parties to the "original position," in which principles of justice are chosen, act as fiduciaries for other people, whose social and economic position, talents and skills, tastes, and conceptions of the good are hidden from the fiduciaries by a "veil of ignorance."[10] Rawls's strategy for reconciling liberty and equality appears to be a mixed interest and constitutive strategy.[11] Liberty enters into the definition of equality, in the manner of the constitutive strategy, in the following way. A political community treats people with equal concern when it respects the principles of justice that would be chosen by their representatives in the original position, and the conditions of the original position are modeled so as to assume that people have a basic interest in liberty. The fiduciaries of the original position are instructed that their beneficiaries have a compelling interest in developing and exploiting their own capacity for autonomy— their capacity to form, criticize, and pursue conceptions of the good life— and that interest plainly cannot be served in a community whose rules do not provide ample freedom of choice over at least important matters.[12] But Rawls seems to retain at least a small element of the interest strategy: he suggests that the fiduciaries of the original position will rely on empirical instrumental claims about how people's assumed higher-order interests are best served in designing particular rights to liberty. These include, for example, claims about the circumstances in which people will feel the confidence in their own powers necessary for self-respect.

B. The Interest Strategy

The interest strategy, if successful, is appealing for a variety of reasons. It offers to put liberty on a secure footing by deriving rights to liberty from more basic assumptions about justice that do not already include those rights. The constitutive strategy, in contrast, seems dogmatic and unproductive. It simply assumes that stipulated rights to liberty are required by justice, and the strategy therefore cannot be convincing to anyone who begins by disagreeing with that assumption. The constitutive strategy that I described in the hands of laissez-faire egalitarians, for example, tries to win its position by fiat. It stipulates that treating people with equal concern means respecting economic rights that work to the benefit of those with talent and luck and against those with neither. That is hardly self-evident.

But the interest strategy faces a different difficulty I glanced at a moment ago when I described crude contractarianism. No citizen with confidence in his own judgment would prefer to be without some protected liberty for himself, all else equal: I can be no worse off just for having the right to speak in politics, or to make my own choice of willing sexual partners, or to march in unpopular demonstrations, even if I never choose to exercise these liberties in a way that, but for these rights, my society would forbid. As H. L. A. Hart pointed out, however, I may very well think myself worse off for these liberties' being general in my society, that is, for other people's having rights of that sort.[13] I am particularly likely to think so at what we might call the margin of these rights. I would no doubt be worse off if no one in my community was permitted to discuss politics with others, even in private. But it hardly follows that I would be worse off if large and unpopular political demonstrations, which many citizens found deeply offensive, were prohibited in public areas; I might think myself better off, at least on balance, if the public funds necessary for policing such demonstrations were spent toward crime prevention instead, or toward better hospitals. Suppose the various liberties now protected by the U.S. Constitution, on the Supreme Court's interpretation of that document, were separately costed in this way, and people were then asked whether they thought it would be in their own individual interests to trade some of these for other advantages that could be gained by abandoning them. It is extremely unlikely that most Americans would decline all such trades; indeed I fear that the majority would accept a great many of them.

Contractarians wedded to the interest strategy might respond to this difficulty in various ways. They might claim that if people reflected on the issue calmly, with good arguments before them, they would in fact decline to trade part of their liberty for anything else. But that seems just another whistling-in-the-dark act of faith. Contractarians might say that whether or not people would accept trades after reflection, it would be irrational to do so. But that seems too strong a claim; why is it irrational for someone who knows that his own political convictions are conventional to trade off the general liberty of political demonstration for whatever advantages he believes this would bring him?

Rawls's version of contractarianism does not allow people to make choices about fundamental principles of justice on the basis of their own peculiar situation or advantages. Its argument for liberty uses, as I said, a mixed method combining features of a constitutive and an interest strategy. The interest strategy seems at work when the fiduciaries choose a particular scheme of liberties as the scheme calculated, better than rival schemes, to develop the assumed moral powers of their beneficiaries. Rawls argues that fiduciaries following that strategy would establish rights to freedom of conscience and thought, of speech and association, and to various personal liberties that are familiar in our political culture. His arguments show how the interest strategy inevitably makes the place of liberty in justice depend on debatable assumptions about what people's interests actually are. He emphasizes, for example, the fundamental importance of self-respect, which he treats as a primary good that fiduciaries would aim to provide for those whom they represent. Self-respect, he says, has two elements: "our self-confidence as a fully cooperating member of society rooted in the development and exercise of the two moral powers" and "our secure sense of our own value rooted in the conviction that we carry out a worthwhile plan of life."[14] He believes that fiduciaries would protect the priority of liberty, among other reasons, because "self-respect is most effectively encouraged and supported by the two principles of justice, again precisely because of the insistence on the equal basic liberties."[15] But some philosophers and sociologists insist that people are much more likely to think that their lives have value, and that they have been successful in realizing their powers for justice and conviction, in a society with a settled and relatively unquestioned common theory of the good life, on which they can draw for confirmation and reinforcement. These philosophers argue that in a more liberal society, whose public philosophy is avowedly neutral among conceptions of the good, the diversity of conviction and evident lack of irresistible argument for any party's views undermine the confidence that a morally homogeneous society promotes.[16]

Fiduciaries drawn to that theory of the conditions of self-confidence will reject Rawls's argument for the priority of liberty insofar as it relies on his contradictory view of those conditions. Of course, they will want to protect those they represent, who may already have formed unpopular convictions, from savage forms of persecution. But they will see no need to create constitutional barriers that would prevent the community from achieving religious and moral orthodoxy over a few generations in less ruthless ways—perhaps by constraining the freedom of people with unpopular or challenging creeds to spread them by proselytizing speech, for example. They will believe that a community can develop stable self-confidence only by at least aiming in the direction of moral and religious consensus.

Rawls might well be able to show that his own view of the conditions of self-respect, which supposes that genuine self-respect is impossible unless the liberties he regards as fundamental are protected, is more accurate than the competing view I just described. But to the extent that his dispute with that view is an empirical one, about what principles would actually be in the interests of people with the moral capacities he assumes, the place of liberty in justice remains hostage to disputes about what those interests actually require. And though it is of course no decisive argument against Rawls's version of the interest strategy that many actual people disavow the importance of the traditional basic liberties to their own lives, even after reflection and argument, that fact nevertheless threatens any confident assumption that wise trustees would think these liberties in everyone's interests, even from behind a veil of ignorance. For it is far from apparent that all popular opinions about the value of liberty reflect only considerations of special personal advantage that the original position would exclude. Popular opinion may also reflect widespread convictions about what would be people's interests generally. If the rival constitutive strategy can be shown to be less dogmatic than it first appears, it might after all provide a better defense for liberty in an egalitarian world.

III. Can Liberty Be Auctioned?

A. An Interest-Based Argument

We turn at last to our main question. Do liberty and equality conflict under equality of resources? I discussed that conception of equality in Chapter 2, and I need offer only a skeletal summary here. Roughly, it stipulates that an ideal egalitarian distribution will satisfy an appropriately complex version of the "envy" test: no one will envy the property assigned to or controlled by any other person. That test may be met, and equality of resources satisfied ideally, by a distribution in which people nevertheless have very different levels of welfare or well-being. In an actual society, whose citizens differ in productive capacities, the entry test cannot be met fully. Redistributive mechanisms can nevertheless be designed to improve the degree to which it is met. These might take the form, for example, of programs of taxation and redistribution modeled on the insurance decisions that members of the community would make under certain appropriate circumstances. In this and other ways, the envy test provides useful practical guidance.

We gain a better grasp of the envy test in action by imagining an artificial mechanism that could achieve a distribution satisfying that test. People on a desert island bid for various groups of the physical resources found there, from an initially equal stock of bidding resources like clamshells, and the auction is run repeatedly, in successive rounds, until everyone is content that it end. If it does end, the envy test is then satisfied, because no one envies the overall bundle of resources another has acquired, even though different people are happy or successful in different degrees. The auction provides only an initial distribution, which will be altered by all the post-auction decisions the parties make about trade, production, and consumption. The resources each person holds from time to time, as well as the welfare they provide him, will therefore depend not only on his own decisions but on those of others as well. This imaginary auction can serve as a rough model in designing political and economic institutions for the real world in search of as much equality of resources as can be found. If we accept equality of resources as the best conception of the abstract egalitarian principle, then, we want institutions that make the resources available to any one person depend so far as possible on the opportunity costs of those resources to others, in the way the imaginary auction and post-auction transactions make them so depend.

That brief description of equality of resources might seem to suggest that only the interest strategy could succeed in reconciling liberty and equality under equality of resources. Here is the argument that seems to drive us to that conclusion. Equality of resources assumes a fundamental distinction between a person, understood to include features of personality like convictions, ambitions, tastes, and preferences, and that person's circumstances, which include the resources, talents, and capacities he commands.[17] A person's welfare, on familiar conceptions of welfare, is sensitive to both personality and circumstances. But equality of resources aims to make circumstances rather than overall welfare equal, and is in that way different from equality of welfare. It seems undeniable, however, that a person's liberty—the range of actions open to him free from any legal constraint—belongs to his circumstances rather than to his person or personality.[18] The general ambition of equality of resources, which is to make circumstances equal under an appropriate version of the envy test, would therefore seem to apply to liberty as well as to material resources. Legal constraints should ideally be designed and distributed so that no one envies the circumstances of anyone else, taking into account not only his material resources but also the opportunities legal constraints allow him.

If that is a sound account of how equality of resources must treat liberty—if it must treat liberty as a resource like any other—then the liberty people will have in an ideal egalitarian distribution must depend on which rights to liberty people generally value, as in their own interests, and on how much they value those rights. Liberty and equality can then be reconciled, under equality of resources, only if enough people think that the rights to liberty an adequate conception of liberty would identify are so much in their own interests that each would choose to have that liberty, in his own bundle of resources, rather than anything else he could have acquired in its place. Equality of resources cannot appeal, as Rawls's method does, to counterfactual choices that people would make, or that fiduciaries would make for them, under circumstances of radical ignorance. For the envy test is a here-and-now test: it demands, in its account of ideal distribution, that people with full knowledge of their plans, projects, and attachments not prefer the resources assigned to someone else. Equality of resources insists that people be allowed to deploy all aspects of their personality in making the judgments on which the envy test depends.

If equality of resources must use the interest strategy to reconcile liberty and equality, therefore, it faces an extraordinarily difficult assignment, and the most likely consequence of its attempt to reconcile them is the near total defeat of liberty. Suppose freedom is just another resource, and so part of what is to be sold, along with land and raw materials, in the imaginary auction I described. Some ingenuity is needed to imagine how liberty might be auctioned. Here is one suggestion: imagine that the auctioneer draws up a list, before the auction begins, of liberties he believes parties to the auction might find important, and then prints a limited number of cards (something like "get out of jail" cards in Monopoly) each of which allows the bearer to exercise a particular liberty drawn from that list. One card, for example, would entitle the bearer to attend political rallies or demonstrations. Then the auctioneer sets a price for each liberty card by dividing the estimated cost to the community of protecting each liberty (the cost, for example, of policing political demonstrations) by the number of cards for that liberty he has printed; he sells the cards, in the general auction, at that price. If cards for any liberty remain unsold at the end of any auction round, he puts fewer cards up for sale, at a different price reflecting his new cost estimates, in the next round. If, on the contrary, all cards for a particular liberty sell in any round at the price fixed for that round, any party may ask that more cards be printed and sold, at a different price reflecting the increase, in the next round. If the auction finally ends, and this procedure has been followed, the auction has distributed liberties in a way that produces an envy-free distribution of liberties and other goods.

Under this design, each person is forced to decide how important each liberty is to him. If some particular liberty, like freedom of political association, proved to be very expensive, because the cost per card necessary to protect it, for example, was very high, given the number who wished to purchase it, people anxious for that liberty would be in the position of those who want expensive consumer goods like champagne or plovers' eggs. They would be required to pay for the expensive liberty, if they could afford it at all, by having much less of other goods or liberties. Some people would buy more liberties of each sort, and more liberties overall, than others. The envy test would nevertheless be satisfied. A would end the auction with many fewer liberties than B: B might be permitted to speak out on political subjects when A is not, for example. Their circumstances would still be equal overall, judged by the envy test, because A would have material resources that B lacks. The fate of liberty, in any post-auction society, would therefore depend wholly on the mix of preferences, tastes, convictions, ambitions, and other aspects of personality that happened to be found among the population. If the depressing suspicion I expressed earlier is accurate—that most people are indifferent about at least some of the basic liberties our constitutional traditions celebrate—liberty would not survive the auction in any robust form. Some people would pay the price necessary to guarantee the basic liberties for themselves, but not many would, and that fact alone would increase the price of liberty for those anxious to secure it.

No doubt it would be nearly impossible to administer a post-auction society in which people have different liberties. But we cannot appeal to that administrative difficulty as providing any reason to resist the conclusion the present argument seems to have reached: an ideal distribution, under equality of resources, is one in which people have different liberties, some have few liberties, and those who have more liberties have fewer other goods in consequence. If that argument is sound, we must decide which practical schemes of recognizing and denying liberties would come as close as is feasible to that ideal. We could not persuade ourselves that our present constitutional system, which guarantees an important set of liberties for everyone, satisfies that test. Liberty would have a much more modest place in any scheme we could justify as coming as close as possible to the ideal. If equality of resources must treat liberty as just another resource, then, far from showing that no conflict exists between liberty and equality, it demonstrates, in a particularly vivid and alarming way, that the conflict between these political virtues is inevitable, and also why it is a conflict liberty must lose.

B. An Important Mistake

Fortunately, this apparently devastating argument is fallacious. I described it only to show the serious consequences, for equality of resources, of trying to rely on the interest strategy to fix the place of liberty in an ideal distribution. In fact, the interest strategy makes no sense within equality of resources. The argument I constructed supposes that acquiring a particular resource and acquiring rights or opportunities to use that resource are two independent transactions. But no one can intelligently, or even intelligibly, decide what to bid for in an auction, or what price to bid for it, unless he makes assumptions about how he will be able to use what he acquires. When you bid for a painting in an auction of art, you assume that you will be able to hang the painting where you like, look at it when you want, and so forth. Any auction requires a background of parallel assumptions constituting what I shall call a liberty/constraint system for that auction. The background must stipulate what one acquires in acquiring something at the auction in question, that is, what one can and cannot do with or about it. Even if particular liberties were auctioned in the mad, Monopoly-card way I imagined, parties could not intelligently decide how much to bid for a particular liberty unless the background stipulated what they could or could not already do, *without* the special liberty they contemplated buying.

So a background or baseline liberty/constraint system is essential, and that system will specify whether parties do or do not begin the auction with any particular liberty in hand. Different baselines will produce different auction results, even though the goods auctioned and the tastes and projects of the parties remain the same. If the baseline stipulates that though a party can use clay for any other purpose he likes, he cannot use it to make a politically satirical sculpture, someone will want clay much less than he would without that background constraint, and so bid a much lower price for it. Each baseline decision the auctioneer makes reverberates, in that way, through the auction as a whole. So he needs a justification for choosing one baseline rather than another. Someone might object that the auctioneer can design a neutral baseline, for which he therefore needs no justification, if he stipulates that the parties begin the auction with no freedom to do anything at all with the goods they acquire. Then anyone who buys something must also buy separately, in a later part of the auction, whatever control he wants over or about it. Someone might buy a pole, for example, and then later, if he wished, the right to plant it in his own land, hang a flag from it, and so forth.

Is that suggestion coherent? Parties to the auction must often adopt bidding programs in which they bid for one good on the expectation of being able to acquire another later: someone who likes hot dogs, but only with mustard, must anticipate the price of mustard before he bids for hot dogs, and he might wish to rerun the auction if that price turns out to be significantly greater than he expected. But there is a crucial difference between the relation between owning hot dogs and owning mustard, on the one hand, and that between owning a pole and having the liberty to use it, on the other. Hot dogs and mustard are two different goods each of which some people, at least, might value apart from the other. But owning a pole and having some set of rights to control its use are essentially only different descriptions of the same thing, as we shall see by trying to imagine how the suggested auction, from a supposedly neutral baseline of total constraint, would proceed.

The auctioneer is meant to hold the auction in two parts. In the first, goods are auctioned, as it were, *tout court,* with no right to use or touch or even regard what one has bought. When all goods are distributed in that way, the second part begins. The auctioneer specifies some set of liberties and powers over the goods supposedly auctioned in the first part, adequate to make these goods recognizably private property, and the parties bid for whatever sets of liberties and powers he has specified. But the auctioneer must specify, before this second part begins, exactly which liberties and powers are available in the second part and how these map over the goods sold in the first part. However he does this, his specification becomes the effective baseline for the auction as a whole; it replaces the original, supposedly neutral, baseline of total constraint which actually plays no role in the proceedings. The parties make all bidding decisions, in other words, as if the auctioneer's liberty specifications were the original baseline.[19] Of course after the supposedly two-part auction is finished the auctioneer can change the baseline system he has in effect imposed, by specifying the liberties sold in the second part somewhat differently and running the auction again. But the second run then becomes a different auction, an auction from a different background liberty/constraint system. The auctioneer cannot escape deciding which baseline system, from among those that define a recognizable scheme of private property, he is justified in adopting.

C. A Fresh Start

So the interest-strategy argument I constructed, which ends in the doom of liberty, begins in a serious confusion. Though liberty is indeed part of one's circumstances rather than one's person or personality, the liberty an egalitarian state provides cannot be wholly settled by auctionlike private decisions, because any auction presupposes a liberty/constraint system of some kind already in place. So the interest strategy is alien to the general structure of equality of resources. That conception of equality makes people's interests relevant only at the level of the auction it imagines; but fundamental decisions about liberty figure at a prior level, the level at which the auction is designed rather than held.

That technical requirement of the auction device signals a fundamental characteristic of equality of resources. The envy test is itself interest based. People have their own interests in mind when they judge whether they prefer the resources available to anyone else to those available to them. But the envy test presupposes a liberty/constraint system and cannot be used to yield one. For any set of background stipulations we suppose about what people will or will not be free to do with the resources they acquire, the envy test will be satisfied by a successful auction against that background. If the background stipulates that no one may use any of the resources he acquires, except in a few enumerated ways, the envy test will be met: people will make choices with those serious constraints on liberty in mind, and by hypothesis will not prefer any bundle of resources anyone else chooses given the same constraints. If the background stipulates a much larger scope of freedom of choice, the bundle each chooses will be a different bundle, but once again the auction, if successful, will produce an envy-free distribution. Since the envy test is in that way indiscriminate among systems of liberty and constraint, the interest strategy cannot possibly succeed; it is wholly misconceived.

Equality of resources, in other words, requires two stages of analysis, of which the envy test, and the imaginary auction designed to satisfy it, represent only the second. At the first, or baseline, stage, the auction is structured by providing a background baseline system against which the auction unfolds. So the definition equality of resources offers of an ideal egalitarian distribution must include a specification of the liberties essential to equality. The envy test, as we just saw, cannot provide the entire definition of an ideal distribution. Since that test is compatible with an indefinite number of different distributions—since it is compatible, that is, with an indefinite number of distributions a successful auction from equal initial resources might produce—it can provide only a necessary condition for an ideal distribution. A liberty/constraint system is part of what is needed to complete a set of sufficient conditions.[20]

It follows from all this that equality of resources must fall back on the constitutive strategy if it hopes to reconcile its version of equality with any adequate conception of liberty. It must show that the most appropriate baseline liberty/constraint system for achieving equality provides the rights that an adequate conception of liberty requires. We shall consider a constitutive argument with that ambition in the next two sections. If that argument is successful, then an attractive conception of liberty flows from the very definition of an egalitarian distribution, and so liberty and equality cannot conflict.

But we should first tie a loose end. I have been arguing that any auction needs a liberty/constraint baseline, which cannot be neutral and so must be justified as appropriate to equality of resources. But devices can no doubt be found for changing the liberties and constraints the baseline provides by putting at least some of these up for auction. When I was constructing the bad, interest-based argument I later rejected, which supposed that liberty could be auctioned from a neutral base, I imagined special Monopoly-card liberties, and I speculated about how prices could be set and an auction conducted for these. No doubt other devices for varying the baseline scheme could be imagined as well. Does the spirit of equality of resources require the auctioneer to conduct such baseline-modifying auctions?

No, it forbids them. I have labored the point that any baseline will be consequential for the auction: different baselines will provide different results even when resources, tastes, and ambitions remain the same. The auctioneer must select whichever baseline best serves the aims of equality of resources. Suppose he judges that the appropriate baseline system does not include the freedom to discriminate on racial grounds. He must not later auction Monopoly cards permitting racial discrimination. For that would place in an unfair position those who would be put at a disadvantage by others' having that liberty. They must decide whether to buy as many of the liberty cards themselves as they can afford, in spite of the fact that they would not use them. If they buy them all, then the remainder of the auction proceeds from the baseline the auctioneer established, but no longer among people with equal resources, because they have had to use some of their clamshells simply to preserve that baseline. If they do not, then the remaining auction is no longer against that baseline—remember that the loss of liberty for some affects prices and opportunities for others as well—and so is no longer warranted for an egalitarian result.

IV. The Principle of Abstraction

A. *The Bridge Version*

The main objection to the constitutive strategy, as we noticed many pages ago, is its apparent circularity: it seems to begin the argument too close to the end. It defines an egalitarian distribution so that liberty is already present in the very definition of equality, and then declares that, for that reason, equality and liberty cannot conflict. How can we construct a constitutive argument for equality of resources that does not claim victory by fiat in this unhelpful way? How can we build a genuine argument for liberty if we begin in a definition that already secures it?

We do not begin in a definition, because equality of resources is not the foundation of our argument. We begin further back, in the more abstract egalitarian principle, which requires a community to treat each of its members with equal concern. We accept that principle, and, at least for purposes of this chapter, we accept equality of resources as the best interpretation or conception of it. So we can use what I shall call the bridge version of the constitutive strategy. We hold two ideas in place: the abstract egalitarian principle, which demands equal concern, on the one hand, and equality of resources, which proposes that an auction under certain conditions realizes equal concern, on the other. We select the baseline system, from among those we consider, that builds the best bridge between those two ideas. We select the baseline system that gives most plausibility to the claim that an auction from that baseline treats people with equal concern.

This bridge strategy, I shall argue, endorses one powerful and general principle, the principle of abstraction, as a central part of any appropriate baseline. This principle establishes a strong presumption in favor of freedom of choice. It insists that an ideal distribution is possible only when people are legally free to act as they wish except so far as constraints on their freedom are necessary to protect security of person and property, or to correct certain imperfections in markets (or other auction-like distributive mechanisms) that I shall describe in due course. The principle of abstraction does not endorse liberty as license. But it is sufficiently powerful to form the heart of an adequate conception of liberty. Moreover, the bridge strategy also supports, as I shall try to show, more specific rights to liberty that protect people from constraints on their freedom even when the principle of abstraction would yield to other considerations. These more specific rights are sufficient to complete an adequate conception of liberty. If so, the constitutive strategy for reconciling liberty and equality is successful. But that happy result is the upshot of an argument, not a hollow definitional victory won in advance.

The bridge strategy does not, however, yield an exhaustive account of the rights to liberty that equality of resources would require. An exhaustive list would draw on other aspects of equality of resources, beyond its theory of distributional equality, including, particularly, its interpretation of political equality or democracy.[21] I am anxious not to be misunderstood on this point. The arguments I provide here for the principle of abstraction and certain other rights emphasize the importance of liberty for distributional equality. I should not be understood as claiming that arguments of that sort are the only arguments we have or need for all the rights to liberty we should want to recognize. Nevertheless the arguments I shall set out for the principle of abstraction and certain other rights are sufficient in themselves to establish a prominent place for liberty in equality of resources. In the final sections of the chapter we shall consider how those arguments bear on decisions about liberty in the real world of practical politics, including the decisions described in the examples I began by listing.

I make one assumption in my argument for and about the principle of abstraction that I shall not develop. I assume that any competent baseline liberty/constraint system would include a principle of security: this would mandate constraints on liberty necessary to provide people with enough physical security and enough control over their own property to allow them to make and carry out plans and projects. I assume, in short, that an adequate baseline system would have legal constraints forbidding physical asault, theft, deliberate damage to property, and trespass, of the sort that are common to the criminal and civil laws of all developed legal systems.[22] Interesting questions arise about the details of such constraints in an ideal egalitarian distribution, but I shall neglect most of these as removed from our present focus on the problem of liberty, and simply assume that familiar and general constraints of this sort are provided in the baseline.

B. True Opportunity Costs

I shall now describe, in a preliminary way, the key argument the bridge strategy provides for the principle of abstraction. Every conception of equality supplies, through its description of an ideal distribution, a metric of equality, a theory about how resources should be measured in deciding when people have equal shares. Equality of resources uses the special metric of opportunity costs: it fixes the value of any transferable resource one person has as the value others forgo by his having it. It deems such resources to be equally divided when the total transferable resources of each person have the same aggregate opportunity costs measured in that way. The imaginary auction is designed to secure exactly that result; if the auction ends, then aggregate opportunity costs, as defined by that auction, are equal.

But different auctions will identify opportunity costs differently. That is only to repeat, in different language, what we have now several times noticed: auctions from different baselines will produce different results, each of which satisfies the envy test. But the force of that observation is special in this context. It shows that the bridge strategy must find some way of identifying what we might call the *true* opportunity costs of a set of resources. If we can give sense to the idea of true opportunity costs, then we can select baseline provisions about liberty, as providing the best bridge between the abstract egalitarian principle and the envy test, by asking which such provisions are best calculated to identify and reflect true opportunity costs. But if we cannot make sense of the idea, then we cannot say that an auction from one baseline, which yields one set of prices and results, comes any closer to the ideals of equality of resources than another, from a very different baseline, that yields very different prices and results. Equality of resources would then be an empty, because hopelessly indeterminate, conception of equality.

So our project of building a bridge between the abstract egalitarian principle and the envy test with its auction device requires an adequate theory of true opportunity costs. We need such a theory, for example, to attack the baseline issue I mentioned earlier: fixing the form in which goods are auctioned. Suppose some parties to the auction went together to buy enough land for a football stadium. The price they must pay will depend, among other things, on the size of the lots that are auctioned. If the auctioneer sells land in lot-sizes no smaller than exactly the size needed for a stadium, and the baseline prohibits transactions subdividing these lots after the auction is completed, the stadium builders will almost certainly pay less than if the auctioneer offered lots in as small a size as anyone else wanted. The second of these auctions, in which land is offered in smaller lots, seems fairer than the first; it seems better to realize the goals of equality of resources. Bur why?

It is no answer, within equality of resources, to say that welfare will be higher on average, or more nearly equal, under the second auction than under the first. (Indeed, under some circumstances, these claims would be false.) We might be tempted to say that since the stadium builders would have to pay more in the second auction, the first auction, which allows lands to be sold only in large lots, hides costs the second auction reveals, and that the true opportunity costs of the land are therefore understated in the first auction. But the fact that the cost of the land is higher in the second auction cannot itself be the reason why the second is fairer. Why should we not say that in the second auction the cost of the land is overstated? And because the cost of the stadium land would be less in the first auction, the cost of other resources would be higher. Why should we not then say that, with respect to those other resources, the first auction is fairer than the second?

We must find a better explanation for our sense that the second auction is fairer than the first; we must look for some principle that both justifies that intuition and provides an adequate bridge between the abstract egalitarian principle and the envy test. Equality of resources aims that each person have an equal share of resources measured by the cost of the choices he makes, reflecting his own plans and preferences, to the plans and projects of others. That is its understanding of an equal distribution of resources, its interpretation of how a community's scheme of private property treats all members with equal concern. If we accept that understanding, it follows that an auction is fairer—that it provides a more genuinely equal distribution—

when it offers more discriminating choices and is thus more sensitive to the discrete plans and preferences people in fact have. In the first of the two auctions we just imagined, someone must pay the same price for land whether his tastes and ambitions are limited to a small cottage or run to a sizable estate. How much he has left for other resources is not affected by his preferences about housing, and this market insensitivity has consequences not only for his own decision but for those of others as well. Football fans pay a different price for their tickets, for example, and thus compete with others for other goods on different terms, than they would if each person's resources were more sensitive to the precise dimensions of his own preferences. The failure of flexibility is a general defeat for the program of equality of resources.

Equality of resources prefers more abstract to less abstract auctions, not because costs of particular resources will be either higher or lower in more abstract auctions, nor because welfare will be overall greater or more equal, but rather because the general aim of that conception of equality, which is to make distribution as sensitive as possible to the choices different people make in designing their own plans and projects, is better achieved by the flexibility abstraction provides. That is the case for the principle of abstraction. The principle recognizes that the true opportunity cost of any transferable resource is the price others would pay for it in an auction whose resources were offered in as abstract a form as possible, that is, in the form that permits the greatest possible flexibility in fine-tuning bids to plans and preferences. It therefore insists that an auction must offer resources in that abstract form if the auction is to be recognized as identifying an equal distribution.

Difficult questions will arise, of course, in applying this principle. Under some circumstances it might be indeterminate which of two arrays of goods better satisfies the principle of abstraction, and in such cases some further tie-breaker principle might be required. But in many cases, the advice of the principle will be straightforward enough. Remember the auctioneer who traded all the varied resources of the island for only plovers' eggs. The trade was offensive to equality not because it disturbed the original array of goods, but because it violated the principle of abstraction in a fundamental way. It made the array much less sensitive—indeed as insensitive as possible—to the plans and preferences of the parties. If the auctioneer had found only plovers' eggs on the island, and had alone been able costlessly to trade these for a mix of goods from other islands, which would have allowed bids in the auction to be more sensitive to the discrete tastes, plans, and ambitions of the bidders, the principle of abstraction would have required, not forbidden, him to do this. The principle also requires that natural resources be auctioned in as undifferentiated a form as is feasible—that iron ore be auctioned rather than steel, for example, and undeveloped land rather than fields of wheat. It requires, as our stadium example shows, the utmost feasible divisibility in the goods auctioned, so that people can bid on indefinitely small units of each resource (though not, of course, on units so small that no single unit can serve any purpose). It also requires recognizing legal rights in property that improve divisibility, like rights of way over, and temporally bound interests in, land rather than only freehold interests.

So the principle of abstraction plays a central part in fixing the aspect of the auction baseline we are not principally considering now: the form in which goods are presented and lots distinguished. But it also plays a crucial part in fixing the baseline aspect that we are studying: the liberty/constraint system that defines the place of liberty in equality of resources. Abstraction requires some legal limits on total freedom because resources cannot be fine-tuned to plans and projects unless people can count on controlling the resources they acquire. The principle of abstraction might therefore be thought to embrace what I called the principle of security; if so, the latter principle would be interpreted and applied in a special and interesting way. But legal constraints beyond those necessary for security obviously compromise abstraction: clay is not auctioned in its most abstract form if the baseline system forbids satirical sculpture, because people anxious to express themselves in that way cannot tailor their resources to their plans as effectively with that constraint as they could without it. So the principle of abstraction insists that people should in principle be left free, under the baseline system, to use the resources they acquire, including the leisure they provide and protect through their bidding program, in whatever way they wish, compatibly with the principle of security.

The principle of abstraction is crucial, therefore, to our main project. It establishes a general presumption of freedom of choice at the core of equality, and that takes a major step toward reconciling liberty and equality. The principle also has an important immediate consequence we should pause to consider. It seems to endorse the liberal thesis that legal prohibitions cannot be justified on the sole ground that the conduct prohibited is offensive to some dominant religion or moral orthodoxy.

C. The Enforcement of Morals

This liberal conclusion will strike some readers as too powerful; they will think that it violates, rather than draws on, the principle of abstraction. Consider the following argument. "The liberal thesis does not respect abstraction because it does not provide people with as much flexibility as possible in the choice of lives to lead. Many people think that a worthy life can be led only in a community whose public culture identifies and prescribes a shared personal morality, which includes, for example, orthodoxy of religious commitment, circumscribed sexual behavior, and traditional gender and class distinctions of role.[23] In most circumstances a public culture of that sort can be sustained only by outlawing the behavior it deems immoral.

"In one way, of course, enforcing religion and morals in this illiberal way would offend the abstraction principle: it would altogether prohibit, or at least make much more difficult, the lives members of religious, cultural, or social minorities hope to lead. So it would hide the true cost of the opportunities it makes possible for the majority. But any choice the community makes about whether to enforce a common morality offends the abstraction principle in the same way. Failing to enforce morality would deny the majority the opportunities *it* wants, and that would distort the true cost of the opportunities then left available to the minority. We must accept that in this sort of case the principle of abstraction cannot be satisfied in full, or unambiguously, because the choice of any liberty/constraint baseline scheme will distort opportunity costs in one direction or another. So we do the best we can for abstraction by balancing the interests of majority and minority against each other in some way. If these conflicting interests are to be balanced, then numbers must affect that balance, and so at least some legal constraints on minority freedom must be accepted to make possible a way of life the majority wishes to have."

That is an important challenge to my suggestion that abstraction forbids enforcing an orthodox religion or personal morality. The objection claims to find an antiliberal impulse in the idea of opportunity costs and therefore at the heart of equality of resources. It is, in one way, a welcome challenge, because it shows that familiar and important political controversies can be modeled from within that conception of equality, and can therefore be studied from its perspective. The challenge is valuable in another way as well: it calls attention to a possible, indeed tempting, misunderstanding of the kind of neutrality toward which equality of resources aims. The objection supposes that the principle of abstraction aims to make each kind of life equally easy to lead. Then it notices what is certainly true: that this equally-easy form of neutrality is impossible, at least under equality of resources, because any choice of a liberty/constraint system will make some lives easier and others harder to lead. Under these circumstances, it declares, some compromise or balance is necessary between the liberal system I described and a more coercive system a majority might think it needs.

But the equally easy form of neutrality plays no role in equality of resources; it belongs to a version of the different conception of equality I called equality of welfare. Equality of resources aims at neutrality in a different sense: it aims that the resources people have available, with which to pursue their plans or projects or way of life, be fixed by the costs of their having these to others, rather than by any collective judgment about the comparative importance of people or the comparative worth of projects or personal moralities. Neutrality in that sense does not guarantee that any kind of life someone might want will be available to him. Someone who wants a life of imperial connoisseurship, assembling massive collections of masterpieces in a private storehouse, will find this impossible under equality of resources: he will not be able to afford the opportunity costs of that way of life, as these are judged in an auction from equal bidding resources, even if he sacrifices everything else. Equality of resources has that consequence, not because it fails to be neutral toward the connoisseur, but in virtue of the fact that it is neutral between him and others who also want to study and enjoy works of art.

The liberal account of opportunity costs, which is now being challenged, extends that version of neutrality to the social circumstances as well as the discrete resources different ways of life require for success. It allows each persons's social requirements—the social setting he claims he needs in order successfully to pursue his chosen way of life—to be tested by asking how far these requirements can be satisfied within an egalitarian structure that measures their cost to others. Someone who wants a life impossible except under a regime of religious intolerance would find that life unavailable for a reason parallel to the argument that denies the connoisseur all of what he wants. Given that some of his fellow citizens care about their religious or spiritual lives too, but are called to a different religion or none at all, he cannot purchase the environment he believes he needs in an auction whose baseline does not give it to him for nothing in advance.

So the baseline scheme I proposed, in which opportunity costs are identified through an auction whose baseline allows no constraints justified on grounds of religion or personal morality, does achieve the balance between the interests of the orthodox and those of the eccentric that is appropriate to equality of resources. The interests different groups have in the design of the social and cultural environment are accommodated by a price structure from assumptions neutral among their projects in the sense I described. Numbers will indeed count in the auction conducted from that neutral baseline. Those who crave the protection and reinforcement of religious homogeneity will be able to secure, if their numbers warrant this, some part of what they think they need, just as connoisseurs, if they are sufficiently numerous, will be able to provide themselves with brilliant museums to visit. People devout in a particular faith, who need a community of other committed believers in which to flourish, may find that enough other people share their convictions to enable them to join together in creating a special religious community without benefit of the criminal law. Nor is any minority, whether religious, sexual, or cultural, assured of social requirements ideal for them. Numbers count for them as well: they would plainly be better off, in a variety of ways, if more people shared their views or had tastes that made their own activities less expensive. Their prospects, too, and for the same reason, will depend on the opportunity costs to others, neutrally judged, of what they want. The bridge strategy therefore commends the liberal view that the baseline liberty/constraint system should be innocent of any constraints justified on grounds of religious truth or moral virtue. No other conception of true opportunity costs or of moral neutrality fits the basic structure of equality of resources.

D. Correction

I must now mention another principle that the liberty/constraint system of a proper baseline would recognize, because I will leave the wrong impression about the scope of the principle of abstraction if I ignore that further principle entirely. The principle of correction, as I shall call it, is of great practical importance. But I shall discuss it only in the most vague way, neglecting many problems it presents, because any more extended discussion would divert us from our main project.

The auctioneer in the imaginary auction I described faces a serious problem. He knows enough about the projects, ambitions, and plans of the parties to the proposed auction to know that the auction will not be able to achieve and retain a distribution of resources equal in opportunity costs. That aim will be defeated by what economists call externalities. Suppose that one party to the auction (A) intends to build a glass box on a lot in an area otherwise destined to become, because of the tastes and cooperative aims of others who buy lots there, a Georgian square. If his intentions were known, and these others were sufficiently numerous and well organized, they might decide collectively to outbid him for the lot he aims to have. Of course, the auctioneer cannot be sure that they would—A might decide to have the lot at any sacrifice to his other interests—but the auctioneer can know that this is unlikely. The auctioneer also knows that even if that result would be reached in an auction meeting those unrealistic conditions about information and organization, it might well not be reached in the actual auction he is about to commence. For A's intentions might not be transparent. Or A might not have the desire to build his glass box when he acquires his lot, but only form that desire later. Or A might sell the lot at some later time to someone who buys it for that purpose. The result that would be reached with perfect predictive knowledge might not be reached for another reason: the costs of forming groups collectively to bid against A. I have generally ignored transaction costs in the auction story, but they would be particularly large in cases of this sort.

In these circumstances, the auctioneer might decide to limit freedom of choice, in the baseline system of liberties and constraints, just for the purpose of correcting the auction in advance toward a result that better reflects opportunity costs as they would be revealed in an auction of perfect knowledge and costless organizational transactions. His intervention might take a variety of forms, some of which would be better suited than others to that end. He might adopt general zoning ordinances, for example, attempting to anticipate land use as this would be determined by a perfect auction. He might respond to other, different forms of auction imperfection by fixing new, different kinds of constraints in the baseline. He might anticipate, for example, that some parties would use material they acquired in the auction in ways that would pollute the atmosphere to the injury of neighbors who, if they could predict the polluters' actions and could organize efficiently, would collectively outbid them for that material. The auctioneer might use the tort law of the liberty/constraint system to make such pollution an actionable nuisance; this device would correct for externality in a more subtle way, because it would leave open the possibility that a polluter could bargain with those affected for a right to pollute. The ground I am now haphazardly racing over is, of course, familiar terrain to students of the literature of law and economics. I mean only to suggest the connection between that literature and the principle of correction. Constraints on freedom of choice are required and justified, according to that principle, if they improve the degree to which equality of resources secures its goal, which is to achieve a genuinely equal distribution measured by true opportunity costs.[24]

Improving the accuracy of the auction in this way would not entail, of course, reaching the exact results that would have been reached if the conditions of ideal knowledge and costless organization had been met. Those who gain from the constraints—those who do not want glass boxes in Georgian squares—would have paid nothing from their initial stock of resources for their success. So a regulatory constraint or an article of tort law is justified under the principle of correction only if there are good grounds for supposing that the corruption of the opportunity-cost test would be less with the constraint in place than it would be without it. It is justified, that is, only if there are good grounds for supposing that people's resources, at the end of the auction and thereafter, would be closer to the results of the superimaginary pre-auction auction we are now contemplating, in which all motives are transparent, all transactions are predictable, and organizational costs are absent. The auctioneer typically does have one reason to suppose that distortion would be less severe if he adopts constraints correcting for externality. In most cases of externality, the windfall that would be produced by a constraint would be spread among more people than the windfall that would result with no constraint. It therefore seems likely that a general practice of correcting for externalities through constraints would roughly even out these windfalls better than a general practice of ignoring the externalities would. Under the former practice, A would benefit from other antinuisance constraints, for example, but under the latter, A's neighbors might be left with no externality windfalls at all to compensate them for their immediate externality loss.

Three cautions seem wise. First, though the principle of correction affects the impact of the principle of abstraction, the former does not qualify or derogate from the latter. On the contrary, correction is an aspect of abstraction, because it aims at an improved discovery of the opportunity costs that abstraction recognizes as genuine. Second, nothing in this brief discussion of correction challenges my earlier claim that baseline liberties and constraints should not be changed by auction transactions. The principle of correction does not attempt to justify constraints by arguing that these would in some way be purchased in any auction. It imagines a purer, pre-auction auction in which the participants have perfect knowledge and predictive power, and in which there are no organizational costs. The constraints recommended by correction are not part of the baseline of that purer auction, to be sure. But they are also not purchased in it. They are justified, as part of the baseline for the auctioneer's actual auction, in which knowledge cannot be perfect, by comparing the speculative results of the purer auction with the likely results of the less pure one.

Nor, finally, does the principle of correction undermine the important result we reached when we considered the principle of abstraction: a proper liberty/constraint baseline cannot make any behavior a crime on the ground that it offends shared or conventional morality. For the purer, hypothetical auction, whose results justify constraints of correction in the auctioneer's actual auction, must itself assume a baseline in which no constraints of that sort are permitted, and that purer auction could not produce results that would justify any such constraints in the actual auction. Though we are imagining that a group of affected neighbors could afford, in combination, to buy lots in the purer auction to prevent incongruous houses from being built on those lots, it is incredible that they could buy resources of such breadth and scope that a homosexual would not be left free to secure a sexual life of his choice with willing partners, for example, or a member of a minority religion not be left free to practice his religion. And even if we could imagine such devastating transactions, these would not be cases in which the distortion would be less with constraints justified by correction than without those constraints.

V. Other Principles

A. Authenticity

Though the principle of abstraction promotes a presumption of liberty, understood in the way just described, it does not discriminate among liberties by ranking some as more basic or fundamental than others, except so far as some particular constraints might be shown to be especially destructive of the flexibility that abstraction aims to secure.[25] The principle of abstraction is qualified, moreover, by a general exception; it recognizes that constraints might be necessary to protect security. An adequate conception of liberty picks out some liberties as stronger than others in the contemplated contest between liberty and the protection of person or property, and promotes these as particularly powerful rights. It insists that a stronger case is needed to justify a prohibition against speech than to justify a prohibition against assault, for example: lawyers often use the familiar "clear and present danger" slogan to suggest the stronger case that is required.

We must therefore consider whether the bridge strategy produces other principles, beyond the principle of abstraction, that establish more distinct rights to freedom of choice. We are studying only the rights to liberty that flow from the view equality of resources takes of equality in private ownership, and, as I warned earlier, we must not suppose that these exhaust the rights that a more general account of equality of resources, which includes its theory of democracy, would support. But the group of rights that flow from equality in private ownership does include more powerful principles, though principles narrower in scope, than the general principle of abstraction. Any auction scheme approved by equality of resources requires, for example, some baseline principle specially protecting the parties' freedom to engage in activities crucial to forming and reviewing the convictions, commitments, associations, projects, and tastes that they bring to the auction and, after the auction, to the various decisions about production and trade that will reform and redistribute their initial holdings.[26]

Personality is not fixed: people's convictions and preferences change and can be influenced or manipulated. A complete account of equality of resources must therefore include, as a baseline feature, some description of the circumstances in which people's personalities will be taken as properly developed so that auction calculations can proceed. The baseline needs, that is, some principle defining authenticity.[27] It cannot be silent on the question of authenticity, nor, of course, can it remit that question in some way to the auction itself. We must choose between different available principles, once again, through the bridge strategy.

Difficult questions arise, of course, about the proper formulation of a principle of authenticity and about the precise limits of the activities a properly formulated principle might be thought to protect. But any acceptable principle must have a certain range. Authenticity has both a passive and an active voice: participants to the auction would want both an opportunity to form and reflect on their own convictions, attachments, and projects, and an opportunity to influence the corresponding opinions of others, on which their own success in the auction in large part depends. So we would expect to find, within the broad dimensions of whatever principle of authenticity the bridge strategy recommends, justification for affording special protection to freedom of religious commitment, freedom of expression, access to the widest available literature and other forms of art, freedom of personal, social, and intimate association, and also freedom of nonexpression in the form of freedom from surveillance.

In the artificial comprehensive-auction story, which in this and other ways assumes Marvel's heaven of world enough and time, the auction would not commence until all parties wanted to exploit these opportunities no further. Ideal authenticity requires the fullest possible opportunity not because people are always more likely to make wise choices with more time but because their choices should not depend on a view of their personality, and of the personalities of others, with whose formation they remain dissatisfied. So the baseline of an ideal distribution would in principle allow no constraint, either before the initial auction or after it, on opportunities to form, to reflect on, or to advocate convictions, attachments, or preferences. Authenticity would have to yield to security, no doubt, on dramatic occasions of emergency in the pre-auction or post-auction world, but the danger would have to be special, because any serious compromise of authenticity would impair the auction, or the equality-preserving power of post-auction transactions, in a particularly fundamental and pervasive way. Violations of the more general principle of abstraction distort prices away from true opportunity costs. But violations of the principle of authenticity are likely to distort prices more fundamentally, because they affect what people decide they want, and therefore change the entire bidding program they decide to pursue. We have that special reason, within the structure of equality of resources, for insisting that authenticity be weighted more heavily than abstraction in any contest between these principles and the requirements of security—for insisting, for example, that free speech be protected except in the case of undeniable and overhanging danger. Authenticity does not supply the only argument of principle we need or have for freedom of speech. And we have more practical arguments for free speech as well—arguments that emphasize the role of a free press in protecting against official corruption, for instance. But equality of resources would require a right of free speech just for authenticity even if we had no other arguments for it.

B. Independence

The principle of abstraction protects from criminal prosecution people who have unpopular moral or religious convictions, and the principle of correction does not undermine that protection. But unpopular people might suffer other disadvantages in the auction as we have so far defined its baseline. Suppose racists are sufficiently numerous that they can combine to buy tracts of land for housing from which they will thereafter exclude blacks. Nothing in the principle of abstraction forbids them to do so. Indeed, that latter principle might, in some circumstances, even argue *for* legally enforced segregation. The auctioneer might be persuaded that racists would combine to that end, over a vast proportion of the community's residential land, if organizational costs did not prevent this, and the principle of correction might then require him to anticipate that result, by racial zoning, in the baseline of the auction.

But a political and economic system that allows prejudice to destroy some people's lives does not treat all members of the community with equal concern. So we need another baseline principle to ensure that the auction's results will not violate the abstract egalitarian principle in that way. The principle of independence speaks to both liberty and constraint. First, it checks the principle of correction by insisting that no baseline constraint can be justified as necessary to reach a result that would be reached in an auction with perfect knowledge and no organizational costs, if that result would be reached only because people's bids would reflect contempt or dislike for those who would be subject to or suffer disadvantage in virtue of the constraint. Next, it checks the principle of abstraction by endorsing baseline constraints necessary to protect people who are the objects of systematic prejudice from suffering any serious or pervasive disadvantage from that prejudice. (In effect, the principle of independence redefines opportunity costs in that way.)

This argument might suggest that we have only an ad hoc case for the principle of independence, that we must design a special bridge between the abstract egalitarian principle and the envy principle just to rule out segregation in an egalitarian distribution. That would, if true, be disappointing, because it would be better if no special additions to the basic structure of equality of resources were needed to rule out arrangements, like either *de jure* or socially coordinated segregation, that seem profoundly inegalitarian. We would hope, that is, to draw the principle of independence from the roots of our conception of equality. In fact we can, because the problem of prejudice is actually an aspect of a more general problem equality of resources must face in a variety of contexts: the problem of handicaps. Equality of resources is challenged by significant differences in talent, understood as the ability to produce goods or services others will pay to have, for example. In Chapter 2 I suggested, as one partial remedy, schemes of compensation based on hypothetical insurance markets.

Prejudice, though obviously different from physical handicaps or lack of skills in any number of ways, is an example of a structurally related problem. Just as some people are at a disadvantage because the tastes of others do not allow their services to command a premium in the market, so other people suffer because they belong to a race, or have other physical or other qualities, that a sizable number of their fellow citizens dislike or for some other reason wish to avoid. True, though equality of resources is neutral about the tastes that impose the disadvantage in the first case, it condemns the attitudes that create disadvantage in the second. But that difference means only that we have more reason to try to reduce the inequality that springs from prejudice than to try to reduce that from other sources. Compensation schemes based on hypothetical insurance markets, useful though they may be in ameliorating other forms of handicap, are plainly inappropriate in combatting the effects of prejudice. We must find some other way, compatible with the other goals and constraints of equality of resources, to place victims in a position as close as possible to that which they would occupy if prejudice did not exist. The principle of independence, with its negative and positive impact on the liberty/constraint system of the egalitarian baseline, seems an appropriate means to choose. So that principle is not, after all, only an ad hoc patch on an isolated leak in equality of resources, but rather a consequence, in the context of prejudice, of a much more general feature of that conception of equality.

VI. Back toward the Real World

A. A Theory of Improvement

We use fantasies, in political philosophy, to sharpen ideals, and we use ideals to choose among failures, to identify the least unjustifiable of practical possibilities. How can we use the fantasies of equality of resources, imagined in a world where everything can be auctioned and auctions can last forever, to choose between practical possibilities in our own world, where most things are already owned, almost no material resources are in anything like their most abstract form, and a comprehensive auction can scarcely even be described?[28] We need counterfactual speculation, and the argument so far should help.

We need, first, to imagine an ideal distribution among us. Suppose people with our tastes and ambitions were somehow able to organize and execute an egalitarian auction of all the resources collectively at our command from a baseline that respected the principle of abstraction and the other principles we identified. What general distribution would result? Of course, it would be absurd to think that we could describe the outcome of such an auction with any precision. It would be impossible to say what each of us would now have, person by person, if such an auction had been held in our youths and we had produced, traded, and consumed from our immediate post-auction position ever since. But we can nevertheless make useful judgments about what our legal and economic structure would be like, and about what patterns of distribution of private property we would have developed. Our criminal law would protect and respect liberty, in the form of the principle of abstraction and the other principles we discussed. Compensatory insurance schemes would be in place, so that the unemployed or underemployed, and the sick and handicapped, would have special resources approaching those that people would provide for themselves in an equal insurance market. People would have different resources, occupations, and savings, but the great extremes of wealth and poverty familiar in most modern societies would not exist.

We can form a picture of the consequences an auction would have produced among us, in other words, which though vague is sufficiently detailed to make us confident that our present legal system and our present distribution of private property are not within the set of arrangements that could have been produced by such an auction. We can also assign many members of the community to one of two classes: those whose circumstances are plainly better, as they would themselves judge, than they would be in any of the arrangements that might have been produced by an egalitarian auction, and those whose circumstances are plainly worse. (Of course, a substantial number of people may not fall into either of these categories.)

A conception of equality is worthless unless it describes not only an ideal egalitarian distribution, but what counts as an egalitarian improvement in a patently unequal distribution. So our next assignment is to compose a theory of improvement that suits equality of resources and can act as a guide for making our own society more egalitarian than it is. We need terms of accounting, though these may seem strange in the context of political philosophy. We might define a person's equity deficit as the amount or degree by which he has less than he would have, or is otherwise in worse circumstances than he would be, under an ideal egalitarian distribution in his community. Since we cannot discover exactly what any particular person would have had under such a distribution, judgments about equity deficit must be rough, and mainly comparative. We would ordinarily feel justified, for example, in saying that a very poor person, whose prior decisions cannot account for any substantial part of his poverty, has a higher equity deficit than a more moderately poor person, and that people in our upper middle class have no equity deficit at all.

The goal of a theory of improvement must be to reduce equity deficit. Several questions arise. How is equity deficit to be measured? I said our judgments must be rough, person by person. But what finer judgments are these rough judgments trying to approximate? Suppose we knew exactly what resources a particular person would have acquired and retained in an ideal distribution. What test would we then use to determine his exact equity deficit now? Would this test allow us always to say, of two people, that one's equity deficit was either greater than or less than or exactly equal to the other's? Let us stipulate that a program improves equality only when it reduces the community's overall equity deficit. This must be some function, presumably, of the discrete equity deficits of its members. But what function? How shall we decide, that is, whether a political program has improved equality of resources if it has reduced the equity deficit of some people but increased the deficit of others?

B. Degrees of Inequality

Each conception of equality must have its own distinct theory of improvement, which must be consistent with its general account of ideal equality; if reducing equity deficit is to be the test of improvement, then the deficit must be measured in the same currency as the ideal. Equality of welfare must define equity deficit as welfare loss: someone's equity deficit is fixed, for that conception, by subtracting his welfare level from the level he would enjoy were welfare equal. But equality of resources cannot use a welfare-based metric of equity deficit; that would introduce, as the right metric for improving equality, a standard that equality of resources rejects for defining it. Equality of resources must calculate equity deficit on the space of resource, in other words, rather than on the space of welfare. But we have discovered that someone's circumstances may be worse than they should be in two respects or dimensions. He may not have the resources he would have acquired in an egalitarian auction from a baseline consisting of the liberty/constraint system actually in force in his community. Or the baseline system actually in force may itself be inappropriate to equality of resources; it may violate the principle of abstraction, for instance, or one or another of the more specific principles we encountered. Of course someone's circumstances may be worse than they should be for both these reasons: the liberty system might be unfair, and he might have fewer resources than he would have in an egalitarian auction even from that unfair system. Most poor people in the real world suffer from that twin injustice.

So we need some further accounting distinctions. A person's resource deficit is the difference between the resources he has and those he would have acquired in an egalitarian auction from a fair baseline. Resource deficit can generally be monetized sufficiently accurately for a practical theory of improvement. Someone's resource deficit is the sum he would need to transform his resources into those he would have had under that auction. A person's liberty deficit, on the other hand, consists in the respects in which he is worse-off, in addition to the respects captured in his resource deficit, because the liberty/constraint system of his community is not what equality of resources requires. Some of the consequences of an unfair baseline, as that definition suggests, figure in resource deficit. I imagined, earlier, a baseline that prohibited dividing land into lots smaller than the size necessary for a football stadium. Some people, as I said, would have fewer resources in virtue of that baseline constraint than they would have had without it, and their resource deficit reflects that difference. But consider another constraint I imagined: no one is permitted to make satirical sculptures. We cannot measure the degree to which that constraint makes any particular person worse off wholly in financial terms: if we set aside the possibility of political bribes, no sum is sufficient to purchase, in the market, the legal right to do what the law prohibits. Nevertheless someone who wants to make satirical sculptures has resources less valuable to him than equality of resources has promised, and that fact must be reflected somehow in any adequate account of his overall equity deficit.

So we need a separate accounting for liberty deficit. Someone's liberty deficit, we might say, is the degree to which he is limited, in what he is able to do or achieve, by some constraint, compared with what he would have been able to do or achieve in the position defined for him by an ideal egalitarian distribution. Liberty deficit is therefore sensitive to other features of circumstance. Suppose a legal system stipulates, for example, that no one may acquire more than half the community's total supply of marble. There would be no such prohibition in the baseline of an ideal egalitarian distribution: it would be forbidden by the principle of abstraction. Nevertheless the prohibition produces no liberty deficit in the real world, for under an ideal distribution no one would be rich enough to buy up more than half the marble. A law wholly prohibiting the acquisition or use of marble, on the other hand, plainly imposes liberty deficit on those who want to sculpt. They cannot lead lives they might well have led following an ideal distribution.

We cannot, as I said, put a money figure on that deficit. We can nevertheless compare liberty deficits in various ways so long as they arise from different constraints. Imagine a fantasy world in which one person is forbidden by law to eat broccoli and another forbidden to read books. Though we have no precise metric for comparing the consequences of these prohibitions, the second is plainly much more serious and consequential than the first; it limits the activities and achievements of those subject to it to a vastly greater degree. When two people are subject to the same illegitimate constraint, however, equality of resources can supply no metric, so far as I can see, for quantifying even informally the difference in the equity deficit created by that constraint for each. Of course, different people will suffer differently from any given prohibition; the marble-using constraint would have been much more serious for Bernini than for me. But these are differences on the welfare space, and we could not deploy them in our accounting of equity deficit without allowing differences in taste, project, and ambition to affect distribution in the way equality of resources denies they should. We want an interpretation of liberty deficit that can guide a theory of improvement, and we cannot accept, within equality of resources, that equality would be improved by assigning more resources to Bernini than to me just because he suffers more from not being free to sculpt.

Equality of resources leaves no basis for interpersonal comparison of liberty deficits rising from the same constraint. It does not follow that such liberty deficits are in some sense identical for everyone. Suppose two people suffer liberty deficits from the same illegitimate legal prohibition, but one has more and the other fewer ordinary resources, in money terms, than they would have in an ideal egalitarian distribution. It is tempting to say that the overall equity deficit of the poorer must be greater than that of the richer, becasue their liberty deficit is identical and only the poorer has a resource deficit. But we have no more right to say that their liberty deficits are identical than that one is greater than the other: both these judgments make sense only as out-of-place judgments about welfare. Two liberty deficits are incommensurate rather than identical, and that incommensurability, as in this example, will sometimes make overall equity deficits incommensurate as well.

C. Overall Gains in Equality

Obviously, equality would be improved overall if an inegalitarian community somehow achieved an ideal egalitarian distribution, if the community actually held a successful comprehensive auction, for example. But since that is never possible, we must consider what to count as a limited or partial improvement in equality, as a step in the right direction. We need an answer that is compatible with the general design of equality of resources, with the view that conception takes of how people are treated with equal concern. Consider this suggestion, for example: a program improves equality if it does not increase anyone's liberty deficit and does reduce the total resource deficit in the community, that is, the total sum that would be needed to erase everyone's resource deficit. Equality of resources cannot accept that test of improvement, because the test assumes that people are treated with equal concern when the resources each has are taken into account, in the same way, in programs designed to maximize such resources. The test would be satisfied, for example, by a program that substantially injured a few people who were already among the poorest in order to make a great many people who were less poor, but still deprived, somewhat better off. That is utilitarian egalitarianism on the resource rather than the welfare space. It defines an ideal egalitarian distribution as whatever distribution maximizes the overall financial value of resources. Since equality of resources rejects the thesis as a general account of equality, it cannot accept it as defining equity improvements.

But when we reject this aggregate-resource-deficit test for defining improvements in equality, and insist that any test for improvement must be sensitive to liberty as well as to resource deficit, we seriously reduce our options. We can certainly accept programs that produce *dominating* improvements in equality. I mean programs that reduce the equity deficit of some people without increasing the equity deficit—either resource or liberty deficit, or both—of anyone else. That is not the same thing as a Pareto improvement. Increasing a progressive income tax to finance a comprehensive welfare program including adequate unemployment relief would not produce a Pareto improvement, because it would leave the rich worse off. But it might well produce a dominating improvement in equality, because it imposes no new constraints on liberty and might make only those who would have no resource deficit, even after the new taxes, worse off. Even programs that do restrict liberty, in ways in which it would not be restricted after an ideal distribution, may produce dominating improvements, as we saw in the case of the imaginary antimarble-monopoly law. Even though they limit freedom, they leave no one worse off, with respect to the value of that freedom, than he would be in an ideal situation. So dominating improvements in equality are much easier to achieve, and are therefore of much greater practical importance, than Pareto improvements.

It would be a mistake to conclude from the argument so far, however, that only dominating improvements count as genuine improvements in equality. But we must take some care in describing genuine improvements that are not dominating, and any list will be incomplete, because nondominating improvements must be generated by a process of proposal and inspection, not by any comprehensive and exhaustive formula. For example: if a program imposes no fresh liberty deficits, and improves the resource position of the group with the largest resource deficit, it plainly improves equality even if other, less substantial resource deficits are increased, but perhaps only provided that no one's deficit loss is greater than the largest deficit gain to a member of that most disadvantaged class.[29] We can no doubt construct similar, more or less untidy, descriptions of programs that would satisfy us as making an inegalitarian society somewhat less so. But there is a general and serious limit to what can count as an overall improvement under equality of resources. No program can count as producing an overall improvement if it adds new and significant constraints on liberty that impose substantial liberty deficits. For since resource and liberty deficits are incommensurate, there is no way to justify the claim that a program that gives more protein to the poor, at the cost of their free speech, is an overall gain in the degree to which the community treats all its members as equals.

D. Defensible Egalitarian Distributions

Our theory of improvement allows us to imagine programs of redistribution, including compensatory insurance against unemployment, low wages, and bad luck, that are technically, as distinct from politically, possible for us, and that would bring our community closer to an ideal distribution. Can we imagine reaching a situation, through such schemes, such that no further technically possible change could bring us even closer to that ideal? Let us call situations of that sort defensible egalitarian distributions, to mark the fact that, though they do not realize perfect equality of resources, they are examples of the best we can manage even with the best political will. We can readily identify distributions that are not defensible because they can plainly be improved, according to our theory of improvement, in the direction of equality judged by opportunity costs. The distributional schemes now in place in the United States and Britain, haphazard and patchwork though they are, could plainly be improved by a more just tax system, for example, and by redistribution toward those at the bottom, that would not impose fresh liberty deficits. Neither Britain nor the United States (nor, I believe, any other country) has yet achieved a defensible scheme of distribution.

I assume that we can also identify the main features, at least, of a situation that would constitute a defensible egalitarian distribution for us. I assume, that is, that we can describe an economic system that is technically possible from our present position and defensible as not open to further plain improvements. But if we can identify any defensible distribution for us, we can undoubtedly identify several, each rather different from the others, because we can imagine our community embarking on very different programs of reform each of which consisted in measures improving equality until no more such measures were available. It makes perfect sense to suppose that some of these programs would be as a whole better than others, because the defensible distribution they would in fact produce would come closer to an ideal distribution. Perhaps we could decide which was best of all, in advance, if we had perfect analytic power and perfect predictive information about the personalities of each member of the community. But of course we do not have that power and that predictive information, particularly since, as the auction story itself emphasizes, people's personalities and ambitions would change as any program tending toward equality unfolded.

So even if we know, for example, that our community would use compen-

satory insurance mechanisms as part of any program of reform it under-
took, we also know that these mechanisms might take a variety of forms,
ranging from a state-administered national medical scheme to more conventional social insurance programs funded from tax revenues, and we cannot predict with great confidence which of these devices would prove most
valuable given the opinions about risk and other matters people actually
turned out to have. Nor could we predict which forms of commercial organization or transaction our community would develop in its search for
equality, except by making dubious assumptions about the savings, investment, employment, collaboration, and consumption decisions people would
be likely to make with and from the resources assigned to them as reform
developed. Even a community thoroughly dedicated to equality of resources
would have to proceed toward that ideal gradually, through a series of
political decisions each of which was judged most reasonable at the time.
These decisions would themselves limit what was technically feasible immediately thereafter, and so historical contingencies, including accidents about
the order in which decisions were made, would cumulatively restrict the set
of initially available defensible distributions toward which any particular
community converged. The process of seeking equality, in other words,
would not be path-independent.

The best we can do now, therefore, by way of identifying defensible distributions for our community, is to imagine a set of such schemes each of
which is technically feasible through a series of steps we might begin to take
at once. So I shall hereafter speak of a defensible distribution, meaning a
member of that set, rather than of the defensible distribution. We might
nevertheless rank defensible distributions in various ways. I shall be particularly interested in one ranking: we might rank them in order of plausibility,
in the order of the probability that our community, if it were converted to
equality of resources, would achieve that distribution. If we did try to rank
distributions in that way, we should have to speculate about the likelihood
that we would turn out to have and retain the convictions, projects, tastes,
and attachments a particular distribution assumes, that we would collectively judge the policies and devices necessary to reach that distribution to
be reasonable under the circumstance, and that we would pursue these
policies and devices in the order necessary to reach it. We could not hope, of
course, to achieve a complete ranking of the plausibility of the defensible
distributions we recognize; we could not hope to be able to decide, for each
pair of them, either that one is more plausible than the other or that they are

equally plausible. Nevertheless, we could reasonably hope for an incomplete ranking of plausibility: we should be able to decide that some defensible distributions are much more plausible than others.

I shall now defend one claim about all but the most implausible defensible distributions for us. No one would be forbidden by law, in a defensible distribution, to use his resources in whatever way he chooses, except insofar as necessary to protect security or to correct for different sorts of auction or market imperfections. Equality of resources, in defining its ideal distribution, insists that the principle of abstraction be strictly observed in any auction baseline and in the transactions and events of post-auction life. If any actual distribution, in the real world, did not reflect the principle of abstraction, as it would not if its criminal law forbade people to use their resources as they wished except on grounds of security or correction, then that distribution could presumably be improved in the direction of the ideal by steps that included removing all such constraints. It would not count as a defensible distribution, therefore, so long as it retained any constraint forbidden in the ideal.

This claim will probably strike some readers as plainly wrong. In many countries an unfair distribution of wealth allows rich people to buy much better medical care than poor people can. Suppose one country remedies this particular injustice by forbidding the private practice of medicine altogether. That is an improvement in equality, even though it has introduced a constraint that would not be permitted in an ideal egalitarian distribution, provided that the constraint imposes no new liberty deficit, as it would not if no one is thereby prevented from obtaining the medical care he could obtain with the resources he would have in an ideal distribution. But just removing that constraint would not be a further step toward equality, but a retrograde step away from it, back to the less egalitarian status quo ante. That fact does not contradict my assumption, however, which is that a community could always advance toward equality by a series of steps that *include* removing any constraints that the principle of abstraction condemns.

The community just described could redistribute wealth generally and adopt, as part of that project, a generous program of tax-financed medical care. Then, as part of the same overall strategy, it could remove constraints on private medicine. That comprehensive change would plainly be an improvement, from the point of view of equality, over the position it had reached in my story, which left great inequality of wealth and ameliorated only the impact of that inequality on medical care. And it would also be an improvement, from that perspective, over a less comprehensive change that redistributed wealth and provided generous medical insurance but left in place the constraint forbidding private medicine. Permitting private transactions in medicine allows people to make their own choices about the relative value of immediate and therefore expensive medical care as against less immediate care and other goods. Permitting private medicine therefore makes distribution more sensitive to opportunity costs in the way equality of resources approves. So my assumption holds except when a community is technically (which does not include politically) incapable of advancing equality through general programs that include removing constraints objectionable to the principle of abstraction and imposing no new constraints of that sort. No doubt we could imagine, with sufficient ingenuity, communities in that technical position. But I believe it very unlikely that our own familiar communities would find themselves in that situation, and so I shall assume that in all but the most implausible defensible distributions the liberties the principle of abstraction requires would be fully protected.

VII. Liberty and Injustice

A. The Real Real World

We began our study of equality of resources in the ideal ideal world of fantasy, of comprehensive and almost eternally drawn-out auctions. We have now followed that study into the ideal real world, only somewhat less fantastic, where inequality survives and technical problems are formidable, but where people are nevertheless fully committed to making distribution more equal. We stayed in that world long enough to define improvements in equality and defensible egalitarian schemes, and to compose an incomplete ranking of the latter according to their plausibility. Now we move again toward reality, toward the real real world in which political difficulties are, if anything, more menacing than technical ones. This is our world, the world in which we must train theory and conviction on practical politics.

We can use the idea we formed in the ideal real world, of a defensible distribution, to judge our performance so far in the real real world. We criticize ourselves, not because we have not achieved an ideal egalitarian distribution, as we might have done in some fantastic comprehensive auction, but because we have not achieved, or even approached, a defensible distribution for us. We have not done even what we technically can to ameliorate distributional inequality; our failures have been failures of will, imagination, and, mainly, justice. Citizens and officials who want to do more for equality face a vast variety of issues and problems.

We must now study one of these. Rich people in the United States and Britain are much better off and most poor people much worse off than equality of resources would permit. Wealth should and could be redistributed by a general program of reform, perhaps through higher taxation and improved social programs of familiar sorts, perhaps in more radical or original and effective ways. But there are serious political limits to any such program; indeed, effective reform seems more remote now, at least in those countries, than it has for some time. The unfair advantages of unjust wealth can be limited, however, through other, more feasible, means: by prohibiting the rich from exploiting their wealth in certain directions, for example. That would require legal constraints, such as constraints on liberty of political activity, on private medicine, and on contracts of employment, that deny people the freedom of choice that the principle of abstraction requires. No plausible defensible distribution, I just said, would contain such constraints. No such scheme would include laws prohibiting people from spending as much as they wished on political campaigns rather than on luxury electronics. None would prohibit people from buying expensive medicine rather than expensive holidays. None would make it impossible for bakers to agree to work long hours rather than watch football on television. Or rather, none would prohibit these decisions unless that was necessary in the interests of security or health or, what is unlikely, for market-correcting purposes. Are constraints on liberty nevertheless justified in a society of very imperfect equality? Does equality of resources insist, even there, that abstraction must not be compromised? Or is limiting freedom of choice a legitimate means of improving equality in a very unequal society?

We have finally returned to the examples of political controversy that I set out at the beginning. We are now able to study these examples in the right way, as cases testing not the standing of liberty in some ideal egalitarian fantasy but how liberty is treated in a realistic theory of improvement fit for our own shabbier world. Some pages ago, I said that equality could be improved by programs that violate the principle of abstraction. Some readers who were persuaded by my earlier arguments might have been troubled by that observation. Earlier I argued, strenuously, that the principle of abstraction is at the core of equality of resources, a crucial part of the baseline from which any version of the envy test must be applied. But once the layers of our argument have been distinguished, any sense of contradiction disappears. I argued, at the first stage of analysis, that we cannot identify an ideal egalitarian distribution, even in principle, except by supposing freedom of choice already in place. We cannot have perfect equality without the freedom that the bridge version of the constitutive strategy endorses as baseline liberties.

In the next stage of our argument, the ideal real stage, we used the idea of unattainable perfect equality to imagine defensible egalitarian distributions for our own community. I argued, at that level, that no plausible defensible distribution would permit constraints disapproved by the abstraction principle. Now we are in the real real world, however, and our question is different. We are no longer considering whether constraints on liberty are required by perfect equality, or even whether they are required by equality as an ideal that could technically be realized by us. We assume that we already know what a defensible distribution would be, and that we do not have one. Now we ask whether constraints on freedom are a permissible means of bringing us closer to a defensible distribution, even though no such distribution would itself allow those constraints.

Nevertheless the suggestion I am now mooting—that constraints on liberty might be justified as promoting equality in the real real world—does seem backsliding in another way. It will be cold comfort to those who love liberty to be told that equality demands liberty in some ideal world if they are also told that it may readily be sacrificed to equality here and now. For they will suddenly be aware of a new, and darker, side of the constitutive strategy I have been promoting over the interest strategy that is more familiar in political philosophy. The interest strategy, if it is successful at all, allows liberties to be ranked in importance. It allows us to say that people do (or would or should) care more about freedom of conscience or speech or choice in sexual orientation than about other freedoms, so that these more fundamental freedoms, at least, should be protected even in the imperfect real real world.

The constitutive strategy, in contrast, seems more an all-or-nothing affair. The bridge version I used does recommend that some liberties be given a special place as rights in the baseline of ideal equality. I sketched a constitutive argument for what I called the principle of authenticity, which gives freedom of speech that special place, for instance. But that special role is internal to the calculations of ideal equality: it justifies only the claim that in ideal equality a stronger argument from security is needed to limit freedom of speech than to limit other freedoms. It seems to provide no reason why any particular freedom should be immune from compromise when our goal is the much more modest aim of approaching a defensible distribution that we cannot, for political reasons, actually reach. The constitutive strategy therefore seems to leave all liberties equally vulnerable in our own political situation, where the shield of rights, undentable in the world of fantasy, turns to tin.

That conclusion might drive some readers back to the interest strategy. But suppose the interest strategy cannot, after all, be successful in protecting our basic liberties in the real real world, as I suggested it could not. Then those who are drawn to liberty will be tempted by a still more radical option. They may take a new, and sharper, look at the humanist ideal that accepts the abstract egalitarian principle either as an absolute requirement of just government or as qualified only in ways not relevant to liberty. Perhaps we should, after all, try to find some value in liberty that leaves it at once independent of equality and also independent of the benefit it brings to particular lives. So a great deal turns on how equality of resources answers our new question. Can freedom properly be compromised, in the real real world, as a means of reducing the inequality found there?

B. The Principle of Victimization

We might reformulate our accounting concept of a liberty deficit in the following way. A liberty deficit is a loss of power, in virtue of legal constraint, to do or achieve something that one would have had power to do or achieve following a defensible distribution. A community victimizes one of its members, let us say, when it imposes a liberty deficit on him. Now we can identify a principle that any acceptable theory of improvement must contain, which I shall call the principle of victimization. The principle speaks to both sides of the liberty-equality equation. It denies that liberty is violated when no one is victimized, that is, when the value of the liberty citizens retain is at least as great as the value of the unconstrained freedom they would have had in a defensible distribution. How can a plausible conception of liberty require that anyone have more power than he would have if freedom of choice was unlimited and resources fairly distributed? But it also denies that equality can be improved when someone is victimized. How can equality be improved when the equity deficit imposed on some is incommensurate with the reduction of equity deficit for others? So the principle reconciles liberty and equality in the real world of practical and imperfect politics. Liberty, it insists, demands nothing but the freedom of genuine equality, and equality cannot be served by any outrage to liberty.

The principle of victimization is incomplete as I just introduced it, however, because it does not identify the range of defensible distributions that must be consulted in applying it. Different versions of the principle are therefore available. The strongest requires that no one's position be made worse, with respect to the value of any aspect of his liberty, than it would be in whichever defensible distribution, no matter how implausible, would provide him the greatest value for that liberty. I shall test the principle in a weaker and more sensible form: I shall assume that it requires that no one's position be made worse, with respect to the liberty in question, than it would most likely have been in a defensible distribution. I assume, as I said, that we can rank defensible distributions in order of plausibility, and identify some set of such distributions as most plausible. If someone's position would be worse, in virtue of a legal constraint, than it would be in most members of the set of most plausible defensible distributions, then it is worse than it would most likely have been in such a distribution.[30]

We may test this version of the victimization principle by applying it to our initial sample cases. Is anyone victimized, first, by limits on the amounts a single person can spend promoting a political candidate? No such limits would be imposed in any plausible defensible distribution. People would have as close to equal resources, judged by the opportunity-cost test, as is technically possible, and each would be free to decide how much of his resources to spend addressing his fellow citizens rather than on other goods he might also want. Nevertheless the limits on election expenses that the Supreme Court struck down in *Buckley v. Valeo*,[31] had they gone into effect, would not have made the value of the freedom that remained less for anyone than the value of the unconstrained freedom he would have had in at least most plausible defensible distributions. For no one in a community that had reached a defensible distribution could have the impact on political decisions, just in virtue of money spent in politics, that the rich can now have in the United States, or even the impact that the rich would still have had if the Supreme Court had left the legislation intact. Disposable wealth would be much more evenly distributed, and though some people would presumably choose to spend a high proportion of their wealth in politics, many others, some of differing political views, would be ready and able to spend a similar proportion of theirs in the same way. The law the Supreme Court struck down therefore victimized no one.

This is the easiest of the examples I listed, because the constraint in question is directly and exclusively financial. The proposal to outlaw private medicine raises more complex issues. I assume, once again, that no such constraint would be imposed in any plausible defensible distribution, though of course constraints designed to assure competence and safety would be. In Britain, only two groups can now afford private medicine: those who are, relative to others, very rich, and those who have jobs in industries whose unions have secured private health insurance, funded largely by the employer, in collective bargaining. The proposed ban on private medicine would of course reduce the freedom of these groups. Would it make the value of their freedom, with respect to choice in medical care, less than it would be under the most-plausible defensible distributions?

Consider two programs a defensible distribution might use for providing medical care. In the first, medicine is wholly private, but an adequate health insurance plan, funded through taxation and available to everyone, provides resources sufficient to pay for the care the average person would insure to provide for himself in a private insurance market. In the second, medical care is offered through something like the British national health service, which is financed, again through taxation, at a sufficient level to provide everyone who uses the service with that same degree of care, though people are left free to make their own arrangements with willing and competent private doctors and hospitals if they prefer. I doubt that either of these possibilities could be shown to be distinctly more plausible than the other, though nothing here turns on that assumption. Other possibilities might be equally likely, but they would then be sufficiently similar to these two to raise no independent issues. So I shall assume that these two descriptions constitute the set of most-plausible defensible distributions.

Let us also assume that the national health service, as it now stands in Britain, would not itself be improved as a result of abolishing private medicine. Under that assumption, would the value of people's liberty be less if private medicine were outlawed than it would be in both of the two defensible distributions I just described? We must compare the medical care now available under the national health service with the care that would be provided under these defensible distributions, and we must distinguish three heads of comparison. Would anyone receive better medical care in either defensible distribution? Would he be able to receive faster service, avoiding the long queues for treatment of non-life-threatening disease in the present health service? Would he have more choice among particular doctors and specialists, a choice he might well value for its own sake? The answer to one or another of these questions, and perhaps to all three, might well be yes. Perhaps, if people had equal resources, they would all have better or speedier care, at prices they could afford, than is now offered by the health service. Perhaps they would have more choice of doctors and specialists whose services they could afford. If so—if any of these hypotheses is persuasive—then government would victimize people by outlawing private medicine and leaving only the national health service, as it now stands, in place.

But the government may nevertheless abolish private medicine as part of a program in search of equality if it is willing and able, concurrently, to improve the national health service in whatever dimension it now fails the test we just constructed. It should, after all, be possible to provide that service with the level of resources a national health service, or a scheme of tax-funded insurance for private medicine, would have available to it under a defensible distribution of wealth, though to do this it would probably be necessary to tax more heavily many of those who now enjoy the benefits of private medicine. Nor does it follow that government may not, even without substantially improving the national health service, restrict freedom of choice in the provision of medical services in ways short of abolishing private medicine altogether. It seems highly likely, for example, that in the most-plausible defensible distributions no one would in fact be able to jump the queue for treatment of crippling though non-life-threatening conditions. Therefore government does not victimize anyone by limited constraints designed only to forbid such queue-jumping through private medicine now. (We are considering, of course, only whether various constraints on freedom would victimize, not whether any of these is, overall, a good idea.) So the victimization principle is valuable beyond its role in forbidding certain constraints on liberty in the real real world: it helps point toward a more inclusive program of reform by identifying a package of measures, in which constraints might figure, that a government might legitimately adopt in pursuit of a defensible distribution of the community's resources.

The example I drew from the Supreme Court's infamous *Lochner* decision, in which the Court struck down a New York statute limiting the number of hours bakers might work a week, is complex in yet a different way. (If I am right, it is a nice paradox that the *Buckley* decision, which many people think right, seems a much clearer mistake than the *Lochner* decision, which everyone agrees was wrong.) Of course the employer bakery firms were not victimized: it is hard to imagine plausible defensible distributions in which they would find people willing to work the hours they wanted at wages that would make such hours profitable for them. But perhaps the New York statute would have worked to the disadvantage of immigrants who were desperate enough for work to accept the terms the bakeries actually offered. It might have cost them their jobs, and so left them worse off with respect to the value of their liberty of contract than they would have been under any defensible distribution counting them as participants. If so, and if New York had made, or would make, no compensating arrangement for alleviating unemployment, the statute victimized them, and I suggest that we should accept the conclusion that follows on the scheme we are exploring. It is wrong in principle for the state to deny people the right to work on terms they are willing to accept, in order to improve the economic situation of workers generally, unless it provides unemployment compensation or other relief for those who cannot obtain employment on the stipulated terms, relief sufficient to make their circumstances plausibly as good as they would be if people held a job under the outlawed terms.

Was *Lochner* therefore rightly decided after all? The Supreme Court gave much too short shrift to the arguments about health and safety from which I am prescinding, and anyway does not appear to have been moved by the egalitarian considerations we are inspecting. But suppose the arguments from health and safety were indeed too speculative alone to justify a constraint on liberty that worked to the disadvantage of those already most severely disadvantaged. I would still think the *Lochner* decision wrong, as a piece of constitutional interpretation, for reasons I develop elsewhere and will not restate here except summarily.[32] New York's action was not wrong if it was part of a more general program advancing its conception of equality without victimizing any person or section of its community. The Constitution cannot be understood as demanding that all parts of a social program interpreting a state conception of equality be adopted at once, nor as permitting the Supreme Court to impose one conception of distributional equality on other departments of government. The Constitution, in other words, treats social legislation of the form struck down in *Lochner* as a matter of policy, not principle. In the absence of any showing that New York had abandoned equal concern for those who would lose jobs under one stage of its program, the Court's decision was unjustifiable.

C. Fundamental Freedoms

We have now canvassed a variety of restrictions on freedom of choice, none of which would be found in any defensible distribution of resources, but each of which might nevertheless legitimately be imposed, at least as part of a larger program, to improve a distribution of resources that is far from defensible. But I began this section by describing a great and understandable fear: that though equality of resources protects liberty in some ideal world, it undermines it altogether in the actual world of our politics, because it puts all liberties, even those we deem fundamental, at risk in this way. We must therefore consider whether the principle of victimization sufficiently protects what we believe to be the most fundamental of our liberties.

In all the examples just considered, the most direct consequence of some suggested constraint is to remove part, though not all, of the advantage someone gains over others just in virtue of economic power he would not have in any defensible distribution. In some of the examples, the constraint has other or more diffuse consequences as well, and we worried over these examples for that reason. The case is very different when the constraint wholly removes a general liberty of considerable importance to some people's lives, because the value of their freedom is then sharply reduced from what it would be under any plausible defensible distribution. If people for whom politics is important are forbidden to speak, under a genuine or (more likely) fancied argument that this will reduce the material resource deficit of those worst-off, they are victimized, whether or not they themselves have more or fewer material resources than any defensible distribution would provide them. So equality of resources cannot be improved by that step. If homosexuals are forbidden sexual intimacy altogether, they are also victimized, again whether they are now rich or poor. So these fundamental liberties are not put in jeopardy by my argument here, even in a deeply inegalitarian society. On the contrary, the argument helps to show just why they are fundamental.

VIII. Looking Back

What is the place of liberty in equality of resources? If my argument is mainly sound, that place is fundamental and secure. I rejected the interest strategy, which makes the role of liberty in a general scheme of justice contingent in one way or another on the convictions or preferences that people happen to have, or would have under specified conditions, or should have. The constitutive argument I described does not make liberty contingent in any such way. Though the outcome of the auctionlike procedures equality of resources imagines is of course sensitive to the projects and convictions people bring to the auction, liberty is not part of that outcome, but is instead fixed in the baseline of any auction that equality of resources accepts.

So my argument has not relied on any claim that most people think liberty more important than other aspects of their circumstances. (Of course many people do think liberty crucially important for their own lives, as I believe everyone should.) Nor have I relied on any instrumental claims about the long-term consequences of protecting any particular liberty. The priority of liberty, under equality of resources, is established at a level that makes it independent of such considerations. Liberty is crucial to political justice because a community that does not protect the liberty of its members does not—cannot—treat them with equal concern on the best understanding of what that means.

It belongs to our political culture not only that liberty is important but that some liberties are more important than others; these more important liberties, we believe, deserve special protection in constitutional arrangements. My argument rejects the interest technique for identifying these more important liberties, which requires that they be shown to be liberties people all or in the aggregate specially value, or would specially value if they reflected upon them. Nevertheless the constitutive argument does capture the intuition that some liberties are more important than others. The principle of authenticity, for example, argues that the freedoms it sponsors, like freedom of speech and conscience, are central, because any compromise of those principles has particularly corrupting consequences for equality of resources. In the last section, when we designed and applied the principle of victimization, we found additional grounds for ranking some liberties as fundamental. We noticed that someone wholly denied those liberties is particularly likely to be victimized, in the real world of our own politics, no matter what his social or economic circumstances otherwise are. It is, of course, a further and difficult question, well beyond our project here, how these important rights should be protected in a constitutional structure. But equality of resources does provide a strong case that they should be protected in some way.

I close by returning to an important matter I mentioned near the beginning. I worried that some readers would find my argument for liberty demeaning to that virtue, because my argument would seem to them to make liberty only instrumental or subordinate to equality, as though we cared for liberty only as a useful circumstance for achieving a fair distribution of resources. I made the following reply to that objection. My argument here encompasses no more than a compatibility claim: liberty and equality cannot conflict, as two fundamental political virtues, because equality cannot even be defined except by assuming liberty in place, and cannot be improved, even in the real world, by policies that compromise the value of liberty. That argument, in itself, makes no claim about the ground of liberty. It is entirely consistent with the claim that liberty is essential for other reasons quite independent of equality; it insists only that even if we had no other reason for protecting liberty we would at least have that egalitarian reason.

I can now, however, expand on a further reply I also made. The interest strategy assumes that liberty and equality are two conceptually distinct political virtues. If they are, then questions naturally arise about the connection between the two virtues and about the priority of one over the other in any case of conflict. I assumed this part of the interest strategy's foundation—the conceptual independence of liberty and equality—when I argued that if the two virtues do conflict, equality must have priority. But the constitutive argument insists, on the contrary, that liberty and equality are not independent virtues but aspects of the same ideal of political association, so that when we declare our faith in liberty we are only affirming the form in which we embrace equality, only declaring, that is, what we mean by it.

The bridge strategy presupposes that liberty and equality are aspects of a single political virtue because that strategy uses liberty to help define equality and, at a more abstract level, equality to help define liberty. I did not argue the straightforward instrumental claim that a general presumption of liberty is a formal requirement of any auction that satisfies the envy test. Indeed, as I emphasized, a general baseline scheme of illiberalism, in which people are permitted to do almost nothing with what they acquire in the auction, would satisfy the formal requirements of such an auction just as well. Liberalism is appropriate to equality of resources, I argued, not because it is formally necessary to a successful auction, but because a liberal baseline expresses equality of resources' interpretation of the abstract egalitarian principle better than any alternative baseline.

The crucial notion of true opportunity costs lies at the intersection of what are traditionally regarded as egalitarian and liberal concerns. It unites the two because it assumes both that a system of private property treats people as equals when it secures them equal resources, judged by the true cost of those resources to others, and also that the true cost to others must be gauged, so far as possible, by assuming a norm of liberty, by assuming, that is, that others would have been free to use the resources in question as they wished if these were theirs instead. Opportunity cost is a Januslike idea: it looks toward equality with one face, toward liberty with the other, and fuses the two virtues.

Of course the integrity of liberty and equality holds, at least in that way, only for equality conceived as equality of resources. That is what I meant when I said that when we declare for liberty we identify the sense in which we are egalitarian. Equality of resources is, we might say, an *inherently* liberal conception of equality. The other conceptions I described, which do not use opportunity costs as the metric of equality, must fall back on the riskier interest strategy to find liberty's place. So our argument has disclosed a further and intriguing contrast between equality of resources and these other interpretations of equality. The interest strategy, which other conceptions use, locates the worth of liberty entirely within individual lives, one by one. The constitutive strategy distinctive to equality of resources does not deny the importance of liberty within lives. But it hazards nothing on it. It appeals instead to the role liberty plays in fixing the overall character of a society, in redeeming its commitment to equal concern for all. So perhaps the constitutive strategy, so far from making liberty seem mean and instrumental, finally offers an account of that virtue that matches our enthusiasm for it.

4

Political Equality

I. Two Strategies for Democracy

A. Democracy and Equality

In Chapters 1–3 I have been studying the idea of equality beginning in a principle—the abstract egalitarian principle—that states the idea in its most abstract form. This principle stipulates that government must act to make the lives of citizens better, and must act with equal concern for the life of each member. We reach a useful, practical theory about what equality requires by constructing and testing concrete interpretations—conceptions—of that principle, to decide which conception is, all things considered, the best. Of course the abstract egalitarian principle cannot decide all matters: government and politics face a variety of issues, at every level of abstraction and concreteness, that cannot be answered simply by selecting among different interpretations or conceptions of abstract equality. And yet the influence of the egalitarian principle will be pervasive for any society that accepts it. The preferred interpretation of equal concern will affect not only the design of all fundamental institutions of government, but also the particular decisions each of these institutions makes.

Here I consider how the abstract principle bears on the foundational question of the distribution of political power within such a community. What political institutions and processes should an egalitarian community have? I assume that the community is large and complex and so must be governed by the decisions of representative officials rather than by separate decisions, case by case, of the whole community. How would a community based on equal concern choose its representative officials? What powers would these officials have, and what powers would the community as a whole retain?

It may seem self-evident that a society committed to equal concern must be a democracy rather than, for example, a monarchy or dictatorship or oligarchy. But though it is clear enough how a democracy differs from these other structures of government in general, democracy is itself an idea of great abstraction if not ambiguity. Democracy requires that officials be elected by the people rather than chosen through inheritance or by a small group of prominent families or electors. But that abstract statement does not decide which officials if any should be chosen not by the community as a whole but by sections or groups within it, how powers should be distributed among officials chosen in these different ways, how far elected officials should be permitted or required to appoint other officials to exercise some of their powers, which responsibilities should be held by elected and which by appointed officials, how long officials of either sort should serve, whether their terms of office should be fixed or subject to early termination by those who elected them, how far elected or other officials should themselves be free to change the constitutional arrangements under which officials are elected, whether a constitution should set limits to the powers of officials, so that the officials cannot themselves alter these limits, and so forth. Though we are all democrats, these are lively political questions among us, and some are matters of heated controversy. Both Britain and the United States are democracies, but they give very different answers to many of these questions, as do, for some of them, the different states within the United States. So the bare observation that a society committed to equal concern must be a democracy is not much help. That observation is better understood as a restatement of our original question: What form of democracy is most appropriate to an egalitarian society?

B. Dependent and Detached Conceptions

We should begin by noticing a crucial distinction between two very different approaches to that question. Each offers to interpret our central assumptions about democracy—that a democracy gives political power to the people as a whole rather than to any individual or group, that in a democracy free speech and expression are protected, and so forth—by providing a general strategy or goal for politics that explains and justifies these central assumptions and also serves as a standard for deciding more detailed and controversial questions, like those I described, about the best form of democracy. The first approach offers what I shall call a *dependent* interpretation or conception of democracy, because it supposes that the best form of democracy is whatever form is most likely to produce the substantive decisions and results that treat all members of the community with equal concern. On that view, the main features of a democracy—near-universal suffrage, free speech, and the rest—are justified because a community in which the vote is widely held and speech is free is more likely to distribute material resources and other opportunities and values in an egalitarian way. So it recommends, when controversial cases arise about the best detailed form of democracy, that a consequentialist test be used: Which decision of these controversial issues seems most conducive to advancing or protecting these substantive egalitarian goals? The second approach produces what I shall call, in contrast, a *detached* interpretation or conception of democracy. It insists that we judge the fairness or democratic character of a political process by looking to features of that process alone, asking only whether it distributes political power in an equal way, not what results it promises to produce. A detached conception hopes to explain and justify our central assumptions about democracy in that austere way. So it argues that freedom of speech, as well as widespread suffrage, helps to make political power more equal. And it argues, when controversial questions of detail arise about our political process, that these should be resolved by asking which decision is best calculated to improve equality of political power still further.

A detached conception of democracy, in other words, supplies an input test: democracy is essentially a matter of the equal distribution of power over political decisions. A dependent conception supplies an outcome test: democracy is essentially a set of devices for producing results of the right sort. We must be careful not to confuse that distinction with a different one, between two types of outcomes or consequences of a political process. Any democratic political process will have both distributive and participatory consequences. Its distributive consequences will be fixed by the decisions it makes dividing resources into public and private ownership, regulating the acquisition, transfer, and taxation of wealth and other forms of property, and determining when and to what degree people should be compensated for injuries to different forms of property, and how far people should be constrained, by the criminal law, in using their property, or otherwise in acting as they wish. A community that accepts the abstract egalitarian principle will aim at distributive decisions that treat people as equals according to the best interpretation of that idea.

The participatory consequences of a political process are the consequences that flow from the character and distribution of political activity itself. An egalitarian community will take an interest in at least three kinds of participatory consequence: symbolic, agency, and communal. Symbolic consequences are declarative. The community confirms an individual person's membership, as a free and equal citizen, by according him or her a role in collective decision. In contrast, it identifies an individual who is excluded from the political process as someone not fully respected or not fully a member. (Penal systems have shaped and exploited this symbolic consequence for many centuries, by attaching loss of vote to criminal conviction.) Agency consequences connect politics, for each individual, to his or her own moral experience; a decent political structure will allow people to participate not merely as voters but as moral agents who bring reason, passion, and conviction to the role. An egalitarian community will recognize that for many of us, politics present moral issues of greater complexity and importance than any other aspect of our lives, and it will therefore take considerable interest in agency consequences. Communal consequences are more difficult to describe. From an individual's perspective, they are the various personal consequences of participating in a process whose success and value are communal in the strong sense that he or she shares fully in the pride or shame of the collective decision. From the collective perspective, they consist in the impact of the political process in nourishing a cohesive and fraternal political community.

A pure dependent conception would obviously be a poor interpretation of our common central assumptions about democracy if it ignored participatory consequences, and counted only distributional consequences among the substantive goals of an egalitarian state. For a benevolent tyranny, in which none of our assumptions about democracy held, might nevertheless produce a just property scheme, and might otherwise respect the distributional goals of the right conception of equality; indeed it might produce a more egalitarian distribution than a democracy could. But no tyranny could advance the participatory goals any egalitarian community would also aim to secure. So any plausible dependent conception of democracy will recognize the importance of participatory consequences and explain central features of democracy, at least in part, on that ground. It will offer an interpretation of universal suffrage, free speech, and other aspects of democracy that tries to show how these can be understood as helping to advance all the goals of equality, taken together, and it will propose changes or improvements to our political process in that spirit.

The contrast between the two conceptions of democracy is not, then, that one emphasizes the participatory and the other the distributional consequences of politics, but rather that one ignores while the other makes crucial all the consequences. The dependent conception blurs the distinction between input and outcome, between political equality and the other aspects of egalitarian theory, including its participatory goals. It supposes that these must be developed and inspected together, as interlocking parts of an overall conception no part of which stands entirely on its own. The detached conception, on the other hand, insists on a sharp split between political and all other forms of substantive equality. It treats political equality as a distinct dimension of equality, with its own distinct metric, which is political power. Suppose state electoral districts can be divided in such a way that residents of very poor urban districts could elect more representatives to the state legislature than they could if all districts contained the same number of residents. Assume that this districting arrangement in fact produces more just (because more genuinely egalitarian) political decisions, and also that it in no way deprives more prosperous residents of moral agency, symbolic recognition, or sense of community. The dependent conception might then endorse the arrangement, as furthering its view of democracy, all things considered. But the detached conception must reject the arrangement as undemocratic, because it concededly aims to give some people more political power than others.

Each of the two conceptions has been put to polemical use, though in different circumstances. People who dislike the policies of a government add force to their criticism when they can plausibly call it undemocratic. That charge seems essential, or at least particularly helpful, in justifying civil disobedience, for example.[1] The dependent conception will be useful, as supporting the charge, when the policies under attack seem plainly unjust, for on that conception critics can appeal to the injustice as evidence that the political process is itself flawed. The detached conception will be useful, on the other hand, when the decision, however just or unjust, does not seem to reflect the will of the majority, as a decision to abandon capital punishment might not. For on that conception critics can object to the process while professing neutrality about the result. Similarly, in some circumstances the dependent conception will be more helpful to people anxious to defend legislation as democratic, and in other circumstances the detached conception will be more helpful to them.

My concern here, however, is not with the practical or polemical consequences of the choice between the two conceptions, but with the choice itself. Which provides a better interpretation of political equality or democracy? The detached conception, in a pure form, is much the more popular. Almost everyone assumes that democracy means equal voting power among competent adults, that majority rule is therefore the nerve of democracy, and that any failure in majority rule is antidemocratic, whether or not it can be justified by appeal to some principle that overrides democracy in some circumstances. These unspoken assumptions dominate the contemporary debate among American constitutional lawyers about the legitimacy of the United States Supreme Court's power to overrule the decisions of elected legislators, for example. Even the most ardent partisans of that judicial power accept that it is an undemocratic feature of American political practice, and must be defended as valuable in spite of that defect. That is, they assume that a detached conception offers the right account of what democracy really is.

Part of the appeal of the detached conception lies, no doubt, in its apparent neutrality. In our society people disagree radically about questions of substantive justice; they disagree, for example, about whether a progressive income tax is official theft, whether laws against pornography are unfair, and whether special benefits for formerly disadvantaged groups are immoral. Divisive issues like these must be settled through the political process, and because the losers in that process will be expected to accept the decision the process reaches, even though they think it unjust, it seems fair that each citizen have equal control over what the decision is. In contrast, the dependent conception multiplies division. Because people have very different ideas about which substantive decisions are egalitarian in the abstract sense— about which decisions treat people with equal concern—they are likely, for that reason, to have very different ideas about which political procedures and institutions are genuinely democratic on the dependent conception.

We must not exaggerate this objection to the dependent conception. On both conceptions the character of democracy is controversial, because, as we shall see, the question of how political power should be measured, to decide whether it is equal, is itself controversial. The difference is rather this: on the dependent conception, controversial questions of substance may well reappear, in much the same form, as controversial questions about process.

Political theorists and philosophers must develop and defend comprehensive theories embracing both substance and procedure at the same time. But on the detached conception, controversies about process, if they break out at all, are more likely to be different controversies. So theorists who accept that conception can develop and defend discrete theories of democracy without touching substantive issues, and then propose that the latter be resolved through the democratic procedures they recommend.

I shall argue that in spite of its popularity and its apparent advantages, a detached conception of democracy cannot be successful in a pure form. We must reject it in favor of either a mixed conception of democracy, which draws features from both a detached and dependent strategy, or a pure dependent conception. I shall describe the main outlines of a pure dependent conception, which I believe provides the most attractive choice, and then consider the important political controversy I mentioned—is judicial review undemocratic?—as an illustration and test of that conception.

II. What Is Equality of Power?

A. *Vertical and Horizontal Dimensions*

Equal voting power is not an inevitable, or even a likely, feature of a dependent conception of democracy. As our districting example demonstrated, a scheme that does not aim at equality of political power may offer a better prospect of achieving the distributive goals of equality than a scheme that does, and may even, as we shall see later, provide a better prospect of realizing the participatory goals as well. But a detached conception of democracy must take equality of power to be fundamental. For if political equality is a separate, independent dimension of equality, then power is the only intelligible metric for that dimension. An egalitarian political process must be a process that distributes political power equally. The appealing argument for the detached conception I described—that if substantive issues of justice are disputed within a society, each citizen should have an equal role in the resolution of those disputes—assumes that any detached conception will have just that feature.

But what *is* equality of political power? How is political power to be measured? Under what circumstances is it equal? These questions will occupy us for several pages. But we should notice, first, that any adequate theory of political equality must compare political power along two dimensions: not only horizontally, by comparing the power of different private citizens or groups of citizens, but also vertically, by comparing the power of private citizens with individual officials. If democracy is a matter of equal political power, both dimensions must figure in the accounting. Horizontal equality of power is hardly enough to provide anything we would recognize as a genuine democracy. In totalitarian dictatorships private citizens have equal political power: none. Cynical pretend-democracies with a single political party are usually scrupulous in providing each citizen with one and only one vote for that party. So the vertical dimension must come into play.

It seems incredible, however, that any genuine vertical equality of power could exist even in apparently genuine democracies like Britain and the United States. How could our political structures and practices be revised, short of destroying representative government altogether, so as to give every citizen of voting age the same power over national affairs as a junior congressman, let alone as much as the president? So a detached conception of democracy, based on equality of power, might seem caught in a dilemma at the start. If it insists on horizontal equality only, equality among the governed, its most stringent requirements might be satisfied by plainly undemocratic tyrannies. If it demands vertical equality as well, then it is wholly unrealistic.

B. Impact and Influence

We must bear in mind that threatened dilemma when we consider what equality of power might mean. We should distinguish two interpretations: equality of impact and equality of influence. The intuitive difference is this: someone's impact in politics is the difference he can make, just on his own, by voting for or choosing one decision rather than another. Someone's influence, on the other hand, is the difference he can make not just on his own but also by leading or inducing others to believe or vote or choose as he does. We need a somewhat more technical account of impact and influence than that, however, because we want to compare the political impact or influence of different people. So let us define degree of impact and influence in the following way, which makes use of the idea of subjective probabilities. Suppose you know everything there is to know about the political structure of a particular community, including the voting rights of all citizens, the jurisdictional structures of representation, and the constitutional power of each official. But you know nothing about the nonconstitutional powers of charisma or reputation or association or skill or threat or bribe or other advantages that give any one person influence over the political acts of anyone else. You know nothing, at the start, about the views or opinions or the voting or choosing intentions of anyone about some matter that the political process must soon decide, like, for example, whether to reduce taxes. In these circumstances you cannot assign any more than an equal probability to the community as a whole's reaching either decision. Now you learn my firm voting or choosing intentions; you learn that I will cast every vote I have against reducing taxes, for instance. By how much should you increase your estimate of the probability of that result? The answer gives my political impact, with respect to that decision.

We can define political influence in a similar way. Now we suppose you know everything there is to know not only about the constitutional structure of powers and rights, but also about the nonconstitutional powers of influence I excluded from your knowledge in the preceding paragraph. Once again you initially know nothing about anyone's opinion or voting intentions about reducing taxes, and so can assign neither community decision greater probability than the other. Now, when you learn that I oppose tax reduction and will do everything I can to defeat it, the degree to which you should increase the probability of that decision in virtue of that information states my political influence over the issue.[2]

The distinction between political impact and political influence suggests an escape from the dilemma I described. Obviously, vertical equality of political power is impossible if that means equality of political impact. You would certainly have decreased the subjective probability of tax reduction by an incomparably greater extent, when you learned of my intention to cast any vote I had against it, if you had thought I was a senator rather than an academic lawyer. Indeed, it makes no sense, even as an unattainable ideal, to call for vertical equality of impact in a structure of representative government, because a representative structure is necessarily one in which impact is sharply different, from a vertical perspective. But it does make sense to call for vertical equality, as an ideal, if the equality in question is equality of influence. We can even describe a fully representational system in which equality of influence holds, at least to the degree of precision to which it can be measured anyway. Suppose that officials accept that they have a duty to vote as a majority of those they represent wish. Suppose that elections are held sufficiently frequently, communication between officials and constituents is good enough, and recall mechanisms sufficiently efficient and inexpensive, so that officials do in fact hold to that duty. In those circumstances rough vertical equality of influence is realized. Because Senator X will vote for tax reduction when but only when he believes that a majority of his constituents favor it, the information that he would personally prefer a reduction does not increase the probability that he will vote for it any more than the information that any other of his constituents would prefer it increases that probability.

So it seems that the detached conception, which takes equality of power to be the sole index of democracy, can succeed as a plausible interpretation of our central assumptions only if it takes equality of power to mean equality of influence, because only that reading would offer a plausible account of the vertical dimension of equality. Now look at the matter from the horizontal perspective. Here, too, it would be implausible to understand equality of power to mean equality of impact, but now for the opposite reason. Equality of impact is not too demanding a goal but one not demanding enough. Equal impact does require that each competent citizen have a vote and the same vote, and it also requires one-person-one-vote districting. Equal impact would condemn the districting arrangement I offered as an example earlier, which provides more political impact, per person, for poor inner-city residents. (It also condemns the American constitutional scheme for electing senators, which gives each resident of Wyoming much more impact over decisions the Senate takes than each resident of California has.) But equality of impact does nothing to justify a central assumption we make about democracy, which is that democracy requires not only widespread suffrage but freedom of speech and association, and other political rights and liberties, as well. My impact in politics is no less than yours when special censorship denies me the right to present my views to the public but allows you to do so. We need to reach beyond the idea of equal impact to equal influence even to begin to explain why censoring the views of some denies equality of political power.

We need to reach beyond equal impact, moreover, to explain a serious complaint against American democracy most people accept to some degree: that some private citizens have disproportionately more political power than others, because they are richer or control media or for some similar reason. That is a complaint not about unfair impact but about unfair influence. No Rockefeller who votes in your jurisdiction has any greater impact on political decisions than you do; his vote counts for no more than yours. All this confirms what we gathered by considering equality of power on the vertical dimension. On the horizontal dimension as well, the equal power that the detached conception demands cannot be equality of impact. If the idea of equal political power is to provide a conception of democracy sufficiently comprehensive to detach that conception from substantive aims, then equal power must be understood to mean equal influence.

C. Should Influence Be Equal?

But is equality of influence really an attractive ideal? Would we not hesitate to improve vertical equality of influence in the way in which we just saw this to be possible: by insisting that officials always act in whatever way a majority of their constituents wished, and adopting electoral devices that would punish those who do not? Of course, even if we did schedule elections frequently enough and provide recall mechanisms sufficiently terrifying to make officials generally obedient, we could not make them always so, if only because they would sometimes be mistaken about what a majority of their constituents wanted, or because in their last planned terms they might depart on frolics of their own. But do we want to come even as close as we can to making sure of their obedience? That question will remind you of Burke's famous letter to the sheriffs of Bristol, in which he denied any responsibility, even in principle, to vote for what those who elected him favored.[3] History has generally credited his opinion, even though depressingly few officials seem actually to follow it.

   Nor do we seem to object to parts of our constitutional structure that are now obstacles to vertical equality of influence. Senators are elected for six-year terms. Presidents and all other elected federal officials are guaranteed fixed terms, no matter how unpopular they become. (In England, by contrast, a very unpopular government falls, and new elections must be held.) Judges have great power; many are appointed rather than elected and, once appointed, have lifetime tenure. And so on. Someone defending vertical equality of political influence as an ideal might respond to these facts in different ways. He might condemn the features of American practice that impair vertical equality as outrageously undemocratic, and call for radical reform. Or he might insist that though these features are indeed undemocratic and unfair, they are justified overall as compromises necessary to achieve other political goals like efficiency and stability. (This latter reply, of course, would mark a retreat from a pure detached conception of democracy because it concedes that political institutions should serve goals other than equality of power, and that these other goals are sometimes important enough to justify compromises of political equality.)

The doubts I mainly want to press here, however, are doubts about equality of influence on the horizontal dimension, where it will seem to most readers, I believe, a much more attractive ideal than it does on the vertical dimension. The main appeal of horizontal equality of influence lies in the conviction that it is unfair that some private citizens have much more influence in politics than others just because they are much richer. But we can explain that intuition in two ways. We can, indeed, explain it as resting on the assumption that any great lapse from equality of influence among private citizens is a serious lapse in democracy. Or we can explain it in a way that does not appeal to equality of influence, as a general ideal, at all. We can say, for example, that it is unjust that some people have as much money as a Rockefeller because that violates the distributive principles of equality, and then add that the disproportionate political influence their wealth gives them is a particularly deplorable consequence of the injustice because it allows them, among other things, to perpetuate and multiply their unfair advantages.

These two ways of objecting to a Rockefeller's political influence are, of course, very different. The first is insensitive to the source of his disproportionate influence; it supposes that aggregate influence, from all sources, must be equal. The second makes no assumptions about aggregate influence; it condemns a Rockefeller's influence only because of the particular source of that influence. We can contrast the two objections by imagining a world in which the first would hold but the second would not. Suppose the distributional goals of equality were met, but some people still had more influence in politics than others. They might have more influence for a variety of reasons, but I shall assume reasons unobjectionable in themselves, because we are considering whether we should object to unequal influence as such. They might have decided to spend more of their initially equal wealth on political campaigns, for example, than others have. Or they might have invested more in study and training, which made others more likely to consult them or listen to their advice. Or they might have led lives of such conspicuous achievement or virtue that others trust them more or are more ready to follow them. The first form of objection to a Rockefeller's influence would nevertheless apply to such people. We would regard the greater influence of politically motivated or experienced or charismatic people as a defect in political organization, and take whatever steps we could to eliminate or reduce it. But the second form of the objection would lapse unless we had some other reason, quite independent of any assumption that political influence should be equal, for objecting to a situation in which some people are more politically motivated or trained or charismatic than others.

Which form of objection is more precise? When we object to the distribution of power in our society, is power really the root of our complaint? Or are we really objecting to other, independently unjust features of our economic or political or social organization in a forceful way, by calling attention to a very unfortunate consequence of these features? Consider the common, and wholly justified, complaint that women have too little power of all kinds in most societies. Someone who takes that view might think that social organization is defective unless the average woman has the same influence over affairs (measured in some specified way) as the average man does. But someone else who makes the same complaint might mean something very different: not that men and women should, as a matter of right, have the same influence on average, but that the smaller influence women now have is the result of a combination of economic injustice, stereotype, and other forms of oppression and prejudice, some of which, perhaps, are so fundamental as to be carried in the community's culture. The difference between these two positions emerges most clearly, once again, if we try to imagine a society in which economic, social, and cultural discrimination against women has been removed. If the average power of men and women is unequal in such a society—as it might be, in either direction—would that fact, just in itself, count as a defect in social organization?

These rhetorical questions are meant to tempt you away from the ideal of equality of power. But I expect that many of you will remain drawn to that ideal, if not in every sphere of life, then at least in politics. I shall therefore try to show how accepting equality of influence as an ideal would conflict with other egalitarian goals, by asking you to consider the steps that would be needed to approach that ideal further once we had corrected the independent injustices that we anyway condemn. I imagined that even in an egalitarian society differences in interest, commitment, training, and reputation might be sources of differences in political influence. Of course, many people would have a much better education in such a society than they do now. And people who now have no interest in politics, because they rightly feel ignored in its processes and excluded from its gains, would then be more likely to seek a political life. But I assume that these plainly desirable consequences of a more egalitarian distribution of resources would not wholly eliminate differences in influence from the sources I mentioned. Some people would remain politically much more interested and informed, and much more effective in convincing and leading others. What could we do to iron out these remaining differences in influence, which might well be substantial?

By far the most effective means, if that were our only goal, would be to reduce the role of influence in politics overall, that is, to reduce the opportunity citizens have to reflect together on what to urge or do. So long as politics is collectively reflective, in ways we now think admirable, it is inevitable that some citizens will have more influence than others. But we can make politics less reflective only by prohibiting political speech and association in the manner of the most savage totalitarian regimes, and I shall assume that any such prohibition would be unacceptable. A second strategy would be much less effective. We might try to make people less unequal in their political influence by setting a top limit to the funds anyone might invest or spend in education or training for politics, or in political campaigns. Limits on campaign expenditures are of course appealing when these compensate for unjust differences in wealth; just as both of the arguments I distinguished earlier object to a Rockefeller's disproportionate political influence, so both recommend limits on political expenditure in present circumstances. But if resources were distributed equally, limits on campaign expenditure would be inegalitarian because they would prevent some people from tailoring their resources to fit the lives they wanted though leaving others, who had less interest in politics, free to do so.[4] Such limits would also be perverse, for they would be protecting equality of influence on behalf of those who put a low value on their own influence but who could have had greater influence if they had valued that higher.

A third strategy would be so ineffectual that it is worth mentioning only because the objections to it are instructive. We might try to educate people not to attempt to influence others, with respect to political decisions, except in ways that do not rely on special advantages they might have, in experience or commitment or reputation, and also to attempt to resist being influenced by other people whose arguments might have special force traceable to such advantages. People could not succeed in following that advice, because in political argument it is impossible to separate dancer from dance. But the suggestion is anyway objectionable, because it encourages people deliberately to ignore what, by hypothesis, seem to them the best arguments, the most convincing reasons for taking up or working for one political cause rather than another. Indeed, it encourages them, sometimes deliberately, to pursue what they think would be the worse decision on substantive grounds.

Of course I do not imagine that anyone would actually recommend any of these three strategies; each is preposterous. But they are preposterous in ways that suggest that equality of influence is incompatible, even in principle, with other attractive aspects of an egalitarian society. Everyone concedes, of course, that conflicts might arise between equality of influence and distributional equality. We anticipated that possibility early in this chapter, in considering the districting arrangement that gave the inner-city poor greater political impact, at least, over certain issues in order to achieve a more egalitarian distribution of resources. However, that kind of conflict is only contingent: there is nothing in the character of equality of influence, as an ideal, that seems at war with distributive equality. But there is a more pervasive and fundamental conflict between that ideal and participatory goals that it would seem natural for an egalitarian society to endorse.

An egalitarian society wishes its citizens to engage in politics out of a shared and intense concern for the justice of the results, out of a shared and intense concern that distributional decisions treat everyone with equal concern. It encourages citizens to take pride or shame in the community's success or failure as if it were their own; it aims at that communal goal of political activity. The ideal of equal influence defies that ambition, however. When people are fastidious not to have too much influence, or jealous that they do not have enough, their collective concern is only a matter of show; they continue to think of political power as a discrete resource rather than a collective responsibility. An egalitarian society also cherishes an agency goal for political activity: that citizens should have as much scope for extending their moral life and experience into politics as possible. But people who accept equality of influence as a political constraint cannot treat their political lives as moral agency, because that constraint corrupts the cardinal premise of moral conviction: that only truth counts. Political campaigning under some self-imposed limit of influence would not be moral agency but only a pointless minuet of deference.

D. Taking Stock

Equality of impact cannot furnish a pure detached conception of democracy. It asks much too much on the vertical dimension of politics, and much too little on the horizontal. Equality of impact may well play an important role in a mixed detached and dependent conception, as a goal to be sought when and as other considerations permit. And, as we shall see, it has a role to play in any plausible pure dependent conception. But if a pure detached conception is to succeed, it must use influence rather than impact as the metric of political power. Equality of influence, however, does not seem desirable, as an exclusive standard, on the vertical dimension. It would require too much sacrifice of official independence and other values. Nor does it seem desirable as an exclusive standard on the horizontal dimension. We should, of course, remedy the distributive injustices that account for a great deal of the inequality in political influence of our own time. But we could not pursue equality of influence beyond remedying those distinct injustices, because the means we should have to use would violate other features of a desirable egalitarian society that seem more important.

It follows that we cannot maintain a pure detached conception of democracy. Should we therefore construct a mixed conception in which equality of influence figures as an attractive though unattainable ideal compromised by consequentialist considerations drawn from a dependent strategy? We would then have a deep dilemma to deplore in the abstract principle of equality. We would have decided that we cannot treat people as equals unless we make their political influence equal, and that we cannot treat them as equals if we do. But why should we accept equality of influence as a discrete ideal? What is to be said for it? I suggested one argument early in this chapter, and we should return to it now. It seems unfair to ask people to accept substantive results they think wrong unless they have had as great a role in the decision as anyone else. When I first advanced that argument, as explaining the intuitive appeal of the detached conception of democracy, we had not yet distinguished the two modes of power: impact and influence. The argument has some force as an argument for equality of impact, and that force is preserved in the limited argument for that form of equality that we will discover later in a dependent conception of democracy. But the argument fails altogether as an argument for equality of influence. It seems quite irrelevant, when I am asked to accept a majority decision I opposed, whether my opponents were more skillful in arguing than I was; I cannot plead my lack of influence as showing the illegitimacy of the vote against me unless I can trace my lack of influence to a source that is itself illegitimate.

We are left, I believe, with only one argument for equality of influence: that we must accept it as an ideal, and must therefore settle for a mixed conception of democracy, because we cannot develop an adequate conception that ignores it. In the remainder of this chapter I shall take up that challenge, by sketching a dependent conception of democracy that provides an important though limited place for equality of impact but none for equality of influence. I hope to show that a dependent conception can account, in a natural and unstrained way, for what we take to be the central features of democracy, and that it can justify those features through principles we can and should use in debates about what democracy, in detail, really means.

III. Participatory Values

A. Symbolic Goals

We must reconstruct and expand the list of substantive political goals that a successful dependent conception of democracy would reflect. We cannot rule out, in advance, that some of the goals we list will conflict with others, in which case the dependent conception must be in some sense a compromise among these goals. Nevertheless, I shall consider the demands of the different goals separately until conflicts do emerge, if they do.

I shall start with participatory goals. The symbolic consequences of a political structure are largely fixed by the assignment of vote, which is a matter of political impact. Elections in large political communities are typically structured by dividing the overall community into electoral districts of different size and character. There are no national undistricted elections in the United States, and such elections are very rare in Britain. We elect officials and decide affairs by states or parliamentary districts, and also by cities and wards and school districts. Equality requires that voting assignments carry a symbolic declaration of equal standing for all. The political decisions that divide the overall political community into districts, and that assign votes within each district so created, must not be motivated by, or be capable of interpretation as reflecting, any lower standing of, or less concern for, one citizen as against others.

So we have, in this symbolic goal, a compelling reason for taking horizontal equality of impact across the political community as a whole as at least the prima facie standard of democratic political structures. But only prima facie, because the symbolic goal permits deviations from that standard when these deviations cannot plausibly be understood as reflecting adversely on the standing or importance of those whose impact is made less. History and convention play an important role in applying these considerations in practice. Our own history is such that no deviation from equal impact within a district—no deviation, that is, from equal vote—is tolerable for us. That strict requirement would not necessarily hold in a community whose history showed that unequal voting did not itself display contempt or disregard. We can imagine, for example, a society in which people gain votes as they grow older, or in which people acquire more votes by pursuing a course of study genuinely open to everyone, or something of that sort. But in a society like our own, in which the vote has traditionally been an emblem of responsibility, weight, and stake, any violation of equal vote would reflect a denial of the symbolic attachment equal vote confirms. That is why loss of vote has so often been used as one of the consequences of a criminal conviction.

Our history does not give equality of impact the same symbolic role in considering how a large community should be districted into smaller voting jurisdictions. Part of the reason is obvious. For practical reasons only rough equality of impact could be established by districting decisions, because these could not be mathematically perfect and would in any case become outdated between periodic redistricting efforts. American history, in particular, has furnished dramatic examples of districting decisions in which equality of impact was disdained for reasons obviously not reflecting less concern for those whose political impact was thereby reduced. The scheme of districting that gives citizens of Wyoming more impact than those of California in the Senate was not originally motivated by, nor could it now plausibly be interpreted as reflecting, contempt for the latter or lack of respect for their views. So our history does not condemn, as incompatible with the symbolic goals of equality, districting decisions denying equal impact if these are equally obviously innocent in that way. The districting scheme I imagined earlier, which aims to give inner-city poor somewhat more impact than they would otherwise have, is hardly incompatible with those symbolic goals, for example, though that scheme might offend other parts of an attractive dependent conception of democracy.[5]

B. Agency Values

The agency values of politics are more diffuse and elusive. But there is an obvious connection between these values and free speech and the other political liberties. We cannot make our political life a satisfactory extension of our moral life unless we are guaranteed freedom to express our opinions in a manner that, for us, satisfies moral integrity. Opportunity to express commitment to our convictions is just as important, for that purpose, as the opportunity to communicate those convictions to others; indeed the two often merge. Just as someone denied opportunity to worship according to his or her own lights is denied a foundational part of religious life, so someone denied opportunity to bear witness to his concern for justice, as he understands what the concern requires, finds his political agency stultified not merely bounded.

But the demands of agency go beyond expression and commitment. We do not engage in politics as moral agents unless we sense that what we do can make a difference, and an adequate political process must strive, against formidable obstacles, to preserve that potential power for everyone. It must, that is, insure a degree of political leverage for each citizen. Districting has a role to play in that ambition, and it is important to notice the difference between mediate and final districting. Districting is mediate when elections pick representatives who together reach a single decision for the political community as a whole, as in the case of statewide elections for the Senate. Districting is final when elections finally decide something for the jurisdiction of the election, as in the case of bond-issue referenda. Both give individual citizens in a large county more leverage, though in different ways. Mediate districting gives somewhat more leverage on important issues of national consequence, and so improves moral agency within the community as a whole. Final districting gives more leverage over issues of correspondingly less dramatic consequence.

Of course, districting is not the only means an egalitarian political process can and should use to provide leverage. In large districts, or in mediate districts in large nations, the leverage of vote is negligible. So the agency goal of politics can be properly served only by providing everyone enough access to influential media, if he or she wishes, to give each person a fair chance to influence others if he or she can. That, we might say, is the other side of the liberties of free speech and audience, judged from the point of view of agency. In our inegalitarian society, the most prominent source of inequality of access is inequality of wealth. If resources were more equally distributed, leverage would automatically be improved for large numbers of citizens. But if, nevertheless, the economics of the media gave only those who chose to invest or work in that industry access to a political audience, the agency goals of democracy would then require access to be guaranteed or provided in some other way for citizens more generally.

Readers will wonder whether I am now introducing, through the idea of leverage and access, the same equality of influence that I rejected before. Moral agency is possible for all citizens in politics only if each has an opportunity to make some difference. In a large district, the opportunity to vote, without more, may not satisfy this requirement. So the opportunity for influence, and not merely impact, is necessary to agency. But this says nothing about *equality* of influence. We encountered that latter idea in the course of a very different argument, which we began by assuming that democracy requires equality of power and wondered what that meant. We discovered that it must mean equality of influence, and we grew doubtful about equality of power mainly for that reason. In the present discussion we encounter the idea of influence in a very different context, in the course of building a dependent conception of democracy. The emphasis is now on the opportunity for some influence—enough to make political effort something other than pointless—rather than on the opportunity to have the same influence as anyone else has. We design a dependent conception of democracy so that it permits anyone who wishes it enough leverage or engagement to make it possible for him or her to treat politics as an extension of his moral life. That is a threshold notion, and nothing in it takes equality of influence to be an ideal toward which we should strive.

So the symbolic values of participation require equality of vote within districts, at least for us, and presume equality of impact across districts. The agency values require liberty and leverage. The communal participatory values send us in a somewhat different direction that I shall not explore here except by suggesting, cryptically, that a political society improves its members' sense of politics as a joint venture by adopting the right conception of distributive equality—equality of resources—and by insisting, in its substantive political and legal decisions, on the second-order political virtue of integrity.

IV. Distributive Values

A. Two Kinds of Issues

We now have some sense of an adequate dependent conception of democracy. It requires equality of vote within districts, and presumes equality of impact across them. It requires liberty and leverage. These requirements leave much open. They hardly speak to questions of vertical equality at all;

they do not stipulate the size of districts, the form of representation, or which decisions must be left to which class or kind of officials, for example. Now we turn to the distinctly substantive goals of an egalitarian political process: the decisions we believe the process should make about the distribution of resources and opportunities into private ownership, about the use of collective power and resources in public programs and foreign policy, about saving and conservation, and about the other topics of public principle and policy that confront a modern government. How would we design a dependent conception of democracy if we wanted to improve the accuracy of these various decisions? I use that provocative word deliberately. Though it might seem odd to speak of a decision about whether to raise taxes or to enforce capital punishment or to give aid to the Contras as either accurate or inaccurate, I am supposing that it is sensible to do so. Or at least to speak (as people skeptical about "right answers" to moral questions prefer to do) about a class of better decisions and a class of worse ones. We want our political process, among other things, to be one well designed to make accurate judgments about which decision is best, or at least in the group of better decisions.

It is now essential that we notice an important distinction between two types or classes of political decisions: those involving mainly what I shall call *choice-sensitive* issues, and those involving mainly *choice-insensitive* ones. Choice-sensitive issues are those whose correct solution, as a matter of justice, depends essentially on the character and distribution of preferences within the political community. The decision whether to use available public funds to build a new sports center or a new road system is typically choice-sensitive. Though a variety of issues may merge in that decision, from issues of distributive justice to those of sound environmental policy, information about how many citizens want or will use or will benefit directly or indirectly from each of the rival facilities is plainly relevant, and may well be decisive. The decision whether to kill convicted murderers or to outlaw racial discrimination in employment, on the other hand, seems choice-insensitive. I do not believe that the right decision on these issues depends in any substantial way on how many people want or approve of capital punishment or think racial discrimination unjust. The case against capital punishment, I believe, is just as strong in a community where a majority of members favor it as in a community of people revolted by the idea.

Of course people will disagree about which issues are choice-sensitive and which, if any, are choice-insensitive. But the second-order question whether any particular first-order question is choice-sensitive or -insensitive is itself choice-insensitive. It makes no sense to say that a particular question is choice-sensitive if, but only if, a majority of people think it is or want it to be. Some readers will recognize, in the distinction between choice-sensitive and -insensitive issues, a distinction I have described differently in the past as one between issues of policy and issues of principle. I do believe that what I call issues of policy are choice-sensitive, and that issues of principle are choice-insensitive. But I do not assume that in the present discussion; I assume only that readers will agree that some political issues are choice-insensitive even if they disagree about which issues are.

B. Accuracy, Impact, and Influence

A political process that distributes political impact roughly equally is generally better suited to the accurate decision of choice-sensitive issues than one that distributes it very unequally. If the question arises whether a new sports stadium or a new road system will better match the needs and desires of the population as a whole, then a process in which the wishes of most people are recorded directly, as through a referendum, or indirectly through the decisions of representatives elected and reelected by popular majorities, is obviously better, at least in ordinary circumstances, than a process in which only a small and possibly unrepresentative section of the community participates in any way. That argues in the direction of horizontal equality of impact with respect to choice-sensitive decisions within the community affected. It does not argue for complete equality of impact, however, even as an ideal, because it is easy to imagine variations in impact that would seem to improve ex ante accuracy in the decision of choice-sensitive issues. The residents of sparsely settled sections of a country or state, for example, might have interests special to them that would be neglected or overridden in an election in which equality of impact was enforced to as great a degree as is technically possible. Over the course of many such elections or political decisions, their interests would be less well served than any plausible account of accuracy in the decision of choice-sensitive issues would allow. We might do better, in deciding such issues, to use some judicious gerrymandering in which the impact of each citizen of a sparse area would be greater, one by one, than the impact of an individual citizen of a denser area. We might do better for the ex ante accuracy of choice-sensitive decisions, in other words, by adopting districting decisions that preserved the equality of vote within districts that we need for symbolic reasons but that reduced equality of impact, in the ways just described, by a deliberate choice for special and limited inequalities. My former example, about districting in favor of poor inner-city residents, is only another case of the same strategy.

What about equality not of impact but of influence? How far would we aim at equality of influence as a device for improving ex ante accuracy in the decision of choice-sensitive issues? Of course we would want to prevent false advertising and other forms of deception whose likely effect would be to hide facts people need in order to judge whether a particular program would be in their own interests. We would also want to prevent manipulation designed to create tastes that are at odds with people's more foundational ambitions or values. But we can justify constraints necessary to these ends without appealing to equality of influence as itself an ideal, and other features of choice-sensitive decision counsel against that ideal as a device for accuracy. For just as some people or groups use their political influence to deceive or manipulate, so others use their influence to teach, reform, and ennoble, to suggest ranges of value and ambition that might, for example, lead some people to favor a theater over both a sports stadium and a road system who would not otherwise have even considered the choice. We have no general reason to rid the political forum of the latter forms of influence, and we therefore have no general reason to try even to achieve as much equality of influence as possible. We must target the constraints we design to bad or inappropriate influence, by reducing the importance of wealth in politics, and by encouraging the forms of political debate in which deception is most likely to be exposed, rather than by taking even the minimal steps we might to insure that no one's views turn out to be more moving than anyone else's.

There is much more to be said about ex ante accuracy in choice-sensitive decisions. But our concern here is schematic, and we should therefore turn instead to the second part of our accuracy study: ex ante accuracy in the decision of choice-insensitive issues. We do not, of course, have the argument for widespread dispersal of political impact here that we had in the case of choice-sensitive issues. For by definition the accurate decision of choice-insensitive issues does not depend on information a wide poll can be expected to provide. If we were to accept certain assumptions, cardinal among which is the assumption that people are on average more likely than not to decide choice-insensitive issues correctly, then we would conclude that the more people who voted on a particular such issue, assuming equal impact, the more likely it would be that the majority would vote for the right side.[6] But there is no a priori ground for accepting those assumptions; whether I think it more likely than not that any particular person will reach the right decision about capital punishment depends on what I think the right answer is, not on any general observations about the average man or woman's skill in moral philosophy.[7]

I conclude that we have no reason to think, ex ante, that anything approaching equality of either impact or influence, in either the vertical or horizontal dimension of politics, is best geared to produce right answers to choice-insensitive issues across the board. But, as we noticed, the participatory and other substantive goals of egalitarian politics are not so indiscriminate. They do argue for particular structures. The symbolic goals argue for equal vote within districts, the agency goals for liberty and leverage, and the choice-sensitive accuracy goal for a large degree of equality of impact. So the right overall dependent conception of democracy has already taken on fairly concrete shape, and we should therefore use the same structure to decide choice-insensitive issues as well, unless two conditions are met. We must have some positive reason to think that a different procedure would considerably improve ex ante accuracy in deciding choice-insensitive issues, and these different procedures must not outrage any of the other goals of egalitarian politics we have canvassed. It would be outrageous, for example, to suggest that only lawyers and moral philosophers should be allowed a vote on choice-insensitive matters, because that suggestion, in addition to its other manifest defects, wholly ignores the symbolic goals that require equality of vote.

I shall briefly discuss, in the final section, a special arrangement for the decision of certain choice-insensitive issues that I believe does satisfy the two conditions I described, and that should therefore be part of our developed dependent conception of democracy. But I should first take up a question I postponed earlier, which the preceding paragraph invites us to consider now. Do the different goals a dependent conception should recognize conflict, so that we must compromise or subordinate some of these to others? It makes a difference whether we have in mind ex post or ex ante conflict. It might well turn out that enforcing equality of vote on some occasion on some issue—whether to build a new sports stadium, for example—will lead to the wrong decision though a more restricted electorate would in fact for some reason have produced the right one. The possibility of such ex post conflict does not require any compromise or subordination of values in the design of political institutions, however, unless the conflict is also ex ante, that is, unless we could have designed a different set of institutions that would have made the wrong decision of such issues less likely but at the cost of injuring competing symbolic or other values. The question whether a dependent conception must acknowledge the more serious, ex ante, form of conflict is necessarily complex, and can hardly be decided in advance of a more detailed examination of institutional design than we are now undertaking. But nothing has yet emerged, in our limited study here, to show that ex ante conflict between the different goals a dependent conception should recognize is inevitable. In that respect the dependent conception of democracy seems to stand on firmer ground than the more popular, detached conception we first studied. For as we noticed, the ex ante conflict that conception embraced, between equality of influence and the participatory goals of egalitarian politics, is evident, profound, and unavoidable.

V. Constitutionalism and Principle

I shall close, as a kind of recapitulation, by considering an important example of how accuracy in the decision of choice-insensitive issues might be improved through special arrangements, at the cost of equality of both impact and influence, but without introducing ex ante conflict with any of the other goals we studied. In the United States (and increasingly in other countries as well) courts test legislation against their understanding of what their nation's constitution requires and hold legislation invalid if it offends that understanding. That practice strikingly compromises vertical equality of both impact and influence. A few judges have profoundly greater power than anyone else over the decision whether, for example, capital punishment or affirmative action or laws restricting abortion are to be permitted. That is why judicial review is generally regarded as undemocratic, even by its sometime friends, and even by its passionate admirers.

If we adopt a dependent conception of democracy, however, rather than a detached conception that makes democracy a matter of vertical and horizontal equality of impact or influence, it is far from evident that judicial review is in any way an undemocratic institution.[8] We must test the democratic character of judicial review by asking whether it does any violence to the ideals of a dependent conception we have been developing. I have not before mentioned what we might call the executive goals of the political process—efficiency of government and political stability, for example—and so I cannot consider the argument made in some quarters that judicial review threatens those goals, except to observe that history provides little support for that view. But it seems plain that, in the form in which it exists in the United States, judicial review does not offend any symbolic or agency goals. It does not impair equality of vote, because it is a form of districting and does not, in itself, reflect any contempt for or disregard of any group within the community. Nor does judicial review damage the agency goals of democracy. On the contrary, it guards those goals, by giving special protection to freedom of speech and to the other liberties that nourish moral agency in politics. It does more: it provides a forum of politics in which citizens may participate, argumentatively, if they wish, and therefore in a manner more directly connected to their moral lives than voting almost ever is. In this forum, moreover, the leverage of the minorities who have the most negligible leverage in ordinary politics is vastly improved.

So constitutionalism seems to do well when tested against the participatory goals of egalitarian politics. It is a crucial question, therefore, whether constitutionalism improves the accuracy of political decisions. If it does, then it would seem, on that ground, to deserve a place in a dependent conception of democracy. But here the distinction between choice-sensitive and choice-insensitive issues is particularly important. I have argued elsewhere that it would corrupt rather than promote accuracy if a court enforcing judicial review were to set aside choice-sensitive decisions legislatures make. I have also argued that it enhances accuracy when a court reviews certain choice-insensitive decisions of a legislature, namely those that reject putative rights against majority decision.[9] It is these choice-insensitive issues, of course, that the federal courts claim jurisdiction to decide, including the choice-insensitive issue of which issues are choice-insensitive. I will not repeat my arguments here. If my views can be sustained, however, then constitutionalism is an improvement in democracy so long as, but only so long as, its jurisdiction is limited to choice-insensitive issues of principle.

VI. Coda

There is much more to be said on this subject, including qualifications of what I have said here, some of which can be found in *Freedom's Law* and later in this book. But I want, in closing, to emphasize one central theme of this chapter. If a community is genuinely egalitarian in the abstract sense—if it accepts the imperative that a community collectively must treat its members individually with equal concern—then it cannot treat political impact or influence as themselves resources, to be divided according to some metric of equality the way land or raw materials or investments might be divided. Politics, in such a community, is a matter of responsibility, not another dimension of wealth.

5

Liberal Community

In the last two chapters we have been considering what place two central political ideals—liberty and democracy—play in a society that is committed to equality when equality is understood as requiring equal resources rather than equal welfare or well-being over a lifetime. In this chapter we consider the place, in such a society, of the further political ideal of community. We shall focus on an old problem: Should conventional ethics be enforced through the criminal law?[1] Was the Supreme Court right, in *Bowers v. Hardwick*, to uphold, against constitutional challenge, Georgia's law making sodomy a crime?[2] It is widely thought that liberal tolerance, which insists that it is wrong of government to use its coercive power to enforce ethical homogeneity, undermines community because the heart of community is a shared ethical code. I shall argue that if liberal tolerance is understood against the background of the conception of equality I have been defining, then such tolerance is not only consistent with the most attractive conception of community but indispensable to it.

Very different arguments, using very different concepts of community, have been used to attack liberal tolerance in different ways. I distinguish four such arguments. The first is an argument from democratic theory which associates community with majority. In *Bowers*, Justice Byron White suggested that the community has a right to use the law to support its vision of ethical decency:[3] it has a right to impose its views about ethics just because it is the majority. The second is an argument of paternalism. It holds that in a genuine political community each citizen has a responsibility for the well-being of other members and should therefore use his political power to reform those whose defective practices will ruin their lives. The third is an argument of self-interest, broadly conceived. It condemns atomism, the view that individuals are self-sufficient and emphasizes the wide variety of ways—material, intellectual, and ethical—in which people need community. It insists that liberal tolerance undermines the community's ability to serve these needs. The fourth, which I shall call integration, argues that liberal tolerance depends on an illegitimate distinction between the lives of individual people within the community and the life of the community as a whole. According to this argument, the value or goodness of any individual citizen's life is only a reflection and function of the value of the life of the community in which he lives. So citizens, in order to make their own lives successful, must vote and work to make sure that their fellow citizens lead decent lives.

Each of these arguments uses the concept of community in an increasingly more substantial and less reductive way. The first argument, that a democratic majority has a right to define ethical standards for all, uses community only as a shorthand symbol for a particular, numerically defined, political grouping. The second argument, which encourages paternalism, gives the concept more substance: It defines community not as just a political group, but as the dimensions of a shared and distinct responsibility. The third argument, that people need community, recognizes community as an entity in its own right, as a source of a wide variety of influences and benefits not reducible to the contributions of particular people one by one. The fourth argument, about identification, further personifies community and describes a sense in which a political community is not only independent of, but prior to, individual citizens. In this chapter I concentrate on this fourth argument, partly because I have not discussed it before, but also because I find its root idea, that people should identify their own interests with those of their political community, true and valuable. Properly understood, the idea furnishes no argument against liberal tolerance, and no support for *Bowers*. On the contrary, liberalism supplies the best interpretation of this concept of community, and liberal theory the best account of its importance.

I. Community and Democracy

Some liberals have thought that liberal tolerance can be fully justified by John Stuart Mill's harm principle, which holds that the state may properly restrain someone's liberty only to prevent his harming others, not himself.[4] In *Law, Liberty, and Morality*, H. L. A. Hart argued that this principle rules out legislation making homosexual acts criminal.[5] But Hart's argument is sound only if we limit harm to physical injury to person or property. Every community has an ethical environment, and that environment makes a difference to the lives its members can lead. A community that tolerates homosexuality, and in which homosexuality has a strong presence, provides a different ethical environment from one in which homosexuality is forbidden, and some people believe themselves harmed by the difference. They find it much harder, for example, to raise their children to absorb instincts and values of which they approve.

The first argument against liberal tolerance declares that questions about the shape of a democratic community's ethical environment should be decided in accordance with the majority's will. It argues not merely that whatever decisions the political officials elected by the majority make should be accepted as law, but that these political officials should make decisions that reflect the preferences of a majority rather than any minority.[6] This is substantive rather than merely procedural majoritarianism. The argument does not assume that any minority's moral views are base or wicked, but only that when opinion divides about the proper ethical environment for a community, it is unfair to allow a minority to dictate to majority will.

The argument does assume, however, that the contours of a community's ethical environment must be decided collectively, in a winner-take-all fashion, so that either the majority or some minority must determine its shape. If that assumption were true, then the argument would plainly be powerful. Some issues must indeed be decided in close to a winner-take-all way, and in those instances one group's view must prevail entirely, to the total exclusion of any other. One such issue is hotly debated now: should the nation adopt a particular version of a Strategic Defense Initiative (SDI). But democracy does not demand that all political decisions be winner-take-all. On the contrary, in one central sphere of life—the economic environment—justice requires exactly the opposite.

The economic environment in which we live—the distribution of property and preferences that creates supply, demand, and price—affects us even more obviously than our ethical environment does. I am harmed by the fact that I own less property than I might, and that others have different tastes from those I might want them to have. The economic environment may frustrate my efforts to raise my children to have the values I might wish them to have; I cannot, for example, raise them to have the skills and experience of collecting Renaissance masterpieces. But even if a majority of citizens wanted to assign all economic resources to themselves, it would not be just for them to do so. Justice requires that property be distributed in fair shares, allowing each individual his or her fair share of influence over the economic environment. People disagree, of course, about what constitutes a fair share, and a good part of modern political argument reflects that disagreement.[7] But my present point does not depend on any particular conception of distributive justice, because any remotely plausible theory will reject the principle of exclusive majoritarian control.

If we take a parallel view of the ethical environment, then we must reject the claim that democratic theory assigns a majority complete control of that environment. We must insist that the ethical environment, like the economic, be the product of the choices individual people make. Of course neither of these environments should be left completely to unregulated individual choices. We need laws to protect the economic environment from theft and monopolization, for example, and zoning regulations that respond to market externalities. These laws help insure, so far as possible, that the economic environment has the shape it would have if resources were fairly distributed and markets were perfect.

The ethical environment requires regulation in the same spirit, to limit a minority's impact on the ethical environment to the impact its numbers and tastes justify. Zoning regulations which restrict the practice of potentially offensive acts to special or private places serve that purpose, for example. But restricting a minority's impact on the ethical environment through zoning is very different from cheating a minority of any impact at all, which is what the majoritarian argument proposes.

If we treat the ethical environment in the same way we treat the economic environment—allowing it to be fixed by individual decisions made against the background of a fair distribution of resources—then we reject the majoritarian claim that the majority has a right to eliminate whatever it finds harmful in the ethical environment. Each member of the majority has a right only to a fair impact on his environment—the same impact as any other single individual. He has no right to the environment that would make it easiest for him to raise his children to hold his favored opinions. He must try to do his best, to that end, in the environment fairness provides.

Can we find any reason to treat the ethical environment differently from the economic environment? Some economic issues, such as SDI, must be decided collectively, all one way or the other, rather than as a resultant of individual forces. And our sense of integrity and fairness requires us to decide some issues of principle in the same way for everyone.[8] For example, officials should not aim to execute some proportion of convicted murderers to match the proportion of citizens who favor capital punishment. But neither of these reasons for making some political decisions collectively provides any argument for fixing a community's ethical environment that way. There is no practical reason why that environment must be exactly what some group thinks best. And since the various individual acts and decisions that contribute to forming an ethical environment are no more the acts of government than the various individual economic decisions that fix the economic environment are, there is no question of government's violating integrity by letting individuals make these decisions in different ways.

We should not subject the ethical and economic environments to different regimes of justice, because they are not two distinct environments, but interdependent aspects of the same one. The value of the resources someone controls is not fixed by laws of property alone, but also by other departments of law, stipulating how he can use that property. So moralistic legislation, which discriminates among some uses of property or leisure, always affects price and value to some degree. In some circumstances that effect is significant: morally inspired prohibition laws are an example. The judgment whether a particular distribution of a community's resources is just must therefore take into account the degree of liberty citizens have.[9] If we insist that the value of the resources people hold must be fixed by the interaction of individual choices rather than by the collective decisions of a majority, then we have already decided that the majority has no right to decide what kinds of lives everyone must lead. Once we accept that the economic and ethical environments are unified, in other words, we must accept liberal tolerance in matters of ethics because any contrary view denies the unity.

The majoritarian argument we have been considering is politically the most powerful argument against liberal tolerance. It was allowed a conspicuous place in the majority opinion in *Bowers*. This part of our overall discussion is therefore of considerable practical importance. But it is important to bear in mind its limits. It is aimed only at the majoritarian argument; it should not be taken as a statement of the exclusive ground of liberal tolerance, or as resting the entire value of liberty on an economic analogy. Nor does it purport to define any special rights to particularly important liberties, such as freedom of speech or association. It only denies the majoritarian argument's essential premise that the shape of the ethical environment as a whole must be fixed winner-take-all by the majority's wishes. If the concept of community has an important role in the criticism of liberal tolerance, it must be in a more robust sense than simply as a name for a political unity over which majority rule roams.

II. Community and Concern

The second communitarian argument, the argument of paternalism, appeals to the idea of community in a more robust sense. It begins in the attractive idea that a true political community must be more than a Hobbesian association for mutual benefits in which each citizen regards all others as useful means to his or her own ends; it must be an association in which each takes some special interest in the well-being of others for its own sake. The argument adds that people who are genuinely concerned about others take an interest in their critical as well as their volitional well-being. I must explain that distinction, because it is crucial to the argument of paternalism.[10]

There are two senses in which people have interests, two ways in which their lives can go better or worse. Someone's volitional well-being is improved whenever he has or achieves something he wants.[11] But his critical well-being is improved only by his having or achieving those things that he should want, that is, achievements or experiences that it would make his life a worse one not to want. We can make this distinction subjectively, as a distinction between two ways in which a person might understand or regard his own interests. I myself, for example, consider some of the things I want very much as falling under my volitional interests. I want good food, and fewer visits to the dentist, and to sail better than I do, and my life therefore goes better when I have them. But I do not think that I ought to want these things, or that my life would be a poorer one if for some reason I did not. But I take a different view of other things I want, such as having a close relationship with my children and achieving some success in my work. I do not think that having a close relationship with my children is important just because I happen to want it; on the contrary, I want it because I believe a life without such relationships is impoverished. We make the same distinction objectively, that is, as a distinction not between two ways in which people might regard these interests, but between two classes of interests people actually have. People can fail to recognize their own critical interests. It makes sense to say that someone who has no regard for friendship or religion or challenging work, for example, leads a poorer life for that reason, whether he agrees or not. We also make critical judgments about ourselves; people all too often come to think, toward the end, that they have ignored what they only then realize is really important to their lives.[12]

The distinction is complex and can be explored and criticized in many different ways. Some, for example, will be skeptical about the whole idea of critical interests or well-being. They may think that since no one can prove that it is in anyone's critical interests to want something he does not, then the whole idea of critical well-being is mistaken. I shall not try to answer that skeptical objection here. I shall assume, as I believe most of us do in our ordinary lives, that we all have both kinds of interests. We can use the distinction between volitional and critical interests to distinguish two forms of paternalism. Volitional paternalism supposes that coercion can sometimes help people achieve what they already want to achieve, and is for that reason in their volitional interests. Critical paternalism supposes that coercion can sometimes provide people with lives that are better than the lives they now think good and is therefore sometimes in their critical interests.

The second communitarian argument appeals to critical rather than volitional paternalism. It forces us to confront a philosophical issue about critical well-being. We can evaluate someone's life in two ways. We can look, first, at the components of that life: the events, experiences, associations, and achievements that make it up, and ask whether in our view these components, in the combination we find them, make a life good. We can look, second, at the attitudes of the person whose life it is. We can ask how he judges those components; we can ask whether he sought them or regards them as valuable, in short, whether he endorses them as serving his critical interests.

What view should we take about the relationship between these two ways of looking at the critical value of a life? We should distinguish two answers. The additive view holds that components and endorsements are separate elements of value. If someone's life has the components of a good life, then it has critical value. If he endorses these components, then their value increases. The endorsement is frosting on the cake. But if he does not, the value of the components remains. The constitutive view, on the other hand, argues that no component contributes to the value of a life without endorsement: If a misanthrope is much loved but disdains the love as worthless, his life is not much more valuable for the affection of others.

The constitutive view is preferable for a variety of reasons. The additive view cannot explain why a good life is distinctively valuable for or to the person whose life it is. And it is implausible to think that someone can lead a better life against the grain of his most profound ethical convictions than at peace with them. If we accept the constitutive view, then we can answer the argument from critical paternalism in what we might call its crude or direct form. Suppose someone who would lead a homosexual life does not, out of fear of punishment. If he never endorses the life he leads as superior to the life he would otherwise have led, then his life has not been improved, even in the critical sense, by the paternalistic constraints he hates.

We must recognize a more subtle aim of critical paternalism, however. Suppose the state deploys a combination of constraints and inducements such that a homosexual is converted and does in the end endorse and appreciate the conversion. Has his life then been improved? The answer turns on an issue I have so far neglected: the conditions and circumstances of genuine endorsement. There must be some constraints on endorsement; otherwise critical paternalism could always justify itself by adding chemical or electrical brainwashing to its regime.

We must distinguish acceptable from unacceptable circumstances of endorsement. The distinction, as we know from the history of liberal theories of education, is a difficult one to draw, but any adequate account of acceptable circumstances would, I believe, include the following proposition. We would not improve someone's life, even though he endorsed the change we brought about, if the mechanisms we used to secure the change lessened his ability to consider the critical merits of the change in a reflective way. Threats of criminal punishment corrupt rather than enhance critical judgment, and even if the conversions they induce are sincere, these conversions cannot be counted as genuine in deciding whether the threats have improved someone's life.[13] The second communitarian argument is therefore self-defeating.

III. Self-Interest and Community

A. Material Needs

It is now a familiar idea in political as well as social theory that people need communities, and that social life is both natural and essential for human beings. The third communitarian argument declares that tolerance makes communities less able to serve their members' various social needs. In the 1950s Lord Devlin offered a straightforward, though very implausible, version of this argument in criticism of the Wolfenden Report, which successfully recommended liberalization of the laws against homosexuality in Britain.[14] Devlin said that a community cannot survive unless it achieves moral homogeneity backed by a sense of intuitive outrage, and that tolerance is therefore a kind of treason.[15] His claim was widely attacked and seems contradicted by the stubborn survival of famously tolerant political communities such as Scandinavia.[16]

There are more-sophisticated versions of the third argument, however. These claim not that tolerance will destroy a community, root and branch, but that it will cripple a community's ability to perform some crucial function. Different versions of the argument cite different functions as crucial, but one set of social needs is obvious: People need security and the economic benefits of division of labor. No one could lead an adequate human life without the mechanisms of community that rationalize production and consumption, provide public goods like police and armed forces, and ameliorate prisoners' dilemmas. But there is no reason to think that these instrumental benefits of community require moral homogeneity. There is no evidence that an illiberal society delivers the goods or the mail more efficiently than a liberal one.

B. Intellectual Needs

But people depend on community in ways that go beyond these evident economic and security benefits. They need a common culture and particularly a common language even to have personalities, and culture and language are social phenomena. We can have only the thoughts, ambitions, and convictions that are possible within the vocabulary that language and culture provide, so we are all, in a patent and deep way, the creatures of the community as a whole. That evident dependence does not, however, suggest that a community must be morally or in any other way homogeneous in order to benefit its members in the right way. On the contrary, cultural and linguistic provision is richer, and therefore apparently more advantageous, in pluralistic and tolerant communities.

Of course some (perhaps a great many) people want to belong to a morally homogeneous society and feel a keen sense of loss, for which we should have sympathy, when traditional ethical patterns are disturbed. But that point, though important, has nothing to do with a community's success in supplying people's intellectual needs of culture and language: It touches distributive justice, the issue raised by the first communitarian argument about the right standards to use in distributing influence over an ethical environment.

Michael Sandel and others have proposed a particularly strong form of the claim that people need community for intellectual as well as material reasons. This argues (so far as I understand it) that people need community not only for culture and language but for identity and self-reference, because people can only identify themselves, to themselves, as members of some community to which they belong.[17] So I cannot but think of myself except as an American, or an Oxford don, or a Red Sox fan. There are two ways to interpret this strong claim. One makes a point of philosophical logic: I am necessarily an American because, were I not an American, I would not be the person I am.[18] But this says nothing at all about the kind of relations I must or should have with other Americans, or about the content or character of our political community. It certainly does not follow, nor does it seem plausible, that any community I am necessarily a member of must be morally homogeneous, or that it must reject moral pluralism in favor of intolerance to protect that intimate connection.

The second interpretation of the self-reference claim seems more pertinent. It makes a claim about phenomenological possibility: people cannot distance themselves, when thinking about their own well-being, from certain kinds of association or connection with community. A profoundly believing Catholic, for example, could not even begin to reflect about whether to regard her Catholicism as important, because Catholicism would be too central to her personality to make questions of that character sensible for her. This interpretation of the third communitarian argument runs as follows. In a community that is morally homogeneous, people identify with the shared morality in just the way that a devout Catholic identifies with Catholicism. The community, for them, is a community of shared beliefs that helps constitute their own identity. If the community tolerates deviation, such citizens will suffer the shock of deracination. They will lose the connection to a moral faith that is essential to proper self-identification.

The phenomenology on which this argument rests seems wrong, or at least overstated. No doubt it is impossible for someone to detach himself from all associations and connections in considering what kind of life to lead. No one can think intelligibly about that question while prescinding from every aspect of the context in which he lives. So no one can put everything about himself in question all at once. But it hardly follows that for each person there is some one connection or association so fundamental that it cannot be detached for inspection while holding others in place. It is an even more serious mistake to think that this is true of the same association or connection for everyone, or that this universally nondetachable connection is to a shared sexual ethic, which must be shared within a political community rather than within some smaller or different community of, say, friends or co-religionists.

Even if we were to accept this odd collection of assumptions in full, the argument would still be vulnerable, because it relies on a further set of doubtful assumptions about the consequences of toleration. It assumes, first, that when a political community tolerates breaches of some principle of conventional ethics or morality, this tolerance must inevitably shake the citizens' own attachment to that principle since their sense of being people is partly defined by their adherence to it. But the strength of people's convictions need not depend on the enforcement or even the popularity of those convictions in their political community. Many American Catholics are as deeply committed to their Catholicism as are most Spanish Catholics. Second, the argument assumes that if people become detached from formerly unquestioned convictions their personalities will disintegrate. But why should people not be able to reassemble their sense of identity, built around a somewhat different and more tolerant set of conditions, when their faith in the morality they associate with their family or community is for some reason shaken?

C. The Need for Objectivity

So far we have considered communitarian arguments built on claims that people need the material and intellectual resources that a community provides, and that they need some attachment to community to constitute their identity. We must now notice a more subtle argument: people need a morally homogeneous community as a necessary conceptual background to a moral and ethical life. They need that background because, in Philip Selznick's illuminating phrase, ethics must have an anchor—some objective standing outside the convictions of the agent—and the only possible anchor is the unquestioned, shared convictions of the agent's political community.[19] The first of these two propositions, that ethics and morality must have an anchor, seems right. Our ethical experience treats the question of how to live well as a question calling for reflection and judgment, not just choice. We think it possible to be mistaken about what sort of life is good, and that a serious mistake is a tragedy.

But what does the second proposition, that a morally homogeneous community is the only possible anchor, mean? It might mean that people will feel that their ethical and moral judgments are grounded—are true independently of their thinking them true—only when their judgments are confirmed by an unquestioned, conventional morality. But people who hold unconventional, even eccentric, views are characteristically convinced that these views are objectively sound. (Indeed, the more unconventional the view the more likely its holder is to claim transcendent authority for it.) So we must understand the second proposition in a different way: We must understand it to mean that anyone who does claim objectivity outside convention is making a philosophical mistake. So understood, the second proposition might be thought to support the following communitarian argument. If the only available form of objectivity in ethics and morality is the objectivity of conventional practice, a tolerant, pluralistic community robs its members of the only possible source of the ethical and moral anchor they need.

There is a difficulty evident in that argument, however. The objectivity people want (and assume they have) for their moral and ethical convictions is not the watered-down version this argument offers: Most people implicitly, if not explicitly, reject the offered anchor. Paradoxically for the present argument, the single firmest part of our conventional morality, shared across every other division, is the second-order conviction that ethical and moral judgments cannot be made true or false by consensus, that they have force across cultural boundaries, that they are not, in short, creatures of culture or community, but rather judges of them. The wide popularity of this full-blooded objectivism does not, of course, argue for its truth or even its philosophical coherence, and I do not consider either here. My point is only that when a society develops this critical attitude, which insists that its own customs and conventions are constantly vulnerable to test and revision against some higher and more independent standard, it irretrievably forfeits the convention-rooted kind of objectivity available within a less critical, simpler community.

IV. Integration with Community

A. Integration

I come finally to the fourth (and in my view the most important and interesting) communitarian argument against liberal tolerance. Liberalism, according to many of its critics, presupposes a sharp distinction between people's own welfare or well-being and the well-being of the political community to which they belong. The fourth argument against tolerance denies that distinction. It claims that the lives of individual people and that of their community are integrated, and that the critical success of any one of their lives is an aspect of, and so is dependent on, the goodness of the community as a whole. I shall call people who accept this view (adopting a fashionable term) civic republicans. They take the same attitude toward the moral and ethical health of the community as they do toward their own. Liberals understand the question whether the law should tolerate homosexuality as asking whether some people have the right to impose their own ethical convictions on others. Civic republicans understand it as asking whether the common life of the community, on which the critical value of their own lives depends, should be healthy or degenerate.

According to the argument from integration, once the distinction between personal and communal well-being is recognized as mistaken and civic republicanism flourishes, citizens will necessarily be as concerned for the soundness of the community's ethical health, including the views of sexual morality that it sponsors or discourages, as for the fairness or generosity of its tax system or foreign-aid program. Both are aspects of the community's overall health, and an integrated citizen, who recognizes that his own well-being is derived from the community's well-being, must be concerned with the community's overall health, not with one selected aspect of it. This is an important argument, even though it ends in serious error. I should say at once what I regard as good in the argument, and where, in my view, it goes wrong. Its most fundamental premise is right and important: political communities have a communal life, and the success or failure of a community's communal life is part of what determines whether its members' lives are good or bad. The argument's most fundamental mistake lies in misunderstanding the character of the communal life that a political community can have. The argument succumbs to anthropomorphism; it supposes that a communal life is the life of an outsize person, that it has the same shape, encounters the same moral and ethical watersheds and dilemmas, and is subject to the same standards of success and failure as the several lives of the citizens who make it up. The illiberal force of the overall argument depends on this fallacy, which forfeits much of the advantage gained by the argument's sound and attractive premise.

B. A Community's Communal Life

We need, to begin, a more detailed account of what the phenomenon of integration is supposed to be. The civic republican, who recognizes that he is integrated with his community, is not the same as the altruistic citizen for whom the interests of others are of capital importance. This is a crucial distinction, because the argument from integration, which we are now considering, is different from the argument of paternalism and other arguments that begin in the idea that a virtuous citizen will be concerned for the well-being of others. The argument from integration does not suppose that the good citizen will be concerned for the well-being of fellow citizens; it argues that he must be concerned for his *own* well-being, and that, just in virtue of that concern, he must take an interest in the moral life of the community of which he is a member. So the integrated citizen differs from the altruistic citizen, and we need some further distinctions to see how and why.

We associate actions with what I shall call a unit of agency: the person or group or entity treated as the author of and held responsible for the action. We normally consider ourselves, as individuals, to be the agency unit of—and only of—actions or decisions we initiate or take on our own. I take myself to be responsible for only what I do. I take no pride or satisfaction or remorse or shame in what you do, no matter how interested I might be in your life or in its consequences. Often a person directs his actions at his own well-being, in either a volitional or a critical sense. The unit of agency and what we might call the unit of the agent's concern are then identical. When someone acts altruistically, whether out of charity or a sense of justice, he continues to regard himself as the unit of agency, but the unit of his concern migrates or expands. Paternalism, including moral paternalism, is a subcase of altruism. If I believe that homosexuals lead degraded lives, I might think that I act in their interests when I campaign for laws making their conduct criminal.

Integration is a different phenomenon, according to the argument I am considering, because it supposes that the appropriate unit of agency, for some actions affecting the well-being of an individual, is not the individual but some community to which he belongs. He belongs to that unit of agency *ethically:* He shares in the success or failure of acts or achievements or practices that may be completely independent of anything he himself, considered as an individual, has done. Some examples are familiar; many Germans born well after World War II feel shame, and a responsibility to compensate, for Nazi atrocities, for instance. John Rawls offers, in a slightly different context, an example that is much more illuminating for our purposes.[20] A healthy orchestra is itself a unit of agency. The various musicians who compose it are exhilarated, in the way personal triumph exhilarates, not by the quality or brilliance of their individual contributions, but by the performance of the orchestra as a whole. It is the orchestra that succeeds or fails, and the success or failure of that community is the success or failure of each of its members.

So integration is strikingly different from altruism and paternalism. It is also different from vicarious or indirect pride or regret. When parents take pride in the achievements of their children, or friends rejoice in each other's success, or brothers (in some cultures) are dishonored by a sister's shame, the unit of agency—the actor whose acts have brought pride or rejoicing or dishonor—remains individual. The vicarious emotion is second-order and parasitic; the success or failure, achievement or disgrace, remains primarily and distinctly that of someone else, and the vicarious concern reflects not participation in any act but a particular connection with the actor.

The argument from integration escapes the objection I made to the second, paternalistic argument because it rejects the whole structure of agency and concern on which the paternalistic argument rests. The argument from integration forbids us to think in Mill's terms about whether we intervene to protect other people, or only the agent himself, from some harm the agent's conduct inflicts. It rejects that whole, individuated way of thinking. Its unit of agency is the community itself, and it asks only how the community's decisions about liberty and regulation will affect the community's life and character. It insists that citizens' lives are bound up in their communal life, and that there can be no private accounting of the critical success or failure of their individual lives one by one. So the personification latent in the idea of integration is genuine and deep. The more familiar ideas of altruism, paternalism, and vicarious emotion are built around individual units of agency and concern. Integration supposes a very different structure of concepts, in which the community, and not the individual, is fundamental.

All this may suggest that integration depends on a baroque metaphysics which holds that communities are fundamental entities in the universe and that individual human beings are only abstractions or illusions. But integration can be understood in a different way, as depending not on the ontological primacy of the community, but on ordinary and familiar facts about the social practices that human beings develop. An orchestra has a collective life not because it is ontologically more fundamental than its members, but in virtue of their practices and attitudes. The musicians recognize a personified unit of agency in which they no longer figure as individuals but as components; the community's collective life consists in the activities they treat as constituting its collective life. I shall call this interpretation of integration, which assumes that integration depends on social practices and attitudes, the practice view, to distinguish it from the metaphysical view, which assumes that integration depends on the ontological primacy of community. I do not mean to suggest that the practice view is reductionist. When an integrated community exists, the statements citizens make within it about its success or failure are not simply statistical summaries of their own successes or failures as individuals. An integrated community has interests and concerns of its own—its own life to lead. Integration and community are genuine phenomena, even on the practice view. But on that view they are created by and embedded in attitudes and practices, and do not precede them.

On the practice view, therefore, a special kind of case must be made before integration can be claimed. It must be shown that social practice has in fact created a composite unit of agency. It would be nonsense for someone to claim integration with some community or institution by personal fiat, that is, simply by declaring and believing that he is part of it. I cannot just declare myself integrated with the Berlin Symphony Orchestra and thereafter share in that institution's triumphs and occasional lapses. Nor can I bring a common unit of agency into existence by fiat. I may declare and believe, for example, that philosophers whose surname starts with "D" are a common unit of agency in philosophical work, and that I can properly take pride and credit in Donald Davidson's and Michael Dummett's work the way a cymbal player can take pride and credit in his orchestra's performance. But I would be wrong. There must already be a common unit of agency, to which I am already attached, for it to be appropriate for me to regard myself as ethically integrated with its actions.

So the argument from integration must rely on some theory about how collective units of agency are established, and how individual membership in them is fixed. On the metaphysical view of integration, collective units of agency just exist: They are more real than their members. But on the practice view collective units of agency are not primitive; they are constituted by social practices and attitudes, and anyone defending this view of integration must identify and describe these practices. Our orchestra example is instructive, because it indicates the features that provide a common unit of agency in central or paradigmatic cases. First, collective agency presupposes acts socially denominated as collective, that is, acts identified and individuated as those of a community as a whole rather than of members of the community as individuals. An orchestral performance is treated as a collective act, in that sense, both by its members and by the community as a whole. Second, the individual acts that constitute collective acts are concerted. They are performed self-consciously, as contributing to the collective act, rather than as isolated acts that happen to coincide in some way. The orchestra performs a particular concerto only when its members play with a cooperative intention; it would not perform at all if its musicians played exactly the notes assigned to them in the score, at exactly the designated moments, and in the same room, but with no intention of playing together as an orchestra. Third, the composition of the community—who is treated as a member of it—is tailored to its collective acts, so that a community's collective acts explain its composition, and vice versa. Since an orchestra is a common unit of agency for the production of music, its members are musicians.

The collective acts of a community constitute its communal life. On the metaphysical view of integration, a community is a superperson, and its collective life embodies all the features and dimensions of a human life. But the practice view defines a community's communal life more narrowly: it includes only the acts treated as collective by the practices and attitudes that create the community as a collective agent. The communal life of an orchestra is limited to producing orchestral music: it is *only* a musical life. This fact determines the character and limits of the ethical integration of the musicians' lives into the communal life. The musicians treat their performances together as the performance of their orchestra personified, and they share in its triumphs and failures as their own. But they do not suppose that the orchestra also has a sex life, in some way composed of the sexual activities of its members, or that it has headaches, or high blood pressure, or responsibilities of friendship, or crises over whether it should care less about music and take up photography instead. Though the first violinist may be concerned about a colleague's sexual habits or deviance, this is concern for a friend that reflects altruism, not self-concern for any composite unit of agency which includes him. His moral integrity is not compromised by the drummer's adultery.

C. A Political Community's Communal Life

How far can we regard a political community—a nation or a state—as having a communal life on the practice view? The formal political acts of a political community—the acts of its government through its legislative, executive, and judicial institutions—meet all the conditions of collective agency we identified when we considered why an orchestra has a communal life. Our practices identify these formal political acts as acts of a distinct legal person rather than of some collection of individual citizens. The United States, rather than particular officials and soldiers, fought a war in Vietnam. The United States, rather than particular officials or citizens, imposes taxes at particular rates, distributes some of the funds it collects in welfare programs, and declines to distribute funds for other programs. The acts of particular people—votes of members of Congress, for example, and commands of generals—constitute these collective acts only because these officials act self-consciously under a constitutional structure that transforms their individual behavior into national decisions. There is at least a rough fit, moreover, between the membership of a decent, democratic political community and those formal collective acts. In a creditable democracy, every citizen who reaches a certain age and meets other conditions can participate indirectly in formal political decisions by voting, speaking, lobbying, demonstrating, and so forth.[21] And the citizens of a political community are those who are particularly affected by its formal political acts. So treating the legislative, executive, and judicial decisions as a political community's communal acts helps to explain the community's composition; it is composed of those who play some role in those decisions and who are most directly affected by them.

That much seems relatively uncontroversial. If a community has a communal life at all, its formal political decisions must be part of that life. But we must ask what else, in addition to those formal political acts, is part of its communal life. The communitarian argument from integration which we are exploring claims that formal political acts do not exhaust the nation's communal life. The argument supposes that the political community also has a communal sex life. It supposes that the sexual activities of individual citizens somehow combine into a national sex life in the way in which the performances of individual musicians combine into an orchestral performance, or the distinct acts of the citizens and officials of a political community combine in legislation. For only if this were true could one citizen's life be defiled by the sexual practices of another.

If we accept the anthropomorphic, metaphysical view of the political community, then we can begin, at least, to persuade ourselves that a state or nation has a sex life toward which the sexual activity of individual citizens contributes in some mysterious way. But if we insist instead on the practice view, then the argument from integration must defend the proposition that the community has a sex life in a very different way. It must show that our social practices and attitudes and conventions in fact create and recognize a national sexual act. You will have anticipated my judgment about that project. Consider the three features we identified as supporting the claim of a communal musical life in the case of an orchestra. None of them is satisfied for the claim of a national sex life. Our conventions recognize no distinctly collective national sexual activity. When we speak of a nation's sexual preferences and habits we speak statistically, not, as in the case of an orchestra's performance, of some collective achievement or disgrace.[22] Nor do we have conventions or practices that provide structures for cooperative sexual activity on a national scale, in the way our constitution provides a mechanism for electing presidents.

Nor is the composition of a political community in any way related to the idea that its communal life has a sexual side. The criteria of citizenship can neither explain nor be explained by the assumption of any collective sexual venture. Citizens are by and large born into their political communities, and most have no real prospect of leaving the one they are born into.[23] People of every race, faith, and ambition may be born into the same political community, and it is deeply implausible that the characterization of communal life that best fits such a community could be one that assumes that it must choose one faith or set of personal ambitions or ethnic allegiance, or one set of standards of sexual responsibility, as a healthy individual person must. That characterization not only does not fit the criteria of citizenship; it makes them close to nonsensical.

Perhaps we cannot rule out, a priori, the possibility that some other social grounds might be found to support the claim that a nation has a collective sex life—grounds very different from those to which we naturally appeal in explaining why a symphony or a piece of legislation is a collective, communal act. But I cannot see what those other grounds could be. If none can be suggested, then the communitarian argument from integration can succeed, if at all, only by falling back on the anthropomorphic view of a political community most readers would be anxious to disavow.

I should add two clarifications here. First, I have not claimed that there are no communities whose collective life has a sexual aspect. There are all kinds of communities—there are associations of stamp fanatics who engage in collective projects of collection, for example—and some might be in the nature of sexual rather than musical orchestras. It has been suggested, for example, that some families do—and that others might—see themselves as communities for propagation, in which case the sexual acts of family members might well be seen as collective in the sense that the integration argument assumes. My point is only that neither the United States nor its several states are communities that have a communal sex life, and that the argument from integration, used to justify illiberal political decisions by and across those political communities, accordingly fails.

Second, I have not considered the argument that the members of a political community should develop whatever practices would be needed in order that it would *then* be true that the community had a collective sex life. I have no idea how such an argument could be defended or made to seem plausible. Someone might say, for example, that people should try to expand the communal life of their political community because the phenomenological sensation of integration is itself desirable in the way some people think sensual pleasure or the exhilaration of danger is desirable. But if the value of integration lies in a particular sensation, it would hardly be necessary to seek integration with a political community to achieve it. People belong to a variety of communities, and most people can belong to many more if they choose. They belong—or may belong—to families, neighborhoods, alumni groups, fraternal associations, factories, colleges, teams, orchestras, ethnic groups, expatriate communities, and so forth. So these would provide ample opportunities for people to have whatever degree of the experience of integration they might think valuable without having to seek that experience in the political community, where it is inevitably harder to secure. In any case, the argument that we should try to create a community with a collective sex life is very different from the integration argument we have been considering. For the latter argument begins in, and draws its force from, the claim that we are already in such a community—that we have no choice now but to look after the sex life of others because if their lives are degraded, ours are too.[24]

V. Liberal Community

A. *Liberal Civic Republicans*

The illiberal argument from integration assumes that a political community has a life that includes a sex life. This assumption is half right. A political community does have a life, but not *that* life. If so, the argument from integration collapses as a critique of liberal tolerance in sexual matters. I shall now explore the part of the argument that is right: its important underlying premise that political integration is of great ethical importance. I shall try to show that although liberals have not emphasized the ethical importance of integration, recognizing its importance does not threaten, but rather nourishes, liberal principles.

First, I must caution against a misreading of my argument so far. I have not said that people should not fully identify with their own political community, or that full identification is impossible because its conditions cannot be met. I have argued rather for a particular view of what identifying with community means. Citizens identify with their political community when they recognize that the community has a communal life, and that the success or failure of their own lives is ethically dependent on the success or failure of that communal life. So what counts as full identification depends on what the communal life is understood to be. The liberal view of integration I shall describe takes a limited view of the dimensions of a political community's communal life. But it is not therefore a watered-down conception of identification with community. It is a full, genuine, intense conception exactly because it is discriminatory. Those who argue that identification with community requires illiberal legislation are not arguing for a deeper level of identification than liberalism allows. They argue only for a different account of what a community's collective life really is. If the liberal account is correct, and theirs is wrong, liberalism provides a more genuine form of identification than its critics can.

What then is the communal life of a political community? I said that the collective life of a political community includes its official political acts: legislation, adjudication, enforcement, and the other executive functions of government. An integrated citizen will count his community's success or failure in these formal political acts as resonating in his own life, as improving or diminishing it. On the liberal view, nothing more should be added.

These formal political acts of the community as a whole should be taken to exhaust the communal life of a political body, so that citizens are understood to act together, as a collective, only in that structured way. This view of a political community's communal life will seem too meager to many, and it is not necessary to the argument for liberal tolerance I have been developing. But it is worth exploring why the meager view might be enough after all.

The idea that a community's collective life is only its formal political life appears disappointing because it seems to eviscerate the idea of integration, to leave it with no work to do. The idea that people's lives should be seen as integrated with the life of their community suggests, at first sight, an exciting expansion of political theory. It seems to promise a politics devoted to advancing the collective good as well as, or perhaps instead of, protecting individual rights. The anthropomorphic conception of communal life—that the life of the community reflects all aspects of the lives of individuals, including their sexual choices and preferences—appears to fulfill that promise. It claims that an integrated citizen will reject liberal tolerance in favor of a commitment to healthy sexual standards imposed on all, because caring for community means caring that its life be good as well as just. But my suggestion—that communal life is limited to political activities—does not expand political justification beyond what liberals already accept. If the life of a community is limited to formal political decisions, if the critical success of a community therefore depends only on the success or failure of its legislative, executive, and adjudicative decisions, then we can accept the ethical primacy of the community's life without abandoning or compromising liberal tolerance and neutrality about the good life. We simply repeat that success at political decisions requires tolerance. Of course that proposition can be and has been challenged. The argument for integration presents a new challenge to those for liberal tolerance, however, only if it assumes an anthropomorphic picture of community, or at least one that includes more than the community's purely formal political activities. If we limit a political community's communal life to its formal political decisions, integration offers no threat to liberal principles, and it seems disappointing exactly for that reason.

It would be a mistake, however, to conclude that integration is an idea of no consequence, that it adds nothing to political morality. A citizen who identifies with the political community, by accepting the community's ethical priority, will offer no new arguments about the justice or wisdom of any political decision. He will, however, take a very different attitude toward politics. We can see the difference by contrasting his attitude, not with the selfish individual of invisible-hand fantasies, but with the person supposed to be the paragon of liberalism by its critics, the person who rejects integration but is moved by a sense of justice. That person will vote and work and lobby only for the political decisions he believes justice demands. He will nevertheless draw a sharp line between what justice requires of him and the critical success of his own life. He will not count his own life as any less successful if, in spite of his best efforts, his community accepts great economic inequality, or racial or other forms of unfair discrimination, or unjust constraints on individual freedom, unless, of course, he is himself the victim of these various forms of discrimination.

The integrated liberal will not separate his private and public lives in that way. He will count his own life as diminished—a less good life than he might have had—if he lives in an unjust community, no matter how hard he has tried to make it just. That fusion of political morality and critical self-interest seems to me to be the true nerve of civic republicanism, the important way in which individual citizens should merge their interests and personality into political community. It states a distinctly liberal ideal, one that flourishes only within a liberal society. I cannot assure you, of course, that a society of integrated citizens will inevitably achieve a more just society than a nonintegrated community would. Injustice is the upshot of too many other factors—of failures of energy or industry, of weakness of will, of philosophical error.

A community of people who accept integration in this sense will always have one important advantage over communities whose citizens deny integration. An integrated citizen accepts that the value of his own life depends on the success of his community in treating everyone with equal concern. Suppose this sense is public and transparent: everyone understands that everyone else shares that attitude. Then the community will have an important source of stability and legitimacy even though its members disagree greatly about what justice is. They will share an understanding that politics is a joint venture in a particularly strong sense: that everyone, of every conviction and economic level, has a personal stake—a strong personal stake for someone with a lively sense of his critical interests—in justice not only for himself but for everyone else as well. That understanding provides a powerful bond underlying even the most heated argument over particular policies and principles. People who think of justice in the nonintegrated way, as requiring necessary compromises of their own interests for the sake of others, will tend to suspect that those who resist programs that require evident sacrifices from them, because they reject the conception of justice on which those programs are based, act out of self-interested bias, whether deliberate or subconscious. Political argument will then degenerate into the sullen trading that destroys civic republicanism.

That kind of suspicion has no place to root among people who take political disagreement to be disagreement, not about what sacrifices are required from each, but about how to serve the common interests of all in securing a genuinely just solution. Disagreement persists against that background, as it is desirable that it should. But it is a healthy disagreement among partners whose interests coalesce, who know that they are not antagonists in interest, who know that they win or lose together. Integration, so understood, gives a fresh meaning to the old idea of a commonweal, a genuine interest people share in politics, even when political disagreements are profound. Of course all this is utopian. We can scarcely hope that a thoroughly integrated political society will ever be realized. It will not be realized in coming decades. But we are now exploring utopia, an ideal of community we can define, defend, and perhaps even grope our way toward, in good moral and metaphysical conscience.

B. Ethical Priority

The consequences of civic republicanism in the liberal mode are therefore attractive. But there is a considerable gap in the argument I have offered, because I have offered no reason, so far, why people should accept integration in the liberal sense, why they should regard the success of their lives as dependent, in the way I just described, on the justice of their community's political decisions. We cannot hope to provide a knock-down demonstration by way of answer to that question. But we can try to make the idea of liberal community more attractive by identifying aspects of the good life that are made possible or are nourished in a just state.[25]

I shall describe only one strand of that project—and that in skeletal form. It begins in a weak form of Plato's view, articulated in the *Republic*, that morality and well-being are interdependent in an adequate ethics, that someone who behaves unjustly leads a worse life in consequence. That is hardly a plausible view if we have in mind what I call volitional well-being. There seems no inherent connection between my being just and my having what I want. But Plato's view seems more plausible when we have critical well-being in mind. The criteria of a life good in the critical sense cannot be defined acontextually, as if the same standards held for all people in all stages of history. Someone lives well when he responds appropriately to his circumstances. The ethical question is not how human beings should live, but how someone in my position should live. A great deal turns, therefore, on how my position is to be defined, and it seems compelling that justice should figure in the description. The ethical question becomes: what is a good life for someone entitled to the share of resources I am entitled to have? And against that background Plato's view of critical success is appealing. Someone does *pro tanto* a poorer job of living—responds *pro tanto* more poorly to his circumstances—if he acts unjustly. We need not accept the strong view that Plato in fact defended, that no one ever profits from injustice. Perhaps the great lives of some artists would not have been possible in a fully just society, and it would not follow that they had bad lives. But it does follow that it counts against the goodness of any life, even theirs, that it was supported by injustice.

Now notice what might seem to be a contradiction between two ethical ideals most of us embrace. The first dominates our private lives. We believe we have particular responsibilities toward those with whom we have special relationships: ourselves, our family, friends, and colleagues. We spend more of our time and other resources on them than on strangers, and we think this right. We believe that someone who showed equal concern for all members of his political community, in his private life, would be defective. The second ideal dominates our political life. The just citizen, in his political life, insists on equal concern for all. He votes and works for policies that he thinks treat every citizen as an equal. He shows no more concern, in choosing among candidates and programs, for himself or his own family than for people who are only statistics to him.

A competent overall ethics must reconcile these two ideals. They can be reconciled adequately, however, only when politics actually succeeds in distributing resources in the way justice requires. If a just distribution has been secured, then the resources people control are morally as well as legally theirs; using them as they wish, and as special attachments and projects require, in no way derogates from their recognizing that all citizens are entitled to a just share. But when injustice is substantial, people who are drawn to both the ideals—of personal projects and attachments on the one hand and equality of political concern on the other—are placed in a kind of ethical dilemma. They must compromise one of the ideals, and each direction of compromise impairs the critical success of their lives.

Acting justly is not entirely a passive matter; it means not only not cheating, but also doing what one can to reduce injustice. So someone acts unjustly when he fails to devote resources he knows he is not entitled to have to the needs of those who have less. That failure will hardly be redeemed by occasional charity, limited and arbitrary in the way charity inevitably is. So if the critical value of a life is diminished by a failure to act as justice requires, then it is diminished by ignoring the injustice in one's own political community. A life entirely devoted to reducing injustice so far as one can, on the other hand, would be at least equally diminished. When injustice is substantial and pervasive in a political community, any private citizen who accepts a personal responsibility to do whatever he possibly can to repair it will end by denying himself the personal projects and attachments, as well as the pleasures and frivolities, that are essential to a decent and rewarding life.

Someone with a vivid sense of his own critical interests is inevitably thwarted when his community fails in its responsibilities of justice, and this is so even when he, for his own part, has done all he personally can to encourage it to succeed. Each of us shares that powerful reason for wanting our community to be a just one. A just society is a prerequisite for a life that respects both ideals, neither of which should be abandoned. So our private lives, our success or failure in leading the lives people like us should have, are in that limited but powerful way parasitic on our success together in politics. Political community has that ethical primacy over our individual lives.

6

Equality and the Good Life

I. Can Liberals Live Well?

In the preceding chapters I defended a particular conception of liberalism. That conception—liberal equality—insists that liberty, equality, and community are not three distinct and often conflicting political virtues, as other political theories on both the left and right of liberalism declare, but complementary aspects of a single political vision, so that we cannot secure or even understand any one of these three political ideals independently of the others. That is the emotional nerve of liberalism, the idea that seems so arresting in eastern Europe and parts of Asia now, and seemed so natural to revolutionaries in Europe and America two centuries ago. It is realized, however, only when we understand liberty, equality, and community in the way I have argued we should. Equality must be measured in resources and opportunities, not in welfare or well-being. Liberty is not the freedom to do whatever one wants no matter what, but to do whatever one wants that respects the true rights of others. Community must be based not on the blurring or melding of individual freedom and responsibility, but on shared and effective respect for that freedom and responsibility. That is liberalism conceived as liberal equality.

In this chapter I try to answer a special and historically powerful objection to liberal equality. Since the Enlightenment, when many of the political ideals of liberalism were formed, its critics have charged that these ideals were fit only for people who did not know how to live. Nietzsche and the romantic iconoclasts said that liberal morality was a prison made by the jealous to lock up the great. Only small people, they thought, would bother with liberal equality; poets and heroes with new lives to invent and new worlds to rule would treat it with contempt. Later this complaint was reversed. Marxists charged liberals with caring too much rather than too little about individual triumphs, and conservatives said that liberalism ignored the importance of the social stability and rootedness provided by conventional morality. These three vectors of criticism share an overall objection, however, which is often stated in a runic slogan: Liberalism pays too much attention to the right, by which is meant principles of justice, and too little to the good, by which is meant the quality and value of the lives people lead. The romantics think that liberalism is insensitive to the importance of the creative individual's breaking free of petty morality. Marxists think that it overlooks the alienated and impoverished character of life in liberal capitalist democracies. Conservatives claim that it fails to understand that life can be satisfying only when it is rooted in community-defining norms and traditions. Liberal justice, they all agree, leaches the poetry out of life.

We should distinguish three charges latent in this rhetoric. The first declares that a genuinely good life would be impossible in a liberal society. That objection, if sustained, would of course be mortal. If life in a liberal society is bound to be mean—bound to produce a stunted, disappointing failure of a life for everyone—then liberalism is a perverse political vision fit only for masochists and the ethically blind. The second objection accuses liberalism not of altogether precluding the possibility of good lives, but of subordinating that private goal to social justice by insisting that justice always comes first, even when this means that some people must sacrifice the quality and overall success of their own lives. That is a less threatening objection, but it is still an important one, because if liberals accept it, they must find a justification for their political vision that is sufficiently compelling to explain why people must sometimes—perhaps often—sacrifice what strikes many of them as their most commanding responsibility, which is to make the best lives they can for themselves and their families. The third objection accuses liberals only of wholesale ethical neutrality—of supposing that a theory of political justice can be developed independently of any sustaining account of what it is to live well. This third objection seems weaker still: indeed liberals often claim themselves that liberalism is ethically neutral, and that this is a virtue not a defect.[1] But that supposed virtue carries a practical cost. If almost any theory of the good life is compatible with liberalism, then liberalism cannot appeal to any such theory in its own defense—it cannot campaign for a liberal state on the ground that only in such a state can people live good as well as fair lives.

Is liberalism actually guilty of any of these charges? Does it preclude living well, or subordinate that goal, or ignore it? No; but we cannot understand why until we recognize that a theory of the good life, like any other important department of thought, is complex and heavily structured. Liberalism can and should be neutral at some, relatively concrete, levels of ethics. But it cannot and should not be neutral at the more abstract levels at which we puzzle, not about how to live in detail, but about the character, force, and standing of the very question of how to live.

We can distinguish at least three such abstract issues. First, what is the source of that ethical question? Why should we worry about how to live? Is there a difference between people's living well and people's simply enjoying their lives? If so, is it important that people live well rather than just enjoyably? Is that important only to the person whose life it is? Or is it important in some broader, more objective way, so that it remains important even if, for some reason, it is not important to him? Is it more important that some people live well than that others do? Or is this equally important in the case of everyone? Second, whose responsibility is it to make lives good? Who, if anyone, is charged with seeing that people do live well? Is this a social, collective responsibility? Is it part of the responsibilities of a good and just state that it identify good lives and attempt to induce or even force its members to lead lives so identified? Or is the responsibility an individual one? Third, what is the metric of a good life? By what standard should we test a life's success or failure? How far is this a matter of the pleasure or happiness that the life has provided for the person whose life it is? How far is it a matter of the difference that person's life has made to other people's lives or to the world's stock of knowledge or art? In what other way or dimension should the overall success or value of someone's life be judged?

These three issues—of source, responsibility, and metric—have generated much controversy, not particularly among philosophers, but among cultures and societies. They are nevertheless more abstract than the detailed questions we have in mind when we say that modern societies are deeply pluralist about ethical and moral matters. For any plausible set of answers to the abstract issues would leave open almost all the more concrete controversies about how to live that divide people in, for example, the United States now. We might all agree, for instance, that it is objectively important that people live well, that people have primary responsibility, as individuals, for the success of their own lives, and that living well means leaving the world a better place, with more value in it, without taking sides between those who insist that a good life is necessarily a religious one and others who count religion as the only dangerous superstition; or between those who insist that a valuable life is one rooted in tradition and those who think that the only decent life is one of rebellion against tradition.

I do not mean that answers to the more abstract questions have no impact on the more concrete ones. On the contrary, abstract ethical theories require people to see and test their concrete opinions in a certain light. Someone who accepts that it is objectively important how he lives, and that living well means improving the world, could not also believe that the best life is the most pleasant one, unless he also thought that pleasure has intrinsic and objective value, which he may not find plausible. Nor do I mean that people, even in a single society, agree on answers to the abstract questions. People disagree about abstract ethics—particularly, as we shall see, about metric— even in Western democracies. But these disagreements are not as striking or heated as many of the more concrete disagreements are, and we might more realistically hope to convert opinion on these abstract issues, through argument, than we could hope for conversion on the more passionately divisive concrete issues.

Would identifying distinctly liberal answers to the abstract ethical questions help liberalism to reply to the three tangled objections that I described? That depends on how appealing those liberal answers, after reflection, turn out to be. In the Introduction I argued that liberal equality reflects and enforces two principles that are very widely accepted in Western democracies now and that offer attractive answers to the questions of source and responsibility. The first of these principles holds that once a human life has begun, it is of great and objective importance that it be successful rather than wasted, and that this is of equal importance in the case of each human life. The second holds that the person whose life it is has primary and nondelegable responsibility for that success. In this chapter I explore the third abstract question I identified: the question of metric. I distinguish various models of ethical value and defend one of these—the "challenge" model, which supposes that a life is successful insofar as it is an appropriate response to the distinct circumstances in which it is lived. This model, I claim, has more intuitive appeal than its main rival and helps to expose what truth there is in the Platonic idea that justice is not a sacrifice that impairs a person's ability to live a successful life but is rather a precondition of a successful life.

I should admit now, however, that I believe I have less chance of persuading readers that they already accept this challenge model of ethics than I do of persuading them that they already accept the principles of equal objective importance and of individual responsibility that I just described. I must therefore emphasize that though I find the case for the challenge model compelling, and also find that it matches and explains my own ethical intuitions, I do not mean to rest the ethical case for liberal equality on that model. I believe the argument of the forthcoming book mentioned in the Introduction, which does not depend on any answer to the question of metric, but depends rather on principles much less controversial among us, is compelling on its own. I press the case for the challenge answer to the question of metric, nevertheless, for two reasons. First, the question of metric is important for its own sake. Our ordinary intuitions about how to live are, as I shall try to show, confused, and I believe that the confusion reflects ambivalence about the right answer to that question. Second, I want to show the ethical appeal behind Plato's view that justice and goodness cannot conflict, and how that view provides a particularly strong defense, not only of liberalism in general, but of liberal equality as the best conception of liberalism.

I assume throughout this chapter a positive answer to one aspect of the question of source I described. I assume that the ethical question—what life would be a successful life for me?—is a genuine and important question, and that it is different, in content though perhaps not in the answer it invites, from both the psychological question—what life will I enjoy or find satisfying?—and the moral question—what obligations or responsibilities do I have toward other people? I reject without comment here what I have elsewhere described as the "externally" skeptical view that the ethical question has no sense. But I do take seriously the claim of "internal" skeptics about ethics, who insist that, in fact, no life really is a good or successful one.[2] I do not address separately the question whether and when a human life has meaning or is meaningful. I cannot understand that question in any way that does not take it to be essentially the same question as the question I do discuss, which is when and why a particular life is good or successful.

I shall end this introductory section with a challenge of a different kind. As I said, the various rivals to liberal equality that are now popular—postmodern romanticism, economic conservatism, communitarianism, perfectionism, and the rest—claim the ethical high ground. They denigrate liberalism for its lack of ethical authority. But the literature of these schools is surprisingly deficient in any serious attention to the issues of philosophical ethics that I have described and will shortly try to engage. I shall argue that the most plausible philosophical ethics grounds a liberal faith, that liberal equality does not preclude or threaten or ignore the goodness of the lives people live, but rather flows from and into an attractive conception of what a good life is. Liberalism's rivals should take up the challenge and try to form answers to the deep questions of ethics that point away from liberalism and in their direction instead. Until they do, their charge that liberals pay inadequate attention to the good life remains bluster.

II. Philosophical Ethics

A. Volitional and Critical Interests

What makes a life a good or successful one? Philosophers in the utilitarian tradition assume that the success of different lives can be measured and compared in respect of a single elemental carrier of ethical value. They debate the merits of two competing claims: first, that ethical value consists in an identifiable felt experience, such as pleasure, and, second, that it consists in the phenomenon of having one's desires satisfied. It now seems plain that though each of these events—pleasurable experiences and the satisfaction of aims and desires—must find some place in an acceptable overall philosophical account of well-being, neither tells the whole story, nor even the most interesting part of it.

We must suppress the reductionist impulse of these philosophers and accept not only complexity but structure within the idea of well-being. We must recognize, first, a distinction between what I shall call volitional well-being and critical well-being. Someone's volitional well-being is improved, and just for that reason, when he has or achieves what in fact he wants. His critical well-being is improved by his having or achieving what it makes his life a better life to have or achieve.[3] Sailing well and freedom from dentistry are part of my own volitional well-being: I want them both, and my life therefore goes better, in the volitional sense, when I have them. I take a different view of other things I want: having a close relationship with my children, for example, securing some success in my work, and—what I despair of attaining—some minimal grasp of the state of advanced science of my era. These I regard as critical interests because I believe that my life would be a less successful one if I failed to have, or wholly failed to achieve, these goals.

My life is not a worse life to have lived—I have nothing to regret, still less to take shame in—because I have suffered in the dentist's chair. And though I do want to sail well, and am disappointed because I do not, I cannot think that my life would be a worse one if I had never conceived that desire. It is important for me to sail well because I want to sail well, not vice versa. But all this is reversed when I consider the importance of being close to my children. I do think my life would have been worse had I never understood the importance of this, if I had not suffered pain at estrangement. I do not think that having a close relationship with my children is important only because I happen to want it. I think that it really is important, and would be even if I did not want it.

The distinction between volitional and critical well-being is not the distinction between what is sometimes called subjective and objective well-being, however. It is true that a critical interest has an objective dimension that a volitional interest does not: it makes perfect sense to suppose that I have made a mistake about my critical interest, though not, at least in the same direct sense, that I could be wrong in my volitional interests. But that is not to say that my volitional interests are only my present judgments, which I may later decide are mistakes, about where my critical interests lie. The two kinds of interests, the two modes of well-being, are distinct. I can intelligibly just want something without thinking that it makes my life a better life to have it; indeed a life in which someone wanted only what he thought it was in his critical interests to want would be a sad mess.

Nor is critical interest the same as motive. Many people share my view that it is important to their lives that they have a close relationship with their children. But most of them do not want that relationship, or strive to secure it when necessary, out of even enlightened self-interest. They want a good relationship with their children for its own sake and their children's, not their own. That is also true of much else that they care about—when they work for justice in politics and in their own lives, for example, it is justice and its beneficiaries they care about, not themselves. Indeed it is undoubtedly part of what makes such interests critical that they are *not* pursued out of self-interest. But these motivational facts do nothing to diminish the ethical role of such interests—their role, that is, in making the life of the person who has those interests, and pursues them for their own or other people's sake, a better life for him. Nor does it preclude his understanding this, and taking satisfaction in it; nor preclude his puzzling over whether or why it is so. The question—what is his *real* reason for dedicating his life to helping the poor?—is, like most questions that lean on the word "real," too crude. People have different sorts of reasons, and these operate at different strata of their moral and ethical imagination.

Critical and volitional interests are interconnected in various ways. Critical interests often track volitional interests. If I have invested some desire with great importance—to sail well, for example—it is normally in my critical interest to succeed, not because sailing well is critically important but because a fair measure of success in what I happen very much to want is critically important. And volitional interest normally tracks opinion about critical interest: people generally want what they think it is in their critical interests to have. If they think it in their critical interest to have a close relationship with their children, they will want to do so, even though (as I just insisted) they do not want this for that reason. But that is not inevitably the case. The common assumption among philosophers that people cannot think something best, all things considered, without wanting it seems to ignore the distinction between the two kinds of well-being. At least part of the complex problem philosophers call *akrasia* arises because people do not actually want what they believe it in their critical interest to have. So I might be convinced that my life would be a better life, in the critical sense, if I worked less and spent more time with my family, and yet I find that I actually don't want to, or don't want to enough.

Are the categories of volitional and critical well-being only components of a larger, more inclusive category that we might call well-being all things considered? We might think that well-being, all things considered, consists in the right mix or trade-off between success in volitional and critical interests. That is a tempting idea, because it supposes a standard for resolving possible conflicts between the two modes of well-being. But the idea makes no sense, however tempting it is. There can be no standards for judging whether the right mix or trade-off has been achieved between volitional and critical well-being except the standards of one of the two modes of well-being themselves. We can ask what we should do, in order to have the right sort of life. Then the answer is the answer given by reflecting on our critical interests alone. Or we can ask what we most want to do, and then the answer is given by consulting (if that is the right word) our volitional interests. But if the two conflict, as when I want to do something I know is against my critical interest, there is no third or higher-order concept of my interest to which I can appeal. What I should do in these circumstances, in order to lead a good life, is to follow my critical interests, and there is no other, higher-order, sense of my best interests that might require or permit me to set my critical interests aside. We must therefore accept that dualism of perspectives, recognizing that practical conflicts between the two perspectives can be frequent and vivid. So far as morality provides different standards for conduct from the standards of critical well-being, then morality offers a different perspective yet. But of course morality is not a more comprehensive category of well-being that includes volitional and critical interests as well.

So we have volitional and critical interests and no more inclusive category of well-being that can adjudicate conflicts between them. I shall from this point assume that any attempt to find ethical foundations for liberalism must concentrate on critical as distinct from volitional well-being. We need an account of what people's critical interests are that will show why people who accept that account and care about their own and other people's critical well-being will be led naturally toward some form of liberal polity and practice. I do not mean, of course, that liberals should care about improving people's lives only in the critical as distinguished from the volitional (or biological) sense. Fighting pain and disease is important no matter in which of these categories it figures. Nor am I making the mistake I have twice warned against, of assuming that people care only about their critical interests; nor the different mistake of assuming that most people often consciously reflect about their critical interests.

Of course it is a sensible question—and a politically crucial one—whether liberal political principles would serve the volitional interests of most people in a democracy and, if so, how liberal politicians can convince a majority that this is so. Our question is not so immediately political, though it is perhaps of more far-reaching political importance. Political principles are normative in the way critical interests are: the former define the political community we should have, the latter how we should live in it. Our search for ethical foundations is therefore a search for normative integrity. We ask whether people who do take their critical interests seriously would have that reason for adopting the liberal political perspective. In the long run that question is, as I just suggested, a practical one, because in the long run political programs fail unless they find space in people's self-image and not just in what they happen to want.

B. Worries and Puzzles about Critical Interests

Most people believe that they have critical interests. They think it important to make something of their lives, whether or not that conviction much affects how they actually live. But most of us are also aware how problematic and obscure the idea of critical interests is, and many fear that it is a cosmic illusion. People who believe in an afterlife are not troubled by that worry, of course, because heaven and hell convert ethics into prudence. But most of us lack that comfort, and though we manage to shake off our skeptical moments, and regain whatever ethical conviction we had before, we have not come to terms with our anxieties but only postponed them. In the next several pages, I offer a kind of catalogue of these anxieties. I do not list, among these, external skepticism about the sense or coherence of the idea that one way of living can produce a better, more successful, life than another.[4] I assume that the idea makes sense, and I consider only substantive puzzles about its application. I begin with the familiar dead-of-night worry of internal skepticism—that life is meaningless, that no life is in fact good or better than any other. Then I add a series of further issues or puzzles about ethics that, while not so intimidating or familiar, are nevertheless of philosophical dimension and personal importance.

Significance.   People who are self-conscious about living well treat this as a matter of capital importance; they think it very important not merely (or even) whether their lives are enjoyable, but whether their lives are good or bad lives to lead. But in what sense or from what perspective could that be important? How can it matter what happens in the absurdly tiny space and time of a single human life? Or even in the almost equally tiny episode of all sentient life taken together? The universe is so big and has lasted so long that our best scientists struggle even to give sense to the question of how big it is or how long it has lasted. One day—any second now in the history of time—the sun will explode, and then there may be nothing left that can even wonder about how we lived. How can we reconcile these two ideas: that life is nothing and that how we live is everything?

Transcendent or indexed?   Critical interests are not just a matter of what someone happens to want, but of what he should want, and he can be deeply mistaken about what his critical interests are. That fact might seem to suggest that ethical values are transcendent, that is, that the components of a good life are always and everywhere the same. But that thought conflicts with another assumption that many of us find irresistibly reasonable: that there is no such thing as the single good life for everyone, that ethical standards are in some way indexed to culture and ability and resource and other aspects of one's circumstance, so that the best life for a person in one situation may be very different from the best life for someone else in another. Which of these two views, each supported by strong intuitions and convictions, is correct, and which must be abandoned? Can we reject the transcendent view of ethical value and still retain our conviction that ethics is not merely subjective, that it is not merely a matter of discovering what we really want?

Ethics and morality.   Now consider Plato's question. What is the connection between self-interest and morality? It is plain that morality and volitional interests often conflict: I can often have more of what I want by cheating or stealing or lying. But the matter is more complex when we take self-interest in the critical rather than the volitional sense. Then three views seem possible. First, we might think that living well, even in the critical sense, is wholly independent of living justly. Someone who believes that the truly good life is the life of great power over others, for example, may well think that his critical interests constantly conflict with justice because he could often increase his power by doing what justice forbids. Second, we might think that justice is a component of critical well-being, but not the whole story. Injustice (we might say) counts against a successful life in the overall balance sheet, so that a person who is forced to choose between extending his power and acting justly has a choice to make within ethics, and not just between ethics and morality. He must decide whether, all things considered, his life goes better with more power at the cost of some injustice, or vice versa. Third, we might take Plato's view: that there is never a conflict between justice and self-interest because one can never lead a critically better life through unjust acts. If it is necessary to act unjustly to gain more power, then gaining more power cannot count, even *pro tanto*, as an improvement in the success of one's life. There are two versions of this third view. The first holds that justice is only one component of the good life, as the second view does, but insists that it is dominantly more important than any other component, so that no gain in any other component could outweigh even the smallest compromise of justice. The second holds that the connection between justice and the good life is more intimate still. But I cannot explain in what way the second view claims a greater intimacy until I have developed (as I do later in this chapter) what I called the model of challenge.

Most people's intuitions seem to favor one of the first two views over the third. Paul Cézanne was a draft dodger not out of conscientious objection but from a desire to paint, and many people think that even if he acted wrongly he had a greater life as a result.[5] But how can we explain this? Suppose someone builds a fortune in a ruthless and immoral business career, and then uses it to finance a dazzling life of refined and exotic experience, artistic creation and patronage, and exploration and discovery. It is hard to resist the view that he has indeed, even in the final analysis, profited from his wrongs—that he has led a successful as well as an immoral life. But it is also hard to resist an apparently decisive argument to the contrary. No doubt he has enjoyed his life, and taken great satisfaction from it. But how can we say that he has lived well—that he has made something good of his life—if all his wealth and achievements grew out of something that he ought not to have done, that we condemn him for having done? Our intuitions are in disorder yet again.

Additive or constitutive? We can reflect on someone else's life with two questions in mind. We can ask, first, how far his life includes whatever experiences or relationships or events or achievements we count as components of a good or decent life. We can ask, second, how far he recognizes whatever components of the good life his own life contains, whether he sought them, regarded them as valuable, in short endorsed them as serving critical not just volitional interests. But how should we combine these two types of question? Two views are possible. The *additive* view holds that we can judge his life a good or bad one without consulting his opinions of its value. If his life has the components of a good life, then it is good for that reason. If he endorses those components, then this increases the goodness of his life; it is frosting on the cake. But if he does not, the ethical value of the components remains. He may have a very good life in virtue of experiences and achievements he does not endorse, though not so good a life, perhaps, as if he had endorsed them.

The *constitutive* view, on the other hand, argues that no component may even so much as contribute to the value of a person's life without his endorsement. So if a misanthrope is much loved but disdains the love of others as worthless, his life is not more valuable for their affection. The constitutive view is not the skeptical view that someone's life is good or bad in the critical sense only when and because he thinks it good or bad. Someone might be wrong in thinking his life a good one, and wrong because he counts something as a component of a good life that in fact is not. And he might be wrong in not recognizing and endorsing some feature of his life that, had he recognized it, would have made his life better. The constitutive view denies only that some event or achievement can make a person's life better against his opinion that it does not.

Which of these views should we adopt? Once again, each seems to be supported and assumed by familiar intuitions and convictions. Ethical value is objective not subjective: that fact, which seems to support the transcendent view of ethical standards, also seems to support the additive view. If it is not just up to me to decide what kind of a life is good, then why should it matter, for the value of my life, what I think about it? In some extreme cases common sense confirms that argument. Would Hitler not have led a better life if he had been locked up from adolescence, even if he spent the rest of his life dreaming of the horror he could have caused? But other, less dramatic, examples provoke contrary intuitions. Even if we think that religion must be part of a good life, can it improve someone's life to force him into a religious observance that he counts worthless? Can it really make sense to say that the misanthrope's life was improved by having the love he did not want? In these cases, we do not feel just that the value of something good—religion or the love of friends—is diminished when it is not appreciated. We feel that its value is obliterated, that there is no value at all unless that value is in some way sponsored by recognition. Once again some of our intuitions seem in conflict with others, and ethics seems more mysterious as a result.

Ethics and community.   Our final set of puzzles concerns the unit of ethical value, that is, the entity whose life ethics aims to make good. On the one hand, we feel that ethics is entirely personal. Each of us has ultimate responsibility for deciding what kind of life is right for him; even a person who unreflectively settles into social grooves is responsible for that choice (or nonchoice) if less conforming lives were available. And each of us has a personal stake in the life he lives, whether or not he chose it. It is *my* life that is at stake when I decide where to live or what career to take up or whether to lie for advantage. But yet on some occasions and in some circumstances that confident division of the ethical world into our own life and the lives of others fails. We sense that the most fundamental ethical unit is collective not individual, that the question of whether my life is going well is subordinate to the question whether, for some group of which I am a member, *our* life is going well.

We must take care not to dissipate this apparent conflict by confusing it with other connections between personal and social concerns that, however important, do not challenge the distinctly individual character of ethics. Of course the lives of other people are important to me; I know that a good life cannot be a selfish or self-centered one. And of course I know that my ethical convictions are socially conditioned and constrained, that I cannot even contemplate lives that seem natural in other cultures. If I believe that ethics is indexed rather than transcendent, moreover, I will think that the connection between conviction and culture is not merely psychological but ethical as well, because the right life for me depends in part on which time and nation and culture I live it in. There is no conflict between believing that the success of my life is fully and only my responsibility and that it is connected to community in these various ways.

I have in mind, as raising a puzzle for ethics, a different and more radical way of connecting my ethical life to my community. This supposes that a community has an ethical life of its own and that the critical success of any individual's life depends to some degree on the critical success of the life of his community. That assumption is, for many people, a common part of their political sensibility. They feel a personal failure when their own nation acts unjustly or wickedly, even when they have played no part in the injustice and have even tried to prevent it—a failure they do not feel when some other nation acts in the same way. The most notorious and powerful example in our time is the responsibility Germans who were not alive during the Holocaust, or who played no part in it, nevertheless feel for the sins of their political community. Most people fuse their lives in a parallel way to nonpolitical communities. Partners in joint projects—people thrown together in a rescue operation, for example—do not distinguish personal success from the success of the venture. If the venture fails they have failed, no matter how well they played their own part.

Mysteries teem. Does this kind of ethical integration, in which an individual's critical interests are dependent on and merged into the critical interests of some group, presuppose ontological priority as well? Does it suppose that the fundamental human units of the universe are groups rather than the individual people who make them up, as some philosophers have thought? If not, how else can ethical integration be explained? Is it consistent to believe, as many of us seem to do, that ethics is both individual and communal? If this is consistent, then which perspective—personal or communal—is the appropriate one to adopt when?

C. Models of Critical Value

These various puzzles and worries arise, I believe, because our ethical instincts and impulses reflect different and in some respects antagonistic ways of conceiving the metric of ethical value. I shall describe two strikingly different models of value that we use in other spheres or to form more limited judgments, both of which, I believe, play a role in forming our ethical convictions as well. Both models have some grip on us, and our ethical intuitions will remain divided and inconclusive until we settle on one or the other, or on some different or more comprehensive model. The first of these models—the model of impact—holds that the value of a good life consists in its product, that is, in its consequences for the rest of the world. The second—the model of challenge—argues that the goodness of a good life lies in its inherent value as a performance. I shall try to show how these two abstract ideas about the fundamental character of ethics guide our reactions to the worries and puzzles I listed, and how far the perplexing character of ethics arises from unnoticed conflicts between the two, and our failure, or perhaps our inability, to resolve them.

Neither of these two philosophical models of ethical value purports to offer any general argument for ethical value from the ground up, that is, against someone who has a settled and unchallenged conviction that it does not matter what he does with his life so long as he enjoys it. The two models are rather interpretations of the ethical experience of those of us—the great majority—whose ethical convictions or intimations presuppose that it does matter. The models try to organize our convictions, so far as possible, into a coherent account. The puzzles I described arise because we have too many rather than too few ethical convictions; some of these seem to conflict with others. On the one hand we believe that something's significance depends on proportion, so that nothing of infinitesimal size relative to the universe can be really important, for example. On the other hand we believe—most of us cannot help believing—that it is crucially important how we live in spite of our insignificance. Any skeptical force that this and the other puzzles I described may have is internal rather than external to ethics—it uses one set of convictions to attack another, rather than attacking ethics from outside as a whole.[6] The philosophical models try to defend ethics from that dangerous internal attack by showing how most of our convictions, at least, can be saved if we look at them all in a certain light.

The model of impact.   The impact of a person's life is the difference his life makes to the objective value in the world. Impact plainly figures in our judgments about whose life was a good one. We admire the lives of Alexander Fleming and Mozart and Martin Luther King Jr., and we explain why we do by pointing to penicillin and *The Marriage of Figaro* and what King did for his race and his country. The model of impact generalizes from these examples; it holds that the ethical value of a life—its success in the critical sense—is parasitic on and measured by the value of its consequences for the rest of the world. The model hopes to dissipate the mysteries of ethical value by tying it to another, apparently less mysterious, kind of value: the value that objective states of affairs of the world can have. A life can have more or less value, the model claims, not because it is intrinsically more valuable to live one's life in one way rather than another, but because living in one way can have better consequences.

We all have opinions about when the world is going better or worse, though of course our opinions differ. Most of us think that things are better when disease is cured or great works of art are created or social justice is improved. Some people—they are almost all philosophers—think that the world goes better when the sum of human happiness or pleasure has been increased. The model of impact does not in itself declare for or against these various opinions about which states of affairs are objectively valuable. It merely fuses anyone's opinions about the critical value of his or other people's lives to whatever opinions he has about objective value in states of the world. If I think that a particular painting has added value to the world, then, according to the model of impact, I must think the life of its author a better life for his having painted it. If, more controversially, I think that the world is better when commerce thrives, I will also think that successful entrepreneurs live distinguished lives for that reason. The model connects not just the type but the quantity of ethical value to the value of a life's consequence. If I think that one artist's work is, as a whole, much greater than the art of another, then I must think the former's life is a much greater life, at least so far as value is given to the lives of each by their art.

The model of impact finds support, as I said, in much conventional ethical opinion and rhetoric. It has great difficulty fitting and explaining other common ethical views and practices, however. Many of the goals that people regard as very important are not matters of consequence at all. I said earlier that I believe my own critical interests include having close relations with my children and securing at least some feeble grasp of contemporary science. Other people have parallel convictions: they think it important to do at least something well—to master some field of learning or craft or to learn to play a musical instrument, for example—not because they will make the world better by so doing—what can it matter that one more person can do something with average skill that other people can do much better?—but just in order that *they* have done it. Many people set wholly adverbial goals for themselves: they want to live, they say, with integrity, doing things their way, with the courage of their convictions. These various ambitions make no sense in the vocabulary of impact. It will make no positive difference to anyone else how much or little grasp I have of cosmology, for example: I will contribute nothing to knowledge of the universe in any case. The model of impact makes many popular views about critical interests seem silly and self-indulgent.

The model of challenge. The impact model does not deny the phenomenon of ethical value: it does not deny that people have critical interests and that their lives are better or worse depending on how far these interests are satisfied. But it describes those critical interests in a way that, as we have seen, is constricting of ethical value. It claims that lives go better only in virtue of their impact on the objective value of states of affairs. The alternate model that I shall now develop—the model of challenge—rejects that limitation. It adopts Aristotle's view that a good life has the inherent value of a skillful performance. So it holds that events, achievements, and experiences can have ethical value even when they have no impact beyond the life in which they occur. The idea that a skillful performance has an inherent value is perfectly familiar as a kind of value *within* lives. We admire a complex and elegant dive, for example, whose value persists after the last ripple has died, and we admire people who climbed Mount Everest because, as they said, it was there. The model of challenge holds that living a life is *itself* a performance that demands skill, that it is the most comprehensive and important challenge we face, and that our critical interests consist in the achievements, events, and experiences that mean that we have met the challenge well.

The model of challenge therefore offers room for the convictions about critical interest that the model of impact rejects as self-indulgent. It makes sense to suppose, even though it is by no means obvious or uncontroversial, that part of living well is acquiring some flavor of the scientific knowledge of one's time. Nor does the model of challenge reject the intuitions that the model of impact accepts. For it also makes sense to think—indeed this seems obvious—that one way brilliantly to meet the challenge of living well is to reduce the world's suffering by conquering disease. The ecumenical character of the model of challenge might strike you as a weakness, as showing that the model is empty or at least uninformative. The model of impact ties ethical value to objective world value, and so seems at least to offer some guidance as to the actual substance of a good life. The model of challenge, by comparison, allows the idea of ethical value to float free of any other kind of value. If we are free to count doing or having anything at all as meeting the challenge of living well, then the model (it might seem) is not so much a model as a truism: living well is doing whatever counts as living well.

That complaint is misjudged. Both models rely on convictions that they assume we already have. The model of impact assumes that we have convictions about what states of the world are independently valuable; it does not offer to judge these, but simply to explain our ethical values by showing the connection between our opinions about the two kinds of value. The model of challenge also assumes we have convictions about how to live; it does not judge these but tells us that we will understand our ethical life better if we see them in the way it recommends, as opinions about the skillful performance of an important self-assignment, rather than just as opinions about how we can change the world for the better. It is true, as we saw, that the model of impact makes certain ethical convictions that some people have seem silly: these convictions would probably not survive if the model were taken to heart as exclusive. But the model of challenge also makes certain convictions seem odd, as we shall see. The difference between the two models, in this respect, is that the convictions the model of challenge makes odd are anyway convictions that few if any people would actually hold.

D. Ethics and Significance

We must now consider the different responses the two models suggest to the various puzzles of ethics, and I begin with the first puzzle I listed: the problem of significance. Since the model of impact locates the value of living a particular way in the independent value of its consequences, it is particularly vulnerable to the charge that the difference even the most powerful human being can make to the state of value in the universe is indescribably puny. Impact can rescue ethics from this objection only by deploying some theory about objective value that stands up to infinity—some theory, that is, that makes the difference people can make to the universe seem much greater than the objection claims it can be. Perhaps that fact explains the appeal, for some people, of the romantic claim that the greatest value in the universe is aesthetic value, so that the transcendent value of a great work of art is in no way undercut by the fact that it is surrounded by billions of light-years of aesthetic nullity. That theory of value, connected to the model of impact, could explain why artistic geniuses have great lives. But if art were the only significant value in the universe, it would not matter how most people lived. Ethics would be only for great souls.

There are other, less relentlessly elitist, theories of value, however, that might also stand up to the universe. One is theological anthropocentrism. Suppose there is a God who, in spite of the amplitude of his creation, takes special interest in human beings, made in his own image, whose lives can please or displease him mightily. If that were true, then people's lives could make an important difference, judged objectively, to the universe. Or consider a currently much more popular view: hedonistic anthropomorphism. On this view, human pleasure or happiness is the only objective value, even if human beings exist only on a tiny mote and only for a tiny moment. This view of consequent value, tied to the model of impact, produces a recognizably utilitarian ethics: our lives are good, in the critical sense, to the degree to which we create pleasure or happiness for ourselves and others. Theological and utilitarian ethics are, in most versions, elitist to some degree but not in the obviously unacceptable way in which the aesthetic theory is elitist. Some people, because they are chosen or blessed or gifted or lucky, will be able to lead critically better lives, measured in the theological or utilitarian way, than others can. But no one is frozen out of ethics, since we can all have some impact on God's satisfaction or on the general level of happiness in the world. Someone can lead a perfectly good life, on the utilitarian version, simply by living in a way that produces great pleasure for himself. So the model of impact can provide an answer to the first puzzle of ethics if we can accept some theory of objective value that makes what people can do seem genuinely important to the universe, like aestheticism or theological anthropomorphism or human utilitarianism.

The model of challenge responds to the problem of significance in a very different way, for the value of a performance, as an exercise of skill in the face of a challenge, is complete in itself and does not depend on any distinct and independent value. We do not need to think that the stock of lasting value in the world has increased whenever an impressive dive has occurred or whenever Everest has been climbed in order to see the point of diving or climbing. This response does not acknowledge and try to meet the objection that nothing human beings can do is important in the face of infinity, as the model of impact does. The model of challenge sets the objection aside as based on a misconception of the kind of value ethical value is.

Nor does this model rely on the independent importance of some event even when it recognizes the importance of making a difference in the world. It is obviously compelling that making great music and conquering pneumonia and reducing racial injustice are among the good ways to live, and we could not accept the model of challenge if it could not find as comfortable a place for these judgments as the model of impact can. It does not distort the idea of performance or challenge to say that someone who has eliminated a great deal of misery in the world has done a skillful job of leading his life. That is not, however, simply a way of incorporating the model of impact within the model of challenge, as a compartment, because the former will not, as the latter must, make the independent value of the achievement the measure of its ethical value. For the contribution someone's invention or discovery or creation makes to the goodness of his life, on the challenge model, is sensitive to much besides the independent value of what he has created. The ethical value of an invention might be thought to depend, for example, on the degree of difficulty involved in its making, or in its originality, or in the degree to which its author made full use of or stretched his abilities, or in the intensity of his dedication, or in the way in which his work flowed from his sense of his role in or his dedication to a particular community or tradition. The model of challenge does not, of course, in itself stipulate which of these or hundreds of other possible considerations should enter into deciding how great a contribution a particular achievement makes to the overall skill with which someone has lived his life. My point is the same one again: that treating achievements as having ethical value in that way, rather than just in virtue of their impact alone, allows more subtlety in our judgments of the success of our own and other people's lives.

The challenge model also allows us to celebrate some kinds of achievement—the creation of great art, for example—without the elitist consequence that only lives capable of that kind of success are really worth leading. Or that, if the lives of two artists are good lives in virtue of the art they have created, the one who has created better art has for that reason had a greater life. I recognize that, in this respect, the name "model of challenge" might be misleading. I do not mean that only lives full of internal challenge, given over to heroic deeds like climbing impossible mountains, can be successful lives on this model. I mean rather that life itself is to be seen as a challenge; skill at that challenge might be thought to require avoiding rather than embracing arduous exploits in favor of a life more suited to one's talents or situation or satisfactions or cultural expectations. The point, yet again, is formal. Seeing ethical value as the value of a performance rather than as tied to the independent value of a product allows a further range of considerations and beliefs to enter ethical judgment, though it does not itself select among any particular set of these as more appropriate than others.

E. Transcendent or Indexed?

Since the model of impact ties ethical value to the independent value of states of affairs, ethical value must be transcendent under that model, because it is very implausible that the independent value of the kinds of impact that make lives good depends on the time or location of the impact. We might, perhaps, imagine bizarre theories of value that would index the value of states of affairs temporally or geographically. But any plausible or familiar theory would be immune to indexing. If we think that the only objective good is God's pleasure or the happiness of human beings, then we cannot think that the same amount of God's pleasure or overall human happiness could be less valuable at one moment of the world's history than at another. That must also be true of more complex theories about objective value that assign, for example, different value to different components of an overall state of affairs. Any particular complex structure of independent value must have the same total value whenever or wherever it occurs. So the model of impact, on any plausible interpretation of the value or values it assumes, implies that ethical value is transcendent. Of course what creates ethical value, according to any particular interpretation, will depend on circumstances. What makes people happy in developed economies may be different from what makes them happy in economically simpler societies. But the metric of value, of how far someone's life has succeeded in being good, must remain everywhere the same. How much objective and timeless value, on the right theory of independent value, has he added to the world's stock?

The model of challenge, on the other hand, tempts those who accept it to the view that ethical value is indexed rather than transcendent. Someone who accepted the model could conceivably, it is true, adopt a transcendent view of what a good performance of living is. He might think, for example, that living well only means living with style, and he might hold some timeless view about what style consists in. But any such timeless account would be fatally superficial. It seems irresistible that living well, judged as a performance, means among other things living in a way responsive and appropriate to one's culture and other circumstances. A life of chivalrous and courtly virtue might be a very good one in twelfth-century Bohemia but not in Brooklyn now.

An analogy to art will be useful, though dangerous, here. I mentioned earlier the opinion some people have that great art has independent and timeless value, so that the world is objectively better for having a brilliant painting in it no matter how that painting arrived. But that opinion, we should now notice, overlooks an important feature of art. A painting does have an independent value that we might call its product value: this is the power it has to excite aesthetic and other forms of valuable experiences. But a painting's product value is different from its *artistic* value, which is the value it has not independently but in virtue of how it was produced. We need the distinction between product and artistic value to explain the different values of an original and of a perfect and undetected copy. The value we attach to great art reflects not just its value as a product, but our respect for the performance that produced it, considered as a skillful response to a well-judged artistic challenge.

Art offers a better analogy to living, according to the challenge model, than the analogies I used earlier. For the challenge of art, unlike the challenge of diving well or climbing a difficult mountain, includes the challenge of defining as well as securing success, and if living well is regarded as a challenge, defining what it is to live well must be part of that challenge too. Artists are not furnished with blueprints, even in the most academic or conventionalized moments. When Duccio drew the Siennese tradition out of the Byzantine, or Duchamp hung his urinal on a gallery wall, or Pollock dripped paint over a canvas on the floor, each made a claim about the character of artistic achievement. There is no settled view about what artistic achievement is, as there is (I imagine) about achievement in diving. We expect artists to make claims that, if successful, will expand or at least change what the tradition counts as good. The most daring of these claims (we might say) offer to make something of nothing, to make artistic value out of a kind of performance in which none was recognized before. If we treat ethical value as the value of a performance rather than as the independent value of a product, then we will take the same view of a skillful performance of living. There is no settled canon of skill in living, and some people's lives, at least, make claims about ethical skill that if widely accepted would change prevailing views on the subject, and might even launch what would seem a new mode of living well, making, once again, ethical value from nothing. I do not mean that living a life well requires breaking with an ethical custom or tradition or even developing it in some particularly original way. The model of challenge makes room for that suggestion: it makes room for the romantic injunction that one should make of one's life an original work of art. But it does not insist on that romantic ideal or presuppose that less original lives must be less successful ones.

I offer the analogy between ethics and art not to endorse the romantic ideal, but to make a very different point. It is remarkably implausible, and foreign to almost everyone's aesthetic impulses, to suppose that artistic value is transcendent, that painting in the same way always has the same artistic value, that there is, in principle, one absolutely greatest way to make art against which all others must be judged. Artists enter the history of art at a particular time, and the artistic value of their work must be judged in that light, not because their circumstances limit how close they can come to the perfect ideal of artistry, but for the opposite reason that their circumstances help to fix what is, for them, the ideal toward which they must struggle. An artist's situation in the history of art, and the political, technological, and social conditions of his age, enter we might say into the *parameters* of the challenge he faces. Duccio's challenge was very different from Duchamp's or Pollock's. Even if we think that contemporary art must explore and comment on the materials of modern technology, we do not count it a limitation on an artist of the trecento that he did not have resin or epoxy available. Even if we think that Christian mythology would be an impoverished religious subject now, we do not count Duccio's work banal.

So the artistic analogy reminds us that the value of a performance can be indexed without being subjective, because the indexing can be provided by parameters of challenge that change with time and situation, but that nevertheless pose categorical demands. Living well, like painting well, means responding in an appropriate way to one's situation, though of course the ethical challenge of a particular time and place is very different from its artistic challenge. Art and ethics, on this view, are indexed in the same way. Both call for a decision, as part of the challenge they present, about the right response to the complex circumstances in which the decision must be made. It is, in both cases, a further question what the right ethical response for any particular person in any particular circumstances actually is, or whether there is a single right response even for a particular person or circumstance or only a set of these. The model of challenge, at the level of abstraction we are exploring, does not attempt to answer these further questions. It only emphasizes what kind of questions they are—that they require a personal response to the full particularity of situation, not the application, to that situation, of a timelessly ideal life.

F. Limitations and Parameters

We must now explore the distinction we have just noticed. Under any plausible version of the model of impact, all the circumstances of any person's actual life act as limitations on the quality of the life he can have. The ideal life is always the same: it is a life creating as much independent value—as powerful a pleasing of God or as much human happiness—as it is conceivable for a human being to create. Circumstances act as limits on the degree to which the ideal can be achieved. Mortality, for example, is a very important limit: most people could create more pleasure if they lived longer. Talent, wealth, personality, language, technology, and culture provide other limits, and their force as limits will be much greater for some people, and in some times and places, than others. If we adopt the challenge view of ethics, however, and treat living well as responding in the right way to one's situation, then we must treat some of the circumstances in which a particular person lives in a different way—as parameters that help define what a good performance of living would be for him.

Someone's living well, according to the challenge model, includes his sensing what the challenge he faces in making a life really is, just as an artist's painting well includes his sensing which aspects of his overall circumstances define the right tradition for him to continue or to defy. We have no settled template for that decision, in art or in ethics, and no philosophical model can provide one, for the circumstances in which each of us lives are enormously complex. These circumstances include our health, our physical powers, our tenure of life, our material resources, our friendships and associations, our commitments and traditions of family and race and nation, the constitutional and legal system under which we live, the intellectual and literary and philosophical opportunities and standards offered by our language and culture, and thousands of other aspects of our world as well. Anyone who reflects seriously on the question which of the various lives he might lead is right for him will consciously or unconsciously discriminate among these, treating some as limits and others as parameters. I might treat the fact that I am an American, for example, as just a fact that in some cases might help and in others hinder my leading the life I think best. Or I might treat my nationality as a parameter and assume, whether or not self-consciously, that being an American is part of what makes a particular life the right one for me.

No philosophical model can adjudicate this distinction; certainly not in any detail. Most people will sort their circumstances into the two camps almost automatically, and those who do reflect on the distinction are unlikely to draw from any overall theory the conclusions they reach. But if I do not think ethics transcendent—if I do not think that one life would be the greatest for all human beings who will ever have lived—then I must treat some of the facts that distinguish my situation from that of other people as parameters rather than limitations. My biological, social, and national associations—those I was born or fell into, not those I chose—seem obvious candidates to me, though they may not to others. The fact that I am a member of the American political community is not a limitation on my ability to lead a good life that I could describe in isolation from that connection. It rather states a condition of a good life for me: it is a life appropriate to someone whose situation includes that connection.

But of course I cannot treat everything about my situation as a parameter without destroying ethics for myself altogether. Suppose I took my own character, desires, resources, opportunities, and predilections to mark parameters for me; I say that the life good for me is a life good for someone with exactly my present material wealth, education, tastes, and ambitions. I would have indexed my account of the good life so thoroughly to my own immediate situation that it could no longer offer a challenge at all. So living well requires more discrimination about limits and parameters than either of the two extreme views that counts everything as limitation or everything as parameter.

It is fortunate that most of the discriminations we need are, as I said, more or less automatic, carried in our culture like so much else about ethics. But we can nevertheless identify some of the decisions we have covertly made, and we can force ourselves to consider whether they have been made in the right way. Someone might come to think, for example, that his professional or religious or some other connections are even more fundamental in defining the challenge he faces in living than his political ones are, and he may therefore seek citizenship in some other nation. When we reflect on the structure of our ethical convictions in this way we notice important complexities. We notice, for example, that many of our parameters are normative: they define our ethical situation not in terms of our actual situation but in terms of our situation as we suppose it should be. Our lives may go badly, in other words, not just because we are unwilling or unable properly to respond to the circumstances we have, but because we have the wrong circumstances. We do not even face the challenge we identify as the right one. Even if we do the best we can in the circumstances we do face, we do badly measuring our success against the chance we believe we ought to have been given, and it is the latter that defines a good life for us.

Consider, for example, the way most of us treat our mortality. We do not count the fact that we will die someday, much as we might fear or resent it, as a limitation on the value of the life we can have. We do not think that our lives can be at best only a tiny fraction as good as the lives people could lead if they lived to biblical ages or forever. We count a life good on that score if it lasts long by human standards, so that it can have the kinds of interrelatedness of age and generation and the other kinds of internal complexity that our cultural standards of a good life presuppose.[7] But we do not judge the goodness of someone's life only by asking how well it occupied whatever span of years it in fact had. We make assumptions about how long a human life can reasonably be expected to be, given appropriate resources of nutrition and medicine, and if someone dies very young by that standard, we count that a tragedy. His life, all else equal, was only partly as good as it might have been. Many of our ethical parameters are normative in that way: they help to define the challenge that people should face. A life not permitted that challenge is for that very reason a worse one.

That fact points the way to a further complexity. We must distinguish between what I shall call hard and soft parameters. Parameters enter into the description of any challenge or assignment: they describe the conditions of successful performance. Hard parameters state essential conditions of a specified performance: if these conditions are violated the performance is a total failure, no matter how successful it is in other respects. The formal structure of a sonnet imposes hard parameters: it ruins a sonnet to add an extra line, no matter how beautiful it is. Soft parameters also define an assignment, but though any violation of a soft parameter is a serious, compromising flaw—a crack in the golden bowl—that compromise is not fatal, and can be overcome. Compulsory figures in competitive figure skating are, I believe, soft parameters. It is part of the assignment that the skater execute a particular figure, and any deviations, no matter how beautifully executed, count as faults that necessarily cost points. But deviations do not mean winning no points at all, and a performance that includes a particularly brilliant deviation may win more points overall than a lackluster but perfectly faithful one.

Most of us, at least, believe that the parameters that define success in living a life are all soft. It counts against the goodness of someone's life that it was cut short by an early death because a good life for a human being is a life that occupies and makes good use of at least a normal life span. But a short life can nevertheless be a brilliant success, as Mozart's was. Some soft parameters require choices, and these may pose conflicts or dilemmas. Suppose I think that my life must be a life appropriate for an American and also for a Zionist, and then I come to think—rightly or wrongly—that accepting both these allegiances fully would tear my life apart. I might then think that the best life for me required some compromise, or that it required accepting one parameter and rejecting the other. Or I might think that no choice, in these circumstances, could really be thought better than the other, that I must just choose knowing that my life will be marred either way. The challenge model gives more sense and point to all these circumstances and dilemmas than the impact model can.

G. Justice as Parameter

The fourth set of puzzles I described is generated by the interplay between ethics and morality. Can someone lead a better life in virtue of injustice? I want now to distinguish two versions of that question. First, how is the critical value of someone's life affected by his own unjust acts? Second, how is it affected by the fact that his society is unjust, though not through his own acts? The impact model, in its abstract form, takes up no position on the first of these questions, about the ethical consequences of one's own unjust acts, because we can find interpretations of it that are compatible with either answer. On one interpretation, for example, we do good for the world only when we make it less unjust, and on that interpretation no one could have a better life through behavior that produced more injustice in the world. On another interpretation the greatest life is a life of producing great art; on that interpretation Cézanne's draft dodging made his life unambiguously a greater one, even if that life was indefensibly unjust.

But the model of impact, even in its abstract form, does take up a position about the second question. It holds that the fact that someone lives in an unjust society makes no difference, in itself, to the success or failure of his own life. It seems undeniable that in the United States now some people—I shall call them the rich—have more wealth than justice allows and others—the poor—have less. A rich man may use his wealth to make a positive impact on the world, however. He may use it to create or sponsor great art, or to finance his own or others' research into antibiotics, or to work in politics for greater equality, or even to help the poor more directly by giving his money to them. However we interpret objective value, the impact of his life is likely to have more value than it would have had if he had only average wealth, and, since the unjust situation (we are assuming) is not of his making, there is no negative impact value, in his own life, to set against the gain. Now consider the poor man. He almost undoubtedly will have a worse life, measured by its impact, than he could have had if he had more wealth. But that is in no way the consequence of the fact that his having less wealth is unjust: it is not the injustice of his share of resources, but the absolute amount of that share, that sets limits to the impact he can have. We would not judge his life a better one if we changed our mind about justice and decided that his share was just after all.

The model of challenge suggests a very different approach to the two questions. Someone who accepts that model, and so accepts that some aspects of our circumstances must count as normative parameters of living well, will find it difficult not to regard justice as figuring among those normative parameters. Certainly resources must figure as parameters in some way. They cannot count only as limitations, because we cannot think that the ideally best life is the life of someone with all the resources available to him that imagination might conceive. We cannot describe the challenge of living well, that is, without making some assumptions about the resources a good life should have available to it. We must therefore find some suitable account of the way in which resources enter ethics as parameters of the good life, and we have, I think, no alternative but to bring justice into that story by stipulating that a good life is a life suited to the circumstances that justice requires.

If living well includes assigning ourselves the right challenge in living, and that in turn means stipulating the right resources by way of parameter, then any normative convictions we have about the right distribution of resources seem inescapably pertinent. It would be bizarre to declare, as our considered moral judgment, that it is appropriate for people each to have a fair share of resources, defined in some particular way, and not also to think, in making an ethical judgment about what circumstances we should treat as appropriate in deciding what life would be good for us, that fair circumstances, so defined, are the appropriate ones. We cannot avoid that conclusion by saying that what is morally appropriate is not necessarily what is ethically appropriate, because the idea of normative parameters would make no sense if we insisted on that distinction. We must set the resource parameters of a life well lived, so far as we can, so that these respect our sense of justice.

If living well means responding in the right way to the right challenge, then someone's life goes worse when he cheats others for his own unfair advantage. It also goes worse when, even through no fault of his own, he lives in an unjust society, because then he cannot face the right challenge whether he is rich, with more than justice allows him to have, or poor, with less. That explains why, on the challenge model, injustice, just on its own, is bad for people. Someone who is denied what justice entitles him to have leads a worse life just for that reason; he leads a worse life than he would with the same absolute resources in, say, a poorer age when no one had more than he does. I do not mean, of course, that the absolute value or quality of the resources a person commands makes no difference to the life he can lead, so long as he has a just share of whatever there is. Someone who lives in a richer community or age, with a just share of its wealth, faces a more interesting and valuable challenge, and can lead a more exciting, diverse, complex, and creative life just for that reason, much as someone playing chess has a more valuable opportunity than someone playing tic-tac-toe. Lives can be better in different ways, and facing a more valuable challenge is one of them. Recognizing justice as a parameter of ethics does, however, limit the goodness of the life someone can lead in any given economic circumstances. I could have a better life, I assume, if circumstances changed so that justice allowed me more resources. It does not follow, however, that I could have a better life with an unjustly larger share of resources now.

But is it really true that no one can ever, in any circumstances, lead a better life by having more than justice permits? Plato's view has some plausibility if we understand him to mean that justice is a hard parameter of living well, that no one can improve his life in the critical sense by using more resources than he is entitled to have, any more than someone can improve a sonnet by adding more lines to it. Once we accept that the best life means a life responding well to the right circumstances, and that the right circumstances are circumstances of justice, we become aware of how difficult it is to lead anything like the right life when circumstances are far from just. We become aware, indeed, of how difficult it is even to imagine a wholly good life then.

Our own society is unjust. So our culture offers no examples of lives that flourished or were deemed successful in circumstances as they should be. Those of us who are rich cannot establish the relations with other people, particularly those who are poor because we are rich, that would be important to a good life in a just society. We may try to live with only the resources we think we would have in a fair society, doing the best we can, with the surplus, to repair injustice through private charity. But since a just distribution cannot be established counterfactually, but only dynamically through just institutions, we are unable to judge what share of our wealth is fair. On the other hand, simply ignoring the fact of injustice, and spending what we have in satisfying the volitional interests our culture recommends to people of our means, hardly seems an appropriate response. We may work in politics. But we will be unlikely to do much good, and our failure to make the community more just will make our own lives worse, because the community's failure is then ours as well. So once we identify the conditions of a really good life, in a clearheaded way, we may have considerable sympathy with Plato's view that justice is a hard parameter of ethics, that nothing can redeem a life spoilt by the misfortune of living in an unjust state.

Nevertheless that hard view does seem too strong. An alternative position, that justice is a soft rather than a hard parameter, would also make justice constitutive of ethics, but would be less destructive of recalcitrant ethical intuitions. On this view, though someone supported by unjust wealth cannot succeed fully in meeting the appropriate challenge, which is to live a life suited to someone in a just community, his life is nevertheless not automatically worthless, and might be a very good life. Indeed, like a skating performance that deviates from compulsory figures, it might even, in rare cases, be a better life than he could have led in a society perfectly just. That will not be true of most people who have more wealth than they should, however. They will do nothing so brilliant or amazing with the surplus over what justice would allow them that it will compensate for their inability to lead a good life in a just community. Some of them may enjoy their life more than they would in a such a community, of course. That does not mean that their lives are any better in the critical sense. We nevertheless concede that some genius financed by unjust wealth—Michelangelo by the Medici—may achieve a life greater than anyone could in a more just state. (As Harry Lime told us in *The Third Man*, the Italian quattrocento produced tyranny and the Renaissance. Switzerland in the same period produced democracy and the cuckoo clock.) A child whose life is saved by hideously expensive medical treatment available to him only through his parents' unjust wealth—treatment that would not be available to anyone in a just society—will very likely lead a better life in consequence. These concessions seem required by our sense of ethical possibility. But though they qualify Plato's insight, they do not undermine it. On the model of challenge, Plato was nearly right.

H. Additive or Constitutive?

Our next set of puzzles worries about the connection between our convictions and the goodness of the lives we lead. How far and in what way does my having a good life depend on my thinking it good? We instinctively assume that ethical standards are objective: a particular life, we think, cannot be good for someone just because he thinks it is. He can have made a mistake in thinking it good. But we know that convictions play a more important part in ethics than that flat statement suggests. How could it be in someone's interests, even in the critical sense, to lead a life he despises and thinks unworthy? So we are also tempted to say, on reflection, that ethical value must be subjective after all—having a good life must be a matter of ethical satisfaction, which means, in the end, that it must be a matter of thinking one's life good. But then the rope turns back on itself again: I cannot think my life good unless I think that its goodness does *not* depend on my thinking it so.

The model of impact cuts that knot by insisting that ethical value is fully objective, so that someone can indeed lead a better life than some alternative life he might have led, even when he thinks it a much worse life. Ethical value is additive rather than constitutive on the impact model, because ethical value is a matter of the independent value a life adds to the universe, and that cannot depend on how much value a person thinks he is adding. Creating great art does not require the artist's belief that he is creating great art. Nor does someone's improving the happiness of others require that he believe he is doing so, let alone that he believes he is leading a better life by doing so. In some cases the ethical convictions of the actor might add to the impact of what he does. Perhaps I can create more pleasure by what I do if others know that I believe it does me good, too. But that extra impact is incremental. The impact model would therefore have no trouble explaining the common feeling I reported earlier: that Hitler would have had a better life for himself, as well as for the rest of the world, if he had been locked up or even killed soon after birth. The impact of Hitler's life would then have been much more favorable, even if he would then have had no impact at all, and so his life would have been a much better one, in the critical sense, for him as well.

The challenge view resolves these puzzles differently. On any plausible interpretation of that model, the connection between conviction and value is constitutive: my life cannot be better for me in virtue of some feature or component I think has no value. Even in its abstract form the model presses toward that constitutive view. For intention is part of performance: we do not give credit to a performer for some feature of his performance that he was struggling to avoid, or would not recognize, even in retrospect, as good or desirable. An art student's performance is not improved when his teacher pushes his hand across the canvas, or drags it back from a stroke that would ruin what he has already done. The misanthrope's life is not made better by the friendship he thinks pointless. Of course it would have been better for everyone else if Hitler had died in his cradle. But on the challenge view it makes no sense to say that his own life would have been better, as distinct from no worse, if that had happened. There is nothing comparable under that model to a negative impact on the world.

It might be useful to consider, at this point, how this difference between the two models affects a standard issue in political philosophy—the legitimacy of coercive critical paternalism. Is it proper for a state to try to make people's lives better by forcing them to act in ways that they think make their lives worse? A good deal of coercive paternalism is not critical in character. The state makes people wear seat belts in order to keep them from harm that it assumes they already think bad enough to justify such constraints, even if they would not actually fasten their seat belts if not forced to do so. But some states claim a right or even an obligation to make people's lives better in the critical sense, not only against their will, that is, but against their conviction. That motive for coercion has not been of much practical importance in our time. Theocratic colonizers aim at their own salvation, not at the well-being of those they force to convert, and sexual bigots act out of hatred, not out of concern for those whose behavior they find immoral. Nevertheless some philosophers do claim paternalistic motives: some so-called communitarians or perfectionists want to compel people to vote, for example, on the ground that civic-minded people lead better lives.

The model of impact accepts the theoretical basis of critical paternalism. I do not mean that anyone who accepts that model must approve paternalism. He might think that officials would misuse their power or make worse judgments about ethical value than ordinary people would on their own. But he would see the point of ethical paternalism: it could make sense to him, for example, that people's lives would go better if they were forced to pray, because in that case they might please God more and so have a better impact, even though they remained atheists.

The challenge view, on the other hand, rejects the root assumption of critical paternalism: that a person's life can be improved by forcing him into some act or abstinence he thinks valueless. Someone who accepts the challenge model might well think that religious devotion is an essential part of how human beings should respond to their place in the universe, and therefore that devotion is part of living well. But he cannot think that involuntary religious observance—prayer in the shadow of the rack—has any ethical value. He may think that an active homosexual blights his life by a failure to understand the point of sexual love. But he cannot think that a homosexual who abstains, against his own convictions and only out of fear, has therefore overcome that defect in his life. On the challenge model, that is, it is performance that counts, not mere external result, and the right motive or sense is necessary to the right performance.

It overstates the point to say that the challenge model rules out any form of paternalism, because the defect it finds in paternalism can be cured by endorsement, provided that the paternalism is sufficiently short-term and limited so that it does significantly constrict choice if the endorsement never comes. We know that a child who is forced to practice music is very likely later to endorse the coercion by agreeing that it did, in fact, make his life better; if he does not, he has lost little ground in a life that makes no use of his training. In any case, however, endorsement must be genuine, and it is not genuine when someone is hypnotized or brainwashed or frightened into conversion. Endorsement is genuine only when it is itself the agent's performance, not the result of another person's thoughts being piped into his brain.[8]

The examples of critical paternalism I have used so far are cases of *surgical* paternalism: coercion is justified on the ground that the behavior implanted is good or the behavior excised is bad for people. Now consider a more sophisticated form of paternalism. *Substitute* paternalism justifies a prohibition by pointing not to the badness of what it prohibits but to the positive value of the substitute lives it makes available. Suppose people in power think that a life of religious devotion is wasted and therefore prohibit religious orders. Citizens who might have spent their lives in orders will then lead other lives with other experiences and achievements they find valuable, even though (unless they change their convictions and endorse the paternalism) they will think these lives worse than the life they were denied. Someone who would have spent his life in monastic orders might, for example, take up a life in politics that is eminently successful and valuable to others in ways that he agrees make his life a better one. Now the dilemma we noticed earlier reappears. Suppose we agree that a life of religious devotion is wasted. The politician's life has plainly not been wasted. He cannot take credit, it is true, for the decision to give up devotion for politics, because that is not something he did or endorsed. But he can take credit for the various acts and decisions that made his life in politics a success; he chose that life and made those decisions with a sense of their value. How can we not think that the decent life he in fact led was better than the life we believe would have been worthless, whatever he thinks? But yet the oddness remains: how can the life he led be better when he goes to his grave thinking it has been worse? In what sense was a life more successful that left its owner bitter, believing that he was leading a false, distorted life, at war with his own ethical sense?

The model of challenge (though not the model of impact) has the resources to resolve this dilemma. If we accept the challenge model we can insist on the priority of ethical integrity in any judgments we make about how good someone's life is. Someone has achieved ethical integrity, we may say, when he lives out of the conviction that his life, in its central features, is an appropriate one, that no other life he might live would be a plainly better response to the parameters of his ethical situation rightly judged. The priority of integrity makes a stronger claim than merely that disappointment and regret mar a life, that these are features of a life that *pro tanto* make it worse. If that were all, then these negative components might easily be outweighed by the positive features of the substitute life. We would be comfortable saying that even though the politician would much have preferred a life in religious orders, his political career was nevertheless, on balance, even taking his own feelings into account, a better life than the wasted life he would have had. If we give priority to ethical integrity, we make the merger of life and conviction a parameter of ethical success, and we stipulate that a life that never achieves that kind of integrity cannot be critically better for someone to lead than a life that does.

Of course ethical integrity may fail for many reasons. It fails when people live mechanically, with no sense of having and responding to ethical convictions at all. It fails when people set their convictions aside and serve their volitional interests with a vague but persistent sense that they are not living as they should. It fails when people believe, rightly or wrongly, that the correct normative parameters have not been met for them, when they have fewer resources than justice permits, for example. And it fails conspicuously when people are made to live, by the fiat of other people, in a way they regret and never endorse.

So recognizing the priority of ethical integrity does not make ethics subjective in the first person, that is, for someone considering how he himself should live. Even in the first person, however, ethical integrity sometimes acquires an independent force. I cannot agonize over ethics all my life; I must come to terms, at least temporarily, with convictions that survive a decent and honest scrutiny. Then I treat these convictions no longer just as hypotheses about ethical value but, right or wrong, as stipulating what ethical integrity requires of *me*. I claim a distinct virtue in holding to them for that reason. But there are limits to when and how far I can stand pat on earlier decisions in that way. For living out of conviction requires, if not continuing self-conscious reflection, at least taking seriously any doubts or twinges that might emerge, as well as the admonitions of teachers and friends.

The role of ethical integrity is different in the third person. When I consider what life is best for someone else, I must take his settled convictions into account, just as facts, in my judgment about what kind of life he should lead. If my friend, after much self-examination, and after having opened his mind to arguments the other way, decides to enter religious orders, I can imagine his life then going three different ways. He might change his mind (perhaps after reflecting on further argument) and enter politics, successfully, for the good of the country, and with full satisfaction and confidence in the value of what he does and the wisdom of his choice. Or he might hold to his course and live a life of religious devotion, again with full satisfaction and confidence in his choice. Or he might for some reason bow to the advice of his friends and enter politics against his own instincts and convictions; he will be successful there but will find no genuine satisfaction or self-approval, and will therefore never cease regretting his choice. I have no doubt that the first life is better, for him, than either of the other two. But I equally have no doubt that the second is better than the third, and that reflects my commitment to the priority of integrity in the third person. There is no skepticism in my ranking. I do not mean that the life of religious devotion is the best for him because he thinks it best. I have not changed my view that his life will be less successful than it might have been, and I will continue to argue with him if I think I can change his mind on that score. I mean that, given his unshaken convictions, it is the only life he can lead at peace with himself, and it is therefore the best he can do in meeting the challenge of his situation now understood to include that fact. Of course some ethical convictions are so terrible or base that we would not encourage someone who was unable to shake them off to live at peace with them. But that is because a wicked life is bad for other people, not because we think a life against the grain would be better for him.

If we accept the priority of ethical integrity, why are we concerned at all about how good a life other people lead, so long as they find it satisfying? Why should we try to persuade someone who finds value only in wealth and power to think again, if he has no doubt that his materialistic convictions are sound? The answer may lie simply in what seems a very abstract benevolence: that we believe people should lead better lives, find integrity at a higher level, even if the satisfaction they take in their new lives is no greater than that which they took in their lives before. The principle of priority offers no reason why we should *not* try to improve people's lives, by persuasion and example, in that way. But in most circumstances the principle provides a more positive reason why benevolence should take that form. For we suspect that the materialist and the misanthrope will not in the end find their lives fulfilling or satisfactory; we suspect that their ethical sense will one day reveal their lives as barren and unrewarding, though perhaps tragically too late. We also know that integrity, over some range, is a matter of degree: even if they think their lives successful now, and would continue to do so, we think they could unite life and conviction even more successfully with different convictions in place.

But does the priority of integrity therefore recommend a deeper form of paternalism than those we have so far been considering? I have in mind *cultural* paternalism: the suggestion that people should be protected from choosing wasteful or bad lives not by flat prohibitions of the criminal law but by educational constraints and devices that remove bad options from people's view and imagination. People do not make decisions about how to live in a cultural vacuum. They respond in various ways to what their culture makes available by way of possibility and example and recommendation. Why, then, should we not try to make that cultural environment as sound as we can, in the interests of people who will decide how to live influenced by it?

Of course our circumstances, including the ethical vocabulary and example of our culture, affect our ethical responses. But to some degree these circumstances are up to us, collectively, and when they are we must ask what these circumstances should be. We must ask, that is, what circumstances are appropriate for people who give value to their lives by showing skill in living. In the last section we saw how justice becomes an ethical as well as political question in that way. We need normative parameters to define the challenge of living, and justice enters ethics when we ask how resources should figure in people's understanding of what that challenge is. Questions about critical paternalism enter ethics, on the challenge model, in a similar way. Those who defend cultural paternalism claim, in effect, that the circumstances appropriate for ethical reflection are those in which bad or wasted lives have been screened out collectively so that the decisions each individual is to make are from a deliberately restricted menu. If that were a sensible view of what ethical reflection should be like, then my argument that paternalism undermines ethical value, because it destroys ethical integrity, would be entirely misplaced. Living well would mean making the best choices from a culled list, and paternalism would be indispensable rather than threatening to ethical success. But that view is not sensible: A challenge cannot be more interesting, or in any other way a more valuable challenge to face, when it has been narrowed, simplified, and bowdlerized by others in advance, and that is as much true when we are ignorant of what they have done as when we are all too aware of it.

Suppose someone replies that the challenge is more valuable when the chances of selecting a truly good life are improved, as they would be if the list of possibilities was filtered by wise collective rulers. That reply misunderstands the challenge model profoundly, because it confuses parameters and limitations. It assumes that we have some standard of what a good life is that transcends the question of what circumstances are appropriate for people deciding how to live, and so can be used in answering that latter question, by stipulating that the best circumstances are those most likely to produce the really correct answer. On the challenge view, living well is responding appropriately to circumstances rightly judged, and that means that the direction of argument must go in the other way. We must have some independent ground for thinking it is better for people to choose in ignorance of lives other people disapprove; we cannot, without begging the question, just argue that people will lead better lives if their choices are narrowed in that way.

Once that point is grasped, any temptation toward cultural paternalism must disappear. That does not mean that government has no responsibility for the cultural background against which people decide how to live. A government anxious to provide the right circumstances for citizens' choosing how to live might well strive that its community's culture provide opportunities for and examples of lives that have been thought good by reflective people in the past, and that might sensibly and properly be lived now, particularly if popular culture provides few examples of those lives. My arguments for government support of the arts in *A Matter of Principle* did not include that argument, because I was attempting there to reply to the objection that such support is unjust when the funds could be used to help relieve disease and unjustified poverty.[9] But a state that has fulfilled the requirements of justice may properly use public funds to support art that the market will allow to perish, on the substantive ground that art improves the value of lives available in the community.

The issue of paternalism therefore adds a new dimension to the differences between the impact and challenge models of ethical value. The impact model allows a defense of surgical paternalism because that model divorces ethical value from ethical choice. The challenge model fuses value and choice. It insists that nothing can improve the critical value of a life unless it is seen as an improvement by the person whose life it is, and that makes surgical paternalism self-defeating. It makes substitute paternalism self-defeating as well when the substitute life lacks ethical integrity. The challenge model undermines cultural paternalism, finally, because that form of paternalism assumes an independent, transcendent picture of ethical value, and the challenge model rejects any such picture. The model does not rule out the possibility that the community should collectively endorse and recommend ethical ideals not adequately supported by the culture. Nor does it rule out compulsory education and other forms of regulation which experience shows are likely to be endorsed in a genuine rather than manipulated way, when these are sufficiently short-term and noninvasive and not subject to other, independent objection. All this follows from the central, constitutive role the model of challenge assigns to reflective or intuitive conviction. Ethical value is objective, but it has features, which we have now noticed, that tempt us to call it subjective as well. We do better, however, to resist that dangerous temptation and take care, instead, to expose the complex phenomenology of ethical judgment—particularly the differences between judging for ourselves and judging for others.

I. Ethics and Community

The last set of problems I described raises the question whether and how far ethics can be social rather than individual. Does ethical integration—the idea that someone's critical interests involve not only his own experiences and achievements but also those of groups to which he belongs—make sense? The impact model supposes that each person's critical good consists in the impact that he makes on the world. It can defend ethical integration only by arguing that an individual sometimes has a more valuable impact, on his own, when he thinks not of his own impact but of the impact of a group to which he belongs. Games theory, and moral and political philosophy in its wake, have defined one situation—the so-called prisoners' dilemma—in which this is true. In these situations individuals each acting rationally to advance his own interests will together do what is worse for each, and this may be true not only when people aim at what is in their own interests in the narrow, volitional sense, but when they aim to have an objectively valuable impact on the world.[10] In these circumstances, each would do better to ask, not how he could have the maximum impact, but how some group might, and then to do his part in that group's project. In that way each secures a greater impact by what he himself does, and so he produces, according to the model of impact, a critically better life for himself.

But the impact model cannot explain our actual convictions by appealing to the structure of a prisoners' dilemma because the most common convictions or intuitions of ethical integration do not match that structure. We feel ethically integrated only into groups to which we already belong in some other way, and then only for acts of those groups that are already established in the group's practices as collective—only into those political communities of which we are citizens, and only for the acts of those communities, like their political decisions, that are institutionally collective.[11] So we recognize ethical integration on many occasions when there appear, at least, to be no advantages to projects we favor in our doing so. I have no games-theoretical reasons for thinking my life goes worse if my community does what I want it not to do: the collective rationality of a prisoners' dilemma solution cannot explain my personal shame at Vietnam. Moreover, we often have no sense of ethical integration when cooperation is plainly appropriate. Both my fellow prisoner and I have a strong reason to sign an enforceable agreement not to confess, and each of us may have a moral reason not to confess even in the absence of such an agreement. But unless we are partners or friends or relatives or are acting together in some joint project, neither of us is likely to feel the reason of ethical integration: that his own life goes badly unless the group of the two of us prospers. So the order of explanation of any argument that the model of impact might offer for ethical integration would go the wrong way. Ethical integration sometimes provides the motivation needed for collective rationality. But not vice versa.

The model of challenge puts ethical integration in an entirely different light. It need not show, in order to make sense of such integration, that an individual has more impact through a community's collective action than on his own. It need only show how ethical integration might sensibly seem an appropriate response to an important parameter of an individual's circumstances—the fact that he lives bound up with other people in a variety of communities. That is, in fact, a very widely shared view about living well, and so the challenge model is able to make sense of ethical integration in a natural rather than strained way. I should probably repeat, once again, that the challenge model is not a mechanism for supporting convictions like that one. I do not cite the abstract claim of that model, that the goodness of living well is a matter of performance not of impact, as part of the case for ethical integration. I mean only to point out, for the final time in this long section, that interpreting the convictions we already have as convictions about a skillful response to a complex challenge gives them more sense and coherence than the alternate general interpretation—that they are convictions about having the best impact—can give them.

III. From Ethics to Politics

I said that I had two aims in this chapter: to study the question of metric in ethics, as important for its own sake, and to show that one response to that question—the model of challenge—provides an important reply to the arguments against liberalism that I began by reciting. I turn now to the second of these aims. I shall assume, in what follows, that we have self-consciously embraced that ethical model of challenge, and also embraced what I called an irresistible consequence of it—that justice is at least a soft parameter of a good life for us. (I assume, as I shall put it, that we have become ethical as well as political liberals.) I shall try to show that, on those assumptions, we have special reasons for adopting liberal equality as our political morality and rejecting its various rivals.

A. Justice and Resource

It is a theme of the early chapters of this book that the justice of an economic distribution depends on its allocation of resources rather than of welfare or well-being. Ethical liberals cannot accept any goal of justice defined in the latter terms, because government could not hope to realize any such goal except in one of two ways both of which such people would regard as intolerable. We live in ethically pluralist societies: People disagree about how, concretely, to live well. Government might try to surmount this difficulty by choosing one conception of living well—say, the hedonistic conception—and using that conception to judge everyone's success. But ethical liberals could not accept this, because government would then usurp the most important part of the challenge people face in leading a life, which is identifying life's value for themselves.

Or government might hope to avoid the difficulty by radically divorcing ethics from justice through some two-stage procedure. At the first stage each citizen would report what level of well-being he would reach, according to his personal standards of living well, under different proposed institutional and economic arrangements. At the second stage officials would select that arrangement in which they judged (I ignore how they possibly could judge) that people's well-being, as they themselves measured it, matched what the officials took to be the right distribution—that well-being so measured is equal, for example, or maximized overall. This two-stage procedure separates ethics from justice. In its first stage citizens decide for themselves what makes a life successful for them, and in its second stage officials contrive to distribute success, so defined, according to some formula they take to be fair. But ethical liberals cannot participate in any such process, because they cannot separate ethics from justice in the way it requires. For they must rely on assumptions or instincts of justice—about whether what we have or do is fair given its impact on our neighbors' and fellow citizens' lives—in order to decide which ways of living are ways of living well. (This point is developed further in Chapters 2 and 7.)

B. Equality

So, once we accept the challenge model, we must insist that distributive justice is a matter of what resources people have, not of what well-being they achieve with those resources. But what share of resources is a just share? Do we have some reason, just in that model of challenge, to accept that the only just share is an equal share? Is the challenge model of ethics inherently egalitarian?

We face a difficult threshold question before we can begin any answer to that substantive one, however. What strategies do ethical liberals have for reasoning about justice? Much contemporary liberal political philosophy is built around what seems a natural, even compelling, assumption—that the interests of the different citizens who make up a political community can be identified in advance of any decision about what distribution of resources among them is just. That is the premise of contractarian theories of justice, which suppose that principles of justice can be derived from thought experiments asking what principles people would agree upon either in their own interests, or in virtue of a motive that makes them want to find a reasonable compromise among different people's interests. Rawls's argument for his "difference" principle assumes, for example, that people's interests can be defined in at least a "thin" way in advance of any decision about what justice requires; even people who are ignorant of their more concrete interests can sensibly assume, he says, that the more resources they have the better for them—so that they can aim, even behind a veil of ignorance about those more concrete interests, to insure themselves against too great a sacrifice of their "thin" interests so conceived.

But ethical liberals believe that the character of people's critical interests, at least, depends upon justice: they cannot know, in adequate detail, what their critical interests are until they know, at least roughly, what distribution of resources among them is just. Each ethical liberal might hope that the just share for him is a large share, but he knows that a large share is unlikely to be good for him unless it is also a just one. So he cannot accept even a "thin" theory of the good that holds that the more resources he has the better it is for him, or any theory that asks him what it is reasonable for him to surrender, by way of his own interests, out of respect for the interests of others.

The impact of the challenge model of ethics on political philosophy is therefore profound. If we are ethical liberals, we find the most basic assumptions and strategies of contemporary liberal political theory both unnatural and unworkable, because our challenge model integrates justice with ethics in a way that defeats those strategies and assumptions. We must think about justice and the good life in a more integrated way: we must arrive at a conception of what justice requires and what our interests are through some argument that does not presuppose that we can have a full answer to either of those questions independently of an answer to the other. We must therefore begin (as we might put it) further back, in a more general theory of value. Ethical liberals assume that it is important how people live—important that they lead successful or good lives rather than bad or wasted ones. Can this sensibly be thought more important in the case of some people than in others'—not more important to or for them, but more important as a matter of objective value?

It is true that for centuries some people have claimed special importance for their own lives by pointing out, for example, that they belong to a nation favored by God, or that they are people of special lineage or talent or beauty or even wealth. Such claims are, happily, out of fashion among us now, and we need not make any great effort to refute them. But it is worth noticing that ethical liberals have a special reason for resisting any such claim. The challenge model makes a deep claim—that the value of a life well lived does not depend on any antecedent circumstance in which the life begins but on the performance of living itself—and that claim offers no purchase for the idea that any antecedent circumstance can add to or detract from that value. A Jew who accepts the challenge model might think it crucial to decide whether he should make his religion central to his life. But he cannot think that it is crucial that he make that decision correctly only because he *is* a Jew. The embracing character of the challenge that the challenge model sets, that is, makes sense only if we understand the challenge as addressed to people generally, to anyone at all who has a life to live. So ethical liberals begin with a strong ethical reason for insisting on an egalitarian distribution of resources. If it is equally important how each person lives, then the lives we lead should reflect that important assumption, and they can do so only if resources are distributed in a way consistent with it.

The argument that has led us to this point has a certain symmetry. It begins in the idea that justice limits ethics, that someone leads a less good life with the same resources when and because these are unjustly low or great. Now we see how ethics limits justice. A scheme of justice must fit our sense of the character and depth of the ethical challenge, and that requirement supports equality as the best theory of justice. I do not mean that a different view of ethics—the impact view, for example—could not support equality, though any strict equality is likely to seem an extreme and doctrinaire position on that view. I mean only that the challenge view supports equality directly, as flowing from people's sense of their own best interests critically understood. Living well has a social dimension, and I live less well if I live in community with others who treat my efforts to lead a good life as less important than theirs. Indeed, everyone is insulted by a political and economic system dedicated to inequality, even those who profit in resources from the injustice. On the challenge model, critical self-interest and political equality are allies. Hegel said that masters and slaves are prisoners together; equality unlocks the chains of both.

C. Ethics and Partiality

But now we have a further issue to face. Ethical liberals reject equality from the personal perspective. They think that someone who tried to show no more interest in his own fate, and in the fate of family and friends, than he shows for strangers would be an ethical idiot. Is it inconsistent to insist on equality in politics and to condemn it in ordinary life? Must ethical liberals be embarrassed by their apparent ambivalence about equality?

Political equality and personal partiality would indeed be inconsistent if equality meant equality of welfare or well-being. If we struggle together in politics, for a decade, to make the welfare of each person in the community equal as of a particular date, but then lapse back into a private life in which each of us spends whatever resources he has improving his own well-being and that of his family and friends, then only by the most freakish coincidence could welfare remain equal among us. We would have undermined individually what we achieved collectively, and we should have to start again. But that is not true, at least not in principle, if for us equality means equality of resources. On that theory of justice, I show equal respect for others when I do not appropriate resources that are properly theirs—when I do not exceed my fair share at their expense. Suppose the auction that I described in Chapter 2 begins in equal bidding resources and ends in a shared recognition that no further rounds of the auction would be helpful. Then my decision, once the auction had finished, to look after my own well-being in my plans and investments, and to work for the welfare of family and friends, could not on its own impair the equality the auction had achieved.[12] Equality of resources in that way licenses partiality.

We might put this point another way: under equality of resources there is a division of labor between the political and the private perspectives. People are free to take up personal aims and attachments in their private lives with complete conviction, if and because politics has secured a distribution that is egalitarian publicly. Of course this division of labor must not be taken to mean that private individuals have no concern with distributive justice, that they are entitled simply to consume whatever resources the reigning system distributes to them indifferent to the demands of others who have less, as if distributive justice were always someone else's business. It would be incredible, for example, that a theory of justice should make no private demands on citizens living in great affluence in an unjust society. But, as we noticed when we first considered the connection between justice and ethics, it is a complex and perhaps unanswerable question what equality of resources asks of us, as individuals, in our own unfair society. That is part of the reason why, according to the challenge model, our lives go worse if we live amid injustice. So we should say, of our own indelible partiality in the private perspective, not that it conflicts with a genuinely egalitarian politics but rather that it conflicts with any other kind of politics.

D. Neutrality of Appeal

We come finally to what is, for many people, the most problematic feature of liberal equality, which is its particular version of neutrality or tolerance. We should distinguish two ways in which a political theory might be neutral or tolerant about different ethical convictions. First, it might be neutral in its appeal, that is to say, ecumenical. It might set out principles of political morality that can be accepted by people from a very great variety of ethical traditions. Second, it might be neutral in its operation, that is to say, tolerant. It might specify, as one principle of political morality, that government must not punish or discriminate against people because it disapproves of their ethical convictions. Obviously these two aspects of neutrality are very closely connected. In many (though by no means all) circumstances the best hope of attracting wide support from different groups lies in some general guaranty against the persecution of any. But the two aspects are nevertheless different.

Is the challenge model of ethics ecumenical? It does not take sides, as a formal matter, among concrete ethical convictions. People who think the good life lies in religious devotion and others who think that it requires unconventional sexual variety may all treat their convictions as opinions about the most skillful performance of living. But I conceded, right at the start, that the challenge model captures and organizes only some of the intuitions people have about ethics, and the model has certain implications that few people have yet embraced. Most people would be puzzled, for example, at least as a matter of first impression, by the proposition that justice is a parameter of good lives, so that most people's lives go worse if they have more resources than justice would allow. We must settle for the weaker claim that the challenge model of ethics could be generally accepted without many people's having to abandon the convictions that seem most important to them. Embracing that model would not force them to change their minds, for example, about which aspects of their circumstances—their religion or nation or vocation, for instance—supply the most basic parameters of a life good for them.

E. Liberal Tolerance

Liberal equality is tolerant in the following sense. It distinguishes two kinds of reasons that a political community might offer as justification for denying liberty. The first is a reason of justice: a community must outlaw some conduct when and because the best theory of justice so requires. It must outlaw theft, for example, to protect people's rights to security of property. The second is a reason of ethics: a community might think that the conduct it outlaws, though not against justice, is demeaning or corrupting or otherwise bad for the life of its author. It might think, for example, that the life of a homosexual is a degrading one, and it might outlaw homosexual relations on that ground. Liberal equality denies the legitimacy of the second, ethical, reason for outlawing conduct.

That does not mean, of course, that liberal equality is ethically neutral in result, or that it aims to be. Any political and economic scheme will make some kinds of lives more difficult or expensive to lead than they would be under other schemes. It is much less likely that anyone will be in a position to gather a great collection of Renaissance masterpieces under liberal equality than under unrestrained capitalism. But liberal equality jeopardizes such a life only because a just distribution of resources has that consequence, not because it deems art collecting to be intrinsically unworthy or degrading. So liberal equality rejects the view the Supreme Court once said was part of American constitutional law: that a majority may properly make homosexuality a crime just because most people think homosexuals lead bad lives.[13]

Can people with strong ethical convictions be ethical liberals? Some people think that homosexuals lead very bad lives. Others think that businessmen are contemptible, that atheists waste their lives, that America has become a nation of pitiful couch potatoes, that welfare benefits rust people's souls, that people need to return to nature, that it is imperative to preserve ethnic or religious identities, that patriotism is the most fundamental of the virtues, and so forth. Some people hold these views passionately; they live and preach them, and they despair when their children reject them. How could they endorse the tolerance of liberal equality? Why should people with such strong convictions not attempt to persuade others to what they think is the good?

They should. The question is not whether they should campaign for the good as they see it, but how. Liberal tolerance denies them only one weapon: they must not use the law, even when they are in the majority, to forbid anyone to lead the life he wants, or punish him for doing so, just on the ground that his ethical convictions are, as they believe, profoundly wrong. If people are drawn to ethical liberalism—even people of very strong personal ethical conviction—they will have no reason to resist that single constraint on their power to propagate their opinions. Ethical liberals know that they cannot make other people's lives better by the coercive means that liberal tolerance forbids, because they know that someone's life cannot be improved against his steady conviction that it has not been. Even if they think someone's life would be better if he changed his convictions, they know they cannot make it better unless he does change them, and in the right way. They accept that he leads a better life at peace with his own settled convictions than he can live, under external pressure, at war with them. This point is a companion to the one I shall emphasize in Chapter 7. Just as no one deserves extra compensation because his ethical beliefs are (as we judge) mistaken, so no one should be denied liberty on the same ground. In both cases, paternalism is misguided because it wrongly treats convictions as limitations or handicaps.

It is important to remember, in assessing this argument for liberal tolerance, that such tolerance falls short of what might be considered absolute neutrality. As I said, liberal equality cannot be neutral in consequences: it must have the result that some kinds of lives are more difficult to lead than others. And liberal equality leaves room, in appropriate circumstances, for short-term educational paternalism that looks forward, with confidence, to free and genuine endorsement. Nor can liberal equality be neutral toward ethical ideals that directly challenge its own. It is not neutral about third-person ethics: it insists, for example, on the proposition I just cited: that no one can improve another's life by forcing him to behave differently, against his will and his convictions. Not everyone accepts that proposition, but liberal equality must nevertheless insist on it.

IV. Epilogue

I am very much aware that the argument of this chapter lacks a historical dimension. I have made no effort (nor am I in any way competent) to ground my central argument in intellectual history. I believe that the challenge model dominates Greek ethics, particularly Aristotelian ethics, and that in the modern period it has played a crucial part (in indistinct battle with ethical skepticism) in the development of humanist ethics. The model of impact, on the contrary, seems to me prominent in theological ethics and in various forms of utilitarian ethics. Whatever sense or cogency these glib historical remarks might have, I do not mean them to suggest what I earlier denied: that religious or utilitarian ethics can have no place in the model of challenge. The idea that living skillfully means recognizing and entering into an appropriate relationship with a God, or that it means recognizing and responding to human misery, is not the only possible interpretation of the challenge model but, for many people, the compelling interpretation of it. But many of the political implications that some scholars have drawn from theological or utilitarian ethics do depend on the model of impact, and would have to be abandoned, in favor of more liberal positions, if those ethics were reformulated in the challenge model's mold.

7

Equality and Capability

⁂

I. Two Objections

I must now discuss two objections to the general account of equality we have been constructing. In Chapter 1 we distinguished two ways in which we might compare different people's situations. We might compare the resources each has available with which to lead his life, or we might compare the welfare or well-being that each has achieved with whatever resources he does have available. I used that distinction to distinguish, in turn, two very different political goals each of which might be thought an egalitarian goal. A political community might aim that its members be equal in their resources or in their welfare.

That description of the two aims is very abstract, however, and many different ideals fit under each of these two general aims. Equality of welfare or well-being is subject to different interpretations. People disagree about what genuine well-being really is; some people think that they achieve it when their lives are full of excitement, for example, and others think that well-being is more a matter of lasting achievement than of transitory absorption. Equality of welfare does not become a concrete political goal until some particular understanding or conception of welfare is specified. I argued, in Chapter 1, that equality of welfare has gained whatever appeal it has precisely by remaining abstract and therefore ambiguous: the ideal loses its appeal whenever a particular conception of welfare is specified, which presumably explains why those who defend it rarely attempt any such specification.

Equality of resources also needs further specification. A person's resources might be understood to include his wealth alone, or his wealth together with his personal qualities of strength, talent, character, and ambition, or both of these together with his legal and other opportunities. In Chapter 2 and subsequent chapters I defined equality of resources as embracing, in different ways, all these categories of resource, and I tried to describe a metric of equality, through the hypothetical auctions, insurance markets, and legal structures described in Chapters 2 and 3, that would unite them in an overall account of equal resources. I made a further crucial distinction within the broad category of personal qualities, however: between a person's personality, understood in a broad sense to include his character, convictions, preferences, motives, tastes, and ambitions, on the one hand, and his personal resources of health, strength, and talent on the other. I said that a political community should aim to erase or mitigate differences between people in their personal resources—should aim to improve the position of people who are physically handicapped or otherwise unable to earn a satisfactory income, for example—but should not aim to mitigate or compensate for differences in personality—for differences traceable to the fact that some people's tastes and ambitions are expensive and other people's cheap, for instance.

The objections I discuss in this chapter insist that equality of welfare and of resources do not exhaust the pertinent possibilities, and that a third ideal—equality of "opportunity" or "capability" of some sort—is preferable to both. In fact, as we shall see, these supposed alternatives are not genuine. One group of critics—I shall use G. A. Cohen's version as representative—proposes that citizens should be equal, not in the welfare they achieve, but in the opportunity that each has to achieve welfare. As we shall see, that supposedly different ideal turns out to be equality of welfare under another name. Another prominent critic—Amartya Sen—proposes the different ideal that citizens should be equal, not in their resources, but in their "capability" for different "functionings"—in their capacity, that is, to act or achieve in specified ways. Sen's statement of this ideal is ambiguous, however. If the apparent ambiguity is resolved in one of two possible ways, his equality of capabilities also collapses into equality of welfare. If it is resolved in the other way, then equality of capabilities is identical with equality of resources. The failure of these two objections to establish genuine alternatives to the two conceptions of equality I began by describing suggests that the distinction between those two conceptions is a particularly deep one. I shall argue that it signals a polar division between two visions of the role political philosophy should play in a democracy.

II. Chance and Choice

Our judgments about personal and collective responsibility are dominated by a key distinction between chance and choice (a distinction that I also explore, in the context of genetic discovery and manipulation, in Chapter 13). We distinguish, for a thousand reasons, between what part of our fate is open to assignments of responsibility, because it is the upshot of someone's choice, and what part is ineligible for any such assignment because it is the work not of people but of nature or brute luck. The whole network of our moral and ethical convictions shifts when technology or discovery makes any dramatic change in the boundary between the two. There was a seismic change when people began to attribute natural disasters to chance rather than to the choices of supernatural gods or demons, whom they might have provoked. We will suffer another seismic change, in the opposite direction, if biotechnology one day allows parents to determine in detail the physical and mental properties of their children.

The choice/chance distinction figures in assignments of a variety of kinds of responsibility. It figures in causal responsibility: my choices are among the causes of my acts, but not among the causes of my genetic predisposition to particular diseases. In this book we have been concerned mainly with the different idea of consequential responsibility. When and how far is it right that individuals bear the disadvantages or misfortunes of their own situations themselves, and when is it right, on the contrary, that others—the other members of the community in which they live, for example—relieve them from or mitigate the consequences of these disadvantages? I used the choice/chance distinction in replying to these questions. In principle, I said, individuals should be relieved of consequential responsibility for those unfortunate features of their situation that are brute bad luck, but not from those that should be seen as flowing from their own choices. If someone has been born blind or without talents others have, that is his bad luck, and, so far as this can be managed, a just society would compensate him for that bad luck. But if he has fewer resources than other people now because he spent more on luxuries earlier, or because he chose not to work, or to work at less remunerative jobs than others chose, then his situation is the result of choice not luck, and he is not entitled to any compensation that would make up his present shortfall.

Cohen and others challenge that way of drawing the line between choice and luck. They point out that even when someone's unfortunate situation is the result of his deliberate choice, that choice might have been dictated by features of his person or personality that he did not choose. Suppose someone cannot stand the taste of ordinary water from the tap—it tastes unbearably sour to him—and he therefore chooses to buy more expensive bottled water. It is true that he has a choice whether or not to do that. But he did not choose to have the property—a special sensory reaction—that made the choice not to do so distasteful. That physiological condition is his bad luck, and he should therefore be compensated for his misfortune: he should be given extra resource so that he will not be worse off buying bottled water than others are who make do with tap water. Now suppose someone yearns to be a photographer but finds that if he is to realize his dream he must spend the greater part of his income buying expensive cameras and lenses. Once again, he could choose not to buy the equipment. But that choice would make him miserable, at least for a time, and once again he did not choose to have the ambition that has that consequence. Surely (the critics argue) it is just as unfair to make him bear the consequential responsibility for his choice to buy the equipment as it would be to make someone handicapped in some other way—born blind or without talent or unable to stand tap water—bear the financial consequences of that condition.

It is important to notice that this argument does not appeal to any general form of metaphysical or psychological determinism. It does not deny that people are free to choose: it does not deny that the would-be photographer is free not to buy expensive equipment, for example, but only insists that he should not be forced into a worse financial position if he does decide to buy it. In fact the critics rely heavily on the assumption that people are free to choose, because they insist that people *should* take consequential responsibility for their expensive tastes when they have deliberately cultivated those tastes. Cohen puts the point this way: "To the extent that people are indeed responsible for their tastes, the relevant welfare deficits do not command the attention of justice. We should therefore compensate only for those welfare deficits which are not in some way traceable to the individual's choices." That is why, he declares, society should compensate the photographer, whose taste for photography, as he stipulates, arose from no choice, but not Louis, a character with champagne tastes whom I discussed in Chapter 2, and who (in Cohen's summary) "did not just get stuck with his taste: he schooled himself into it."[1]

Cohen agrees, for that reason, that equality of welfare is an improper political ideal. It fails to distinguish between expensive tastes that people are

simply landed with and expensive tastes that they have deliberately cultivated. So he and other critics who make similar arguments reject both
equality of welfare and equality of resources in favor of a supposedly third
ideal: equality in people's *capacity* or *capability* or *opportunity* to secure
welfare or some other form of advantage. Since Louis had as much opportunity for welfare as anyone else before he cultivated his expensive tastes, it is
not necessary to reward or compensate him for having done so. But the
photographer did not choose his burning ambition: it simply stole up upon
him. He did not have an equal opportunity for welfare, and he deserves
compensation for that reason.

This last distinction, which Cohen claims to be fundamental, is illusory.
Louis did not cultivate his grand tastes to get more "welfare" in the way of
buzzes of pleasure or ticks of desire satisfaction: that would have been
irrational because, even in a community committed to equality of welfare,
he would have less buzz or fewer ticks in consequence.[2] He cultivated refined
tastes because, given his royal Bourbon heritage, he thought such tastes
appropriate to him: he had, we might say, a taste for refined tastes. But that
background taste, out of which he acted, is no more "traceable" to choice
than the photographer's taste for photography. (Nor does that fact turn on
Louis's royal pedigree or upbringing: I might have called him Jay rather than
Louis.)

It would not help if Cohen were to describe Louis's operative taste as
"second order," and then propose a principle that compensated for unculti-
vated first-order but not second-order expensive tastes. Cohen's "cut" between choice and luck is meant to be a deep one, and in whatever way he
supposes that his photographer would suffer if he could not afford expensive lenses, so Louis would have suffered if he found, to his dismay, that he
continued to enjoy TV dinners.[3] So equality of opportunity for welfare or
advantage, understood as Cohen understands it, is not after all a distinct
political ideal. It collapses back into the simple equality of welfare he wants
to abandon. If we are not responsible for the upshot of some of our "expensive" tastes, on the ground that we did not choose those tastes, then we are
not responsible for any of them, and the community is obliged, according to
his principle, to see that we suffer no comparative financial disadvantage in
virtue of any of them.

Cohen's argument is actually an argument for simple equality of welfare,
and that argument depends on drawing the chance/choice distinction differently from the way I do. My distinction tracks ordinary people's ethical

experience. Ordinary people, in their ordinary lives, take consequential responsibility for their own personalities. We know that when we make the decisions, grand and small, that will shape our lives, we must often struggle against or accommodate or submerge or otherwise come to terms with our inclinations, dispositions, habits, and raw desires, and that we must do this in the service of our judgments and convictions of various kinds, including moral convictions about what is fair to others and ethical judgments about what kind of life would be appropriate or successful for us. We do not think that we have chosen these various judgments and convictions from a menu of equally eligible alternatives, the way we might choose a shirt from a drawer or dishes from a menu. True, it is up to us what to read, or listen to, or whether to study or ponder, and for how long and in what circumstances. But it is not up to us what, having done what we have done in that way, we conclude. We nevertheless do not count the fact that we have reached some particular moral or ethical conclusion as a matter of good or bad luck. That would be to treat ourselves as dissociated from our personalities rather than identified with them—to treat ourselves as victims bombarded by random mental radiation. We think of ourselves differently—as moral and ethical agents who have struggled our way to the convictions we now find inescapable. It would strike us as bizarre for someone to say that he should be pitied, or compensated by his fellow citizens, because he had the bad luck to have decided that he should help his friends in need, or that Mozart is more intriguing than hip-hop, or that a life well lived includes foreign travel.

Philosophers who are drawn to the language of eighteenth-century psychology and twentieth-century economics refer to the great variety of human motives, simple and complex, crude and sophisticated, as "desires" or "preferences." Those terms suggest a sharp split between those motives, on the one hand, and reasoned judgment and conviction on the other. In fact, most of the motives that people cite, in explanation of behavior, are not the raw emotions that judgment confronts, but the consequence of that confrontation.[4] People's large-scale hopes for their lives—their ambitions—are plainly suffused with judgment. Someone who hopes to change the face of architecture, or to become president, or to help house more of the homeless, does not just desire but *values* that achievement. He would no doubt glow with satisfaction if his dreams were realized, but it is the importance of the achievement not the prospect of a glow that sustains his efforts, and the glow is explained by the achievement's importance to him not the other way around. Even most of what we might more naturally call "tastes" are soaked in judgment. Some are not; some really are just bad luck. The unfortunate man whose tap water tastes sour would prefer not to have that disability: his condition is a handicap, and equality of resources would regard it as such. But more complex tastes are interwoven with judgments of endorsement and approval. A passionate photographer, it is true, savors the technology and skill of his craft and the exhilaration of capturing light forever, and he might cite these sensations in explanation of his passion. But he savors these in some measure—often in large measure—because they fit so well with other, more general, opinions he has about the value of aesthetic judgment and response, technical mastery, visual insight, and a large variety of other pertinent values, and these more general opinions are in turn drawn from and play into a yet more general picture of the kind of life that is right, if not for everyone, at least for him. None of this need be (or often is) a matter of self-conscious assessment. But a network of interlocking and mutually reinforcing tastes, beliefs, and judgments is nevertheless at work in the photographer's psyche, and that network explains the revulsion he would feel if he were offered a pill that would drain away his interest in his art. It would seem just as bizarre for him to call his commitment bad luck as it would be for someone else to describe his loyalty to his friends that way.

III. Addicts and Us

It is hard to conceive how creatures otherwise like us would behave if they did treat their beliefs, convictions, tastes, judgments, and ambitions as lucky or unlucky accidents. But we should try to imagine such creatures, in hopes of better understanding the presuppositions of Cohen's argument. Imagine, then, a buzz addict whose sole aim is to create for himself a series of emotional highs or buzzes; experience teaches him, perhaps by trial and error, that he finds the buzz he craves in certain activities and events but not in others—in driving sleek cars fast or in learning that a homeless family has been housed, for example. He describes the activities and events that he finds to cause that buzz as his "preferences." He only means, by that description, that they serve that instrumental purpose, and he values his preferences only because and so far as they do serve him in that way.

His preferences are no more intrinsically valuable to him than the state of the organs of his body; indeed he thinks of them *as* states of his body, and he might find a medical analogy appropriate. It is a feature of his neural system, he might say, that he gets more pain relief from certain medications than from others, and just another feature of it that he gets more of the buzz he wants from certain activities than from others. Just as he has no independent preference for one form of medicine over another, apart from its impact on his pain, so he has no independent preference for one kind of experience or achievement over another, apart from its buzz-producing capacity. He knows that if his psychological and physiological constitution were different, so that he had different tastes and ambitions, these might be more efficient buzz-creating vehicles, either because any single act of satisfying the taste or advancing the ambition would produce a greater buzz, or because it would produce a comparable buzz so much more cheaply that he could afford more such acts and buzzes. He would prefer to have those preferences to his own, and he counts himself unlucky that they are not his. If he were offered an effective preference-changing pill, he would leap at the chance to take it, just as someone on a particular course of pain-relieving medicine would leap at the chance for cheaper or more effective drugs.

We can also imagine a similar though different creature: the tick addict. His driving aim is not a buzz but the satisfaction of getting whatever it is that he finds he wants. His mission is to tick off as many instances as possible of "desire satisfaction," as he calls these achievements and events. (He has, perhaps, a scale of achievement that awards him more tick-points when the desire is, as he puts it, a stronger one.) He finds that he has a variety of desires: he loves opera, for example, and is a fanatic about the conservation of great forests and beautiful old buildings. Like the buzz addict, he treats these desires as only instrumental: since these are, as it happens, what he wants, it is their satisfaction that is important to him. But it is a matter of critical indifference to him which desires these are: they are only contingent facts about the state of his neural system, and important only for that reason. He regards his present set of desires as advantages to the degree that they are easier to satisfy than other desires he might have had, and as disadvantages to the extent that they are harder to satisfy than others he can conceive. He can imagine desperately wanting to collect matchbook covers, for example, and is sorry that he does not, because he could easily become a champion at that activity. He, too, would take a pill to change the object of his desire from opera to matchbook covers if such a pill were available, and he, too, counts himself unlucky that, in the absence of such a pill, he finds himself stuck with the more expensive desire that he has. Try as he will to want to collect matchbook covers, he finds that he does not, and therefore that collecting them would not count, for him, as an incident of preference satisfaction.

These addicts (I am sorry to report) have played an important role in philosophy and economics, and still flourish in some of those quarters. It is therefore worth noticing that they would find Cohen's argument entirely compelling. It would indeed seem arbitrary to them to draw any important distinction, in calculating people's entitlement, between disabilities and handicaps, on the one hand, and tastes, convictions, and ambitions on the other. According to the addicts, tastes and ambitions that are relatively expensive to satisfy or fulfill *are* handicaps, and it makes no sense to treat them differently from other handicaps. You and I are different from addicts because almost everything that we would count as an ambition or a preference or even a taste is suffused, as I said, with judgments of independent value.[5] If you love jazz, it is jazz that you love, not some sensation that you happen to realize at a jazz concert but that you might hope to obtain in some different and perhaps less expensive way. If you want to help save a species or a building, that is what you want, not another desire-satisfaction notch on your belt. Of course you get a thrill from jazz, and you do feel a tingle when some bulldozer is turned away from its unwholesome work. But those sensations are predicated on judgments—that good jazz is wonderful, for example, and that saving certain buildings is desperately important.

The interconnections among tastes, preferences, ambitions, motives, convictions, and judgments of different sorts that distinguish us from addicts make it impossible for us to treat most of what the critics call tastes as handicaps. We cannot think that we would be better off if we gave up some ambition or no longer found satisfaction in what we now find deeply satisfying. On the contrary, it is our various tastes, convictions, and ambitions that define for us what a satisfying or gratifying life would be, and treating these as impediments to our realizing such a life would be incoherent. Resources and handicaps—including cravings and obsessions that we wish we did not have, and struggle to conquer or dispel—enable or limit us in their ability to do what we wish to do. Beliefs, convictions, ambitions, projects, and tastes of the ordinary kind—those that we do not struggle against or hope to eliminate but rather take satisfaction in—determine what it is that we wish to do. We enjoy or labor under the former. But we reason or feel or puzzle our way to the latter, and it is among the most basic of our ethical assumptions that the responsibility for such judgment is our own.

Cohen is not a buzz or a tick addict, so we must speculate about his enthusiasm for an argument that would appeal only to such addicts. He and others who make parallel arguments might have one of two reasons. They might take the radical view that our conventional personal ethics are founded on a serious philosophical mistake, that we ought to try *not* to take responsibility for our own convictions, but should instead think and act as the addicts do. But the critics make no argument to support that bizarre suggestion, and it is hard to imagine what argument they could make. They cannot appeal to any general psychological determinism, for two reasons: first, they themselves do not challenge our general freedom of choice in action, and, second, the conventional distinction we all make between circumstances and personality does not assume that we have chosen our personality, and so would not be undermined by any argument, no matter how general or metaphysical, that we could not have chosen it. Moreover, any argument that could hope to undermine the foundation of our sense of personal responsibility would have itself to be a moral or ethical argument: it would have to demonstrate some unappealing consequence of that foundation or otherwise give us some normative reason to abandon it, and it seems unlikely that any such argument would have the power to shake so fundamental a part of our ethical economy.[6] The critics could not just appeal to a supposed normative principle holding that people should never be held responsible, in any sense of responsibility, for what they have not deliberately chosen. That principle would be contradicted not only by our practice of taking consequential responsibility for our convictions, but by much else in ethical and moral experience besides, including, for example, the obligations and responsibilities most people believe they have toward their political community, their parents and their siblings.[7]

It is more likely that the critics' argument stands on an entirely different footing: that they assume that a political theory need not or should not track the familiar structure of our personal morality and ethics. Equality of resources does track that familiar structure; it carries it into politics intact. It proposes a politics that we can embrace as flowing from the rest of our convictions, a politics in which citizens can make and respond to claims of justice without switching to a special, made-for-politics morality. It allows us to cite, as disadvantages and handicaps, only what we treat in the same way in our own ethical life. The critics might prefer to see politics in a different light: as imposed from outside by external agents using an independent morality that may contradict what their subjects believe. Cohen, for example, says that although someone whose religion imposes strenuous burdens on his life would not regard his faith as a handicap or wish to lose it if he could, there is nevertheless no reason why "we," who do not accept his religion, could not treat it as a handicap, and compensate him for its extra costs.[8] "We" apparently refers to a political majority that adopts a system of redistribution whose premises would be rejected as abhorrent by those it is designed to benefit. But any such procedure seems incompatible with the basic presuppositions of partnership democracy, which insist that citizens be able to see themselves as joint authors of collective decisions.[9] In any case, on this explanation of their argument, the critics propose to override the personal ethics not just of a small minority but of everyone. They propose that we should all pretend, in politics, that we are addicts—that we should all act collectively in ways that we would find demeaning individually. There may be a reason for such collective self-degradation, but I do not know what it is.

We ordinary people, moreover, could not achieve the discontinuity between our personal ethics and our political morality that the critics, on this hypothesis, advise even if we wanted to. Since our preferences and ambitions are infused with judgments of value, and since, at least for most of us, these judgments include both ethical convictions about the shape of an overall successful life and moral judgments about the reasonableness, fairness, and justice of any particular assignment of resources, we could not separate ambition and judgment in the way that any scheme of justice defined in a welfare vocabulary requires. Addicts can neatly separate their single value—buzz or tick—from any knowledge or convictions they might have about either the foreseen or the proper distribution of resources. Their preferences reflect no independent value or judgment, but are simply neurological facts about what will produce a buzz in or a tick for them, and these preferences are therefore insensitive to the distribution of resources that they either expect or approve. If they prefer champagne and architecture to beer and construction work, they know that they will have less buzz or fewer ticks than if they had the opposite preference. But which of these preferences they have will not in any way depend on what level of wealth they predict they will enjoy, let alone on any judgments about what level of wealth it is appropriate for them to have. (They may, of course, have preferences on the latter score, and these may have causally affected the other preferences they have formed, but the latter will nevertheless have a neurological existence and life of their own.) Since their preferences are stable in that way, they can report these preferences to a committee or computer that can use those reports to calculate which distribution of resources would make preference satisfaction overall equal (or, what comes to the same thing, opportunity for preference satisfaction equal, or, if utilitarianism were back in fashion, would maximize total preference satisfaction overall). I am not suggesting that this ludicrous process would actually be feasible, even in a community of addicts.

But we real people cannot participate in any such exercise, even in our imagination, because almost all our preferences, including all the important ones, are soaked in judgments that make these preferences sensitive, to a vast degree, to assumptions about the wealth that we are likely to have. Whether I endorse—and therefore have—a particular ambition turns on my judgment about the consequences for the rest of my life of pursuing that ambition, and those consequences depend on the overall resources that I can predict, at least within an order of magnitude, will be available to me. I might, it is true, think some ambition so important that I am willing to pauperize myself just for a chance to realize it: that is what we like to think that great artists thought in their youth. But even that judgment requires some expectation of the degree of poverty I will suffer, and its consequences for other people who might be dependent on me. Since real people's expectations play into the formation of their tastes and ambitions in this way, it is not possible for them to form stable preferences in advance of distribution, and so not possible for them to tell the computer or committee what it needs to know. For many people, moreover, the connection between preference and resource has a moral dimension as well: they take justice to be at least a soft parameter of well-being, and so they must take a view not only about what resources they are likely to have available, but also about what resources they should have available, before their ambitions and preferences can be fixed in any stable way. So even if such people were themselves committed, as a matter of their own sense of justice, to welfare egalitarianism, they could not report their preferences until they knew what the calculations based on their and other people's preferences would produce, and so, like Zeno's arrow, the process could never begin its flight.

IV. People and Luck

Cohen has two other objections to equality of resources that do not depend, at least in his view, on any addictlike assumption that people's preferences and ambitions are matters of good or bad luck. He devotes several pages of an essay to the first of these, but I believe it rests on a misunderstanding. He says that equality of resources would not permit a community, in the name of equality, to make special provision for people who need expensive medicine to relieve pain that, while serious, does not disable them from pursuing their plans, or for people who, because they are particularly susceptible to cold, need expensive sweaters, or for people who suffer from enduring and serious (but somehow not disabling) depression or gloominess that spoils their lives but that they are unable to shake off.[10] Cohen's claim raises two separate questions. First, are people who suffer from these unfortunate conditions eligible in principle for compensation under the scheme described in Chapter 2? Second, if such a scheme were put into practice in the real world, would it be likely, as a practical matter, to provide compensation for those conditions? (I employ the same distinction later in this chapter, in considering Amartya Sen's objections to equality of resources.)

The answer to the first of these questions is plain enough. Almost everyone would agree that a decent life, whatever its other features, is one that is free from serious and enduring physical or mental pain or discomfort, and having a physical or mental infirmity or condition that makes pain or depression or discomfort inescapable without expensive medicine or clothing is therefore an evident and straightforward handicap. Someone with such an infirmity did not choose it; he would cure it if he could, and none of his beliefs, judgments, convictions, or commitments would argue against such a cure. A pain-producing infirmity is a canonical example of a lack of personal resources for which equality of resources would, in principle, provide compensation. The second question cannot be answered in the abstract. But if the pain that Cohen imagines were serious and, as he also imagines, medicine could relieve it, then a hypothetical insurance arrangement would almost certainly provide funds adequate to purchase that medicine. We would need to assume many more facts than Cohen provides to decide whether gloomy people or people who need heavier sweaters would have wished to secure insurance against these misfortunes at the premium that such insurance would cost. But, once again, if their situation was grave, and money would help, we might well think that they would have.[11]

Cohen's final objection to equality of resources is revealing in a different way. He says that even if people cannot sensibly claim that they have suffered bad luck in having the tastes and ambitions that they do, they can certainly claim that they have suffered bad luck when, in virtue of other people's competing tastes and ambitions, what they want is expensive. How much I can have of what I want does indeed depend on what others want. In some cases I can have more of what I want if others want the same thing, because the unit cost of manufacturing it will then be lower; in other cases people's like preferences will make what I want more expensive—in an auction room, for example. But the preferences of others (or the scarcity of certain objects or raw materials that governs how those preferences affect prices) are certainly not matters of either my choice or my judgment. They are matters, Cohen insists, of brute luck, and hence should call for compensation under even my own views.

This argument, if successful, would certainly undermine my claim that expensive tastes should not entitle anyone to extra resource. But it would also, on its own, sweep away Cohen's own distinction between equality of opportunity for welfare and plain equality of welfare. Even if we accepted his claim that some people, like Louis, have chosen their own champagne tastes, we would also have to concede that such people have not chosen that these tastes be expensive: They can sensibly complain that it is their bad luck that, in virtue of the scarcity of soil of the right kind and orientation, champagne is more expensive than beer. Indeed everyone, no matter how cheap his tastes and ambitions are to satisfy, can complain that it is his bad luck that other people's tastes, or the fortunes of supply and demand, are not such that his own tastes would be cheaper still.

The indiscriminate force of Cohen's new argument points to its flaw. Once again we should begin in ethics, reflecting again on how luck, choice, and judgment shape our personal sense of responsibility. We then see the error in supposing that other people's tastes and preferences are matters of the *kind* of luck that can relieve us of consequential responsibility for our acts or circumstances. The mix of personal ambitions, attitudes, and preferences that I find in my community, or the overall state of the world's resources, is not in itself either fair or unfair to me; on the contrary, that mix is among the facts that fix what it is fair or unfair for me to do or to have.[12] This is plain in politics: it would be absurd for me to claim unfairness or injustice in the fact that so few others share my tastes in civic architecture or my views on foreign policy that I am on the losing side of every vote on these matters. It is also plain in morality: I cannot avoid culpability by pointing to my bad luck that the victim of my theft lacked a preference—to give me what I stole—that would have made theft unnecessary. Other people's needs and opinions are not resources that can be justly or unjustly distributed among us: they are, to repeat, part of what we must take into account in judging what injustice is or what justice requires. They are, in the vocabulary of Chapter 6, parameters of justice.

V. Equality and Capability

Sen also rejects resource-based accounts of equality in favor of a conception written in the vocabulary of opportunity or capacity or (Sen's own term) capability. His objection to resource-based theories is not, however, as Cohen's is, that these take us too far from equality of welfare, but that they do not take us far enough from it. Sen says that philosophers who want to measure equality in resource terms—he names John Rawls and me—aim at the right thing, which is the personal freedom of individuals. "It is not unreasonable," he says, "to think of [their] moves as taking us *towards* freedom—away from attention being confined exclusively to evaluating achievement. If we aim at equality in the space of resources or of primary goods, this can be seen as moving the evaluative exercise towards the assessment of freedom away from that of achievement as such."[13]

But, according to Sen, these advances stop short of genuine equality of freedom because they ignore the crucial fact that different people have very different levels of ability actually to do what they want—they can achieve, in his vocabulary, different levels of "functioning"—with the same material resources. "But it must be recognized at the same time," he adds, "that equalizing ownership of resources or holdings of primary goods need not equalize the substantive freedoms enjoyed by different persons, since there can be significant variations in the *conversion* of resources and primary goods into freedoms." These variations may reflect "complex social issues," but they may also arise from "simple physical differences." "A poor person's . . . freedom from undernourishment," he writes, "would depend not only on her resources and primary goods . . . but also on her metabolic rates, gender, pregnancy, climatic environment, exposure to parasitic diseases, and so on. Of two persons with identical incomes and other primary goods and resources (as characterized in the Rawlsian or Dworkinian frameworks), one may be entirely free to avoid undernourishment and the other not at all free to achieve this."[14]

Sen believes that equal freedom would be more fully served by comparing not people's resources but their capability to engage in various functionings or activities. He appreciates the obvious difficulty. Different people rank different activities differently in order of importance. Some people think that a high level of intellectual or artistic achievement is more important than physical skill, for example, while others think the opposite. This is the difficulty that I said faces any version of equality of welfare: whatever conception of welfare is specified, any attempt to make people equal in welfare so specified would aim to make them equal in something they value very differently. Sen suggests that it might be possible to construct an objective ranking of activities, though he concedes that any such ranking must suffer from some indeterminacy. But, as I pointed out in Chapter 1, an objective ranking would be controversial, even one with a generous helping of indeterminacy, and basing distribution on such a ranking is not consistent with equal concern for all.

I shall set that objection aside for now, however, to consider, first, whether Sen's criticism of resource-based theories of equality is sound, and, second, whether his "equality of capabilities" really does provide, as he thinks, a genuine and attractive alternative to such theories. I shall not try to defend Rawls's version of resource-based distributive justice here, because, as has emerged at several points in this book, my own position is different in ways that might be thought to make his more vulnerable than mine to Sen's critique.[15] But Sen's criticism of my own account of equality is mysteriously misjudged. I have stressed, beginning in the earliest chapters of this book, that a person's resources include personal resources such as health and physical capacity as well as impersonal or transferable resources such as money, and that though different batteries of techniques are required to correct or mitigate inequalities in these two major domains of resource, both must command the attention of egalitarians. The hypothetical insurance auction for illness and physical handicaps described in Chapter 2 and illustrated in Chapter 8 aim, for example, at increasing the impersonal resources of those whose personal resources are in different ways impaired.

Sen does describe physical differences between people at a finer-grained level than I did in illustrating personal resources: he calls attention, for instance, to the possible importance of differences in people's metabolic rates. But it is important to distinguish between two questions in considering how far his greater level of detail marks a theoretical divergence. First, what kinds of differences between people should count, in principle, as justifying measures aimed at compensating for or mitigating those differences? Second, which differences are such that a feasible, real-world, scheme for improving equality would actually mitigate or compensate for them?

Sen's criticism is misguided at the first, theoretical, level. Metabolic rates are plainly personal resources, and equality of resources therefore counts them, in principle, as matters of egalitarian concern. The second question is more difficult to answer in the abstract. Whether any practical and justified scheme for seeking equality of resources would compensate people for an inefficient metabolic rate—by supplying them with extra food stamps, for example—must depend on a host of facts, including, most conspicuously, the gravity of the inefficiency. A redistributive scheme modeled on the hypothetical insurance market would compensate for any metabolic disorder that made particularly expensive or copious food necessary for survival. But it would not, I believe, fine-tune metabolic needs by awarding marginally more money for food to marginally larger people, for example, because the administrative costs of such a program would be disproportionately great. Sen does not himself propose any concrete and politically realizable scheme for instituting his conception of equality, however, and the tone of his discussion suggests that he takes his criticism to be theoretical rather than practical.

Is Sen's own positive conception of equality—equality of capabilities—really different from equality of resources? If it is, is it really different from equality of welfare? Consider this statement of his position:

> A person's achievement in this respect can be seen as the vector of his or her "functionings," consisting of beings and doings. The relevant functionings can vary from such elementary things as being adequately nourished, being in good health, avoiding escapable morbidity and premature mortality, etc., to more complex achievements such as being happy, having self-respect, taking part in the life of the community, and so on. The claim is that functionings are constitutive of a person's being, and an evaluation of well-being has to take the form of an assessment of these constituent elements. Closely related to the notion of functionings is that of the capability to function. It represents the various combinations of functionings (beings and doings) that the person can achieve. Capability . . . represents a person's freedom to choose from possible livings.[16]

This paragraph is most naturally read, I fear, as suggesting that people should be made as nearly equal as possible in their capacity to realize the "complex" achievements of happiness, self-respect, and a significant role in the life of the community. But it if is read in that way, then it advocates not something new, but only a form of equality of welfare—and a particularly chilling form at that. People vary in their capability for "happiness" for a thousand reasons, including their wealth, their personality, their ambitions, their sensitivity to the suffering of others, and their attitudes toward Milton's rival muses. Molière's misanthrope lacks the capacity for happiness of Voltaire's Pangloss. People vary in their capacity for "self-respect" for all those and countless other reasons, including their opinions about what kinds of lives justify self-respect. (Tolstoy's Ivan Ilych had a formidable capacity for self-respect for most of his life, but none at all close to its end, for example.) People's capacities for "taking part in the life of the community" or for attracting the high opinion or respect of other people in the community vary for most of these reasons, and for a vast additional dimension of reasons as well. Other people in my community also have tastes, convictions, standards, and attitudes; their opinion of me and my various convictions, and the degree to which they wish to make common cause with me, will reflect these. Of course, it is good when people are happy, think well of themselves, and are thought well of by others. The idea that people should be *equal* in their capacities to achieve these desirable states of affairs, however, is barely coherent and certainly bizarre—why would that be *good?*—and the idea that government should take steps to bring about that equality—can you imagine what steps those would be?—is frightening.

Why is all this not obvious? Because we know that what makes it impossible for most people to achieve happiness, self-respect, and a decent role in community life is a lack of resources—largely impersonal resources, including education, but also, in many cases, personal ones. So we are tempted to say that what we aim to achieve, by redistributing resources and creating opportunities, is an improvement in people's ability to secure these important goods. But there is nevertheless a danger in putting the matter that way—the danger of sliding into the fallacy of supposing that our ultimate political goal is not simply to make people equal in the resources they need to achieve happiness, self-respect, and like desiderata, which is an attractive and compelling goal, but to make them equal in their overall capacity to achieve these goals, whatever ambitions, projects, tastes, dispositions, convictions, and attitudes they might have, which is the false goal of equal welfare or well-being.

Fortunately, we have excellent reason to reject this "natural" reading of Sen's suggestion, because it is central to his purpose, as I said, to move even further from equality of welfare than he takes Rawls and me to have done, not closer to it. So we should adopt the following very different understanding of what he means. Government should strive to insure that any differences in the degree to which people are not equally capable of realizing happiness and the other "complex" achievements should be attributable to differences in their choices and personality and the choices and personality of other people, not to differences in the personal and impersonal resources they command. If we do understand equality of capabilities in that way, it is not an alternative to equality of resources but only that same ideal set out in a different vocabulary. Of course people want resources in order to improve their "capabilities" for "functionings"—that is, in order to improve their power to do what they want. But (on this reading of Sen's position) it is their personal and impersonal resources, not the happiness or well-being that they can achieve through their choices, that are matters of egalitarian concern. So Sen's efforts to achieve an objective ranking of "functionings" is not, after all, either necessary or helpful. It is enough to distribute impersonal resources equally, and find devices, like the hypothetical insurance market, to mitigate differences in personal resources so far as this is possible. Then we can allow people, through their choices against that more nearly equal background, to make their own rankings of "functionings" important to them.

Even if Sen's theory is only equality of resources in a different vocabulary, that vocabulary does italicize the point I just called obvious—that people want resources not simply to have them but to do something with them. That emphasis is an advantage, however, only so long as we are careful to make the further point I just labored: that the equality we seek is in personal and impersonal resources themselves, not in people's capacities to achieve welfare or well-being with those resources. The difference in these egalitarian goals is profound: it is the difference between a nation of equals and a nation of addicts.

II

PRACTICE

8

Justice and the High
Cost of Health

᠊ᛉ᠊

I

Everyone agrees that the United States now spends too much on health care. Medical services accounted for 14 percent of our gross domestic product in 1991—France and Germany spent 9 percent and Japan and Britain 8 percent—and economists predict that without reform medical expenses will grow to 18 percent by the year 2000. But how much should a nation like ours spend on its citizens' health? How do we know that other nations are not spending too little, rather than that we are spending too much?

Most people also agree that health care is unjustly distributed in America. Forty million Americans have grossly inadequate medical coverage or none at all, and many who now have adequate insurance will lose it, because they will lose their jobs or develop a disease or condition that makes them uninsurable. In all, without reform, a quarter of all Americans will be without health insurance for some period during the next five years. But how much health care should a decent society make available for everyone? We can't provide everyone with the medical care that the richest among us can buy for themselves. How do we decide what lesser level of health care justice demands even the poorest should have?

The health-care plan that President Clinton presented to Congress in 1993, but was never adopted, would have instituted a form of health-care rationing. It provided a basic package of health care that would be guaranteed to almost everyone. The plan specified some components of this basic package in considerable detail: the package included, for example, a comprehensive schedule of immunization for infants and children, routine screening and physical examinations at different intervals for different age groups,

and mammograms to detect breast cancer for women every two years starting at age fifty. The plan also specifically excluded some kinds of treatment
from the basic package altogether—most cosmetic surgery, for example.

The plan's most important rationing provision, however, was not detailed
but extremely abstract: it provided that medical treatment be part of the
basic package only if it was "necessary and appropriate," and it would have
created a National Health Board charged with the responsibility of determining what kinds of treatment were necessary and appropriate and in what
circumstances. That board would have had to decide, for example, whether
bone-marrow transplants or other experimental forms of treatment were
necessary and appropriate for particular diseases; it would have had to
determine whether most people could have such expensive procedures when
doctors told them that was their only chance, slim though it might be.

How should an agency charged with such a responsibility make such
decisions? When should expensive magnetic resonance imaging be provided
to those who cannot afford it on their own? Should speculative bowel and
liver transplants ever be provided? If so, to which patients suffering from
which diseases? If a nation cannot buy all the tests and treatment that its
citizens might want or need, how should it decide, as a nation, how much it
should spend, collectively and on each citizen?

Some critics deny that any such rationing of health care is really necessary: they argue that if the waste and greed in the American health-care
system were eliminated, we could save enough money to give men and
women all the medical treatment that could benefit them. But though administrative expenses account for a significant part of hospital costs,[1] and
American doctors' salaries are extremely large by other nations' standards,[2]
the greatest contribution to the rise in medical costs in recent decades has
been the availability of new, high-tech means of diagnosis like magnetic
resonance imaging and new and very expensive techniques like organ transplants and, on the horizon, monoclonal-antibody treatment for cancer.
America is not paying all that much more for the medicine it formerly
bought more cheaply; rather, it now has so much more medicine to buy.

Many politicians and some doctors say that much of the new technology
is "unnecessary" or "wasteful." They do not mean that it provides no benefit
at all. They mean that its benefit is too limited to justify its cost, and this is
an argument for rationing, not an argument that rationing is unnecessary.
There is an emerging consensus among doctors that routine mammograms
for women under fifty, which are expensive, do not save many women's lives.

But they do save some.[3] Heroic transplants that rarely work do work rarely. So we cannot defend the rationing decisions that any health-care plan would make as simply avoiding waste. We cannot avoid the question of justice: what is "appropriate" medical care depends on what it would be unfair to withhold on the grounds that it costs too much.

II

For millennia doctors have paid lip service, at least, to an ideal of justice in medicine which I shall call the rescue principle. It has two connected parts. The first holds that life and health are, as René Descartes put it, chief among all goods: everything else is of lesser importance and must be sacrificed for them. The second insists that health care must be distributed on grounds of equality: that even in a society in which wealth is very unequal and equality is otherwise scorned, no one must be denied the medical care he needs just because he is too poor to afford it. These are understandable, even noble, ideals. They are grounded in a shared human understanding of the horror of pain, and, beyond that, of the indispensability of life and health to everything else we do. The rescue principle is so ancient, so intuitively attractive, and so widely supported in political rhetoric that it might easily be thought to supply the right standard for answering questions about rationing.

In fact, however, the rescue principle is almost wholly useless for that purpose, and the assumption that it sets the proper standard for health-care reform has done more harm than good. The principle does offer an answer to the question of how much America should spend on health care overall: it says we should spend all we can until the next dollar would buy no gain in health or life expectancy at all. No sane society would try to meet that standard, any more than a sane person would organize his life on that principle. In past centuries, however, there was not so huge a gap between the rhetoric of the rescue principle and what it was medically possible for a community to do. But now that science has created so many vastly expensive forms of medical care, it is preposterous that a community should treat longer life as a good that it must provide at any cost—even one that would make the longer lives of its people lives barely worth living.

So the rescue principle's answer to the question of how much a society should spend on health care overall must be rejected as incredible. Once that answer is rejected, the principle has no second-best or fallback level of advice: it simply is silent. That is worse than unhelpful, because it encourages the idea that justice has nothing to say about how much a society should spend on health care, as against other goods, like education or controlling crime or material prosperity or the arts.

The rescue principle does have something helpful, though negative, to say about the other question of justice, which is how health care should be distributed. It says that if rationing is necessary, it should not be done, as it now largely is in the United States, on the basis of money. But we need more positive advice: What should the basis of rationing be? The egalitarian impulse of the principle suggests that medical care should be distributed according to need. But what does that mean—how is need to be measured? Does someone "need" an operation that might save his life but is highly unlikely to do so? Is someone's need for life-saving treatment affected by the quality his life would have if the treatment were successful? Does the age of the patient matter—does someone need or deserve treatment less at seventy than at a younger age? Why? How should we balance the need of many people for relief from pain or incapacity against the need of fewer people for life-saving care? At one point the procedures of an Oregon commission appointed to establish medical priorities ranked tooth-capping ahead of appendectomy, because so many teeth can be capped for the price of one operation. Why was that so clearly a mistake?

We need a different, more helpful statement of ideal justice in health care, and we should start by noticing one problem that seems to make reform mandatory. Why does America spend so much—so much more than other nations—on medicine? In large part because individual decisions about how much health care to buy are made by patient and doctor but paid for by a third party, the insurance company, so that those who make the decisions have no direct incentive to save money. Insurance premiums are tax-deductible, moreover, and an employer's contribution is not treated as part of the employee's taxable income. So health insurance makes patients insensitive to cost at the moment of decision, and the real price of that insurance is subsidized by the nation. People would probably spend less on their own or their family's care if they had to pay the actual cost themselves, at the expense of other goods and opportunities they might also want or want their families to have.

Of course, in the long run most people do pay the true costs of their health care, but they do so indirectly and unwisely, because employer contributions and tax funds could be used to buy what they would choose to have if they made the choice themselves: better schools for their children, for example, or economic investments and programs that would improve America's competitiveness and give them greater job security. Our medical expenditures are therefore irrational: the system makes choices for people that they would not make for themselves, and the result is that our collective expenditures are too high—measured, as they should be, by how much care we really want, taken together, at the price we really want to pay.

Conservative economists seize on this fact: they say we should create a free market in health care by removing all tax benefits and subsidies so that people can have only the care they can afford. While that is, of course, an unacceptable solution, it is important to see why. It is unacceptable for three reasons. First, wealth is so unfairly distributed in America that many people would be unable to buy any substantial health insurance at market rates. Second, most people have very inadequate information about health risks and medical technology; they do not know what the risk of breast cancer is before the age of fifty, for example, or how many years having routine mammography before that age would add to their life expectancy. Third, in an unregulated market, insurance companies would charge some people higher premium rates because they were greater health risks (as, indeed, many insurance companies now do) so that people with a poor health history, or who were members of ethnic groups particularly susceptible to certain diseases, or who lived in areas where the risk of violent injury was greater would be charged prohibitive rates.

This analysis points to a more satisfactory ideal of justice in health care—the "prudent insurance" ideal. We should allocate resources between health and other social needs, and between different patients who need treatment, by trying to imagine what health care would be like if it were left to a free and unsubsidized market, and if the three deficiencies I have just described were somehow corrected. So try to imagine that America is transformed in three ways. Suppose, first, that the distribution of wealth and income is as fair as it possibly can be. In my view, that means that the resources people can initially command, in making their decisions about education, work, and investment, are as nearly equal as possible; but you should imagine an economic distribution that is fair according to your own views, whatever these are. (I shall assume, however, that on your views, as on mine, the wealth of everyone in a fair society would be much closer to the average than is true in America now: the great extremes between rich and poor that mark our economic life now would have largely disappeared.)

Second, imagine that America has also changed so that all the information that might be called state-of-the-art knowledge about the value and cost and side effects of particular medical procedures—everything, in other words, that good doctors know—is generally known by the public at large as well. Third, imagine that no one—including insurance companies—has any information available about how likely any particular person is to contact any particular disease or to suffer any particular kind of accident. No one would be in a position to say, of himself or anyone else, that that person is more or less likely to contract sickle-cell anemia, or diabetes, or to be the victim of violence in the street, than anyone else.[4]

The changes I am asking readers to imagine are very great, but they are not, I think, beyond the reach of the imagination. Now suppose that health-care decisions in this transformed community are left simply to individual market decisions in as free a market as we can imagine, so that doctors and hospitals and drug companies are free to charge whatever they wish. Medical care is not provided by the government for anyone, nor are medical expenses or health-insurance premiums tax deductible. There is no need to subsidize medical care in any such way, because people have enough resources to buy, for themselves the medical care they decide is appropriate. What kind of health-care institutions would actually develop in such a community? Would most people join health maintenance organizations that provided care by staff doctors at a relatively inexpensive rate? Would any substantial number choose more-expensive insurance arrangements that allowed more freedom of choice in doctors or hospitals? Would the average plan or policy provide coverage for routine medical examinations or diagnostic screenings? What kind, how often, and at what age? How many plans or policies would provide, at appropriately high rates or premiums, experimental or very expensive or high-risk or low-expected-benefit procedures of different kinds? How much of its aggregate resources would the community devote to medical care through these various individual decisions?

It is impossible to answer these questions with any precision.[5] But we can nevertheless make two crucial claims about justice. First, whatever that transformed community actually spends on health care in the aggregate is the morally appropriate amount for it to spend: it could not be criticized, on grounds of justice, for spending either too much or too little. Second, however health care is distributed in that society is just for that society: justice would not require providing health care for anyone that he or his family had not purchased. These claims follow directly from an extremely appealing assumption: that a just distribution is one that well-informed people create for themselves by individual choices, provided that the economic system and the distribution of wealth in the community in which these choices are made are themselves just.[6]

These important conclusions help us to decide what health care we should aim to provide for everyone in our own, imperfect, and unjust community. We can speculate about what kind of medical care and insurance it would be prudent for most Americans to buy for themselves if the changes I imagined had really taken place; and we can use those speculations as guidelines in deciding what justice requires now—in deciding, for example, which medical tests and procedures the National Health Board should decide are "necessary and appropriate" if the Health Security Act is passed.

Consider a twenty-five-year-old with average wealth and prospects and state-of-the-art knowledge of medicine. Suppose he can choose from a wide variety of possible arrangements to provide for the health care he might want, under various contingencies, over the course of his life. What arrangements would it be prudent for him to make?[7] He might be tempted, initially, to buy insurance providing every form of treatment or care that might conceivably be beneficial for him under any circumstance. But he would soon realize that the cost of such wildly ambitious insurance would be prohibitive—he would have nothing left for anything else—and decide that prudence required a much less comprehensive insurance program.

Of course, what is prudent for someone depends on that person's own individual needs, tastes, personality, and preferences, but we can nevertheless make some judgments with confidence that they would fit the needs and preferences of most contemporary Americans. We can be confident, for example, about what medical insurance it would not be prudent for most people to buy, because some insurance would be a mistake no matter what happened in the future, including the worst outcome. It would be irrational for almost any twenty-five-year-old to insure himself as to provide for life-sustaining treatment if he falls into a persistent vegetative state, for example. The substantial sum he would have to spend in insurance premiums, year by year, to provide that coverage would be much better used in other ways to enhance his actual, conscious life. Even someone who lived only a few months after purchasing the insurance before he fell into a vegetative state would have made, in retrospect, a mistake, giving up resources that could have made his short remaining conscious life better in order to buy a longer unconscious state.

We can enlarge this claim to include dementia as well as unconsciousness: it would not be prudent, for almost anyone, to purchase insurance providing for expensive medical intervention, even of a life-saving character, after he entered the late stages of Alzheimer's disease or other form of irreversible dementia. The money spent on premiums for such insurance would have been better spent, no matter what happens, in making life before dementia more worthwhile. Of course, most prudent people would want to buy insurance to provide custodial care, in conditions of dignity and adequate comfort, if they became demented; providing for such care would be much less expensive than providing for life-saving treatment—for example renal dialysis or an organ transplant—if it were needed.[8]

Now consider a somewhat more controversial suggestion. In most developed countries, a major fraction of medical expense—over a quarter of Medicare payments in the United States, for example—is spent on people in the last six months of their lives. Of course, doctors do not always know whether a particular patient will die within a few months no matter how much is spent on his care. But in many cases, sadly, they do know that he will. Most young people on reflection would not think it prudent to buy insurance that could keep them alive, by expensive medical intervention, for four or five more months at the most if they had already lived into old age. They would think it wiser to spend what that insurance would cost on better health care earlier, or on education or training or investment that would provide greater benefit or more important security. Of course, most people would want to live those additional months if they did fall ill: most people want to remain alive as long as possible, provided they remain conscious and alert and the pain is not too great. But prudent people would nevertheless not want to guarantee those additional months at the cost of sacrifices in their earlier, vigorous life, although, once again, they would certainly want insurance to provide the much less expensive care that would keep them as comfortable and as free of pain as possible.

We can use these assumptions about what most people would think prudent for themselves, under fairer conditions than those we now have, as guides to the health care that justice demands everyone have now. If most prudent people would buy a certain level of medical coverage in a free market if they had average means—if nearly everyone would buy insurance covering ordinary medical care, hospitalization when necessary, prenatal and pediatric care, and regular checkups and other preventative medicine, for example—then the unfairness of our society is almost certainly the reason some people do not have such coverage now. A universal health-care system should make sure, in all justice, that everyone does have it.

On the other hand, if even under fair conditions very few prudent people would want to insure themselves to a much higher level of coverage—if, as I said, very few people would insure to provide life-saving care when demented, or heroic and expensive treatment that could prolong their lives only by a few months, for instance—then it is a disservice to justice to force everyone to have such insurance through a mandatory scheme. Of course, any judgment about what most prudent people would do is subject to exceptions: some people have special preferences and would make very different decisions from those that many other people would. Some people might think, even on reflection, that guaranteeing a few extra months of life at the end was worth great sacrifice earlier, for example.[9] But it seems fair to construct a mandatory coverage scheme on the basis of assumptions about what all but a small number of people would think appropriate, allowing those few who would be willing to spend more on special care to do so, if they can afford it, through supplemental insurance.

If we substituted the prudent insurance approach for the rescue principle as our abstract ideal of justice in health care, we would therefore accept certain limits on universal coverage, and we would accept these not as compromises with justice but as required by it. Expensive treatment for unconscious or demented or terminally ill patients would be relatively easy cases to decide if we adopted that approach. Other decisions would be more difficult to make, including, for example, heart-wrenching decisions about the care of babies born so deformed or diseased that they are unlikely to live more than a few weeks even with the most heroic and expensive medical intervention. A few years ago doctors in Philadelphia separated newborn Siamese twins who shared a single heart, though the operation would certainly kill one baby and give the other only a one-in-a-hundred chance of surviving for long, and though the total cost was estimated to be a million dollars. (The twins' parents had no medical insurance, but Indiana, where they lived, paid

$1,000 a day toward the cost, and the Philadelphia hospital absorbed the rest.) The chief surgeon justified the procedure by appealing to the rescue principle: "There has been a unanimous consensus," he said, "that if it is possible to save one life, then it is worth doing this."

But the different standard I am defending would probably have recommended against the operation. Suppose people of average wealth, when they marry, are offered the opportunity to buy one of two insurance policies: the first provides that if any of their children is born with a life-threatening defect, neonatal treatment will be covered only if it offers a reasonable (say, 25 percent) chance of success, and the second—much more expensive— provides that such treatment will be guaranteed even if it offers only the barest hope. Most potential parents would decide, I believe, that it would be better for them and their families to buy the first policy, and to use the premiums they would save each year to benefit their healthy children in other ways—to provide better routine medical care, or better housing, or better education, for example—even though they would be giving up the chance for a desperate gamble to save a defective child if they ever had one.

Any public body charged with overseeing the distribution of health care would have to decide what medical procedures are "necessary and appropriate" and thus should be part of a comprehensive package of benefits everyone is guaranteed. Some of these decisions would be particularly difficult: deciding when very expensive diagnostic techniques or experimental organ transplants with a low chance of success are appropriate, for example. Such decisions must of course be based on the best and latest medical evidence, and must constantly be reviewed as that evidence changes. But they, too, should be guided by the standard of individual prudence: Would it make sense for someone to insure himself when young to guarantee a vastly expensive blood test which would improve the diagnosis of a heart attack by a very small percentage of accuracy if he should ever have doubtful symptoms of cardiac disease? Or to provide a risky, expensive, and probably ineffective bowel and liver transplant if doctors decided it would give him a small chance to live?

The rescue principle insists that society provide such treatment whenever there is any chance, however remote, that it will save a life. The prudent insurance principle balances the anticipated value of medical treatment against other goods and risks: it supposes that people might think they lead better lives overall when they invest less in doubtful medicine and more in making life successful or enjoyable, or in protecting themselves against other risks, including economic ones, that might also blight their lives. An agency might well decide that while prudent people would provide their family with the prenatal and well-child care that so many Americans lack, and would insure against serious medical risks at all stages of their lives by providing tested and reasonably effective treatment should they need it, they would forgo heroic treatment of improbable value if they needed it in return for more certain benefits like education, housing, and economic security. If so, then justice demands that a universal health scheme not provide such treatment.

In summary, the prudent insurance test helps to answer both questions of justice I mentioned at the beginning: How much should America spend overall on its health care, and how should that health care be distributed among its citizens? The test asks what people would decide to spend on their own medical care, as individuals, if they were buying insurance under fair free-market conditions, and it insists, first, that we as a nation should spend what individuals would spend, collectively, under those conditions; and, second, that we should use that aggregate expenditure to make sure that all have now, as individuals, what they would have then.

Of course some of the decisions I have been discussing would be made differently by different people trying to apply the prudent insurance test. It is very important that any agency charged with those decisions should be made up of representatives of different groups that might be expected to make such judgments differently; it should have doctors and health-care specialists, of course, but it should also have ordinary people of various ages drawn from different parts of the country and, if possible, different ways of life. Such an agency could draw on the experience of countries with "single-payer" government-run health services which have had systematically to ration health care.

In Britain, for example, doctors in the national health system have been forced to allocate scarce resources like renal dialysis machines and organs for transplant, and they have worked out informal guidelines that take into account a potential recipient's age, general health, life quality, and prospects, as well as prospects for adequate care by family or friends. Though this supposed cost-benefit test is different from the prudent insurance test, the decisions doctors have made under the former presumably reflect their judgments, guided by experience, about the relative value of different kinds of treatment at different ages and in different circumstances, and these are also judgements that a prudent insurer would be required to make.

The prudent insurance test also makes plain why it is so important to consult public opinion before rationing decisions are made. Since rationing should reflect not just technical cost-benefit calculations but also the public's sense of priorities, consultation is essential. When Oregon sought to establish priorities in health care under Medicaid, it organized a series of "town meetings," and a "parliament" to discuss the matter, and though the meetings were criticized by some because they were attended by very few of the poor whose health care was being debated, the meetings were nevertheless valuable sources of information about what those who did participate thought would be prudent insurance decisions.

Still, no matter how much information an agency seeking to apply the prudent insurance test is able to gather, its results must be provisional, open to revision on the basis of further evidence of public preference as well as of medical technology and experience. Clinton's failed health-care plan would have allowed people covered by the plan to purchase supplemental health insurance at market prices, with no tax deduction or subsidy. That provision would have fitted the prudent insurance approach particularly well.[10] If, after an agency has established a basic coverage package, a very substantial number of people of average income buy supplemental insurance, in spite of its expense, the basic package should be expanded. If most men of average wealth bought supplemental coverage providing yearly prostate examinations beginning at a younger age than the basic package specified, for example, the prudent insurer test would require that the age specified in the basic package be lowered.

III

Clinton's health-care plan failed, and conventional political wisdom now holds that no health-care reform even approaching the scope of that plan will be adopted in the United States for at least a generation. If that is true, our national disgrace will continue: it is disgraceful that so prosperous a nation cannot guarantee even a decent minimum of medical care to all those over whom it exercises dominion. Clinton's plan was, in retrospect, too complex, in some respects ill judged, and in any case artlessly presented. But some of the plan's most forceful opponents argued, not just that the scheme was wrong in detail or even in design, but that it was rooted in the unacceptable "socialistic" idea that government should watch over people from cradle to grave rather than allow them to take responsibility for themselves.

If the argument of this chapter—and indeed of this book as a whole—is sound, then this objection is wholly misguided. A community that is committed to equality of resources, so that people can make their own decisions about what lives are best for them, enforces rather than subverts proper principles of individual responsibility. It does accept that the intervention of government is sometimes necessary to provide the circumstances in which it is fair to ask all citizens to take responsibility for their own lives. But it respects the personal judgments of need and value that citizens have actually made, or would be likely to make under appropriate conditions, in the exercise of this responsibility. That goal is at the heart of the resource conception of equality, and of the hypothetical insurance strategy it recommends. A health-care scheme constructed to respect the decisions of citizens as prudent insurers is indeed egalitarian. But it is the very opposite of paternalistic.

9

Justice, Insurance, and Luck

⚜

I. Introduction: Bad Day for Justice

The 1996 welfare reform act was a plain defeat for social justice.[1] The president had campaigned on the promise, among others, to "end welfare as we know it," and he insisted, in signing the act, that a radical revision of the long-standing federally financed welfare scheme was necessary. Though some of the more punitive provisions of this bill were regrettable, he said, the bill as a whole was the best that could be expected from the Republican Congress, and some reform was better than none at all.

Clinton's claim that the existing welfare scheme had failed and must be replaced by something else was unchallenged, even by those who urged him to veto the bill. But no one has made adequately clear what was wrong with the old federal programs, and what tests should be used to decide whether any proposed replacement is an improvement. In many ways the national debate about welfare reform was like the debate a few years earlier about health care. It was said that as a nation we spend far too much on welfare, just as it was said that we spend far too much on health. But that is mysterious as an independent claim: it makes little sense unless we are given some explanation of how much a nation *should* spend on its poor. Why should we think that we now spend too much rather than too little? It was also widely claimed that the existing welfare system had been abused, that unworthy people, who could support themselves, were instead supported by taxes extracted from hard-working people. That complaint was fueled by images of gloating scroungers taking taxis to the welfare office and of immoral teenagers having babies at the public expense because it beat working. Race dominated those images, as it does so much in our politics, and that is cause

320

for great suspicion that the claims of abuse were overblown. But of course there was, and is, abuse. That obvious fact is not in itself decisive that the old welfare programs were fundamentally wrong, however. Rather it raises mixed questions of legislative strategy and social justice. We want to avoid two evils: a welfare program so porous that it allows extensive abuse and one so stringent that it denies welfare to many people who need and deserve it. Which of these two evils is the worse? Can we design a welfare scheme that improves on past programs in both respects? If not, what balance should we seek?

The liberals who attacked the bill and pleaded with the president not to sign it conceded that there are grave problems in the existing structure. They disagreed with the conservatives only in thinking that the Reform Act went too far. But they have done little better than the conservatives in defending the answers they give to the questions just raised. They have not provided a standard for deciding, even roughly, how much a just society would spend on welfare for the poor, what form such welfare payments should take, or what conditions should be attached to them. Can we do better in defining a fair redistributive scheme?

We would have to confront and answer a variety of more specific questions, which we might divide into these categories.

Merit.   Who, in all justice, is entitled to public support? Is support owed— as some liberals still insist—to those who cannot find work they think fulfilling? What about someone who can find only distasteful work, or work of low status, or work that does not exploit or challenge his talents and training? Or someone who can find work but only at the cost of relinquishing the care of her children to others?

Level.   To how much support is someone who is entitled to support entitled? What the average person in employment makes? What the nation has defined as a minimum wage? What it has defined as the line of poverty? Something more or less? On what principle, other than political compromise, can these questions of level be answered?

Administration.   Suppose we have adequately distinguished the properties that entitle someone to welfare relief from those that disqualify him. How much should we spend deciding into which of these categories a particular welfare claimant falls, assuming that every dollar spent on these administrative decisions leaves less for actual welfare payments? Can we afford to define entitlements so as to capture the finest moral discriminations we might make? If not, how should we define them so as to achieve the right balance between administrative savings and individual justice? What procedures—what presumptions and allocations of burden of proof, for example—would a just society use to test whether a particular claimant is entitled to succeed?

Dependency.   In many cases, those who claim welfare are responsible for the care of others: infants and children, for example. Is it just to limit what such a claimant receives on grounds that his behavior has disqualified him, when the impact will be severe or catastrophic for his dependents? Conservatives say that government should not encourage teenagers to have children by supplying them with welfare assistance when they do. But can we accept a policy that punishes the babies that will inevitably still be born?

These are among the difficult questions that a useful account of social justice must acknowledge and try to address. It would be foolish to expect any philosophical theory to answer them in detail, and even more foolish to expect it to provide answers that everyone in the relevant political community would accept. Nevertheless we should try to provide a structure within which a public debate could usefully take place, a structure that both sets the terms of argument and provides limits to the range of answers that any side could in good faith take to be plausible.

II. The Strategic Problem

People's fates are determined by their choices and their circumstances. Their choices reflect their personality, which is itself a matter of two main ingredients: ambition and character. I mean ambition in a very broad sense. Someone's ambitions include all his tastes, preferences, and convictions as well as his overall plan of life: his ambitions furnish his reasons or motives for making one choice rather than another. Someone's character consists of those traits of personality that do not supply him with motives but that nevertheless affect his pursuit of his ambitions: these include his application, energy, industry, doggedness, and ability to work now for distant rewards, each of which might be, for anyone, a positive or negative quality. Someone's circumstances consist of his personal and his impersonal resources. His personal resources are his physical and mental health and ability—his general fitness and capacities, including his wealth-talent, that is, his innate capacity to produce goods or services that others will pay to have. His impersonal resources are those resources that can be reassigned from one person to another—his wealth and the other property he commands, and the opportunities provided him, under the reigning legal system, to use that property.

Distinctions of this sort are essential to our personal ethics, that is, to our own sense of how we should live and when we are living well or badly. We take responsibility for our choices in a variety of ways. When these choices are freely made, and not dictated or manipulated by others, we blame ourselves if we later decide that we should have chosen differently. We evaluate and criticize the ambitions out of which our choices are made. We try to reform or overcome those character traits that have led us to make choices we would prefer not to have made. Our circumstances are a different matter: It makes no sense to take responsibility for these unless they are the upshot of choices. On the contrary, if we are dissatisfied with our impersonal resources and do not blame ourselves for any choices that affected our share of these, it is natural for us to complain that others—often the officials of our political community—have been unjust to us. The distinction between choice and circumstances is not only familiar in first-person ethics but is essential to it. We might think ourselves persuaded, intellectually, of the philosophical thesis that people have no free will, and that we are no more causally responsible for our fate when it is the upshot of our choices than when it flows only from a handicap or from society's distribution of wealth. But we cannot lead a life out of that philosophical conviction. We cannot plan or judge our lives except by distinguishing what we must take responsibility for, because we chose it, and what we cannot take responsibility for because it was beyond our control.

We need one more distinction: between two types of theories of justice. Ethically sensitive (or "continuous") theories grow out of our internal lives because they base their judgments about the justice or injustice of any distribution of impersonal resources on assignments of responsibility drawn from ethics—assignments that distinguish between choice and circumstance in the way just described.[2] The theory of distributive justice that I have been defending in this book—equality of resources—is continuous. It aims to make people's impersonal resources sensitive to their choices but insensitive to their circumstances. Ethically insensitive ("discontinuous") political theories, on the other hand, deploy standards of just distribution that are special to politics and that do not reflect the distinctions and assignments of responsibility we make in leading our lives from the inside. A utilitarian theory of justice, for example, is discontinuous because it makes no room, at the ultimate level of assessment, for any distinction between choice and circumstance as causal determinants. If average welfare would be maximized by a welfare scheme that awarded everyone who is unemployed the same benefits, without regard to whether he is able to find work if he chooses, that scheme would be commended by a utilitarian political theory.

I argued, in Chapter 2 and elsewhere in this book, that we should insist on a continuous theory of justice that is drawn from and respects two main ethical principles. The first holds that, from the objective standpoint appropriate to the government of a political community, it is important that the lives of people go well, and it is equally important that each person's life go well. The second insists that nevertheless each person has a special responsibility for his own life, a responsibility that includes deciding what kind of life is appropriate to him, and how best to use his resources to secure it. Any society faithful to these two principles must adopt legal and institutional structures that reflect equal concern for everyone in the community, but it must also insist, out of respect for the second principle, that the fate of each must be sensitive to his own choices.

The distinction between choice and circumstances, however, is problematic in many ways. There are often formidable difficulties in deciding whether someone's failure to find employment at a decent wage is a consequence of his lack of wealth-talent or his lack of industry and application, for example. In some cases the difficulty is more than epistemic. Some traits of character may be so pronounced and disabling that they seem more like handicaps: indeed many of them—extreme indolence, for example—may be symptoms or consequences of mental disease. Most people's personal resources, on the other hand, are much affected by past choices and attitudes about health care, physical risks, education, and training. But such choices and attitudes are themselves much affected by unchosen domestic and cultural influences. These latter influences can, however, often be overcome, and though it seems preposterous to suppose, as some conservatives say they do, that hard work can rescue everyone no matter what his circumstances, it is equally obvious that hard work and dedication can help many who would be unemployable without it. These interactions pose a strategic problem for any continuous political theory. How, more precisely, should it draw the distinction between those influences on an agent's fate for which he must take responsibility and those whose influence the community has a responsibility to mitigate? How, in practice, is that distinction to be enforced?

III. The Conservative Arguments

We can distinguish two important arguments for eliminating or sharply reducing welfare payments to the unemployed. (I use "unemployed" to include those employed only part-time and at low wages involuntarily.) The first argument hopes to bypass the strategic problem jut described. It claims that people who make money in a market economy deserve to keep what they earn because wealth-talent is a kind of merit. The second accepts the strategic problem and insists on a particular solution. It holds that long-term unemployment is so dominantly the result of work-aversion or other negative traits of character that it is better for everyone, including the unemployed, simply to presume that all long-term unemployment is avoidable by self-help.

A. The Argument from Merit

Any continuous theory faces the strategic problem I described because such theories do not aim to reward people for their innate abilities, including their wealth-talent. High native talent, on that assumption, is good luck, not a matter of merit that deserves tribute. The first conservative argument—the argument from merit—challenges the assumption. It does not suppose that talent is chosen, but rather that it should be rewarded in spite of not being chosen. Conservatives who take that position—and many do, in at least an inarticulate way—insist that the wealth some people attract in virtue of their talent is as much deserved as what they earn by sheer industry and application.

We must be careful to distinguish that claim from others that are not now in point. In another culture it might be said, for example, that people with more wealth-talent are intrinsically more important people, that it matters more how their lives go, and that they should have more resources at their disposal for that reason. That position challenges a basic ethical principle of our culture, because it denies that everyone's life is of equal objective importance. The argument from merit, on the contrary, does not deny that proposition. It urges instead an independent ground of entitlement: government should maintain institutions that reward wealth-talent, not because those who have it are inherently more important but because they have some attribute worthy of praise.

The argument from merit is also different from another familiar argument: that people with wealth-talent deserve more because they contribute more to our collective wealth. That latter argument is not apposite when the question is the basic one of what economic structure a just society would create. Only some structures would encourage or even permit people with more of a certain talent to contribute more to overall wealth. If production was centrally directed, for example, as it has been in some socialist countries, then wealth-talents as I defined them—talents to produce what people actually want—might contribute very little to overall wealth. So the claim that wealth-talent produces wealth presupposes rather than argues for a particular economic structure—a market structure in which that claim is true. Of course, it might be argued on instrumental grounds—for example, on utilitarian grounds—that communities should have economic systems of that sort. But the claim that people with wealth-talent deserve more wealth would then play no part in the argument.

The present claim is that talent deserves reward in virtue of some intrinsic relationship between the two—that is, that people with wealth-talent deserve more wealth in the way that the fastest runner deserves to win the race. But the analogy is instructive against the claim. Races and other contests are designed to make a particular property a matter of desert: the relationship they create is not deep—we have no duty to organize races—but manufactured for and by the occasion. No one would have a right to anything, in virtue of having the property of speed over terrain, if races had never been invented. But the present claim about wealth-talent, if it is to be effective, must be a deep one: it must claim that people with the talent to produce what other people want are entitled to financial success—that they are entitled to an economic race that they will win. But when the claim is put that way, it does not seem possible to sustain it.

First, it does not follow from the fact that we ought to admire certain qualities of mind or taste or physical skill that the admiration should take a material form. A society that awarded inexpensive medals to its great scientists and artists would in no way be inferior to one that added a check to the medal. (Unless, perhaps, the social vocabulary of the community was such that only money could signal respect. In that case, however, the connection between the virtue and that particular reward would be contingent not intrinsic.)

Second, it is deeply implausible to suppose that wealth-talents, as such, are virtues, that is, qualities that ought to be admired. What counts as a wealth-talent is contingent in a hundred dimensions: Until recently, the ability to project a ball into a hoop from a distance ranked low among wealth-talents, and the qualities of mind that have made Bill Gates the richest person in the world were once dismissed as unattractive. True, some more durably admired qualities of mind are widely thought important in producing wealth, such as intelligence, courage, and that encompassing virtue, judgment. But these qualities themselves have dimensions, and which dimension will secure great wealth in a market economy and which only the admiration of selective friends is itself the slave of contingency. Luck is, anyway, by far the most important wealth-talent in the catalogue—being in the right place is often more important than being anything else at all—and though many of us do admire good luck, we know we shouldn't.

Even if wealth-talent were a virtue, finally, and even if virtue's reward should be cash, it would still be mysterious why the metric and vehicle of the reward should be a commercial market—why, that is, the right reward should be what the person with the virtue can earn before taxes. Why shouldn't it be the smaller but still ample reward that a CEO can earn after taxes that are used in part to reduce poverty? There is no such thing as a "natural" market: we use "market" to designate a range of economic mechanisms all of them regulated and therefore defined in some way. Government must regulate markets in some way, and the rental value of a particular corporate officer's "judgment" will be a function, among myriad other things, of whether laws discourage monopolies, regulate industries for safety and conservation, or restrict enterprise in other ways quite unconnected to welfare programs. If there is no canonical choice among these different "markets," how can it be clear that the reward appropriate to a financier's virtues must be determined free of redistributive taxes?

B. The Psychological Argument

The second conservative argument—the psychological argument—accepts the challenge of the strategic problem. It agrees that personality and circumstance interact. But it insists that personality is almost always the dominant factor, that people with pluck and stamina "make the most" of their native abilities and create decent lives for themselves and their families. Those without those qualities—the indolent or feckless among us—fail. It is a mistake to force the successful to bail out the failures, for two reasons. First, it is unfair that the ants of the community should be made to support the grasshoppers. Second, it is unwise, because it perpetuates a "culture of dependency." People find and show application when they have to, but not when it doesn't much matter if they don't. Ending welfare is good for the poor. It is "tough love" that will help them to "shape up" and allow them to lead lives of more dignity and self-respect by supporting themselves, through work, rather than slouching through life on other people's handouts. This conservative argument confronts the strategic problem by declaring a presumption that a lack of application—laziness, irresponsibility, or some other defect of character—is responsible for all long-term unemployment, and then suggesting, as a response to the problem, a policy of granting welfare benefits only to those people who can overwhelmingly rebut that presumption. The Welfare Act's decision to terminate all unemployment benefits after two years is a refinement of that policy.

The psychological argument rests, therefore, on a series of factual premises about the proportion of scroungers among welfare recipients and of predictive judgments about the motivational and behavioral consequences of welfare. It also relies on a judgment of controversial morality: that it is acceptable to deny welfare to those who really need it, however few they may be, in order to punish or coerce those who do not. Liberals respond mainly by challenging the premises and the predictions. But that liberal response suffers from two defects. It does not offer a competing welfare strategy, and it does nothing to reduce the troubling ambiguities of behavioral responsibility that I described. It only matches the conservative presumption with contrary presumptions of its own: it presumes that scroungers are few rather than many. Can we construct an alternate strategy that has more structure? A strategy that relies less on controversial psychological presumptions that are easy for opponents to dismiss, or on homilies about tolerating cheats for the sake of the worthy that are easy for opponents to resent? We might be tempted to turn to discontinuous theories of justice, because these make no fundamental use of the distinctions whose difficulties pose the strategic problem.

IV. Familiar Discontinuous Responses

A. *Utility*

A utilitarian analysis of the welfare problem asks which welfare scheme would manufacture most utility across the community, on some suitable conception of what utility is like—"happiness" or "people's having what they want," for example. I argued, in Chapter 1, that no suitable conception of utility can be found—that whatever appeal utilitarianism has depends on *not* specifying what utility means, since once any more detailed specification such as "happiness" or "success in one's aims" is chosen, it becomes plain that the goal of maximizing utility so defined, even when feasible, is unfair, because at least some people would not take utility so characterized as of dominant importance for their lives. Utilitarianism, once utility is specified, violates the second principle of ethical individualism.

Even if we leave the content of utility unspecified, however, utilitarianism seems particularly inappropriate as a model for welfare reform just because it is discontinuous: it fails to take behavior and choice into account in the way that both politics and fundamental fairness require. Perhaps overall utility would be improved by a scheme that allowed substantial benefits to people who chose not to work because they preferred leisure. A utilitarian would reply that a sophisticated utilitarian analysis could not reach that result, because any such policy would reduce the productive labor force of the community, lower its wealth, and therefore lower its average utility. But that reply is unsatisfactory, because it is not just contingently wrong to reward those who choose not to work with money taken in taxes from those who do work—it is not just wrong, that is, when we have reason to think that doing so will have some undesired social consequence. That policy is inherently wrong because it is unfair. It might well be, as a utilitarian might now claim, that we would not think it unfair to compensate the indolent unless we supposed, at least unconsciously, that rewarding them was bad for the overall utility of the community in the long run. But that reply confuses the source with the content of our convictions. So long as we do think that forced transfers from the ant to the grasshopper are inherently unfair, we cannot accept an explanation of why it is wrong that turns on a contingent economic prediction.

I just imagined that a utilitarian analysis might award too much compensation to the wrong people. It is far more likely that it would award too little to the right ones. For it is not only conceivable but plausible that the prosperity of the United States, and the average welfare of its citizens, would suffer if it were to institute an effective welfare program that provided a decent living for everyone who could not find work or who had children to care for. It is hard to construct any impressive argument to the contrary. Liberals insist that the long-term negative effects of neglecting the education of poor children, or of sustaining an underclass that might one day be driven to violence, outweigh the short-term benefits of improving present wealth even when measured on a utilitarian scale. But these predictions are hugely speculative. They appeal to us because we think that it would be unjust to deny many thousands of children a chance to make something of their lives, not vice versa.

B. The Difference Principle

John Rawls's difference principle declares that no inequality in primary goods is justified unless it improves the position of the economically worst-off group, and those who accept that principle may suppose that it offers a good response to the conservative claim. But there are serious difficulties in using the principle in that way. First, the concept of the worst-off group is too malleable to generate any detailed welfare scheme, because it is likely to make a considerable difference, in applying the difference principle to the welfare problem, how large a band at the bottom we select as making up that group. Measures that improve the prospects of the worst-off decile of the population, for example, may injure those of the lowest quintile, which will include many more low-paid workers, and also the prospects of the worst-off one percent—the severely handicapped and the permanently unemployable, for example—because a program designed only for them would presumably help them more. The difference principle, however, as least as commonly stated, offers no advice about where the ceiling defining the class should be drawn.

If we were to stipulate a percentile as defining the class, then the strategic problem I described would present no conceptual difficulties for the difference principle, because that principle is discontinuous. But, like utilitarianism, its discontinuous character prevents it from taking account of choice and conduct in the right way. Compare, for example, the following two welfare programs. Under the first only those who attempt to work receive welfare, but under the second everyone who does not work, for whatever reason, receives benefits. It might be that no group in the second program is as badly off as the stipulated worst-off group in the first one, in which case the difference principle would recommend the second program. It may be said, in reply, that this could not happen, because the worst-off group in any society would be better off if its economic system provided incentives to work for all who can work. But that is not necessarily true: it may be that some people (how many would depend on how the worst-off group is defined) would so strongly prefer idleness that they would be financially better off under a scheme that did not punish that choice.

The difference principle attends, moreover, only to the position of those who have fewest primary goods. It demands that their position be improved no matter what the consequences for those who will still have more. It seems unfair wholly to ignore the impact of a welfare scheme on people who are not in the worst-off group, however that is defined, but who nevertheless must struggle to secure a decent living for their families, and who unsurprisingly feel resentment when part of their hard-won wage is taken in taxes and paid over to those who do not work at all. The difference principle seems most appropriate in times of rising general expectations. It seems fair to use the steadily increasing wealth of the community, so far as possible, to help those whose prospects are particularly poor, when this means only a lessening in the slope of the increase in the resources of everyone else. But global capital mobility now threatens steadily to decrease the general level of wages throughout any prosperous community's nontechnical and nonmanagerial ranks. In these circumstances, it seems callous to say that the only people for whom a theory of justice has concern are those whose lives are the most damaged, even though others, who work as hard as they can, are also seriously injured. Rawls has never been able satisfactorily to explain why the members of his original position, ignorant of their own future status, would choose the difference principle out of their own self-interest, and the politics of the welfare problem show the practical shadow of that theoretical failure. Politicians who preach fairness to the "hard-working middle classes" are of course fishing for votes, but they are also giving voice to a widespread instinct of justice.

V. The Hypothetical Insurance Scheme

A. The Story

Ethically insensitive theories of justice are unhelpful in addressing a problem so connected to individual responsibility as welfare. Can we construct an ethically sensitive account of a just welfare scheme that does not rely as much on presumptions about causal responsibility as familiar liberal appeals do, and that does not rest on the unsurprisingly resented proposition that hard-working wage-earners should subsidize fraud in order to insure that the genuinely needy are supported? I begin with a utopian story.[3] Imagine the United States transformed in the following ways. Wealth and other opportunities have been fairly distributed as of some particular moment. Everyone is aware at that moment, however, of global competition, technological instability, increasing average age, and all the other factors that contribute to our own contemporary economic insecurity. Everyone is offered the opportunity to buy insurance providing a stipulated income if unemployed, or employed at a wage lower than that income, and such insurance is offered at community rates, that is, at the same premium for the same coverage package for everyone, because—this is the only nearly impossible assumption—everyone assumes that each person, including himself, is equally likely to lose his job. People make their individual insurance decisions prudently; that is, they decide whether to insure against low income, and what income to insure against not earning, in a way appropriate to their dominant hopes, fears, tastes, and values.

In a moment I will speculate about the shape of that imagined commercial market—about what sort of policies would be written, with what coverage and at what rates. But I want first to make an important claim about whatever distribution of wealth would result. No matter what happened, there would be no ground for objecting that undeserving people, who could work but didn't, or who could have trained themselves earlier or better but didn't, were unfairly capitalizing on the efforts of those who did work. For whatever benefits were received would be the upshot of market decisions of various kinds that reflected the impact of everyone's choices on everyone's opportunities. No one could object, for example, if a woman who had purchased insurance received a stipulated compensation if she chose to quit her job during pregnancy because that is what the policy she purchased provided. She would have paid a premium reflecting the cost of that option to others. True, insurance policies might be offered that would provide an opportunity for cheating: a policy might provide that an insurance recipient had an obligation to search for work, for example, and someone might lie about having done so. But though others would presumably condemn his behavior, they could not complain that the institutional arrangement that offered him that opportunity was unfair to them. If a policy that would provide greater protection against fraud had been overall profitable for the insurer, it would have offered that policy, at a lower premium, either in place of or in addition to the policies that the "cheaters" bought. If such a policy was not in fact profitable, an insurer who insisted on offering it would have had to make up his loss by charging more for other policies. It might be in everyone's interests, that is, that the detection system be porous.

So in these imagined circumstances no one could sensibly complain that the scheme was unfair to him because it compensated others. We can make that claim, moreover, without any assumptions about the distribution of causal influences—between choice and circumstance—on people's educational and employment opportunities, behavior, or success. No one would recover compensation unless he had made the decision to insure; if he had insured in a way that covered unemployment due to lack of technological skills, for example, no one could justly complain that he ought not to be compensated because his character had contributed to his not acquiring those skills. Of course, a mixture of ambition, character, and native resourcefulness might play an important role in someone's decision whether to insure. If someone decided not to purchase insurance he later regretted not buying, he might complain that his choice was influenced by a personality disorder over which he had no control, and that his society should therefore treat him as if he had bought the insurance. But that is not the complaint I am now considering: I am ruling out only the charge that the structure of the insurance market might be unfair to those who do not receive any payments.

Contemporary America is different from the America I just imagined in two crucial ways: wealth is not fairly distributed among us, and the antecedent risk of sustained unemployment is vastly greater in some parts of the population than in others. But we might nevertheless capitalize on the imaginary exercise by asking what unemployment insurance people with a representative mixture of the tastes and ambitions most Americans have (we need not assume that everyone who is representative has the same tastes and ambitions) would buy if they had the wealth that is average among us and were acting prudently. There is no single right answer, I agree, to hypothetical questions like that one. Which insurance opportunities people would be offered, and which of these they would take up, would depend on hosts of contingencies and market and personal decisions that we can sensibly imagine in different ways. But if we could construct a narrow range of unemployment insurance policies such that it is plausible to assume that almost every American who was acting rationally would buy a policy within that range, whatever other insurance he added to it, we could design the core structure of an eminently defensible welfare program based on that information.

If it is true that almost everyone would have bought unemployment insurance to a particular general level, in the imagined case, then we can confidently assume that some particular person's failure to do so in our world is attributable to circumstances—the circumstances that either make such insurance unavailable in our community or make it unaffordable for him. For the differences between our world and the imagined ones are unambiguously differences in people's circumstances—differences in wealth and in the educational and social opportunities that make one part of our community—one actuarial group—antecedently more likely to suffer an insured risk. So the general goal of equality of resources—that distribution should be sensitive to choice but not to circumstance—is satisfied by a welfare scheme that places people in the circumstances we assume they would have enjoyed had insurance been available to them on equal terms.

A scheme of welfare benefits generated in this way would have several other advantages over other proposed schemes. It would leave scope for the play of personal choice, the influence of character, and the attraction and utility of gambles. It would not (as more drastic egalitarian suggestions would) squeeze the differences out of persons or lives. It would not dampen initiative or flatten society or compromise any sensible conception of liberty.[4] It would only insist on what seems an undeniable tenet of fairness: that a society comes closer to treating people as equals when it adds, to the choices they have, choices they would have had were circumstances more nearly equal. It is, moreover, a realistic scheme. Since its calculations are modeled on hypothetical decisions of actual people choosing among various calls on their resources, those calculations would never require a community to spend more on welfare benefits than it should given its responsibilities to provide other services essential to its members' lives. Since income taxes used to finance those benefits would be modeled on assumed premiums in that market, those taxes would be both fair and feasible.

B. The Shape of the Market

So we should speculate about the shape of the unemployment insurance market in the imagined world. It might seem, at first blush, that a hypothetical insurance approach would justify (contrary to what I just said) a wholly unrealistic level of welfare, because rational people in the imagined world would pursue a "maximin" strategy—that is, a strategy that would set the floor of their prospects as high as possible. In fact, prudent people would not adopt that strategy. All insurance is, in one familiar sense, a bad buy: the premiums must cover the insurer's administration and profits as well as providing the fund out of which compensation is paid, and premiums must therefore substantially exceed expected return. That is particularly true in the case of unemployment insurance, which inevitably carries, as we shall see, a high "moral hazard"—the risk insurers run of fraud, including, for example, false claims about attempts to secure employment. Unemployment insurance makes sense, therefore, only when it protects, not just against having less wealth than one otherwise might, but against being in such a significantly worse position that it is worth a technically bad investment to avoid any chance of it. A maximin low-income policy is therefore imprudent for all except those (if any) for whom any drop from the specific sum it would guarantee would be both salient and grave.

It seems equally evident, however, that the consequences of protracted unemployment or extremely low income are sufficiently serious that most prudent people of average means would insure against those consequences to some degree: they would attempt to buy coverage that would at least enable them to sustain life with some dignity—provide food, decent shelter, and a minimum level of medical care for themselves and their family. Most nations now calculate that sustenance level, for various purposes, by defining a "poverty line," and we might assume that almost everyone who could afford the necessary premium would insure at least to the level of his community's poverty line. Could people afford such a policy in the imagined community? That depends on the state of its economy, but so long as employment remained the norm across the community as a whole, sustenance coverage would not require a major fraction of average income to purchase, and we can assume that most people would purchase it.

We now come, however, to more complex issues about the definition of the insured risk. How would popular policies define the covered risk of unemployment or low-wage employment? It would not, of course, be possible to insure against not having the job one wants: the premium for such insurance would presumably approach the coverage. On the contrary, any affordable policy would stipulate that the beneficiary attempt to mitigate his position by seeking employment. But how would that provision be framed and enforced? It would be possible, of course, for the claims adjusters simply to take people's word, and in certain communities that might well be efficient. But let us assume that in America an affordable policy would require more by way of claims review than that.

Now consider the following four insurance policies against unemployment. Each policy requires the claimant to seek employment, and under each policy benefits terminate if it is proved that he had been offered and declined a job. The *severe* policy provides, further, that coverage for each incident of unemployment ceases if the claimant has not secured a job in two years, whether or not he has been able to secure one, and that, in any case, no one may claim more than five years of benefit in the aggregate during his lifetime. The *generous* policy has no cutoff or other form of restriction beyond the provision that the claimant must seek and accept employment. The *optional-interventionist* policy provides no flat cutoff, but it does provide that the insurer may require the claimant to pursue job training, at its expense, while unemployed, and that he must take any job that it provides or finds for him, forfeiting compensation if he refuses a stipulated number of such offers. The *mandatory-interventionist* policy copies the optional- interventionist one but also provides that the insurer must provide training and use its best efforts to find jobs.

The severe policy could presumably be offered at the lowest premium of the four policies (assuming otherwise identical coverage) because it allows the insurer to economize in two important ways. First, since "scroungers" will in any case receive coverage for only two years, the insurer need spend less than it otherwise would on the expensive and uncertain process of identifying them. Second, some of those who remain without jobs for two years will not be scroungers, but people who lack the skills or training or luck to find work in an economically insecure environment. The insurer therefore saves by offering, in effect, much less than full coverage—it offers not insurance against unemployment, but insurance against a few incidents of short-term unemployment. So the severe policy would certainly be cheaper than the generous policy, and it might also—though this would depend on additional facts—be cheaper than either of the interventionist policies. But it would presumably also be very unappealing, in spite of its more attractive cost. People, we are assuming, would buy unemployment insurance at some low level—say, at the poverty line—not as a novel form of lottery, but because they are frightened of what they deem a catastrophe. They are driven to insure at that level not because insurance becomes a better buy in investment terms when the coverage is low, but because the risk of not having even that much is terrible, and they would therefore find a policy that does not eliminate the worst of the risk—long-term unemployment—very unattractive. We might therefore suppose that the severe policy would sell badly unless the alternatives were prohibitively expensive.

The generous policy would be much more attractive, of course. In common with other policies, it requires claimants to seek and accept work, but that does not in itself impair the coverage most people want. However, the generous policy would also be very costly. An insurer offering it would have to adopt stricter review procedures, and these, if effective, would be expensive. It might find itself managing an unwieldy claims bureaucracy. No matter how elaborate and expensive its review process, it would harbor some scroungers who were attracted to the policy exactly because it offered them a chance of a work-free life, and the less the insurer spent on claims examination and review, the greater its scrounging loss would be. If the other forms of policy were also offered, the generous policy would also suffer from adverse selection—the propensity of people to choose this policy only if they were would-be scroungers or fatally unskilled—and that would force the price of the policy still further up.

The optional-interventionist policy could not be more expensive than the generous one, because the insurer that offered the former would not provide or finance training or attempt to arrange jobs unless it was in its commercial interests to do so, that is, unless its expected savings from reduced payments exceeded the cost of those services. Since it seems likely now, and in the foreseeable future, that those savings would exceed the cost in the case of some claimants, and perhaps many of them, the optional-interventionist policy would be cheaper than the generous one. So if that policy were offered in the imagined community, it would drive the generous plan from the field. For most people—all but would-be scroungers—the interventionist features of the plan would themselves add to its value, because training might enable them to get a job paying much more than the covered level, and because many and probably most welfare claimants prefer to work, particularly at skilled jobs.

Whether the optional-interventionist policy would also be cheaper than the severe policy would depend on a complex calculation. Presumably some claimants under the severe policy who would receive compensation until its cutoff point was reached could find jobs before that point if training and job assistance were provided. The optional-interventionist policy would be cheaper than the severe one if the additional compensation that would have been paid to such claimants under the latter policy was in aggregate greater than the cost of the training and assistance program under the former. The longer the cutoff period under the severe policy, therefore, the more likely that the optional-interventionist policy would be cheaper, and, since that policy is otherwise much more attractive, that fact puts a limit on the length of cutoff a severe policy could propose. It follows that the only such policies in the market would be the least desirable and presumably least popular ones.

The mandatory-interventionist policy would be even more attractive for most people than the optional-interventionist one, because it promises an even greater chance at a better life. True, the mandatory version would be more expensive for insurers in the short term. But in the long term this equation would presumably change: over a generation, for example, barring economic catastrophe, an initially expensive training-and-jobs program could be expected to be cheaper for insurers than a de facto generous policy would be, and to approach the cost of an optional-interventionist package. So insurers might do well to offer a mandatory version of the policy stipulating long-term commitments, and this might prove more popular than the optional version even if somewhat more expensive.

C. Dependency

Women seeking unemployment insurance would be particularly anxious to secure sufficient coverage to care for dependent children, and would seek some exemption from any work or training requirement during the late stages of pregnancy and while their children were very young. But insurers would worry that the availability of such insurance would itself increase pregnancy among those with low income. This suspicion—that welfare is in good part responsible for increases in the number of teenage single parents—was one of the prime political forces behind the welfare "reform" that ended the federally sponsored Aid for Families with Dependent Children program and stipulated that states cannot compensate single parents for more than two years. Many politicians declare such stringency necessary to break the cycle of dependency that, they say, has made many teenagers indifferent to pregnancy and led some of them deliberately to seek it, as a means of leaving an unappealing home to establish an independent residence. But though the consequences of the "reform" are unlikely to include a significant drop in teenage pregnancy, they will almost certainly produce great harm to infant children, many of whom will be taken from their parents and put into foster-care programs.

If we follow the hypothetical insurance approach we have been exploring, and try to design a welfare scheme by asking what insurance people would buy in the imagined community, and if we restrict our attention to the insurance that people facing a risk of unemployment might buy for themselves, we will reach a depressing conclusion. Insurance policies written for potential parents, providing coverage sufficient for raising a family as well as maintaining themselves, would be likely to contain a provision denying such coverage to unmarried (or otherwise economically unqualified) parents, placing on them the risk of neglected or unsuccessful contraception. If we modeled welfare provision in our own society on that insurance, welfare would be denied to many single parents who now receive it. The hypothetical insurance approach seems, at least in this instance, to endorse the austere strategy of the recent legislation.

But that is a misunderstanding, because the hypothetical insurance approach is designed to serve the needs of an ethically sensitive theory of justice by making distribution sensitive to choice and conduct, and it must therefore not be used to condition distribution to one group—children—on the conduct of another—their parents. We must ask a different question: how much insurance would children buy, and on what terms, against being born to indigent and unemployed parents? We need not imagine fetuses negotiating insurance policies to try to answer that question. We can ask: How much insurance, at what terms, would prudent guardians buy on their behalf, on the understanding that premiums were to be paid later, on some long-delayed installment plan, by the children themselves? It seems plain that a prudent guardian would buy insurance to provide enough coverage to allow an infant to live with its own parents, and to receive enough medical care and education to survive and qualify for employment when appropriate. Insurers would approach the design of such a policy statistically, as they would any other form of health insurance, since they could not condition compensation on anyone's behavior without destroying the point of the insurance. They would be alive to the commercial importance of discouraging poor and unmarried women from becoming pregnant, however, and it would probably behoove them to set aside part of their profits for education campaigns, as insurers now do for information about smoking. They might also require, as a provision in the policy, that they be subordinated to an infant's legal rights against an absent parent: it might possibly act as some deterrence if insurance companies were to pursue absent fathers with paternity claims.

D. Summary

The hypothetical insurance approach attempts to bracket a range of welfare programs that a reasonable person or legislature might think required by the twin principles that people's lives are of equal importance and that each person has a responsibility to take control of his own life. The approach confirms a conviction that I believe a great many readers already have: that a welfare scheme with no cutoff, that either may or must provide training and job assistance, and that conditions compensation on good-faith endeavor to find employment, is preferable either to a more severe or a more generous program. If so, that is good news for the insurance approach and good news for that conviction, because each stands up for the other.

Several states have in fact been pursuing such welfare schemes, though only as special pilot programs under waivers granted by the federal government. But the provisions of the new Welfare Reform Act do not fall within the range licensed by the insurance approach. They are modeled on the severe policy, and that policy would be distinctly unpopular among prudent insurers. The provisions that terminate poor parents' welfare after two years, and so doom children to the bleakest poverty or to foster care, are particularly deplorable. The hypothetical insurance approach, as we just saw, would condemn those provisions, not so much for supplying the wrong answer, but for posing the wrong question.

VI. The Luck of the Draw

The conservative arguments I discussed earlier insist that the welfare schemes authorized by the hypothetical insurance device are too generous. We must now consider the deeper and more serious objection that, on the contrary, the device is too mean. Transfers modeled on hypothetical insurance will mitigate but by no means erase the inequality generated by unemployment, because no hypothetical prudent person would buy insurance that would guarantee him even the average wage of those in employment, let alone wages equal to those that the highest earners gather.

The hypothetical insurance device, the new objection complains, makes too much still depend on luck: Those born with less wealth-talent, or into a background where wealth-talent is less likely to be honed, will have fewer resources throughout their lives, even after they receive the benefits that the insurance device would justify. We need, according to this complaint, a more thorough and radical welfare program. We need, perhaps, a welfare program that would fully satisfy the "envy" test discussed in Chapter 2 by making the resources that equally industrious people command over their lives equal no matter what native talent they are born with.

There are a variety of conceptual difficulties in that last ambition, all described in Chapter 2, and the strategic problem we considered earlier in this chapter adds further difficulties, because any political program that aimed at making the income of the involuntarily unemployed equal to that of those who work would, in practice, inevitably and seriously violate the principle that distribution should be sensitive to choice. It is no more possible to erase all differences in wealth that derive from inequality in talent without also erasing some of those that derive from choice than it was for Shylock to take his pound of flesh without drawing a drop of blood. But we should set aside these serious conceptual and practical difficulties now, to focus on the underlying question of principle that the objection raises. Is the hypothetical insurance device defective because it undercompensates those who genuinely want work but are unable to find it? When I introduced that device, in Chapter 2, I did so with reservations: I said that egalitarians could defend at least as much compensation as the device would recommend, but that we might hope to be able to find a different analytical tool that would justify greater compensation. The objection we are now considering provides an opportunity to return to those reservations. How far were they justified?

The effect of the hypothetical insurance strategy is not to eliminate the consequences of brute bad luck—bad luck that flows not from a gamble deliberately taken but from life itself—but only to mitigate it to the degree and in the way that prudent insurance normally does. The strategy aims to put people in an equal position with respect to risk, rather than to negate risk altogether. Does that aim show equal concern for all citizens? Or does genuine equal concern require what I called, in Chapter 8, a "rescue" approach, which would require the community to provide any medical treatment, no matter how speculative or expensive, that increases, no matter how marginally, a patient's life expectancy. I pointed out that no community could actually keep that promise without crippling itself: it would have to spend so much on medical care that it would have nothing left with which it might try to make the lives of its members—the unlucky as well as lucky— good as well as long. It is harder to stipulate what the rescue approach would require by way of compensation not for illness but for unemployment, but it might be thought to require, for example, that anyone unemployed through no fault of his own should continue to receive his last wage in employment, adjusted from time to time for any inflation. The manifold costs to the community of that policy, and the damage it would inflict on the community's economy, would be very great.

The insurance approach reflects a very different understanding of how a community with equal concern for all treats risk. That different conception seems clearly superior to the rescue approach in some contexts. Imagine a disabling disease that is in no degree either genetic or class biased, and that strikes people randomly but only after the age of forty, and suppose a community in which wealth is distributed fairly and all citizens are below that age. The insurance approach requires the community to offer insurance against contracting the disease, at market rates, either privately through commercial insurers or publicly through a state program, so that citizens can decide for themselves whether to buy such insurance and at what level of coverage. That approach is ex ante better for everyone (except, perhaps, citizens who are imprudent) than a rescue approach, because it gives each the choice as to how much future protection he wishes as against how much sacrifice, in the form of insurance premiums, he is willing and deems it right to make now, rather than forcing on him a collective decision that no one would make for himself. That policy seems the ideal way, at least in these circumstances, to show equal concern for all, but it does require that the community limit its help to those who do later contract the disease to the coverage they purchased (except, perhaps, for paternalistic aid to the very imprudent). If the community were to switch to something closer to the rescue approach when the first victim fell ill, it would then in effect have imposed on everyone, for the future, an insurance regime vastly more expensive than its citizens deemed it wise and appropriate to buy for themselves.

Now imagine a different story: suppose that the disease is in fact genetically skewed—people with a certain genetic structure are much more likely to contract it—but that no one, including himself, knows that any particular citizen has the dangerous genes until after the disease strikes. Now we must distinguish between subjective and objective interests. It is still in everyone's subjective interests—his interests so far as he or anyone else knows—that the community choose the insurance rather than a rescue approach, but not (or at least not equally) in everyone's objective interests. Why, however, should that make a difference? Why should it matter *when* fate intervenes in our lives? There seems no difference, in the justice of the matter, whether bad luck falls on us a moment after the insurance decision is made or whether it has already fallen on us, unawares, at some earlier time. There are varieties of poker in which players bet on cards they have been dealt but have not seen, and these are no less fair than games in which they bet on cards to come. So the insurance approach still seems fair even when the story is changed in this way. The community treats people with equal concern when it allows them all to insure, on the same terms, and at the level of coverage each chooses, even when the bad luck against which they insure has already secretly struck.

Now change the story again: imagine now that the genetic information needed to predict who will develop the disease is easily available, so that everyone knows who the victims will be. Indeed, suppose that some of the victims have already developed the disease when the community first begins to consider what policy of compensation it will follow. There is now no possibility of an ordinary insurance market against the disease. Even if insurers offered policies on the same terms to everyone, only people who knew they were at risk would buy it, and insurers would go bankrupt unless they charged premiums so high that the insurance would be useless to future victims. But government can nevertheless follow the hypothetical insurance device: it can in that way transform the story so that it becomes, counterfactually, like the first two stories we considered. Government can pay those who contract the disease, or those who have already done so, in accordance with policies it seemed reasonable to assume most people would have bought in the first or second stories. Would the insurance approach, understood in that counterfactual way, be less appropriate—less a display of equal concern for everyone—in this case than in the others?

There are two pertinent differences between the first two stories and this third one. In the first two stories, government makes its initial decision to pursue an insurance approach rather than a rescue one when no citizen can complain that the opposite decision would be more in his favor; in the third story, on the other hand, some citizens can make that charge whenever government's initial decision is made. In the first two stories, moreover, individual citizens themselves decide whether to insure and for how much: the decision as to which risks are worth running is theirs. In the third story, however, government must make that decision, collectively, for everyone, and some victims may insist that they would have insured for more if they had had the chance to make the decision themselves.

The first of these two differences might seem the more important, but it is in fact illusory, because any political decision once made is constantly re-made. Once the first victim developed the disease, in the first story, it was open to the community to change its mind and to adopt the rescue policy on his behalf, and the community's decision not to do that, in the face of his then identifiable special needs, was a fresh decision needing a fresh justification. True, any victim in the first story would already have had the benefit of the insurance approach before he fell ill—he would have profited from the expenditures the community was able to make on education, job-producing capital investment, and the rest of what it could do because it was not setting money aside to finance the rescue approach. But that is also true in the third story, because even those who are doomed from birth nevertheless share the benefits of communal expenditures that would not have been made if a rescue approach had been established long ago. It may well be that a victim in the third story would have been better off, all things considered, if the rescue approach had been adopted, say, just before his birth. But that may also be true for a victim in the first story, as things turned out for him. Just as the difference in the moment of objective vulnerability makes no difference in what justice requires when we move from the first to the second story, so the difference in subjective vulnerability should make no difference in what justice requires when we move from the second to the third. The insurance approach makes sense only if we treat it as the standing policy of a community into which individuals enter: it insures them against bad luck even when they bring that bad luck into the world with themselves.

The other difference I mentioned—that in the third story citizens do not make the pertinent insurance decisions for themselves—is more important. It is a great strength of the insurance approach in the first two stories, as against the rescue one, that it allows people to make decisions about the relative importance of various risks for themselves, so that they can tailor their use of their own resources to their own judgments, ambitions, tastes, convictions, and commitments. That makes the insurance policy both more egalitarian and more liberal than the rescue policy in those two stories: the approach illustrates a central claim of this book by serving equality and liberty together. In the third story, however, it is not possible for people to make the judgment for themselves. The community must make it for them; it does so in a counterfactual spirit, attempting to recapitulate what they are likely to have decided for themselves if they did have that opportunity. In practice, however, that cannot be a matter of individualized psychology—

how could we decide what a particular individual who has carried knowledge of his vulnerability all his life would have decided about insurance if he had not had that knowledge?

A community that adopts the insurance understanding of equal concern must treat the counterfactual question as statistical rather than individualized. It must ask roughly what level of coverage against risks of the character in question would seem reasonable to the majority of people in the community, or to the average person, or something of that sort, given the likely premium structure and given most people's needs, tastes, and ambitions. Judgment is required to answer even so loose a question, of course, and different citizens and officials would answer it somewhat differently. But their answers would almost all fall within a certain range. The average person would insist on some insurance—enough to provide medicine that could reliably be expected to cure the disease or sharply mitigate its consequences, for example—but would not purchase a "rescue" policy that would provide coverage for highly speculative or marginal treatment, because the cost of a rescue policy would mean that his life would be crippled even if he never contracted the disease. Of course, no matter what counterfactual judgment the community makes about what an average person would have done, someone born with the disease or with a genetic propensity toward it might well believe that he would have bought more coverage than that even if he were ignorant of his affliction. But he could hardly argue that he would have bought anything approaching a rescue policy, and, given the impossibility of establishing what coverage less than that but greater than the supposed average coverage he would have bought, it seems fair enough to ask him to be satisfied with the latter.

The main subject of this chapter is not disease, however, but unemployment, and there is an important difference between the two topics. While it seems right to suppose that illness—even when it has a genetic base—is a matter of bad luck, that does not seem entirely right in the case of unemployment. Genetic luck does play a role in fixing how likely someone is to find a desirable job, since wealth-talents are in some measure, and perhaps in a large measure, innate. But class and prejudice are matters of injustice not luck, and they also play an important role in the distribution of jobs and income in modern democracies.

For the purpose of our analysis, however, we must try to separate these two factors—luck and injustice. If the central features of equality of resources were realized, then class would disappear, at least over time. If proper civil rights laws were enacted and enforced, the influence of prejudice on employment would wane—there is much less systematic discrimination against women and minorities in the workplace in the United States now, three decades after discrimination in employment was outlawed, than before that legislation. The objection to the insurance approach that we are now considering is broader, and would still be pertinent even if class and prejudice were no longer significant, for it would still be true that some citizens were unemployed, or employed at a relatively low wage, through no fault of their own but only because they lacked the pertinent talent or were not in the right place at the right time. That is their bad luck, and the argument we just outlined for an insurance rather than the rescue policy in the case of disease applies with equal force to unemployment for those reasons. The objection that we have been considering in this section—that the insurance approach fails to show equal concern—is understandable but wrong.

VII. Luck, Class, and Generation

I must now say something about why equality of resources would not generate class distinctions. For reasons we have already noticed, that conception of equality would not equalize citizens' impersonal resources over time. Some people will earn more than others through their choices for higher-paying jobs or for more work and less leisure, or through investment gambles that prosper rather than disappoint. The insurance device that we have been studying, moreover, aims to make people equal in their ex ante risk of bad luck, but not in their ex post circumstances once bad luck strikes. So as time passes some citizens will grow richer than others. Income taxes modeled on hypothetical insurance, and used to compensate the unemployed and others who have suffered from brute bad luck, will make differences in income and wealth much less striking than they are in the United States and other mature economies now. But nevertheless some citizens will accumulate more wealth than others, and if they are free to pass on their greater wealth to their children, either by gift during their lives or by bequest, the differences will tend to increase and to take on the familiar character of a class system.

What legitimate policy could prevent that? Many nations impose capital transfer taxes on gifts and bequests, and these have often been steep and highly progressive—in some cases approaching 100 percent at the margin of a wealthy decedent's estate—though the trend in many nations has been toward lower capital transfer taxes in recent years. But it is not immediately clear that these taxes are justified under equality of resources and, if they are, at what level. If income taxes modeled on hypothetical unemployment insurance have been enacted and are enforced, and if the proceeds of that taxation are redistributed to victims who could claim under that hypothetical insurance, then no citizen has an unjustly large income after taxes. If so, then citizens are morally free to spend their wealth as they wish—on expensive cars or art or travel, for example—without incurring further taxes. Why should they be unable to spend their wealth, free of further taxes, in one specific way—giving it away, while alive or after death—in accordance with their wishes?

We want to say: people may be taxed on what they give or leave to others because this one form of expenditure, unlike all others, produces injustice in the next generation. But we must take care to specify what that injustice is, and why an inheritance or other form of capital transfer tax is the right remedy for it. It is a ruling principle of equality, we have decided, that it is unjust when some people lead their lives with less wealth available to them, or in otherwise less favorable circumstances, than others, not through some choice or gamble of their own but through brute bad luck. It is bad luck to be born into a relatively poor family or a family that is selfish or spendthrift. We need not fantasize, to adopt that idea, that people enjoy some ghostly preexistence before they are conceived, and that some such speculative persons have the good fortune to be conceived by industrious, lucky, and generous parents while others the bad luck to be conceived by poor or unlucky or selfish ones. For we have been treating genetic structure as a matter of luck—the luck, good or bad, that people bring into the world with them—as we must if we accept the commonsense view that handicaps of various kinds are a misfortune. Luck, for purposes of our analysis, includes what might be thought to be matters of identity as well as accidents that happen once identity is fixed, and the situation and properties of one's parents or relatives are as much a matter of luck, in that sense, as one's own physical powers.

If inheritance is, for our purposes, a matter of luck, then we can justify inheritance and other capital transfer taxes in the now familiar way. In a more nearly equal world, people would be able to insure against bad inheritance luck as much as against bad genetic luck, and we may therefore justify such taxes, and fix the band of their acceptable levels, by constructing another hypothetical insurance market in which hypothetical people may all buy such insurance on equal terms. Just as we imagined guardians contracting for handicap and unemployment insurance on behalf of people yet to be born, so we can imagine guardians contracting for insurance against their charges' having the bad luck to be born to parents who can give or will leave them relatively little.

It is more difficult, however, to specify the properties of a hypothetical market in inheritance insurance. We should begin by asking why people would want such insurance and what considerations would affect how much they would be willing to pay for it. The harm such insurance protects against is, we might say, relative rather than absolute. We assume that people have decided how much health and unemployment insurance to buy: they have decided, let us assume, that it makes sense to provide for helpful but not speculative medical care, and for income, if unemployed, somewhat above the poverty line in their community. They have decided that further insurance to guarantee more medical care or a higher income would not be worth its premium cost. Inheritance insurance would make sense, therefore, to guarantee not a higher standard of living in absolute terms, but against the different and distinct harm of occupying a low tier in a class system— against, that is, a life in a community where others have much more money, and consequently more status and power, than they do and their children will. But it does not make sense for them to pay premiums out of current income to guard against that relative disadvantage, because, as I just said, they have already decided that spending more to guarantee a higher absolute income would be unwise.

We can now see why an inheritance tax, at a steeply progressive rate, seems a natural response to the problem: in this case we work back from the properties of a familiar tax to the structure of a hypothetical insurance market that would justify that tax to test whether that structure is plausible. We construct a hypothetical market in which no premiums are due until the insured dies or makes a voluntary gift, any premiums then due are measured by the assets given or bequeathed, and the premium rate rises steeply from zero in the case of modest gifts or a modest estate to a very high marginal proportion of very great wealth. That structure allows someone to insure with no premium impact on his own life, that is, no sacrifice in his goals or ambitions for himself and for those, including his spouse, for whom gifts or bequests are normally premium-free.

Of course most people care about their children's welfare, often more than they care about their own, and they want to save and even sacrifice, if necessary, for their children. But that motive is double-edged. It provides someone with some reason for not wanting the premiums on inheritance insurance, when these finally fall due, to exhaust all assets remaining at death. But it also provides a strong reason for insuring that they themselves will have a fairly equal start in their own lives, that they will not begin handicapped by their own parents' failure or bad luck in their desire to make a good life for themselves and therefore for their children as well. In any case, a steeply progressive premium schedule would assure them that their own work and success would benefit their children; the only sacrifice they would risk, by insuring at a high progressive premium, would be an inability to make their children very much richer than their contemporaries.

So the character of familiar inheritance taxes does suggest a hypothetical insurance market that is counterfactually plausible. The most plausible form of that market, moreover, in turn suggests the more concrete form that inheritance taxation should take: it suggests that inheritance taxes should be both progressive and at a high enough level to protect against economic stratification. That is, after all, the point of the insurance. In many countries inheritance taxes have decreased from historically high levels, and our analysis shows that this decrease, however popular politically, may well be unjust. Our exercise also suggests how government should spend the money raised from gift and inheritance taxation. It should not use those funds to pay for the medical and unemployment benefits that, on our analysis, it falls to income taxes to finance. Government should rather use the proceeds of inheritance tax for improved public education, education and training loans for would-be professionals, and other programs that ease the impact of whatever economic stratification remains after the tax has been levied.

VIII. Insurance and Utility

It remains to emphasize, as a caution against misunderstandings, that though the conception of equal concern developed in this chapter does emphasize the ex ante benefits of the insurance approach, it does not transform equality of resources into any form of welfarism, including utilitarianism. A community that followed the insurance approach to the various problems we have been discussing would indeed secure greater collective welfare, on any conception of welfare we might choose, than one that tried to follow a rescue approach. But the point of the strategy is fairness to individuals rather than any collective goal, and in the result is very unlikely to match what programs designed to maximize collective utility would recommend. A utilitarian would find it unreasonable to stipulate that taxes for redistribution should mimic an insurance market in which each individual is offered insurance at parallel rates. Differences in objective and subjective risk among actual people would be of prime importance in any utilitarian calculation, but of no importance for equal concern as we have now understood it.

10

Free Speech, Politics, and the Dimensions of Democracy

I. Introduction

American Politics at Century's End

Our politics are a disgrace, and money is the root of the problem. Our politicians need, raise, and spend more and more money in each election cycle. The candidate who has or raises the most money, as the 1998 midterm elections demonstrated once again, almost always wins. Officials begin raising money for the next election the day after the last one, and often put more time and industry into that task than into those for which they were elected. They spend the bulk of the campaign money they raise, moreover, on television ads that are often negative and nearly always inane, substituting slogans and jingles for argument.

The more money politicians need to be elected, the more they need rich contributors, and the more influence such contributors then have over their political decisions once elected. Federal law does limit how much individual citizens and groups can give to political campaigns. But new and larger loopholes make these limits less and less effective year by year. In recent years candidates and anxious donors have exploited the "soft money" loophole, which permits donors—not just individuals but corporations and unions, which are otherwise prohibited from making political contributions—to make unlimited donations to political parties or committees. The parties spend that money on "issue advocacy" media campaigns that do not technically, in explicit terms, urge a vote for or against any candidate, but praise or denounce candidates with uninhibited vigor, and often end by advising their audience to "tell" the denounced candidates to mend their ways. The "issue advocacy" device has eviscerated long-standing legal controls on political contributions. In the 1996 presidential election both major party candidates used that loophole to avoid not only the contribution limits but their legal obligation to observe voluntary spending limits on campaign expenditures in return for federal funding, and the *New York Times* called that election, for that reason, one of the most corrupt in American history.

The staff of the Federal Election Commission recommended that both the Clinton and Dole campaigns be forced to refund contributions, but the full commission refused to accept the staff's advice, and their decision helps to guarantee that the 2000 presidential election will see yet another major escalation of the "soft money" device. Would-be presidential candidates in both parties have established political action committees of their own so that corporations, unions, and rich private individuals can donate huge sums to run issue ads for them and against their primary or general election opponents.

Other democracies, appalled by the overweening importance of money in American elections, wonder why we do not simply place a ceiling, as they do, on the total amount that a candidate may legally spend in a particular election campaign. The most effective way to prevent money from dominating politics, and to prevent powerful corporations, unions, and other groups from receiving favors for contributions, is to lessen politicians' need for money, and the most effective way to do that is to limit what the politicians may spend. Congress did enact expenditure limits in 1974, following the Watergate scandals. But in less than two years, in *Buckley v. Valeo*,[1] the Supreme Court ruled that expenditure limits are unconstitutional because they violate the First Amendment of the United States Constitution, which provides that Congress shall "make no law" abridging the freedom of speech or association. Prohibiting a politician or anyone else from spending as much money as he wishes to express his political convictions and policies, the Court said, is restricting his freedom of speech. Regulating campaign expenditures would have raised many problems even if the Court had upheld spending limits. But the experience of the other democracies I just mentioned, which do severely limit election expenditures, shows that such limits are workable.

Many constitutional scholars (though by no means all) believe that the *Buckley* ruling striking down expenditure limits was a mistake, and they hope that it will be overruled. It is optimistic to suppose, however, that *Buckley* will be flatly overruled, as least for some time. It is more plausible to imagine that as conviction spreads that the decision was a mistake, it will be reinterpreted and narrowed so as to permit more regulation. It is nevertheless important to pause over the question whether and, if so, why *Buckley* was a mistake, because much of the criticism of the decision ignores the most powerful arguments in its favor. Until we identify those arguments we cannot understand why the decision, which seems so wrong to so many scholars and lawyers, seemed so right to the Supreme Court and to so many other scholars and lawyers who continue to defend it. In fact, the legal and political disagreement over *Buckley* is both deep and important, because whether we think the decision right or wrong depends on how we conceive the character of American democracy and the role of the First Amendment in defending and perfecting that democracy. Our answer to a philosophical question—what is the best conception of democracy?—is likely to be decisive of whether we endorse or reject not only campaign expenditure limits but other ways of regulating our electoral process.

The Argument to Come

The strongest case for *Buckley's* ruling that expenditure limits are unconstitutional depends on a popular strategic assumption about the best way to realize and protect democracy. I call this assumption (following the famous federal judge Learned Hand) the "democratic wager." It holds that democracy is best protected by a principle that forbids government to limit or control political speech in any way for the purpose of protecting democracy. So it forbids laws that attempt to make elections fairer by limiting what rich candidates or parties can spend. That principle may seem paradoxical: How can it improve democracy to prevent government from restricting political speech when government believes that the restriction will itself improve democracy? But the wager supposes that constraints on political speech are likely to harm democracy even when they are enacted with the intent, real or feigned, of improving it. That is what Hand called the bet "on which we have staked our all." So it adopts the prophylactic technique of forbidding government to attempt to make our political system more democratic through that device. Even though government may regulate and restrict speech for other reasons—to protect national security, for example, or private reputation—it cannot regulate or restrict it for that particular reason. As the Court said in *Buckley*, in as explicit a statement of the democratic wager as any in the legal record, restricting "the speech of some elements of our society in order to enhance the relative voice of others is wholly foreign to the First Amendment."

If we accept the democratic wager, then we must acknowledge that very strong argument for the *Buckley* ruling. Should we accept it? Perhaps we should if we conceive democracy, as many political theorists have, only as a political arrangement designed to enforce the will of the majority. But if we reject that majoritarian conception of democracy, in favor of a more ambitious one that understands democracy as a partnership in collective self-government in which all citizens are given the opportunity to be active and equal partners, then we should reject it. We should adopt instead a finer-grained and more discriminating, though still rigorous, test for deciding when government should be permitted to regulate political speech in the interests of democracy. That test would permit reasonable expenditure limits on political campaigns; it would make plain why *Buckley* was wrong in principle and should now be overruled.

I am not supposing that freedom of speech has only instrumental value, that it is nothing but a means to a more important end. On the contrary, that freedom is in itself a fundamental human right. Free speech and democracy are connected not instrumentally but in a deeper way, because the dignity that freedom of speech protects is an essential component of democracy rightly conceived. We cannot hope fully to understand either free speech or democracy, or properly to interpret the First Amendment as part of the Constitution as a whole, unless we interpret those values together, trying to understand the role each plays in a full account of the other.[2] The assumption that the two ideas are bound together in that way is itself part of American constitutional practice: We treat the Constitution as constructing a distinctive form of democracy, and we assess the First Amendment as both contributing to and helping to define that form. Of course, free speech serves other purposes as well. Many people suppose, as John Stuart Mill did, that a society that adopts the free-market strategy will be more effective in discovering truth, for example, than a society that rejects or qualifies it. But it is the connection between free speech and democracy that has been the nerve of First Amendment jurisprudence.

I shall try to mitigate the abstraction of this jurisprudential discussion in two ways. First, I shall describe, at the outset, the general form of various proposals that critics have made for reforming American election law. The proposals can serve as both illustrations and tests of principles I discuss, and at the end, we can consider how we might evaluate these proposals if *Buckley* were no longer an obstacle to their implementation. Although Congress is unlikely to enact any of these proposals in the present political climate, it will be revealing to examine how the choice among the different conceptions of democracy that I shall describe affects the desirability, in principle, of reforms of these different kinds. Second, in the discussion to come we need to ask not merely which conception of democracy, and of the role of free speech in protecting democracy, is superior as a matter of abstract political morality, but which conception and role offers a better interpretation of American constitutional and legal practice. So I shall illustrate and refine the theoretical claims by attempting to interpret selected Supreme Court decisions, including *Buckley*, in their light.

II. Proposed Reforms

Familiar proposals for reform can be grouped under four headings.

1. *Expenditure caps.* Overall expenditures by parties and candidates should be limited to stipulated sums during each election period. The expenditure ceiling must be generous enough to enable little-known candidates and parties to bring themselves and their positions to the public's attention, but low enough that candidates and parties without access to enormous funds are not driven from the field.
2. *Contributions and coordinated expenditures.* Individuals should continue to be limited in their contributions to political campaigns and parties, and expenditures that are coordinated with a particular candidate's campaign must count against that limit. Coordination is defined, for this purpose, to include any consultation with or solicitation of advice from a candidate's advertising, polling, and strategic organizations, as well as other parts of the campaign staff. The "soft money" loophole should be eliminated.
3. *Independent expenditures.* Individuals and PACs should of course continue to be free to spend their own funds on political advocacy. But during an election period, each individual's expenditure on advocacy that mentions a political party or a candidate for national office should be subject to a further and distinct limit. Such expenditures made during an election period by an advocacy committee or group to which an individual has contributed should be charged, to the extent of that contribution, to that individual's overall limit.
4. *Conditional public funding for political broadcasts.* Generous public campaign funds should be made available to candidates and parties, but only to those who agree not to run, during the election period, ordinary

campaign commercials—the short advertisements run in breaks in regular programming on radio or television that have become a staple of our elections. Those who accept such funds would be free to run longer, more substantive political broadcasts on behalf of a candidate or party during that period. Such political broadcasts would be free-standing programs not broadcast in commercial slots within other broadcasts, of at least three minutes' duration, in which a candidate or officer in a political party speaks to camera or microphone for the bulk of the broadcast. Such funds should be offered, subject to that condition, equally to the major parties, and to other parties in a proportion fixed by evidence of public support.

The first three proposals directly address the role of money in our elections by imposing limits on campaign expenditures and contributions. The fourth proposal goes further, imposing conditions designed to affect the form of electronic media politics. It draws a line between some media of expression—television and radio—and the rest, and it aims not just to reduce the impact of money on elections overall, but to improve the character and quality of the political debate by eliminating sound-bite political commercials. The fourth proposal is therefore more troublesome than the first three, because the First Amendment is particularly hostile to efforts to regulate the content of political speech, and encouraging politicians to substitute substantive argument for sound-bites might be considered an attempt to regulate content. Though expenditure caps do limit the quantity of political speech, they are nevertheless neutral as to the form of the political messages that the permitted expenditures may be used to publish. The conditions imposed in the last proposal are not neutral in that sense. They pick out electronic media for special restriction—not through flat prohibition, to be sure, but as a condition on a public grant—and the restriction is designed to affect the form of political speech by making it more argumentative, though not to discriminate in favor of or against any particular political party or position or conviction. The last proposal raises First Amendment issues that might well be thought grave even if *Buckley* were overruled.

III. What Is Democracy?

Democracy is extraordinarily popular now, around the world. But people disagree about what democracy is. When these disagreements cross cultures, they are often formidable: Some leaders claim, for example, that a one-party state with only state-controlled press and media, whose elections are formalities, comes closest to realizing the democratic ideal. Even within the mature Western democracies the disagreements are considerable. Some Americans believe that judicial review of legislation by courts, which have the power to declare such legislation unconstitutional, undermines democracy; others hold that judicial review helps to perfect it. Americans and Europeans disagree about whether proportional representation or federalism or voter initiatives of various kinds, make representative government more or less democratic.

The near universal agreement that democracy is the only acceptable form of government hides deeper disagreements of that character. Many of the disagreements among constitutional lawyers about the proper understanding of the First Amendment, including the argument about the constitutionality of campaign expenditure limits, are best explained as consequences of these more general disagreements about democracy. Of course, few lawyers have formulated an explicit conception of democracy; they rely on an intuitive sense of what democracy is. But some of these intuitive understandings are strikingly different from others.

Democracy, we all say, means government by the people rather than by some family or class or some tyrant or general. But "government by the people" can be understood in two radically different ways. On one view—the "majoritarian" conception—it means government by the largest number of the people. On this majoritarian view, the democratic ideal lies in a match between political decision and the will of the majority or plurality of opinion. We can construct different versions of that general account of democracy. One is a populist version: A state is democratic, according to that version, to the degree to which government enacts the law or pursues the policy that is actually favored by the largest number of citizens at the time. A more sophisticated version of the majoritarian conception, however, insists that the majority's opinion does not count as its will unless citizens have had an adequate opportunity to become informed and to deliberate about the issues. A state is democratic, on that more sophisticated account, when its institutions give citizens that opportunity, and then allow a majority of citizens to select the officials whose policies match their will. That sophisticated account is plainly more attractive than the populist one, and I shall have the sophisticated account in mind when I refer, in the rest of this chapter, to the majoritarian conception of democracy.

I shall call the rival, very different, conception of democracy the "partnership" conception. According to the partnership conception, government by "the people" means government by *all* the people, acting together as full and equal partners in a collective enterprise of self-government. This is a more abstract and problematic conception than the majoritarian one, and, as we shall see, it is more difficult to state crisply what it takes to be the democratic ideal. But we should note, immediately, one fundamental and relevant difference between the majoritarian and partnership conceptions of democracy.

Citizens play two main roles in a mature democracy. They are, first, the judges of political contests whose verdicts, expressed in formal elections or in referenda or other forms of direct legislation, are normally decisive. "Public opinion" means the relevant opinions of citizens acting in this capacity. Citizens are also, however, participants in the political contests they judge: they are candidates and supporters whose actions help, in different ways, to shape public opinion and to fix how the rest of the citizens vote. The majoritarian conception of democracy pays exclusive attention to the first of these roles. It insists, in the more sophisticated version I described, that, so far as this is feasible, the informed and reflective opinions of the largest number should be decisive of who is elected to government and of what government once elected does. But it says nothing further about the role that individual citizens and groups must be allowed to play in shaping the opinions of others. The partnership conception recognizes both roles, because it supposes that in a true democracy citizens must play a part, as equal partners in a collective enterprise, in shaping as well as constituting the public's opinion.

IV. Democracy and Free Speech

A. Free Speech and the Majoritarian Ideal

Free speech plays an evident role in the majoritarian conception. That understanding of democracy requires that citizens be given an opportunity to inform themselves as fully as possible and to deliberate, individually and collectively, about their choices, and it is a compelling strategic judgment that the best way to provide that opportunity is to permit anyone who wishes to address the public to do so, in whatever way and at whatever length he wishes, no matter how unpopular or unworthy the government or other citizens deem his message to be. Of course, that strategy cannot be absolute. Free speech must sometimes yield to other values, including security and, perhaps, a private interest in reputation. In such cases, laws forbidding or regulating speech may have the incidental result of influencing the public's verdict on officials or their policies. But this is a regrettable side effect of constraints adopted for reasons quite independent of that effect.

Regulations that are intended to improve democracy, however, like the various proposals for electoral reform that I described earlier, deliberately aim at changing public opinion in some way. They do not aim that the public reach a different overall verdict in any particular election. But since they attack what they take to be defects in the formation of public opinion, they do aim that the content of public opinion be different from what it would otherwise have been. Reformers want to limit campaign spending, for example, because they think that rich candidates and groups now have too much power to mold public opinion their way. They therefore assume that limiting what the rich can spend would make a difference in what at least some members of the public come to believe or want. Such limits would not, perhaps, favor one party or one political perspective: They might well be, in the language of constitutional lawyers, viewpoint neutral. But they would certainly alter public opinion. That is, after all, their point. So the proposals raise the following question for the majoritarian model: Is it consistent with that conception of democracy to permit legal restrictions that decrease the overall volume of electoral speech when such restrictions have, as their goal, that public opinion be different from what it would be without such restrictions?

The majoritarian conception tests any proposed electoral structure by asking whether that structure reveals what a majority of citizens would choose after the fullest possible opportunity for information and reflection. If we are to make that test workable, however, we need to specify more precisely what conditions provide that fullest possible opportunity. What structure of public debate and argument would be ideal for that purpose? How close does any particular structure come to meeting that ideal?

We might consider a result-oriented answer: Ideal conditions, we might say, are those that make it most probable that citizens will vote in accordance with their "true" or "authentic" interests. We can make some sense of this suggestion if we limit our concern to citizens' narrow economic interests. We might think that certain tax or other economic policies would actually work against the economic interests of most citizens, for example, even though we know that politicians with enough money to spend on advertising might persuade them of the contrary, and we might intelligibly consider which forms of electoral regulation would best guard against such deception. It is hard to predict what such a result-oriented study might indicate. We might decide, for example, that a scheme that gave all parties and candidates equal time to argue their case would give citizens the best chance of reaching the right conclusions. Or we might reach some more surprising and unattractive conclusion—for instance, that a scheme that disqualified rich candidates from speaking at all would provide the best protection. We need not pursue these possibilities, however, because in any case a result-oriented strategy could not take account of the interests and convictions citizens have beyond their own narrow economic self-interest—it could not take account of their convictions about economic justice, or foreign policy, or abortion, for instance. For it makes no sense to think that there is an underlying fact of the matter about what a particular citizen's "true" or "authentic" political or social or moral convictions are, a fact that can be determined without his answering a question or voting. Since any such poll or vote must take place after a particular, even if minimal, public discussion, we cannot establish which structure of discussion is most likely to produce "true" answers without begging the question in favor of some such structure.

So we need a different strategy for refining the test the majoritarian conception deploys, and we must seek this in some combination of two areas: first, assumptions about the conditions of good reasoning generally and, second, assumptions that underlie the majoritarian conception of democracy itself. We know from experience, first, that certain intellectual practices and environments are more likely than others to produce good reasoning about a wide variety of matters. Scientists, historians, and people facing practical decisions all do better, for example, when they base their conclusions on a wide rather than a restricted set of pertinent data, and when they have reflected on and tested these conclusions over time rather than settling on them precipitously. We have no reason not to assume that these general conditions of good reasoning apply to political judgments as well as to everything else. So the majoritarian conception can endorse any government intervention in the political process—subsidies for publicizing underfinanced or unpopular opinions, for example—that provides the public with access to information, argument, or appeal that it would not otherwise have.

It might seem tempting to use a similar argument in favor of expenditure limits: We might argue that the public will reason better if it hears no more from one side than from any other. But that argument, on reflection, is very weak. True, we can imagine circumstances in which limiting the advertising of a rich candidate would prevent voters from being misled in some way: such limits might prevent a well-financed candidate from broadcasting mendacious advertisements in so many areas that less-well-financed rivals could not reply to all of them, for example. But we can as easily imagine circumstances in which such limits would prevent some voters from receiving information they would value. Even a political message endlessly repeated on television is seen on each repetition by at least someone who had not yet seen it, and that message might seem valuable to that voter. So we cannot say, in general and in advance, that reducing the overall quantity of political information in order to make the influence of all candidates more equal would improve the ability of voters to think clearly.

In any case we could not support that suggestion, as we can support the idea that the more information voters have the better, by appeal to general principles about good methods of reflection. No scientist or historian or practical decision maker would avoid reading all material arguing for one hypothesis or decision just because more literature was available for that hypothesis or decision than for its rivals, even if he knew that the group that had produced more literature was for some irrelevant reason better financed. He might well take that latter fact into account in evaluating what he read, but he would not limit his reading for that reason. He would trust his own tutored judgment.

It is true that in some contexts—appellate legal arguments and formal debates, for example—each side is given equal time. But those contexts are special in two pertinent ways. First, the overall time set aside for an appellate argument or a formal debate is fixed, so that time taken by one side is necessarily lost by the other. In contrast, though as a practical matter the time any particular voter has available for politics is limited, no such limit is formal or rigid, and allowing rich candidates to broadcast more often does not mean that voters are unable to pay as much attention to whatever advertising a poorer candidate can offer as they could if expenditure were equal. Second, equal-time regulations in legal arguments and formal debates are mainly justified by independent concerns about fairness to the parties or participants: It is fair to the participants that no side have a greater opportunity to make its case than any other. That concern for fairness is distinct from any concern for accuracy or good reasoning. It is recognized by the partnership conception of democracy, but not by the majoritarian conception whose implications we are now considering.

The second body of ideas on which a majoritarian conception might draw to help define ideal conditions of political argument is democratic theory itself. The democratic claim that the people must be left free to judge for themselves, and not have their minds made up for them by any official or caste, means that citizens must have that freedom as individuals. It is not consistent with that assumption to allow the legislature, even representing the will of the majority, to dictate to individual citizens what it is appropriate for them to attend to in considering how to vote. It is not consistent for the legislature to prevent individual citizens from watching as many political advertisements of a particular candidate as that candidate is willing and able to provide. The *Buckley* Court put the point, once again, with the clarity that makes its decision such a crisp endorsement of the majoritarian conception. "In the free society ordained by our Constitution it is not the government, but the people—individually as citizens and candidates and collectively as associations and political committees—who must retain control over the quantity and range of debate on public issues in a political campaign." On the majoritarian conception, the only argument for limiting the quantity of political debate is the paternalistic and unacceptable one that people will think more clearly if government limits what they hear. (No such assumption is necessary on the partnership conception, because that conception justifies expenditure limits by appealing to an independent concern for fairness among political contestants.)

So neither of the two grounds that a proponent of the majoritarian conception might consider for accepting expenditure limits—general assumptions about the conditions of good reasoning and general presumptions embedded in the majoritarian conception itself—offers any persuasive argument for such limits. On the contrary, together they make a powerful—and some might think a compelling—case for the democratic wager that I described earlier, the wager on which the *Buckley* decision was premised.

B. The Partnership Conception: The Three Dimensions of Democracy

The majoritarian conception of democracy is very popular—it is the conception most frequently endorsed by political scientists and philosophers—and it is therefore hardly surprising that the *Buckley* ruling against expenditure limits should have struck many lawyers and judges as correct. The equally widespread impression that the *Buckley* ruling is wrong, however, suggests that many other lawyers and laymen reject that conception of democracy, at least intuitively. I have elsewhere argued that the majoritarian conception is radically defective.[3] Almost all of us think that democracy is a valuable, even indispensable, form of government. We think that it is worth fighting, and perhaps even dying, to protect. We need a conception of democracy that matches that sense of democracy's value: We need an understanding that shows us what is so *good* about democracy. The majoritarian conception fails to do this, because there is nothing inherently valuable about a process that allows a larger number of people to impose its will on a smaller number. Majority rule is not fair or valuable in itself: It is fair and valuable only when certain conditions are met, including requirements of equality among participants in the political process through which majority will is determined.

So we must now explore the rival, partnership conception of democracy, which insists on recognizing these conditions as essential to true democracy. On the partnership conception, institutions are democratic to the degree that they allow citizens to govern themselves collectively through a partnership in which each is an active and equal partner. That aim, as I conceded, is a very abstract one, and it might be realized, more or less well, through very different packages of institutions. British democracy is differently structured from American democracy, and both are differently structured from South African democracy. But they all grant some measure of partnership democracy, even though none grants a full measure. We test how well any society has succeeded in creating a partnership democracy not by holding its institutions to a single standard, like the standard I constructed to illustrate the majoritarian construction, but against a more complex set of ideals encompassing different dimensions.

The first dimension of partnership democracy is popular sovereignty, which is a relation between the public as a whole and the various officials who make up its government. Partnership democracy demands that the people rather than the officials be masters. The revolutionary slogans that demanded equality when modern democracy began in the eighteenth century had that kind of equality in mind: Democracy's enemy, then, was privilege by inheritance or caste. The majoritarian conception demands popular sovereignty too, but it defines this not as a relation between the people generally and their officials but as the power of the largest number of citizens finally to have their way.

The second dimension of partnership democracy is citizen equality. In a democracy, citizens though collectively sovereign are also, as individuals, participants in the contests they collectively judge. Citizen equality demands that they participate as equals. The distinct importance of that dimension of equality became evident only later in democracy's story, when it was no longer controversial that the people as a whole rather than some monarch or despot should have the final power of government, but it nevertheless remained unclear how that collective power should be distributed among citizens individually—who should be allowed to vote and speak in the various processes through which collective political decisions are made and public opinion and culture are formed. It is now settled among mature democracies that, in principle, all mature citizens, with very few exceptions, should have equal voting impact. The majoritarian conception of democracy insists on equal suffrage because only in that way can elections hope to measure the will of the largest number of citizens. The partnership conception insists on equal suffrage too, but it requires that citizens be equal not only as judges of the political process but as participants in it as well. That does not mean that each citizen must have the same influence over the minds of other citizens.[4] It is inevitable and desirable that some citizens will have greater influence because their voices are particularly cogent or moving, or because they are particularly admired, or have devoted their lives to politics and public service, or have taken up careers or investments in journalism. Special influence that is gained in these ways is not in itself incompatible with the partnership understanding of democracy.[5] (On the contrary, democracy could not succeed on its third dimension, which I introduce in the next paragraph, unless it encouraged special influence on at least some of those grounds.) But partnership democracy is damaged when some groups of citizens have no or only a sharply diminished opportunity to appeal for their convictions because they lack the funds to compete with rich and powerful donors. No one can plausibly regard himself as a partner in an enterprise of self-government when he is effectively shut out from the political debate because he cannot afford a grotesquely high admission price.

The third dimension of democracy is democratic discourse. Genuine collective action requires interaction: If the people are to govern collectively, in a fashion that makes each citizen a partner in the political enterprise, then they must deliberate together as individuals before they act collectively, and the deliberation must center on reasons for and against that collective action, so that citizens who lose on an issue can be satisfied that they had a chance to convince others and failed to do so, not merely that they have been outnumbered. Democracy cannot provide any genuine form of self-government if citizens are not able to speak to the community in a structure and climate that encourages attention to the merits of what they say. If the public discourse is crippled by censorship, or collapses into a shouting or slandering match in which each side tries only to distort or drown out what the others say, then there is no collective self-government, no collective enterprise of any kind, but only vote counting as war by other means.

This brief account of partnership democracy is a tripartite idealization, of course. No nation has achieved or could achieve perfect control of officials by citizens, perfect political equality among citizens, or a political discourse unsullied by irrationality. America does not have full popular sovereignty, because our government still has great powers to keep dark what it does not want us to know. We do not have full citizen equality, because money, which is unjustly distributed, counts for far too much in politics. We do not have even a respectable democratic discourse: Our politics is closer to the war I described than to any civic argument. But we must keep the tripartite ideal in mind in judging, as now we must, what role the First Amendment could sensibly be assigned in improving democracy on the partnership conception, in bringing it at least closer to the unattainable pure case of that form of government.

C. Free Speech in a Democratic Partnership

Each of the three dimensions of a nation's democracy, on the partnership conception, is affected by the constitutional and legal arrangements it makes to encourage and protect political speech. Popular sovereignty demands that the people rather than officials have final power of government. But if officials are allowed to punish criticism of their decisions as "sedition," or to forbid the publication of information that might lead to such criticism, or to shut down new parties or newspapers that might expose their mistakes or crimes, then the people are not, or not fully, in charge. So a constitutional structure that guarantees freedom of speech against official censorship protects citizens in their democratic role as sovereigns.

Free speech helps to protect citizen equality as well. It is essential to democratic partnership that citizens be free, in principle, to express any relevant opinion they have no matter how much those opinions are rejected or hated or feared by other citizens. Much of the pressure for censorship in contemporary democracies is generated not by any official attempt to keep secrets from the people, but by the desire of a majority of citizens to silence others whose opinions they despise. That is the ambition of groups, for example, who want laws preventing neo-Nazis from marching or racists from parading in white sheets. But such laws disfigure democracy, because if a majority of citizens has the power to refuse a fellow citizen the right to speak whenever it deems his ideas dangerous or offensive, then he is not an equal in the argumentative competition for power. We must permit every citizen whom we claim bound by our laws an equal voice in the process that produces those laws, even when we rightly detest his convictions, or we forfeit our right to impose our laws upon him. Freedom of speech enforces that principle, and so protects citizen equality.

Some argue that the expression of opinions derogatory of a race or ethnic group or gender—often called "hate speech"—itself injures citizen equality because it not only offends the citizens who are its targets but damages their own ability to participate in politics as equals. Racist speech, for example, is said to "silence" the racial minorities who are its targets. The empirical force of that large generalization is uncertain: It is unclear how great an impact such speech has and on whom. But in any case it would be a serious misunderstanding of citizen equality, and of the partnership conception of democracy in general, to suppose that allowing even psychologically damaging political opinions free circulation offends the equality in question. Citizen equality cannot demand that citizens be protected by censorship even from those beliefs, convictions, or opinions that make it more difficult for them to gain attention for their views in an otherwise fair political contest, or that damage their own opinion of themselves. We could not possibly generalize a right to such protection—a fundamentalist Christian, for example, could not be protected in that way—without banning speech or the expression of opinion altogether. We must collectively attack prejudice and bias, but not in that way.

Citizen equality does require, however, that different groups of citizens not be disadvantaged, in their effort to gain attention and respect for their views, by a circumstance so remote from the substance of opinion or argument, or from the legitimate sources of influence, as wealth is. Experience has shown—and never more dramatically than in recent elections—that any group's political success is so directly related to the sheer magnitude of its expenditures, particularly on television and radio, that this factor dwarfs others in accounting for political success. That is the heart of the democratic argument for expenditure limits in political campaigns.

The connection between freedom of speech and the third dimension of democracy—democratic discourse—is also complex. Some regulations of speech that a government might be tempted to adopt, including laws limiting the investigative powers of the media, would damage the democratic discourse by denying it information and diversity. But the degradation of our public discourse by moronic political commercials that make no arguments beyond repetitive slogans and jingles also compromises the argumentative character of our discourse, and certain forms of indirect regulation of that discourse, such as the last proposal in my list, might help to arrest that damage.

So the connection between a constitutional guarantee of free speech and the quality of a partnership democracy, on its different dimensions, is a complicated and delicate one. If we were constructing such a guarantee as part of a new constitution, we would have to choose among three strategies: the democratic wager I described earlier, a "balancing" approach that would permit regulations of political speech that damaged democracy on one of its dimensions but improved it on another when the combined effect was thought to enhance democracy overall, or a more discriminating approach that combined elements of each of these two strategies.

Should we permit a balancing approach that allows regulations that impair democracy on one dimension when these are calculated to improve democracy overall? The case for such balancing might seem, in the abstract, a strong one. A guarantee of free speech cannot, in any case, be absolute: We cannot prohibit otherwise reasonable regulations that are necessary to protect national security or, perhaps, private reputation. We would be likely to sustain regulations for less urgent reasons, moreover: we would presumably permit "time and place" restrictions, like those forbidding broadcasting from sound trucks at night. If constraints like these are acceptable, because they serve a useful purpose and do not detract from democracy overall, then why should we not make exceptions for other regulations that actually improve democracy overall?

But there are two powerful answers to that simple argument. First, the different dimensions of democracy cannot be collapsed into one overriding goal that allows trading off violations on one dimension for overall gains. In particular, citizen equality is a matter of individual right, and we could not justify violations of that right—by censoring racists on the ground that this would improve democratic discourse, for example—through any aggregating calculation. Second, any such exception would be peculiarly open to abuse: There would be a standing danger that government would attempt to crush strident new parties or powerful critics in the name of democratic discourse or citizen equality, as, after all, totalitarian governments have often done elsewhere. Congress or a state legislature might disqualify a party whose message it declared dangerous to popular sovereignty because it was confusing, for example.

These fears justify rejecting a balancing strategy. Should we then accept the democratic wager? Are the dangers I just described so great that we should insist that though government may regulate political speech for a number of compelling reasons, it may never do so in order, in its judgment, to improve democracy itself? Our Constitution, we might say, should commit us to the prophylactic judgment that democracy is best served, in the long run, by a rule that forbids government any power to try to improve it, from time to time, by compromising the freedom of people to say what they like when and as often as they like. Justice Scalia set out that argument in characteristically vivid language in 1990. He referred to the idea that "too much speech is an evil that the democratic majority can proscribe," and he declared that that idea "is incompatible with the absolutely central truth of the First Amendment: that government cannot be trusted to assure, through censorship, the 'fairness' of political debate."[6] If we accepted this caution, we would make the democratic wager part of our constitutional law.

This argument for the democratic wager has two parts. The first is a diagnosis of danger: that the most significant threat to democracy, even now, lies in government's desire to protect itself, and to cheat citizens of their democratic sovereignty, by filtering and choosing what the public may watch or read or learn, and by attempting to justify that illegitimate control by claiming, as many tyrannies have indeed claimed, that this control is necessary to protect democracy on some other dimension. The second part is a maxim of strategy: It supposes that the best protection from that threat lies in prophylactic overkill, that is, in a doctrine that absolutely forbids government to appeal to that kind of justification for constraining speech even when the legitimacy of the appeal seems obvious. But though history supports both the plausibility of that fear and the wisdom of such a strategy, we can no longer afford to ignore the opposite dangers—particularly in the electronic age—of a wholly unregulated political discourse. We must compare the danger that a less rigid constitutional guarantee will allow an ingen-ious government to cheat the public of information and argument it should have, even if the courts are vigilant to prevent such abuse, with the rival danger that more rigid protection will allow wealth and privilege grossly undemocratic power, and allow the political discourse to be so cheapened as altogether to lose its argumentative character.

The signs of exactly that decay are now too obvious to be set aside: We have as much a parody of democracy as democracy itself. In the 1996 and 1998 elections, political expenditures ballooned to formerly incredible sums, and politicians at every level, including the president and vice president, were forced to abase themselves before rich donors. Politicians continue the relentless, draining chase for money even while they call for rules that would make this unnecessary. For many politicians the situation is a classic prison-ers' dilemma. Each would prefer expenditures to be limited, but if they are not limited, each must struggle to raise and spend as much as possible. Poorer would-be candidates are driven from the field at every level, and groups representing convictions unpopular among the rich are not able even to begin assembling wide political support. Elected officials must begin the search for fresh money the morning after their election, and the intense and continuing effort seriously erodes the time they have for the public's busi-ness. The money these politicians raise is spent under the direction of pollsters and consultants who have no interest in principle or policy and whose skills lie only in the seduction of consumers by repetition, jingle, and sound-bite.

The consequence is the most degraded and negative political discourse in the democratic world. Public participation in politics, measured even by the number of citizens who bother to vote, has sunk below the level at which we can claim, with a straight face, to be governing ourselves. The public traces its own disaffection to the process itself: It reports that the power of money in politics has made it cynical and that the coarseness of television politics has made it sick. The prophylactic overkill of the democratic wager is now far too expensive in genuine democracy. It is now foolish rather than cau-tious, blind rather than wise.

So we have powerful grounds for trying to construct a strategy for the protection of political speech that has something of the flexibility but not the danger of the balancing strategy. The "discriminating" strategy (as I shall call it) acknowledges that danger and forbids any regulation of speech that appreciably damages either citizen sovereignty or citizen equality. It does not allow government to compromise popular sovereignty by forbidding the press to discuss the sexual lives of officials, for example, even though it is highly plausible that the third dimension of democracy—democratic discourse—would be improved by that constraint. It rejects, as incompatible with citizen equality, the argument I mentioned that racist or sexist speech should be forbidden in order to avoid "silencing" minority groups or women or in order to improve the character of political discourse.[7]

But the discriminating strategy does permit regulations of political speech that improve democracy on some dimension when the defect that they aim to repair is substantial, and when the constraint works no genuine damage to either citizen sovereignty or citizen equality. So it permits ceilings on campaign expenditures when these help to repair significant citizen inequality in politics, provided the ceilings are set high enough that they do not dampen criticism of government, and that no new inequality is introduced by foreclosing unfamiliar parties or candidates.

V. The Legal Record

A. *The Issue Framed*

I have been examining the philosophical basis for the "democratic wager" on which the Supreme Court based its *Buckley* ruling. That prophylactic strategy flows naturally from the majoritarian conception that takes the nerve of democracy to lie in government according to the informed and reflective will of the majority. Some critics of *Buckley* have said that the decision represents a return of the *Lochner*[8] mentality that once led the Supreme Court to reject progressive social and economic legislation on the ground that people had a right to use their property and spend their money as they wished. But the *Lochner* analogy misunderstands the true appeal of the prophylactic reading, which rests, not on the almost universally rejected view that people with money should always be free to spend it as they wish, but on the much more popular idea that democracy means government by majority will. If democracy has only that single dimension, then the democratic wager might well be deemed a good bet.

The majoritarian conception is not, however, the only available conception of democracy. The partnership conception is a more attractive alternative: That conception offers at least three dimensions on which democracy must be tested, and it recommends not the democratic wager but the more discriminating interpretation of free speech that I described. If we were constructing a new constitution, on a clean slate, we would have powerful reasons for constructing it with a partnership democracy in mind, and for drafting a discriminating protection of free speech. But we are not drafting a new constitution. We are attempting to interpret the Constitution we have, and the history of practice and adjudication under it. So we must ask: Which conception of democracy provides a better interpretation of our own constitutional structure and practice?

I have elsewhere argued that the partnership conception does, because that conception explains, while the majoritarian conception cannot, the Constitution's provision of individual rights against a democratic majority.[9] True, some of those rights could be explained as necessary to create and protect even a majoritarian democracy.[10] If we read the First Amendment as incorporating the democratic wager, then we could treat a citizen's right to free speech as a right protecting a majoritarian democracy in spite of the fact that it limits what a democratic majority can do. But the Constitution contains individual rights—like the right to equal protection of the laws as this has been interpreted by the courts—that cannot be reconciled with the majoritarian conception of democracy in that way.

We would do well, however, for this occasion, to frame our interpretive question more narrowly. We should confine ourselves to First Amendment jurisprudence and distinguish between two readings of the free speech clause. The first is a prophylactic reading modeled on the democratic wager. It declares that political speech may never be restricted or regulated in the interests of democracy. The second is a more flexible reading drawn from the partnership conception. It allows regulation of free speech that improves citizen equality provided it meets the rigorous standards of the discriminating strategy that I described. Which of the two readings seems better to explain what the Constitution says or what the courts have done about free speech?

B. Text and Rhetoric

We get little help, in choosing between those two interpretive readings, from the Constitution's text. The First Amendment provides that "Congress shall make no law . . . abridging the freedom of speech." It is possible to read that language in an absolutist way as forbidding regulation of speech for any reason whatsoever. But both the democratic wager and the discriminating strategy reject that absolutist interpretation, as do almost all scholars and judges, and the text provides no further guidance as to the choice between those two readings. If the text permits regulation of speech to protect national security or the peace and quiet of neighborhoods, then it also permits, just as a matter of the bounds of language, regulation to protect or perfect democracy.

Nor is judicial rhetoric decisive in either direction. The flat declaration in *Buckley* that concerns for equality are "foreign" to the First Amendment is, as I said, a clear endorsement of the democratic wager. But we can find even better-known statements that equally clearly endorse the rival discriminating strategy. Chief among these is Justice Brandeis' famous statement in his *Whitney* opinion.

> Those who won our independence believed that the final end of the state was to make men free to develop their faculties, and that in its government the deliberative forces should prevail over the arbitrary. They valued liberty both as an end and as a means. They believed liberty to be the secret of happiness and courage to be the secret of liberty . . . that the greatest menace to freedom is an inert people; that public discussion is a political duty; and that this should be a fundamental principle of the American government.[11]

This statement recognizes the importance of popular sovereignty. But it also lays particular emphasis, as part of an overall justification of the First Amendment, on the other dimensions of democracy: on the importance of citizen equality and, above all, on the value of a deliberative democratic discourse. It declares that the point of freedom of speech is not just to stop government from oppressing the people, but to allow individual citizens to develop their faculties, that liberty is for this reason a democratic end as well as a means to other democratic purposes, and that civic deliberation with others is a "political duty" that stands beside the duty, as citizen-sovereign, to vote. It would be bizarre to accept that strong endorsement of the varied goals of the First Amendment and yet to insist that it must never be interpreted or applied to further those goals.

So we must look beyond text and rhetoric to evaluate our rival readings as interpretations of judicial practice. We must look to the actual decisions in those cases in which the two readings compete. There are not many such cases: Most First Amendment decisions are consistent with both readings. Both readings justify *New York Times v. Sullivan*,[12] the Pentagon Papers decision,[13] the Skokie case,[14] the flag-burning cases,[15] and most of the other First Amendment landmarks. I shall concentrate on a number of those relatively few cases in which the two readings do pull in opposite directions, to see which reading's gravitational force proved the stronger in each case. That question is not settled by the language of the opinions in question, which almost never addresses our question directly. We shall have to look at what American courts have actually done in these cases, against the background of the facts presented to them, to judge which of the two readings better explains what they did.

C. Contribution Limits

As we have already seen, one part of *Buckley*—its holding that expenditure caps are unconstitutional—is supported only by the prophylactic reading. The Court declared, in its argument for that holding, that the purpose of the First Amendment is limited to protecting popular sovereignty—to providing the public with "the widest possible dissemination of information from diverse and antagonistic sources"—and it specifically rejected the argument that government could regulate speech to protect citizen equality. We must take the same view of some of *Buckley*'s progeny—the cases, like *Colorado Republican*,[16] that were decided by appealing to that *Buckley* ruling as a precedent.

But another ruling was also part of the *Buckley* decision—the Court's ruling that permitted Congress to impose limits on the contributions that people might make to political campaigns of others—and that ruling is just as much a part of the constitutional record. It presupposes not the prophylactic but the discriminating reading, because it can be justified only on the assumption that Congress has the power to limit the political activity of some people in order to safeguard the citizen equality of others. The Court denied this rationale for its decision: it said that preventing people from speaking indirectly, by contributing as much as they wish to help finance the speech of other people, is different from preventing them from spending their own money to speak for themselves, and that contribution limits were therefore subject to a lower constitutional standard than expenditure limits. But that supposed distinction is illusory, as Justice Thomas pointed out forcefully in the *Colorado Republican* case.

The most effective means most people have of expressing their political convictions is contributing to an organization or campaign dedicated to publicizing or acting on those convictions. Contribution limits offer as great—or as little—a threat to popular sovereignty as expenditure limits. If the rich are prevented from contributing all they would wish to political campaigns, then politicians will not be able to broadcast their messages as often as they would like, and citizen-sovereigns will not hear a message they would otherwise have heard. Government would have limited the flow of campaign information and appeal just as directly as it would have done had it limited what the politicians might spend. Though contributors conceivably could spend as much in other ways and forums as they would have contributed to particular campaigns, had they been allowed to do so, few are likely to do so, for a variety of reasons, including the evident fact that independent expenditures are less likely to attract the gratitude of powerful public officials. Nothing in the prophylactic reading justifies testing laws limiting political contributions by a less exacting standard than laws limiting direct expenditures.

The conclusion that many commentators have reached—that the *Buckley* Court sought a compromise by striking down expenditure limits and accepting contribution limits—seems irresistible. But it was a compromise of the wrong kind, a checkerboard compromise that applies one reading of the First Amendment to the first of these issues and a different reading to the other. The *Buckley* decision, which in one aspect is the strongest available authority against the discriminating reading, is in its other aspect a strong argument for it.

D. Fairness Doctrine

The First Amendment is pertinent not only when government seeks to stop a publisher from printing or broadcasting what he wishes, but when it forces him to publish what he otherwise would not, because in such a case government also intervenes in the political discourse by altering what information is available to citizens, and that, too, offends the principle of popular sovereignty that government must not choose what citizens hear. In *Red Lion*,[17] however, the Supreme Court upheld the FCC's "fairness doctrine" then in force, which required broadcasters who chose to editorialize on a controversial political issue to present opposing views as well. The Court cited the "First Amendment goal of producing an informed public capable of conducting its own affairs," and said that it was perfectly consistent with that goal for government to require more balanced programming. That idea fits comfortably with the discriminating reading of the First Amendment. But it is anathema to the prophylactic reading, because it rests on exactly the kind of judgment—that citizens are better informed and more responsible if opposing views are presented to them by the same broadcaster than if they are left to seek out opposing opinions on their own if they so wish—that the prophylactic reading condemns.

It is often said, however, that the *Red Lion* decision was based on what is called a "scarcity" rationale: that because only a relatively small number of broadcast stations can operate within any particular geographical area, government has a stronger interest in forcing those few outlets to broadcast opinions contradicting their own. If so, then the decision would be inapplicable in the cable and satellite age, when a much larger number of outlets is available throughout the country. But a concern for scarcity could not have figured in the decision in any way that suggests a prophylactic reading, because scarcity is not pertinent under that reading. If it is in principle wrong for government to attempt to control the flow of political information and argument to the public, then the fact that the outlets it seeks to control are scarce, or that it has licensed the use of those outlets, would be beside the point. For it would nevertheless be government, rather than the combined force of individual decisions, that had decided what information and argument would flow out of that scarce medium. Since government had the option of licensing broadcast bands without such intervention, the First Amendment, on the prophylactic reading, would demand that it do so.

In fact the Court cited scarcity only to support the proposition that entry into the broadcast medium is very expensive—it cited the commanding position of early entrants, which, it said, was minatory even when gaps in the spectrum were still available. But of course speakers who are denied the use of television for these economic reasons are free to seek other, less scarce, and in any case less expensive media through which to publish their views. The Court's argument actually depended on the assumption, almost explicit in its opinion, that it is unfair and undemocratic when access to a medium so dominant in politics as broadcasting has become is restricted—either by license grant or by economic power—to a very few and therefore very powerful people, and that government therefore had a right to intervene to make the political process more equal. The decision presupposes the discriminating reading: that citizen equality in politics is so central to the

Constitution's overall conception of democracy that the First Amendment must recognize that improving equality is sometimes a compelling reason for appropriate regulation.

Of course it does not necessarily follow, even if we accept the discriminatory reading, that the *Red Lion* Court correctly applied that reading. Someone might argue that citizen sovereignty is significantly impaired when broadcast editorialists are dissuaded from stating controversial opinions because it would be expensive or otherwise distasteful for them to allow conflicting views to air, and that the decision was wrong, even assuming the discriminating reading, for that reason. That is not a powerful argument in the case of broadcast companies, whose editorial content rarely constitutes a significant part of their programming in any case, however, and I believe that the decision was correct. In other circumstances, however, such an argument would be more persuasive: In the *Tornillo* case,[18] for example, the Court struck down a Florida law requiring newspapers to grant equal space for a response by candidates they had criticized. Since judges might well think that such a law would have a chilling effect on the critical zeal of newspaper editors, that decision is consistent with the discriminating reading as well as the prophylactic one.

E. Must Carry Rules

In the two *Turner* decisions,[19] the Supreme Court upheld "must carry" regulations requiring cable companies, under certain circumstances, to carry broadcast stations. Justice Breyer, who provided the swing vote in a five-to-four decision in *Turner II*, began his analysis by remarking that First Amendment interests were to be found on both sides of the case. It is difficult to make sense of that claim on the prophylactic reading. The First Amendment, on that reading, commits the nation to the strategy of protecting democracy by keeping government out of the various decisions that determine what the public is offered by way of speech. If so, then there is a First Amendment issue only on one side—on the side of the cable companies who wish to be free of government's interference in their decision what mix of programming to offer. The consideration Breyer stressed—that requiring cable companies to carry broadcast stations improves political discourse because it provides local news and argument that cable subscribers would otherwise have to seek elsewhere—is irrelevant. According to the discriminating reading, however, Breyer was right, because that reading acknowledges the democratic importance of informed discourse and accepts that government may intervene in media decisions to help secure it. He embraced the discriminating view when he declared that the policy in question "seeks to facilitate the public discussion and informed deliberation which, as Justice Brandeis pointed out many years ago, democratic government presupposes and the First Amendment seeks to achieve." He underlined his reliance on the discriminating reading, moreover, by citing not only Brandeis' *Whitney* opinion, but *Red Lion.*

Breyer's was only one opinion in *Turner II*, and he did not participate in *Turner I*. But his opinion makes much more sense than the plurality's opinion, which relied on economic analysis, as Justice O'Connor remarked in her dissenting opinion in *Turner II*. The complicated *Turner* litigation is best read, overall, as recognizing one of the most basic claims of the discriminating reading: that government may intervene in the powerful electronic media in order to improve the public political discourse, when the intervention favors no point of view, popular or unpopular, and does not otherwise compromise citizen sovereignty or citizen equality.

F. Campaign-Free Polling Zones

In *Burson*,[20] the Supreme Court upheld state election laws forbidding political canvassing on election day within a stipulated distance from polling places. Though the Court attempted to justify its decision in the way that a prophylactic reading of the First Amendment would require, the decision can in fact be supported only on a discriminating reading. The Court said that barring political speech from a large area around voting booths on election day was not neutral, because it touched only political and not other forms of speech or solicitation. But it also said that the regulations met the exacting "compelling justification" standard for overriding the First Amendment's prohibition on such content-sensitive regulation, because a state has a compelling interest in election procedures that eliminate intimidation. This argument has the right form for the prophylactic reading, because it does not appeal to informed discourse, or to any other dimension of democracy, to justify a constraint on political speech. It appeals instead to people's distinct interest in not being intimidated.

But though that argument has the right prophylactic form, it is a silly argument, and it was properly ridiculed by Justices Stevens, O'Connor, and Souter in their dissent in the case.[21] The state did not need to prohibit political speech over an area of 30,000 square feet (or, in the case of some states, over 750,000 square feet) in order to prevent intimidation. Once again, the decision is much better justified if we suppose that the Court actually rejected the prophylactic reading and embraced the discriminating one. If we read the First Amendment to permit regulations of speech that further its assumed goal of protecting democracy, by improving citizen equality or the character of political discourse, the case becomes an easy one. It is fairer to citizens as participants not to allow any candidate or group the special and unseemly advantage of a last-second appeal at the crucial moment of voting, and it improves democratic deliberation to allow citizens a space for final reflection, free from importuning, before they vote—to allow them freedom *from* politics when that freedom is most important.

The First Amendment, on the discriminating reading, does not prohibit government from intervening to aid citizens in that way, so long as such regulations do not offend the core principles of political impartiality or any other aspect of popular sovereignty. The importance of that qualification is underscored by an earlier decision in which the Supreme Court struck down a state law that might initially seem similar to the one it upheld in *Burson*. In *Mills v. Alabama*,[22] the Court declared unconstitutional a law forbidding newspapers to publish editorials endorsing or opposing any candidate on election day. That law would have deprived citizens of a traditional source of political argument and advice that could be read and reflected on at home, away from the bustle of the actual voting booth, even on election day. Its impact on consumer sovereignty was therefore greater, and its contribution to deliberative deliberation nonexistent.

G. Corporate Electioneering

In *Austin v. Michigan Chamber of Commerce*, the Court upheld a statute that prohibited corporations from using their general assets to support or oppose political candidates, though it permitted them to use segregated funds they raised expressly for political purposes. The Court's argument almost explicitly endorsed the discriminating reading and rejected the prophylactic one. It conceded that, according to *Buckley*, states need a "compelling" interest to justify constraints on political speech, and acknowledged that the only such interest recognized in that case was an interest in protecting against corruption. But, the Court said in *Austin*, the kind of "corruption" that states may guard against is not limited to the familiar contribution-for-favors kind, but includes "a different kind of corruption in the political arena: the corrosive and distorting effects of immense aggregations of wealth that are accumulated with the help of the corporate form and that have little or no correlation to the public's support for the corporation's political ideas."

The "distortion" in question has nothing to do with the familiar kind of corruption. It is not a compromise of popular sovereignty: The fact that a political commercial has been paid for by a corporate contribution does not make the information or appeal it contains any less valuable to the public who watches that commercial. The "corrosive" impact of large corporate spending is entirely its impact on citizen equality, that is, on the dimension of democracy that *Buckley*'s prophylactic interpretation of the First Amendment declared irrelevant. Nor does it matter, from the perspective of that prophylactic understanding, how the corporation's profits are earned. It is irrelevant, on that understanding, that these profits do not reflect popular political convictions: The value of the information to the public as sovereign is the same whether the corporate contributions are from a segregated political action fund or from the corporation's general treasury. That is not, however, irrelevant to the discriminating reading, because that reading permits government to regulate electoral speech so as to protect citizen equality when the regulation does not damage democracy on any other dimension, and citizen equality is seriously impaired when corporations are free to use their vast general wealth to wield political influence that few if any individual citizens can.

The discriminatory reading provides not only a persuasive justification for *Austin*, but a persuasive distinction between that decision and an earlier decision that has struck many commentators as contrary to *Austin* in spirit. In the *Bellotti*[23] case, the Court declared unconstitutional a Massachusetts statute forbidding corporations to spend any funds at all campaigning for or against a state ballot initiative. That restriction posed a much more serious threat to citizen sovereignty than the statute upheld in *Austin* did, because it threatened to deprive citizens of information that might not otherwise be available to them. Many ballot initiatives concern complex economic issues, and corporations often have an incentive that individuals lack for presenting a particular side of the argument. The *Bellotti* statute did not allow such corporations even the use of segregated funds raised specifically to present that argument. The *Austin* statute, on the contrary, was limited to elections, in which political parties and other groups have a lively interest in offering any argument for their candidates and against their opponents, and it did permit corporations the use of segregated funds to make whatever case for or against a candidate they believed had not been effectively made by others.

VI. The Epistemic Argument

So the discriminating reading that I associated with the partnership conception of democracy fits the pertinent precedents as well as the prophylactic reading associated with the majoritarian conception. If the analysis of the preceding section is sound, it fits those precedents, on the whole, even better. Constitutional interpretation, however, is not just a matter of fit: A compelling interpretation should not only fit the record but justify it as well. Is the prophylactic or the discriminating reading superior on that score? It is true that the discriminating reading is at least marginally more open to abuse by a government anxious to protect itself from criticism or to solidify its position. Such a government might regulate political speech, claiming to protect democracy when it is really only protecting itself. But the discriminating reading runs no serious risk of such abuse, because, unlike the balancing reading I distinguished, it does not permit regulations of political speech that damage either citizen sovereignty or citizen equality in any significant way, and, in any case, the risk of abuse is more than outweighed by the evident damage to democracy that the prophylactic reading requires us to bear.

But the prophylactic reading might seem more appealing for a very different reason. It is a popular rationale for the First Amendment that freedom of speech helps the public not only to govern but also to discover the truth about how best to govern. Proponents of that claim often refer to John Stuart Mill's argument that a competition of ideas, from which no idea is excluded, is the best means of discovering truth across both science and value—not just truth about what people want but truth about what they should want. The prophylactic reading seems more deeply committed to such a competition, because it rejects any regulation of speech in the supposed interests of improving democracy. So Mill's epistemic hypothesis might seem to argue for that reading. In fact, however, both readings find support in Mill's epistemic claim, though the claim takes different forms in the two readings and is actually more plausible under the discriminating reading than under the prophylactic one.

If we accept Mill's claim as a justification for the prophylactic reading, we must take that claim to endorse the sheer *quantity* of speech as having, in itself, epistemic value. On this view, the value of a public debate is overall improved, at least in the long run, by enforcing the principle that the more speech-acts the better, so that repetitions of substantially the same claims or ideas are to be valued as contributing, at least marginally, to the epistemic promise of the debate, and by rejecting any qualification of that principle designed to improve the *quality* of the argument. If we offer the claim as a justification for the discriminating reading, on the other hand, we emphasize the epistemic importance of a principle holding, not that no speech-act be excluded, but that no *idea* be excluded. On this different view, what is important is the cognitive and emotional mix of what is presented, not the quantity in itself, and it is mix rather than quantity that is served when we declare, as the discriminating reading does, that no speech may be censored or constrained because what it says or expresses is deemed dangerous or offensive. Rigorously enforcing *that* principle is the best way of insuring that the debate is exposed to the widest variety of ideas possible; it is not also necessary to maximize the sheer quantity of speech.

The discriminating reading permits an expanded and even more plausible epistemic claim to be made, moreover, which is that a discourse from which no idea is formally excluded is even more likely to secure truth if the discourse is further structured to encourage ideas to be inspected on their merits. The prophylactic reading cannot make that expanded claim, because it insists on the sole epistemic virtue of the highest quantity of speech unstructured by any regulation. That idea—that quality as well as quantity counts—is widely accepted in other contexts, as in appellate arguments or formal debates where we insist on argument rather than multimedia performances. The prophylactic model, on the contrary, places all its epistemic eggs in one unsound basket: It must rely, for any claim that its rigidity serves the discovery of truth, on the hugely doubtful assumption that an unstructured debate is more effective as a means of discovery than a structured one with just as many ideas but fewer speech-acts.

VII. The Proposals Revisited

The discriminating reading of the First Amendment allows legislation that limits and regulates political speech when such legislation does not keep information or argument from the public that would otherwise be available to it, when it is not designed to favor government or to favor any party or ideology or policy over any other, when it does not reflect any assumption about the truth, falsity, danger, or offensiveness of any message or display, and when it is likely to improve the democratic character of public political discourse by making participation available to more citizens on an equal footing, or by improving the quality of public discourse, or both.

It would be difficult to defend the constitutionality of any of the proposals set out at the start of this chapter, including the limits on campaign contributions already in force, if we accepted the prophylactic reading of the First Amendment. We must now examine those proposals against the discriminating reading I have been defending. It might be helpful to notice, first, that though some of the proposals might seem radical to Americans, they are familiar in other democracies. Adopting all the proposals would make the American system much more like the British electoral scheme, for example, which according to general international opinion works very well. It is true that elections in a parliamentary system, with strong party control, are in many ways different from those in our own complex federal system, which separates executive and legislative offices. But the differences do not defeat the comparison. President Clinton, calling for campaign reform, suggested in November 1997 that the election in which Tony Blair defeated John Major was both fairer and better reasoned and argued than the one in which he defeated Robert Dole.[24] The proposals would also bring our electoral system closer to those in place in the other major democracies. None of these allows unlimited expenditure, and all regulate television and radio politics.

The proposals that limit campaign expenditures are, of course, contrary to the *Buckley* holding. If that holding were overruled in deference to the discriminating reading, then the First Amendment would permit expenditure ceilings high enough that they do not increase the advantage that incumbents already have over challengers and do not prevent candidates with no name recognition or groups with novel policies from securing enough public interest to engage the attention of journalists and other broadcasters. Unless these conditions were satisfied, expenditure limits would compromise citizen equality, and they would injure popular sovereignty too, because the public would be denied the ideas that such candidates or groups would offer if they could. The discriminating reading does not permit significant damage to any dimension of democracy.

The final proposal grants generous public funds for political campaigns but prohibits candidates who accept those funds from running political commercials on radio and television, except in the form of political broadcasts whose format encourages argument and discourages subliminal and other nonargumentative techniques. This proposal is more novel and unsettling, and would be controversial even if the discriminating reading had been recognized and adopted. The legislation would prohibit nothing. It would merely impose conditions on the use of public funds and leave any politician who prefers to pay for ordinary political commercials out of his limited campaign budget free to do so by refusing any public funds. But the pressure on both candidates and broadcasters to accept the public's shilling would be so strong, particularly on the assumption that other candidates and broadcasters had done so, that the conditions imposed would have a coercive bite. The discriminating reading therefore requires proponents of these proposals to show that they would not, in practice, damage democracy on any of its dimensions.

It might be objected, for example, that a grant program that imposed such conditions would offend citizen sovereignty because it would induce politicians not to produce political appeals in the form that the public prefers. After all, politicians swamp programming with thirty-second negative sound-bites not out of personal taste, but because they judge that such advertising has the most impact. We must be careful to distinguish, however, between what the public deems appropriate, by way of political discourse, and what it in fact responds to—the advertising industry is largely built on the difference between these two phenomena. We learn, from polls as well as from politicians, that the public disapproves the genre of political commercials, and that distaste is thought in part responsible for the alienation of so many people from politics.

That does not, however, fully answer the objection, because it remains true that in consequence of the condition imposed on public financing, at least some people would not have political appeals available to them in the volume and form they prefer and that politicians would otherwise provide. But it is a mistake to think that citizen sovereignty, or either of the other two dimensions of democracy, requires that every citizen be entitled to receive political information in his preferred form. Even on the prophylactic reading, government is permitted to regulate the time, place and manner of political appeals. Some citizens might prefer political appeals delivered by sound truck at home at three in the morning: That might fit their occupational schedule or diurnal rhythm perfectly. But democracy is not compromised by regulations that make middle-of-the-night sound-truck campaigns impossible, so long as these regulations in no way diminish the information that is ultimately and reasonably available to each citizen. The political broadcast regulations I described have only the same limited effect. They do not diminish the information or argument that would be available to any citizen who is willing to make a reasonable effort, by tuning in on political broadcasts at the scheduled time, or by watching other election coverage, to learn what a candidate or group has to say. The First Amendment hardly demands, on any reading, that a citizen so unconcerned that he will not make that effort can have a cheap and inadequate substitute in time-out commercials while watching his favorite football team.

It might now be said, however, that the restrictive conditions on the use of public funds for electronic politics, which are designed to make politics more argumentative, offend citizen equality, because they are not after all neutral among political perspectives. They favor an elitist form of political discourse. Once again, however, we must be careful not to misunderstand the form of neutrality that citizen equality, properly understood, demands. It does not demand that political procedures be constructed so that bad arguments can be as effective as good ones and jingles as powerful as reasons, or so that candidates without knowledge or convictions or qualifications have maximal opportunity to hide those embarrassing failings. The neutrality at which we should aim is almost exactly the opposite: It requires a scheme that allows citizens to judge the structure, merits, and appeal of all candidates and ideas, including the worst financed and initially most unpopular of these, and the proposed scheme would serve that conception of neutrality much more effectively than unregulated television and radio politics can. I do not mean now to claim that the discriminatory reading would plainly permit that scheme, but only that the argument that it should is both more complex and plausible than it might first appear to be.

VIII. Conclusion

I began by reporting the widespread view that our democracy has been seriously damaged by the curse of money. We can use the different dimensions of the partnership conception of democracy that we have now distinguished to make that charge more explicit. It is not obvious that unlimited campaign expenditures, which give the rich more influence in politics because they can finance vast media advertising campaigns, offend citizen sovereignty. Their money is spent in forming majoritarian opinion, not in evading what majority opinion commands. It is arguable that vast disparities of wealth can mislead the public into thinking it wants what it is not in its real economic interests, narrowly defined, to want. But we have no basis for supposing that its votes would more accurately reflect its "authentic" overall convictions if campaign expenditures were limited, in part because we have no independent way of defining or discovering those "authentic" convictions. So if popular sovereignty were our only concern it would seem reasonable to allow the public as much information or advertising as anyone wished and was able to supply to it, and then to rely on the public to discount repetitive or misleading messages, and to seek out information about small and underfinanced candidates through journalism and less expensive media like small cable stations. Popular sovereignty is not threatened by such a policy, and whatever appeal the *Buckley* ruling has lies in the policy's apparent reasonableness.

When we adopt the partnership conception of democracy, however, we add two more dimensions to the democratic metric, and on each of these two further dimensions the defects of our present democracy are evident. Citizen equality is destroyed when only the rich are players in the political contest, and no one could mistake our huckster politics for democratic deliberation. The partnership conception makes plain, too, what is at stake in these defeats. We take pride in the democratic legitimacy of our form of government: we pride ourselves that ours is a nation in which the people govern themselves. But self-government means more than equal suffrage and frequent elections. It means a partnership of equals, reasoning together about the common good. We can never fully achieve that ideal—no nation could. But when politics are drenched in money, as our politics now are, then we risk not simply imperfection but hypocrisy.

II

Affirmative Action:
Does It Work?

▲

I

For over thirty years America's best universities and colleges have used race-sensitive admissions policies to increase the number of their black, Hispanic, Chicano, Native American, and other minority students.[1] Conservative writers and politicians have attacked this policy of "affirmative action" from its inception, but the policy is now in the greatest danger it has yet faced—on two fronts, political and legal. In 1995, by a fourteen-to-ten vote, the regents of the University of California declared that race could no longer be taken into account in admissions decisions at any of the branches of that university. In 1996 California voters approved Proposition 209, which ratifies and broadens that prohibition by providing that no state institution may "discriminate against, or grant preferential treatment to, any individual or group on the basis of race, sex, color, ethnicity or national origin in the operation of public employment, public education, or public contracting."[2]

The effect of the regents' decision was immediate and, in the view of many of the university's faculty, disastrous: the Boalt Hall Law School at Berkeley—the state's premier public law school—had enrolled an average of twenty-four black students each year for the last twenty-eight years. In 1997 it enrolled only one, and he had been admitted the previous year but had deferred entering.[3] The political campaign against affirmative action will continue, encouraged by the success of the California initiative, in other states. A similar prohibition was enacted in Washington in 1998, and other states are likely to follow.

The second danger may be even more menacing. In 1978, in the famous *Bakke* case, the Supreme Court in effect ruled that race-sensitive admissions plans do not violate the Fourteenth Amendment of the United States Constitution, which declares that "no state may deny any person equal protection of the laws," so long as such plans do not stipulate fixed quotas for any race or group, but take race into account only as one factor among others.[4] In 1996, however, in the *Hopwood* case, the Fifth Circuit Court of Appeals declared the admissions program of the University of Texas Law School at Austin unconstitutional, and two of the three judges who made up the majority in that case declared that the *Bakke* rule had been overruled, even though not expressly, by more recent Supreme Court decisions.[5]

The immediate consequences of the Fifth Circuit decision were, once again, dramatic: though the Texas Law School had enrolled thirty-one black students in 1996, it could enroll only four in the following year. The Supreme Court declined to review the Fifth Circuit's decision, which therefore stands as law in Texas and the other states of that circuit. In October 1998, the Washington, D.C.–based Center for Individual Rights, which had spawned the attack on the University of Texas in the *Hopwood* case, filed a similar suit in Michigan, arguing that the University of Michigan's admissions program is also unconstitutional, and similar suits are expected in other states. Sooner or later the Supreme Court will be required to take some such case for review, and if the Court does overrule or substantially restrict *Bakke*, affirmative action henceforth will be crippled across the country. Without a constitutional amendment or another change of heart in the Court, not even a shift in the political climate could bring it back.[6]

Much of the political and legal attack on affirmative action has centered on its consequences: critics say that it has lowered educational standards by admitting students who are unqualified to benefit from the education they receive, and that it has exacerbated rather than relieved racial tension. It is therefore opportune that the first comprehensive and statistically sophisticated examination of the actual effects of thirty years of affirmative action in American universities has just been published. *The Shape of the River*, by William G. Bowen, who was president of Princeton University, and Derek Bok, the former president of Harvard, analyzes an enormous data base of records, called the College and Beyond (C&B) data base, which was compiled by the Mellon Foundation, of which Bowen is the president, over four years.[7]

That data base contains information about each of more than 80,000 undergraduates who matriculated at twenty-eight selective colleges and universities in 1951, 1976, and 1989; these institutions are representative of the elite schools that have used affirmative action, and they range, in their selectivity in admitting students, from Bryn Mawr and Yale to Denison and North Carolina (Chapel Hill).[8] In the case of the 1976 and 1989 cohorts, the data base records the undergraduates' race, gender, high school grades, SAT scores, college majors and grades, extracurricular activities, any graduate or professional school record, and, for many, family economic and social background. It also presents information about the post-university experience of all those in the sample who answered detailed questionnaires sent out when the data base was being compiled. An unusually high number of those surveyed did so—80 percent for the 1976 and 84 percent for the 1989 cohorts.

Bowen, Bok, and their colleagues have used advanced statistical techniques to analyze, so far as possible, the distinct impact of each of the great range of variables the study isolates. They have done so in an attempt to chart the consequences affirmative action has actually had, over its now substantial career, for individual students and graduates, for their colleges and universities, and for race relations in the country as a whole. Their book is an extremely valuable sociological study quite apart from its specific findings about affirmative action, and it offers, in detailed appendices, a clear description of the complex statistical techniques it employs.

The *River* study has limitations, of course, which its authors are careful to acknowledge. A statistical survey, no matter how substantial its data or careful its techniques, is not a laboratory experiment, and though the authors show considerable ingenuity in finding and using controls and other checks on their conclusions, certain conclusions, as they point out, inevitably include some surmise. The study is confined to affirmative action in higher education, and its results may have little bearing on the effects of racial classifications for other purposes—in hiring, for example, or in awarding opportunities to minority-owned businesses. Most university affirmative action plans are designed to increase the enrollment of a variety of minority groups, but, except for some discussion of Hispanic students, the study presents and analyzes mainly data about black students and graduates. The institutions in the C&B list are representative of highly selective universities and colleges, moreover, and the study's findings may not hold for less selective sectors.

The authors have not been able to answer all the questions that their data raise. They concede that they are unable fully to explain, for example, the particularly worrying fact that black students as a group underperform in college grades compared to white students in the same institution who had the same SAT scores and other academic qualifications.[9] None of these limitations compromises the force of the conclusions the study reaches, however, and many of these conclusions, as we shall see, flatly contradict premises and assertions that have become staples of the affirmative action debate in recent years.

In order to gauge the importance and the limits of the *River* study, we must take care to distinguish the two main strands of that debate.[10] The first is an issue of principle: Is affirmative action for blacks unfair because it violates the right of every applicant to be judged on his or her individual merits? The second is a matter of policy or practical consequence: Does affirmative action do more harm than good, because it enrolls some blacks in studies beyond their capacities, or stigmatizes all blacks as inferior, or makes the community more rather than less conscious of race? These two questions are connected, because many people think that affirmative action is fair if it does substantial good, either for those it is intended to benefit or for the community as a whole, but unfair if it does not, because the damage it does to the admissions prospects of other applicants (who include not only whites but other minorities, like Asian Americans, whose test scores as a group are relatively high) is then pointless. The questions are nevertheless independent, however, because race-sensitive admission policies may be unfair to rejected applicants or to blacks as a group even if they achieve exactly what they are designed to achieve.

The practical question has been the more sharply debated in recent years. Advocates of affirmative action often insist that race-sensitive policies of different sorts are essential, in the short run, if we are to have any genuine hope of eradicating or diminishing the impact of race in the longer term. The most prominent critics of such programs, both white and black, reply that affirmative action has been in every way counterproductive: that it has "sacrificed" rather than helped the blacks admitted to the programs, perpetuating a sense of black inferiority among both whites and blacks themselves, and promoting black separatism and a race-conscious society rather than black integration and a genuinely colorblind community.[11]

Both advocates and critics rely, however, on only sketchy factual evidence to support their large claims. They cite newspaper accounts of isolated incidents of interracial cooperation—or of racial disharmony—in universities. They rely on introspective or anecdotal reports of successful blacks who credit affirmative action with having given them a chance, or blame it for stigmatizing, insulting, or cheapening them. Most of all they appeal to supposedly commonsense assumptions about how whites and blacks "must" or "may" feel or react.

It would be wrong to blame proponents and critics for relying on such thin evidence for their large claims, however, because though some excellent studies have been produced on particular issues—Bowen and Bok refer to several of these—there have been few studies of the scope needed. That is why *The Shape of the River* is so important: it offers much more comprehensive statistics and much more sophisticated analysis than have been available before. It has already made a considerable impact: its findings have been widely reported and discussed in the press.

We must be careful, of course, not to accept even such an apparently imposing study uncritically. The statistical analysis it offers may later be shown to be flawed. Or even more comprehensive studies may later be published that refute some or all of its main conclusions. But it would be surprising and shaming if *The Shape of the River* did not sharply improve the character of the long political and legal debate. Its analysis has significantly raised the standard of argument. Impressionistic and anecdotal evidence will no longer suffice: any respectable discussion of the consequences of affirmative action in universities must now either acknowledge its findings or challenge them, and any challenge must match the standards of breadth and statistical professionalism that Bowen, Bok, and their colleagues have achieved.

II

The two former university presidents are cautious and judicious scholars, and they are careful to limit their claims to what the evidence justifies. Yet they have no doubt as to the most important result of their study.

> If, at the end of the day, the question is whether the most selective colleges and universities have succeeded in educating sizable numbers of minority students who have already achieved considerable success and seem likely in time to occupy positions of leadership throughout society, we have no problem in answering the question. Absolutely . . .
>
> Overall, we conclude that academically selective colleges and universities

have been highly successful in using race-sensitive admissions policies to advance educational goals important to everyone.[12]

We cannot evaluate that overall conclusion, however, without noticing the large variety of distinct findings on which it is based. I cannot, of course, adequately summarize all of these, or describe the often ingenious techniques used to obtain and defend them. I shall concentrate instead on those findings that seem most germane to the political and legal argument.

Does affirmative action accept unqualified blacks? In 1951 there was a total of sixty-three blacks—only an average of 0.8 percent per school—in the entering classes of the nineteen C&B institutions for which records are available. In 1989 blacks accounted for 6.7 percent of the entering class in all C&B schools, and for 7.8 percent in the most selective group. Much of this increase must be attributed to race-sensitive admissions. Bowen and Bok estimate, by factoring out the impact of other variables, that a race-neutral admissions policy would have reduced the number of black entrants to between 2.1 and 3.6 percent for all schools in the study (depending on different assumptions about how many of the blacks admitted decided to attend). The decline would be greatest at the most selective schools.

It would be a serious mistake, however, to assume that these "retrospectively rejected" blacks were unqualified for the education they received.[13] White applicants to the schools did have significantly higher test scores, as a group, than the black applicants. The difference narrows sharply, however, when we compare the scores of blacks who enrolled with the lowest decile of the scores of whites admitted: a study of law school admissions showed a difference, in LSAT scores, of only 10 percent. The difference in scores between white and black applicants is better explained, in any case, by the extraordinary improvement in recent decades in the academic qualifications of white applicants to selective schools—Bowen and Bok call these applicants "spectacularly" well qualified—than by any assumption that the black applicants were not qualified. Five of the C&B schools, which were otherwise representative of them all, retained full information about all their 1989 applicants, and more than 75 percent of the black applicants had higher math SAT scores, and more than 73 percent had higher verbal SAT scores, than the national average of white test-takers. The professional success of black graduates from C&B schools, discussed below, in itself rebuts any assumption that these blacks were, as a group, unqualified for their education.

It is a striking fact, moreover, that the average SAT scores of black entrants to the most selective schools in 1989 were higher than the average of all matriculants in the same institutions in 1951. As the authors observe, middle-aged and elderly graduates should reflect on that fact before insisting that blacks accepted through affirmative action programs are unfit for their universities. It is also striking that the test scores of the retrospectively rejected blacks—those who the study predicts would not have been admitted had race-neutral tests been used—were not much different from the scores of the blacks who would have been accepted anyway. In the five schools just mentioned, the average SAT score of the former was 1145 and of the latter 1181. So while abolishing affirmative action would very greatly decrease the number of blacks who attended selective schools, it would not much improve the average scores of those who did.

Do blacks waste the opportunity they are offered? Would they be better off in less demanding institutions where they would "fit" better? In their recent book *America in Black and White,* Stephan and Abigail Thernstrom report that at some 300 "major" colleges and universities between 1984 and 1987 the dropout rate was 43 percent for white students and 66 percent for black students. They quote an article in the *Journal of Blacks in Higher Education* describing this fact as "disastrous," and they cite the same fact as justifying their own conclusion that "Affirmative action admissions policies . . . did work to increase enrollments, but if the larger aim was to increase the number of African Americans who would successfully complete college, preferential policies had disappointing, even counterproductive, results."[14] But (as would have been evident had they quoted the two sentences immediately following the *Journal* sentence from which they did quote)[15] their argument is highly misleading. The figures they cite are drawn from records of 301 schools in Division I of the National Collegiate Athletic Association (NCAA), and though these schools do include some institutions that are plainly "major," they include a great many that are equally plainly not.[16] Though the dropout figure for blacks in the 301 schools taken together is indeed much greater than that for whites, even the figure for whites is so alarmingly high that it suggests that affirmative action cannot be the main problem. The Thernstroms provide no evidence, in any case, as to how many of those 301 institutions practice affirmative action. (Bowen and Bok refer to a study that suggests that only the top 20 percent of all four-year institutions do.) If many do not, the difference in graduation rates would be unaffected even if that practice were eliminated elsewhere.[17]

The *River* study is much more discriminating and useful than the study cited by the Thernstroms. It shows that the black dropout rate in the C&B schools is small by national standards: 75 percent of the 1989 black C&B cohort graduated from the school they entered within six years compared with 59 percent of white students at the 301 schools that belong to Division I of the NCAA. Even so, the black graduation rate is lower than the white rate even at the C&B schools—by 11 percent in the 1989 group.

Some of the gap can be explained by obvious factors—blacks come, on average, from worse-off households, and are more likely to be forced to leave college for financial reasons, for example—but not all of it can be explained in that way. However, the black graduation rate, for blacks at each level of SAT scores, is progressively higher at more selective schools in the C&B group. Even blacks with the lowest SAT scores (1000 and less) graduated at higher rates when they attended more selective and demanding schools in the C&B group, where the difference between their scores and the average of other classmates was greater.[18]

Bowen and Bok consider a variety of explanations for these results. The more selective schools are also richer schools with more resources available for scholarships and other forms of student aid. Since the economic value of a college degree increases with the prestige of the school, moreover, all students have a greater financial incentive to remain in a more selective school. Such schools also have the resources to set up "mentoring" and other programs designed to help blacks with less adequate prior training in study and research skills to cope, and the study demonstrates the value of that help in other ways. In any case, these findings are of great importance because they seem to refute the "fit" hypothesis that the Thernstroms and others defend: that blacks would graduate in higher numbers if affirmative action were abolished and they attended less selective and competitive schools as a result.

That dismal hypothesis is also contradicted by much of the other data and analyses in the *River* study. Blacks as a group do not suffer, financially or otherwise, when they have attended a more selective school. At each SAT level, blacks earn more after having attended a more selective school, and report themselves as more satisfied with their careers. Nor do most blacks

who attended more selective schools report any discomfort or regret when
they reflect on their undergraduate experience, or otherwise suggest that
they were "sacrificed" by affirmative action programs. Black graduates of
C&B schools report satisfaction with their university experience at the same
very high rate—in the 1989 cohort, 91 percent declared themselves either
"very" or "somewhat" satisfied—as that of all other students. At every SAT
level, moreover, blacks who attended the more selective C&B schools, where
the gap between their SAT scores and the norm for the school was greater,
reported a higher degree of satisfaction, which is the contrary of what the
"fit" hypothesis claims. That hypothesis has played a very prominent part in
the affirmative action debate in recent years: the *River* study—at least until it
is challenged by evidence rather than shoddy scholarship or anecdote—
should put an end to its role.

III

Has affirmative action produced, as hoped, more successful black businessmen, professionals, and community leaders? If we measure success by income, it certainly has. Black male graduates from the twenty-eight C&B
schools in the 1976 cohort found less-well-paid jobs than their white classmates who had parallel test scores and college or professional school
grades,[19] and that sad fact is alone enough to refute any suggestion that
racism has disappeared from our economy. But black C&B graduates earn
considerably more than the average black with a B.A. degree: black women
in the 1976 cohort earn on average 73 percent, or $27,200, more than the
average of all black women with B.A.s, and black men in the cohort earn 82
percent, or $38,200, more than the average of all black males with B.A.s.

Several factors help to explain those differences: blacks in the C&B cohort
had on average better test scores, and came on average from higher socioeconomic backgrounds, than black graduates generally. But the selectivity of
the school they attended is nevertheless an important part of the story: the
more selective a black graduate's school, the higher his or her anticipated
income, even with all other factors held equal. As the authors point out,
"While graduation from a selective college hardly guarantees a successful
career, it may open doors, help black matriculants overcome any negative
stereotypes that may still be held by some employers, and create opportunities not otherwise available."[20]

The income advantage for blacks of attending a more selective school is revealing, not only because it shows that these admissions policies have helped, not harmed, their intended beneficiaries, but because it provides further evidence that the beneficiaries were fully qualified to profit from the education they received. Black graduates of the C&B institutions would not get or retain their well-paid positions in business, law, and medicine if their ability and education did not enable them to earn those salaries, in competition with others, by genuine contributions to their firm or profession.

We cannot measure the success of affirmative action by concentrating only on salaries, however, or only on the increased numbers of black executives, lawyers, doctors, and professors the study shows that the policy has helped to produce. Affirmative action, Bowen and Bok write, "was also inspired by a recognition that the country had a pressing need for well-educated black and Hispanic men and women who could assume leadership roles in their communities and in every facet of national life."[21] In this respect, too, the study reports success. Nationwide, black and white college graduates are equally likely to participate in various kinds of civic and professional groups. But among C&B graduates, black men are strikingly more likely to do so, especially in those activities that seem most important to black communities, including social service, youth clubs, and elementary and secondary school organizations. Almost twice as many blacks as whites from the 1976 cohort have participated in community service organizations, for example. In every type of activity cited, moreover, black males were more likely than white ones to hold leadership positions.

These findings are particularly interesting in view of the widespread fear, voiced by Henry Louis Gates and Orlando Patterson, among others, that educated middle-class blacks will take up new lives at a distance from the concerns of the larger black community.[22] That fear remains, but the study's statistics offer hope. "The fact that this group is consistently providing more civic leadership than its white peers indicates that social commitment and community concerns have not been thrown aside at the first sign of personal success."[23]

Does racial diversity in a university's student body help to break down stereotyping and hostility among the students, and, if so, does the benefit endure in post-university life? Or does racial preference generate animosity on campus, and a backlash that increases rather than decreases racial tension in the community generally? Critics cite well-publicized incidents of racial hostility on campus, and practices like "black tables" in university dining halls, to suggest that racial diversity has done nothing to reduce racial isolation and hostility, and may even have exacerbated it.

It is difficult to test attitudes and emotions, but the Bowen-Bok study has produced impressive statistics about them. The *River*'s questionnaire asked graduates in the cohorts it studied how important they thought race relations are, whether they thought their undergraduate education contributed to improving their own relations with other races, what interactions they had with members of other races as undergraduates, and whether they thought their university's admissions policies had emphasized racial diversity too much, too little, or in about the right degree. Answers to multiple-choice questions can only partly capture the complexity of personal experience and opinion, but the results are nevertheless telling.

Predictably, more blacks than whites thought knowing people of other races particularly important. In the 1976 cohort, 45 percent of whites thought it was "very important" to get to know people of "different beliefs" and only 43 percent to know people of different races, while 74 percent of blacks in that cohort thought the latter very important and only 42 percent the former. The number of both whites and blacks who thought race relations very important increased in the 1989 cohort, however—by a modest 2 percent for blacks but by a dramatic 13 percent for whites. (For those white graduates occupying leadership positions in civic organizations, the increase was even greater—to 59 percent.)

When asked to rank the value of their college experience in improving their ability to "get along with" people of other races, 46 percent of white and 57 percent of black respondents in the 1976 cohort rated that value at either 4 or 5 (5 indicated "very important"), and 18 percent of white and 30 percent of black respondents rated it at 5. In the 1989 cohort, these figures had jumped: 63 percent of the white respondents ranked the value at either 4 or 5, and 34 percent at 5; 70 percent of blacks ranked it either 4 or 5, and 46 percent at 5. These are significant differences between the two cohorts: the authors speculate that students might have become more aware of the importance of racial interaction by 1989, or that universities might have become more adept at creating an environment that facilitates that interaction, or, most likely, both.

It is important to try to confirm these subjective judgments of the importance of diversity by seeing how far they were actually reflected in behavior, particularly in view of the widespread belief that student groups are often racially isolated from one another. The study asked its respondents whether they had "known well" two or more students different from themselves in each of several categories, including geographical and economic background, general political orientation, and race. Even though black students made up less than 10 percent of the student body (except in one school, where they were 12 percent), 56 percent of the white respondents in the 1989 cohort said they knew two or more black students well. (Eighty-eight percent of the black students said that they knew two or more white students well.) The authors conclude that even though there was undoubtedly some self-segregation of races on these campuses, in clubs and dining arrangements, for example, "the walls between subgroups were highly porous." [24]

The further question the study put to respondents, about whether they approve of the level of concern for racial diversity that they believe their institution has shown, is doubly important, because it helps us to assess not only the value graduates place on that diversity in their own lives, but also the degree to which they, as members of the general public, resent racial preferences. Most of the whites in the 1976 cohort think that their institution places too much emphasis on alumni concerns, intercollegiate athletics, and faculty research. But only 22 percent of them think it places too much emphasis on racial and ethnic diversity, compared to 39 percent who think it places too little. Blacks in that cohort agree with their white classmates about alumni, athletics, and research, but, understandably, many more of them think their institution places too little emphasis on race. (The opinions of the 1989 cohort are surprisingly similar to those of the 1976 one, except that the later graduates think that their university places a greater emphasis on racial diversity than the earlier ones do.)

The study also reports interesting figures for the 1951 cohort, who are now in their mid-sixties. That group might be expected to be more conservative about affirmative action, which did not exist in their college years, than later cohorts. But 41 percent of the 1951 cohort (as compared to 37 percent and 48 percent of the 1976 and 1989 cohorts) believe that a great deal of emphasis should be placed on seeking racial diversity. Though roughly a third of its members think that their institution now places too much emphasis on it, half think the present emphasis right, and 17 percent would prefer more.

It might seem plausible to assume that white students with relatively low SAT scores, who might have worried more about the impact of race-sensitive admissions standards on them before they were admitted, would disapprove of them more. But there is no significant difference in approval or disapproval of such policies across the full range of SAT levels. Perhaps even more surprisingly, those white students who were not admitted to their first-choice school, and might well be expected to blame their failure on racial preferences, do not disapprove of seeking racial diversity any more than their initially more successful classmates do. The figures for the once-rejected white graduates in both the 1976 and 1989 C&B cohorts are nearly identical with those of all white graduates.

These statistics seem important in any attempt to assess the degree of general backlash against affirmative action in the United States generally. The political wars against affirmative action have concentrated on racial preferences in hiring, which many working-class voters believe they have personal cause to resent, and some commentators have doubted whether there is a genuinely deep national resentment against affirmative action even over hiring. Louis Harris, for example, has argued that the success of the California proposition banning all affirmative action was determined by a misleading presentation; his own polls suggest, he reports, that a fairer presentation of the proposition would have led to its defeat.[25] In any case, the *River* study gives some reason to doubt whether there is any general and deep-seated antagonism to affirmative action specifically in university admissions. Of course, many rejected university applicants (including, presumably, the plaintiffs in the lawsuits I mentioned) are indeed resentful. But the study estimates the number of once-rejected students who are resentful as relatively low.

Does affirmative action damage blacks by insulting or mortifying them, or destroying their self-respect, or poisoning the black image? The most moving arguments against affirmative action are made by those blacks who feel insulted or damaged by the assumption that blacks need special favors. Anyone, whether a black graduate or a successful child of rich or prominent parents of any race, will resent any suspicion that undervalues his personal achievements, and the fact that many prominent blacks fear that affirmative action has encouraged such suspicion is an undoubted and regrettable cost of the policy.

It is obviously important, however, in estimating the extent of that cost, to discover how many blacks hold this view. If many do, then the cost is great. But if the view is firmly rejected by most black graduates of elite institutions, who are especially likely to suffer professionally and personally from any assumption that their credentials or achievements are tainted, or from any damaged black image in the nation—if most such graduates believe, on the contrary, that the pursuit of racial diversity through race-sensitive admissions policies has been good for them and for their race—then the pain suffered by the small minority who disagree, while genuine, cannot be thought significant enough to outweigh the advantages the majority believe the race has gained. In fact, the overwhelming majority of blacks canvassed in the *River* study applaud the race-sensitive policies of their university. They think that their universities should now place more, not less, emphasis on racial diversity, and they accept what the study confirms: that affirmative action has been good for them, both in raising their income and in other, less material ways.

Could the proportion of blacks in prestigious institutions be maintained if affirmative action was abandoned and race-neutral standards used instead? The *River* study calculates, on the basis of plausible assumptions, that a strict race-neutral admissions policy would have reduced the number of blacks in the C&B schools by between 50 percent and 75 percent.[26] The impact of race-neutral policies on the professions would be particularly dramatic and damaging: blacks would have made up only 1.6 to 3.4 percent of the total number of students accepted to the 173 law schools approved by the American Bar Association if those schools had relied only on college grades and test scores, and less than 1 percent in the most selective law schools.[27]

Some scholars, including many who are anxious not to reduce the number of blacks in elite schools, have suggested that roughly the same number would be admitted if schools gave preference to low-income applicants instead of to black applicants, because so many black applicants are poor. The study shows that this suggestion is based on a fallacy: though black applicants are disproportionately poor, poor applicants are still dominantly white, and even race-neutral tests that aimed at economic diversity would result in greatly decreased numbers of blacks.[28]

That calculation assumes, it is true, that institutions like those in the C&B list would be content to accept so dramatic a reduction in black presence in their classrooms, and would not try to escape whatever political or legal decisions had forced them to use race-neutral standards. That assumption is not necessarily valid. Boalt Hall and other branches of the University of California are studying changes in admissions procedures, including treating top grades at much less selective colleges as just as important as top grades at Harvard, and relying less on test scores altogether.[29]

The Texas state legislature, responding to the Fifth Circuit's *Hopwood* decision, enacted a new program requiring the public universities of the state to accept all graduates of state high schools in the top 10 percent of their classes: since some high schools are almost exclusively black, this change can be expected to increase black enrollment at the formerly most selective Texas universities. Even if such adjustments succeed in their goal, they may well do so by substituting less qualified black matriculants for those that an open and acknowledged affirmative action program would have selected. Some former opponents of affirmative action, worried by that possibility, are having second thoughts. Professor John Yoo of Boalt Hall, who campaigned for Proposition 209, now says he realizes that conventional affirmative action is a useful way of maintaining racial diversity while still, as he puts it, "limiting the damage" to academic standards generally.[30]

Is the United States better off, judged strictly by the outcome, because its most selective universities and colleges have practiced affirmative action over the past thirty years? Most of the 700 "retrospectively rejected" black students from the 1976 cohort, who would not have attended a C&B school if race-neutral standards had been used, would have attended other, less selective, universities. But the high correlation the study establishes between the selectivity of the school attended and later success, for every level of SAT score, high school grades, and socioeconomic background, suggests that many fewer of them would then have become prominent professors, doctors, or lawyers, or high-salaried and powerful business executives, or political or community service leaders, than the actual graduates have become. The 1,000 "retrospectively rejected" black students of the 1989 cohort give promise, already, of even greater success. So we can rephrase the question: Would America be better off if many fewer such important positions were held by blacks now and over the next generation? It seems incredible to suppose that it would. In all the dimensions in which our society is stratified—income, wealth, power, prestige, and authority—blacks are greatly underrepresented in the top levels, and the resulting de facto racial stratification is an enduring shame, waste, and danger. How could we think ourselves better off if that racial stratification were even more absolute than it is, and if we saw no or fewer signs of its lessening?

IV

Still, if affirmative action is unfair, because it violates the rights of white and other candidates who are refused places or of the few blacks who feel insulted, then it would be improper even if it does make the nation better off. We should notice, before we begin to examine that possibility, that the damage affirmative action inflicts on any particular nonpreferred candidate is very small: the *River* study suggests that if race-neutral standards had been used in one set of schools it studied, and fewer blacks therefore admitted, the antecedent probability of admission of any particular white applicant who was in fact rejected would have risen only from about 25 percent to about 26.5 percent, because there were so many rejected white candidates at approximately the same level of test scores and other qualifications that adding a few more places would not much have improved the chances of any of them. When the Fifth Circuit declared the Texas Law School's admission scheme unconstitutional, and remitted the case to a lower court to award damages to the rejected white plaintiffs who had brought the lawsuit, the lower court awarded each only one dollar because it was so unlikely that any of them would have been admitted even under race-neutral standards.

Does affirmative action violate the right of candidates to be judged only on the basis of their individual qualifications? What counts as a qualification in this context? In some competitions, such as a beauty contest or a quiz show, qualification is a matter only of some physical or intellectual quality: the winner should be the most beautiful or knowledgeable candidate. In others, such as a book prize or a medal awarded for bravery, qualification is a matter of prior achievement: the winner should be the candidate who has produced the best work or product, or shown special character in some way, in the past. In still other competitions, however, qualification is a matter of forward-looking promise rather than backward-looking achievement or natural property: a rational person does not choose a doctor as a tribute to her skill or to reward her for past cures: he chooses the doctor whom he expects to do best for him in the future, and he takes the doctor's innate talent or past achievements into account only because, and so far as, these are good indicators of the doctor's value to him in the future.

Competitions for university places are, of course, competitions of the last sort. Admissions officers should not award places as prizes for past achievements or effort, or as medals for inherent talents or virtues: their duty is to try to choose a student body that, as a whole, will make the greatest future contribution to the legitimate goals their institution has defined. Elite higher education is a valuable and scarce resource, and though it is available only to very few students, it is paid for by the community generally, even in the case of "private" universities that are partly financed by public grants and whose "private" donors benefit from tax deductions. Universities and colleges therefore have public responsibilities: they must choose goals to benefit a much wider community than their own faculty and students. These need not be economic or social or political goals in any narrow sense: on the contrary, we expect all our educational institutions, and particularly the best-financed and most-prestigious ones, to contribute to science, art, and philosophy, whose advancement we take to be part of our collective public responsibility, and to select students and faculty very much with that goal in mind.

But the advancement of knowledge is not the only goal that we allow or expect educational institutions to pursue. We expect them all, particularly the best financed, to help both their students and the larger community in other, including more practical, ways as well—a great university may properly decide to study the treatment of AIDS or Alzheimer's disease even when it knows that different, more basic research would be theoretically more rewarding. Nor do we expect all schools to adopt the same goals or to attach the same relative importance to the goals they do select. The great research universities in the C&B data base have different priorities from the smaller liberal arts colleges in that base, and both of these have different goals from small agricultural colleges, community colleges, and other institutions of a kind not represented in the base at all. The academic freedom we prize means, among much else, that each institution is free, within broad limits, to set goals for itself and to define the academic strategies, including admissions strategies, that it believes most appropriate to those goals.

All the C&B schools have traditionally regarded impressive high school or college grades and high SAT and other test scores as important qualifications for university and professional education. But none of them has treated these distinctly academic qualifications as exclusive: they have all from time to time rejected candidates with top SAT scores and grades—even black candidates—in favor of other students with lower grades and scores. The list of other qualifications is long: it includes motivation for public service, athletic ability, unusual geographical background, and, in the case of some of these schools, "legacy status," which means having parents who are graduates of that university. Admissions officers regard each of these attributes, and many more, as indicators (though far from perfect ones) that a particular applicant will contribute to one or more of the institution's traditional goals. The *River* study shows, and the great American universities and colleges have recognized for thirty years, that at least two of these traditional goals are well served by including, as one among the myriad factors that admissions officers take into account, a candidate's race.

First, as I said, American schools have aimed at student classes that are diverse in several ways. They have plausibly assumed that students are better equipped for commercial and professional life, and better prepared to act as good citizens in a pluralistic democracy, if they have worked and played with classmates of different geographical background, economic class, religion, culture, and—above all, now—race. Critics argue that selecting on the basis of race is an inappropriate means of pursuing diversity because it wrongly, and insultingly, assumes that all black students do, and only black students can, provide desirable diversity in class, political attitudes, or culture: it would be better, according to these critics, to accept students of whatever race whose parents are poor or who appreciate soul music, rather than seek black students, some of whom have rich parents or prefer Bach.

But this objection misses the aspect of diversity that is in question, which is not what race may or may not indicate, but race itself. Unfortunately the worst of the stereotypes, suspicions, fears, and hatreds that still poison America are coded by color, not by class or culture. It is crucial that blacks and whites come to know and appreciate each other better, and if some of the blacks turn out not to have the class or cultural or other characteristics that are stereotypically associated with them, that obviously enhances rather than undermines the benefits of racial diversity.

Second, our schools have traditionally aimed to help improve the collective life of the community, not just by protecting and enhancing its culture and science or improving its medicine, commerce, and agriculture, but by helping to make that collective life more just and harmonious—those are, after all, among the main ambitions of our law schools and schools of politics and public administration, and they should form part of the goals of the rest of the academy as well. Our universities and colleges are surely entitled to think that the continuing and debilitating segregation of the United States by race, class, occupation, and status is an enemy of both justice and harmony, and it is one of the most dramatic conclusions of the

River study that affirmative action has begun to erode that segregation in ways no other program or policy probably could. We expect educational institutions to contribute to our physical and economic health, and we should expect them to do what they can for our social and moral health as well.

So affirmative action, in pursuit of either or both of the twin goals of student diversity and social justice, in no way compromises the principle that student places should be awarded only on the basis of legitimate and appropriate qualifications. No student has a right to a university place in virtue of past achievements or innate virtues, talents, or other qualities: students must be judged only by the likelihood that each, in combination with others selected on the same standards, will contribute to the various goals that the institution has legitimately chosen. I do not mean (as some critics have accused defenders of affirmative action of supposing) that black color is in itself a virtue or an aspect of merit. But it is nevertheless a qualification in the sense I have been describing. We do not count a person's height as a virtue or a merit. But someone who is tall may just for that reason be better able to contribute, on a basketball court, to one of a university's traditional goals, and in the same way, though for sadder reasons, someone who is black may for that reason be better able to contribute to its other goals, in the classroom and dormitory and in the course of his or her later career.

Why, then, is affirmative action so widely thought unfair? Why do even many of its supporters concede that it is a distasteful remedy, even if, in their view, a necessary one? We must take care to distinguish and consider a variety of answers to those questions, because each has had an important though sometimes inarticulate part in the public's response. It is often said, first, that race-sensitive admissions policies do not judge applicants as individuals, but only as members of large groups. That objection was strongly pressed against early and relatively crude forms of affirmative action, such as the quota system declared unconstitutional in the *Bakke* case, because, as Justice Powell said, once the white quota had been filled, no further white candidate could be compared, even on an all-things-considered basis, to a black who was accepted instead.[31] Under contemporary versions of affirmative action in university admissions, however, no quotas are used: these plans are in that respect like the Harvard plan that Powell expressly approved. Admissions officers now do make case-by-case, all-things-considered judgments, and they sometimes accept a white student with lower SAT scores than a rejected black applicant. No one is accepted or excluded simply by virtue of race.

Many people do feel very strongly that even if universities should view a wide variety of properties as among the qualifications for admission they recognize, race, for special reasons, should not be among these. It is crucial, however, to distinguish different ways in which race might be thought special, and to consider the implications of each. We have already discussed one: many people believe that race-sensitive admissions standards exacerbate rather than help relieve racial tension. But we may set that claim aside, in the light of the *River* study, unless that study is somehow impeached. Many people also believe, however, that racial classifications are always wrong in principle, even when their results are in themselves desirable. They point out that we would not accept a law school's argument that it rejects all black applicants because it aims to help the community's economy by producing graduates who will function effectively in local law firms that do not welcome blacks. They insist that we cannot in principle distinguish that invidious use of race to achieve results in themselves creditable from a so-called "benign" use. And even if we could do so in principle, we could not realistically do so in practice, because invidious uses might easily masquerade as benign ones.

The first of these arguments is the easier to answer: we can make the distinction between affirmative action and malign uses of race, at least in principle, in two ways. First, we can define an individual right that the malign forms of discrimination violate but that properly conceived affirmative action programs do not: this is the fundamental right of each citizen to be treated by his government, and by institutions acting with the support of his government, as equally worthy of concern and respect. A black citizen is denied that right when schools justify discriminating against him by appealing to the fact that others are prejudiced against members of his race.

But the case for affirmative action does not reflect, either directly or indirectly, prejudice against white citizens; seeking racial diversity no more reflects a prejudice against whites than seeking geographical diversity expresses prejudice against people from large urban centers. Second, though it is important to allow universities ample latitude in designing their own purposes and goals, we can nevertheless insist that some goals a university might conceivably adopt are illegitimate and unacceptable, and we can dismiss, as such, a goal that panders to and reinforces the racial stratification of our society.

It is true, however, that these distinctions of principle may be hard to enforce in practice, particularly because they rely on judgments about institutional motives that are often hard to identify. How could we be sure, for example, that a program that gives preference to some minorities, like blacks and Hispanics, is not motivated by hostility to other groups of citizens—Asian Americans or Jews, for example—who score well on tests and who would be admitted in greater numbers if admission policies were race-neutral? Or by an even cruder desire on the part of admissions officials in some institutions, who might themselves be black, to favor their own people at the expense of others? Would it not be better to guard against this possible corruption by flatly forbidding all use of race in university admissions?

That argument has been pressed in nonuniversity situations, as an argument, for example, against allowing city councils, which might well be dominated by black members or dependent on black support, to set aside a quota of construction contracts for black-owned firms, or allowing a state legislature, which might be influenced by racial politics in these and other ways, to design electoral districts so as to elect more black officials.[32] But however forceful this argument for a flat prohibition on racial classifications might or might not be in these other situations, it seems fanciful and misplaced when applied to higher education. The faculty and academic administrators who stipulate and use race-sensitive admissions standards are in no way beholden for power or financial support to any of the communities these standards benefit. They act in pursuit of traditional goals that the *River* study shows are most efficiently served in that way.

Moreover, any suspicion of hidden hostility to another group that has also been the target of prejudice could easily be tested by seeing whether that group is disproportionately represented among those who would probably have been admitted under race-neutral standards. True, these considerations do not wholly eliminate any conceivable possibility that illegitimate motives have played a role. But denying all universities the power to do what they can to improve diversity and social justice and stability, on the remote chance that some one or two institutions would abuse that power and escape undetected, would be like denying any use of public funds for medical research on the ground that a few researchers might be plagiarists or embezzlers.

So we may set aside these mistaken arguments of principle and policy. We must nevertheless recognize the important psychological fact that many people do think that being rejected by a university because they are not of the "right" race is far worse—more outrageous and more insulting—than being rejected because they lack some other quality, like a skill or physical ability, or even because their parents did not graduate from the school. That special outrage is understandable, however, not because race has some special importance in the metaphysics of personal identity—one's skin color is no less a matter of choice, and no more genetically grounded, than the raw abilities that insure that some adolescents will never be able to score above 1400 on an SAT test no matter how hard they prepare. It is understandable because we are all so familiar with the character and consequence of invidious racial classification.

Racial discrimination expresses contempt, and it is deeply unjust and wounding to be condemned for one's natural properties; racial discrimination is, moreover, wholly destructive of its victims' lives—it does not merely close off to them one or another opportunity open to others, but injures them in almost all the prospects and hopes they might conceive. In a racist society people are indeed rejected absolutely and for who they are, and it is therefore natural that racial classifications should be seen as capable of inflicting a special form of injury. But it would nevertheless be perverse to disallow the use of such classifications to help combat the racism that is the true and continuing cause of that injury. The special psychological character of race is not a fixed fact to which policy must always defer. It is a product and sign of racism, and it must not be permitted to protect the racism that has generated it.

We should consider one final reason why race might be thought special, which lies at the intersection of moral and legal concerns. It is often argued that America's social and constitutional history has committed us, as a people, to a society that is colorblind as a matter not just of our ultimate goals but also of the means that we are entitled to use toward any goal. According to this argument, the constitutional amendments adopted after the Civil War, which include the Fourteenth Amendment's guarantee of "equal protection of the laws," were a national commitment—moral as well as legal—to refuse race any official role in our affairs whatever. If so, then university affirmative action programs are wrong in principle, whether or not they violate anyone's rights as an individual, because they cheat on that important national commitment.

But this argument, though popular, is unpersuasive. Some critics of affirmative action do argue, as we have seen, that a colorblind commitment would be a wise strategic decision: that we would do a better job of confronting and eliminating racism in the long run if we always avoided any racial classification, even those that might seem, in the short run, effective against racism. But they have offered no argument for that strategic hypothesis, and the *River* study seems to prove it false. Nor is there any ground for supposing that the Constitution, or anything else, has committed the nation to that strategy. The Fourteenth Amendment does not mention race, and no plausible interpretation of that amendment shows it automatically to rule out all racial classifications as means to greater justice. Nor have the American people, by any long-standing or sustained consensus, ruled out all such classifications for that purpose. The supposed national commitment is an illusion.

So, according to by far the best evidence yet available, affirmative action is not counterproductive. On the contrary it seems impressively successful. Nor is affirmative action unfair: it violates no individual rights and compromises no moral principle. Is it nevertheless unconstitutional, as the Fifth Circuit judges ruled in the *Hopwood* case?

In Chapter 12 I consider the arguments of constitutional principle and the analysis of recent Supreme Court decisions on which those judges relied. There I argue that both principle and precedent continue to support the *Bakke* principle that properly drafted race-sensitive admissions standards are constitutional. Of course affirmative action has had its costs—both to disappointed white applicants and to those successful black ones who resent any suspicion that they needed special preference to succeed—and the policy has undoubtedly provoked more general resentment, even if the scale of that resentment remains unclear. But the moral and practical costs of forbidding it would be far greater. The systemic racial discrimination of the past has created a nation in which positions of power and prestige have been largely reserved for one race. It was not irresponsible for critics to oppose affirmative action, on the ground that it would do more harm than good, when the consequences of the policy were still uncertain. But it would be wrong for the nation to prohibit that policy now, when comprehensive statistics and analysis have apparently demonstrated its value. Unless and until the *River* study has been impeached by a better—larger or more sophisticated—study, we have no reason to forbid university affirmative action as a weapon against our deplorable racial stratification, except our indifference to that problem, or our petulant anger that it has not gone away on its own.[33]

12

Affirmative Action:
Is It Fair?

⋀

I

Is affirmative action unconstitutional? Does it violate the Fourteenth Amendment's guarantee of "equal protection of the laws" for universities to give preference to blacks and other minorities in the fierce competition for student places, as the best of our universities have done for thirty years? In 1978 Justice Lewis Powell, in his opinion in the Supreme Court's famous *Bakke* decision, ruled that racial preferences are permissible if their purpose is to improve racial diversity among students, and if they do not stipulate fixed minority quotas but take race into account as one factor among many.[1] Since four other justices in that case would have upheld even a quota system, five of the nine agreed that plans meeting Powell's tests were constitutional.

Many lawyers fear that the Supreme Court will soon reconsider its *Bakke* ruling, however, and declare that any racial preference in an admissions process is, after all, unconstitutional. In 1996 the Fifth Circuit Court of Appeals, in the *Hopwood* case, struck down the Texas Law School's affirmative action plan, and two of the three judges in the panel declared that recent Supreme Court decisions about affirmative action policies in areas other than education have already in effect overruled *Bakke*, so that all university affirmative action is now unconstitutional.[2]

The Fifth Circuit's decision had immediate and, in the view of the Texas Law School's faculty, disastrous results: that school had admitted thirty-one black students in 1996, but it enrolled only four in 1997. The Supreme Court refused to review the decision, but the Center for Individual Rights, a Washington, D.C.–based organization that had facilitated the *Hopwood* litigation, filed a new lawsuit in Michigan in 1998 challenging the University of Michi-

409

gan's affirmative action plan, and other suits can be expected in other jurisdictions. The Supreme Court will have to rule on the matter soon.

It will be not only ironic but sad if the Court reverses its own long-standing ruling now, because dramatic evidence of the value of affirmative action in elite higher education has just become available. Critics of the policy have long argued, among other things, that it does more harm than good, because it exacerbates rather than reduces racial hostility, and because it damages the minority students who are selected for elite schools, where they must compete with other students whose test scores and other academic qualifications are much higher than their own. But a new study—*The Shape of the River,* by William G. Bowen and Derek Bok—draws on a huge data base of information about student records and histories, and on sophisticated statistical techniques, not only to refute those claims but to demonstrate the contrary.[3] According to the *River* study, affirmative action has achieved remarkable success: it has produced higher rates of graduation among black college students, more black leaders in industry, the professions, and community and neighborhood service, and more sustained interaction and friendship among different races than would otherwise have been possible. (I have discussed the findings and implications of this study in detail in Chapter 11.) If the Supreme Court declares affirmative action unconstitutional, the study declares, black enrollment in elite universities and colleges will be sharply reduced, and scarcely any black students will be admitted to the best law and medical schools.[4] That would be a huge defeat for racial harmony and justice. Will the Supreme Court rule that the Constitution requires us to accept that defeat?

The Fifth Circuit judges are convinced that it will, and if we are to understand why they think so, and why so many commentators fear that they are right, we must explore the apparatus of legal doctrines and distinctions that the Court has developed, over the last several decades, to assist it in applying the equal protection clause; for this is one of those instances, created by our constitutional system, in which America's social and political future hinges on careful legal analysis.

The equal protection clause does not, of course, protect citizens from all legal distinctions or classifications that work to their disadvantage. Government must decide which medical research to support, which art to subsidize, which industries or products to protect by tariffs or other trade policy, which businesses to regulate for environmental reasons, where to locate a new army base or airport or a new nuclear waste dump, and thousands of other matters that will affect the fates and fortunes of different citizens very differently. Officials make such decisions for a variety of reasons. In principle, they should aim at decisions that, though they benefit some citizens and disadvantage others, are in the general interest of the community as a whole. In practice, interest-group politics often play a crucial part: an industry that is denied protection or selected for regulation may have lost its legislative battle, not because a different decision would have been less in the public interest, but because it lacked the political power, on this occasion, to force that different decision.

The equal protection clause is violated, not whenever some group has lost an important decision on the merits of the case or through politics, but when its loss results from its special vulnerability to prejudice or hostility or stereotype and its consequent diminished standing—its second-class citizenship—in the political community. The clause does not guarantee each citizen that he will benefit equally from every political decision; it guarantees him only that he will be treated as an equal—with equal concern and respect—in the political processes and deliberations that produce those decisions.

But the Fourteenth Amendment therefore poses a special difficulty for the courts that must enforce it: it requires them to judge not merely the consequences of legislation for different groups, but the motive behind that legislation. Was the law that injures this or that group the product of a forbidden, prejudiced attitude toward that group or of more benign motives? It is extremely difficult to attribute motives and attitudes to general legislation, not just because it is difficult to identify the psychological states of individual legislators and other officials, but for the deeper reason that it is often unclear how we should translate those individual motives—and the motives and attitudes of the constituents in whose interests the legislation has supposedly been adopted—into an overall motive that we can attribute to the legislation itself.[5]

In some cases, that judgment seems easy, at least in retrospect. The Court rightly decided, in 1954, that racial school segregation violated the equal protection rights of black children, because segregation signaled their inferiority and exclusion. It rightly decided, in 1996, that a Colorado state constitutional amendment forbidding any local antidiscrimination protection for homosexuals violated the equal protection rights of members of that group, because, as Justice Anthony Kennedy said, "the amendment seems inexplicable by anything but animus toward the class it affects."[6]

Other cases, however, are much more difficult to assess. Does a local rent-control ordinance, for example, express a theory about wise and fair housing management or a special hostility toward landlords as a class? It seems silly to invite judges to review the political sociology of every piece of legislation that anyone challenges, because they have neither the time nor the equipment for such studies. It also seems dangerous to democracy, because judges might overrule democratic decisions on the barest speculation of improper motives.[7]

The courts have instead tried to approach the question of motive indirectly, through doctrines intended to "smoke out" improper motives by concentrating on the apparently more objective question of a law's actual effects. They subject all political decisions that are challenged on equal protection grounds to an initial threshold classification. If a decision imposes serious disadvantages on what the Supreme Court has called a "suspect" class—a class, according to one prominent definition, that is "saddled with such disabilities, or subjected to such a history of purposeful unequal treatment, or relegated to such a position of political powerlessness as to command extraordinary protection from the majoritarian political process"[8]—then the decision is to be subject to "strict scrutiny." This means that it must be rejected as violating the equal protection clause unless the disadvantage can be shown to be essential in order to protect some "compelling" governmental interest. But if those whom a law disadvantages do not form such a "suspect" class—if they are only the members of a particular business or profession or the residents of a particular area, and are not different from their fellow citizens in any way historically associated with prejudice or antipathy—then that law is subject to only a "relaxed" scrutiny: it is constitutional unless it can be demonstrated to serve no purpose or point at all.

The initial assignment of any particular law or decision to one or the other of these "levels of scrutiny" has almost always proved final. As one leading commentator put it long ago, strict scrutiny is "'strict' in theory and fatal in fact," because almost no interest has seemed sufficiently "compelling" to justify imposing further disadvantage on a suspect class,[9] and "relaxed" scrutiny is in effect no scrutiny at all, because some purpose or other can always be attributed to even the most inane legislation.

So lawyers considering the constitutionality of affirmative action programs naturally begin by asking whether such programs should be initially classified as requiring strict or only relaxed scrutiny. But they have great difficulty answering that question, because neither choice seems fully appropriate. On the one hand, affirmative action plans seem entitled to relaxed scrutiny, because though they use racial classifications, the group they mainly disadvantage—white applicants to colleges and universities—do not constitute a "suspect class," that is, a class that has been the victim of prejudice. But race is so closely associated with bias and favoritism that some racial classifications that seem benign on the surface might turn out, after a closer look, to be constitutionally offensive. Black municipal councils might conceivably have acted to favor black businesses out of racial solidarity, for example, or to punish innocent whites for the racial crimes of their ancestors; a university admissions scheme that gives preference to blacks might conceivably have been constructed to reduce the number of Asian Americans or Jews admitted.

Careful inspection would almost always disclose such improper motives—statistics could show whether any such group was disproportionately represented among the applicants displaced by affirmative action—but relaxed scrutiny would not permit that inspection. On the other hand, subjecting racial classifications that benefit "suspect" groups to the same standards of strict scrutiny as those classifications that impose further damage on those groups seems insensitive to the important moral differences between those two aims. It also seems perverse, because, as the *River* study apparently demonstrates, affirmative action is one of the most effective weapons we have against the racism that strict scrutiny is designed to thwart.

So affirmative action presents a great challenge to the conventional doctrine, and lawyers and judges have suggested different responses to that challenge. The most direct—and, I believe, the most appealing—response would be to declare the level-of-scrutiny strategy inapposite to the problem. That strategy, as it has historically been understood and used, is designed to identify types of legislation that by their nature involve either so high a risk of invidious discrimination that invidiousness should be nearly irrevocably presumed or so low a risk that its possibility should be nearly irrevocably dismissed. Race-sensitive programs that are, on their face, designed to help a disadvantaged racial group fall into neither of these categories, and it is procrustean to try to force them into one or the other.

Instead, judges should inspect such plans, when they are challenged in litigation, on a more case-by-case basis: they should use, as Justice Thurgood

Marshall once recommended, a "sliding-scale" approach in order to decide whether there is any convincing evidence that the racial classification actually does reflect prejudice or hostility of the kind forbidden by the equal protection clause.[10] Such an approach would take into account, among other pertinent factors, the character of the groups benefited and disadvantaged by the program, the racial or other character of the officials who have designed and will administer the plan, and whether the plan aims at a goal—like educational diversity, for example—that has historically been recognized as appropriate for the institution in question. It is true that this case-by-case approach to the affirmative action problem would require more judicial work and provide less predictability and guidance for lower courts, at least initially, until new rules of thumb and doctrinal strategies began to emerge. But any initial loss in predictability would be more than outweighed by the more accurate discrimination between valuable and invidious policies that greater flexibility would allow.

Supreme Court justices have disagreed for many years about whether to abandon the levels-of-scrutiny approach for affirmative action and, if not, about which level to choose. In two cases, the Court tried to solve the problem by defining an "intermediate" level of scrutiny, which requires that an affirmative action plan be shown to serve an "important" but not necessarily a "compelling" interest.[11] But in recent cases, chiefly through a series of opinions written by Justice Sandra Day O'Connor, the Court has decided that all racial classifications, including those that are apparently designed to favor rather than injure suspect groups, are subject to strict scrutiny. In 1986, in the *Croson* case, the Court struck down a Richmond, Virginia, city council plan that required city contractors to subcontract at least 30 percent of the dollar amount of any contract to minority-owned firms.[12] Richmond called its plan "remedial" and said it had adopted the plan "for the purpose of promoting wider participation by minority business enterprises in the construction of public projects."

O'Connor ruled that Richmond could properly claim a "compelling" interest in rectifying the continuing effects of past discrimination only if it had itself been the author of the injustice, either directly, by its own discriminatory practices, or "as a 'passive participant' in a system of racial exclusion practiced by elements of the local construction industry";[13] and she held that the city had not shown that its plan was carefully tailored to rectify only the effects of its own direct or passive discrimination. It could not satisfy strict scrutiny, she said, by claiming an interest in achieving a racially more diverse local construction industry, because there might be many reasons, other than the continuing effects of past discrimination, why a particular race was underrepresented in a particular industry, and it was not a permissible aim of government to pursue racial diversity or proportionality for its own sake.

The Fifth Circuit judges, in their *Hopwood* opinion striking down the Texas Law School plan, relied mainly on the Supreme Court's *Croson* decision to justify their claim that university affirmative action plans are now unconstitutional. The Texas Law School argued that its affirmative action plan was justified, even under a strict scrutiny test, because, among other things, affirmative action was necessary in order to produce a racially diverse student body—the goal that Powell had approved in *Bakke*. But the judges said that *Croson* and other cases had in effect overruled Powell's principle. These decisions had established the new rule that no state institution may use a racial classification for any purpose except to remedy the continuing effects of its own direct or indirect discrimination. The law school could not satisfy that test, the judges said, because it had ceased discriminating against minorities many years ago. Are those judges right that *Croson* and later cases have had that dramatic and devastating consequence? That is a crucial question for the future of American education and society, and it is important that the public understand the actual force of these Supreme Court precedents.

II

In fact the strict scrutiny test, as it has often been formulated in textbooks and judicial opinions, can be interpreted in two very different ways. One of these (which I shall call the "overriding necessity" version) supports the Fifth Circuit judges' opinion that the Supreme Court has already in effect declared all university affirmative action unconstitutional. The other (which I shall call the "rebuttal" version) refutes that opinion. When we inspect the recent Supreme Court decisions that the Fifth Circuit judges cited with the distinction between these two interpretations of strict scrutiny in mind, we find that though three of the present Supreme Court justices—Chief Justice Rehnquist and Justices Scalia and Thomas—prefer the overriding-necessity version, O'Connor's key opinions presuppose the rebuttal version. We also find that the rebuttal version much better fits the opinions of the five remaining justices.

The two versions are based on strikingly different assumptions about the constitutional status of racial classifications. According to the first version, that of overriding necessity, any racial classification imposed by any branch of government for any purpose whatever automatically violates the equal protection clause in principle. A racial classification can therefore be tolerated only if it is absolutely necessary either as the only available means for that branch to end its own past and continuing racial discrimination, or to forestall some danger of such dramatic urgency—in Justice Scalia's words, "a social emergency rising to the level of imminent danger to life and limb"[14]— that we must overlook a grave constitutional wrong in order to avoid that danger. If the *Croson* decision is properly understood as endorsing that version of the strict scrutiny test, then the Fifth Circuit judges were right. Racial diversity in a student body may be an important academic and social goal, but pursuing that goal would not justify overlooking a serious violation of the Fourteenth Amendment. Underrepresentation of minorities in a law school class does not present an "imminent danger to life and limb."

The second, rebuttal, version of the strict scrutiny test rests on very different premises. It does not presuppose that every racial classification violates the Fourteenth Amendment, even in principle, and it therefore does not assume that no racial classification is tolerable unless it is required by some emergency sufficiently grave to justify overlooking a constitutional wrong. It assumes that racial classifications violate the equal protection clause only when they have been generated by the unacceptable attitudes of prejudice or stereotyping that the clause outlaws. But it also supposes that since race has so often proved a ground of prejudice and favoritism, it is a wise constitutional strategy to impose a strict burden of proof on any institution employing such a classification, by demanding that the institution produce evidence of a proper motive that is sufficiently compelling to rebut any realistic suspicion that unacceptable motives were actually responsible.

This rebuttal version is much more demanding than the sliding-scale test I said that I prefer, because the rebuttal version sets the standard of proof very high.[15] But it is much more flexible than the overriding-necessity version, because whether an institution is able to rebut all suspicion by pointing to some legitimate goal or interest that its racial classification serves depends not just on the intrinsic urgency of that goal, considered abstractly, but on all the concrete circumstances. It depends, among other things, on whether the goal has been part of the institution's traditional responsibilities—for example, diversity among university students—whether the classification seems carefully designed to serve that goal, whether the institution might have other, less respectable, motives for what it has done, and on any other factors that might arouse or quiet suspicion given all the facts of the case. So a Supreme Court decision that Richmond could not satisfy strict scrutiny by declaring that it was aiming to improve racial diversity in the construction industry would not entail, or even strongly suggest, that the Texas Law School could not satisfy that test by pointing out that its admissions policies improve racial diversity in its classrooms. The grounds and character of suspicion might be so different in the two cases that a goal that fails to rebut the suspicion in one case would not fail in the other.

The rebuttal reading is much easier to justify on constitutional principle than the overriding-necessity reading. The latter assumes that the equal protection clause automatically forbids all racial classifications no matter what purposes they serve, and there is no warrant for that understanding in any plausible theory of constitutional interpretation. The Fourteenth Amendment does not mention race, and we have no reason to think that those who drafted and endorsed that amendment meant to forbid all racial classifications outright. On the contrary, many of them voted for and endorsed a variety of racial classifications, including even racial segregation in public schools.

It is true that the equal protection clause lays down a general principle of political morality, and that its contemporary interpreters must make moral judgments if they are to remain faithful to that general principle.[16] If racial classifications were inherently morally wrong, then they might well be deemed unconstitutional for that reason. But (as I argued in Chapter 11) racial classifications are not inherently wrong, any more than are any other classifications based on physical or genetically grounded properties. The rebuttal version of the strict scrutiny test is therefore the strongest version that the text and point of the Constitution can plausibly be thought to authorize: if the circumstances of some otherwise lawful government action that employs racial criteria are such as to rebut all genuine trace of suspicion that improper motives have been at work, the Court has no license for intervening to halt that action.

The three justices I cited—Scalia, Rehnquist, and Thomas—have nevertheless indicated that they will insist on something like the overriding-necessity reading. In his concurring opinion in the *Croson* case, Scalia, for example, said that the only interest he would recognize as compelling, apart from the "life and limb" emergency, is a community's interest in eliminating "their own maintenance of a system of unlawful racial classification."[17] But there is ample evidence that the six other current justices—so far as they would subject affirmative action to strict scrutiny at all—would prefer a reading much closer to the rebuttal one.

O'Connor's *Croson* opinion was starkly different from Scalia's. True, she said that "classifications based on race carry a danger of stigmatic harm. Unless they are strictly reserved for remedial settings, they may in fact promote notions of racial inferiority and lead to a politics of racial hostility."[18] But that is carefully guarded language—"may" is not "will," and the *River* study suggests that O'Connor's concern was not justified in the case of higher education—and it is best understood as explaining why racial classifications that are not remedial in the narrowest sense must be subjected to particularly careful examination.

In any case, it would certainly be wrong to conclude that O'Connor meant that no institution could ever use racial classifications except in that narrowly remedial way.[19] For she made plain that the strict scrutiny she proposed was not intended to replace a careful, case-by-case examination, designed to "smoke out" illegitimate uses of race, with a flat, mechanical rule striking down all plans that did not meet a simple a priori test. "Absent searching judicial inquiry into the justification for such race-based measures," she said, "there is simply no way of determining what classifications are 'benign' or 'remedial' and what classifications are in fact motivated by illegitimate notions of racial inferiority or simple racial politics."[20]

O'Connor took special pains to point out the features of the Richmond plan which, in her view, invited the suspicion that the plan was indeed motivated by "simple racial politics."

> In this case, blacks constitute approximately 50 percent of the population of the city of Richmond. Five of the nine seats on the city council are held by blacks. The concern that a political majority will more easily act to the disadvantage of a minority [on the basis of] unwarranted assumptions or incomplete facts would seem to militate for, not against, the application of heightened judicial scrutiny in this case.[21]

She rejected the city's claim, that is, not through a blanket ruling that none of the interests it cited could ever be deemed compelling, in any circumstances, but because citing those interests was not enough to dispel all trace of the suspicion raised by other features of the actual circumstances. Richmond's plan gave preference, for example, not only to local minority firms, for whose fate it might plausibly have taken some civic responsibility, but to firms controlled by "black, Spanish-speaking, Oriental, Indian, Eskimo, or Aleut" people anywhere in the nation. That alone left room for suspicion that Richmond was not pursuing a realistic civic purpose important enough to justify a significant deviation from the normally wise rule, intended to protect the city from illegitimate favoritism of all kinds, that contracts should be awarded to the lowest bidder. "The random inclusion of racial groups that, as a practical matter, may never have suffered from discrimination in the construction industry in Richmond suggests that perhaps the city's purpose was not in fact to remedy past discrimination," O'Connor said.[22]

In her later opinion in the *Adarand* case (which held that the Small Business Administration's regulations providing special benefits to business controlled by, among others, "black, Hispanic, Asian Pacific, Subcontinent Asian, and Native Americans," are subject to the strict scrutiny test), O'Connor was even more explicit in disclaiming any mechanical understanding of that test. She reacted strongly to the suggestion that her approach could not discriminate between invidious and genuinely benign discrimination: strict scrutiny, she insisted, does "take 'relevant differences' into account—indeed, that is its fundamental purpose," and

> does not "treat dissimilar race-based decisions as though they were equally objectionable" . . . To the contrary, it evaluates carefully all governmental race-based decisions *in order to decide* which are constitutionally objectionable and which are not. By requiring strict scrutiny of racial classifications, we require courts to make sure that a governmental classification based on race . . . is legitimate.

"Finally," she added, "we wish to dispel the notion that strict scrutiny is 'strict in theory, but fatal in fact.' The unhappy persistence of both the practice and the lingering effects of racial discrimination against minority groups in this country is an unfortunate reality, and government is not disqualified from acting in response to it."[23]

Five other justices of the present Court have been even more explicit than O'Connor in rejecting any mechanical version of strict scrutiny. In his concurring opinion in *Croson,* Justice Stevens said that racial classifications should be judged in terms of their impact on the future, and he expressly rejected any implication that "a governmental decision that rests on a racial classification is never permissible except as a remedy for a past wrong."[24] Justice Kennedy, in his concurring opinion in the case, conceded that Scalia's position, which "would strike down all preferences which are not necessary remedies to victims of unlawful discrimination, would serve important structural goals, as it would eliminate the necessity for courts to pass upon each racial preference that is enacted." Nevertheless, Kennedy said, he believed that so rigid a policy was unnecessary, and preferred what he called O'Connor's "less absolute rule" that racial preferences must face "the most rigorous scrutiny."[25]

Justices Souter, Ginsburg, and Breyer all dissented in the *Adarand* case, along with Stevens. Souter wrote that "the Court has long accepted the view that constitutional authority to remedy past discrimination is not limited to the power to forbid its continuation, but extends to eliminating those effects that would otherwise persist."[26] Ginsburg, in an opinion Breyer joined, emphasized her view that the Court should now be using strict scrutiny not mechanically, but as an aid to discovering actual legislative motives that are illegitimate because they offend the equal concern required by the equal protection clause. The strict scrutiny test, as defined in O'Connor's majority opinion, Ginsburg said, is a device "to ferret out classifications in reality malign, but masquerading as benign."[27]

III

So the two-judge opinion in *Hopwood* was wrong in assuming that the Court has already adopted a mechanical strict scrutiny test that makes university affirmative action plans in the *Bakke* mold automatically unconstitutional.[28] It does not follow, however, that the Court will not strike down race-sensitive admission standards, in the test case that many commentators now predict, even on a less mechanical, rebuttal reading of strict scrutiny.

So we must ask whether and how university affirmative action plans can meet a strict scrutiny test construed in that way. The *River* study suggests two main justifying purposes for race-sensitive admissions tests: the universities' own need for racial diversity in their student bodies, and the community's need for a larger presence of minority members in important political, business, and professional roles. Are either of these needs sufficiently "compelling" to justify the use of race as one factor among many in evaluating applicants? Does the record rebut any scintilla of reasonable suspicion that the schools surveyed in the *River* study have used race for illegitimate purposes?

Powell himself insisted, in *Bakke,* that affirmative action plans were subject to strict scrutiny, and his decision that universities may seek racial diversity was therefore a ruling that diversity was a sufficiently compelling interest to survive that scrutiny. It is true that O'Connor has rejected a diversity justification in other contexts, not only in *Croson,* but in a dissenting opinion in the *Metro Broadcasting* case, in which the Supreme Court sustained policies of the Federal Communications Commission that gave preference to minority-owned firms in applications for licenses for new radio and television stations—the FCC claimed that such preferences were necessary in order to improve diversity of viewpoint in programming.[29] But neither of these O'Connor opinions forecloses allowing universities to use racial classifications to produce racial diversity in the classroom.

The overriding question, for a rebuttal reading of strict scrutiny, is whether an institution's appeal to diversity is sufficient to dispel any genuine trace of suspicion that it has acted out of constitutionally forbidden motives. Richmond's appeal to diversity was compromised not only by the factors I mentioned earlier, but because diversity has not been a traditional goal of officials in charge of awarding municipal construction contracts. On the contrary, a city that claimed, say, geographical diversity as a reason for denying construction contracts to the lowest bidders would raise deep suspicion of corruption. The FCC regulations that O'Connor condemned in her *Metro Broadcasting* dissent were open, as she emphasized, to a grave though different kind of suspicion: the argument that diversity in ownership is necessary to achieve diversity in broadcasting, she said, relied on racial stereotypes because it assumed that people's "race or ethnicity determines how they act or think."[30]

O'Connor argued that the asserted interest in diversity of programming is, in any case, "too amorphous, too insubstantial" to rule out any possibility of racial preferences or prejudices. The FCC, she said, might, under cover of this alleged interest, identify a "black" or "Asian" or "Arab" viewpoint, and then deny licenses to races or ethnic groups it deemed less likely to present the favored view. She particularly feared that recognizing a general interest in diversity would allow great and indiscriminate use of racial classifications not just for particular purposes and a limited time, but for all purposes and for all time. Because it is impossible to define a particular racial viewpoint, or to assess how diverse one viewpoint is from another, she said, "Members of any racial or ethnic group, whether now preferred under the FCC's policy or not, may find themselves politically out of fashion and subject to disadvantageous but 'benign' discrimination."[31]

Universities are in a much stronger position than Richmond or the FCC was to dispel any suspicion that they seek racial diversity for improper underlying motives or on stereotypical assumptions. University admissions policies are not set by politicians, who might hope to court the votes of a racial bloc, but by faculty members, who are not running for office. Their interest in diversity is not novel or unusual, as Richmond's was, but traditional and recognized: no one disputes that large, mainly white universities have a social and educational responsibility to seek a student body that is diverse in many ways, and any such university that abandoned that aim altogether would be behaving irresponsibly. Elite universities believe that it would now be irrational to seek diversity in geographical origin, in social class, and in cultural orientation, and not also to seek racial diversity.

Indeed, their failure to seek the latter dimension of diversity as well would make their general concern with diversity seem arbitrary. They have decided, and the *River* study amply confirms their view, that they cannot achieve racial diversity indirectly by relying on economic class as a proxy for race, or by using otherwise less efficient means to the hoped-for end. Any such policy would be not only disingenuous but harmful. Nor do universities rely, as O'Connor said the FCC did, on any presumed connection between race and belief, conviction, taste, culture, or attitude.

They seek racial diversity, as I said in Chapter 11, because race is itself important, unfortunately but inescapably, in contemporary America: it is vital that students of each race meet and work with, not just other students with other attitudes or cultures, but students who are in fact of a different race. Nor would the courts be risking open-ended and indiscriminate racial preferences by continuing to permit affirmative action on the *Bakke* model. Universities have used such programs judiciously for a third of a century, with no tendency to expand them beyond sensible proportions.

These institutions have, moreover, a crucial stake in their academic reputations, both absolutely and relative to other comparable institutions, that would check any desire significantly to expand an admissions policy or curriculum that might threaten that reputation. Nor is there any genuine risk that race-sensitive admissions programs will be used as a pretense for disfavoring any other particular group of applicants. Any suspicion of that could be tested, as I said, using statistical means like those used in the *River* study, by analyzing the retrospectively rejected students to see whether they were disproportionately members of any suspect group.

There is ample evidence, moreover, that O'Connor, as well as several other members of the present Court, has already accepted that the search for racial diversity among students is a compelling interest that survives strict scrutiny. In 1986, in the *Wygant* case, the Supreme Court struck down a Michigan school board's collective bargaining agreement that gave minority schoolteachers special protection against layoffs: it rejected the school board's claim that its interest in correcting the effects of past discrimination in the community at large, or in providing black faculty "role models" with whom black students might identify, justified this racial classification.[32] O'Connor wrote a separate opinion in which she noted that the board had not claimed that it had acted to protect racial diversity on its faculty, and that the Court was therefore not to be understood to have ruled out that interest as compelling.[33] "Although its precise contours are uncertain," she said, "a state interest in the promotion of racial diversity has been found sufficiently 'compelling,' at least in the context of higher education, to support the use of racial considerations in furthering that interest."[34]

O'Connor has several times, moreover, cited Powell's *Bakke* opinion, which declared diversity in higher education a compelling interest, as authority for her view that any racial classification must be subjected to strict scrutiny. She would hardly rely on that opinion with such force if she thought that Powell did not himself understand the implications of his strict scrutiny approach, or intended to lay down, under that name, a different doctrine from the one for which she cited his authority.

The argument is therefore strong that the *Bakke* principle, in force for over twenty years, remains good constitutional law, and that American colleges and universities may continue to rely on that principle to justify using race-sensitive admissions policies to secure a diverse student body. If I were defending such schemes in the courts, I would certainly emphasize that interest in student diversity, which seems enough, on its own, to ensure that the programs survive strict scrutiny. I must add, however, that I believe that the other institutional interest I mentioned—helping to redress the still-deplorable absence of blacks from key positions in government, politics, business, and the professions—is at least an equally important one that should also be recognized as sufficiently compelling to sustain race-sensitive admissions policies. One of the gravest problems of American society is the de facto racial stratification that has largely excluded blacks and other minorities from the highest ranks of power, wealth, and prestige; and past racial discrimination, as well as the vicious circle that robs black children of successful black leaders to emulate, has contributed substantially to that stratification.

Nevertheless, many statements sprinkled throughout the various Supreme Court opinions I have been discussing might well be read as hostile to that further, and different, justification of race-sensitive admissions policies, including Powell's statement, in *Bakke,* that medical schools may not use affirmative action just in order to increase the number of black doctors.

Several of the justices have declared that racial classifications cannot be justified as helping to cure the lingering effects of past "societal discrimination," and the *Wygant* decision rejected the claim that they can be justified as providing "role models" for black children. It might be, however, that these statements have not paid sufficient attention to the distinction that Justice Stevens has several times made—between backward-looking justifications of racial classifications as compensatory and forward-looking justifications that argue that such classifications may, in some circumstances, be in the general interest of the community as a whole.

Compensatory justifications suppose that affirmative action is necessary, as Scalia put it, to "make up" to minorities for damage done to their race or class in the past, and he was right to point out the mistake in supposing that one race "owes" another compensation. But universities do not use race-sensitive admission standards to compensate either individuals or groups: affirmative action is a forward-looking, not a backward-looking, enterprise, and the minority students whom it benefits have not necessarily been victims, as individuals, of any distinct injustice in the past. Great universities hope to train more blacks and other minority students not to repay them for past injustice, but to make the future better for everyone by helping to lift a curse that the past laid on us all.

O'Connor and other justices have worried that any broad and general remedial justification for affirmative action is too "amorphous" and "open-ended" because it would license racial preferences until every industry or social or professional stratum had the same racial and ethnic composition as the nation as a whole. But however genuine or inflated that concern might be as a worry about the consequences of government-imposed hiring or contracting regulations, it is distinctly out of place as an objection to university affirmative action plans. If any branch of government—whether Congress or a local city council—requires employers or contractors to hire a quota of black employees or to set aside a quota of contracts for black firms, its decision ensures a particular racial representation in some segment of employment or industry. No more natural process of decisionmaking can alter or shape that racial structure so long as the government's program is in place. In such cases, government, and only government, decides how many members of each of the racial or ethnic groups it designates will fill which jobs in which sectors or roles or offices. Judges who are particularly sensitive to the danger that some of these decisions might be made out of improper motives will be reluctant to accept so broad a justification for them as the claim that they are necessary to prevent excluding one or another race from power, wealth, and prestige.

But colleges, universities, and professional schools use race-sensitive standards not in response to any central government mandate but through individual decisions by individual schools. They act, not to fix how many members of which races will occupy what roles in the overall economy and polity, which is in any case beyond their power, but only to increase the number of blacks and other minorities who are in the pool from which other citizens—employers, partners, patients, clients, voters, and colleagues acting in their own interests and for their own purposes—will choose employees, doctors, lawyers, and public officials in the normal way.

The distribution of position and power that affirmative action helps to achieve, that is, flows and changes naturally in accordance with millions of choices that people make for themselves. If the policy works to improve the overall position of any minority—as the *River* study suggests it has helped to improve the position of blacks—it does so only because other people have chosen to exploit the results of that policy: the greater range and variety of graduates with the motive, self-respect, and training to contribute effectively to their lives. Affirmative action in universities, in that way, makes the eventual economic and social structure of the community not more artificial but less so; it produces no balkanization, but helps to dissolve the balkanization now sadly in place.

If the justices recognize this aspect of what our best universities aim to do, as well as their academic need for educational diversity, then they will have served us particularly well. They will have acted not just as judges allowing a crucial educational initiative to continue, but as teachers helping to explain to the nation the true and continuing costs to everyone of our racist past, and the distinct promise of an educational policy that can help us all to achieve, if we really want it, a more perfect union.

13

Playing God:
Genes, Clones, and Luck

⁂

I. Introduction

No other department of our science, including cosmology, has been more exciting in recent decades than genetics, and none has been remotely as portentous for the character of the lives our descendants will lead. We need to improve our understanding of these rapid changes in the basic science of genetics and also of the developing techniques for applying that basic science in medical diagnosis, prognosis, and therapy. We must hope better to appreciate how government and commerce—interacting in ways that range from funding grants to patent policy to statutory prohibitions and regulations—fuel, restrain, and shape these developments.

We need, above all, to try to identify and assess the great variety of moral, social, and political problems that the new technology will present to the new century. To some degree, those problems are evident and pressing now. Tests can identify genetic predictors of disease or predisposition to disease, and new tests of that kind are coming on line with increasing speed. So we already face extremely difficult issues about how far and when these tests should be allowed, or required, or forbidden, and how far, if at all, employers and insurance companies should be allowed to demand or ask for their results. Some problems are more speculative, because we shall face them only if science develops in a particular way. If it becomes possible to clone human beings, for example, or radically to alter the chromosomes of an early fetus to make the later child more intelligent or less aggressive, then people will have to decide whether, in some or all circumstances, these interventions are undesirable, and, if so, whether they should be forbidden by law.

427

I shall concentrate on certain of the moral and political problems, both evident and speculative, that the new genetics may generate in the twenty-first century. I shall not discuss all such problems: in particular I will not say much here about the feasibility, propriety, or character of government regulation of research and commerce. Instead I shall discuss the issues that seem to me fundamental and pervasive.

I will make use of an important distinction that has not been much canvassed in the moral or philosophical literature, at least in the terms in which I shall draw it, and which I should therefore introduce here. This is a distinction between two kinds of values to which we might appeal in evaluating the implications of new technology.[1] The first set of values, which I shall call derivative values, are parasitic on the interests of particular people. We must ask, in considering whether any new technique should be permitted or regulated or forbidden, about the likely impact of any such decision on individual interests. Who will be better off and who worse off in virtue of any such decision? Then we must evaluate the implications of that technique in that dimension: we must ask whether any particular decision or practice is "cost-benefit efficient." Do the gains to some outweigh, on some scale of interpersonal comparison, the losses to others? We must also ask, in that dimension, whether the outcome is "fair" or "just"—is it *right* that some should lose and others gain in that way?

The second set of values that will figure in our argument constitute what I have elsewhere called "detached" values: these are values that do not derive from the interests of particular people, but are rather *intrinsic* to objects or events in some other way. Many people think that great works of art have detached value, that their value does not depend on whether they actually give pleasure or enjoyment. Many people think that animal species have detached value: they think it is intrinsically wrong when a distinctive animal species becomes extinct, that this is bad quite apart from the impact on the interests of actual people.

The controversy over abortion brings out the importance of the difference. If, as I have elsewhere argued, an early fetus can have no interests of its own, then the argument that abortion is wrong because it is against someone's interests is indefensible. But it nevertheless makes sense to believe, as a great many people do, that abortion is always morally problematic, and at least in some cases morally wrong, because it offends an intrinsic or detached value—the "sanctity" of human life in any form. Advances in genetic science raise many problems, as we shall see, about derivative interests: these are problems of efficiency and justice. But I shall argue that the sharp negative reactions that both people and governments have displayed to some of the more speculative genetic techniques, particularly cloning and radical genetic engineering, are not best understood as appealing to derivative values of that kind, though they are often, rather lamely, presented in that dress. They are much better understood as deep and instructive appeals to intrinsic, detached, value.

II. Diagnosis and Prognosis

A. Should Tests Be Offered?

It is a large question (taken up, in part, in Chapter 8) how much of its treasure any society should devote, through public or private vehicles, to health care, how much of that to research rather than to treatment or public health, and how much of that to research into any particular medical condition or disease. No doubt many people object to large-scale programs in genetic research, like the genome project, on grounds of cost: they think the money would be more usefully spent in other ways. My discussion will be limited, however, to the nonbudgetary reasons that people have offered for not developing genetic tests for disease or predisposition to disease, or not making these tests widely available if they are developed.

Some of the diseases that can be predicted by genetic testing, either with certainty or with an important degree of probability above the norm, are in different ways treatable: a course of treatment, or of monitoring, or of changes in diet or life style can reduce the probability or the seriousness of the disease. These include certain bowel cancers and rarer diseases, like phenylketonuria. It is difficult to imagine good arguments against making testing for those diseases both legal and readily available. It is true that the availability of such tests might further increase the advantages of the rich over the poor, either because the tests could be afforded only by the rich, or because the treatment that capitalizes on the information—frequent colonoscopy or a very expensive special diet—is itself too expensive for some. It is also true that test results may fall into the hands of others—employers or insurers—to the patient's damage. But these disadvantages cannot outweigh the value of an increased life expectancy. Genetic tests can identify the certainty or likelihood of other diseases, however, like Huntington's disease and, it appears, certain breast cancers, that cannot be cured or alleviated, at least at the present stage of medical knowledge. We must consider the argument, about these diseases, that genetic testing can do no good, and may well do harm, because a death sentence is very likely to be demoralizing, and because it will often be catastrophic if the information falls into the hands of employers, insurers, or others from whom the subject wishes to keep that information. My own view, however, is that adults who wish the tests, and have been given as clear an understanding as is possible of their import, and of the risks that the information will be available to others, must be permitted to have them. Some such people—in whose family, for example, Huntington's disease has occurred—will already be terrified that they will be victims as well, and they must be permitted to judge whether the potential relief from a negative result is worth the risk of a positive and devastating one. Many people, too, would want to know that their life is doomed to be a short one, in order to capitalize on that short life more effectively, and they should be permitted that opportunity. We have more general reasons, as we shall see, for restricting the access that third parties may have to genetic tests. But whatever limitations on third-party access the community decides are feasible and desirable, adult patients must be allowed to gauge for themselves the risk of whatever danger remains.

What about children, however? Should blanket genetic tests be permitted soon after birth, if not before, that would reveal any genetic abnormalities? It might seem unfair for a child to grow up in a world in which others know he is doomed, even if this information is somehow limited to his own family, who would inevitably treat him differently. But would it be right to deny a family such information, which it might use not only to help prepare for his life but to avoid the worst consequences for other members of the family? A legal prohibition on blanket testing might have a deleterious effect on research, moreover, and hinder the search for treatment of diseases now intractable. On balance, I believe that families should be allowed blanket testing of infants, but that the practice underscores the need for effective limits on the dissemination of genetic information.

B. Prenatal Testing

The major objection to prenatal testing is a fear of abortion, or of abortion for the wrong reasons. Of course, parents might wish to have as full a genetic profile as possible of a fetus, just as many are now anxious to know its sex, for less minatory reasons. But abortion is the main worry, and we shall therefore have to face a particularly difficult and frightening question. Under the law now in force in the United States and, at least in practice, elsewhere in democratic societies, there is no legal prohibition of early abortion for any reason, and it is unlikely that more stringent legal restrictions will be adopted soon. In these circumstances, it strikes the fiercest opponents of abortion as particularly important that no information be available that would be likely to increase the number of abortions. They—sensibly, given their convictions—think that any means, including bans on discovery, are justified that will reduce the number of what they believe to be murders. But those of us who reject their general position, because we do not believe that it even makes sense to suppose that a fetus has interests of its own before sentience has developed, have more difficult choices to make. We face a series of questions. Is abortion ever a moral mistake? If so, does whether it is a mistake depend on the motive for the abortion? If so, is it appropriate for us, if we are in the majority, to enforce our conviction that abortion is wrong through the criminal law? If so, is the means now under discussion— restricting the discovery by a woman of facts about a fetus she is carrying— an appropriate means of enforcing that conviction?

We must remember that under the hypothesis that an early fetus has no interests, we are considering a moral question on the second dimension I distinguished: a question of detached not derivative value. Opinions about such values are notoriously varied, even within a particular democratic culture, in large part because they are sensitive to the very different religious convictions that coexist in such cultures. I myself believe that an abortion is morally wrong when it does not show respect for the intrinsic value of every human life, in no matter what stage or form, and that the moral rightness or wrongness of an abortion therefore depends critically on its motive.[2] An abortion shows the proper respect for human life, in principle, in two circumstances: first, when the life of the child, if carried to term, would be a frustrating one, in which the ambitions common to the full range of normal lives, which include freedom from pain, ample physical mobility, the capacity for an intellectual and emotional life, and the capacity to plan and execute projects, could be realized, if at all, only to a sharply reduced degree; second, when bearing a child is foreseeably likely to have so catastrophic an impact on the success of other lives—of the mother and of other children in the family, for example—that concern for the intrinsic value of the latter lives might plausibly be thought to outweigh concern for the life of the fetus, in which no investment beyond the biological had as yet been made.

The second of these circumstances, though of enormous moral and political importance, is not in point here. The first distinguishes between conditions so threatening to a prospective life that they justify abortion out of
concern for the value of that life, and those that are not so threatening. How
shall we make that distinction? The devastating genetic defects that take
hold immediately, or in infancy, and insure an early death seem to me
unproblematic. I would, myself, include diseases whose crippling or fatal
onset occurs later in life though at an age almost everyone attains, like
Huntington's disease, but not a predisposition to diseases that occur primarily at an age that many people do not attain in any case, like many cancers
and heart diseases. I would include diseases that impose serious barriers to
intellectual and emotional development, like Down's syndrome; and this
disease, which has aroused passionate division of opinion, makes it important to remember that we are discussing when abortion is morally wrong,
not when it is morally wrong not to abort, which is of course a very different
question. I would not include properties, like below-average height, that are
sometimes resented by those who have them but that plainly do not fall
within the description I gave. I would of course not include sex. No matter
how much one wants a child of one sex, it shows inadequate respect for a life
in being to end it because its sex is the other one.

I distinguished the question whether abortion for some motives is wrong
from the question whether, if it is, it is right for the state to forbid it. My own
view is that when the state's only justification for prohibiting the exercise of
an important freedom is the protection of a detached value with a religious
dimension, then the state has no right to forbid, no matter what the motive
in play. If so, then the state has no right to forbid indirectly, by denying
people information, what it must not forbid directly. I should emphasize
that I believe that a state does have the right, and indeed has a responsibility,
for educating and urging its members to make decisions touching important
detached values responsibly, and that officials may therefore forcefully express their opinion that abortion that discriminates against one sex, or is
motivated by other improper considerations, is offensive even though not
illegal.

C. Embryonic Selection

In vitro fertilization requires a selection of some zygotes to implant, allowing others to perish. For that reason, some opponents of abortion, who

regard any zygote as a person, condemn the practice. Those who do not have that conviction, however, must once again be discriminating. If—some would say when—we are able to prepare a comprehensive genetic profile of a zygote after only a few cell divisions, are we justified in using that information to select which to implant? It seems obvious that if we identify in a candidate embryo a genetic defect so serious that it would be morally permissible to abort a fetus with that defect, then it is morally permissible, and perhaps morally mandatory, to select against that embryo. But is the opposite true: if it is wrong to abort a fetus because it can be predicted to grow to less than normal height or because it is of an unwanted sex, is it therefore wrong to select against embryos with those qualities?

It does not follow that it is. We accept in vitro fertilization as a reproductive technique because we do not believe that it shows disrespect for the human life embodied in one zygote to allow it to perish when the process that both created and doomed it also produces a flourishing human life that would not otherwise have existed. When one zygote has already been implanted, a decision to terminate its life because it is female shows a disdain for its life, because the question is then whether a single, isolated human life will continue or cease. But before implantation some zygotes must inevitably perish, and using sex as a ground seems no more to disrespect life than using chance. I do not mean that there are no other reasons for not permitting sex, or some other particular property, to be used as the ground of the selection. We shall consider such other reasons later, when we consider genetic engineering.

D. Who May Know?

I must now turn to a very different set of issues. What restrictions should be imposed on the use of genetic information by others than its subject? Critics of genetic testing have cited various kinds of harm that might result from dissemination of test results. If it is widely known that someone will die early or is particularly vulnerable to a particular disease, others will treat that person differently in consequence. They will regard marriage, and may even regard friendship, with such a person as much less attractive, for example. At the opposite extreme, people may be overly solicitous or attentive, and this behavior might be equally undesirable. In some cases, particularly in those of employers and insurers, the consequences might be financial and devastating: someone might be unemployable, at any rate in a preferred occupation, or uninsurable, except perhaps at discriminating and prohibitive rates, in consequence of what others know about his genes. How far are these devastating consequences fair?

We should begin by recognizing that the unfairness, if any, is already part of our lives. People who are visibly disabled suffer social and emotional harm in consequence, and employers and insurance companies have a right to ask for, and act on the basis of, much information about medical history. Nevertheless access to a comprehensive genetic profile or even selective information about genetic disposition to cancer, heart disease, aggressive behavior or, so long as the AIDS epidemic continues, sexual orientation would measurably increase many people's vulnerability to different forms of discrimination.

Some people's first, instinctive response to the danger is to suppose that the dissemination of genetic information must be under the sole control of its subject. But this requirement seems too strong, even in principle, and extremely difficult, if not impossible, to secure in practice. Should DNA evidence never be used in criminal investigation and prosecution? The deplorable O. J. Simpson case at least educated the public in both the power and the fragility of such evidence. But we should be reluctant to forgo its use entirely, particularly as techniques of storage and testing become more reliable. What about occupations in which a propensity to disease poses a genuine threat to the public—a disposition to heart attack in a pilot, for example, or any grave illness in a president? And is it really right that people who actually pose very different risks to insurers should pay the same premiums for their insurance? Doesn't this mean that some are subsidizing others? We think it right that smokers should pay higher rates for life insurance. Suppose we find a set of alleles that dispose someone to nicotine addiction. Would we then be unjustified in continuing to ask smokers to pay higher rates? If not, why should the fact that the danger posed by a genetic profile has been expressed in visible behavior, rather than still lying latent in the chromosomes, call for different treatment?

How can we discriminate, in practice, between a proper and an improper use of genetic information? Suppose life or health insurance companies are forbidden from either requiring genetic tests as a condition of insurance or asking whether candidates have had such tests. Then insurers will be destroyed by "adverse selection": people who had had genetic tests would insure heavily if most at risk and not at all if much less at risk, and insurance bankruptcy would follow. Should insurance companies be entitled, then, to ask for information from candidates for insurance who have had their own tests? Then more people would be discouraged, by that fact, from having such tests, and their own and the public health will suffer. (This might be called the "insurance dilemma.")

These questions and comments only hint at the complexity of the issues, which display, in a much more dramatic form, puzzles about social justice that have long been with us, and that we have not adequately understood or faced before. We need to attack the problems, at least in the genetic context, on two fronts. First, we need to continue to develop standards of fair employment practice, administered by competent agencies, that adjudicate between public and commercial interests. Airlines should be entitled to demand appropriate tests, at their expense, for pilots, because the balance of public interest falls in favor of such tests. But though few businesses would wish to hire and train somehow who they knew would die of Huntington's disease in early middle age, we should prevent most employers from asking for information that would reveal a predisposition to that disease. The impact of permanent unemployment on the short life of someone already doomed is too great not to require employers to continue to run the kinds of risk they have always run, in spite of the fact that genetic advances now make it technically possible for them to reduce those risks.

The insurance problem should be attacked more directly. The insurance dilemma provides, I think, a finally irresistible argument that basic health and life insurance should no longer be left in the private sector. The United States is alone among prosperous democracies in not having yet learned that lesson for health insurance. (Life insurance is less important but still consequential, and it remains private in most countries.) If I am right that the insurance dilemma will seem more and more problematic as more genetic information becomes available, then genetic research may have the unanticipated but welcome effect of striking a more general blow for justice in that way. Basic health insurance must be provided for everyone, and it must be financed out of taxation computed by modeling a hypothetical insurance market in which insurance is offered to everyone at "community rating," that is, at prices assuming that each candidate presented the average risk. (This scheme for modeling health care is the subject of Chapter 8.) Genetic information will be invaluable in calculating community rates, but it should not be used to discriminate among people. Should private insurers be permitted to offer extra health or life insurance, at market rates, beyond the basic package? I believe so, and the possibility shows the importance of the question, discussed next, of fixing a fair and adequate basic package. Should insurers be entitled to demand genetic tests, in accordance with actuarial and commercial efficiency, in setting discriminatory rates for such additional insurance? I believe so.

E. Justice and Genetic Medicine

Nations that offer single-payer health insurance to everyone, financed out of taxation, should not discriminate against the genetically unfortunate simply because they have the power, through genetic testing, to do so. (Nice questions will arise about how the line between behavior that generates greater risk, like smoking, and genetic predisposition that creates such risk is to be drawn. But I set these aside for now.) So a further question becomes imperative: how far should a national health insurance not only provide standard treatment for diseases whose risk can be anticipated by genetic testing, without discrimination against those who might be shown predisposed to that disease, but also provide the new, and undoubtedly expensive, diagnostic techniques and therapies that genetic research and commercial development will make available?

Available genetic medicine includes new diagnostic techniques that can help doctors decide, for example, which form of cancer a particular patient has, and how the cancer-producing genes interact with other parts of his genetic profile, in order more efficiently to design and direct chemotherapy and gene therapy. Scientists are developing revolutionary techniques, some of which may have dramatic medical effects, for altering a patient's protein chemistry by introducing cells taken from his body and then engineering them to produce an improved genetic profile. Should these dramatic new techniques of diagnosis and therapy be made available to everyone? We might be tempted to say that whatever saves lives must be made available to everyone, as soon as possible, and that it is disgraceful when lives are lost because the community is unwilling to spend the money necessary to save them.

But as I said in Chapter 8, a community that actually tried to live up to that "rescue principle" (rather than just endorsing it in rhetoric and ignoring it in practice) would have nothing left to spend on resources other than health care, like education and job training and culture, and would end only by enabling citizens to live somewhat longer in misery. If we accept that sad fact, and deny some care that would save lives on the ground that it would be too expensive to provide it, should those who can afford the expensive treatment be allowed to buy it for themselves? Or should they be denied that opportunity, in order to prevent the injustices arising from unequal wealth from growing steadily worse?

If we are to consider these questions adequately, we need to revisit some of the issues I set aside at the beginning. How much should a nation spend, in all fairness, on its health care, and how should that expense be distributed? I shall summarize here the answer I gave in Chapter 8. Consider this thought experiment. Suppose that all the citizens of any particular political society, with their present tastes and ambitions, had the average wealth now found in that society, as well as full, state-of-the-art information about what benefits genetic engineering might bring them, under imagined circumstances, and what the cost of insuring to provide it in those circumstances would be. If we think that citizens generally would purchase insurance to provide a particular kind of therapy—say, genetic tests to improve the effectiveness of chemotherapy should they need it—then we should insist that a national health service provide that treatment. If, on the contrary, we think that citizens would not purchase insurance providing for a particular therapy—say, growth treatment for a marginally short child they might conceive—because they would think they had better uses for the money the premiums would cost, given how unlikely they were to need the treatment, then a national health service should not provide that treatment, so that the collective wealth saved could indeed be spent elsewhere. My own opinion, however, once again, is that rich people should be allowed to purchase therapy, at market rates, beyond what that calculation would mean providing for everyone. We do not in general seek equality by leveling down, and even a diminished demand for a particular therapy will stimulate research, with possibly unanticipated general benefits, that would not otherwise take place.

III. Cloning and Engineering

A. Why Not?

So far we have been occupied with familiar problems of personal and social justice in a new context: these problems are exacerbated, but their character is not fundamentally changed, by genetic discoveries and inventions. We have also been concerned, except in our brief discussion of abortion, with what I called derivative rather than detached values. We have been worrying about how the new technology should be used and regulated so as to protect people's interests. Our next discussion will reverse this emphasis: we will henceforth be worried mainly by dramatically new issues and by values of a different and detached character.

The most arresting of the possibilities geneticists are now exploring would give scientists and doctors the power to choose which human beings there will be. People gained that power long ago, in a broad and clumsy way, when they came to understood that allowing certain people rather than others to mate would have consequences for the kind of children they produced. Eugenics, which was supported by George Bernard Shaw and Oliver Wendell Holmes as well as Adolf Hitler, was modeled on that simple insight. But genetic science now holds out the possibility, at least as comprehensible fantasy, of creating particular human beings who have been designed, one by one, according to a detailed blueprint, or of changing existing human beings, either as fetuses or later, to create people with chosen genetic properties.

Even the fantasy of this, when the technology was first described, was greeted with shock and indignation, and that shock crystallized when scientists in Scotland cloned an adult sheep, and other scientists and publicists speculated that the technique could be used to clone human beings. Committees hurriedly appointed by governments and international bodies all immediately denounced the very idea. President Clinton ruled that federal funds could not be used to finance research into human cloning, and the United States Senate considered forbidding, through preposterously overbroad and panicky legislation, any and all such research. The possibility of comprehensive genetic engineering—altering a zygote's genetic composition to produce a battery of desired physical, mental, and emotional propensities—has also aroused great fear and revulsion, and any success in engineering mammals, comparable to the creation of the sheep Dolly, would undoubtedly provoke a similar official response. (In this discussion I shall often use the word "engineering" to include both comprehensive genetic alteration and human cloning, the latter being treated as a special case of the former. Of course engineering and cloning are very different techniques, but many of the social and moral issues they raise are the same.)

The rhetoric of the European Parliament is not untypical of the reaction that prospects of genetic engineering have produced. In its "resolution on the cloning of the human embryo," that body declared its "firm conviction that the cloning of human beings, whether on an experimental basis, in the context of fertility treatments, preimplantation diagnosis, for tissue transplantation, or for any other purpose whatsoever, is unethical, morally repugnant, contrary to respect for the person, and a grave violation of fundamental human rights which can not under any circumstances be justified or accepted." How might we justify, or even explain, this blunderbuss reaction? We might explore three grounds of objection that are frequently mentioned. First, genetic research is said to pose great danger, and extreme caution is therefore urged. If human cloning or other comprehensive genetic engineering is possible at all, research into it or attempts at it might result in an unacceptable number of miscarriages or in the birth of an unacceptable number of deformed children, for example. Second, some people resist research into genetic engineering on grounds of social justice. Cloning, if available, is bound to be hideously expensive for a long time, and hence would be available only to rich people who would want, out of vanity, to clone themselves, increasing the unfair advantages of wealth. (Opponents horrified by the prospect of cloning have cited the specter of thousands of Rupert Murdochs or Donald Trumps.) Third, much of the hostile reaction has been generated by a detached and reasonably familiar aesthetic value. Engineering, if available, might well be used to perpetuate now desired traits of height, intelligence, color and personality, and the world would be robbed of the variety that seems essential to novelty, originality and fascination. We must discuss each of these supposed justifications for a ban on research and development, but in my own view they do not separately or together explain the dogmatic strength of the reaction I described.

Security. It is unclear how far the Dolly precedent should be relied on in predicting the likely results of experimentation into human cloning. On the one hand, technical skill will presumably improve; on the other, human cloning may prove exponentially more difficult than cloning sheep. Several hundred attempts were necessary to produce one sheep, but, as I understand it, the rest were lost through early miscarriage, and no deformed but viable sheep was produced. Nor is there much reason to think that either cloning or engineering would produce germ-line damage threatening generations of deformity, or deformity that would not appear for generations. In any case, however, these dangers are not enough, on their own, to justify forbidding the further research that could refine our appreciation of them, and perhaps our ability to forestall or reduce whichever threats are in fact genuine. True, the sudden appearance of Dr. Seed, in the headlines and on the screen, promising to clone anyone for a high price, was enough to terrify anyone. But regulation can rein him in, along with the thousands of other cloning cowboys who would be bound to appear, without closing down research altogether. If we are assessing the risks of damage that experimentation or testing might produce, moreover, we must also take into account the hope that advancing and refining the techniques of genetic engineering will vastly decrease the number of defects and deformities with which people are now born or into which they inexorably grow. The balance of risk might well be thought to tilt in favor of experimentation.

Justice. We can easily imagine genetic engineering's becoming a perquisite of the rich, and therefore as exacerbating the already savage injustice of both prosperous and impoverished societies. But these techniques have uses beyond vanity, and these uses may justify research and trials, even if we decide that vanity is an inappropriate and forbidden motive. We noticed, earlier, the important medical gains that have already been achieved through selective engineering, and more comprehensive engineering can confidently be expected to expand these enormously. Cloning may prove to have particularly dramatic medical benefits. Parents of a desperately sick child might want another child, whom they would love as much as any other, but whose blood or marrow might save the life of the sick child from which it was cloned. Cloning individual human stem cells to produce a particular organ for transplant, rather than an entire organism, might have even more evident benefits. A reengineered and then heavily cloned cell, taken from a cancer patient, might prove to be a cure for that cancer when the clones were reintroduced. We must also count benefits beyond the narrowly medical. Childless couples, for example, or single women or single men might wish to procreate through cloning, which they might think better than the alternatives available. Or they may have no alternative at all.

Perhaps we could regulate engineering to screen out all but approved motives. If this is possible, does justice demand it, even if we assume that there are no other objections to it? I do not believe so. We should not, as I have already said, seek to improve equality by leveling down, and, as in the case of more orthodox genetic medicine, techniques available for a time only to the very rich often produce discoveries of much more general value for everyone. The remedy for injustice is redistribution, not denial of benefits to some with no corresponding gain to others.

Aesthetics. We already have clones—genetically identical multiple births (which have increased as a result of infertility treatment) produce clones—and the history of genetically identical children shows that identical genes do not produce identical phenotypes. We may have underestimated nature in years past, but nurture remains important too, and the reaction to the prospect of engineering has underestimated its importance in turn. Nevertheless, people do fear that if we replace the genetic "lottery" with engineered reproduction, the welcome diversity of human types will be progressively replaced with uniformity dictated by vogue. To some degree, of course, greater uniformity is unambiguously desirable: there is no value, aesthetic or otherwise, in the fact that some people are doomed to a disfigured and short life. But it is widely believed better that, within limits, people look different and act differently in ways that might well be the consequence of different alleles. This thought appeals to a derivative value: that it is better for everyone to live in a world of differences. But it might also be seen as appealing to a detached value: many people think that diversity is a value in itself, so that it would remain valuable even if, for some reason, people came to prefer uniformity.

What is not plain, however, is how far engineering, even if it were freely and inexpensively available, would actually threaten desirable diversity. Presumably all parents, if given a choice, would wish their children to have the level of intelligence and other skills that we now regard as normal, or even that we now believe superior. But we cannot regard that as undesirable: it is, after all, the object of education, ordinary as well as remedial, to improve intelligence and skill levels across the board. Do we have good reason to fear that if parents had the choice they would often prefer cloning one of them—or cloning a third person—to sexual reproduction that produces a child bearing the genes of both? Or that they would choose cloning for reasons other than to exclude damaging alleles, or because they were incapable of sexual reproduction? That seems unlikely. Do we have reason to fear (as many people do fear) that parents will engineer a reproductive zygote in order to make it a male rather than a female child, for example? It is true that in certain communities—in northern India, for example—male children are apparently preferred to female ones. But that preference seems so sensitive to economic circumstances, as well as to shifting cultural prejudices, that it offers no reason for thinking that the world will suddenly be swamped with a generation dominated by males. Selective abortion for sex has been available, as a result of amniocentesis and liberal abortion laws, for some time now, and no such general trend seems to have been established. In any case, we would not be justified in stopping experimentation on the basis of such thin speculation.

The fear, however, goes beyond a fear of sexual asymmetry: it is a fear that one phenotype—say, blond, conventionally goodlooking, nonaggressive, tall, musically talented, and witty—will come to dominate a culture in which that phenotype is particularly valued. We should pause to notice the scientific assumptions embedded in that fear: it supposes not only that comprehensive genetic design is possible, but that the various properties of the preferred phenotype can be assembled in the same person through that design, as if each property were the product of a single allele whose possession made the property at least very highly likely, and that could be specified, and would have that consequence, independently of the specification of or phenotypic expression of other alleles. Each of those assumptions seems improbable, and their combination highly so. It seems much more likely that even parents with state of the art engineering at their disposal would have fewer combinations to choose from, and more risks to run about the impact of nurture and experience, and that they would make these choices differently in response to the very differences among them that we now celebrate. The later impact of differing personal choices by their offspring themselves, perhaps in search of individuality, would enlarge on those differences.

The basic motivational assumptions behind the fear seem equally as dubious as the scientific assumptions, moreover. Most people delight in the mysteries of reproduction—that value is, after all, at the root of the very objection we are considering—and many, and perhaps the great bulk, of people would forgo engineering, beyond trying to eliminate obvious defects and handicaps, as distasteful. If all this is right, the aesthetic objection is overblown or, at best, premature. We would need much more information, of a kind that could be produced only through research and experimentation, before we could even judge the assumptions on which the objection is founded, and it would therefore seem irrational to rely on that objection to prevent that research.

B. Playing God

The arguments and objections we have so far been canvassing do not provide what T. S. Eliot called an "objective correlative" for the immediate and largely sustained revulsion that I described. People feel some deeper, less articulate ground for that revulsion, even if they have not or perhaps cannot fully articulate that ground, but can express it only in heated and logically inappropriate language, like the bizarre reference to "fundamental human rights" in the European Parliament resolution I quoted earlier. We will not adequately appreciate the real power of the political and social resistance to further research into genetic engineering, or the genuine moral and ethical issues that such research presents, until we have better understood that deeper ground, and we might begin with another familiar piece of rhetoric. It is wrong, people say, particularly after more familiar objections have been found wanting, to play God.

This objection appeals to what I called a detached rather than a derivative value. Playing God is thought wrong in itself, quite apart from any bad consequences it will or may have for any identifiable human being. Nevertheless it is deeply unclear what the injunction really means—unclear what playing God is, and what, exactly, is wrong with it. It can't mean that it is always wrong for human beings to attempt to resist natural catastrophes, or to improve upon the hand that nature has dealt them. People do that—always have done that—all the time. What is the difference, after all, between inventing penicillin and using engineered and cloned genes to cure even more terrifying diseases than penicillin cures? What is the difference between setting your child strenuous exercises to reduce his weight or increase his strength and altering his genes, while an embryo, with the same end in view?

These are not rhetorical questions. We must try to answer them, but we must begin at some distance from them, in the overall structure of our moral and ethical experience. For that structure depends, crucially, on a fundamental distinction between what we are responsible for doing or deciding, individually or collectively, and what is given to us, as a background against which we act or decide, but which we are powerless to change. For the Greeks, this was a distinction between themselves and their fate or destiny, which was in the hands or the laps of the gods. For people, even today, who are religious in a conventional way, it is a distinction between how God designed the world, including our natural condition in it, and the scope of the free will he also created. More sophisticated people use the language of science to the same effect: for them the fundamental distinction falls between what nature, including evolution, has created, by way of particles and energy and genes, and what we do in that world and with those genes. For everyone, the distinction, however they describe it, draws a line between who and what we are, for which either a divine will or no one but a blind process is responsible, and what we do with that inheritance, for which we are indeed, separately or together, responsible.

That crucial boundary between chance and choice is the spine of our ethics and our morality, and any serious shift in that boundary is seriously dislocating. Our sense of a life well lived, for example, is fundamentally shaped by supposed givens about the upper limits of human life span. If people could suddenly be expected to live ten times as long as we now do, we would have to recreate the whole range of our opinions about what an attractive kind of life would be, and also our opinions about what activities that carry some risk of accidental death for others, like driving, are morally permissible. History already offers, in our own time, less dramatic but nevertheless profound examples of how scientific change radically dislocates values. People's settled convictions about the responsibilities of leaders to protect their own soldiers in war, at any cost, changed when scientists split the atom and vastly increased the carnage that those convictions could justify. People's settled convictions about euthanasia and suicide changed when deathbed medicine dramatically increased a doctor's power to extend life beyond the point at which that life had any meaning for the patient. In each case a period of moral stability was replaced by moral insecurity, and it is revealing that in both episodes people reached for the expression "playing God," in one case to accuse the scientists who had dramatically increased our powers over nature by cracking what had been thought fundamental in God's design, and in the other to criticize dying patients for taking upon themselves a decision that the past limits of medicine had made it easy to treat as God's alone.

My hypothesis is that genetic science has suddenly made us aware of the possibility of a similar though far greater pending moral dislocation. We dread the prospect of people designing other people because that possibility in itself shifts—much more dramatically than in these other examples—the chance/choice boundary that structures our values as a whole, and such a shift threatens, not to offend any of our present values, derivative or detached, but, on the contrary, to make a great part of these suddenly obsolete. Our physical being—the brain and body that furnishes each person's material substrate—has long been the absolute paradigm of what is both devastatingly important to us and, in its initial condition, beyond our power to alter and therefore beyond the scope of our responsibility, either individual or collective. The popularity of the term "genetic lottery" itself shows the centrality of our conviction that what we most basically *are* is a matter of chance not choice. I do not mean that genetic continuity provides the key to the technical philosophical problem of personal identity, though some philosophers have indeed thought this. I mean to make a psychological point: people think that the very essence of the distinction between what God or nature provides, and what they are responsible for making of or with that provision, is to be defined physically, in terms of what is in "the genes" or, in a metaphor reflecting an older science, "the blood."

If we were to take seriously the possibility we are now exploring—that scientists really have gained the capacity to create a human being having any phenotype that they or their prospective parents choose—then we could chart the destruction of settled moral and ethical attitudes starting at almost any point. We use the chance/choice distinction not simply in our assignments of responsibility for situations or events, for example, but in our assessments of pride, including pride in what nature has given us. It is a striking phenomenon, now, that people take pride in physical attributes or skills they did not choose or create, like physical appearance or strength, but not when these can be seen to be the results of the efforts of others in which they played no part. A woman who puts herself in the hands of a cosmetic surgeon may rejoice in the result but can take no pride in it; certainly not the pride she would have taken if she had been born into the same beauty. What would happen to pride in our physical attributes, or even what we made of them, if these were the inexorable results not of a nature in whose pride we are allowed, as it were, to share, but of the decision of our parents and their hired geneticists?

But the most dramatic use of the fundamental chance/choice distinction is in the assignment of personal and collective responsibility, and it is here that the danger of moral insecurity seems greatest. We now accept the condition in which we were born as a parameter of our responsibility—we must make the best of it that we can—but not as itself a potential arena of blame, except in those special cases, themselves of relatively recent discovery, in which someone's behavior altered his embryonic development, through smoking, for example, or drugs. Otherwise, though we may curse fate for how we are, as Richard Crookback did, we may blame no one else. The same distinction holds, at least for most people, and for many reflective moral philosophers, for social responsibility as well. We feel a greater responsibility to compensate victims of industrial accidents and of racial prejudice, as in both cases victims, though in different ways, of society generally, than we feel to compensate those born with genetic defects or those injured by lightning or in those other ways that lawyers and insurance companies call "acts of God." How would all this change if everyone was as he is through the decisions of others, including the decision of some parents not to intervene but to let nature take its course?

Change it must. But how and why? Once again, these questions are not rhetorical. I do not know the answers, and can hardly guess at them. But that is the point. The terror many of us feel at the thought of genetic engineering is not a fear of what is wrong; it is rather a fear of losing our grip on what is wrong. We are not entitled—it would be a serious confusion—to think that even the most dramatic shifts in the chance/choice boundary somehow challenge morality itself: that there will one day be no more wrong or right. But we are entitled to worry that our settled convictions will, in large numbers, be undermined, that we will be in a kind of moral free-fall, that we will have to think again against a new background and with uncertain results. Playing God is playing with fire.

Suppose that this hypothesis, at least as it might be corrected and improved, makes sense, and accounts for the powerful surd in people's emotional reaction to genetic engineering that is not accounted for by the more discrete grounds we first examined. Have we then discovered not only an explanation but a justification for the objection, a reading of "don't play God" that shows why, at least in this instance, we shouldn't? I think not. We would have discovered a challenge that we must take up rather than a reason for turning back. For our hypothesis implicates no *value*—derivative or detached—at all. It reveals only reasons why our contemporary values, of both kinds, may be wrong or at least ill considered. If we are to be morally and ethically responsible, there can be no turning back once we find, as we have found, that some of the most basic presuppositions of these values are mistaken. Playing God is indeed playing with fire. But that is what we mortals have done since Prometheus, the patron saint of dangerous discovery. We play with fire and take the consequences, because the alternative is cowardice in the face of the unknown.

IV. Postscript: The Impact of Ethical Individualism

If the dramatic techniques of cloning and genetic engineering that I have been discussing are, as many biologists think, only science fiction, they are nevertheless already popular fiction, and the public's hostile reaction, which is presented as based on moral and ethical conviction, may stand in the way of independent and genuine scientific advance. Even if it is never possible to clone entire human beings, research into the processes of cloning may yet produce enormous medical benefits—in the generation of immune-reaction-proof organs for transplant into a patient whose somatic cell produced the organ, for example. The hostile popular reaction has been indiscriminate, however, and threatens to generate across-the-board bans on all such research, so it might be helpful to debate whether the moral and ethical objections would provide sound reasons for halting research even if, as popular imagination fears, the most dramatic consequences were in fact realized. Moreover, the questions raised by the specter of cloning and dramatic genetic engineering are morally instructive even if these techniques are not genuine possibilities. Once the techniques are in the air, they provide fresh and valuable tests for the coherence and adequacy of established and conventional assumptions. Many of us regard reproductive freedom as a fundamental human right, for example. Can we continue in that conviction once we acknowledge even the bare possibility that such a right, once granted, would extend to the freedom to clone oneself or to design a child according to some supposed standard of perfection?

Whether such questions seem important may well depend on one's views about the character of morality. Some people take a pragmatic attitude toward moral conviction: morality, they think, is a device for coordinating our behavior in useful and peaceful ways in the face of potential conflicts. Such people will not see the point in worrying about the adjustments in our coordinated behavior that might conceivably be required, but not for many years if ever. Others think that morality has a more independent status and authority: they would be reluctant to base any argument, even one of immediate practical consequence, on the claim that a principle like the principle of reproductive autonomy had overriding authority if they had to concede that they would not endorse that principle in imagined even if unlikely circumstances. I believe that most people take the latter—philosophers call it a "realist"—attitude toward their moral principles and convictions rather than the former, more instrumental attitude, and the explanation I offered of the ground of the deep-seated hostility toward the more dramatic genetic technology presupposes that latter attitude.

I suggested that even the bare possibility of achieving dramatic control over our children's genetic structure undermines our most basic assumptions about the boundary between what we are responsible for choosing and what, for better or worse, lies beyond our control because it is fixed by chance or nature or the gods. Our genetic identity—who we and our children are—has been a paradigm of nature's responsibility and not ours, and any substantial reallocation of that decision to the sphere of our own responsibility would destabilize much of our conventional morality. Once we understand that it is up to us, at least collectively, whether we allow and encourage our scientists to pursue such technical possibilities and whether we exploit whatever technology they develop, then it is already too late to wish the old boundary back in place, because a decision to turn away from what science may provide is itself a choice we might have made differently. For better or worse, when even the possibility of genetic engineering has been impressed upon us, a basic assumption of much of our conventional morality and attitude has been challenged, and we stand in danger of what I called a state of moral free-fall.

If we are to respond to that danger, we must rely on a more critical and abstract part of our morality. We must try to identify what we might call a critical moral background: a basic set of convictions that we hope can guide when the moral practices and assumptions that we took for granted have been challenged. Do you have a set of background convictions that emphasize individual freedom? Would you require some positive showing of a serious danger to health or safety before you would be ready to endorse legal limits on genetic testing or research or experimentation? Or is your instinct more conservative: would you require a positive showing that some program of testing or line of research is safe and helpful before you would permit it? Of course, these two background positions are only crude paradigms; any actual background morality is likely to be more complex, more deeply grounded, and harder to articulate. But that kind of critical moral backdrop or default is nevertheless indispensable.

My own critical morality rests on a pair of humanist ethical ideals that I call ethical individualism and that define the value associated with human life. The first principle holds that it is objectively important that any human life, once begun, succeed rather than fail—that the potential of that life be realized rather than wasted—and that this is equally objectively important in the case of each human life. I say "objectively" important to emphasize that the success of a human life is not important just for the person whose life it is or for those close to him. We all have a reason to care about the fate of any human life, even that of a stranger, and to hope that it will be a successful life. The second principle acknowledges this objective importance, but insists nevertheless that one person—the person whose life it is—has a special responsibility for each life, and that in virtue of that special responsibility he or she has a right to make the fundamental decisions that define, for him, what a successful life would be. If we take these two principles of ethical individualism as fundamental guides in constructing a theory of political morality, it will be an egalitarian theory, because it will insist that government must treat the life of each person it governs as having great and equal importance, and construct its economic and other structures and policies with that egalitarian principle in mind, and it will also be a liberal theory, because it will insist that government must leave people finally free to make decisions that set the parameters of success for their own lives for themselves.

This book is an attempt to describe the general implications of these two principles for political morality. In this postscript I shall try to suggest their more specific implications for this chapter. I shall use again the distinction between two types of issues—"derivative" and "detached." Derivative issues are raised when government must decide how best to protect the interests of particular people and how to resolve conflicts among such interests fairly. Should tests that might reveal genetic propensity to disease be available to the public? There are causes for concern. Tests might be offered by "cowboy" firms by mail order, for example, and these firms would provide no very accurate information about the reliability or implications of the tests they offer, and no counseling at all to help a woman decide whether to take a test for a gene disposing her to breast cancer, for instance, or how to respond to a positive result. Some diseases that can be predicted by accurate tests have no cures. Should someone be encouraged to submit to a test that might tell him that he has a near certainty of developing Huntington's disease? In other cases, the experimental data justify much less confidence in the result: the research so far may assign probabilities, for example, on the basis of population classifications that may be superseded by more precise classifications with wide probability differences.

We can choose various policies in the face of these difficulties, ranging from total prohibition of genetic testing, at least until research is much further developed, to total commercial freedom that would allow any vendor to provide tests in a wholly unregulated market. If neither extreme is justified, which strategy, somewhere between the two, should we choose? Our answer will very likely depend on our background critical morality. The principle of special responsibility I endorsed argues against any deep form of paternalism. It argues, therefore, for regulation rather than flat prohibition, and regulation that seeks accurate disclosure and licensing rather than even limited prohibition. It would accept that tests should be provided only through doctors with sufficient training and experience to provide professionally competent counseling and interpretation. But it would not accept banning a test, for competent people, only because its accuracy is speculative, provided that its speculative character is fully disclosed.

Should tests ever be required? It might seem that the principle of special responsibility rules that out. But sometimes tests protect the interests of others than the person whose consent would normally be thought necessary. Suppose it were possible to correct serious genetic defects of different kinds in embryos, for example, either through genetic engineering or through more conventional forms of therapy. Then the principle of special responsibility would no longer justify allowing a pregnant woman to refuse tests to discover such a defect in an embryo she carries, and the first principle of ethical humanism—an objective concern that any life, once begun, be a successful one—would counsel mandatory testing. It is true that modern democracies share a visceral distaste for requiring anyone to submit to a medical procedure to which she objects, particularly when the objection is founded, as an objection to genetic testing and the treatment that follows might well be founded, on religious conviction. This flat principle of bodily integrity may, however, be one of those artifacts of conventional morality that seemed well justified before the possibilities suggested by modern genetic medicine were plausibly imagined, but not after. If we are to accept a more fundamental principle of concern for the lives of everyone, that principle of bodily integrity may one day have to be qualified.

How would our attitudes about a fair insurance market have to be revised if genetic testing became sufficiently widespread to affect the economics of that market? Should life insurers be permitted to require genetic tests that they deem good predictors of life expectancy? Or to charge higher premiums to those who refuse such tests? If not, should they be allowed to ask whether applicants for insurance have had such tests, and to demand the results if they have? The Association of British Insurers has decided not to demand tests, or even to ask whether an applicant has had tests, for life policies of less than £100,000 when the policy is taken out in connection with a mortgage. But that is only a temporary and voluntary restriction.

Should it be made mandatory and permanent? Should it apply to all policies?

That is a derivative issue, because it asks about the appropriate resolution of a conflict of interests between the genetically lucky, who would pay less for insurance if premiums reflected genetic propensity to disease, and the genetically unlucky, who would pay more. There are several candidates for a principle to resolve that conflict. One, which might be called a principle of actuarial accuracy, objects to the use of genetic testing in insurance decisions on the ground that insurance companies would rely on crude classifications for genetic prediction because refining those categories to establish a more finely graded premium structure would be too expensive in administration costs. Many people would then be charged at higher rates than their actual predisposition to disease would justify. That is unfair, however, only if fairness requires that people pay in proportion to the risk that they impose on the risk pool, no matter how expensive it would be to discover that risk. That seems an irrational definition of fairness, because a fair system, on that account, would be an economically wasteful one. If fairness really means that each applicant should pay in proportion to the antecedent cost to the pool of insuring him, then that cost must include administrative and other secondary costs, so that it would not, after all, be unfair to lump people together who actually fall into different categories of genetically signaled risk. If that practice does seem unfair to you, then you may actually reject the idea that fairness demands that people who pose higher risks, through no fault of their own, should pay a higher share of the overall insurance premium.

The default system of ethical individualism, which demands equal concern for the situation of everyone, recommends a different account of fairness. It insists that a fair distribution of risks and benefits is one that is sensitive to different people's choices but insensitive to their brute bad luck, including their luck in what is still, at the present stage of technology, a genetic lottery. (This analysis of fair insurance might have to be revised, of course, along with almost every other relatively concrete judgment of fairness, if the most extravagant promises of genetic engineering were realized. We would then have to consider, in our "moral free-fall" state, how far children should be held to account for choices their parents made.) So, though it might be fair to charge smokers more for health or life insurance—I set aside problems that might arise if we found that certain genes "forced" smoking the way that other genes "force" disease—it would not be fair to charge people more because their chromosomes contain an allele threatening breast or prostate cancer. Fairness, understood in the light of ethical individualism, would therefore require "community rating" in the face of discoveries about the genetic basis of disease susceptibility: premiums should be based on the average risk in the relevant community, and the same premium (adjusted only for risks knowingly and voluntarily assumed) should be offered to every applicant.

But if insurers offered community rates, and applicants were permitted to discover their own genetic situation through appropriately regulated genetic testing, then applicants would engage in what insurers call "adverse selection." Those at most risk would insure heavily, those at least risk would not insure at all, and insurers would have to raise their rates sharply (which would in effect reintroduce discrimination) or face bankruptcy. If, on the other hand, insurers were allowed to charge higher rates to applicants who had chosen to test themselves before insuring and had learned that they were genetically unlucky, this would discourage testing and doom individuals whose lives could have been saved or repaired by such tests. I said earlier that the only solution to this "insurance dilemma" lies in the nationalization of insurance—life as well as health insurance—in those societies that have not yet taken that step.

Even deeper divisions emerge around the detached issues provoked by the possibility of cloning and other dramatic genetic engineering. These issues are detached because they mainly concern not the interests of particular people but rather which kind of people, produced in which way, there are to be. How far and how fast should scientific research continue in these areas? Here, too, ethical individualism offers guidance. There is nothing in itself wrong with the detached ambition to make the lives of future generations of human beings longer and more full of talent and hence achievement. On the contrary, if playing God means struggling to improve our species, bringing into our conscious designs a resolution to improve what God deliberately or nature blindly has evolved over eons, then the first principle of ethical individualism commands that struggle, and its second principle forbids, in the absence of positive evidence of danger, hobbling the scientists and doctors who volunteer to lead it.

14

Sex, Death, and the Courts

⚹

I

May a "moral majority" limit the liberty of individual citizens on no better ground than that it disapproves of the personal choices they make? Though almost all Americans agree that human life is sacred in some way, they disagree about whether it follows that people must never kill themselves, even to avoid terrible pain or crippling indignity, and even when they will soon die anyway. Some think it degrades life to end it prematurely, even in those circumstances; others think it degrading not to die in dignity when further life would be appalling. Should that decision be made individually, each person deciding for his own life out of his own conviction? Or should it be made collectively, so that the convictions of the majority are imposed even on those whose most basic beliefs are thereby compromised?[1]

Sexual morality is also central to people's lives and personality. Should adults be free to make their own decisions about sex when these decisions have no direct impact on others? If so, how far should others then be free, as private individuals, to express their disapproval of those decisions in their own choice of employees, associates, or teachers for their children? Americans have accepted that some forms of private discrimination are matters of public concern, and that the law should guarantee equality of treatment for blacks, women, and the handicapped in many spheres. Why not for homosexuals as well? Does it matter that sexual behavior, unlike race or gender or handicap, is finally a matter of choice? Scientists disagree about how far genetic factors fix sexuality, though it seems undeniable that they play at least a significant role. In any case, abstaining from homosexual sex would

453

mean no sex at all for many people, or living a lie. Should society allow discrimination against people who refuse to make a choice with such costs?

In the United States—and in many other nations and international communities that have followed our lead in establishing constitutional rights—these questions are also legal questions, because the American Constitution provides that individuals have certain rights that a majority may not invade. The most abstract source of these rights is the Fourteenth Amendment, which provides that no state may constrain any citizen's liberty without "due process of law," and that no state may deny anyone "the equal protection of the laws." The due process clause forbids compromising certain basic rights altogether, except for a particularly compelling reason. The equal protection clause requires only that states not discriminate unfairly in the liberties and other privileges it chooses to allow. Both clauses have been interpreted to give citizens at least some rights to make personal moral decisions for themselves. In 1963, for example, in *Roe v. Wade*,[2] the Supreme Court held that the due process clause gives women a right to abortion in the early stages of pregnancy; and in 1996 it appealed to the equal protection clause to strike down an amendment to the Colorado constitution that made it illegal for cities and towns in that state to grant homosexuals protection against discrimination. In 1997, however, it refused to declare unconstitutional state statutes prohibiting doctors from assisting in the suicide of terminally ill patients: it declined to hold that either the due process clause or the equal protection clause gives citizens a constitutional right to control the manner of their own deaths.[3]

How should judges decide which liberties the due process clause treats as basic, and what kinds of discrimination the equal protection clause treats as unfair? For over a century two sharply opposed views have been fighting a constitutional War of the Roses, with first one side and then the other achieving temporary dominion. One party, anxious to restrict the power of judges to adjudicate moral issues, insists that the due process and equal protection clauses give legal protection only to a limited list of rights that have been recognized and enforced over the broad course of America's post–Civil War history. In the Supreme Court's 1986 decision in *Bowers v. Hardwick*,[4] in which the Court declined to strike down Georgia's law making sodomy between consenting adults a crime, Justice Byron White set out this view of the due process clause in a passage that has become talismanic for this party of history. He adopted the view that the clause protects only those rights that are "deeply rooted in this Nation's history and tradition," and he said that it was therefore decisive against the alleged right of homosexuals to be free to practice sodomy that until 1961 all 50 American states outlawed that sexual act; the suggestion that "a right to engage in such conduct" meets either of the two tests is therefore, he said, at best "facetious."[5]

On this view, logic and consistency in principle play little role in identifying constitutional rights. The fact that the Court has recognized one right—a right to abortion, for example—provides no argument why it should also recognize any other right—the right of homosexuals to sexual freedom or of dying patients to control their own death, for instance—even if no principled reason can be given why people should have the former right but not the latter ones. The only issue is whether the particular right in question has been historically recognized, and that test must be applied independently to each suggested right, one by one. Only in that way, as White made plain, can the power of judges to expand constitutional rights in the name of consistency be curtailed. "Nor are we inclined," he said, "to take a more expansive view of our authority to discover new fundamental rights imbedded in the Due Process Clause. Otherwise, the Judiciary necessarily takes to itself further authority to govern the country without express constitutional authority."[6] It is better, on this view, to tolerate inconsistency in the rights the Court recognizes than to expand the list of those rights.

The opposite party in the constitutional wars—the party of integrity—denies that order of priority. It insists if the constitutional rights acknowledged for one group presuppose more general principles that would support other constitutional rights for other groups, then the latter must be acknowledged and enforced as well.[7] In 1961 a conservative justice—John Harlan—offered one of the strongest judicial statements of this view, and just as White's formulation in *Bowers* has become an anthem for the party of history, Harlan's has become one for the party of integrity. The liberty protected by the due process clause, Harlan said, "is not a series of isolated points . . . it is a rational continuum which, broadly speaking, includes a freedom from all substantial arbitrary imposition and purposeless restraints."[8] Though Harlan made that statement in a dissenting opinion, it has often been cited in later decisions of the Court. Justices Kennedy, O'Connor, and Souter relied on it, for example, in their crucial plurality opinion in 1993, in *Casey v. Planned Parenthood of Pennsylvania*,[9] in explaining why the Supreme Court was right to recognize a right to abortion in *Roe v. Wade*, even though most states had outlawed abortion for decades before that decision. We should examine the two latest Supreme Court decisions I mentioned, about homosexuality and assisted suicide, with this great doctrinal dispute in mind.

II

Many Americans have become ashamed and embarrassed at the legal, economic, and social disadvantages that homosexuals still suffer in their country, and in recent decades they have supported laws and industrial and academic regulations prohibiting or limiting such discrimination. The Colorado cities of Aspen, Boulder, and Denver, for example, enacted legislation that protected homosexuals, along with minority races and women, from discrimination in housing, education, employment, and health and welfare services. Other Colorado voters were outraged, however, by the suggestion, implicit in such legislation, that homosexuality is a legitimate way of life. In a 1992 statewide referendum, they adopted "Amendment 2" to their state constitution, which was titled "No Protected Status Based on Homosexual, Lesbian, or Bisexual Orientation." It declared:

> Neither the State of Colorado, through any of its branches or departments, nor any of its agencies, political subdivisions, municipalities or school districts, shall enact, adopt or enforce any statute, regulation, ordinance or policy whereby homosexual, lesbian or bisexual orientation, conduct, practices or relationships shall constitute or otherwise be the basis of or entitle any person or class of persons to have or claim any minority status, quota, preferences, protected status or claim of discrimination.

This provision, if valid, would have a catastrophic effect on the political situation of homosexuals in Colorado. It would annihilate the protection that some cities had already given, and forbid any political subdivision of the state, and indeed the state itself, from enacting any protective legislation in the future. Homosexuals could thereafter secure antidiscrimination legislation only by further amending the state constitution itself, to repeal or amend Amendment 2. That struck many people, within the state and outside it, as monstrously unfair. They assumed that such a blatant piece of discrimination must violate the U.S. Constitution, and a group of Colorado homosexuals and others sued in a Denver court, in the case of *Evans v. Romer*, asking for a ruling to that effect. Many constitutional lawyers were dubious, however, that they could win. Supreme Court precedents over many years seemed to indicate that Amendment 2 violated neither the due process nor the equal protection clauses.

We need some doctrinal history to understand why lawyers doubted that the Supreme Court would hold that Amendment 2 violated the due process clause. When litigants challenge some law on due process grounds, judges characteristically rule on that challenge by asking two questions. First, does the law compromise a "liberty interest"—that is, a right that the Constitution in principle protects from state action? Second, if so, are the purposes and effects of the statute so important that they nevertheless justify a state's invading that liberty interest? The first question divides the parties of history and integrity in the way I described: the former insists that constitutional rights are limited, even in principle, to the concrete rights established in history, while the latter insists that such rights also include as-yet-unrecognized rights that would follow from the principles that justify the historically recognized ones. The second question, which arises only if it is decided that the law does compromise a constitutional right, requires a balance. A court must assess the strength of that right and consider whether the state's alleged interests are sufficiently strong to justify compromising a right of that strength.

So the *Bowers* decision I mentioned seemed decisive against the claim that Amendment 2 violated the due process clause. White had explicitly declared that homosexuals do not have, even in principle, a constitutional right that states invade when they make homosexual activity a crime. It therefore seemed impossible to argue that they have a constitutional right that would bar the less serious disadvantage of Amendment 2, which merely prevents them from obtaining special legislation in their favor.[10] As the District of Columbia Circuit had observed in 1987, "If the Court . . . was unwilling to object to state laws that criminalize the behavior that defines the class, it is hardly open . . . to conclude that state sponsored discrimination against the class is invidious. After all, there can hardly be more palpable discrimination against a class than making the conduct that defines the class criminal."[11]

The equal protection clause might seem a more promising basis for challenging Amendment 2, because that law denied homosexuals a political opportunity—attempting to secure local legislation protecting their basic interests—open to all other groups. But once again, precedent stood in the way of using the equal protection clause to invalidate that discrimination; once again we need some history to see why. The provision that states must not deny any person "the equal protection of the laws" might conceivably have been understood to impose only a very weak requirement on states: that they could discriminate among their citizens only if they first enacted laws describing and authorizing that discrimination. But that banal reading would leave a state free to create a caste system in which blacks (for example) were denied any civil or legal rights, so long as it did so through explicit legislation. Since the Fourteenth Amendment was enacted after the Civil War, with the expectation of preventing any further racial castes, that A reading is unacceptable. But so is the opposite reading, which would declare that states must never enact laws that discriminate in any way among groups of citizens, awarding advantages to some at cost to others. For almost every national or state law has precisely that effect—the North American Free Trade Agreement worked against the interests of some workers and in favor of others, environmental legislation injures some industries though not others, and state banking, securities, and professional regulations help some people but disadvantage others. So the Supreme Court has developed a more sophisticated reading of the equal protection clause that avoids either of these extreme and unacceptable readings. It has done this through a set of rules and distinctions that, taken together, are calculated to serve an attractive conception of political equality.[12]

The underlying rationale of these rules and distinctions is a theory about when a democracy is working well, so that those who lose out in a political contest cannot complain of procedural inequality or unfairness, and when it is defective, so that losses to some groups cannot be accepted as fair. In the normal circumstances of ordinary politics, groups that lose—as the timber industry, for example, might lose through environmental legislation—have had a fair opportunity to present their case and exert an influence on the result in rough proportion to their numbers and the strength of their interests. The Court will therefore scrutinize ordinary legislation challenged on equal protection grounds only in a "relaxed" way: it will declare such legislation unconstitutional only if it finds that the distinction it draws, between those it benefits and those it harms, is plainly irrational, because it does not serve, even in a speculative or problematical way, any legitimate purpose of government. So the Court has approved, for example, a law subjecting oculists and optometrists to different regulatory schemes, even though no very impressive reason could be given why they should be treated differently. Only rarely, in fact, has any statute been found to violate this "relaxed" test of rationality.

In some circumstances, however, the general presumption that the political process has worked in a fair way is doubtful. That presumption cannot rescue legislation that deprives some group of the very political rights it needs in order to participate in the process on fair terms—when the legislation reduces the voting power of some group, for example, so that its political impact is made less than its numbers would otherwise justify. The Court has therefore created a different, "strict" or "heightened," level of scrutiny for laws that have that effect. It declares such laws unconstitutional, even if they are rationally related to some legitimate state purpose, unless they can be shown to be necessary to prevent some grievous result that cannot be avoided in any other reasonable way. The Court relied on the strict test, for example, in its series of "reapportionment" decisions in which it struck down state schemes for drawing boundaries of electoral districts whose effect was to deny equal impact of all citizens, on a one-person, one-vote basis.[13] Just as the "relaxed" test is rarely failed, so this "strict" test is rarely passed.

The presumption of a fair political process is also doubtful when the group that loses is one that has historically been the victim of a prejudice or stereotype that makes it likely that its interests will be discounted by other voters. Blacks have often lost out in politics, for example, not because their own interests were outweighed by those of others in a fair contest, but for a combination of two other reasons: because they were economically and socially marginalized, and lacked the training and means needed to command the attention of politicians and other voters, and because many white citizens voted for discriminatory laws not just to protect their own competing personal interests but because they held blacks in contempt and wanted them subjugated. So the Court has created another special category attracting "heightened" scrutiny: it declared that blacks form a "suspect" class, and that any legislation that works to their special disadvantage must be struck down unless it can be defended as serving some absolutely compelling purpose. That strict test, too, has rarely been met. The Court has added other groups to the list of "suspect" classes deserving this special protection: ethnic minorities and immigrants. It has, moreover, created a further category of "quasi-suspect" classes—these now include women and illegitimate children—and declared that legislation working against them will also receive "heightened" (but not as "strict" as in the case of fully "suspect" classes) scrutiny.

So an equal protection challenge to any legislation must show either some reason why "heightened scrutiny" of that legislation is appropriate, or that the legislation is irrational because it does not bear even a speculative relation to a legitimate governmental purpose. Heightened scrutiny is appropriate if the group that is disadvantaged counts as a "suspect" or "quasi-suspect" class, and homosexuals are certainly targets of prejudice and irrational hatred. In the years following the *Bowers* decision, however, several federal courts held that homosexuals nevertheless do not count as a suspect or quasi-suspect class. Suspect groups, they said, are those that lack the political power necessary to make the political process a fair and democratic one for them. But a group might lack that power for either of the two reasons that I distinguished earlier, in discussing the case of blacks.

First, it might be so marginalized financially, socially, and politically that it lacks the means to attract the attention of politicians and other voters to its interests, and so cannot wield the power at the polls, or in alliances or horse-trading compromises with other groups, that its numbers could otherwise be expected to produce. Second, it might be the victim of bias, prejudice, hatred, or stereotype so serious that a majority wants it constrained or punished for that reason, even when this does not serve any other, more respectable or legitimate, interests of other groups.[14] Blacks and the other classes the Supreme Court has hitherto treated as suspect or quasi-suspect arguably suffer from both these systemic disabilities, and so it has not been necessary to decide whether one of the two disabilities is enough, on its own, to justify a "suspect" classification. But (at least in the view of the judges who have spoken on the issue) homosexuals suffer only from the second.[15] Justice Scalia has insisted that homosexuals have at least the political power their numbers would warrant: "those who engage in homosexual conduct," he said, "tend to reside in disproportionate numbers in certain communities . . . have high disposable income . . . and of course care about homosexual-rights issues much more ardently than the public at large, they possess political power much greater than their numbers, both locally and statewide."[16] If a state like Colorado rejects the homosexuals' case, he said, it is not because they have not had a chance to organize their political efforts or to speak effectively to their fellow citizens, but because, in spite of the fact that they have had those opportunities, the majority has found against them.

It is therefore crucial to decide whether the second disadvantage—the prejudice and contempt of a potential majority—is an independent defect in the proper functioning of a democracy that is sufficiently serious to justify heightened scrutiny of legislation that harms those who suffer from such prejudice. *Bowers* answered that question negatively. The groups who challenged the Georgia antisodomy law in that case argued that a state has no right to enact criminal legislation when its only reason is that the majority morally disapproves of those it makes criminals. White replied: "The law, however, is constantly based on notions of morality, and if all laws representing essentially moral choices are to be invalidated under the Due Process Clause, the courts will be very busy indeed." White's reply missed the point. Of course most of the criminal laws that a community enacts express a moral choice: laws against murder express a moral condemnation of that activity. The challengers argued only for the narrower principle that a criminal law is unconstitutional if it is enacted only to condemn some people morally, and not to protect anyone else's direct interests. Laws against murder do more than denounce murderers: they protect the most basic interests of innocent people. Making consensual adult sodomy a crime, on the other hand, serves no interests that are independent of the moral condemnation, and those who challenged Georgia's antisodomy law argued that that is not a legitimate justification for a criminal penalty.

White clearly meant to reject that narrower principle as well, however, and *Bowers* therefore stands for the principle that it is permissible for government to prohibit freedom of choice in private sexual behavior even if that behavior harms no one in any direct way, so long as the condemnation expresses popular morality. Since *Bowers*, judges have therefore uniformly rejected the suggestion that homosexuals form a suspect or quasi-suspect class for equal protection purposes, and every judge who expressed an opinion on that issue in the course of the *Evans v. Romer* litigation agreed. There is another kind of legislation that also attracts the "heightened scrutiny" test, however, as we noticed at the beginning of this history: legislation that compromises a fundamental political right. The claim that Amendment 2 violated a fundamental political right does not depend on supposing that homosexuals are a suspect or quasi-suspect class. On the contrary, it could be sustained only by showing that it would be unconstitutional to treat any group of citizens—people who rent houses, for example, as opposed to owning them—as Amendment 2 treated homosexuals. But, just for that reason, it is enormously difficult to define what the right in question is.

The Denver trial judge who first considered the case, H. Jeffrey Bayless, decided that the amendment did violate a fundamental right: the right "not to have the State endorse and give effect to private biases." But that is exactly the right that White, in *Bowers*, said that no one has. So when Colorado appealed the trial judge's decision to the Colorado Supreme Court, that court upheld the trial judge's decision but cited a different fundamental right—the right of all groups to "participate equally in the political process." There is an evident difficulty in that suggestion as well, however. Amendment 2 did not diminish or dilute anyone's voting power. It did put one group—homosexuals—at a particular legislative disadvantage: they would have to amend the state constitution again to secure legislation of particular concern to it. But no one has a right not to have to amend the constitution to obtain legislation it favors or believes it needs. It would not be unconstitutional, in principle, for Colorado's constitution to forbid municipalities to adopt rent-control legislation, for example, even though that would pose special problems for people who rent. Indeed, the national constitution has parallel disabilities: groups who fervently want prayer back in their schools would have to repeal the First Amendment before petitioning the local school board.

So many lawyers were fearful, when Colorado appealed from its own supreme court to the national one, that even if a majority of the justices wanted to strike down Amendment 2, they would not find room to do so within the network of doctrine and precedents they had themselves constructed. But an all-star group of some of America's most distinguished constitutional law scholars submitted an ingenious brief, as *amici curiae*, or friends of the court, which pointed a way out of these doctrinal difficulties.[17] The academic brief bypassed the elaborate structure of categories and distinctions that I described, about suspect classes, fundamental rights, and different levels of scrutiny, by insisting that it is an automatic (or "per se") violation of equal protection for the state to declare that any group of citizens is simply ineligible for any protection whatever from any form of the terrible harm of discrimination. Such a declaration, the brief said, in effect outlaws the group, and it was the central point of the equal protection clause to prevent that kind of caste distinction.

This argument, the brief insisted, assumes nothing about homosexuals' being a suspect class. A state constitutional provision would violate equal protection, it said, if it forbade any legislation protecting any group of citizens against any form of discrimination. It offered this example: a state constitution would not provide equal protection for people who rent homes (surely not a suspect class) if it provided that any local or state legislation that protects renters from any imaginable harm or loss is invalid. But this comparison reveals how limited an argument the brief was making, and how carefully it had tailored that argument to the facts of this particular case. It made the unconstitutionality of Amendment 2 depend on its great breadth, and, as the example of home renters shows, its argument would not invalidate a narrower but still destructive state constitutional provision aimed at homosexuals permissible. For the brief conceded that it would not be per se violation of equal protection for a state constitution to forbid a specific form of protection for renters—for it to forbid rent-control legislation, for example. So, by a parity of reasoning, it would not be a per se violation for a constitution to forbid a single form of antidiscrimination legislation—local laws banning discrimination against homosexuals in hiring, for example, or in hospital admissions. We might be tempted to say that these are very different matters: a provision forbidding rent control might express an economic theory, while one forbidding even a specific and limited form of help to homosexuals would express only bias. But the academic brief's argument was careful, for reasons I have tried to make clear, not to rely on that distinction, because that would have been tantamount to declaring homosexuals a suspect class, or to affirming the right Bayless had cited but the state supreme court had feared to endorse—a right to be free from legislation motivated by bias against one's group.

When the Supreme Court delivered its long-awaited verdict, in May 1996, Justice Anthony Kennedy's opinion for the six-justice majority was surprisingly bold—bolder than the opinions of either of the lower courts and bolder than even the academic brief. (As Justice Scalia wryly noticed, the Court has the luxury, as other judges and lawyers do not, of overruling its own precedents.) Kennedy did accept, in general terms, the argument of the academic brief. He emphasized, as that brief did, that Amendment 2 was wholly novel in the sheer breadth of the potential damage it worked on homosexuals, by depriving them of any possible opportunity to secure protection, except by constitutional amendment, against any form of discrimination no matter how harmful or wrongful. But, perhaps understanding the limitations of that argument, he also made a much broader and potentially more reforming claim. He said that Amendment 2 violates even the most relaxed form of scrutiny under equal protection doctrine, because it is not even rational. "In the ordinary case," Kennedy said, "a law will be sustained if it can be said to advance a legitimate government interest, even if the law seems unwise or works to the disadvantage of a particular group, or if the rationale for it seems tenuous." But, he said, "[Amendment 2's] sheer breadth is so discontinuous with the reasons offered for it that the amendment seems inexplicable by anything except animus toward the class that it affects; it lacks a rational relationship to legitimate state interests."[18]

That statement is of crucial importance, because it flatly contradicts White's pivotal assumption in *Bowers*. White, you recall, declared that it was legitimate for a state to impose a disadvantage on a particular group just to express the majority's moral contempt for that group's practices, even when no other proper purpose, such as protecting anyone's economic or security interests, is served. Kennedy, in the passage just quoted, said that this is *not* legitimate. It is true that White spoke in terms of moral disapproval and Kennedy in terms of "animus." But there can be no difference in what these words mean in this context.[19] For Colorado could certainly declare, in perfect good faith, that the amendment's "sheer breadth" was justified by the depth of its citizens' moral disapproval of homosexuality. Nothing less than a complete ban on any law that suggests that homosexuality is an acceptable form of sexual union, it might say, would be enough to express the profoundness of the majority's rejection of that moral opinion. By describing that justification as one appealing to "animus," and declaring it illegitimate, Kennedy reached back to Judge Bayless' original judgment in the trial court, and drew the sting from *Bowers* without even mentioning it.

Kennedy did not put homosexuals in as secure a position as they would enjoy if they were designated a suspect or quasi-suspect class. They have the burden of proof in showing that a particular rule or law that harms them serves no legitimate purpose, but only the illegitimate one of expressing "animus," and they might find that burden difficult to sustain in many cases—in challenging the military's opposition to retaining openly homosexual soldiers, for example. But they would presumably not find it difficult to show that the outright criminalization of all homosexual sex serves no purpose beyond that illegitimate one. Scalia was right, in his biting dissent, that the combination of the results in *Romer* and *Bowers* is ludicrous: practicing homosexuals can be jailed but not put at an electoral disadvantage that many other groups, including religious fundamentalists, suffer. But the inevitable resolution of that conflict may not be the one he would prefer. The majority in *Romer v. Evans* may have done more than simply ignore *Bowers:* they may have begun the process of isolating and finally overruling it altogether, an event that would have an enormous impact not only on the civil liberties of homosexuals but on constitutional theory generally.

In its ten-year life, *Bowers*, the flagship decision of the party of history, has frequently been damned by scholars and commentators for its cramped view of what a free society is and does. It was a five-to-four decision, and Justice Powell, who tipped the balance, said after his retirement that his vote was the worst mistake of his career. Justice O'Conner, another member of that slim majority, joined Kennedy's opinion in *Romer*, which may suggest that she, too, has changed her mind. Perhaps *Bowers* would win only three votes if it were directly challenged now: Justices Scalia and Rehnquist, who were also members of the original *Bowers* majority; and Thomas, who joined in Scalia's dissent in *Romer v. Evans*. In any case, that decision was a victory for the party of integrity, and for the conviction that equality is a principle not only of justice but of constitutional law as well.

III

Was the Supreme Court's later assisted-suicide decision an offsetting victory for the party of history? The Court, in that decision, reversed the decisions of two circuit courts of appeal that had declared that statutes making assisting suicide a crime were unconstitutional: the Ninth Circuit had said that such statutes violate the due process clause, because dying patients have a liberty interest in controlling the timing and manner of their death; and the Second Circuit had said that the statutes violate the equal protection clause because the Supreme Court had held, in its *Cruzan* decision in 1990,[20] that patients who are on life support have a constitutional right to terminate that support, and forbidding dying patients who are not on life support an alternate means to hasten their deaths denies them equal treatment. In *Compassion*, the Supreme Court overturned both these circuit court decisions by an apparently crushing nine-to-nothing vote. But the unanimity of the vote was deceptive. Five of the six justices who wrote opinions made it plain that they did not altogether reject the claim that dying patients have a constitutional right to a willing doctor's help in hastening their death, suggesting that the Court might well change its mind in a future case when more evidence of the practical impact of any such right was available.

The opinions of the six justices make up the fullest and most candid debate between the historicist and the integrity understandings of the due process clause for many decades. In his majority opinion, on behalf of himself and four other justices, Chief Justice William Rehnquist defended the historicist view.[21] He insisted that the due process clause protects only those specific liberties that have historically been respected by American states. The clause does protect citizens from unwanted and invasive medical treatment, he said, because the common law of most states has for a long time granted that protection, but it does not condemn laws prohibiting a doctor from helping people dying in great pain to die sooner, because almost all states have long prohibited such help. Rehnquist acknowledged that his historicist approach might well produce anomalies of principle, because it might well be that no principled distinction can be drawn between liberties that American states have historically protected and those that they have denied. He said that the Supreme Court's suggestion, in its earlier *Cruzan* decision, that the due process clause gives people a right to have life-saving apparatus removed from their bodies was drawn only from common-law practice, and was "not simply deduced from abstract concepts of personal autonomy . . . The decision to commit suicide with the assistance of another may be just as personal and profound as the decision to refuse unwanted medical treatment, but it has never enjoyed similar legal protection."

Justice David Souter, on the other hand, in his separate opinion concurring in but not joining Rehnquist's majority opinion, offered a classic statement of the integrity view. He said that the nation's history and traditions include not just the specific rights that have been recognized in the past, but the "basic values" that are revealed when we interpret those rights to see which more general principles of political morality they represent. It may be, he said, that states have not always been wholly faithful to those basic values, and that some of even the oldest legal practices, like the long prohibition on abortion, can now be seen to offend them and so to violate the due process clause. Judges, he said, must take care in deciding which principles of political morality do underlie the nation's history, because such principles can be identified at varying levels of generality, and judges must not state them more broadly than a sound interpretation would justify. He conceded that identifying principles at the right level of generality is "not a mechanical matter." Selecting among such competing characterizations demands "reasoned judgment about which broader principle, as exemplified in the concrete privileges and prohibitions embodied in our legal tradition, best fits the particular claim asserted in a particular case." He drew, from his understanding of the due process clause, very different conclusions from Rehnquist's about assisted suicide. If we apply reasoned judgment to the assisted suicide issue, Souter argued, we can identify arguments of what he called "increasing forcefulness for recognizing some right to a doctor's help in suicide."

The strongest of these arguments, he said, rests on a general principle, embedded in past traditions, that guarantees a "right to medical care and counsel, subject to the limiting conditions of informed, responsible choice when death is imminent . . . There can be no stronger claim to a physician's assistance than at the time when death is imminent, a moral judgment implied by the State's own recognition of the legitimacy of medical procedures necessarily hastening the moment of impending death [e.g., terminating life support and allowing pain relief that advances death]."

So Rehnquist's and Souter's views of the due process clause are dramatically different: the former protects individuals only from laws that few states have seen any reason to enact, and offers no protection at all against historically popular invasions of individual freedom. The second holds out the possibility that even long-standing and popular legal rules, like the ban on assisted suicide, might be held unconstitutional when they can be seen to violate more general and established principles of freedom. It is therefore important to try to gauge the popularity of each of these views in the present Supreme Court. Rehnquist, as I have said, had no difficulty in using his historicist approach to reject any right to assisted suicide out of hand. Four other justices—Justices Anthony Kennedy, Sandra Day O'Connor, Antonin Scalia, and Clarence Thomas—joined Rehnquist's opinion, and we may safely assume that Scalia and Thomas do in fact embrace the historicist assumptions of that opinion.

O'Connor and Kennedy, however, were two of the three justices—the other was Souter—who wrote a joint opinion in the 1992 *Casey* abortion decision endorsing the interpretive view of due process that Souter defended in this case, and it is therefore puzzling why they joined Rehnquist's opinion. Perhaps they did so out of institutional courtesy, so that one opinion—Rehnquist's—could attract five votes and so count as the opinion of the Court, avoiding the inelegant result of a unanimous decision with no minority opinion. In any case, however, O'Connor wrote a separate opinion that makes it plain that she does not accept Rehnquist's historicist understanding of the due process clause. She identified the question posed by the cases as "whether a mentally competent person who is experiencing great suffering has a constitutionally cognizable interest in controlling the circumstances of his or her imminent death." She said that she saw no need to decide that question because, even if such a patient had such a right, the state laws challenged in the cases did not violate it because they allowed doctors to administer pain-relieving drugs even when these hastened death. She left open, that is, the crucial question—whether patients have some right to control how they die—that the historicist understanding would have answered, negatively and immediately. Kennedy did not write a separate opinion. But it is unlikely that he accepts the historicist account, given not only his opinion in *Casey* but also his explicitly interpretive reading of the equal protection clause in *Romer*.

Ginsburg said simply that she agreed with O'Connor. Breyer said pointedly that he joined O'Connor's opinion "except insofar as it joins the majority." He added that he would formulate the patient's claim in these cases, not as Rehnquist had, but rather in "words roughly like a 'right to die with dignity,' " and he said that "our legal tradition may provide greater support" for such a right. He added that he did not have to decide the question whether the due process clause actually does require judges to recognize such a right, because "the avoidance of severe physical pain (connected with death) would have to comprise an essential part of any successful claim," and he agreed with O'Connor that pain can be avoided under the statutes the Court was considering because these statutes do not prohibit pain-relieving treatment that advances death. He concluded with the important observation that if states did interfere with the "administration of drugs as needed to avoid pain at the end of life," then, "as Justice O'Connor suggests, the Court might have to revisit its conclusions in these cases."

The remaining justice—Stevens—wrote an eloquent separate opinion to explain that his vote to reverse the lower court decisions was based on procedural rather than substantive grounds. He said that since the patients who were plaintiffs in the cases at hand had all died before the Supreme Court decision, the question before the Court was not whether the anti–assisted suicide laws could constitutionally be applied to patients who were dying when they asked for relief. Instead, he said, once the patients had died, the case required the Court to decide whether the antisuicide laws could constitutionally be applied to anyone at all, including, for example, a depressed but otherwise healthy person who had expressed a wish to die. Since he thought that a state could properly prevent doctors from aiding some people who wanted to die, he voted to sustain the statutes as not "facially" invalid. His opinion left little doubt, however, that in what he deemed an appropriate case he would vote to overrule a statute that prevented doctors from helping competent and informed dying patients—not just those whose pain could not otherwise be relieved—to die sooner. He emphasized that different people have different religious and ethical convictions about what kind of death most respects the value of their lives, and that individual freedom demands that dying patients be permitted to die according to their own convictions. He ended with the uncompromising statement: "In my judgment . . . it is clear that [the states'] so-called 'unqualified interest in the preservation of human life' . . . is not itself sufficient to outweigh the interest in liberty that may justify the only possible means of preserving a dying patient's dignity and alleviating her intolerable suffering." Stevens' opinion, though technically a vote against those who challenged the prohibitory statutes, was in fact a vote for all that they asked. So the narrow, historicist view of the due process clause is now probably confined to a core group of the three most conservative members of the present Court—Rehnquist, Scalia, and Thomas—and that is welcome news for those who favor a principled construction of the individual rights that American citizens enjoy against their government. It is also welcome news that though the Supreme Court refused to recognize a right to assisted suicide in these cases, five justices took care not to foreclose the constitutional debate over such a right for the future.

IV

So the assisted suicide decisions cannot be counted a victory for the party of history. Stevens declared his readiness to recognize a right to assisted suicide that had not been recognized before whenever an appropriate case arose. Souter's opinion said three times that his vote was only "at this time." O'Connor and Breyer each said that changed circumstances might cause them to reconsider. And Ginsburg, joining O'Connor's opinion rather than that of the Court, made it clear that she agreed. It is therefore important to consider why each of these justices, except Stevens, declined to recognize the right "at this time."

O'Connor, Ginsburg, and Breyer argued, as I have said, that any constitutional right would be limited to relief from pain. But that limitation seems arbitrary, for several reasons. These justices did not explain why what Breyer called a right to die "with dignity" means only dying without pain when, as Souter noted, many people dread a drug-induced stupor just as much, and understandably think it just as offensive to their dignity.[22] Though these justices declared themselves satisfied that pain could be prevented in all but a very few cases, moreover, they did not attempt to respond to the substantial evidence, cited by Stevens, to the contrary. And it seems odd that they should be ready to overrule carefully considered decisions of the lower federal courts recognizing a limited right to assisted suicide by appealing to a factual claim vigorously contested in the briefs without themselves supplying any argument for that claim.

Nor did these justices explain why people whose pain cannot be relieved except by rendering them unconscious, no matter how few or many they are, do not have a right to assistance in dying. Breyer did acknowledge that many patients, particularly poor patients, do not receive the palliative treatment, which is often expensive, that would benefit them. But, he said, that is for "institutional reasons or inadequacies or obstacles, which would seem possible to overcome." It is unsatisfactory, however, to argue that poor patients have no right to assisted suicide even when they are dying in great pain because their state could provide the expensive pain relief that it does not, in fact, provide.

Souter offered a more elaborate set of reasons for not recognizing any constitutional right at this time. He mentioned the argument, pressed by opponents of assisted suicide, that it would prove impossible to design any system of regulatory control that would protect people whose death was not in fact imminent, or who did not really wish to die, from being coaxed into suicide by relatives or hospitals who did not want to bear the expense of keeping them alive, or by compassionate doctors who thought them better off dead. He cited, in particular, books and articles purporting to show that the only documented program of assisted suicide and euthanasia—the Dutch one—had failed to prevent many such mistakes. He noted that these analyses of the Dutch case were contradicted by other reports, and that many writers did think that states could develop an effective regulatory scheme that would reduce mistakes to the level that was unavoidable in any grave medical procedure. But, he said, judges should not declare laws enacted by almost all the states unconstitutional on the basis of disputed and controversial judgments of fact, particularly in circumstances when legislatures, who can deploy investigative committees, are in a better position to assess the facts than judges are. So, he concluded, the Court should not declare anti–assisted suicide laws unconstitutional "at this time," though it might be right to do so later, when and if better evidence is available or more persuasive studies have been made.

That seems reasonable in principle. But, as Souter candidly acknowledged, the Court has assumed that dying patients have a constitutional right to terminate life support even when this means that they will die immediately; and there is as much danger that such patients will be coaxed into a request to die in that way as by requesting lethal pills, particularly since life-support techniques are typically very expensive.[23] In any case, the question whether a factual issue is too difficult or uncertain for judges to decide, so that they ought to defer to legislative decisions for that reason, is itself a complex and difficult one, and the courts should answer it only after very careful review of the evidence, particularly when putatively fundamental rights of individual citizens are at stake. Careful review would seem particularly crucial, moreover, in the assisted suicide debate, because many of the social scientists who have compiled the relevant evidence have strong ethical opinions, including religious convictions or convictions about proper medical ethics, that might impair their scientific independence. Many opponents of assisted suicide argue that in the Netherlands—where doctors are not prosecuted if they help patients to die, provided the doctors follow guidelines approved by the courts—people have been, in the words of the psychiatrist Herbert Hendin, "seduced" into death.[24] (Hendin is the executive director of an organization called the Suicide Foundation, which he describes in his book as "working to prevent suicide.")[25] Souter cited Hendin's book, among others, as supporting his own argument that American courts are not now in a position to dismiss the view the books defended.

It is unclear, however, why, even if Hendin and other critics are right about "the Dutch experience," it follows that American states, which would be free to impose much stricter regulations than the Dutch courts have, could not offer much greater protection to patients who might be pressured into death. It is also unclear, moreover, that a closer look at the books critical of Dutch medical practice would not have revealed serious methodological flaws. Three scholars in Groningen University in the Netherlands—John Griffiths, Alex Bood, and Heleen Weyers—have offered a balanced and to some degree critical account of Dutch practice, suggesting ways in which enforcement of the court-approved guidelines for euthanasia might be improved.[26] But they are highly critical of Hendin's methodology. They allege that his book contains many mistakes, and that several of his reports of his conversations with Dutch doctors, on which many of his arguments are based, misinterpreted those conversations.[27]

Souter referred, particularly, to Hendin's claim that in the Netherlands doctors have ended the life of fully competent patients without a request from, and without consulting, the patients. Rehnquist also referred to the apparently shocking fact that "The Dutch government's own study revealed that in 1990, there were . . . more than 1,000 cases of euthanasia without an explicit request." In fact, an official report on that study published in English in 1992, which neither Souter nor Rehnquist cited, shows that the cases described as euthanasia "without a patient's request" were of many different types. They included, for example, cases of patients who could not consent because they were in the final throes of death, and whose death the doctors made easier with drugs that hastened the dying process by minutes, cases of people who had earlier expressed a wish to die but not in terms conforming to the strict Dutch test for a technically explicit request, and cases of just-born infants who would have died within days anyway, and whose prompt death, at their parents' request, saved those parents agony.[28] If American states believe such practices offensive or undesirable, they could prohibit them with straightforward legislative provisions, and it is hard to see how allowing assisted suicide for those who do request it, subject to strict regulations and reporting, would make such practices more likely. I do not mean to suggest that the Groningen scholars' criticism of Hendin is justified. But it is regrettable that Souter and the other justices were not able to inspect Hendin's research techniques, and those of the other critics of Dutch practice they cited, more thoroughly before deciding that their books raised issues that judges are now incapable of resolving. Perhaps there really is no sound research suggesting that the Dutch experience demonstrates the danger these authors claimed.

In any case, these outstanding factual issues make it even more likely that the constitutional debate will continue. What effects will the Court's decisions have in the meantime? The Court made plain that citizens are free to press for permissive reforms in the present law in the ordinary way, through legislation or referendums, and, since the idea that dying patients should have a chance for a doctor's help in easing their death remains popular, such efforts might well succeed in some further states. But the more immediate consequences of the Court's decision may be medical rather than political: the combination of opinions I described strongly suggests that the Court, though perhaps by a divided vote, would be ready to recognize that dying patients do have a right to pain relief even in doses, if necessary to stop pain, that bring death. It is, of course, very difficult to judge whether a doctor and patient who agree on such high doses of painkilling drugs aim at the death that follows or only at pain relief. But thousands of doctors have been prescribing such drugs in lethal doses, for dying patients whose families they know and trust, in order to hasten death.[29] The effect of the present decisions may well be not only to confirm but to extend that practice.

That is paradoxical, because the administration of very high levels of morphine and other drugs is not regulated in the way that any state that permitted assisted suicide would certainly require. Any assisted-suicide statute that could be enacted in the United States would demand full information for and informed consent by patients who seek such assistance. It would also require hospitals to satisfy supervising authorities that all options for treatment and palliation had been explained and offered to them. Such a scheme might improve the situation of such patients, and might well extend their lives. A policy that encourages financially stretched hospitals routinely to recommend morphine in potentially lethal doses, for the ostensible purpose of relieving pain, subject to no specific code of regulation at all, may seem less a violation of established medical practices. But it hardly offers less danger to poor patients dying in pain whose relatives or doctors might prefer them dead at once.

Sources

∧

Chapters 1 and 2 were first published in *Philosophy and Public Affairs* in 1981. Chapter 3 was published in the *Iowa Law Review* in 1987, Chapter 4 in the *University of San Francisco Law Review* in the same year, and Chapter 5 in the *University of California Law Review* in 1991. Chapter 6 is a revised and shortened version of "Foundations of Liberal Equality," delivered as the Tanner Lectures at Stanford University and published in volume XI of *The Tanner Lectures on Human Values* (University of Utah Press, 1990). Chapters 8, 11, and 12 first appeared, under other titles, in the *New York Review of Books,* on January 13, 1994, October 22, 1998, and November 5, 1998, respectively. Chapter 10 first appeared in *If Buckly Fell,* edited by E. Joshua Rosencrantz (New York: Century Foundation, 1999). Chapter 13 was first prepared for a 1998 meeting of the Twenty-first Century Foundation and was distributed to the participants. Chapter 14 combines two articles that first appeared in the *New York Review of Books,* one under a different title, on August 8, 1996, and September 25, 1997.

Notes

Introduction

1. For my own account of the objectivity that moral judgments may claim, see Ronald Dworkin, "Objectivity and Truth: You'd Better Believe It," *Philosophy & Public Affairs* 25 (1996): 87.

1. Equality of Welfare

1. I owe this last suggestion to Derek Parfit, and through him, I understand, to J. P. Griffin and J. McMahon.
2. In the case of some people, but not Jack, we might be able to find an amount of resources such that their actual regret at not having more is so weak that we do not need to compute their reasonable regret at that amount to say that the latter must be less than the actual regret that others would have if the former had that amount. But many questions arise even then. Is it not necessary still to compute the reasonable regret, as distinguished from the actual regret, of the latter group, before deciding that the former group may not have more than that amount? Can this be done without regress? In any case, the total of amounts fixed as maxima for particular people, in this way, would undoubtedly exceed the total available for distribution. I shall not pursue these complexities further.
3. See Bernard Williams, "Egoism and Altruism," in *Problems of the Self* (Cambridge: Cambridge University Press, 1973), p. 262.
4. Kenneth J. Arrow, "Some Ordinalist-Utilitarian Notes on Rawls's Theory of Justice," *Journal of Philosophy* 70, no. 9 (10 May 1973): 254.
5. If the chosen conception is some objective version of equality of success, rather than the subjective version discussed in this paragraph, the situation is different still. If the change in Louis's tastes has the consequence that his life is now objectively more successful, then he should have fewer rather than more resources. If (because Louis's

convictions are mistaken) the change makes his life objectively worse, then the claim that someone might make on his behalf, for still further resources for reeducation, seems especially strong. But I am assuming that the objective version of equality of overall success has little appeal for a liberal society, so I shall not pursue this line.

6. See T. M. Scanlon's discussion of this problem in "Preference and Urgency," *Journal of Philosophy* 72, no. 19 (6 November 1975): 659–661.

7. A. K. Sen, "Utilitarianism and Welfarism," *Journal of Philosophy* 76, no. 9 (September 1979): 463–489.

2. Equality of Resources

1. D. Foley, "Resource Allocation and the Public Sector," *Yale Economic Essays* 7 (Spring 1967); H. Varian, "Equity, Energy and Efficiency," *Journal of Economic Theory,* September 1974, pp. 63–91.

2. I mean to describe a Walrasian auction in which all productive resources are sold. I do not assume that the immigrants enter into complete forward contingent claims contracts, but only that markets will remain open and will clear in a Walrasian fashion once the auction of productive resources is completed. I make all the assumptions about production and preferences made in G. Debreu, *Theory of Value* (New Haven: Yale University Press, 1959). In fact the auction I describe here will become more complex in virtue of a tax scheme discussed later.

3. The process does not guarantee that the auction will come to an end in this way, because there may be various equilibria. I am supposing that people will come to understand that they cannot do better by further runs of the auction, and will for practical reasons settle on one equilibrium. If I am wrong, then this fact provides one of the aspects of incompleteness I describe in the next section.

4. See, however, the discussion of handicaps below, which recognizes that certain kinds of preferences, which people wish they did not have, may call for compensation as handicaps.

5. The averaging assumption is a simplifying assumption only, made to provide a result in the absence of the detailed (and perhaps, for reasons described in the text, indeterminate) information that would enable us to decide how much each handicapped person would have purchased in the hypothetical market. If we had such full information, so that we could tailor compensation to what a particular individual in fact would have bought, the accuracy of the program would be improved. But in the absence of such information, averaging is second best, or in any case better than nothing.

6. The hypothetical insurance approach does not require any stipulation of "normal" powers, because it allows the hypothetical market to determine which infirmities are compensable.

7. Robert Nozick, *Anarchy, State, and Utopia* (New York: Basic Books, 1974).

8. Notice that our analysis of the problem that differential talents presents to equality

of resources calls for an income tax, rather than either a wealth or a consumption tax. If people begin with equal resources, then we wish to tax to adjust for different skills so far as these produce different income, because it is only in that way that they threaten equality of resources. Someone's decision to spend rather than save what he has earned is precisely the kind of decision whose impact should be determined by the market uncorrected for tax under this analysis. Of course, there might be technical or other reasons why a society dedicated to equality of welfare would introduce taxes other than income taxes. Such a society might want to encourage savings, for example. But these taxes would not be responses to the problem now under consideration. Should unearned (investment) income be taxed under the present argument? I assume that unearned income reflects skill in investment as well as preferences for later consumption, in which case that argument would extend to taxing such income. Since I am not considering here the problem of later generations, I do not consider inheritance or estate taxes.

9. Other forms for the insurance market we are imagining are possible, but those I have considered seem to produce roughly the same results. Amartya Sen has suggested to me, for example, that the insurer might offer a policy guaranteeing the named level of coverage to every policyholder, but making the premium depend on the economic rent people turn out to have. This would not, I think, produce different results from the arrangement I describe in the next section, and I think it useful to consider, as I do there, why these elaborations would be necessary.

10. If I am wrong in this, the hypothetical insurance argument would insist on radical redistribution and substantial wealth equality. So the scheme would offer an argument for that consequence, on that assumption.

11. I have neglected the question of the technology that will be available for the insurance firms to decide and prove who has what level of talent, and the cost of that technology. I assume that the computer will have that information, as part of its technological data base, and will use it to predict the premium structure and other incidents of the contract of insurance. When I speak of "winning" or "losing" the insurance bet, I mean qualifying for compensation or failing to qualify under the incidents the computer predicts.

12. He may also run the even graver risk of losing under the tests specified in the policy and yet not, in fact, having the ability to earn the covered level. I do not emphasize this risk, because it assumes failures of technology about which it is impossible to speculate. I therefore assume, arguendo, that no one will be in that perilous position.

13. Thomas Scanlon provided this example.

14. As in the case of handicaps, I have chosen to make premiums and therefore tax payments turn on the average coverage level as a simplifying device. I might, of course, have chosen either the median or the mode of coverage selected in the hypothetical market instead of the average or mean. It is an interesting question whether either of these would be better. I chose the average on the assumption that our assessment of the chance of error in particular cases (the chance that the "pre-

mium" extracted differs from what the individual in question actually would have paid in the hypothetical market) should reflect the amount as well as the fact of that difference.

15. John von Neumann and Oskar Morgenstern, *The Theory of Games and Economic Behavior*, 3d ed. (Princeton: Princeton University Press, 1980).

16. As it often does, I think, in hard cases at common law when those who would benefit and those who would lose by the introduction of any new rule of law are or must be assumed to be classes roughly equal in their command over resources. See R. Posner, "The Ethical and Political Basis of the Efficiency Norm in Common Law Adjudication," *Hofstra Law Review* 8 (1980): 487.

17. Ronald Dworkin, "Why Efficiency?" *Hofstra Law Review* 8 (1980): 563.

18. John Rawls, *A Theory of Justice* (Cambridge, Mass.: The Belknap Press of Harvard University Press, 1971), p. 98.

19. Ronald Dworkin, *Taking Rights Seriously* (Cambridge, Mass.: Harvard University Press, 1977), chap. 6.

3. The Place of Liberty

1. See Federal Election Campaign Act Amendments of 1974, Public Law no. 93-443, 88 Stat. 1263 (1974).

2. Buckley v. Valeo, 424 U.S. 1 (1976).

3. See, e.g., John Rawls, "The Basic Liberties and Their Priority," in *Liberty, Equality, and Law: Selected Tanner Lectures on Moral Philosophy*, ed. Sterling M. McMurrin (Salt Lake City: University of Utah Press, 1987), pp. 1–89.

4. Lochner v. New York, 198 U.S. 45 (1905).

5. See Day-Brite Lighting, Inc. v. Missouri, 342 U.S. 421 (1952); West Coast Hotel Co. v. Parrish, 300 U.S. 379 (1937).

6. I mean to doubt that liberty can have inherent or fundamental value independent of its contribution to the value of lives. It can, of course, have instrumental value toward some other goal, like art or knowledge, that is itself thought to be inherently valuable for reasons that make its value independent of its contribution to the value of lives.

7. An attractive and reasonably complete conception of equality—a general theory about how a political community treats its members with equal concern—must be complex: it must describe political equality, for example, and equality under law, as well as equality in the distribution of material resources. I emphasize the latter aspect of equality in considering the conflict between liberty and equality here, however, because the supposed conflict is generally thought to be most serious when that aspect of equality is in play. In each of the examples I offered earlier, for instance, a proposed constraint of freedom of choice is defended as ameliorating the consequences of an inegalitarian distribution of wealth. I shall simplify my discussion further, without, I believe, compromising its value, by assuming that the conceptions of equality in play contemplate only private ownership of resources. A conception of

equality, then, describes the distribution of goods into private ownership that would result from political decisions which together show perfectly equal concern for all, and which therefore count, for that conception, as an ideal egalitarian distribution.

8. It will strike some readers as Pickwickian to call that theory of justice egalitarian in any form; I do so to emphasize the important fact that those who embrace it can also accept the abstract egalitarian principle and claim their theory as the best interpretation of that principle.

9. I make no effort here to discover how far my argument qualifies or expands my discussion of liberty in my book *Taking Rights Seriously* (Cambridge, Mass.: Harvard University Press, 1977), pp. 240–258. It might be wise to point out, however, that my discussion there was aimed at showing why a utilitarian political morality could not recognize a general right to liberty as a trump over utilitarian calculations of overall social advantage, and why to be plausible a utilitarian morality would nevertheless have to recognize certain specific rights to particular liberties. See *Taking Rights Seriously* and Dworkin, *A Matter of Principle* (Cambridge, Mass.: Harvard University Press, 1985), pp. 293–303. Here I am considering the role of liberty in a different political morality based not on utilitarian ethics but on what I believe to be the more attractive morality of equality of resources. The different strategies used here therefore illustrate the methodological claim about rights made in both *Taking Rights Seriously* and *A Matter of Principle:* that rights cannot be identified independently of the overall political morality in which they are meant to figure.

10. See John Rawls, "Justice as Fairness: Political Not Metaphysical," *Philosophy & Public Affairs* 14 (1985): 223–251.

11. In its original formulation, Rawls's strategy seemed to rely much more on the interest strategy; see John Rawls, *A Theory of Justice* (Cambridge, Mass.: The Belknap Press of Harvard University Press, 1971), pp. 195–257. Rawls describes the changes between the original and the present formulation as made in response to H. L. A. Hart's criticisms of the original formulation. See Rawls, "The Basic Liberties"; and Hart, "Rawls on Liberty and Its Priority," *University of Chicago Law Review* 40 (1973): 534.

12. Though this is not entirely clear, Rawls does not seem to rely on empirical claims about the degree to which actual people would in fact acknowledge that compelling interest; in any case, I assume this in suggesting that this aspect of Rawls's argument uses a constitutive rather than an interest strategy.

13. See Hart, "Rawls on Liberty," p. 550.

14. Rawls, "The Basic Liberties," p. 34, n. 4.

15. Ibid., p. 32.

16. Bernard Williams suggests that what might reasonably be considered knowledge in the area of personal morality is possible only in a society whose moral traditions are uncritically accepted as defining right and wrong; *Ethics and the Limits of Philosophy* (London: Fontana Press/Collins, 1985).

17. It may seem linguistically inexact to assign a person's physical and mental capacities to his circumstances rather than to his personality. But drawing the distinction that way is important for reasons discussed later in the text. Treating capacities as part of

circumstances, however, presents complexities for equality of resources. Capacities cannot be auctioned in the way ordinary material resources can be, nor can they be transferred among persons in pursuit of equality of resources. The hypothetical insurance schemes discussed in Chapter 2 are in large part responses to that problem.

18. Felt moral constraints, on the contrary, belong to personality. A complication therefore arises in virtue of the familiar moral conviction many people have, that they ought to obey legal constraints. I avoid this complication by assuming that legal constraints, so far as they belong to circumstances, are to be viewed as Holmes's "bad man" would view them—as threats raising the cost of the actions they forbid.

19. It might help, in appreciating this point, to review various choices the auctioneer has available. Suppose he defines the liberties he auctions in the second part of the auction as liberties to use something one has already purchased in the first part, so that liberties are valuable, with respect to each good, only to the prior purchaser of that good. There will then be no competition for any set of liberties: the holder of any good acquires the specified liberties to use it (all but) free. The auction collapses into its first part: the competition is only about who acquires what goods in the first place, and parties will make their bids, in the first stage, by assuming the liberties to be specified in the second as already attached to goods for which they bid. The liberties specified in the second stage therefore become the effective baseline for the first stage. Suppose, on the other hand, that the auctioneer defines the liberties sold in the second stage as powers to control the use of designated goods no matter who acquired them in the first stage: if I outbid you for rights over your pole, it is I, not you, who decides what can be hung from it. Then the auction collapses into the second part: no one would bid anything for a useless title, whose benefit is wholly at risk, with no advantage to the holder, in a later competition. The liberties sold in the second stage then become, once again, the assumed baseline of the entire auction. In each of these cases, and in any other we could construct, the upshot is the same. No matter how and when liberties are specified, parties make decisions as if these were specified as an original baseline. Since they cannot be specified in a way that has no impact on the auction, any specification needs the kind of justification I explore in the next several sections of the text.

20. An auction baseline must, of course, address questions other than those about liberty and constraint. I emphasized a different aspect of the baseline in Chapter 2, where I said that the baseline for the imaginary auction must specify the form in which the available resources are to be auctioned. Suppose the auctioneer was able to make nonreversible trades with neighboring islands and, in spite of the fact that some of the parties to the forthcoming auction disliked plovers' eggs, traded all the goods of the island, before the auction, into only a large number of those delicacies. The resulting auction would yield an envy-free distribution, but the procedure would be flawed. And the results would not constitute an ideal egalitarian distribution, because proper baseline assumptions about the form of the resources to be

auctioned would have been violated. Some baseline issues about the goods to be auctioned are more difficult than the question whether the auctioneer should trade a mix of resources for plovers' eggs. Do the goods to be auctioned include, for example, parts of the bodies of the parties, so that each party would have to bid for his own eyes against competitors who might wish to use his eyes for their own purposes? In Chapter 2 I made heavy weather of another issue I presented as an issue about what goods are to be auctioned: the question whether rights over labor are among such goods. I now think this is better treated as an issue about the baseline liberty/constraint system. The argument of this chapter provides a better, because less ad hoc, argument for the conclusion I reached earlier: that rights over one's labor and leisure are not included in the auction.

21. See Chapter 4.
22. I do not mean to suggest that all communities have exactly the same rules, or that there is a single, "natural" meaning of "ownership" from which such rules can be drawn.
23. We noticed, when we considered Rawls's use of the interest strategy, that some philosophers and sociologists claim that a truly desirable life can be led only in an environment of moral and perhaps even religious homogeneity.
24. The analysis sketched in this paragraph would seem adequate to justify, within the general framework of equality of resources, constraints serving purposes somewhat different from these examples: for resolving different forms of prisoners' dilemma, for example, and for justifying traffic regulations, like one-way systems, that aim to protect convenience or efficiency rather than only safety or security.
25. It is an interesting question how far the liberties we intuitively consider to be fundamental might be identified and protected by the principle of abstraction in that way. I see no reason, a priori, for any great confidence that they could be; the project would be threatened by the contingency of preferences I described earlier as a problem for the interest strategy.
26. Once again, a dramatic example is available. Suppose the auctioneer, noticing that most parties to the auction would prefer the distribution that would then result, brainwashes a small minority out of their present tastes, which, if they remained, would make certain resources especially expensive for the majority. The resulting distribution, of course, satisfies the envy test, but can hardly be defended as showing equal concern for the parties for whom the auctioneer is initially responsible. Of course most of the constraints on freedom of religion or speech or association we deplore are not cases of brainwashing; I point to this dramatic example only to make plain why equality of resources needs an account of authenticity that respects the abstract imperative of equal concern.
27. I use "authenticity" in a special sense: personalities are authentic, for our purposes, when they have been formed under circumstances appropriate to using an auction among personalities so formed as a test of distributive equality. Of course this is a very different idea from the idea of metaphysical or even psychological authenticity. It focuses, for one thing, on the absence of legal constraints, and most personality-

forming constraints and other influences are, at least for us, cultural rather than legal. But for our special purpose, which is to explore how government treats people as equals, the special concern with legal constraint is legitimate.

28. No actual community, at least no complex community in which production and exchange takes place, can technically reach or sustain an ideal egalitarian distribution on the model of the imagined auction. Some shortfall is inevitable for two very different kinds of reasons. First, distribution is inevitably incomplete in the following way: the liberty/constraint system explicitly established in legal rules and past judicial decisions does not decide all questions that arise about the rights people have to use their property in ways that conflict with the use others make of theirs. In *Law's Empire*, I tried to show how the civil law of negligence and nuisance can usefully be understood as responding to this problem by requiring private citizens to make adjustments to the standing liberty/constraint system so as to carry forward, though in a necessarily imperfect way, the general scheme of equality of resources. See *Law's Empire* (Cambridge, Mass.: Harvard University Press, 1986), pp. 276–312. I shall not discuss this problem here. Second, distribution, even so far as it is complete, cannot wholly satisfy the envy test when people differ not only in personality but in productive ability, as they always do, or when people have different good and bad luck, as they inevitably do. We can—and equality therefore demands that we do—compensate for these differences in ability and luck in various ways. I tried to suggest, by constructing hypothetical insurance markets designed for that purpose, how we might hope to do so. But this compensation cannot wholly cure the disadvantage, so the envy test will continue to fail. I shall not discuss this problem any further, here, either.

29. If we accept that qualification, this version of maximin is more guarded than Rawls's version, which counts any improvement in the situation of the worst-off group a gain in justice.

30. This formulation of the principle of victimization is sufficient for my argument, though it could easily be improved. I ignore problems about the individuation of distributions, for example, though these strike me as manageable. Very different formulations might also be investigated. There is much to be said, for example, for taking the reference point to be the least favorable defensible distribution for the value of the liberty in question. I doubt that the discussion that follows in the text would be different, however, if I had chosen that formulation to test.

31. 424 U.S. 1 (1976).

32. For my account of constitutional interpretation, see Dworkin, *Law's Empire*, pp. 355–399.

4. Political Equality

1. See Ronald Dworkin, *A Matter of Principle* (Cambridge, Mass.: Harvard University Press, 1985), pp. 237–292.

2. Of course, we could not hope to make any judgments about equality of power with

the precision these definitions seem to suggest, I offer them only to provide some sense for the comparisons that must, in practice, be made more roughly.

3. See Edmund Burke, "A Letter to John Farr and John Harris, Esqrs., Sheriffs of the City of Bristol, on the Affairs of America," in *The Writings and Speeches of the Right Honorable Edmund Burke,* ed. J. F. Taylor (New York: Beaconsfield, 1901). Originally published in 1777.

4. I assume, in this claim, that wealth remains equal so that no small group of very rich people could dominate politics through political contributions or expenditures. See Chapter 10.

5. But because the requirement that a districting scheme that imposes significant inequality of impact must not reflect any lack of equal concern is a requirement particularly easy to evade, any attractive dependent conception would insist that a strong and evident case be made for any exemption from the equal impact requirement. Perhaps this is the best justification for the U.S. Supreme Court's one-person, one-vote decisions; we might understand the Court as deciding, as a piece of prophylaxis, that no constitutionally required exceptions should be permitted. See, e.g., Gaffney v. Cummings, 412 U.S. 735 (1973) (reapportionment plan of Connecticut General Assembly challenged under the equal protection clause following the 1970 population census); Reynolds v. Sims, 377 U.S. 533 (1964) (equal protection clause challenge to proposed plan to reapportion voting districts for the two houses of the Alabama legislature).

6. See Lewis Kornhauser and Lawrence Sager, "Unpacking the Court," *Yale Law Journal* 46 (1986): 82.

7. Some famous political philosophers have thought that the right answer to all choice-insensitive issues will be produced by a "general will" that emerges from the people as a whole under favorable circumstances. But that idea, whatever one might think of its metaphysical basis, is not an argument for anything approaching equality in political power. Indeed, the idea of a general will is antagonistic to any concern for either the impact or the influence of individual citizens one by one. Those forms of equality are important, if at all, only when disagreement must be resolved, but a general will assumes the emergence, through discussion not logrolling, of unanimity, or at least of a decision that wins by a knockout not on points.

8. For a more thorough analysis and evaluation of this argument, see Dworkin, *Freedom's Law* (Cambridge, Mass.: Harvard University Press, 1996).

9. See, e.g., Dworkin, *A Matter of Principle,* pp. 33–71; *Law's Empire* (Cambridge, Mass.: Harvard University Press, 1986), pp. 87–113.

5. Liberal Community

1. Throughout this book I distinguish ethics from morality. Ethics, as I use the term, includes convictions about which kinds of lives are good or bad for a person to lead, and morality includes principles about how a person should treat other people. So

the question I consider is whether a political community should use criminal law to force its members to lead what a majority deems good lives, not whether it should use the law to force them to behave justly to others.

2. 478 U.S. 186 (1986).

3. Id. at 192–196.

4. J. S. Mill, *On Liberty* (Harmondsworth: Penguin, 1982), pp. 68–69.

5. H. L. A. Hart, *Law, Liberty, and Morality* (Stanford: Stanford University Press, 1963).

6. We might object to procedural as well as substantive majoritarianism in the case of enforcing morals; we might say that such questions should be decided not by elected officials but by a constitutional court such as the Supreme Court. I am not considering that procedural question here, however. See Chapter 4 and Ronald Dworkin, "Equality, Democracy, and Constitution: We the People in Court," *Alberta Law Review* 28 (1990): 324.

7. In my view, fair shares are those that equalize, so far as this is possible, the opportunity costs to others of the material resources each person holds. See Chapter 2. I restrict the opportunity-cost test to material (or, as I have sometimes said, impersonal) resources, because that test is not appropriate for personal resources such as talents and health.

8. For an account of the requirement of integrity, and of the issues of principle it demands be decided the same for everyone, see Ronald Dworkin, *Law's Empire* (Cambridge, Mass.: Harvard University Press, 1986), esp. chap. 6. For a more extended discussion of the distinction between matters of principle like those cited in the text, and matters of policy like SDI, see Dworkin, *A Matter of Principle* (Cambridge, Mass.: Harvard University Press, 1985), esp. chap. 3.

9. This argument is developed at considerable length, and its consequences for liberalism described, in Chapter 3.

10. The discussion in this section draws on material in lectures I gave at Stanford University under the auspices of the Tanner Foundation. These will appear in a forthcoming collection of Tanner Foundation lectures to be published by the Foundation. See Chapter 6.

11. That characterization of volitional interests ignores the fact that some of the things a person wants may conflict with other things he wants. But the refinements needed to take account of that fact are not necessary for the general distinction between volitional and critical interests I make in the text.

12. The distinction between critical and volitional well-being is not the distinction between what is really in my interests and what I only think is. My volitional interests are genuine, real interests, not merely reflections of my present judgments, which I may later decide are mistakes, about where my critical interests lie. The two kinds of interests, the two modes of well-being, are distinct. I can intelligibly want something without thinking it makes my life a better life to have; indeed a life in which someone wanted only what he thought it in his critical interests to have would be a sad, preposterous mess of a life.

13. I shall not consider a form of critical paternalism more subtle and academic still,

though it raises difficult and important questions about the concept of critical well-being. Suppose critical paternalism is aimed not at the present generation of homosexuals, but at the remote future. Suppose it aims to eliminate homosexuality, as a form of life, from the conceptual menu, so that future generations will not even be able to imagine such a life. It is extremely doubtful such a project could succeed. But assume that it could and also (what many of us would not accept) that a homosexual life is inherently a bad life to lead. Would this kind of conceptual paternalism then be in the interests of people who would have led homosexual lives had these been on their menu? Some conceptual paternalism would certainly be in the interests of justice; the world would be a better place if no one could even imagine a life of genocide or racism, for example. Even so, it seems to me odd to think that a person's own life could be made a better life to have lived, in the critical sense, by constriction of his imagination.

14. Patrick Devlin, *The Enforcement of Morals* (London: Oxford University Press, 1965); see *Committee on Homosexual Offenses and Prostitution: The Wolfenden Report* (1957; Amer. ed. 1963).

15. Devlin, *The Enforcement of Morals,* pp. 9–15.

16. Devlin himself later said that he did not mean to suggest that tolerating homosexuality would subvert the community, but only that society might be threatened by tolerance, and must therefore reject any principle that rules out intolerance altogether. See Patrick Devlin, "Law, Democracy, and Morality," *University of Pennsylvania Law Review* 110 (1962): 635–641 and n. 14.

17. Michael J. Sandel, *Liberalism and the Limits of Justice,* 2d ed. (Cambridge: Cambridge University Press, 1998), pp. 62–65, 179–183.

18. Readers interested in this issue of philosophical logic should begin with Saul Kripke, *Naming and Necessity* (Cambridge, Mass.: Harvard University Press, 1980).

19. See Philip Selznick, "The Idea of a Communitarian Morality," *California Law Review* 75 (1987): 445.

20. John Rawls, *A Theory of Justice* (Cambridge, Mass.: The Belknap Press of Harvard University Press, 1971), pp. 520–529.

21. I do not mean that these participatory acts are themselves collective acts of the political community as a whole: They are not. But they may be collective acts of some smaller community within it; a demonstration, for example, may be part of the communal life of a political action group, which, though political in its aims, is not in itself a political community, because it does not administer its affairs through a monopoly of coercive power over its members.

22. Of course, as I emphasize later, that is not to say that no community does or could recognize a collective sex act.

23. Citizens are not mutually self-selected, like members of a fraternal organization, nor are they chosen for some particular talent or ambition, like musicians in an orchestra, nor are they identified by some independently given religious faith or sexual conviction or even, in the modern world of immigration and boundary shifts, by racial or ethnic or linguistic type or background.

24. It does not follow, of course, from my claim that ethical integration is possible only when social practices create the necessary conceptual background, that ethical integration is mandatory or even defensible on every occasion when they do. No one should think his own critical interests tied to the success or failure of a community that does not recognize him as an equal member, or that denies him the most basic human rights, for example. Compare, in this connection, the parallel conditions of political obligations discussed in Dworkin, *Law's Empire*.

25. The skeletal (and, I fear, somewhat cryptic) discussion in this section borrows from, and is much expanded in, Chapter 6.

6. Equality and the Good Life

1. Myself included. See Ronald Dworkin, *A Matter of Principle* (Cambridge, Mass.: Harvard University Press, 1985), chap. 8, etc.

2. See Ronald Dworkin, "Objectivity and Truth: You'd Better Believe It," *Philosophy & Public Affairs* 25 (1996).

3. A fuller exposition would distinguish a third category of well-being that is more elemental or biological, such as health and freedom from pain and sexual or other frustration. But it will be enough for the arguments I shall make here to see how these biological interests can figure within the two categories I name. Avoiding pain is something I want, and so it counts, for me, as part of my volitional interests. Avoiding pain counts as part of my critical interest as well, though in a different and generally smaller way.

4. See Dworkin, "Objectivity and Truth."

5. I owe this example to A. J. Ayer, who emphatically rejected the third view.

6. See Dworkin, "Objectivity and Truth."

7. See "Age," in *Encyclopedia of the Italian Renaissance* (New York: Oxford University Press, 1981), p. 17.

8. I say a bit more about this issue in Chapter 5.

9. See Dworkin, *A Matter of Principle,* chap. 11.

10. See Derek Parfit, *Reasons and Persons* (Oxford: Oxford University Press, 1984).

11. See Chapter 5.

12. I set aside a more complex problem, whose solution I believe would require elaborating the hypothetical insurance feature of equality of resources beyond what I or others have yet done. Suppose I consume all my resources but you economize and leave most of yours to your children. Or that you have invested skillfully and have more to leave for that reason. Or that I have more children than you, and so must divide their inheritance into smaller shares. Then, although neither of us has invaded resources properly belonging to another, our children will not have equal resources: some will envy what others have. Equality of resources must find some way to identify and at least reduce inequality generated in that way, perhaps, as I just suggested, by regarding one's situation as a beneficiary as an in-principle-insurable

hazard. In the text I consider only the central problem: whether it is inconsistent to work for equality in politics and yet try to improve the situation of only some people close to us in our ordinary life.

13. Bowers v. Hardwick, 106 S. Ct. 2841 (1986).

7. Equality and Capability

1. G. A. Cohen, "On the Currency of Egalitarian Justice," *Ethics* 99 (July 1989): 914, 923.
2. See Chapter 2.
3. Cohen introduces his principle by quoting John Rawls's comment that compensating people for expensive tastes "presupposes that citizens' preferences are beyond their control as propensities or cravings which simply happen. Citizens seem to be regarded as passive carriers of desire" (quoted at Cohen, "Currency of Egalitarian Justice," p. 913). Cohen insists that some "preferences" are indeed of that character because they are not deliberately chosen, and that the implication of Rawls's remark is that such preferences should attract compensation. Rawls did not mean, I believe, that citizens should take responsibility only for values that they choose; he meant that they should take responsibility for the values that, in his words, they "have some part in forming," which suggests the different account I offer later in this chapter.
4. See T. M. Scanlon, *What We Owe to Each Other* (Cambridge, Mass.: The Belknap Press of Harvard University Press, 1998), chap. 1. See also Warren Quinn, "Putting Rationality in Its Place," in *Morality and Action* (Cambridge: Cambridge University Press, 1993). Scanlon makes a useful distinction between what he calls attributive responsibility and substantive responsibility; the former is susceptibility to blame for some action, and the latter is what I have called consequential responsibility, that is, the propriety of someone's being in a better or worse position in virtue of that action. Scanlon believes that these two forms of responsibility sometimes come apart. He gives two examples: a willing cocaine addict who does not regret his addiction but could not conquer it even if he did, and a young man who has no taste for work because he grew up in a culture in which work was regarded as pointless and demeaning. We might well disapprove morally of both individuals, he says, because their craving or disposition is judgmental and not a true handicap, and yet not ask them to bear the financial and other consequences of their acts, because, in the case of the addict, he is not now free to behave differently, and, in the case of the work-shy man, because his situation is the consequence of injustice.
5. Cohen disagrees with this account: he says that "not all ambitions, and few tastes, are informed by beliefs and attitudes: plenty of tastes and ambitions arise without being drawn forth by any sort of doxatic pull" ("Currency of Egalitarian Justice," p. 930). This might suggest that his disagreement with me is primarily one of empirical or perhaps philosophical psychology. But it turns out that he thinks it irrelevant whether tastes and ambitions are intertwined with beliefs and commitments: he acknowledges, for example, that the desires of someone who is driven by religion to

build expensive monuments are generated by convictions, but nevertheless insists that people with such desires have a call on extra resources for that reason, provided only that they do not prefer that their projects be expensive (pp. 935–938).

6. See Ronald Dworkin, "Objectivity and Truth: You'd Better Believe It," *Philosophy & Public Affairs* 25 (1996): 87.

7. See Ronald Dworkin, *Law's Empire* (Cambridge, Mass.: Harvard University Press, 1986), chap. 6.

8. Cohen, "Currency of Egalitarian Justice," pp. 938–939.

9. Scanlon suggests that in certain cases in which it would be proper to blame people for their decisions, their community might nevertheless have reason to relieve them from consequential responsibility for those decisions. See Scanlon, *What We Owe to Each Other*, p. 292. He discusses someone who has grown up work-shy in an environment in which his peers discourage a taste for work. We might not be as ready to refuse such a person unemployment relief, on the ground that he is unwilling to work, as someone not from such a background. We must take care, however, to distinguish two reasons we might think we have for that special treatment. We might think, first, that since he did not choose his distaste for work, he should not be asked to conquer it. Or we might think, second, that if he and his peers developed no interest in work because unjust and inadequate education or poverty or prejudice insured that work was not available to them on reasonable terms, it would be unfair to force him to accept the consequences of his distaste now. We can distinguish the two cases by imagining two different stories: that Scanlon's work-shy person is an upper-class twit raised to think that work was beneath his class and, second, that he grew up in a desperately poor urban slum with high and endemic unemployment. The first of the two reasons just distinguished would treat both these stories alike; the second would treat them very differently. I accept the second reason, and would distinguish the stories. See Chapter 2. So, I believe, does and would Scanlon, because he is clear that someone who does not want to work on fair terms deserves moral condemnation even in the case he imagines, and that does not seem compatible with the first reason.

10. Cohen, "Currency of Egalitarian Justice," pp. 917–921, 930.

11. Cohen apparently believes that this obvious response to his claim that equality of resources would not compensate for pain appeals to well-being or welfare in a way that compromises my arguments against equality of welfare. But I believe he misunderstands the arguments I made in Chapter 1. I did not mean to bar political philosophy from considering people's well-being in any way—that would be mad—but only to deny equality of welfare as a metric of justice. When we consider which features of a person's physical and mental constitution we should count as handicaps eligible for compensation, we must of course consider the consequences of these features for his well-being: mental illness that produces serious and enduring depression is a handicap for that reason. It does not follow that we must accept that any feature of his personality that lessens his happiness, including his tastes and convictions, is a handicap; it is a main purpose of Chapter 1 and of this chapter to explain

why that does not follow. In any case, providing compensation for the unfortunate people Cohen imagines does not assume that we take equality of welfare as a goal. If the community gives someone money for medicine to relieve pain, it does so not in order to make his welfare or well-being equal to anyone else's, but because his physical constitution handicaps his ability to lead the life he wishes to lead.

12. Allowing someone's fate to depend on other people's *external* preferences, including prejudice against people of his race or class, is indeed unfair however. For an account of the difference between personal and external preferences, see Ronald Dworkin, *Taking Rights Seriously* (Cambridge, Mass.: Harvard University Press, 1977), chap. 12; and Dworkin, *A Matter of Principle* (Cambridge, Mass.: Harvard University Press, 1985), chap. 17. For an account of how equality of resources treats external preferences, see Chapter 2.

13. Amartya Sen, *Inequality Reexamined* (Cambridge, Mass.: Harvard University Press, 1992), p. 33.

14. Ibid.

15. Rawls's list of primary goods does not include, for example, physical abilities that might make two people markedly different in their capacities to achieve the same goals. It is important to remember, however, that Rawls attempts to describe principles of justice for the "basic structure" of a political community, and expects that provision for physical disabilities would be the subject, not of that constitutional stage, but of a later legislative stage.

16. Sen, *Inequality Reexamined,* pp. 39–40.

8. Justice and the High Cost of Health

1. According to a *New England Journal of Medicine* study, administrative costs were 25 percent of hospital costs in 1990. See Erik Eckholm, "Study Links Paperwork to 25% of Hospital Costs," *New York Times,* August 5, 1993.

2. The average medical salary in the United States in 1992 was over $160,000. Salary varies dramatically by medical specialty: the average salary of a cardiovascular surgeon was $574,769, that of a family practitioner $119,186. See "Health Plan Would Hurt Most the Doctors Who Make the Most," *New York Times,* November 7, 1993, p. 1.

3. See Gina Kolata, "Mammogram Guideline Is Dropped," *New York Times,* December 5, 1993, sec. 1, p. 30.

4. I am ignoring an important issue that my argument raises but that I will not pursue here. Is it right, in the hypothetical exercise I am constructing, to exclude information relating risk of disease to voluntarily chosen behavior? Should insurance companies be in a position to charge cigarette smokers or mountain climbers higher premiums, for example? That seems reasonable. But if so, what counts as voluntary behavior? Should sexual behavior of a particular kind be treated as voluntary for this purpose? It would seem wrong for insurance companies to charge active male homosexuals higher premiums because they are considered more likely to contract AIDS.

Is this because sexual preference is less under people's control than nicotine addiction? Or because the sacrifice in giving up sex is so much greater than that in giving up smoking?

5. It does seem likely that even though the members of the imagined community would begin by making individual insurance decisions, they would soon develop, through these individual decisions, collective institutions and arrangements like cooperative insurance purchasing agencies or pools, because these would provide economic advantages in a free market among people of roughly equal wealth. The result of the process might very well be something functionally very close to that proposed in Clinton's plan.

6. My claim needs minor qualification. Even in the imagined community, some paternalistic interference might be necessary to protect people from imprudent insurance decisions, particularly when they are young. And some constraints might be necessary to provide adequate resources for later generations.

7. That is different from asking what any particular twenty-five-year-old would in fact do, because many people, particularly when young, do not make prudent decisions. They do not, that is, make the decisions that best serve the plans, convictions, tastes, and preferences they would find, on reflection, that they already have. It is prudent, of course, to provide for change—any prudent long-term insurance policy is written in general clauses rather than precise details of treatment, and is open to revision year by year.

8. See Ronald Dworkin, *Life's Dominion* (New York: Alfred A. Knopf, 1993), chap. 9.

9. People with certain religious convictions might make that choice, for example. But it is worth noticing that even those Catholics and others who think that it is always wrong to refuse available life-prolonging treatment do not necessarily think that all possible sacrifices must be made, in advance, to insure that very expensive life-prolonging treatment *is* available. Someone who thought it would be wrong, as a matter of religious principle, to decline an expensive and arduous operation that he could afford in order to extend his life a few months might nevertheless, with perfect consistency, think it prudent not to pay for the insurance, over his lifetime, that would enable him to afford it. He might think it more sensible to use the money that such insurance would cost to provide better medical treatment for himself or his family earlier, or better education, or some other goods or opportunities his convictions also deemed important. If so, then the prudent insurance test offers no reason why a national health scheme should make available for him what he would not have insured to provide for himself.

10. The rescue principle might hold it unjust for anyone to buy better medical care than everyone can have, and that medical care outside a system of universal coverage should therefore be abolished or, as it is in Canada, seriously discouraged. But the prudent insurance approach begins in a different idea: that no one can complain, on grounds of justice, that he has less of something than someone else does, so long as he has all he would have if society were overall just. Suppose, for example, that if wealth were fairly distributed no one, in view of the cost and the prospects, would

prudently insure to provide a liver and bowel transplant for himself even though it might conceivably one day save his life. If so, then justice does not require that such transplants be provided for everyone now, even when some people, unfairly rich, can buy them for themselves. See Ronald Dworkin, "Justice in the Distribution of Health Care," *McGill Law Journal* 38 (1993): 883.

9. Justice, Insurance, and Luck

1. Personal Responsibility and Work Opportunity Reconciliation Act of 1996, Public Law no. 104-193, 110 Stat. 2105. The Act is popularly known as "The End of Welfare as We Know It." "Welfare" is used in the rest of this book in the more technical sense it has acquired in philosophical and economic literature, but in this chapter I use it in the more familiar political sense to refer to government programs that transfer funds to citizens who are needy.
2. This distinction is amplified in Chapters 2 and 7.
3. What follows is a summary and reformulation of the hypothetical insurance approach described in more detail in Chapter 2.
4. See Ronald Dworkin, "Do Liberty and Equality Conflict?" in *Living as Equals,* ed. Paul Barker (New York: Oxford University Press, 1996), p. 39.

10. Free Speech, Politics, and the Dimensions of Democracy

1. Buckley v. Valeo, 424 U.S. 1 (1976).
2. I expand on the claim that free speech and democracy are conceptually connected in that way in *Freedom's Law* (Cambridge, Mass.: Harvard University Press, 1996).
3. See the introduction to *Freedom's Law.*
4. On this point, and for general observations about equality of influence as a democratic goal, see Chapter 4.
5. In a society of greatly unequal wealth and other resources, some citizens will have much greater opportunity to occupy each of these positions of heightened influence only because they are richer, and that is indeed an insult to citizen equality. But that more general unfairness could not be ended except through a vast redistribution of wealth and what wealth brings. The more specific unfairness that brings influence to the rich only because they can afford large contributions to politicians could be ended or minimized through the simple expedient of expenditure limits.
6. Austin v. Michigan Chamber of Commerce, 494 U.S. 652, 679 (1990).
7. I have argued this point at some length in *Freedom's Law,* chaps. 9 and 10.
8. Lochner v. New York, 198 U.S. 45 (1905) (striking law that imposed a cap on the number of hours an employer could require a laborer to work).
9. See the introduction to Dworkin, *Freedom's Law.*
10. As John Hart Ely argues in *Democracy and Distrust: A Theory of Judicial Review* (Cambridge, Mass.: Harvard University Press, 1980).
11. Whitney v. California, 274 U.S. 357, 375 (1927) (Brandeis, J., concurring).

12. 376 U.S. 254 (1964).
13. New York Times Co. v. United States, 403 U.S. 713 (1971).
14. Collin v. Smith, 578 F.2d 1197 (7th Cir.), *cert. denied,* 439 U.S. 916 (1978).
15. Texas v. Johnson, 491 U.S. 397 (1989); United States v. Eichman, 496 U.S. 310 (1990).
16. Colorado Republican Federal Campaign Committee v. FEC, 518 U.S. 604 (1996) (protecting the right of political parties to spend unlimited amounts of money on electioneering "independent" of their candidates).
17. Red Lion Broadcasting Co. v. FCC, 395 U.S. 367 (1969).
18. Miami Herald Publishing Co. v. Tornillo, 418 U.S. 241 (1974).
19. Turner Broadcasting System, Inc. v. FCC, 512 U.S. 622 (1991) [*Turner I*]; Turner Broadcasting System v. FCC, 520 U.S. 180 (1997) [*Turner II*].
20. Burson v. Freeman, 504 U.S. 191 (1992).
21. 504 U.S. at 217 (Stevens, J., dissenting).
22. 384 U.S. 214 (1966).
23. First National Bank of Boston v. Bellotti, 435 U.S. 765 (1978).
24. *Meet the Press,* November 9, 1997.

11. Affirmative Action: Does It Work?

1. I use the concept of race in this chapter as it has figured in the political and legal debates I discuss. Anthony Appiah, among others, has argued that this use mistakes "race" for "skin color" or "population." See his discussion in Appiah and Amy Gutmann, *Color Conscious: The Political Morality of Race* (Princeton: Princeton University Press, 1996), p. 73.
2. A federal judge in San Francisco stayed the enforcement of Proposition 209, but the Ninth Circuit Court of Appeals removed the stay, the Supreme Court refused to consider an appeal from that decision, and the proposition is now in force. See The Coalition for Economic Equity v. Wilson, 122 F.3d 692 (9th Cir. 1997), *cert. denied,* 118 S. Ct. 397 (1997).
3. See John E. Morris, "Boalt Hall's Affirmative Action Dilemma," *American Lawyer,* November 1997, p. 4.
4. Regents of the University of California v. Bakke, 438 U.S. 265 (1978). The justices wrote a variety of opinions in the case, and the opinion of the late Justice Lewis Powell, which laid down the rule I describe in the text, came to be regarded as stating the views of five justices, which included four others who would have sustained even the quota scheme used by the Medical School at the University of California at Davis, which Powell, in concert with the remaining four justices, struck down. In the *Hopwood* opinion I describe later in the paragraph, two judges declared that Powell spoke for himself alone. But that interpretation has been hotly disputed (see "Recent Case: Constitutional Law," *Harvard Law Review* 110 [1997]: 775), and the contrary view has prevailed in general constitutional understanding. For a discussion of the various opinions in the case, see Ronald Dworkin, "The *Bakke* Decision: Did It Decide Anything?" *New York Review,* August 17, 1978.

5. Hopwood v. Texas, 78 F.3d 932, *cert. denied*, 116 S. Ct. 2581 (1996). Of the five judges who decided the case, two—Judges Smith and DeMoss—ruled that *Bakke* has been overruled and that universities may no longer use racial classifications to produce a racially diverse student body. Another—Judge Weiner—voted to strike down the Texas Law School plan, which had been replaced by a different one anyway, on the much narrower grounds that it was not properly "tailored" to secure its stated goal of racial diversity. But he disagreed with Smith and DeMoss on the larger issue, and declined to rule that racial diversity was not a legitimate goal. The two remaining judges—Chief Judge Politz and Judge King—dissented. So only two of the five judges actually declared *Bakke* overruled, but the full Fifth Circuit, en banc, declined to grant a rehearing of the case.

6. The Fourteenth Amendment applies only to state, not to private, action, and all the defendants in the leading affirmative action cases in higher education have been branches of state universities. But private universities are in effect subject to the same rules, because the Civil Rights Act forbids any university receiving any public funds or grants to discriminate against any race, and because the tax code denies tax-exempt status to any discriminating university. Any Supreme Court holding that affirmative action violates the Constitution would presumably mean that it discriminates within the meaning of these rules. After the *Hopwood* decision, several private Texas law schools stopped using race as a factor in their admissions practices. See "Beyond Hopwood: Texas Schools Consider New Approaches," *Dallas Morning News*, October 26, 1997.

7. William G. Bowen and Derek Bok, *The Shape of the River: Long-Term Consequences of Considering Race in College and University Admissions* (Princeton: Princeton University Press, 1998). The book's title, and the river analogy it perhaps overworks, are taken from Mark Twain's *Life on the Mississippi.*

8. The study divided the C&B schools into three groups according to their levels of selectivity in admitting applicants. I list the schools in their selectivity groups in 1989: there were some variations in selectivity assignments in the 1976 listing. The most selective group (alphabetically listed) included Bryn Mawr, Duke, Princeton, Rice, Stanford, Swarthmore, Williams, and Yale; the next most selective group: Barnard, Columbia, Emory, Hamilton, Kenyon, Northwestern, Oberlin, Smith, Tufts, University of Pennsylvania, Vanderbilt, Washington University, Wellesley, and Wesleyan; the least selective group: Denison, Miami University (Ohio), Pennsylvania State, Tulane, Michigan (Ann Arbor), and North Carolina (Chapel Hill).

9. The authors consider, as contributing factors to black dropout rates, poor high school education in study techniques and continued stereotyping in college.

10. For a more general discussion of the distinction between issues of principle and of policy, with special reference to the affirmative action debate, see Ronald Dworkin, *A Matter of Principle* (Cambridge, Mass.: Harvard University Press, 1985).

11. See, among other material cited in *The Shape of the River,* Stephan Thernstrom and Abigail Thernstrom, *America in Black and White* (New York: Simon and Schuster, 1997) ("The university had wanted to make minority students feel at home. But with

the dramatic increase in minority numbers and with the creation of ethnic theme houses, the level of minority student discomfort actually rose"); and Shelby Steele, "A Negative Vote on Affirmative Action," in *Debating Affirmative Action: Race, Gender, Ethnicity, and the Politics of Inclusion*, ed. Nicolaus Mills (New York: Delta, 1994) ("The effect of preferential treatment—the lowering of normal standards to increase black representation—puts blacks at war with an expanding realm of debilitating doubt, so that the doubt itself becomes an unrecognized preoccupation that undermines their ability to perform, especially in integrated situations").

12. Bowen and Bok, *The Shape of the River*, pp. 284, 290.

13. The gap between average black and white SAT scores narrowed considerably from 1976 to 1989 in the more selective C&B schools; ibid., p. 30.

14. Thernstrom and Thernstrom, *America in Black and White*.

15. The next two sentences read: "But at the top-ranked schools the black graduation rate is very high, in some cases nearly matching the white rate. This refutes the thesis that affirmative action at the nation's elite colleges and universities puts blacks in institutions where they will be over their heads academically and are likely to drop out"; "Graduation Rates of African-American College Students," *Journal of Blacks in Higher Education*, Autumn 1994, p. 44.

16. The NCAA is an association of universities and colleges that compete in various sports. It is often used as a source of data about the graduation rates of blacks, because it requires its members to file graduation data with it by sex and race.

17. A recent study published by the Southern Education Foundation described black admissions to universities in nineteen states—chiefly, though not exclusively, southern states, where blacks make up a very high proportion of college-age youth. It reported a depressing rate of black dropout in the public institutions of those states—blacks accounted for 17 percent of the entering class, but for only 10 percent of those graduating. But the study also reported that many of these institutions have been sharply criticized for insisting on race-neutral admissions standards, and refusing or limiting affirmative action. See Ethan Bronner, "Black Gains Found Meager in the Old Segregated States," *New York Times*, August 28, 1998, p. B8.

18. The *River* study also contradicts another widespread assumption. Some critics it cites charge that black students major mainly in "black" subjects, such as "black studies and multiculturalism," because it is easier for them to get good grades in such subjects. See Lino A. Graglia, "Racial Preferences in Admission to Institutions of Higher Education," in *The Imperiled Academy*, ed. Howard Dickman (New York: Transaction, 1993), p. 135. In fact, blacks at the C&B schools are distributed among majors in roughly the same proportions as white students.

19. The difference was less for women. See Bowen and Bok, *The Shape of the River*, p. 123.

20. Ibid., p. 130.

21. Ibid., p. 156.

22. See ibid., p. 171.

23. Ibid. Bowen and Bok also refer to studies showing that black and Hispanic physi-

cians are much more likely to practice in minority neighborhoods, and to number minorities and poor people among their patients.

24. Ibid., p. 231. The study also asked where the interactions among students of different races had begun. Ninety-three percent of the blacks and 80 percent of the whites who reported two or more close friends of the other race cited "class or study groups" and "same dorm or roommate," and about 67 percent of both groups cited "parties or other social activities" and "extracurricular activities."

25. Louis Harris, "The Power of Opinion," *Emerge,* March 1996, pp. 49–52. The Harris poll is discussed in an important article by Andrew Hacker, "Goodbye to Affirmative Action?" *New York Review,* July 11, 1996.

26. On one analysis, of the 2,171 blacks who entered the C&B schools in 1989, over 1,000 would have been rejected under a genuinely race-neutral admissions policy, and of the 646 entering the most selective group of these schools, 473 would have been rejected; Bowen and Bok, *The Shape of the River,* p. 350.

27. A recent study has estimated that if affirmative action were eliminated from medical school admissions, black enrollment in "the nation's highest-ranked medical schools may be reduced by as much as 90 percent"; "What If There Was No Affirmative Action in Medical School Admissions?" *Journal of Blacks in Higher Education,* Spring 1998, p. 11.

28. The C&B schools, like most large colleges and universities, report that they try to enroll as many applicants from economically disadvantaged backgrounds as possible. But such applicants are, unsurprisingly, very badly prepared, and relatively few, even among blacks, can be accepted by selective schools. The *River* study, using a rough classification of socioeconomic status, found that although 50 percent of American black families with children age sixteen to eighteen fell into the lowest of its three classes (neither parent has a college degree and family income is below $22,000), only 14 percent of the C&B black matriculants in 1989 were from that class, and that although only 3 percent of those black families were in the highest of its classes (at least one parent is a graduate and family income exceeds $70,000), 15 percent of the black matriculants were from that background. As the authors point out, elite schools serve social mobility mainly by providing educational opportunities for the middle class. "It usually requires more than a single generation to move up to the highest rungs of the socioeconomic ladder." See Bowen and Bok, *The Shape of the River,* p. 50. It is nevertheless encouraging that even 14 percent of the black matriculants were from families so deprived.

29. Jeffrey Rosen, "Damage Control," *New Yorker,* February 23 and March 2, 1998.

30. Ibid., p. 58.

31. This purported distinction between the early quota plans and more complex later plans is overstated—see Dworkin, "The *Bakke* Decision"—but the distinction is now firmly embedded in constitutional law.

32. See the Supreme Court's decision, in City of Richmond v. J. A. Croson Company, 488 U.S. 469 (1988), which struck down such a set-aside program created by the black-

dominated Richmond city council; and its decisions in Shaw v. Reno, 509 U.S. 630 (1993) and Miller v. Johnson, 515 U.S. 900 (1995), which declared electoral gerry-mandering schemes designed to increase black representatives unconstitutional. I discuss the *Croson* decision in detail in Chapter 12.

33. Some Supreme Court justices have indeed spoken of the constitutional ideal of America as a colorblind society. But they have done so in considering what constitu-tional rights the equal protection clause provides against racial classifications, not as part of an argument that the Constitution should be read to prohibit such classifica-tions as a matter of strategy. Judges have no authority to make their own policy judgments of strategy in defiance of the collective wisdom of experts, and to use the Constitution to protect those strategic judgments from all test and challenge. See Ronald Dworkin, *Freedom's Law* (Cambridge, Mass.: Harvard University Press, 1996).

12. Affirmative Action: Is It Fair?

1. Regents of the University of California v. Bakke, 438 U.S. 265 (1978).

2. Hopwood v. Texas, 78 F.3d 932, *cert. denied*, 116 S. Ct. 2581 (1996). In Chapter 11 I mentioned two dissenting opinions in the case; in fact these were dissents in a denial of rehearing a month later. The Lexis report of the case is in error in that respect.

3. William G. Bowen and Derek Bok, *The Shape of the River: Long-Term Consequences of Considering Race in College and University Admissions* (Princeton: Princeton Uni-versity Press, 1998).

4. Abigail Thernstrom, who has been a firm opponent of affirmative action, has argued that the *River* study, in reaching its conclusions about the hypothetical consequences of race-neutral admissions policies, ignored the "cascading" effect: that some of the blacks who would have been accepted by highly selective schools under affirmative action, but would be rejected by those schools under a race-neutral standard, would then apply to and be accepted at a somewhat less selective school. See Abigail Thern-strom, "A Flawed Defense of Preferences," *Wall Street Journal*, October 2, 1998. In fact the *River* study called explicit attention to that effect, and it was plainly reflected in the book's conclusion that race-neutral policies would reduce the number of blacks in the schools it analyzed by at least 50 percent. See Bowen and Bok, *The Shape of the River*, pp. 35–42, 349, and appendix tables B.4 and B.5.

5. I try to identify the various puzzles raised by the concept of a legislative intention, and to clarify that concept, in *Law's Empire* (Cambridge, Mass.: Harvard University Press, 1986), chap. 9.

6. Romer v. Evans, 488 U.S. 469 at 511 (Stevens, J., concurring in part and concurring in the judgment). I discuss this decision in Chapter 14.

7. Many constitutional historians believe that the Supreme Court developed in stages the set of doctrines I describe in the next paragraph, mainly in reaction to the hostility the Court aroused when it struck down central pieces of progressive eco-

nomic legislation before and during the New Deal. See, for example, K. G. Jan Pillai, "Phantom of the Strict Scrutiny," *New England Law Review* 31 (1997): 397.

8. Justice Powell in San Antonio Independent School District v. Rodriguez, 411 U.S. 1 at 28 (1973). In that case the Court rejected the suggestion that the poor, as such, constitute a suspect class. The concept of a suspect class is not itself free from serious difficulty and ambiguity; I discuss these difficulties in the concept in Chapter 14. But these problems are not germane to the affirmative action controversy.

9. Gerald Gunther, "The Supreme Court, 1971 Term—Foreword: In Search of Evolving Doctrine on a Changing Court: A Model for a Newer Equal Protection," *Harvard Law Review* 86 (1972): 8. Some of the few exceptions—the "Japanese Internment Cases," in which the Supreme Court upheld the internment of Japanese Americans during World War II—were unfortunate. See Korematsu v. United States, 323 U.S. 214 (1944) and Hirabayashi v. United States, 320 U.S. 81 (1943).

10. Marshall endorsed the "sliding-scale" approach in his dissent in San Antonio v. Rodriguez, 411 U.S. at 98–99; Furman v. Georgia, 408 U.S. 238, 330 (1972); and Dandridge v. Williams, 397 U.S. 471 at 520–521 (1970).

11. See Fullilove v. Klutznick, 448 U.S. 448 (1980) and Metro Broadcasting Inc. v. FCC, 497 U.S. 547 (1990). The "intermediate" standard of scrutiny was applied to gender-based discrimination in Mississippi University for Women v. Hogan, 458 U.S. 718, 722 (1982); Califano v. Webster, 430 U.S. 313, 322 (1977); and Craig v. Boren, 429 U.S. 190, 197 (1976); and to questions of illegitimacy in Clark v. Jeter, 486 U.S. 456 (1988).

12. City of Richmond v. J. A. Croson Company, 488 U.S. 469 (1988).

13. Id. at 492.

14. Id. at 521. The Fifth Circuit judges cited this passage in Scalia's opinion; see Hopwood, 78 F.3d at 945, n. 26.

15. O'Connor made plain, in *Croson,* that part of the point of requiring strict scrutiny for even apparently benign racial classifications was to reflect, in constitutional doctrine, Americans' great suspicion of and distaste for all racial classifications. The rebuttal version of strict scrutiny expresses that suspicion and distaste in the heavy burden of proof it places on institutions that feel compelled to use such classifications. As I suggested, I believe that even the rebuttal version imposes too heavy a burden on branches and departments of government, from Congress to city councils, that are struggling with intractable problems of de facto racial segregation in industry and politics. My point in distinguishing the rebuttal version from the overriding necessity version of strict scrutiny is not to endorse the former, though it is plainly preferable to the latter, but only to clarify what the Court has actually decided, and what its past decisions entail in future cases.

16. See the discussion of equal protection in Ronald Dworkin, *Freedom's Law* (Cambridge, Mass.: Harvard University Press, 1996).

17. Croson, 488 U.S. at 524.

18. Id. at 493.

19. In fact O'Connor cited, as authority for the quoted statement, Powell's opinion in *Bakke,* which accepted that a university has a compelling interest in enrolling a racially diverse student body, whether or not it has itself been guilty of discrimination in the past.

20. Id. at 493.

21. Id. at 481. Opponents of the plan had testified that its adoption would lead to a windfall for the few minority firms in Richmond.

22. Id. at 506.

23. Adarand Constructors Inc. v. Pena, 515 U.S. 200 at 228, 237 (1995).

24. Croson, 488 U.S. at 511.

25. Id. at 518–519.

26. Adarand, 515 U.S. at 269.

27. Id. at 275.

28. The Fifth Circuit judges did concede that a university department might use affirmative action to help put an end to its own past discrimination against minority applicants. But the exception is of no practical importance: as the Fifth Circuit judges noted, the Texas Law School, like all other elite universities, had ceased any discrimination against minorities long ago.

29. Metro Broadcasting Inc. v. FCC, 497 U.S. 547 (1990).

30. Id. at 602.

31. Id. at 615.

32. Wygant v. Jackson Board of Education, 476 U.S. 267 (1986).

33. She said: "The goal of providing 'role models' discussed by the courts below should not be confused with the very different goal of promoting racial diversity among the faculty." Id. at 288.

34. Id. at 289. The two-judge *Hopwood* opinion discounts that statement as merely "descriptive." That is odd, since the same opinion cites another of O'Connor's statements (that "modern equal protection has recognized only one [compelling state] interest: remedying the effects of racial discrimination") as the basis for its own holding; that statement is at least equally plainly "descriptive" on its face, and, if it was intended to have the meaning the two-judge opinion assigns it, false, since *Bakke* recognized diversity as such an interest, as O'Connor has herself several times stated. In any case, O'Connor could hardly have intended a statement that was an important part of her argument that the Court was not deeply divided about affirmative action not to express her own view of the law.

13. Playing God

1. This distinction is elaborated in my book *Life's Dominion* (New York: Alfred A. Knopf, 1993).

2. The discussion of abortion that follows summarizes certain conclusions in *Life's Dominion* and should be read against that background.

14. Sex, Death, and the Courts

1. I discuss these questions at length in *Life's Dominion* (New York: Alfred A. Knopf, 1993).
2. Roe v. Wade, 410 U.S. 113 (1973).
3. The Supreme Court's assisted suicide decision was rendered in two companion cases: Washington et al. v. Glucksberg, 521 U.S. 702 (1997) and Vacco v. Quill, 521 U.S. 793 (1997).
4. Bowers v. Hardwick, 478 U.S. 186 (1986).
5. Id. at 191, 194.
6. Id. at 195.
7. In *Freedom's Law* (Cambridge, Mass.: Harvard University Press, 1996), I described this approach as insisting on a "moral reading" of the Constitution, and I tried to defend it against the objection of the party of history that it is undemocractic.
8. Poe v. Ullman, 367 U.S. 497, 543 (1961).
9. 505 U.S. 833 (1992).
10. The group challenging Amendment 2 did argue that it could be struck down consistently with *Bowers* because though that decision allowed states to outlaw homosexual acts of sodomy, Amendment 2 applied not only to active homosexuals but to everyone of a homosexual orientation, and so disadvantaged people on the basis of their psychological state or disposition rather than their conduct. Colorado replied that the various parts of the amendment could be separated, and suggested that the Colorado Supreme Court could declare unconstitutional only those parts prohibiting antidiscrimination legislation in favor of nonpracticing homosexuals, leaving the prohibition in place for legislation favoring "homosexual, lesbian or bisexual . . . conduct, practices or relationships." The Colorado court made plain, however, that its decision that the amendment was unconstitutional applied to all of its parts, including its prohibition of antidiscrimination legislation for practicing homosexuals, and the Supreme Court considered the appeal on that basis.
11. Padula v. Webster, 822 F.2d 97, 103 (1987).
12. The subtleties of the Supreme Court's interpretation of the equal protection clause are discussed in Chapter 12.
13. See, e.g., Reynolds v. Sims, 377 U.S. 533 (1964).
14. I have elsewhere distinguished between two kinds of preferences that might guide voters in a democracy: "personal" preferences, which concern a voter's own ambitions for his own life; and "external" preferences, which are his preferences about how other people should live or what should happen to them. See *Taking Rights Seriously* (Cambridge, Mass.: Harvard University Press, 1977) and *A Matter of Principle* (Cambridge, Mass.: Harvard University Press, 1985). I argue that it is unfair and undemocratic when people lose in politics because external preferences are arraigned against them, and that the equal protection clause should be interpreted to protect citizens from that circumstance. *Bowers*, as the text makes plain, takes a contrary view.

15. See, e.g., High Tech Gays v. Defense Indus. Sec. Clearance Office, 895 F.2d 563 (1990).

16. Romer v. Evans, 517 U.S. 620, 645 (1996).

17. Professor Laurence Tribe of the Harvard Law School was counsel of record, and he was joined by Professors John Hart Ely, Gerald Gunther, and Kathleen Sullivan of the Stanford Law School, and the late Philip B. Kurland of the University of Chicago Law School.

18. 517 U.S. at 632.

19. Scalia, in dissent, agreed. "Surely that is the only sort of 'animus' at issue here: moral disapproval of homosexual conduct, the same sort of moral disapproval that produced the centuries-old criminal laws that we held constitutional in *Bowers*." Id. at 644.

20. Cruzan v. Director, Missouri Dept. of Health, 497 U.S. 261 (1990).

21. It is worth noticing that Rehnquist did not defend the historicist approach, as other conservative lawyers have attempted to do, by appealing to the "original intention" of those who wrote and enacted the Fourteenth Amendment. He defended it on the different, and I think now much more popular, ground that weakening the due process clause in this (or indeed any other available) way reduces the power of judges to contradict the wishes and convictions of a majority of a state's citizens. For an assessment of that argument, see Dworkin, *Freedom's Law*.

22. Of course, all pain can be relieved by total anesthesia. But I assume that the justices meant that in almost all cases it can be relieved while leaving the patient in some, though perhaps a reduced, state of consciousness. Many people would regard living the rest of their lives under total anesthesia as worse than death.

23. Souter suggested, in a footnote, that the state has a weaker interest in preventing death following the removal of life support, because then "nature" causes the death. *Glucksberg*, at 785. That distinction is not pertinent when the question is only whether a patient's request is genuine or forced. He also said, in the same footnote, that because life support is a bodily intrusion, there is less reason to fear that someone requesting its removal, when the result is death, is not fully responsible than there is in the case of someone requesting lethal pills. That seems a non sequitur: people often request that life support be terminated not because they find its presence particularly offensive, but because they want to die, and the dangers of coaxing someone to make that decision seem equally great in the two cases.

24. Herbert Hendin, *Seduced by Death: Doctors, Patients, and the Dutch Cure* (New York: W. W. Norton, 1997). The book takes issue with my own writing on its subject.

25. Ibid., p. 223.

26. John Griffiths, Alex Bood, and Heleen Weyers, *Euthanasia and Law in the Netherlands* (Amsterdam: Amsterdam University Press, 1997).

27. Five doctors, four of whom Hendin describes as "major sources" of his research, wrote a joint letter to the journal that published his initial article, which had the same title as the later book. The letter read, in part, "The following persons interviewed by dr. [*sic*] Herbert Hendin . . . wish to declare that the texts of the interviews . . . do not contain a truthful description of the interviews. The text contains several

errors and flawed interpretations." They asked that their letter be published with the article. It was not, and though Hendin made some changes in the article before publication, these changes, according to the Groningen scholars and three of the doctors, with whom I spoke on the telephone, did not correct the misinterpretations, which, in their opinion, are perpetuated in Hendin's later writings.

28. See P. J. van der Maas, J. J. M. van Delden, and L. Pijnenborg, "Euthanasia and Other Medical Decisions Concerning the End of Life," translated and printed as special supplement 1 and 2 to Health Policy 22 (1992).

29. A 1997 *New York Times* article described this practice and quoted a University of California professor of medicine and anesthesiology as saying, "It happens all the time"; Gina Kolata, "When Morphine Fails to Kill," *New York Times,* July 23, 1997. That article reports the opinion of several doctors that patients whose dosage of morphine is slowly increased can tolerate, in the end, very high doses. But that has not been proved to be true for all patients, and it would be difficult to challenge a doctor's decision that pain could not be controlled soon enough except through doses that, in fact, caused death. For an example of the wide variation of opinions among doctors on these issues, see the series of articles in *Journal of Palliative Care* 12, no. 4 (1996).

Index